Second Edition

The Social LENS

To Steve O'Boyle, for hopeful monsters,
mad ones, and the core.

Second Edition

The Social LENS

An Invitation to Social and Sociological Theory

Kenneth Allan

University of North Carolina at Greensboro

SAGE | PINE FORGE

Los Angeles | London | New Delhi
Singapore | Washington DC

For information:

Pine Forge Press
An Imprint of
  SAGE Publications, Inc.
2455 Teller Road
Thousand Oaks, California 91320
E-mail: order@sagepub.com

SAGE Publications Ltd.
1 Oliver's Yard
55 City Road
London EC1Y 1SP
United Kingdom

SAGE Publications India Pvt. Ltd.
B 1/I 1 Mohan Cooperative
  Industrial Area
Mathura Road, New Delhi 110 044
India

SAGE Publications Asia-Pacific Pte. Ltd.
33 Pekin Street #02-01
Far East Square
Singapore 048763

Printed in the United States of America

Library of Congress Cataloging-in-Publication Data

Allan, Kenneth, 1951-
The social lens : an invitation to social and sociological theory / Kenneth Allan. — 2nd ed.
    p. cm.
Includes bibliographical references and index.
ISBN 978-1-4129-7834-7 (pbk. : acid-free paper)
  1. Sociology. 2. Sociology—Philosophy. 3. Sociologists. I. Title.

HM586.A44 2011
301.01—dc22   2010004040

This book is printed on acid-free paper.

10   11   12   13   14   10   9   8   7   6   5   4   3

Acquisitions Editor:	David Repetto
Editorial Assistants:	Nancy Scrofano and Maggie Stanley
Production Editor:	Carla Freeman
Typesetter:	C&M Digitals (P) Ltd.
Proofreader:	Theresa Kay
Indexer:	Rick Hurd
Cover Designer:	Janet Kiesel
Marketing Manager:	Erica DeLuca

Contents

Acknowledgments

My most immediate debt continues to be to my students—thank you for your support and especially your questions—and to the Department of Sociology at UNCG (including our unsung champions, Julie Capone and Jean Holliday). And I especially want to acknowledge Steve Kroll-Smith for always believing. The A-team at Pine Forge is amazing: Carla Freeman, Dave Repetto, Karen Ehrmann, and Laureen Gleason—you make it happen. Special thanks to Christine Calabria for a critical reading of the text. And, of course, my continuing thanks to Ben and Jerry. Without the insightful comments of the following reviewers, this book wouldn't be half of what it is; my gratitude for your time, concern for theory (and our students), and wisdom:

Gabriel A. Acevedo
University of Texas at San Antonio

Kurt Borchard
University of Nebraska at Kearney

Nicole Xavier Cauvin
Sacred Heart University

Louis Corsino
North Central College

David R. Dickens
University of Nevada, Las Vegas

Patricia Gagne
University of Louisville

Peter R. Grahame
Pennsylvania State University

Stephen B. Groce
Western Kentucky University

Suzanne E. Tallichet
Morehead State University

Photo Credits

Special thanks to all the rights holders of the following theorists' photographs:

Chapter 2: Herbert Spencer. Wikimedia Commons.

Chapter 3: Karl Marx. Library of Congress.

Chapter 4: Max Weber. Wikimedia Commons.

Chapter 5: Émile Durkheim. Wikimedia Commons.

Chapter 6: George Herbert Mead. Wikimedia Commons.

Georg Simmel. Wikimedia Commons.

Chapter 7:   Charlotte Perkins Gilman. Library of Congress, © C. F. Lummis.

W. E. B. Du Bois. Library of Congress, photo by Cornelius M. Battey, 1918.

Chapter 8:   Talcott Parsons. © Granger Collection.

Robert K. Merton. Reprinted with permission of Columbia University.

Chapter 9:   Lewis Coser. Reprinted with permission of the American Sociological Association.

Ralf Dahrendorf. Hulton Archives/Getty Images.

Randall Collins. Courtesy of Randall Collins.

Chapter 10:   William Julius Wilson. Reprinted with permission of the American Sociological Association.

Janet Saltzman Chafetz. Courtesy of Henry Chafetz.

Chapter 11:   George C. Homans. Reprinted with permission of the American Sociological Association.

Peter M. Blau. Courtesy of Judith Blau.

Randall Collins. Courtesy of Randall Collins.

Chapter 12:   Erving Goffmann. Collections of the University of Pennsylvania Archives.

Harold Garfinkel. Photo by Andrew Clement.

Chapter 13:   Jürgen Habermas. © Ralph Orlowski/Reuters/Corbis.

Chapter 14:   Anthony Giddens. Courtesy of Anthony Giddens.

Pierre Bourdieu. © Alain Nogues/Sygma/Corbis.

Chapter 15:   Immanuel Wallerstein. Courtesy of Immanuel Wallerstein.

Manuel Castells. Photographer: Maggie Smith, 2005.

Chapter 16:   Michel Foucault. © Bettmann/Corbis.

Jean Baudrillard. © Res Stolkiner. European Graduate School EGS, Saas-Fee, Switzerland, 2002.

Chapter 17:   Dorothy E. Smith. Courtesy of Dorothy E. Smith.

Cornel West. Time & Life Pictures/Getty Images.

Patricia Hill Collins. Courtesy of Patricia Hill Collins.

Part I

Modernity and the Sociological Response

CHAPTER 1

Sociology, Theory, and the Modern Agenda

The Making of Modernity—Social Factors and Intellectual Ideas
    Modernity's Two Projects
America and the First Sociologists
Theory and Its Place in Modernity
Building Your Theory Toolbox

We live in a powerful time, a time ripe with potential for good and ill. On the national agenda of most modern states are issues such as global warming, war, nation building, the global economy, human rights, and so on. I think it's significant that the national association of sociologists in the United States (the American Sociological Association) has focused their annual meetings in 2010 and 2011 on such issues. The theme of the 2010 meeting was *Toward a Sociology of Citizenship*. The goal of the meeting was "to stimulate development of sociological approaches to a comparative transnational study of citizenship"; among the specific questions asked were "How are status categories (e.g., gender, age, race) and affiliations (e.g., religion, language, culture) used to define different levels or degrees of citizenship?" and "How has the growth of supra-national entities (e.g., international human rights regimes, global banking and financial systems, and multi-national corporations) affected the role or significance of citizenship in sub-national, national, and supranational communities?" (Footnotes, 2009).

The theme for the 2011 meeting is equally as pointed: *Social Conflict: Multiple Dimensions and Arenas*. In part the call for papers reads,

Sociology is the only social science that takes conflict as a major topic, and the only field that throughout its existence has been crucially centered on class, race, and ethnicity. New fields focused on race, ethnicity, gender, and sexuality are also concerned with conflict, but the intellectual driving force in most of these fields is a sociological perspective. (Collins, 2009)

To me, these themes not only give indication of the concerns of our time, they also point to the way sociology and theory came to exist in the first place. As Collins says, sociology has been concerned with "class, race, and ethnicity throughout its existence." Comprehending these issues, and how sociology came to exist, is paramount for understanding theory, sociology, and in the end society itself and your place in it. All of these are wrapped up in the Enlightenment and modernity.

In this book, we're going to begin thinking about society and your place in it using a specific view of modernity, one that assumes a rational actor and an ordered world that can be directed. It's important that you understand that this approach to understanding modernity and knowledge is just one of many possibilities. So, this story of modernity is simply our beginning; it's our touchstone, the place from which to organize our thinking. As we move through the book, you'll find that many contemporary theorists, and even some classical ones, point to social factors and processes that make it difficult to be a reasoned social actor; and, there are theories that indicate that the social world may not be ordered, but, rather, is a kind of chaotic system. And, more fundamentally, the social world may not be objective, but may simply be a subjective attribution of meaning. Further, some critical theorists argue that the kind of modern knowledge we're starting with is intrinsically linked to power and is thus oppressive. That's why we are starting with this view of modernity and modern knowledge: It's the ideal, and it's the one that many people assume to be alive and well in modern democracy.

The Making of Modernity: Social Factors and Intellectual Ideas

The words *modern* and *modernity* are used in a number of different ways. Sometimes modern is used in the same way as *contemporary* or *up-to-date*. Other times it's used as an adjective, as in modern art or modern architecture. In the social disciplines, there has been a good bit of debate about the idea of modernity. Some argue that we are no longer modern, others that we never were, and still others that we are living in some different form of modernity, like liquid modernity. In the course of our time together you'll find that there aren't any clear answers to these issues. But, rather than attempting to give answers, my hope is that this book will help you ask good questions about our time and society. In fact, I would be most happy if after reading this book you have more questions than you started with.

As a historical period, *modernity* began in the seventeenth century and was marked by significant social changes, such as massive movements of populations from small local communities to large urban settings, a high division of labor, high commodification and use of rational markets, the widespread use of bureaucracy, and large-scale integration through national identities. In general, the defining institutions of modernity are nation-states and mass democracy, capitalism, science, and mass media; the historical moments that set the stage for modernity are the Renaissance, Enlightenment, Reformation, the American and French Revolutions, and the Industrial Revolution.

But modernity is more than a period of time; it's a way of knowing that is rooted in the Enlightenment and positivism. The Enlightenment was a European intellectual movement that began around the time Sir Isaac Newton published *Principia Mathematica* in 1686, though the beginnings go back to Bacon, Hobbes, and Descartes. The people creating this intellectual revolution felt that the use of reason and logic would enlighten the world in ways that fate and faith could not. The principal targets of this movement were the church and the monarchy, and the ideas central to the Enlightenment were progress, empiricism, freedom, and tolerance.

The ideas of *progress* and *empiricism* are especially significant. Prior to the Enlightenment, the idea of progress wasn't important. The reason for this is that the dominant worldview had its basis in tradition and religion. Traditional knowledge is by definition embedded in long periods of time and thus resists change and progress. Religion is based upon revelation, which, again by definition, makes our learning about the world was dependent upon God's disclosure and not upon us developing or advancing it. In order for the modern idea of progress to make sense, the universe had to be seen in a specific light. Rather than a mix of physical and spiritual, as with religion or magic, the world had to be understood as simply empirical; and our knowing of this world was dependent upon our own efforts, our own observations using our five senses, and our own gathering of evidence. Traditional knowledge is valid if it stands the test of time; religious knowledge is valid if it is revealed by God; but modern knowledge is valid if and only if it is empirically tested and works.

The idea of progress is also tied up with what's called *positivism*. The basic tenant of positivism is that theology and metaphysics are imperfect ways of knowing and that positive knowledge is based upon facts and universal laws. The ideal model for positivistic knowledge is science: *Science* assumes the universe is empirical, operates according the law-like principles, and that human beings can discover those laws. Further, the reasons to discover these laws are to explain, predict, and control phenomena for the benefit of humankind. Scientific knowledge is built up or accumulated as theories are tested and the untenable parts discarded. New theories are built up from the previous and those in turn are tested, and so on. It's essential for you to notice that this business of testing is one characteristic that separates positivistic knowledge from all previous forms: The basis of accepting knowledge isn't faith but doubt. It's this characteristic of positivistic knowledge that gives progress its modern meaning.

Modernity's Two Projects

Progress in modernity—and thus the intent of modern knowledge—is focused on two main arenas: technical and social. The technical project of modernity is generally the domain of science. In science knowledge is used to control the universe through technology. While we've come to see science as the bastion for the technical project of modernity, the responsibility for the social project is seemingly less focused, at least in our minds today. Generally speaking, the institutional responsibility for the social project rests with the democratic state and the discipline best suited to provide knowledge for that project is sociology; at least, that was part of the intent.

Before we talk about sociology, there's an important point I want you to see. Sociology is the study of society, but this idea of society is historically specific; it came into existence in and because of modernity. The word *society* came into the English language from French and has a Latin base. The Latin root for *society* means companion or fellowship and up until the middle of the eighteenth century it kept this basic meaning (Williams, 1983, pp. 291–292). Society thus initially referred to a group of friends or associates, like a legal or scientific society. But toward the end of the seventeenth and through the middle of the eighteenth centuries the idea of society was seen in more abstract ways, to refer to something not only bigger than face-to-face social interactions but also an objective entity that could act independently. This is what Durkheim (1895/1938) means when he refers to society as a *social fact,* which "consists of ways of acting, thinking, and feeling, external to the individual, and endowed with a power of coercion, by reason of which they control him" (p. 3). These ideas concerning society began to give people a language they could use to talk about such things as religion, education, family, economy, and so on as separate parts of a larger entity called society. Notice that society not only became more abstract and larger, it was seen in terms of *a system of interrelated parts.*

Along with these changes in the idea of society came an important shift in the use of the word *state* (Williams, 1983, pp. 292–293). In the thirteenth and fourteenth centuries *state* was used to refer to any hierarchical order, such as the state of priests, state of knights, and as referring to the monarchy. In time the idea of state came to be used in the way we generally understand it today, in its political sense. The significance in this seemingly minor shift is that the state and society came to be seen as mutually defining one another. "To the extent there is something called 'society,' then this should be seen as a sovereign social entity with a nation-state at its centre that . . . regulates the life-chances of each of its members" (Urry, 2006, p. 168). But the two aren't synonymous; they are two different but related spheres: the state as the organization of power and society as an organization of free people. The ideas were further differentiated with the use of **civil society,** especially in the political discourse of the seventeenth and eighteenth centuries. Here society is specifically seen as "of or belonging to citizens" (Williams, 1983, p. 57).

America and the First Sociologists

Auguste Comte (1798–1857) is generally seen as the founder of sociology. He was one of the first to use the term *sociology* and he literally wrote the book on positivism. Initially called *The Course of Positive Philosophy,* later translated and condensed by Harriet Martineau, Comte (1854/1898) argued that the progress of knowledge has gone through three phases: theological, metaphysical, and scientific, which he also called positive. He also gave theory a central place in scientific enterprise claiming that while theory is empirically based, the observation and meaningfulness of empirical facts is established theoretically. Equally important is that

Comte considered sociology to be the queen of sciences. He argued that like all knowledge, science progresses by building upon previous work and that sociology was the final expression of science, in that society was the pinnacle, the final step, of evolution. His own empirical motivation in sociology was to understand how society could be reorganized after the French Revolution (1789–1799) destroyed the monarchy. It was during this time, generally the same period as the American Revolution, that France began to embrace the principles of the Enlightenment along with the ideas of inalienable rights and citizenship.

In this use of sociology, the United States held a unique place. The first sociologists did not hold PhDs nor did they go to school to study sociology. They were generally found among the "thousands of 'travelers,' . . . who came to [the United States] to observe how the new revolutionary system worked" (Lipset, 1962, p. 5). In the beginning phases of modernity, the United States was seen as the first and purest experiment in democracy. Unlike Europe, where modern government had to contend with and emerge from feudalism, America was born in democracy. People thus came to the United States not only to experience freedom but also to observe how modern democracy worked. Sociology was and continues to be one of the best disciplines for inquiry into modernity's social goals, precisely because it is the study of society.

Though there were many who came and studied, Harriet Martineau's (1802–1876) work holds a special place, first because of her association with Comte. Of Martineau's work in translation, Comte said,

> Looking at it from the point of view of future generations, I feel sure that your name will be linked to mine, for you have executed the only one of those works that will survive amongst all those which my fundamental treatise has called forth. (as quoted in Harrison, 1913, p. xviii)

Martineau also wrote one of the first books of sociological method: *How to Observe Morals and Manners* (1838/2003), which she then used in her two-year study of American democracy, published in three volumes in 1837. Martineau is also significant because of her gender. She was among the first to bring the gender lens to bear on democracy. Martineau (2005) argued that the test of any democratic nation is the "condition of that half of society over which the other half has power" (p. 291). Her assessment of the condition of gender in the United States in the beginning of the nineteenth century is that "tried by this test, the American civilization appears to be of a lower order than might have been expected" (p. 291).

Of the importance of the United States for the study of society and democracy, Martineau (1838/2003) said,

> The United States are the most remarkable examples now before the world of the reverse of the feudal system—its principles, its methods, its virtues and vices. In as far as the Americans revert, in ideas and tastes, to the past, this may be attributed to the transition being not yet perfected—to the generation which organised the republic having been educated amidst the remains of feudalism. (p. 46)

One of the guiding lights of modernity that directed Martineau's work is the idea of natural law. *Natural law* is the notion that, apart from human institutions, there are laws and rights to which every human being adheres. The U.S. Declaration of Independence contains this idea in the phrase, "We hold these truths to be self-evident, that all men are created equal, that they are endowed by their Creator with certain unalienable Rights, that among these are Life, Liberty and the pursuit of Happiness." This was Martineau's (1838/2003) belief as well: "Every element of social life derives its importance from this great consideration—the relative amount of human happiness" (p. 25). Happiness—and its prerequisite, freedom— are thus a touchstone and concern for modern sociological analysis.

Early positivists, such as Martineau, were impressed with the need to evaluate how well any modern society was doing with regard to its purpose. Again, let me remind you that fundamental shifts occurred in modernity. One of the major changes had to do with government: the shift from rule by monarchy to rule by democracy administered through the nation-state. This shift also implied that people went from being subjects to being citizens with the inalienable rights of life, liberty, and the pursuit of happiness. The Declaration of Independence continues, "to secure these rights, Governments are instituted among Men." Thus, the purpose of the state in modernity is to secure and safeguard civil rights for its citizens. Here is the critical part for our discussion: Early social thinkers felt compelled to evaluate society's progress.

Theory and Its Place in Modernity

Theory is at the heart of modern knowledge and science—theory is the basis of modern control (one of the goals of science)—and, most of your classes, whether it was explicit or not, are based on theoretical understandings. Yet there's a line in pop culture that says, "It's only a theory." The truth of the matter is that apart from tradition and religion, theory is all we have. All scientific work is based on theory— science and technology in all its forms would not exist if it wasn't for theory. Theories aren't accepted on faith, nor are they time honored. In fact, the business of science is the continual attempt to disprove theories! Theories are accepted because they have stood up to the constant doubt and battering of scientists. Furthermore, "facts" are actually a function of theory: Scientific data are produced through testing and using theoretical perspectives and hypotheses. So, having "just a theory" is a powerful thing.

The first and most important function of theory is that it explains how something works or comes into existence—*theory* is a logically formed argument that explains an empirical phenomenon in general terms. I came across two statements that help illustrate this point. A recent issue of *Discover* magazine contained the first one: "Iron deficiency, in particular, can induce strange tastes, though it's not known why" (Kagan, 2008, p. 16). There are many of these empirical observations in science and medicine. For example, it's not known why some people get motion sickness and others don't, nor is it known why more women than men get Raynaud's disease. Observations like these that simply link two empirical variables together are not theoretical.

The second statement appeared in an article about how exercise improves memory and may delay the onset of Alzheimer's. In linking these variables, the article says, "It works like this: aerobic exercise increases blood flow to the brain, which nourishes brain cells and allows them to function more effectively" (deGroot, Redford, & Kinosian, 2008, p. 26). Unlike the first statement, this one offers an explanation of *how things work*. This, then, is a theoretical statement. It describes how the empirical association between exercise and improved memory works. This function of theory is extremely important, especially for civic sociology. So in studying theory, always look for factors that, when connected, explain how something works or exists.

Theory is built out of assumptions, perspectives, concepts, definitions, and relationships. Our word *perspective* comes from the Latin *perspectus,* and it literally means "to look through." Perspectives act like glasses—they bring certain things into focus and blur our vision to others. *Perspectives* thus determine what we see. Joel Charon (2001) explains it this way:

> Perspectives sensitize the individual to see parts of reality, they desensitize the individual to other parts, and they guide the individual to make sense of the reality to which he or she is sensitized. Seen in this light, a perspective is an absolutely basic part of everyone's existence, and it acts as a filter through which everything around us is perceived and interpreted. There is no possible way that the individual can encounter reality "in the raw," directly, as it really is, for whatever is seen can be only part of the real situation. (p. 3)

In other words, we never directly experience the world; we encounter it through our perspectives. For a trained sociologist, every theory is based on a perspective, it is a way of seeing and not seeing the world.

All perspectives are built upon *assumptions*—things that we suppose to be true without testing them. There's an old saying that goes like this: When you *assume*, you make an Ass out of U and Me. That saying is dead wrong. Human beings can't begin to think, let alone act, without making assumptions. What makes an ass out of you and me is when we don't acknowledge and critically examine the assumptions underlying our knowledge and actions.

There are three basic assumptions used in social theory: assumptions about human nature, the existence of society, and the purposes and goals of knowledge. Human nature may be seen as utterly social or egoistic, symbolic and flexible or genetically determined, rational or emotional, freely acting or determined, and so on. While there are a number of variations, the basic assumption about society is whether or not it exists objectively—as something that can act independently of the individuals that make it up. At one end of this continuum are those who assume that social structures are objective and strongly influence (or cause) human behavior. Theory that is based on this assumption seeks to explain and predict the effects of social processes using law-like principles. At the other end of the continuum are those who argue that society does not exist objectively outside of human interpretation and action. These kinds of theories don't try to predict human action at all; instead, they seek to understand and explain contextual social action. The assumption about purpose involves the value or ethics of theory and sociological work. At one end of this continuum are those that believe sociology should be value-free and only explain what exists. This is the ideal of science—knowledge for knowledge's sake. At the other end of the spectrum are those that believe the purpose of theory and sociological work is to critique society and bring about change.

The concepts that theory uses are abstract. The reason for this is that abstract concepts give us explanatory power. For example, in one of Karl Marx's writings he talks about "the discovery of America" and how it gave impetus to the world market. That idea of Marx's can only be used to explain one empirical event. However, if we can see what happened in more abstract terms, we can explain more than one situation. In this case we could substitute "geographic expansion" and the theory would have more explanatory power. The problem with abstract concepts is that they are indefinite, which is why definitions are so important.

Let's use a common table as an example. Any specific table is there for everyone to see and touch. We can assess it using a standard of measurement. So, we can say, "That table is 48 by 24 inches." (Of course, it changes to 121.92 by 60.96 centimeters if we use the metric system.) But a definition of *table* must be general enough to be used to classify all tables, not just this one. Definitions describe ideas and concepts. How, then, do we know where the idea or category of table begins and ends? The only way to limit the idea of table is to specify it through a definition.

If I ask you to give me a definition for table, you might say something like, "A table is a wooden structure that has four legs." But is that general enough? No. Don't we call some metal things tables as well? And some things that count as tables have three rather than four legs. So, you might then say, "A table is a structure made out of any material that has three or more legs that has a flat surface upon which we can place objects." That's better, but is it good enough? Maybe, but this definition could also apply to chairs as well as tables. Obviously, we aren't usually that concerned about the definition of table. We all know what a table is, at least within practical limits, which is all we're really concerned with in everyday life. But I hope you can see the issue for critical thinking and theory: If all we have to build arguments and theory out of are concepts, then definitions become extremely important. They are the basic fodder for critical thinking and are the fundamental building blocks of theory and arguments.

Strong definitions will go beyond a simple description and will explain the conditions necessary for belonging to the concept/class being defined. We were working toward this kind of *stipulative definition* in our discussion of table. In our definitions, we want to fully explain the qualities that make something what it is and not something else. *Merriam-Webster* (2002) defines *table* as "a piece of furniture consisting of a smooth flat slab fixed on legs or other support and variously used (as for eating, writing, working, or playing games)." That strikes me as a fairly good definition. It's general enough to include tables with three, four, six, or eight legs, yet specific enough to exclude other similar objects like chairs (tables are used for "eating, writing, working, or playing games")—the definition stipulates the necessary conditions for a thing to be considered a table.

Theories also need to explain the relationships among the concepts. Keep this in mind: Theoretical concepts do work and it's the relationships that explain how they work. There are at least two concerns in spelling out theoretical relationships. The first is the direction of the relationship. There are two basic possibilities, positive and negative. A relationship is positive if the concepts vary in the same direction (either both increase or both decrease); relationships are negative if they vary in opposite directions (if one increases, the other decreases). Let's use a simple example—education and occupation. The relationship between these two concepts is positive (at least, that's your working hypothesis for being in school): Increasing years of education will produce higher-rated jobs for the individual. Notice that because the relationship is positive, it works the same in reverse: Lower years of education produce lower-rated jobs.

The second concern with relationships is more difficult: We need to explain the relationship. More years of education might equate to a better job, but how does that work? If you think about this a moment, you'll see that the theoretical task just grew tremendously. What is it about education that would affect jobs in that way? How does this relationship work? Historically, it wasn't always true that formal education and occupation were related. Why are they now? Many people in our society know that higher levels of education lead to better jobs, but most can't explain how that works. When you can do that, you're beginning to form authoritative opinions.

But theory can and should do more. Theory should inspire and give insight; it should make us see things we wouldn't otherwise. For example, when Marx says that capitalism breeds its own gravediggers, we see something that isn't possible when giving a technical explanation of the material dialectic. Or, when Durkheim says that the collective consciousness is so independent that it will often do things for its own amusement, our mind is captured in such a way that a technical explanation of social facts can't match. The same is true with Habermas' colonization of the lifeworld, or the idea that money is a pimp, or the notion of plastic sexuality, and many others. It's important to see that this function of theory isn't simply a matter of "turning a phrase." These kinds of theoretical statements get at the essence—they help us see into the core of a social factor or process. Both functions of theory are important, but they can easily overshadow one another. Theory should thus explain how something works or came about as well as inspire us to insight.

One of the things I hope you take from this discussion is that your education in social and sociological theory isn't insignificant. It is an intrinsic part of what we mean when we talk about modernity and democracy. Yet at the same time I've set up an ideal modernity. Through our journey together we'll see that some of the ideals are substantiated in the theories we consider, but we'll also see that many are challenged. Part I of the book presents theorists working in the early stages of modernity, and they have concerns (basically the same ones that Randall Collins notes as previously mentioned). Herbert Spencer is concerned about how complex modern societies can be integrated; Karl Marx, Chapter 3, is concerned with capitalism, initially seen as a vehicle for equality; Max Weber, Chapter 4, is concerned about the effects modern rationality has on society and social relations; in Chapter 5, we'll see that Émile Durkheim focuses on the cultural diversity modernity brings with it; George Herbert Mead and Georg Simmel, Chapter 6, are interested in how modern society affects the person; and in Chapter 7, we meet the challenges of gender and race to the modern social project. In Part II, we turn to theories coming out of twentieth-century modernity, a period of theory cumulation and schools of thought. And in Part III, we'll consider the most contemporary theories, such as postmodernism, poststructuralism, theories of globalization, and identity politics. But to take this journey we have to start here, firmly grounded in modernity, its vision, and most importantly its way of knowing.

BUILDING YOUR THEORY TOOLBOX

At the end of every chapter, I will be giving you exercises and projects. These activities are designed to help you understand and use the theories you've learned. The intent of this chapter is to provide you with a background for the rest of the book. I am thus keeping this toolbox brief. The most important things I want you to take away from this chapter are ideas that you can use to think through and analyze the theories that follow.

- Please define the following terms. Make your definitions as theoretically robust as possible (don't be afraid to consult other sources). You want these definitions to work for you throughout the book: *modernity, progress, empiricism, positivism, science, technical project, social project, democracy, theory, perspectives, theoretical definitions.*

- Please answer the following questions:
  - ○ Explain the projects of modernity and how science as a knowledge system fits in.
  - ○ Describe the work of the first sociologists. What were their concerns? How do you think sociology fits into the projects of modernity?
  - ○ Define theory. In your definition be certain to explain the purpose, building blocks, and goals of theory.
  - ○ What are the three assumptions sociologists usually make? Describe each assumption and why it is important in the work of theory.

CHAPTER 2

The Evolution of Society:

Herbert Spencer

(1820–1903)

As we've seen, sociology was born out of the ferment of modernity and the quest for scientific knowledge. The subject matter of sociology is, of course, society; but in order to study it early sociologists had to define it. One of the earliest and more pervasive definitions was put forth by Herbert Spencer. In order to begin thinking about society, Spencer used the **organismic analogy**—this eventually became the cornerstone of functionalism. The organismic analogy is a way of looking at society that understands the form of society and the way society changes as if it were an organism. For example, in order for you to survive, you need oxygen, and you get your oxygen from air. Because of that need and because of that source, your body has a specific structure built inside it—your lungs. It also has other structures and systems (such as the circulatory system) that aid the lungs in fulfilling this need. Fish don't have lungs and neither do plants. They have other structures and systems that are designed to meet their specific needs within their environment.

There are three specific theoretical ideas that come from looking at society as an organism: the relationship between needs and functions, systems thinking, and systemic equilibrium. Societies have specific needs, just like your body, called **requisite needs**. The term underscores the idea that these needs are required for survival. Societies develop certain structures or institutions that meet those needs. Just as your lungs are built differently than your stomach because they fulfill a different function, so, too, different social institutions are built differently from one another because they function to fulfill diverse social needs. Another similarity with your body is that institutions are taken for granted. That is, they work without our usually being aware of them. In fact, the more we are aware of social institutions, the less power they have over our lives.

Thinking in terms of society as an organism also implies that society works like a system. Systems are defined in terms of relatively self-contained wholes that are made up of variously interdependent parts. That's a mouthful, but it really isn't as daunting as it might seem. Your body is a system and it's made up of various parts and subsystems that are mutually dependent upon one another (your lungs would have a hard time getting along without your stomach), each part contributing to the good of the whole. Thinking about the body also lets us see that systems are bounded. That is, they exist separate from but dependent upon the environment. There's a definite place where your body ends and the world around you begins. In that sense, your body is relatively self-contained. We have to negotiate the boundary between ourselves and the physical environment, but they are separate. As we will see, that negotiation is part of the needs of the system. So, for Spencer, society acts like a system with mutually dependent parts that are separate from but interacting with the environment.

In addition, systems tend toward equilibrium. If you are reading this book, then you are alive. If you are alive, your body is regulating its temperature, among other things. The point is that it is probably either hotter or colder in the environment than your body wants or needs. Your body senses the difference between its goal (98.6 degrees Fahrenheit) and its environment and uses more or less energy in heating itself. Your body keeps itself in balance. Spencer posits that society does the same kind of thing: The social system has internal pressure mechanisms that work to keep society in balance. One of the things that we will notice as we move through Spencer's theory is that change and integration are social responses to system pressures, rather than individual people making decisions. According to Spencer, the mechanisms for integration and change are in the system itself, not in the people who live in the system.

THEORIST'S DIGEST

Brief Biography

Spencer was born on April 27, 1820, in Derby, England, the eldest of nine children, and the only child to survive to adulthood. His father, George (a religious dissenter and Benthamite), was a school teacher and taught Herbert at home until he was 13, after which the boy continued his training with his Uncle Thomas. Part of his schooling was taken up with reading aloud from Harriet Martineau's *Illustrations of Political Economy*. At age 17, young Spencer decided he wasn't cut out for a university education and worked as a railway engineer for about four years. Afterward, he supported himself as a journalist and editor (at *The Nonconformist* and the London *Economist*) until his uncle died and left him money. From that point on, Spencer lived as a private intellectual.

Spencer was one of the most widely read writers of his time—his works sold somewhere between 500,000 and 1,000,000 copies in his day. His works formed the foundation of many intellectual disciplines, including biology, psychology, sociology, physics, and education.

After a lengthy illness, Spencer died on December 8, 1903.

Central Sociological Questions and Issues

Spencer is primarily concerned with how societies change and function. He wants to understand what the basic parts of society do, how they relate to one another, and what force pushes societies to change. Remember, for most of human history, social groups were very slow to change. Modernity, however, is synonymous with progress and change. Thus, Spencer is centrally concerned with explaining modern societies and change in the most general terms.

Simply Stated

Spencer argues that all systems—organic or social—need to draw resources from their environment (operative function), distribute those resources through the system (distributive function), and be well organized (regulatory function). As the population of a society grows, these three system needs are divided up among different structures. Society thus becomes come complex and better able to adapt and survive. However, there is a danger that society can become so complex it's unable to function well because its organization isn't strong enough. The social system thus pushes for increased regulation; but there's a danger of too much regulation, which can stagnate society. In the long run, then, complex societies tend to cycle through periods of growth and stagnation.

Key Ideas

evolution, segregation, multiplication of effects, organismic analogy, requisite needs, regulatory function, operative function, distributive function, differentiation, specialization, structural differentiation, compounding, problems of coordination and control, militaristic and industrial societies, domestic institutions, ceremonial institutions, political institutions, ecclesiastical institutions

Concepts and Theory: Social Evolution

Most social scientists of the eighteenth and nineteenth centuries either assumed an evolutionary point of view or explicated one. Both Marx and Durkheim, for example, assumed an evolutionary-like position. Marx assumed that societies are changing through the material dialectic, though the "evolutionary" change was not seen as progressive until the very last movements when history moves from capitalism to socialism and, finally, to communism. Durkheim argued for a moral–cultural evolution. This evolution moves from particularized to generalized culture and morality. More complex societies demand a more generalized culture and value system. For example, a social group that only has one kind of person in it can afford to have a very specific culture (in fact, it *must* have such a culture). Urban gangs are a good example. But a larger social group that embraces a number of different types of people must have a more general identity and value system. Durkheim argued that religion would facilitate this evolution, particularly in its final phase from nation-state to universal humanity (keep in mind that this kind of religion would be very humanistic and accepting of diversity). In addition, according to Durkheim, improvements in communication and transportation move morals to become increasingly independent of time and space and thus embracing of the "sole ideal of humanity."

Yet both Marx and Durkheim saw problems associated with the evolution of society. Herbert Spencer, on the other hand, saw it more in terms of positive progress coming out of social evolution in general and the Industrial Revolution in particular. Spencer saw evolution as a movement from simple forms to complex forms with greater adaptability. Spencer was born and lived his life in Britain. England, in contrast to France (where Durkheim grew up), had experienced slow and steady growth, politically and economically. There was thus a tendency to see the world in terms of gradual and peaceful change. Spencer, like most British people at the time, saw the Empire as the pinnacle of social evolution. Capitalism and the Industrial Revolution were seen as expressions of this superiority. Spencer therefore saw laissez-faire capitalism, the division of labor, free markets, and social competition as part of the survival of the fittest.

System Needs

Just as every living organism has certain needs that must be met for it to survive, society too has specific needs. For example, every society needs some standardized method of providing food, shelter, and clothing to its members. Every society also needs some agreed-upon method of communication, some way of passing down its culture to succeeding generations, some way of achieving a general but morally binding identity and value system, and so on. Each functionalist has his or her own proposed list of needs. As expected, these lists are pretty similar, but they are usually pretty abstract as well, particularly in the case of a grand theorist such as Spencer.

Spencer argues that because all systems basically work in the same manner, all systems should have the same requisite needs. For Spencer, there are three requisite needs or functions: regulatory, operative, and distributive. The *regulatory function* involves those structures that stabilize the relationships between the system and its external environment and between the different internal elements. In short, it regulates boundaries. An example of a regulatory social structure is government or polity. Governments, both local and national, set and enforce laws that control relationships, whether between internal units (such as individuals or corporations) or between our society as a whole and other external systems (such as a foreign country). The printing and regulation of money is another example of how governments manage relationships. When exchanges occur between individuals or companies or nations, it is money and its determined value that standardize those exchanges.

The *operative function* concerns those structures that meet the internal needs of the system. For a society, these needs could be cultural or material. The cultural needs of a society are met through institutions such as education, and the material needs are met through the economy. The operative system also includes such things as values (we can either value material gain or spiritual enlightenment) and communities (the social networks that meet our emotional needs). The *distributive system* involves those structures that carry needed information and substances. It is the transportation (roads, railways, airlines) and communication (telephone, mail, and Internet) networks that move goods and information through society.

These three different functions are not simply a way to categorize and understand what is going on in society, though they certainly do that. Spencer also says that there are at least two kinds of issues associated with these functions. First, Spencer notes that each subsystem will display the same needs. What that means is that every subsystem acts just like a system and can be understood as having the same needs. So, the distributive system, for example, has needs for distributive, operative, and regulatory functions. Spencer doesn't make subsystem needs and analysis a central feature of his theory; but, as we will see, Talcott Parsons (Chapter 8) does. Another dynamic that Spencer points out is that in social evolution, there is a tendency for the regulatory function to differentiate first. In other words, as we move from simple collectives to more complex societies, the first structure to differentiate and specialize is government.

Differentiation and Specialization

Evolution involves three phases: differentiation, specialization, and integration. The basic premise is that complex organisms have greater chances of survival. Complexity in this case is defined in terms of structure and function: More complex organisms will have a greater number of specialized structures fulfilling the requisite functions of regulation, operation, and distribution. The instability of homogeneous units, segmentation, and multiplication of effects therefore push organisms to differentiate and specialize; once an organism has multiple structures performing specialized tasks, integration becomes a need. Think of single-celled amoebas. Because of their nature, **integration** isn't an issue: If there is only one cell, there is nothing with which that cell can be integrated. Differentiated and specialized structures by definition perform dissimilar tasks and will tend to move in different directions. Thus multicellular animals must create structural solutions to the problem of integration. The human body, for instance, uses the central nervous system to integrate all its different structures and subsystems.

Obviously, when we are talking about social evolution, we have in mind social structures. Before we go any further, I'd like to stop and make sure we have a good definition of **social structure**—I have found that the idea of social structure is something with which most students have trouble. I want you to think for a moment about how you made your way into the room you are in right now. Unless the room you're in is a single room standing all by itself out in the middle of a field with no roads in or out, then you probably got to the room by driving on roads, walking on paths, and stepping through hallways and doorways. Okay, now imagine that you wanted to get into this room using something besides the door or the window. It would be difficult, wouldn't it? Walking through walls is no easy task. The point of all this is that you used different kinds of structures to get around (roads, walls, floors, doors, and so on). Those structures helped you accomplish your goal of getting to this room (which is itself a structure), but they also restricted and guided your options. Social structures are like material structures: They guide our behavior, but they restrict us as well.

Here's an important point about structures to keep in mind: The *structural* parts of structures are the *connections* among the units. For example, the highway system is considered a societal infrastructure precisely because it contains relationships among all the roads in the system. A single road out in the middle of nowhere would not be considered part of the infrastructure. However, I can stand on the road in front of my house and be connected to every other road on the North American continent precisely because they are structured. Using a different analogy, the substructure of a house isn't created simply by piling 2×6s in a haphazard manner. It's putting them together in a specific way that creates the structure.

Social structures, then, both restrict and enable human behavior, and are made up of connections among sets of positions that form a network. The interrelated sets of positions in society are generally defined in terms of status positions, roles, and norms. These social and cultural elements create and manage the connections among people, and it is the connections that form the structure. **Structural differentiation** in society, then, is the process through which social networks break off from one another and become functionally specialized. That is, the network of status positions, roles, and norms becomes peculiar to a specific function. Social evolution has involved a movement from simple social forms (like hunter-gatherer societies) to more complex forms (like postindustrial societies). Just as the human body has developed specialized structures, such as the heart, to meet certain needs, so society has developed dedicated structures. Initially, all the needs of society were met through a single structure, kinship; but as societies grew, they also became more complex and developed specialized structures to meet the requisite needs. I've pictured this progression in Figure 2.1.

Figure 2.1   Social Evolution—Simple to Complex

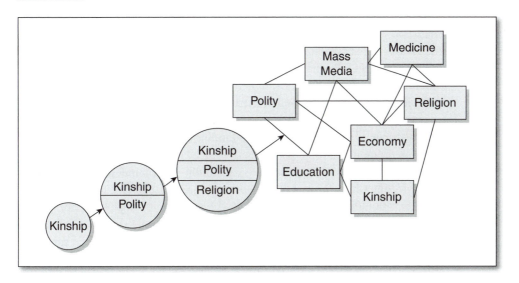

Figure 2.1 is not meant to be a dynamic model, nor does it attempt to map out all the steps. It simply presents a picture of the general idea of Spencerian social evolution. Notice that in the first circle, which would represent hunter-gatherer societies, there is only one structure: kinship. What that indicates is that all the needs of society are being met through one social institution. So, for example, the religious needs of the group are met through the same role and status structure as family. That is, the head of the family is also the "priest."

The second and third circles indicate that there is some differentiation, but the different institutions are still very closely linked. For example, the first-born son would be expected to go into government and the second-born son into religion. The final picture shows a society that is structurally differentiated and specialized, much like our own. In our society, your family role is generally not associated with the role you will play in religion, school, government, or the economy (to the degree that it is, there is another structure at work—a structure of inequality).

Social evolution is fueled by population growth. Notice the line that says "social evolution is fueled by." That means that the principle force in Spencer's theory is population growth. All theories that are dynamic rather than analytic have factors that push the other elements of the theory along. They are the driving forces and important to know and understand. As populations grow, they need to expand their structural base in order to meet the needs of the collective. There are two basic ways a population can grow: through a higher birth rate than death rate and/or by compounding (the influx of large populations through either military or political conquest). Generally speaking, increased population growth increases the level of structural diversity. According to Spencer, the different ways populations grow and gather—dissimilar levels of force, motion, and matter—produce different types of society.

Types of Society: Militaristic and Industrial

Spencer gives us two related typologies of society. Typologies are used to categorize and understand some phenomenon. We think in terms of typologies all the time. For example, we use music typologies: Beethoven falls under classical music, Pete Seeger under folk, and Eminem is hip-hop. One of the big differences between our everyday typologies and those used in sociology is that the ones in sociology are more rigorously constructed and defined. We will see that a number of theorists use typologies to understand various aspects of society. Spencer's first societal typology is defined around the processes of compounding (population growth) that we have been talking about.

There may be simple, compound, and doubly compound societies. A simple society is "one which forms a single working whole unsubjected to any other, and of which the parts co-operate, with or without a regulating centre, for certain public ends" (Spencer, 1876–1896/1975a, p. 539). In this definition of simple societies, we see that the defining feature is that the whole must not be subject to political rule from more than one group. I mentioned earlier that the first structure to differentiate is government. The levels of government that form in response to population compounding are, then, the basis of Spencer's first typology. In simple societies, like hunter-gatherer groups, the vertical dimension of government is flat. In other words, if the group has a chief, there is only one chief with no one above him. Compounded societies, on the other hand, not only have larger populations, they also have "several governing heads subordinated to a general head." In doubly compounded societies, there are additional layers of governing bodies. Obviously we are talking about increasing complexity in social structures; this typology notes the importance the political structure plays.

When all the functions were carried out by one social structure, coordinating the way it fulfilled those functions was easy. However, as structures differentiate, they also become segmented and specialized. Each structure develops its own set of status positions, norms, goals, methods of organizing, values, and so on. This process of differentiation continues as each of the subsystems becomes further differentiated through the principle of segmentation and multiplication of effects. For example, airlines, financial markets, automobiles, the Internet, and newspapers are all part of the distributive system, but each has its own language and values. Spencer identifies these issues as *problems of coordination and control:* As societies become more differentiated, it becomes increasingly difficult to coordinate the activities of different institutions and to control their internal and interinstitutional relations. As a result of these problems, pressures arise to centralize the regulatory function (government). Notice the way that is phrased: It is not the case that the individuals or political parties decide that there needs to be increased governmental control; it is the system itself that creates pressures for this centralization.

Spencer's basic model of evolution is outlined in Figure 2.2. For societies, population growth is the basic matter or mass. The force and motion of the mass is increased dramatically through compounding: the gathering together of large groups of people. Society responds to influxes of population by structurally differentiating. Each of the

Figure 2.2   Structural Differentiation and Integration

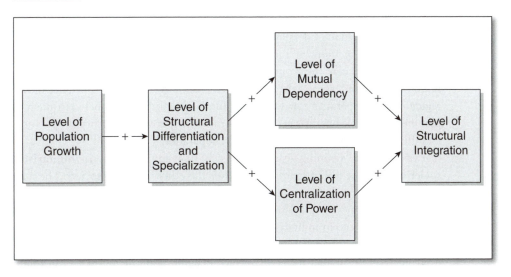

differentiated structures is functionally specialized; each fulfills one rather than several functions. As a result, structures become mutually dependent. So, if the economic system only produces goods and services necessary for collective and organic survival, then it must depend upon another structure like the family for socialization. Because diverse structures require organization, the regulatory sector tends to become more powerful and exert greater influence on social units (both organizations and people). Together, mutual dependency and a strong regulatory subsystem facilitate structural integration. The positive feedback arrow from integration to population growth indicates that a well-integrated **social system** makes possible further population growth and aggregation.

Centralized authority thus solves the problems of coordination and control, but it in turn can create productive stagnation and resentments over excessive control. Increased authority over people's behavior makes them less likely to innovate. It also hampers the exchange of information, the flow of markets, and so forth. Freedom brings innovation; thus stagnation in the long run creates pressures for deregulation. As you might already be able to tell, this is a kind of cycle that societies go through, but there are a variety of complications in the process.

This cycle of centralization and decentralization brings us to Spencer's second societal typology. In some ways, we can think of his first typology as a rough guide to understanding the structural aspect of social evolution. It focuses on the kind of polity or government a society has defined in terms of its structure. That is, the structure surrounding governmental actions can be measured from simple, with one level of governing structure, to complex, with multiple levels of governing structures. Understanding evolution in terms of the regulation function makes a certain amount of intuitive sense. In terms of evolutionary survival, the most complex and adaptive species is humanity, and it is mainly our brain and mind that give us the evolutionary advantage. Evolution, then, can be seen as the progress toward more and more complex regulatory systems.

Spencer's second typology also focuses on the regulatory system. While with the first he is interested in understanding the structural differentiation of polity, in this one he is looking more at the content of government and its relationship to society—in particular, the economic system. There are two types in this scheme—militaristic and industrial—that are defined around the relative importance of the regulatory and operative functions. The fundamental difference between them is that the militaristic operates according to the principle of compulsory cooperation and the industrial according to voluntary cooperation.

I've listed the defining features of each type in Table 2.1. In **militaristic societies**, the state is dominant and controls the other sectors in society. The religious, economic, and educational structures are all used to further the state's interest. The economy's first mission is to provide for military needs rather than consumer products. In militaristic societies, religion plays a key role in legitimating state activities. The religious structure itself is rather homogeneous, as religion needs to create a singular focus for society. Religion also provides sets of ultimate values and beliefs that reinforce the legitimacy and actions of the state. Information is tightly controlled and the government exercises strong control over the media. Public meetings and individual behaviors are controlled as well. Religion in particular provides ultimate sanctions (death and hell) for social deviance. The status structure also assures individual compliance. The status hierarchy in militaristic societies is much more pronounced and the rituals surrounding status (like bowing or using status titles such as *madam, lord, mister*, and so forth) are clear, practiced, and enforced.

As you can see from Table 2.1, industrial societies are less controlled by the state and are oriented toward economic freedom and innovation. Rather than the collective being supreme, the individual is perceived as the focus of rights, privileges, consumer goods, and so forth. Religion is more diverse and there is a greater emphasis on individualistic reasons for practicing religion than on collective ones. Individual happiness and peace is associated with salvation and religiosity. Education shifts to scientific and inclusive knowledge rather than increasing patriotism through selective histories and ideological practices (like the pledge of allegiance). Information is freed and flows from the bottom up.

Both the typology of compounding and the centralization of power are meant as ways of classifying and understanding social evolution. According to Spencer, the typology of compounding is clear: Societies have a tendency to become structurally more complex over time, especially with regards to the regulatory function. This progression is analogously seen in organisms. There has been an overall inclination toward more complex entities because they have a greater chance to survive.

Much less clear is the evolutionary path between militaristic and industrial societies. It seems that there is a general evolutionary trend toward industrial societies. Spencer characterizes the movement from industrial to militaristic as regressive. All societies begin as militaristic. Evolutionary routes are characterized by competition and struggles of life and death. Aggressive and protective behaviors

Table 2.1   Militaristic and Industrial Typology

	Militaristic	Industrial
Dominant Institution	The state: the nation (including all social institutions and actions) seen as synonymous with the army; power is centralized	The economy: freedom of economic exchange and association; profit motivation; regulatory function is diffused
System Equilibrium	Compulsory cooperation	Functional equilibrium maintained through individual choices
Religious Function	Oriented toward legitimating government—direct regulatory function: • Government identified as God-ordained • Homogeneous religious types • Legitimating political myths tend to contain ultimate values • Social deviation is defined as sin	Oriented toward the individual—indirect regulatory function: • Greater separation of church and state • Heterogeneous religious types • Focus on individual salvation and happiness
Status Structure	Greater status differentiation with distinct categories and clear ceremonial practice	Overlapping and vague status positions with unclear and infrequently practiced ceremonial distinctions
Educational Function	Directly controlled by state with strong ideological socialization	Indirectly monitored by state with emphasis on general and scientific knowledge
Mass Media	Information tightly controlled by state	Information freely flows from the bottom up
Conception of Individual	Individual exists for the benefit of the whole; individual behaviors, beliefs, and sentiments are of interest to the state	State exists to protect rights of the individual; duty of individual to resist government intrusion; belief in minority rights

became pronounced for humans once we began to use agriculture for survival; it was also at this point that people became aware of themselves as a society and not simply as a family. Land was paramount for survival and something that could be owned and thus taken or protected. The regulatory function, then, grew to be most important and differentiated from the rest. Early society developed through warfare and eventually standing armies and taxation were created. Once established, it is then functional for society in the long run to move toward the industrial type. However, society can "regress." Having set the general tendency, Spencer delineates the reasons why there is likely to be a "revival of the predatory spirit" and the various complications involved in such a regression.

There are three main reasons why a society would, once it has become industrialized, *regress back to the militaristic type.* First, there is pressure in the system toward militaristic society originating from the military complex itself. A military complex is formed by a standing army and the parts of the economy that are oriented toward military production. It's a fact of evolution: Once an organism comes into existence, it will fight for its own survival; this is no less the case for social entities than for natural organisms. Thus, a military complex by its very existence is not only available for protection; it is in its best interests to instigate aggression: "Of the traits accompanying this reversion towards the militant type, we have first to note the revival of predatory activities. Always a structure assumed for defensive action, available also for offensive action, tends to initiate it" (Spencer, 1876–1896/1975a, p. 569). This is not to deny the existence of legitimate threat, which is the second reason for regression to militarism. Spencer argues clearly that there are times when a system is threatened by other societies, internal pressures, or the natural environment. Under such threat, the system will revert back to militaristic configurations for its own survival. However, a constant pressure toward militaristic society is exerted by the military complex.

The final reason a society might revert is the presence of territorial subjects. A territorial subject is a social group that lives outside the normal geographic limits of the state, yet is still subject to state oversight. A current example of this kind of relationship for the United States is Puerto Rico. Puerto Rico is a commonwealth of the United States with autonomy in internal affairs, yet its chief officer is the U.S. president and its official currency is the U.S. dollar. The United States not only has a vested interest in Puerto Rico, it is also organizationally and politically involved. As such, the United States is ultimately responsible for Puerto Rico's internal stability and external safety. Issues of investments and responsibilities provide opportunity for military action and the creation of a militaristic society.

However, there are complications on the road to regression. The first complexity is social diversity. When Spencer talks about social diversity and societal types, he generally has race in mind. He also, however, acknowledges that what he has in mind is best "understood as referring to the relative homogeneity or heterogeneity of the units constituting the social aggregate" (1876–1896/1975a, pp. 558–559). Race, in this case, is the most stable social difference because it has the clearest visible cues associated with it. Spencer argues that groups have natural affiliations to band together and to create their own social structures. If such different groups do not affiliate with one another in larger collectives, then society will not be internally integrated.

Spencer terms this the "law of incompleteness" and says that it represents a risk to society if an institutional shock were to occur. In other words, segregated societies are unstable because functional unity is difficult to achieve. This situation represents a potential threat: It indicates that the society may not be able to respond quickly enough to changes in the environment (societal or physical). Because of this potential threat, societies with diverse groups that do not associate with one another will tend to be militaristic. However, if the groups *do* affiliate with one another and the differences are perceived to be small, then the society is "relatively well fitted for progress." Such societies tend to produce heterogeneous groups that are functionally linked together, and are thus more flexible and gravitate toward the industrial type.

Another complication of regression is the effects of different institutions and their previous growth. For a society to regress to militarism, it must first have been industrial. Under the conditions of the industrial type, the economy grows and its power can rival or even exceed that of the state; religion diversifies and becomes more focused on the individual; and the culture of individualism grows. Returning to a militaristic posture, then, must counter all of these institutional developments.

I've diagrammed these factors and their relationships in Figure 2.3. As I mentioned before, there is a back-and-forth movement from centralized to decentralized state control. The general evolutionary movement is toward industrial forms, but there are also pressures to revert back to militarism that are themselves countered by other social pressures and complications. In the diagram, both the regressive factors (military complex, threat, and territorial subjects) and impediments (social diversity and institutional configurations) are pictured as mitigating forces. In other words, a society that has moved from militaristic to industrial will tend to stay industrial unless the regressive factors mitigate the general evolutionary trend; and once a revival of the predatory spirit begins, it will continue to move society to militarism unless the impediments mitigate the effects. Thus, modern society is generally seen

Figure 2.3   Militaristic-Industrial Cycle

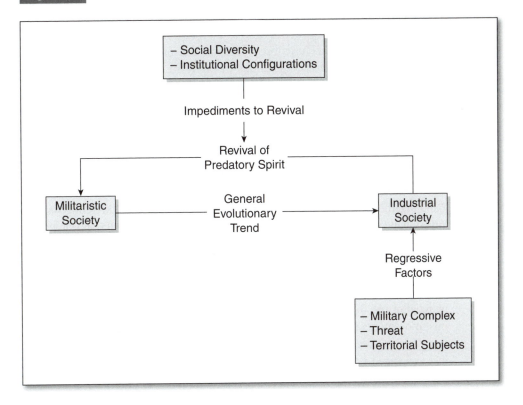

as moving along the continuum from military to industrial forms in response to population pressures, system stagnation, internal or external threats (other nations or changes in physical resources), previous institutional arrangements (such as the military complex or diversified religion), and the level of social integration.

Spencer does allow himself a speculative moment about future types. He says that the change from militaristic to industrial and back again involves a change in belief. In militaristic societies, people believe that the individual exists for the state and common good. Industrial societies represent a reverse of that belief: The state exists for the individual, to protect his or her rights and freedoms. Spencer says that the next type will also require an inverting of belief. In industrial societies, people believe that life is for work. As we'll see when we get to Weber, this is the work ethic of capitalism. The next step in social evolution inverts that belief from life is for work, to work is for life. As an illustration, Spencer (1876–1896/1975a) points to "the multiplication of institutions and appliances for intellectual and aesthetic culture and for kindred activities not of a directly life-sustaining kind, but of a kind having gratification for their immediate purpose"; unfortunately, he also says, "I can here say no more" (p. 563).

Concepts and Theory: Social Institutions

The bulk of Spencer's three-volume set, *The Principles of Sociology*, is dedicated to an analysis of institutions. Spencer, like so many students of sociology, uses the term **social institution** but never provides a clear definition. I'm going to give you a definition that is in keeping with Spencer, but it probably goes a bit beyond him as well. Social institutions have three interrelated elements. First, institutions have functions: They are collective solutions to survival needs that provide predetermined meanings, legitimations, and scripts for behavior. This notion of function is probably the most important defining feature of an institution. In everyday speech, we tend to use the term *institution* in a variety of ways. We use it to refer to someone or something that is firmly established; for example, "George is an institution around this place"; or, we use it to refer to a significant practice, as in "Baseball is an American institution." Yet these don't qualify as social institutions because they do not themselves meet a societal need.

The second defining feature of institutions is that they are not reducible to individual actions or agency. Institutional behaviors aren't something that one person does; they are society-wide. Further, institutions resist modification by the individual or even groups of individuals. For example, a number of years ago it was popular among some to see legal marriage as unnecessary and even detrimental. Marriage was seen as part of the Establishment, part of the baggage forced upon us by religion and the state. These feelings of course came out of the hippie and feminist movements in the 1960s. As a result, many people didn't get legally married. Some had private ceremonies in a field surrounded by family and friends; others just exchanged vows between themselves in the privacy of their own home. As a result of all these countercultural behaviors, nothing happened; marriage didn't go away. It's still a booming business, because institutions resist change from agents.

In addition to not being reducible to individual agency and resisting modification, institutions are not subjectively available. Let's take marriage as our example again. There isn't one of us living that was around when marriage was created. We don't have a subjective memory of it or personal orientation toward it. Everything we know about the reasons why marriage was instituted and the functions it fulfills is contained in stories that we tell each other. These stories legitimate our institutions. They give us a justifiable basis for believing in them. Obviously, the stories are the products of generations of politically motivated groups, but they constitute the reasons we believe in our institutions.

The fourth characteristic of a social institution is that it tends to be wrapped in morality; institutions are moral phenomena. In addition to containing their own legitimations, they also provide beliefs and rituals that imbue the institution with rightness and moral energy. One of the functional reasons for this morality is undoubtedly the necessity to protect our solutions to survival needs. Just as any animal will fight to protect its continued existence, so humans must be motivated to shield their cultural institutions. High levels of moral investment also serve to ultimately legitimate our institutions. We tend to see morality as connected with a higher being. Thus, if our institutional arrangements are moral religious entities, we do not see them as our own creation.

Domestic Institutions

The *domestic institution,* kinship or family, is one of the most basic of all social institutions. Its essential function is to facilitate biological reproduction, without which any species will die. In the long run, family functions to provide for patterned relationships between men and women, emotional and physical support, lines of inheritance, and care and socialization for the young.

In the absence of alternatives, kinship is the chief organizing principle of a collective; before there were state bureaucracies or economic organizations, people were organized by kinship. The roles and status positions found in the kinship system informed people how to act toward one another and what their obligations and rights were; and all social functions were met through the status positions and roles of family. Spencer argues that there is a clear association between the structure of family and the regulation of social action and relationships generally. This idea makes sense when we consider it in the evolutionary model. Humans depend more upon social networks for survival than any other creature. However, these networks aren't created through instincts or sensory experiences (like smell) as they are with most other social animals; they are produced through culture. In fact, it is the inability of humans to generate extensive social networks and behaviors through instinct or the senses that pushes us to move toward monogamy. Maryanski and Turner (1992) explain our problem with creating social structures and networks:

Our central finding is that, compared with most Old World monkeys, the reconstructed blueprint of the social structure of the LCA [Last Common Ancestor] of apes and humans reveals the hominoid lineage as predisposed toward low-density networks, low sociality, high mobility, and strong individualism. This pattern of weak tie formation, low sociality, high mobility, and strong individualism was to pose . . . a difficult problem for hominoid species, especially those on the human line, once they moved from a forest to an open-range habitat. (p. 13)

In the beginning of human history, Spencer argues, there was almost complete and universal promiscuity. However, under general promiscuity, social relationships are weak and can only extend as far as the mother and child. Even the siblings themselves are only half-related. As a result, political subordination and control are limited. Only the strongest will lead, and leadership will be ever-changing based on contests of strength. The development of religion is also hampered. Spencer argues that early forms of religion involved ancestor worship. When human beings first began to see past the objective line of this life, they saw it in terms of social relationships. The thing that connected us to the next life was kinship. We saw ancestors who had gone before as paving the way for us. It was through them that communication with the spiritual world could occur. Further, some of our first inklings of the idea of the soul came through the idea of ancestral reincarnation. Thus, when kinship only extended as far as mother to child, the ability of people to see past this life was limited.

The link between species survival and sociability pushed humans to begin to control sexual behavior and family relationships. However, the two forms that followed general promiscuity, polyandry and polygyny, were also limited. Polyandry is the practice of a woman having more than one husband. The major problem with this type is that it produces fewer offspring than other kinship forms. A woman can only birth and care for about one child per year, no matter how many husbands she has. Therefore, a social structure that is built around polyandry is at an evolutionary disadvantage.

In terms of offspring, one man with many wives (polygyny) is a better model, yet it suffers in its ability to produce social stability. Remember that one of humankind's most basic needs is a subsystem that regulates internal and external social relationships. Thus, stabilizing the political structure is one of the first concerns of society. Most initial forms of government were male dominated, due to ever-present war and the use of men to wage war. The reasons why men were used for war probably had less to do with the differences in strength between men and woman, and more to do with the expendability of men. Men are more expendable in terms of biological reproduction than women. Women were needed to nurse the young; and in terms of reproduction, society can do with far fewer men than women (one man can literally inseminate hundreds of women).

There came to be, then, a clear association among men, war, and political governance (war was generally the outcome of relationships with other groups). The problem with polygyny is that the line of succession from chief to son is unclear (initial forms of stable governance came through family lineage). The relationships among mothers, children, and father are clear in polygyny, but which son is preeminent isn't obvious. So, in the ruling families, a pattern began to develop that privileged one wife above all others; and her children were dominant and in line to succeed their father.

Gradually, monogamy was chosen as the primary form of kinship for a number of evolutionary reasons. To begin with, it added to the political stability of the group as competition among wives and offspring was done away with. Spencer also notes that "succession by inheritance" is conducive to stability because it secures the supremacy of the elder; and the use of elders for ruling tends to create what Weber would later call traditional authority. Further, the practice of monogamy was an important component in the **evolution of religion,** as it favors a single line of ancestral worship. The establishment of religion, of course, also helped to systematize socialization, which led to further social stability. In addition, monogamy tends to increase the overall birthrate and decrease the childhood morbidity rate. We've seen that polyandry results in low birthrates, and when compared to monogamy, so does polygyny. Under polygyny, some men have many wives and some have none; but under monogamy, most men have wives and thus there are more family units capable of producing children. And since monogamy also provides for greater emotional care for everybody concerned, children are better cared for physically and the morbidity rate goes down.

Because of the relationship between family and gender, I want to pause to note that Spencer feels that men and women should have equal rights. He sees them as performing different functions, but the functions themselves are equally needed by society. I must also note that one of the criticisms of Spencer is that he is a social Darwinist, seeing certain societies and races as more advanced—but in his view of equal rights for women, he was in many ways ahead of his time, as the following quotes illustrate.

> Equity knows no difference of sex. In its vocabulary, the word man must be understood in a generic and not in a specific sense. The law of equal freedom manifestly applies to the whole race—female as well as male. (1882/1954, p. 138)

> Perhaps in no way is the moral progress of mankind more clearly shown, than by contrasting the position of women among savages with their position among the most advanced of the civilized world. (1876–1896/1975a, p. 713)

Ceremonial Institutions

Spencer argues that there are three major forms of social control: ceremonial, ecclesiastical, and political. Most sociology students are very familiar with the latter two. Political entities govern human behavior externally through laws, coercive force, and authority. One of the defining characteristics of states is the monopolization of legitimate coercive force. This monopoly serves not only to protect the nation's external boundaries but also to maintain internal peace. Religious, or ecclesiastical, institutions bring about social control internally rather than externally. Religion gives us sets of beliefs about right and wrong behaviors. These moral standards exert their force from inside of the individual. An individual believes that his or her behavior is right and the person wants to please his or her god through proper behavior.

Spencer gives us yet another form of social control in the form of *ceremonial institutions.* Ceremonies are formal or informal acts or series of acts that link people together hierarchically. Ceremonies may be simple, as in an act of politeness, or quite elaborate, as in prescribed rituals. Obviously there are certain protocols that apply when a head of state visits another country. In the protocol, the relationship between the ruler and the ruled is played out in behaviors. Ceremonies also indicate the hierarchical relationship among nations: Some visiting dignitaries are afforded more elaborate ceremonies than others. Ceremonies can also be conventional and every day. In this sense, Spencer has in mind forms of address, titles and emblems of honor, forms of dress, and the like. For example, when we use titles like "Professor" or "Doctor" or "Miss," we are reproducing a hierarchical system of authority and control.

Spencer argues that ceremonial institutions are the earliest and most general forms of social control. The other forms of social control, religion and government, both sprang from this primitive type. The earliest forms of ceremony evolved naturally; that is, there was a natural connection between emotional responses and physical behaviors. Emotions cause physical reactions that vary according to the intensity of the feeling. For example, you can judge the strength and type of emotion that someone has for you by the way the person hugs you. When someone is joyful, the person's body reacts by becoming excited and perhaps jumping around; and feeling inferior is expressed bodily by relaxed muscles and lowered gaze and posture.

Ceremonies evolved further by becoming more symbolic, but they initially still maintained a degree of natural sequence. For example, the Dakota ceremony of burying the tomahawk to symbolize peace is clearly linked to the actual putting away of weapons in order to cease hostilities. Another example that Spencer gives us is the past practice in central South Africa of drinking blood to establish kinship relations. The practice is based on the early belief that all of a person is contained in a part of the person. Spencer traces many of these natural sequences such as the move from taking trophies (such as the head of an enemy) to mutilating some part of an enemy's body to mark conquest.

Ceremonies further changed toward intentional symbolization in societies "which have reached the stage at which social phenomena become subjects of speculation" (Spencer, 1876–1896/1975b, p. 25). Spencer gives us a really interesting idea and relationship here. The idea of social phenomena becoming subjects of speculation is one that would later be important to Weber, and, in a somewhat modified form, important to contemporary theorists such as Anthony Giddens. Something important changes when we go from simply living in society to thinking about society and our social encounters. When we simply live socially, our experience is fairly immediate and all that exists is contained in those kinds of moments. In contrast, when we come to the point in our development when we think more and more about society, when we become reflexive about our place and actions in society, then everything becomes less tied to the moment and more abstract.

Spencer generally argues that as societies begin to use ecclesiastical and political means of control, ceremonial controls become less used and more inconspicuous.

More specifically, this general trend is influenced by the degree of voluntary coop-eration versus enforced structures. The higher the level of voluntary cooperation, the less that ceremonial institutions will be used. On the other hand, the higher the levels of inequality in a society and the greater the need for coercive enforcement, the greater will be the use of ceremonial institutions that mark and re-create the differences among social groups.

The power of ceremonial institutions is that they "spontaneously generate afresh" the forms of rule every time human beings interact and use them. One of the interesting things about this section of Spencer's work is that he anticipated work done by contemporary theorists who emphasize the importance of micro-level interaction for building and preserving society. For example, both Erving Goffman and Randall Collins argue that one of the foundations of society is micro-level interaction rituals. One of the things that Goffman (1967) brings out is the unintentional consequences of ritualized behaviors. During encounters with other people, we engage in what he calls "face-work." In face-work, we strive to avoid embarrassing ourselves or others by maintaining role-specific behavior and not noticing when action doesn't meet expectations. Our intent is to save face; the effect is that we save the interaction and thus the patterned interactions upon which society is built. Collins (1988) argues that behavior such as deference and demeanor rituals produces and reproduces the status hierarchy of society. Our demeanor tells others the level of social honor that we expect in a given situation; and deference refers to the behaviors through which we demonstrate respect to others (e.g., prof-fering titles of respect, exhibiting downcast eyes, and so forth).

Political Institutions

Society is defined through cooperation, and Spencer tells us that there are two principal ways through which cooperation occurs: spontaneous cooperation due to individual motives of exchange, and consciously devised cooperation. When groups consciously create organization, they become aware of public ends or goods for the first time. In other words, it is through political organization that a group becomes reflexively aware of itself. Up until that point, the primary awareness is individual. So, political organization is necessary for society. Through it we become aware of ourselves as a whole, and it provides direction for cooperative efforts and restraint on individual behaviors.

Spencer sets out to understand the fundamental forms of *political institutions* and how they evolved. He argues that undergirding every type of government is a primitive form. The basic political division in society is between strength and age. With age comes experience, but it is usually accompanied by reduction in strength. The most distinguished individuals, then, incorporate both strength and wisdom; and, among those with strength and wisdom, some are more distin-guished than others. Therefore, according to Spencer, there are three divisions to the basic political structure: the masses of young and weak, those who are strong and/or experienced, and those elite few who are the best among the strong and experienced.

Spencer argues that every political structure is but a derivation of this one. What began as distinctions among the predominant man, the superior few, the inferior many, became in successive forms the head chief, subordinate chiefs, and warriors; kings, nobles, and people; and in our own society, the chief executive officer, elected officials, and citizens. Further, Spencer (1876–1896/1975b) proposes that every type of political structure is simply differing combinations in these three areas:

A despotism, an oligarchy, or a democracy, is a type of government in which one of the original components has greatly developed at the expense of the other two . . . the various mixed types are to be arranged according to the degrees in which one or other of the original components has the greater influence. (p. 317)

Thus, in a democracy the citizens are most important; in an oligarchy the power is vested in the middle section of small groups of leaders; and despotism is defined by power exercised exclusively by the chief person.

We have already talked about most of the dynamics through which political forms evolve. The first mechanism is population growth. As populations grow, especially through compounding, the levels of governing structure become more complex. In terms of Spencer's triune political structure, that means that additional levels of strong and/or experienced and elite positions are created (or what we might refer to as upper and middle management). The second influencing factor is the environment wherein the society is located, and this influences the degree of centralization of power. The environment is composed of both other societies and physical resources. These two elements are interrelated for societies. The presence of war is more likely when physical resources are few. Nations with few natural resources must obtain them from others, either through military conquest or political trade affiliations. In earlier times, military conquest was used, since political economic agreements are based on established and rather complex political entities. Thus, the complexity of the political structure is narrowed during times of war or threat (military type) and widened during times of peace and development (industrial type).

In addition to the basic structure of government, Spencer also explains the foundation of power. He notes that we have a tendency to think of political power as a feature of the governing structure itself. But that's incorrect. The political structure was built upon something more fundamental: the public sentiment of community. Spencer is arguing that underneath and prior to the political and judiciary systems that everywhere appear to guide our lives is a feeling of being part of something larger than ourselves; sociologists would later refer to this as social solidarity. This collective sentiment is stronger in more primitive societies and is most clearly expressed through religious sanctions. This argument of Spencer's is strikingly similar to the one Durkheim would make some 25 years later: The source of society is an emotional feeling of attachment that provides moral basis for social identity and action.

According to Spencer, political authority finds its legitimacy in emotion derived from ancestors and its power in socialization. Weber, writing almost 50 years later, would call this kind of legitimation traditional authority. It's an authority based on time-honored customs; it has the weight of time and history in back of it. Again anticipating Weber, Spencer argues that political power that is ascribed to a single individual is unstable. The leader will eventually die and the governing body be re-created. However, linking government to family lineage and traditional authority creates a stable form that can survive from one generation to the next (Spencer, 1876–1896/1975b, pp. 321–344).

Political power is also stabilized through socialization. Spencer doesn't use the word *socialization*, but the process he describes is exactly what contemporary sociologists mean by the term. Through proper training during youth, people come to share similar ideas, sentiments, ideas of right and wrong, language, and so forth. The trick of socialization is that when it is successful, these socially constructed items appear as subjective and natural to the individual.

Ecclesiastical Institutions

We have seen religion referenced in our discussion of other institutions. Particularly, we have seen that religion functions as an agent of social control. Religion infuses values and morals with supernatural power. According to Spencer, religion also functions to reinforce and justify existing social structures, particularly those built around inequality. If social structures are seen as an extension of a god's spiritual order, and if behaviors are seen as holy directives, then questioning social arrangements becomes a matter of questioning the god, and inappropriate behavior becomes sin.

As with all social institutions, Spencer is primarily concerned with tracing its evolutionary development. Any student of religion is faced with one inarguable fact: Through the course of human history, religion has changed. Our initial forms of religion were not monotheistic or ethical. They were, in fact, marked by the presence of many gods displaying quite human behaviors of greed, lust, and so on. The question, then, with which we are faced, is why did our conceptions of deity change over time? Did God reveal herself or himself gradually, or was the idea of God linked to developments in society and human personality? Spencer (1876–1896/1975c) argues for the second alternative: "Among social phenomena, those presented by Ecclesiastical Institutions illustrate very clearly the general law of evolution" (p. 150).

I'd like to take a moment to point out that we are not necessarily faced with an either/or proposition. It isn't the case that God either revealed himself or herself or the idea of God evolved. If God had to progressively reveal the truth to humans, it was because we weren't ready either socially or psychologically. That would imply that there would be corresponding changes in society (and/or personality) and in our idea of God. If God works through history, then we would expect to find similarities between social and personality structures and the type of religion practiced. On the other hand, if there is no God, then we would expect to find similarities between social and personality structures and the type of religion practiced. Either way, the results are the same.

Spencer argues that all religions share a common genesis. Religion began, according to Spencer, as "ghost-propitiation." Spencer argues that human beings became aware of themselves as double. We have the waking, walking self, and we also have a self that can be absent from the body. We became aware of this other-self through dreams and visions. During dreams, we have out-of-body experiences. We travel to far off places and engage in some pretty amazing behaviors. In thinking about these experiences, primitive humans concluded that we are double. There's part of us that is tied to the earth and time, but there is also part of us that can transcend both.

Moving from conceptualizing the other-self from dream states to thinking that the other-self survives death is a short and quite intuitive step. Death seems a lot like permanent sleep; it's a sleep from which we don't awake. If we soul-travel when we are temporarily asleep, then we must also travel when we permanently sleep. This idea led early humans to minister to the dead, especially dead relatives. These dead relatives could cause mischief if not taken care of, but they could also prove to be valuable allies in times of need. Further, these disembodied spirits also came to be seen as the source for life on this earth through reincarnation. Early humans were quite in tune with the cycles of nature. Trees that appear to die in winter came back to life in the spring. Thus it was not a very big step, once souls were seen as surviving death, to see them also as the source for the other-self in life. In this way, early humans began their ancestor worship.

Obviously, ancestor worship is linked to family, and the head of the family was also the head of religious observance. However, two factors that came from military conquest brought about significant social and structural changes. First, the religious function differentiated from family. As human beings moved from nomadic existence to settled farming, war became more and more common. People were tied to the land in a way never before realized and land became a limited resource that had to be protected from other groups who had outgrown the ability of their land to produce enough food. The increased involvement in war by the clan chief meant that he had to shift his priestly responsibilities to another family member. Eventually, these religious functions were separated structurally as well.

The other factor that influenced the development of religion, which was also the result of military conquest, was the incorporation of more and more conquered people into the collective. Each of these groups of people had its own family god and ancestral worship. Polytheism was therefore the natural result of war and conquest. Further, the presence of this competitive chaos of gods created pressures for there to be a professional class of priests. The priests began to impose order on this array of deities, which of course reflected the social order of society: The gods that became most important were the gods of the most important families.

As societies continued to evolve to more complex forms of organization, so did the structure of religion. Organized pantheons developed as the political structure became more centralized and class inequalities increased. The hierarchy of higher and lower gods thus reflected the organized divisions of society. Because polity relies a great deal on religion for legitimation, the more warlike, and thus more successful, societies developed images of vengeful and jealous gods. And as the political structure became more centralized and bureaucratized, the religious structure did as well. When governments rely on religion for legitimation, it is in the best interest of the professional priestly class to organize and unite. As religious leaders organize and unite, they have to simplify the religious belief system, which in turn leads to monotheism. Max Weber gives a more detailed account of the evolution from magic to ethical monotheism, but the basic outline of Weber's thought is here in Spencer.

Summary

- Spencer's perspective is in many ways foundational for sociology. He explicates the basic premises with which most sociologists will either agree or disagree. Spencer's point of view is founded on positivism, the search for the invariant laws that govern the universe. He approaches society as if it were an object in the environment, and his purpose as a theorist is to simply describe how this object works. Notice that, for his time, Spencer had a fairly radical point of view; yet, his is not a critical theory. The reason for this blend of radical yet descriptive perspective is that Spencer sees the dynamics of progress existing within the evolutionary process. It is less important, then, to try and change the way people think about society. For Spencer, society works much like an organic system, with various parts functioning for the welfare of the whole. He extends the analogy to explicate the evolutionary changes in society, from simple to complex structural differentiation. The evolution of society occurs in much the same way that evolution occurs universally: through the motion and force of matter driven by the instability of homogeneous units, segmentation, and the multiplication of effects.

- All systems have universal needs: regulation, operation, and distribution. Every system, including society, meets these needs through various kinds of structures. The ways in which the needs are met produce the unique features of each system and society. Generally speaking, there is an evolutionary trend toward greater structural differentiation and specialization, with system needs being met through separate and distinct structures. For society, this trend is driven by increases in population size. As the population increases, especially through compounding, structures differentiate and specialize in function. This process produces interstructural dependency but also problems in coordination and control. In response, society tends to centralize the regulatory subsystem, which, along with dependency, facilitates system integration. However, too much regulation can cause stagnation and pressures for deregulation. In reaction to these system pressures, societies in the long run move back and forth on a continuum between militaristic and industrial.

- Social institutions are special kinds of structures. They are organized around societal needs, resist change, and are morally infused. All institutions, however, change slowly through evolutionary pressures, and because they are functionally related, change is mutual and generally in the same direction. Generally speaking, family evolves from universal promiscuity to monogamy (monogamy is evolutionarily chosen because it provides more explicit and stable social relations); religion moves from polytheism to monotheism (monotheism has the evolutionary advantage of providing a single legitimating and enforcing mechanism for diverse populations and bureaucratic states); the state generally moves from militaristic with simpler political structures to industrial with more complex structures; and ceremonial institutions generally recede in importance as religion, family, and polity become successful structures. In spite of this, the political and ceremonial structures tend to move back and forth on a continuum in response to vested interests, perceived threat, and the level of social inequality.

- Modernity for Spencer is characterized by high levels of structural differentiation. This increased complexity gives modern societies greater adaptability and increased chances of survival. Postmodernity is characterized by institutional and cultural fragmentation. The main difference between differentiation and fragmentation revolves around unity—in differentiated systems, the different elements are linked together, whereas in a fragmented system, the parts are not as organized and have greater freedom. The effects of postmodernity are themselves contradictory: Culture and self (subjective experience) are simultaneously becoming more important and less real and meaningful. Religion is a case in point: Religion in postmodernity is less centrally organized and thus open to increasingly idiosyncratic interpretations.

TAKING THE PERSPECTIVE—FUNCTIONALISM

Functionalism is a theoretical perspective that began with the work of Herbert Spencer in the nineteenth century and was systematized by Talcott Parsons in the twentieth. Functionalism is built around the organismic analogy and has at least five defining features: concern for requisite needs, structural differentiation, specialization, integration, and system equilibrium. Functionalism came under a great deal of criticism in the latter half of the twentieth century. Some of this criticism was no doubt due to what was seen as functionalism's inability to explain the social upheavals of the 1960s. But part was also due to the place that Talcott Parsons held in mid-century sociology. For much of the twentieth century, Parsons was "the major theoretical figure in English-speaking sociology, if not in world sociology" (Marshall, 1998, p. 480). As Victor Lidz (2000) notes, "Talcott Parsons . . . was, and remains, the pre-eminent American sociologist" (p. 388). A good portion of contemporary theory was penned in reaction to Parsons and thought of as alternative approaches to his question of social order.

But functionalism is still part of contemporary theory. Neo-functionalism reconceptualizes (see Alexander, 1998) some of these issues and is concerned with the integrity and interrelationship of social structures, social change as generated by structural differentiation and by the tension produced by the relationships among various social structures. Equilibrium in neo-functionalism is seen as simply a reference point for studying an empirical system. Perhaps more important has been functionalism's continuing influence on our thinking as sociologists. They taught us to think in terms of social systems and the effects that different structures or social units can have on one another and the system as a whole.

This way of thinking is at the core of our ideas of global systems. Another specific idea that has currency in contemporary theory is what Spencer called the problem of coordination and control, but is more currently termed the problem of steering. This issue is at the heart of modernity, for society must be able to be controlled or guided in order to meet the goals of the social project. One theorist who looks at this issue is Anthony Giddens, who argues that late modern societies can no longer be steered or guided. Giddens (1990) characterizes late modern society as a juggernaut, "which threatens to rush out of our control and which could rend itself asunder" (p. 139).

BUILDING YOUR THEORY TOOLBOX

Learning More—Primary and Secondary Sources

- For primary readings, I suggest Spencer's *The Study of Sociology* (1961) and *The Principles of Sociology* (1975).

- The single best secondary source for Spencer is Jonathan H. Turner's (1985) *Herbert Spencer: A Renewed Appreciation*, Beverly Hills, CA: Sage. (Turner is probably the foremost expert on Spencer.)

- For an overview of functional theorizing, including anthropology, see Jonathan H. Turner and Alexandra Maryanski (1979), *Functionalism*, New York: Benjamin-Cummings.

Seeing the Social World (knowing the theory)

- Write a 250-word synopsis of the theoretical perspective of functionalism. Don't be afraid of using other sources or drawing from different parts of this chapter. This definition should be your own.

- After reading and understanding this chapter, you should be able to define the following terms theoretically and explain their theoretical importance to Spencer's functionalism: *evolution, segregation, multiplication of effects, organismic analogy, requisite needs, regulatory function, operative function, distributive function, differentiation, specialization, structural differentiation, compounding, problems of coordination and control, militaristic and industrial societies, domestic institutions, ceremonial institutions, political institutions, ecclesiastical institutions.*

- After reading and understanding this chapter, you should be able to answer the following questions (remember to answer them *theoretically*):

  ○ Explain how society becomes more complex.

  ○ How are complex societies integrated?

  ○ Explain how modern societies move between militaristic and industrial forms.

(Continued)

(Continued)

Engaging the Social World (using the theory)

- Spencer argues that monogamy developed because of its functional use in creating social relationships. Many people feel that monogamy is currently threatened. If monogamy is in danger, how do you think Spencer would theorize about it? (Remember, he would think about it in progressive, evolutionary terms.)

- Spencer argues that ceremonial institutions are at the heart of social control. Do you think the use of ceremonial institutions has gone up or down since Spencer's time? Theoretically, what do you think this change would indicate?

- Recalling our definitions of structures and institutions, do you think there are more social institutions today than 100 years ago? If so, what does this imply about society's survivability? What does it imply about the state?

- Using Google or your favorite search engine, type in "censored news stories." Read through a few of the sites. Based on your reading, do you think that the news is being censored in this country? If so, or if not, how would Spencer's theory explain it?

Weaving the Threads (building theory)

There are central themes about which most of our theorists speak. These themes include modernity; social institutions such as the state, economy, and religion; culture; diversity, equality, and oppression; social cohesion and change; and empiricism. A good approach to theory is to pay attention to how these themes are developed. As I noted in the beginning chapter, one of the ways we can build theory is through synthesis: Compare, contrast, and bring together elements from different theorists. The following questions are based on Spencer's theorizing and are meant to begin your thinking about these themes:

- What are the functions of kinship in society? How did the structure of kinship aid in the evolution of society? If the structure of kinship has changed since Spencer's time, what do you think that means (remember to think like Spencer)?

- What is religion's function in society? How has religion evolved over time? In other words, what are the social factors that contributed to changes in religion?

- What is the basis of political power in society? What factors bring about changes in the type of state and its structure?

- How do societies differentiate? Once societies differentiate, how do they integrate? Thinking like Spencer, would you conclude that this country has higher or lower structural complexity and differentiation as compared to even 50 years ago?

CHAPTER 3

Contradictions in Capitalism:

Karl Marx

(1818–1883)

Adam Smith is often considered the founder of free market capitalism, the person who more than any other before him explained that modern governments should not interfere with capitalist enterprise. Smith explained that capitalism is the result of social evolution, a superior economic system that would preserve the natural rights of humanity: "The obvious and simple system of natural liberty establishes itself of its own accord. Every man . . . is left perfectly free to pursue his own interest his own way, and to bring both his industry and capital into competition with those of any other man, or order of men" (Smith, 1776/1937, p. 247). The reason that capitalism shouldn't be regulated is because it, like natural evolution, contains a type of natural selection dynamic that Smith called "the invisible hand." Unfettered competition would weed out weaker businesses, regular prices, and result in the best product for the least cost. In this free market capitalism, which Smith termed "economic individualism," the differences in wealth or social standing among people would be the result of their own determination and effort.

That was the hope and the ideal. While capitalism did achieve some of its goals, the reality, especially in the beginning decades of capitalism, was quite different than the ideal. Child labor was common, with children as young as four forced to work in factories and mines, and many lost their lives or were maimed (child labor is a continuing issue in developing nations). There were no safety regulations, no minimum wage, no limit on hours worked, no health insurance, and so on. Rather than producing an even playing field, if left to itself, capitalism produces monopolies and insurmountable gaps between the rich and poor. And rather than uplifting the dignity of humankind, capitalism will push exploitation to its furthest limits. My purpose here isn't to rehash the litany of early abuses of capitalism. Rather, I want you to see the ideal of capitalism in modernity on the one hand, and, on the other, the unanticipated consequences of that system. This world of early capitalism is the one that Karl Marx spoke to. He was among the first to see that capitalism contained intrinsic elements that would create conditions antithetical to its goals and that would in the long run destroy it. He also argued that capitalism produces ideology, false beliefs that keep people from truly seeing the damaging effects of capitalism.

THEORIST'S DIGEST

Brief Biography

Karl Marx was born on May 5, 1818, in Trier, one of the oldest cities in Germany, to Heinrich and Henrietta Marx. Both parents came from a long line of rabbis. At seventeen, Karl Marx enrolled in the University of Bonn to study law. It was there that he came in contract with and joined the Young Hegelians, who were critical of Prussian society (specifically, because it contained poverty, government censorship, and religious discrimination). This association informed much of Marx's thinking. Eventually Marx finished his formal education in philosophy at the University of Jena in 1841.

In 1843, Marx moved to Paris with his new wife, Jenny von Westphalen. In Paris, he read the works of reformist thinkers who had been suppressed in Germany and began his association with Friedrich Engels. During his time in Paris, Marx wrote several documents that were intended for self-clarification (they were never published in his lifetime) but have since become important Marxian texts (*Economic and Philosophic Manuscripts of 1844* and *The German Ideology*, which was finished in Brussels).

Over the next several years, Marx moved from Brussels, back to Paris, and then to Germany. Much of his moving was associated with worker revolutions that broke out in Paris and Germany in 1848. That year also marks the publication of *The Communist Manifesto.*

The workers' movements were quiet after 1848, until the founding of the International Workingmen's Association in 1864. Founded by French and British labor leaders at the opening of the London Exhibition of Modern Industry, the union soon had members from most industrialized countries. Its goal was to replace capitalism with collective ownership. Marx spent the next decade of his life working with the International. The movement continued to gain strength worldwide until the Paris Commune of 1871. The Commune was the first worker revolution and government. Three months after its formation, Paris was attacked by the French government. Thirty thousand unarmed workers were massacred.

Marx continued to study but never produced another major writing. His wife died in 1881 and his remaining daughter a year later. Marx died in his home on March 14, 1883.

Central Sociological Questions

Marx's interests were broad, including such philosophic concerns as human nature, epistemology (the study of knowledge), and consciousness, along with more social science concerns with politics and capitalism. Specifically, Marx was concerned with the unanticipated effects of capitalism. Capitalism was to be an important mechanism through which social equality would come about in modernity. Instead, capitalism tended to produced high levels of inequality and abuse. Marx wanted to understand how these undesirable effects came about; and he wanted to explain how history would move from capitalism to another, more humane, economic system.

Simply Stated

Marx argues that capitalism is based on certain structural factors that create tensions in capitalism—most notably exploitation and overproduction. These tensions invariably create the recurring cycles of economic recession to which capitalism is susceptible. These cycles generate a small class of wealthy capitalists and a large class of dependent and deprived workers. Each economic crisis is deeper than the previous, which in turn concentrates wealth and power in fewer and fewer hands with the working class experiencing greater levels of economic, physical, and psychological suffering. In the long run these cycles will cause capitalism to implode, which, in turn, brings economic and social change.

Key Ideas

species-being, material dialectic, the means and relations of production, class bipolarization, exploitation, surplus value, commodification, overproduction, alienation, private property, commodity fetish, ideology, false consciousness, class consciousness

Concepts and Theory: Human Nature and History

As I mentioned in Chapter 1, one of the assumptions that theorists make is about human nature. Sometimes that assumption is implicit but other times it's quite clear. With Marx his argument about human nature is explicit and I would say imperative for understanding his theory: His ideas of alienation and false consciousness only make sense once we comprehend his argument about human nature, which he calls **species-being**.

Species-Being

Marx argues that the unique thing about being human is that we create our world. All other animals live in a kind of symbiotic relationship with the physical environment that surrounds them. Zebras feed on the grass and lions feed on the zebras, and in the end the grass feeds on both the zebras and the lions. The world of the lion, zebra, and grass is a naturally occurring world, but not so for the human world. Humans must create a world in which to live. They must in effect alter or destroy the natural setting and construct something new. The human survival mechanism is the ability to change the environment in a creative fashion in order to produce the necessities of life. Thus, when humans plow a field or build a skyscraper, there is something new in the environment that in turn acts as a mirror through which humans can come to see their own nature. Self-consciousness as a species that is distinct from all others comes as the human being observes the created human world. There is, then, an intimate connection between producer and product: *The very existence of the product defines the nature of the producer.*

Here's an illustration to help us think about this: Have you ever made anything by hand, like clothing or a woodworking project, or perhaps built a car from the ground up? Remember how important that thing was to you? It was more meaningful than something you buy at the store simply because you had made it. You had invested a piece of yourself in it; it was a reflection of you in a way that a purchased commodity could never be. But this is a poor illustration because it falls short of what Marx truly has in mind. Marx implies that human beings in their natural state lived in a kind of immediate consciousness. Initially, human beings created everything in their world by hand. There weren't supermarkets or malls. If they had a tool or a shirt, they had made it or they knew the person who did. Their entire world was intimately connected. They saw themselves purely in every product. Or, if they had bartered for something, then they saw an immediate social relationship with the person who had made the thing. When they looked into the world they had produced, they saw themselves, they saw a clear picture of themselves as being human (creative producers), and they also saw intimate and immediate social relations with other people. The world that surrounded them was immediately and intimately human. They created and controlled and understood themselves through the world that they had made.

Notice a very important implication of Marx's species-being: Human beings by their nature are social and altruistic. Marx's vision of human is based on the importance of society in our species survival. We survive collectively and individually because of society. Through society we create what is needed for survival; if it were not for society, the human animal would become extinct. We are not equipped to survive in any other manner. What this means, of course, is that we have a social nature—we are not individuals by nature. Species-being also implies that we are altruistic. Altruism is defined as uncalculated commitment to others' interests. Not only are we not individualistic by nature, we are not naturally selfish. If human survival is based on collective cooperation, then it would stand to reason that our most natural inclination would be to serve the group and not the self. The idea of species-being is why Marx believes in communism—it's the closest economic system to our nature state. Further, Marx would argue that, under conditions of modernity/ capitalism, we don't see these attributes in humans because we exist under compromising structures. It is capitalism that teaches us to be self-centered and self-serving. This effect of capitalistic structures is why Marx argues that society will go through a transition stage of socialism on its way from capitalism to communism.

Marx's theory of species-being also has implications for knowledge and consciousness. In the primitive society that we've been talking about, humans' knowledge about the world was objective and real; they held ideas that were in perfect harmony with their own nature. According to Marx, human ideas and thought come about in the moment of solving the problem of survival. Humans survive because we creatively produce, and our clearest and most true ideas are grounded in this creative act. In species-being, people become truly conscious of themselves and their ideas. Material production, then, is supposed to be the conduit through which human nature is expressed, and the product ought to act as a mirror that reflects back our own nature.

Let's try an analogy to get at this extremely important issue. There are a limited number of ways you can know how you physically look (video, pictures, portraits, mirrors, and so forth). The function of each of these methods is to represent or reproduce our image with as little distortion as possible. But what if accurate representation was impossible? What if every medium changed your image in some way? We would have no true idea how we physically look. All of our ideas would be false in some way. We would think we see ourselves but we wouldn't. Marx is making this kind of argument, but not about our physical appearance; he's concerned with something much more important and fundamental—our nature as humans. We think we see it, but we don't.

We need to take this analogy one step further: Notice that with mirrors, pictures, and videos, there is a kind of correspondence between the representation and its reality. What I mean is that each of these media presents a visual image, and in the case of our physical appearance, that's what we want. Imagine if you asked someone how you looked and the person played a voice recording for you. That wouldn't make any sense, would it? There would be no correspondence between the mode of representation and the initial presentation. This, too, is what Marx is telling us. If we want to know something about our human nature, if we want to see it represented to us, where should we look? What kind of medium would correspond to our nature? Marx is arguing that every species is defined by its method of survival or existence. Why are whales, lions, and hummingbirds all different? They are different because they have different ways of existing in the world. What makes human beings different from whales, lions, and hummingbirds? Humans have a different mode of existence. We creatively produce what we need—we make products, and we are the only species that does.

So, where should we look to understand our nature? What is the medium that corresponds to the question? If we want to know how we look physically, we look toward visual images. But if we want to know about our nature, we must look to production and everything associated with it. Thus, according to Marx, production is the vehicle through which we can know human nature. However, Marx says that there is something wrong with the medium. Under present conditions (capitalism), it gives a distorted picture of who and what we are.

If we understand this notion of species-being, then almost everything else Marx says falls into place. To understand species-being is to understand alienation (being cut off from our true nature), ideology (ideas not grounded in creative production), false consciousness (self-awareness that is grounded in anything other than creative production), and we can also understand why Marx placed such emphasis on the need for class consciousness in social change. This understanding of human nature is also why Marx is considered an economic determinist. The economy is the substructure from which all other structures (superstructure) of human existence come into being and have relevance.

Material Dialectic

The second key in understanding Marx's theory is the concept of the **material dialectic**, or what is sometimes called dialectical materialism. There are two components to this idea: The first is materialism and it's a statement about human reality. In Marx's time, there were two important ways of understanding the issue of reality: idealism and materialism. *Idealism* posits that reality only exists in our idea of it. While there may indeed be a material world that exists in and of itself, that world exists for humans only as it appears. The world around us is perceived through the senses, but these sense data are structured by innate cognitive categories. Thus, what appears to humans is not the world itself but our idea of it.

On the other hand, *materialism* argues that all reality may be reduced to physical properties. In materialism, our ideas about the world are simple reflections; those ideas are structured by the innate physical characteristics of the universe. Marx feels that both of these extremes do not correctly consider humans as social animals. He proposes another way of understanding reality and consciousness; he terms this way of thinking naturalism, or humanism.

Marx rejects brute materialism out of hand, but he has to consider idealism more carefully. One of idealism's strongest supporters, Georg Wilhelm Friedrich Hegel, died just four years prior to Marx enrolling at the University of Bonn, and at the time, Hegel still held a significant place in the thinking of German philosophers (in fact, Hegel is still a powerful figure in philosophy). Hegel was an idealist and argued that material objects (like a chair or a rock) truly and completely only exist in our concept of them. But Hegel took idealism to another level, using it to argue for the existence of God (the ultimate concept); he argued that the ideal took priority over the material world. According to Hegel, human history is a dialectical unfolding of the Truth that reality consists of ideas and that the material world is nothing more than shadow. This dialectical unfolding ends in the revelation of God.

A **dialectic** contains different elements that are naturally antagonistic to one another; Hegel called them the thesis and antithesis. The dialectic is like an argument or a dialog between elements that are locked together. (The word *dialectic* comes from the Greek word *dialektikos,* meaning discourse or discussion.) For example, to understand "good," you must at the same time understand "bad." To comprehend one, you must understand the other: Good and bad are locked in a continual dialogue. Hegel argued that these kinds of conflicts would resolve themselves into a new element or synthesis, which in turn sets up a new dialectic: Every synthesis contains a thesis that by definition has conflicting elements.

Marx liked the historical process implied in Hegel's dialectic, but he disagreed with its ideational base. Marx, as we have seen, argues that human beings are unique because they creatively produce materials to fill their own material needs. Since the defining feature of humanity is production, not ideas and concepts, then Hegel's notion of idealism is false, and the dialectic is oriented around material production and not ideas—the material dialectic. Thus, the dynamics of the historical dialectic are to be found in the economic system, with each economic system inherently containing antagonistic elements (see Figure 3.1). As the antagonistic elements work themselves out, they form a new economic system.

Notice that the engine of progress according to the dialectic is conflict. For Hegel, ideas resolve themselves and humanity comes closer to the Truth because there is a natural antagonism within the idea itself. Marx of course sees this occurring in material or social relations, so the way societies change and progress is through conflict—the engine of social change is dialectical conflict. Here we see a general point about the conflict/critical model of society, and of course another element in Marx's thinking.

We can think of this way of seeing society as an upheaval model. According to this perspective, society is not like an organism that gradually and peacefully

Figure 3.1   Marx's Material Dialectic

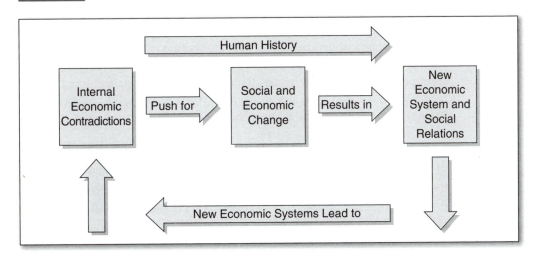

becomes more complex in order to increase its survival chances, as in functionalism. Rather, society is filled with human beings who exercise power to oppress and coerce others. Periods of apparent peace are simply times when the powerful are able to dominate the populace in an efficient manner. But, according to this model, the suppressed will become enabled and will eventually overthrow and change the system. Social change, then, occurs episodically and through social upheaval.

There's an important point here: For Marx, revolution is unavoidable. It is certainly the case that Marx was critical about capitalism because of a personal point of view: He hated the abuses he saw. Remember, at that time governmental controls such as OSHA did not exist and capitalists required their workers to work in abject conditions. But here we can also see a more logical, philosophical reason behind the critical point of view. If history is the result of structural forces locked in a dialectic, then it makes sense and is philosophically consistent to look at society using a conflict perspective.

In mapping out the past of the historical dialectic, Marx categorizes five different economic systems (means of production along with their relations of production): preclass societies, Asiatic societies, ancient societies, feudal societies, and capitalist societies. Preclass societies are like hunter–gatherer groups. These were small groups of people with a minimal division of labor (one that Marx termed the natural division of labor) and communal ownership of property (termed primitive communism). Asiatic societies were a special form in that they had particular problems to overcome due to their large populations. There was thus a tendency to form "oriental despotism" to solve these problems. Ancient societies developed around large urban centers, such as Rome. Private property and slave labor came into existence, as well as significant class inequality. Ancient societies were replaced by feudal systems wherein the primary economic form was serf labor tied to the land of the aristocracy. Feudal systems were replaced by capitalist systems. Eventually, the capitalist system will be replaced by socialism and that by communism. The specific dynamics that Marx says caused these shifts in economic systems are not important in our consideration right now. What is important to see is that for Marx, social change comes about because of inherent contradictions in the economic structure. What this implies is that to think like Marx is to think as a structuralist.

There are a number of *dualisms* in sociology. One of them concerns the tension between agency and structure: How free (agency) are people to be and act apart from social constraints (structure)? As a structuralist, Marx feels that social structures profoundly influence human thought, feelings, and action. Social change comes about not simply because of the free actions of the people, but because of changes in the social structure. These changes are prompted by the dialectical elements within every economic system.

To think like Marx, then, is to be driven by two main ideas. The first is the notion of species-being. Seeing society through this lens means to understand basic human nature as defined through production. It also implies that all true ideas are materially based. If human nature is founded on a unique way of existing in the world through creative production, then our most human (humane and humanistic) ideas must spring from the economy. This means two things. It first implies that true ideas are not abstract concepts with no basis in material reality. Human ideas are grounded and real, if they spring from creative production.

The other implication of this way of understanding consciousness and knowledge concerns false ways of knowing and existing. If ideas come from any other source than creative production, then they are simply counterfeit realities that lead to false consciousness and alienation. We will talk at length about these issues shortly, but for now I want us to see an important repercussion of this concept: To think like Marx means to be concerned about the inner, subjective world that human beings experience.

Marx has often been seen as anti-spiritual. This notion is far from the truth. Marx is deeply concerned with lifting human experience out of the quagmire and placing our feet on higher ground. Species-being implies that humans are altruistic, social beings, but our sociability has been cut off and each person stands alone and naked due to cold capitalistic considerations. Species-being also implies that the individual person is filled with a creative capacity that has been disconnected and denied in the search for profit. Rather than being a cold materialist, Marx gives us a "spiritual existentialism in secular language" (Fromm, 1961, p. 5). To think like Marx, then, is to be critical of humanity's inhumanity. "Marx's philosophy is one of protest; it is a protest imbued with faith in man, in his capacity to liberate himself, and to realize his potentialities" (Fromm, 1961, p. vi).

The second idea that drives Marx's thought is the material dialectic. Thus, to think like Marx also means to think in historical, structural terms. While Marx is overwhelmingly concerned with the authenticity of human experience, he sees that it is the economic structure that moves history and influences our inner person. Society, then, is objective and causative, through the economy and class relations. To think like Marx also means to have a historical perspective. It's easy for us to be weighed down by the demands and problems of our lives. And it is thus easy for us to be concerned only with small segments of time and society. Yet Marxian thought is different; it is bigger. C. Wright Mills (1959) made this distinction clear when he spoke of personal troubles and public issues. He called this point of view the sociological imagination:

> The first fruit of this imagination—and the first lesson of the social science that embodies it—is the idea that the individual can understand his own experience and gauge his own fate only by locating himself within his period, that he can know his own chances in life only by becoming aware of those of all individuals in his circumstances. (p. 5)

Concepts and Theory: Contradictions in Capitalism

Marx forms much of this theory of capitalism in direct contrast to the political economists of his day. For most political economists in Marx's time, commodities, value, profit, private property, and the division of labor were seen as natural effects of social evolution. However, Marx takes a critical perspective and sees these same processes as instruments of oppression that dramatically affect people's life chances.

Value and Exploitation

One of the important issues confronting early political economists concerned the problem of value. We may have a product, such as a car, and that product has value, but from where does its value come? More importantly, why would anybody pay more for the car than it is worth? Well, you say, only a sucker would pay more for a car than it is worth. Yet, as you'll see, there is a way in which we all pay more for every commodity or economic good than it is worth. That was what struck the early economists as a strange problem to be solved.

In order to understand this issue, Adam Smith, an early economist and author of *Inquiry Into the Nature and Causes of the Wealth of Nations* (1776), came up with some useful concepts. He argues that every commodity has at least two different kinds of values: use-value and exchange-value. *Use-value* refers to the actual function that a product contains. This function gets used up as the product is used. Take a bottle of beer, for example. The use-value of a bottle of beer is its taste and alcoholic effect. As we drink the bottle, those functions are expended. Beer also has exchange-value that is distinct from use-value. *Exchange-value* refers to the rate of exchange one commodity bears when compared to other commodities. Let's say I make a pair of shoes. Those shoes could be exchanged for 1 leather-bound book or 5 pounds of fish or 10 pounds of potatoes or 1 cord of oak wood, and so on.

This notion of exchange-value poses a question for us: What do the shoes, books, fish, and potatoes have in common that allow them to be exchanged? I could exchange my pair of shoes for the leather-bound book and then exchange the book for a keg of beer. The keg of beer might have a use-value for me where the leather book does not; nonetheless, they both have exchange-value. This train of exchange could be extended indefinitely with me never extracting any use-value from the products at all, which implies that exchange- and use-value are distinct. So, what is the common denominator that allows these different items to be exchanged? What is the source of exchange-value?

Smith argues, and Marx agrees, that the substance of all value is human labor: "*Labour, therefore, is the real measure of the exchangeable value of all commodities*" (Smith, 1776/1937, p. 30, emphasis added). There is labor involved in the book, the fish, the shoes, the potatoes, and in fact everything that people deem worthy of being exchanged. It is labor, then, that creates exchange-value. If we stop and think for a moment about Marx's idea of species-being, we can see why Smith's notion appealed to him: The value of a product is the "humanness" it contains.

This explanation is termed the *labor theory of value,* and it is the reason why Marx thinks money is so insidious. The book, the shoes, and the potatoes can have exchange-value because of their common feature—human labor. If we then make all those commodities equal to money—the universal value system—then labor is equated with money: "This physical object, gold [or money] . . . becomes . . . the direct incarnation of all human labour" (Marx, 1867/1977, p. 187), which of course adds to the experience of alienation from species-being.

In employing the two terms, Smith tends to collapse them, focusing mainly on exchange-value. Nevertheless, Marx maintains the distinction and argues that the difference between use-value and exchange-value is where profit is found (we pay more for a product than its use-value would indicate). Smith eventually argued that profit is simply added by the capitalist. Profit in Smith's theory thus becomes arbitrary and controlled by the "invisible hand of the market." However, in analyzing value, Marx discovers a particular kind of labor—surplus labor—and argues that profit is better understood as a measurable entity that he calls **exploitation.**

Like Smith, Marx distinguishes between the use-value of a product and its exchange-value in the market. Capital, then, is created by using existing commodities to create a new commodity whose exchange-value is higher than the sum of the original resources used. This situation was odd for Marx. From where did the added value come? His answer, like Smith's original one, is human labor. But he took Smith's argument further. Human labor is a commodity that is purchased for less than its total worth. According to the value theory of labor, the value of any commodity is determined by the labor time necessary for the production or replacement of that commodity. So, what does it cost to produce human labor? The cost is reckoned in terms of the necessities of life: food, shelter, clothing, and so on. Marx also recognizes that a comparative social value has to be added to that list as well. What constitutes a "living wage" will thus be different in different societies. Marx calls the labor needed to pay for the worker's cost of living necessary labor. The issue for Marx is that the cost of necessary labor is less than that of what the worker actually produces.

The capitalist pays less for a day's work than its value. I may receive $75.00 per day to work (determined by the cost to bare sustenance the worker plus any social amenities deemed necessary), but I will produce $200.00 worth of goods or services. The necessary labor in this case is $75.00. The amount of labor left over is the **surplus labor** (in this case, $125.00). The difference between necessary labor and surplus labor is the rate of exploitation. Different societies can have different levels of exploitation. For example, if we compare the situation of automobile workers in the United States with those in Mexico, we will see that the level of exploitation is higher in Mexico (which is why U.S. companies are moving so many jobs out of the country). Surplus labor and exploitation are the places from which profit comes: "The rate of surplus-value is . . . an exact expression for the degree of exploitation . . . of the work by the capitalist" (Marx, 1867/1977, p. 326).

By definition, capitalists are pushed to increase their profit margin and thus the level of surplus labor and the rate of exploitation. There are two main ways in which this can be done: through absolute and relative surplus labor. The capitalist can directly increase the amount of time work is performed by either lengthening the workday, say from ten to twelve hours, or he or she can remove the barriers between "work" and "home," as is happening as a result of increases in communication (computers) and transportation technologies. The product of this lengthening is called absolute surplus labor. The other way a capitalist can increase the rate of exploitation is to reduce the amount of necessary labor time. The result of this move is called relative surplus labor. The most effective way in which this is done is through industrialization. With **industrialization,** the worker works the same number of hours but her or his output is increased through the use of machinery. These different kinds of surplus labors can get a bit confusing, so I've compared them in Figure 3.2.

Figure 3.2 Surplus Labor

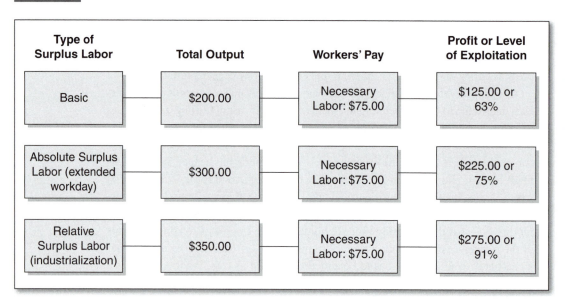

Type of Surplus Labor	Total Output	Workers' Pay	Profit or Level of Exploitation
Basic	$200.00	Necessary Labor: $75.00	$125.00 or 63%
Absolute Surplus Labor (extended workday)	$300.00	Necessary Labor: $75.00	$225.00 or 75%
Relative Surplus Labor (industrialization)	$350.00	Necessary Labor: $75.00	$275.00 or 91%

The figure starts off with the type of surplus labor employed. Since there is always exploitation (you can't have capitalism without it), I've included a "base rate" for the purpose of comparison. Under this scheme, the worker has a total output of $200.00; he or she gets paid $75.00 of the $200.00 produced, which leaves a rate of exploitation of about 63%, or $125.00. The simplest way to increase profit, or the rate of exploitation, is to make the worker work longer hours or take on added responsibilities without raising pay (as a result of downsizing, for example). In our hypothetical case, the wage of $75.00 remains, but the profit margin (rate of exploitation) goes up to 75%. By automating production, the capitalist is able to extract more work from the worker, thus increasing the total output and the level of exploitation (91%). If this seems natural to us (capitalists have a right to make a profit), Marx would say that it is because we have bought into the capitalist ideology. We should also keep in mind that in their search for maintaining or increasing the rate of exploitation, capitalists in industrialized nations export their exploitation—they move jobs to less developed countries.

Industrialization, Markets, and Commodification

As we've seen, capitalists are motivated to increase the level of surplus labor and exploitation, and the most efficient way to accomplish these goals is industrialization. *Industrialization* is the process through which work moves from being performed directly by human hands to having the intermediate force of a machine. Industrialization increases the level of production (by increasing the level of relative surplus labor), which in turn expands the use of markets, because the more product we have, the more points of purchase we need. The relationships among industrialization, production, and markets are reciprocal so that they are mutually reinforcing. If a capitalist comes up with a new "labor-saving" machine, it will increase production, and increased production pushes for new or expanded markets in which to sell the product. These expanding markets also tend to push for increased production and industrialization. Likewise, if a new market opens up through political negotiations (like with Mexico or China, for the United States) or the invention of a new product, there will be a corresponding push for increased production and the search for new machinery.

An important point to note here is that capitalism, to feed the need for continuous capital accumulations, requires expanding markets, which implies that markets and their effects may be seen as part of the dialectic of capitalism. In capitalism, there is always a push to increase profit margins. To increase profits, capitalists can expand their markets horizontally and vertically, in addition to increasing the level of surplus labor. In fact, profit margins would slip if capitalists did not expand their markets. For example, one of the main reasons that you probably have a CD player is that the market for cassette tape players bottomed out (and now there is a push for MP3 and newer technologies). Most people who were going to buy a cassette player had already done so, and the only time another would be purchased is for replacement. So, capitalists invented something new for you to buy so that their profit margin would be maintained.

In general, *markets* refer to an arena in which commodities are exchanged between buyers and sellers. For example, we talk about the grocery market and the money market. These markets are defined by the products they offer and the social network involved. Markets in general have certain characteristics that have consequences for both commodities and people. They are inherently susceptible to expansion (particularly when driven by the capitalist need for profit), abstraction (so we can have markets on markets, like stock market futures or the buying and selling of home mortgage contracts), trade cycles (due to the previous two issues), and undesirable outputs (such as pollution); and they are amoral (so they may be used to sell weapons, religion, or to grant access to health care).

The speed at which goods and services move through markets is largely dependent upon a generalized medium of exchange, something that can act as universal value. Barter is characterized by the exchange of products for one another. The problem with bartering is that it slows down the exchange process because there is no general value system. For example, how much is a keg of beer worth in a barter system? We can't really answer that question because the answer depends on what it is being exchanged for, who is doing the exchanging, what their needs are, where the exchange takes place, and so on. Because of the slowness of bartering, markets tend to push for more generalized means of exchange—such as money. Using money, we can give an answer to the keg question, and having such an answer speeds up the exchange process quite a bit. Marx argues that as markets expand and become more important in a society, and the use of money for equivalency becomes more universal, money becomes more and more the common denominator of *all* human relations. As Marx (1932/1978) says,

> By possessing the *property* of buying everything, by possessing the property of appropriating all objects, *money* is thus the *object* of eminent possession. The universality of its *property* is the omnipotence of its being. It therefore functions as the almighty being. Money is the *pimp* between man's need and

the object, between his life and his means of life. But that which mediates *my* life for me, also *mediates* the existence of other people *for me*. For me it is the *other* person. (p. 102, emphasis original)

The expansive effect of markets on production is called the process of **commodification**. The concept of commodification describes the process through which more and more of the human life-world is turned into something that can be bought or sold. So, instead of creatively producing the world as in species-being, people increasingly buy (and sell) the world in which they live. This process of commodification becomes more and more a feature of human life because it continually expands. Think of a farming family living in the United States around 1850 or so. That family bought some of what they needed, and they bartered for other things, but the family itself produced much of the necessities of life. Today the average American family buys almost everything they want or need. The level of commodification is therefore much higher today.

These three factors, market expansion, industrialization, and commodification, are mutually reinforcing and multiplying—that is, they continue to expand at ever-increasing rates. We have to add one more element to this part of Marx's theory. Modern capitalism is different than any previous type of capitalism. In terms of people making things to sell and get profit, capitalism has been around for ages. Max Weber (Chapter 4) explains how the shift to modern capitalism happened, but for now it's important to know that *modern capitalism is characterized by the endless pursuit of capital.* Capital is defined as resources, usually money, that are invested in order to produce profit that is then reinvested. In other words, capitalists invest capital to get more capital to invest to get more capital, and so on without end. This structured feature of capitalism tends to accelerate the relationships among industrialization, markets, and commodification. But capitalists aren't the only accelerant to this process. One of the more interesting things that Marx points out about human beings is that we have the unusual ability to create their own needs. Animal needs are basically tied to instinct, the natural environment, and survival—but once humans begin to create commodities, we create our own needs (I really do *need* a sub-woofer for my stereo).

Thus, the potential for the production of commodities is endless. There is no natural limit to the ability of humans to create new needs; and there isn't a structure or mechanism in capitalism that will stem the endless pursuit of capital. Taken together, these factors point to what Marx sees as the primary dialectic in capitalism: overproduction. Yet there is one more element we need to bring into this dynamic before putting it all together.

Class and Class Structure

For Marx, class involves two issues: the **means and relations of production**. The means of production refers to the methods and materials that we use to bring into being those things that we need to survive. On a small scale, we might think of the air-hammers, nails, wood, concrete mixers, and so forth that we use to produce a house. Inherent within any means of production are the relations of production: in this case, the contractor, subcontractor, carpenter, financier, buyer, and so forth. In the U.S. economy, we organize the work of building a house through a contracting system. The person who wants the house built has to contract with a licensed builder who in turn hires different kinds of workers (day laborers, carpenters, foremen, etc.). The actual social connections that are created through particular methods of production are what Marx wants us to see in the concept of the relations of production.

Of course, Marx has something much bigger in mind than our example. In classic feudalism, for instance, people formed communities around a designated piece of land and a central manor for provision and security. At the heart of this local arrangement was a noble who had been granted the land from the king in return for political support and military service. At the bottom of the community was the serf. The serf lived on and from the land and was granted protection by the noble in return for service. Feudalism was a political and economic system that centered on land—land ownership was the primary means of production. People were related to the land through oaths of homage and fealty (the fidelity of a feudal tenant to his lord). These relations functioned somewhat like family roles and spelled out normative obligations and rights. The point here, of course, is that the way people related to each other under feudalism was determined by that economic system and was quite different than the way we relate to one another under capitalism: Most of us don't think of our boss as family.

For Marx, human history is the history of **class** struggles. Marx identifies several different types of classes, such as the feudal nobility, the bourgeoisie, the petite bourgeoisie, the proletariat, the peasantry, the subproletariat, and so on. As long as these classes have existed, they have been antagonistic toward each other. Under capitalism, however, two factors create a unique class system. The first thing capitalism does is lift economic work out of all other institutional forms. Under capitalism, the relationships we have with people in the economy are seen as distinctly different from religious, familial, or political relations. For most of human history, all these relationships overlapped. For example, in agriculturally based societies, family and work coincided. Fathers worked at home and all family members contributed to the work that was done. Capitalism lifted this work away from the farm, where work and workers were embedded in family, and placed it in urban-based factories. Capitalist industrialization thus disembedded work from family and social relations. Contemporary gender theorists point out that this movement created dual spheres of home and work, each controlled by a specific gender.

Marx, and more specifically Engels, was actually among the first to write on the issue of gender. In 1877, an American anthropologist, Lewis H. Morgan, published a book that argued for the matrilineal origins of society. Both Marx and Engels felt that this was a significant discovery. Marx planned on writing a thesis based on Morgan's work and made extensive notes along those lines. Marx never finished the work. Friedrich Engels, however, using Marx's notes, did publish *The Origin of the Family, Private Property, and the State* in 1884. The argument is fairly simple, yet it presents one of the basic ways in which we understand how gender inequality and the oppression of women came about.

As with all of Marx and Engels' work, Engels begins with a conception of primitive communist beginnings. In this setting, people lived communally, sharing everything, with monogamy rarely, if ever, practiced. Under such conditions, family is a social concern rather than a private issue, with children being raised by the community at large, rather than by only two parents. As a matter of fact, because identifying the father with any certainty was impossible in pre-modern society, paternity itself wasn't much of an issue. Thus, in Marx's way of thinking, "The communistic household implies the supremacy of women" (Engels, 1884/1978, p. 735).

The key in the transition from matrilineal households to patriarchy is wealth. Primitive societies generally lived "from hand to mouth," but as surplus began to be available, it became possible to accumulate. As men began to control this wealth, it was in their best interest to control inheritance, which meant controlling lineage. Engels (1884/1978) says that the way this happened is lost in prehistory, but the effect "was the *world-historic defeat of the female sex*" (p. 736, emphasis original). In order to control the inheritance of wealth, men had to control fertilization and birth, which meant that men had to have power over women. Control over women's sexuality and childbirth is why, according to Engels, we have developed a dual morality around gender—women are considered sluts but men are studs if they sleep around. Marriage, monogamy, and the paired family (husband and wife) were never intended to control men's sexuality. They were created to control women's sexuality in order to assure paternity. This control, of course, implied the control of the woman's entire life. She became the property of the man so the man could control his property (wealth). Quoting Marx, Engels (1884/1978a) concludes, "The modern family contains in embryo not only slavery . . . . It contains within itself in *miniature* all the antagonisms which later develop on a wide scale within society and its state" (p. 737, emphasis original).

The second unique feature of class under capitalism is that it tends to be structured around two positions—the bourgeoisie (owners) and the proletariat (workers). Marx does talk about other classes in capitalism, but they have declining importance. The petite bourgeoisie is the class of small land and business owners and the lumpenproletariat is the underclass (like the homeless). While the lumpenproletariat played a class-like position in early French history, Marx argues that because they have no relationship to economic production at all, they will become less and less important in the dynamics of capitalism. The petite bourgeoisie, on the other hand, does constitute a legitimate class in capitalism. However, this class shrinks in number and becomes less and less important, as they are bought out and pushed aside by powerful capitalists, as a result of the capitalist investment cycle.

As capitalists reinvest capital, the demand for labor goes up (as the labor theory of value would predict). The increased demand for labor causes the labor pool, the number of unemployed, to shrink. As with any commodity, when demand is greater than the supply, the price goes up—in this case wages. The increase in wages causes profits to go down. As profits go down, capitalists cut back production, which precipitates a crisis in the economy. The crisis causes more workers to be laid off and small businesses (the petite bourgeoisie) to fold. These small businesses are bought out by the larger capitalists and the once small-scale capitalists become part of the working class. The result of this process being repeated over time is that the class of dependent workers increases and capital is centralized into fewer and fewer hands.

Thus, the existing capitalists accumulate additional capital and the entire cycle starts again. "But not only has the bourgeoisie forged the weapons that bring death to itself; it has also called into existence the men who are to wield those weapons—the modern working class—the proletariat" (Marx & Engels, 1848/1978, p. 478).

The *bipolarization of conflict* is a necessary step for Marx in the process of social change, and an important one for conflict theory as a whole. Overt and intense conflict are both dependent upon bipolarization; crosscutting interests, that is, having more than one issue over which groups are in conflict, tend to pull resources (emotional and material) away from conflict. For example, during World War II it was necessary for the various nations to coalesce into only two factions, the Axis and the Allied powers. So the United States became strange bedfellows with the Soviet Union in order to create large-scale, intense conflict. Note that each time the United States has engaged in a police action or war, attempts are made to align resources in as few camps as possible. This move isn't simply a matter of world opinion; it is a structural necessity for violent and overt conflict. The lack of bipolarized conflict creates an arena of crosscutting interests that can drain resources and prevent the conflict from escalating and potentially resolving.

Overproduction

We're now in a position to bring all these factors together. I've diagramed these relationships in Figure 3.3. Note that the plus (+) signs indicate a positive relationship (both variables move in the same direction, either more or less) and the minus (−) signs indicate negative relationships (the variables go in opposite directions). Starting at the far left, the defining feature of modern capitalism (incessant accumulation of capital) is the primary dynamic. As capitalists invest, markets, industrialization, and employment all go up. Notice that all the arrows are double-headed, which means these all mutually influence one another. Industrialization, markets, and employment all produce profit that is then reinvested in those same three factors. Also notice the possible limit of markets is linked to our ability to create our own needs. Markets and human "need" feed off each other. It's also important to note that markets don't simply expand; they can become more abstract. Such markets are the ones associated with the speculation that has been endemic in the world stock markets.

The effects of these first four factors continue to feed one another creating ever increasing levels of commodity production until a threshold is reached—**overproduction**—and there's too much production for the current demand. Since capital accumulation is a structural part of capitalism, capitalists will continue to create new and produce existing commodities until the market will no longer bear it. When this happens, production is cut back, workers are laid off, and the economy slumps. Small businesses collapse and capital is concentrated in fewer hands; capital is thus accumulated and the failures of small businesses push toward the bipolarization of classes. With the renewed accumulation of capital, capitalists reinvest and the market picks back up; and the cycle starts again. However, each economic cycle is larger and deeper than the previous and the working class becomes larger and larger. In the end, Marx argues, this process of accumulation and overproduction will lead to the collapse of capitalism, because

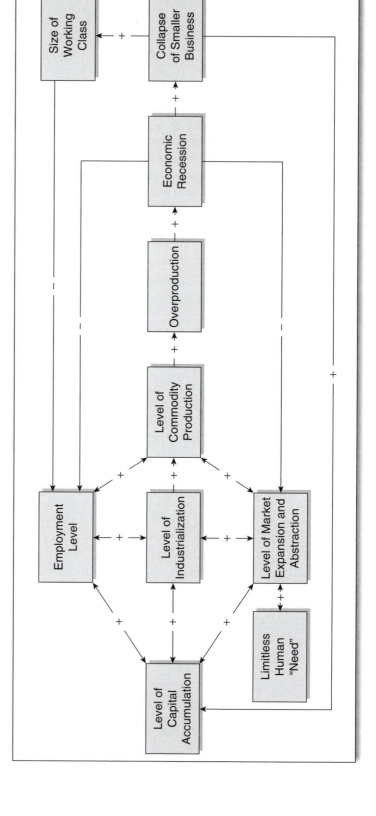

Figure 3.3 Overproduction Cycle

there are no natural limits: "The development of Modern Industry, therefore, cuts from under its feet the very foundation on which the bourgeoisie produces and appropriates products. What the bourgeoisie, therefore, produces, above all, is its own grave-diggers" (Marx & Engels, 1848/1978, p. 483).

Concepts and Theory: The Problem of Consciousness

We arrive at the result that man (the worker) feels himself to be freely active only in his animal functions—eating, drinking, and procreating, or at most also in his dwelling and in personal adornment—while in his human functions he is reduced to an animal. The animal becomes human and the human becomes animal.

—Marx, 1932/1995, p. 99

Marx's theory is clearly structural: The dialectical elements within the economic structure are what bring about change. However, there is something that can impede or facilitate change: human consciousness. As I noted in the beginning of this chapter, one of the most powerful elements of Marx's theory is that he connects a person's social position with her or his knowledge and awareness of the world. And, Marx gave us a material basis for consciousness. Human consciousness, that awareness that makes us unique in the animal world, comes out of our innate ability to economically produce. Putting these ideas together, the things that we think and "know to be true" are in fact a reflection of our place in the economic food chain. As such, the things we're aware of may be false; and we may believe some things that in the end are hurtful for us and work to oppress rather than liberate.

Alienation, Private Property, and Commodity Fetish

We often think of alienation as the subjective experience of a worker on an assembly line or at McDonald's. This perception is partly true. To get a little better handle on it, however, let's think about the differences between a gunsmith and a worker in a Remington plant. The gunsmith is a craftsperson and would make every part of the gun by hand—all the metal work, all the woodwork, everything. If you knew guns, you could tell the craftsperson just by looking at the gun. It would bare the person's mark because part of the craftsperson was in the work, and the gunsmith would take justifiable pride in the piece.

Compare that experience to the Remington plant worker. Perhaps she is the person who bolts the plastic end piece on the butt of the rifle, and she performs the task on rifle after rifle, day after day. It won't take long until the work becomes mind numbing. It is repetitive and non-creative. Chances are, this worker won't feel the pride of the craftsperson but will instead experience disassociation and depression. We can see in this example some of the problems associated with a severe division of labor and over-control of the worker. There's no ownership of the product or pride as there is in craftsmanship. We can also see how the same issues would apply to the worker at McDonald's. All of it is mind-numbing, depressive work, and much of it is the result of the work of scientific management.

Frederick Taylor was the man who applied the scientific method to labor. He was interested in finding the most efficient way to do a job. Efficiency here is defined in terms of the least amount of work for the greatest amount of output. Under this system, the worker becomes an object that is directly manipulated for efficiency and profit. Taylor would go out into the field and find the best worker. He and his team would then time the worker (this is the origin of time-management studies) and break the job down into its smallest parts. In the end, Taylorism created a high division of labor, assembly lines, and extremely large factories.

The problem with understanding our Remington and McDonald's examples as alienation is that it focuses on the subjective experience of the worker. It implies that if we change the way we control workers—say from Taylorism to Japanese management, as many American companies have—we've solved the problem of alienation. For Marx, that wouldn't be the case. While alienation implies the subjective experience of the worker (depression and disassociation), it is more accurate to think of it as an objective state. So workers under the Japanese system are not structurally *less* alienated because they are more broadly trained, are able to rotate jobs, work holistically, and have creative input. Workers *are* alienated under all forms of capitalism, whether they feel it or not. Alienation is a structural condition, not a personal one. Workers are of course more likely to revolt if they experience alienation, but that is a different issue.

Alienation always exists when someone other than the worker owns the means of production and the product itself. Having said that, we can note that Marx actually talked about four different kinds of alienation. Alienation in its most basic sense is separation from one's own awareness of being human. We know we are human; Marx doesn't mean to imply that we don't have the idea of being human. What he means is that our idea is wrong or inaccurate. Recall Marx's argument of species-being: That which makes us distinctly human is creative production, and we become aware of our humanity as our nature is clearly reflected back to us by the mirror of the produced world. At best, the image is distorted if we look to see our nature in the things we own. It's the right place to look, but according to Marx, products should be the natural expression of species-being and production should result in true consciousness. The commodity itself does not reflect humanity, and thus, everything about our commodities is wrong. At worst, the image is simply false. Marx argues that if we look elsewhere for our definition and knowledge of human nature (such as using language; having emotions; possessing a soul, religion, rationality, free-will, and so on), it is not founded on the essential human characteristic—free and creative production. Thus, the human we see is rooted in false consciousness.

From this basic alienation, three other forms are born: alienation from the work process, alienation from the product itself, and alienation from other people. In species-being, there is not only the idea of the relationship between consciousness and creative production, there is also the notion that human beings are related to one another directly and intimately through species-being. We don't create a human world individually; it is created collectively. Therefore, under conditions of species-being, humans are intimately and immediately connected to one another. The reflected world around them is the social, human world that they created. Imagine, if you can, a world of products that are all directly connected to human beings (not market forces, advertising, the drive for profit, and so forth). Either you made everything in that world or you know who did. When you see a product, you see yourself or you see your neighbor or your neighbor's friend. Thus, when we are alienated from our own species-being, because someone else controls the means and ends of production, we are estranged from other humans as well.

Finally, of course, we are alienated from the process of work and from the product itself. There is something essential in the work process, according to Marx. The kind of work we perform and how we perform that work determines the kind of person we are. Obviously, doctors are different from garbage collectors, but that isn't what Marx has in mind. An individual's humanity is rooted in the work process. When humans are cut off from controlling the means of production (the way in which work is performed and for what reason), then the labor process itself becomes alienated. There are three reasons for this alienated labor, which end in the alienation of the product. First, when someone else owns the means of production, the work is external to the worker; that is, it is not a direct expression of his or her nature. So, rather than being an extension of the person's inner being, work becomes something external and foreign. Second, work is forced. People don't work because they want to; they work because they have to—under capitalism, if you don't work you die. Concerning labor under capitalism Marx (1932/1995) says, "Its alien character is clearly shown by the fact that as soon as there is no physical or other compulsion it is avoided like the plague" (pp. 98–99). And third, when we do perform the work, the thing that we produce is not our own; it belongs to another person.

Further, alienation, according to Marx, is the origin of private property—it exists solely because we are cut off from our species-being; someone else owns the means and ends of production. Underlying markets and commodification—and capitalism itself—is the institution of private property. Marx felt that the political economists of his day assumed the fact of private property without offering any explanation for it. These economists believed that private property was simply a natural part of the economic process. But for Marx, the source of private property was the crux of the problem. Based on species-being, Marx argues that private property emerged out of the alienation of labor.

Marx also argues that there is a reciprocal influence of private property on the experience of alienation. As we have seen, Marx claims that **private property** is the result of alienated labor. Once private property exists, it can then exert its own influence on the worker and it becomes "the realization of this alienation" (Marx, 1932/1995, p. 106). Workers then become controlled by private property. This notion is most clearly seen in what Marx describes as *commodity fetish:* Workers become infatuated with their own product as if it were an alien thing. It confronts them not as the work of their hands, but as a commodity, something alien to them that they must buy and appropriate.

Commodity fetish is a difficult notion and it is hard to come up with an illustration. Workers create and produce the product, yet we don't recognize our work or ourselves in the product. So we see it outside of us and we fall in love with it. We have to possess it, not realizing that it is ours already by its very nature. We think *it,* the object, will satisfy our needs, when what we need is to find ourselves in creative production and a socially connected world. We go from sterile object to sterile object, seeking satisfaction, because they all leave us empty. To use a science fiction example, it's like a male scientist who creates a female robot, but then forgets he created it, falls in love with it, and tries to buy its affection through money. As I said, it is a difficult concept to illustrate because in this late stage of capitalism, *our entire world and way of living are the examples.* In commodity fetish, our perception of self-worth is linked with money and objects in a vicious cycle.

In addition, in commodity fetish we fail to recognize—or in Marxian terms, we **misrecognize**—that there are sets of oppressive social relations in back of both the perceived need for and the simple exchange of money for a commodity. We think that the value of the commodity is simply its intrinsic worth—that's just how much a Calvin Klein jacket is worth—when, in fact, hidden labor relations and exploitation produce its value. We come to need these products in an alienated way: We think that owning the product will fulfill our needs. The need is produced through the commodification process, and in back of the exchange itself are relations of oppression. In this sense, the commodity becomes reified: It takes on a sense of reality that is not materially real at all.

Contemporary Marxists argue that the process of commodification affects every sphere of human existence and is the "central, structural problem of capitalist society in all its aspects" (Lukács, 1922/1971, p. 83). Commodification translates *all human activity and relations* into objects that can be bought or sold. In this process, value is determined not by any intrinsic feature of the activity or the relations, but by the impersonal forces of markets, over which individuals have no control. In this expanded view of commodification, the objects and relations that will truly gratify human needs are hidden, and the commodified object is internalized and accepted as reality. So, for example, a young college woman may internalize the commodified image of thinness and create an eating disorder such as anorexia nervosa that rules her life and becomes unquestionably real. Commodification, then, results in a consciousness based on reified, false objects. It is difficult to think outside this commodified box. There is, in fact, a tendency to justify and rationalize our commodified selves and behaviors.

False Consciousness and Religion

Alienation, false consciousness, and ideology go hand in hand. In place of a true awareness of species-being comes **false consciousness**, consciousness built on any foundation other than free and creative production. Humans in false consciousness thus come to think of themselves as defined through the ability to have ideas, concepts, and abstract thought, rather than production. When these ideas are brought together in some kind of system, Marx considers them to be ideology. Ideas function as ideology when they are perceived as independent entities that transcend historical, economic relations: Ideologies contain beliefs that we hold to be true and right, regardless of the time or place (like the value of hard work and just reward). In the main, ideologies serve to either justify current power arrangements (patriarchy) or to legitimate social movements (like feminism) that seek to change the structure.

Though Marx sometimes appears to use the terms interchangeably, in some ways I think it is important to keep the distinction between false consciousness and ideology clear. **Ideologies** can change and vary. For example, the ideology of consumerism is quite different than the previous ideologies of the work ethic and frugality, yet they are all capitalist ideologies. The ideologies behind feminism are different than the beliefs behind the racial equality movement, yet from Marx's position, both are ideologies that blind us to the true structure of inequality: class. Yet false consciousness doesn't vary. It is a state of being, somewhat like alienation in this aspect. We are by definition in a state of false consciousness because we are living outside of species-being. The very way through which we are aware of ourselves and the world around us is false or dysfunctional. The very method of our consciousness is fictitious.

Generally speaking, false consciousness and ideology are structurally connected to two social factors: religion and the division of labor. For Marx, *religion* is the archetypal form of ideology. Religion is based on an abstract idea, like God, and religion takes this abstract idea to be the way through which humans can come to know their true nature. For example, in the evangelical Christian faith, believers are exhorted to repent from not only their sinful ways but also their sinful nature and to be born again with a new nature—the true nature of humankind. Christians are thus encouraged to become Christ-like because they have been created in the image of God. Religion, then, reifies thought, according to Marx. It takes an abstract (God), treating it as if it is materially real, and it then replaces species-being with non-materially based ideas (becoming Christ-like). It is, for Marx, a never-ending reflexive loop of abstraction, with no basis in material reality whatsoever. Religion, like the commodity fetish, erroneously attributes reality and causation. We pour ourselves out, this time into a religious idea, and we misrecognize our own nature as that of god or devil.

> [I]t is clear that the more the worker spends himself, the more powerful the alien objective world becomes which he creates over-against himself, the poorer he himself—his inner world—becomes, the less belongs to him as his own. The more man puts into God, the less he retains in himself. (Marx, 1932/1978, p. 72)

There is also a second sense in which religion functions as ideology. Marx uses the term ideology as *apologia,* or a defense of one's own ideas, opinions, or action. In this kind of ideology, the orientation and beliefs of a single class, the elite, become generalized and seem to be applicable to all classes. Here the issue is not so much reification as class consciousness. The problem in **reification** is that we accept something as real that isn't. With ideology, the problem is that we are blinded to the oppression of the class system. This is in part what Marx means when he claims that religion is "the opium of the people." As we have seen, Marx argues that because most people are cut off from the material means of production, they misrecognize their true class position and the actual class-based relationships, as well as the effects of class position. In the place of class consciousness, people accept an ideology. For Marx, religion is the handmaiden of the elite; it is a principal vehicle for transmitting and reproducing the capitalist ideology.

Thus, in the United States we tend to find a stronger belief in American ideological concepts (such as meritocracy, equal opportunity, work ethic, poverty as the result of laziness, free enterprise, and so on) among the religious (particularly among the traditional American denominations). We would also expect to see religious people being less concerned with the social foundations of inequality and more concerned with patience in this life and rewards in the next. These kinds of beliefs, according to Marx, dull the workers' ability to institute social change and bring about real equality.

It is important to note that this is a function of religion in general, not just American religion. The Hindu caste system in India is another good example. There are five different castes in the system: Brahmin (priests and teachers), Kshatriya (rulers), Vaishya (merchants and farmers), Shudra (laborers and servants), and Harijans (polluted laborers, the outcastes). Position in these different castes is a result of birth; birth position is based on karma (action); and karma is based on dharma (duty). There is virtually no social mobility among the castes. People are taught to accept their position in life and perform the duty (dharma) that their caste dictates so that their actions (karma) will be morally good. This ideological structure generally prevents social change, as does the Christian ideology of seeking rewards in heavenly places.

For Marx, then, religion simultaneously represents the furthest reach of humanity's misguided reification and functions to blind people to the underlying class conditions that produce their suffering. Yet Marx (1844/1979) also recognizes that those sufferings are articulated in religion as the sigh of the oppressed: "*Religious* suffering is at the same time an *expression* of real suffering and a *protest* against real suffering. Religion is the sigh of the oppressed creature, the sentiment of a heartless world, and the soul of soulless conditions. It is the *opium* of the people" (p. 54, emphasis original). Marx thus recognizes that religion also gives an outlet to suffering. He feels that religion places a "halo" around the "veil of tears" that is present in the human world. The tears are there because of the suffering that humans experience when they don't live communally and cooperatively. Marx's antagonism toward religion, then, is not directed at religion and God per se, but at "the *illusory* happiness of men" that religion promises.

Most if not all of Marx's writings on religion were in response to already existing critiques (mostly from Georg Hegel and Ludwig Feuerbach). Marx, then, takes the point of view that "the criticism of religion has largely been completed." What Marx is doing is critiquing the criticism. He is responding to already established ideas about religion, not religion itself necessarily. What Marx wants to do is to push us to see that the real issue isn't religion; it is the material, class-based life of human beings that leads to actual human suffering.

In keeping with that notion, a school of contemporary Marxism, *Humanistic Marxism,* most notably the area of Liberation Theology, sees religion as an agent of social change. Liberation theologians argue that there are two poles of Christian expression. The one pole is the classic ideological version, where religion serves to maintain the establishment. The other pole emphasizes compassion for the human condition and leadership in social change. The first gives importance to the "meek and mild Jesus" who taught that the proper response to oppression was to turn the other cheek. The second stresses the Christ in the temple who in rage overturned the tables of the moneychangers and drove them out with a whip. So, there are some Marxists that argue that religion can function as an agent of social change, but that kind of religion is very specific and is not encountered very often.

Marx also sees ideology and alienation as structurally facilitated by the **division of labor** (how the duties are assigned in any society). Marx talks about several different kinds of divisions of labor. The most primitive form of separation of work is the "natural division of labor." The natural division was based upon the individual's natural abilities and desires. People did not work at something for which they were ill suited, nor did they have to work as individuals in order to survive. Within the natural division of labor, survival is a group matter, not an individual concern. Marx claims that the only time this ever existed was in preclass societies. When individuals within a society began to accumulate goods and exercise power, the "forced division of labor" replaced the natural division. With the forced division individual people must work in order to survive (sell their labor) and they are forced to work at jobs they neither enjoy nor have the natural gifts to perform. The forced division of labor and the commodification of labor characterize capitalism.

This primary division of labor historically becomes extended when mental labor (such as that performed by professors, priests, philosophers) is divided from material labor (workers). When this happens, reification, ideology, and alienation reach new heights. As we've seen, Marx argues that people have true consciousness only under conditions of species-being. Anytime people are removed from controlling the product or the production process, there will be some level of false consciousness and ideology. Even so, workers who actually produce a material good are in some way connected to the production process. However, with the separation of mental from material labor, even this tenuous relationship to species-being is cut off. Thus, the thought of those involved with mental labor is radically cut off from what makes us human (species-being). As a result, everything produced by professors, priests, philosophers, and so on has some reified ideological component and is generally controlled by the elite.

Class Consciousness

So far we have seen that capitalism increases the levels of industrialization, exploitation, market-driven forces such as commodification, false consciousness, ideology, and reification, and it tends to bifurcate the class structure. On the other hand, Marx also argues that these factors have dialectical effects and will thus push capitalism inexorably toward social change. Conflict and social change begin with a change in the way we are aware of our world. It begins with **class consciousness**.

Marx notes that classes exist objectively, whether we are aware of them or not. He refers to this as a "class in itself," that is, an aggregate of people who have a common relationship to the means of production. But classes can also exist subjectively as a "class *for* itself." It is the latter that is produced through class consciousness. Class consciousness has two parts: The subjective awareness that experiences of deprivation are determined by structured class relations and not individual talent and effort, and the group identity that comes from such awareness.

Industrialization has two main lines of effects when it comes to class consciousness. First, it tends to increase exploitation and alienation. We've talked about both of these already, but remember that these are primarily objective states for Marx. In other words, these aren't necessarily subjectively felt—alienation isn't chiefly a feeling of being psychologically disenfranchised; it is the state of being cut off from species-being. Humans can be further alienated and exploited, and machines do a good job of that. What happens at this point in Marx's scheme is that these objective states can produce a sense (or feeling) of belonging to a group that is disenfranchised, that is, class consciousness.

As you can see from Figure 3.4, industrialization has positive relationships with both exploitation and alienation. As capitalists employ machinery to aid in labor, the objective levels of alienation and exploitation increase. As the objective levels increase, so does the probability that workers will subjectively experience them,

Figure 3.4 The Production of Class Consciousness

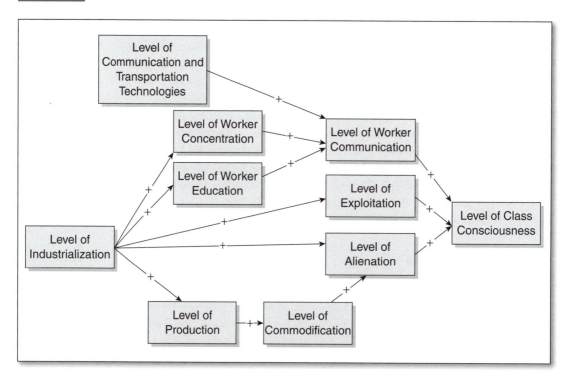

thus aiding in the production of class consciousness. Keep in mind that industrialization is a variable, which means that it can increase (as in when robots do the work that humans once did on the assembly line—there is a human controlling that robot, but far, far removed from the labor of production) or decrease (as when "cottage industries" spring up in an economy).

The second area of effect is an increase in the level of worker communication. Worker communication is a positive function of education and ecological concentration. Using machines—and then more *complex* machines—requires increasing levels of technical knowledge. A crude but clear example is the different kinds of knowledge needed to use a horse and plow compared to a modern tractor. Increasing the use of technology in general requires an increase in the education level of the worker (this relationship is clearly seen in today's computer-driven U.S. labor market).

In addition, higher levels of industrialization generally increase the level of worker concentration. Moving workers from small guild shops to large-scale machine shops or assembly lines made interaction between these workers possible in a way never before achievable, particularly during break and lunch periods when hundreds of workers can gather in a single room. Economies of scale tend to increase this concentration of the workforce as well. So for a long time in the United States, we saw ever-bigger factories being built and larger and larger office buildings (like the Sears Tower and World Trade Center—and it is significant that terrorists saw the World Trade Center as representative of American society). These two processes, education and ecological concentration, work together to increase the level of communication among workers. These processes are supplemented through greater levels of communication and transportation technologies. Marx argues that communication and transportation would help the worker movement spread from city to city.

So, in general, class consciousness comes about as workers communicate with each other about the problems associated with being a member of the working class (like not being able to afford medication). The key to Marx's thinking here is to keep in mind that these things come about due to structural changes brought about simply because of the way capitalism works. Capitalists are driven to increase profits. As a result, they use industrialization, which sets in motion a whole series of processes that tend to increase the class consciousness of the workers. Class consciousness increases the probability of social change. As workers share their grievances with one another, they begin to doubt the legitimacy of the distribution of scarce resources, which in turn increases the level of overt conflict. As class inequality and the level of bipolarization increase, the violence of the conflict will tend to increase, which in turn brings about deeper levels of social change.

However, class consciousness has been difficult to achieve. There are a number of reasons given as to why this is true, but many Marxist approaches focus on the relationships among a triad of actors: the state, the elite, and workers. Marx felt that as a result of the rise of class consciousness, and other factors such as the business cycle, workers would unite and act through labor unions to bring about change. Some of the work of the unions would be violent, but it would eventually lead to a successful social movement. In the end, the labor movement would bring about socialism.

Marx sees two of the actors in the triad working in collusion. He argues that under capitalism, the state is basically an arm of the elite. It is controlled by capitalists and functions with capitalist interests in mind. Many of the top governing officials come from the same social background as the bourgeoisie. A good example of this in the United States is the Bush family. Of course, electing a member of the capitalist elite to high public office not only prejudices the state toward capitalist interests, it is also an indicator of how ideologically bound a populace is.

In addition, as C. W. Mills (1956) argues, the elite tend to cross over, with military men serving on corporate boards and as high-placed political appointees, and CEOs functioning as political advisees and cabinet members, and so on. A notable example of these kinds of interconnections is Charles Erwin Wilson, president of General Motors from 1941 to 1953. He was appointed Secretary of Defense under President Dwight D. Eisenhower. At his senate confirmation hearing, Wilson spoke the words that epitomize the power elite: "For years, I thought what was good for our country was good for General Motors—and vice versa."

In response to the demands of labor unions, certain concessions were ultimately granted to the working and middle classes. Work hours were reduced and healthcare provided, and so forth. Capitalists working together with a capitalist-privileging state granted those concessions. Thus, even when allowances are granted, they may function in the long run to keep the system intact by maintaining the capitalists' position, silencing the workers, and preventing class consciousness from adequately forming.

The state is also active in the production of ideology. Marx sees the state as somewhat ill-defined. In other words, where the state begins and ends under capitalist democracy is hard to say. The state functions through many other institutions, such as public schools, and its ideology is propagated through such institutions, not only through such direct means as the forced pledge of allegiance in the United States but also through indirect control measures like specific funding initiatives. A good deal of the state's ideology is, of course, capitalist ideology. As a result, the worker is faced with a fairly cohesive ideology coming from various sources. This dominant ideology creates a backdrop of taken-for-grantedness about the way the world works, against which it is difficult to create class consciousness.

The movement of capitalist exploitation across national boundaries, which we mentioned before, accentuates the "trickle-down" effect of capitalism in such countries as the United States. Because workers in other countries are being exploited, the workers in the United States can be paid an inflated wage (inflated from the capitalists' point of view). This is functional for capitalism in that it provides a collection of buyers for the world's goods and services. Moving work out from the United States and making it the world's marketplace also changes the kind of ideology or culture that is needed. There is a movement from worker identities to consumer identities in such economies.

In addition, capitalists use this world labor market to pit workers against one another. While wages are certainly higher due to exported exploitation, workers are also aware that their jobs are in jeopardy as work is moved out of the country. Capitalism always requires a certain level of unemployment. The business cycle teaches us this—that zero unemployment means higher wages and lower profits. The world labor market makes available an extremely large pool of unemployed workers. So, workers in an advanced industrialized economy see themselves in competition with much cheaper labor. This global competition also hinders class consciousness by shifting the worker's focus of attention away from the owners and onto the foreign labor market. In other words, a globalized division of labor pits worker against worker in competition for scarce jobs. This competition is particularly threatening for workers in advanced capitalist countries, like the United States, because the foreign workers' wage is so much lower. These threatened workers, then, will be inclined to see their economic problems in terms of global, political issues rather than class issues.

Further, the workers divide themselves over issues other than class. We tend to see ourselves not through class-based identities, which Marx would argue is the identity that determines our life chances; instead, we see ourselves through racial, ethnic, gender, and sexual preference identities. Marxists would argue that the culture of diversity and victimhood is part of the ideology that blinds our eyes to true social inequality, thus preventing class consciousness.

Summary

- Marx's perspective is created through two central ideas: species-being and the material dialectic. Species-being refers to the unique way in which humans survive as a species—we creatively produce all that we need. The material dialectic is the primary mechanism through which history progresses. There are internal contradictions within every economic system that push society to form new economic systems. The dialectic continues until communism is reached, a system that is in harmony with species-being.

- Every economic system is characterized by the means and relations of production. The means of production in capitalism is owned by the bourgeoisie and generally consists of commodification, industrial production, private property, markets, and money. One of the unique features of capitalism is that it will swallow up all other classes save two: the bourgeoisie and proletariat. This bifurcation of class structure will, in turn, set the stage for class consciousness and economic revolution.

- Capitalism affects every area of human existence. Through it, individuals are alienated from each aspect of species-being and creative production. The work process, the product, other people, and even their own inner being confront the worker as alien objects. As a result, humankind misrecognizes the truth and falls victim to commodity fetish, ideology, and false consciousness. However, because capitalism contains dialectical elements, it will also produce the necessary ingredient for economic revolution: class consciousness. Class consciousness is the result of workers becoming aware that their fate in life is determined primarily by class position. This awareness comes as alienation and exploitation reach high levels and as workers communicate with one another through increasing levels of education, worker concentration in the factory and city, and communication and transportation technologies.

TAKING THE PERSPECTIVE—CONFLICT AND CRITICAL THEORY

A knowledge of the writings of Marx and Engels is virtually indispensable to an educated person in our time. . . . For classical Marxism . . . has profoundly affected ideas about history, society, economics, ideology, culture, and politics; indeed, about the nature of social inquiry itself. . . . Not to be well grounded in the writings of Marx and Engels is to be insufficiently attuned to modern thought, and self-excluded to a degree from the continuing debate by which most contemporary societies live insofar as their members are free and able to discuss the vital issues.

—Tucker, 1978, p. ix

The above quote isn't exaggerated in the least, especially when it comes to contemporary social and sociological theories. A good way to talk about his influence is to see that Marx made two kinds of arguments, one philosophical and the other structural. Marx's structural argument was based on his view of history. The engine of history—the dynamic that brings historical change—is the dialectic inherent in noncommunistic economic forms. This is decidedly a structuralist argument: The dynamics of social structures bring about change. And it's also a conflict model: The structural system is built around conflict. Marx's structural argument, then, is the basis for modern conflict theory.

In general, *conflict theory* seeks to scientifically explain the general contours of conflict in society: how conflict starts and varies, and the effects it brings. Conflict theorists generally see power as the central feature of society, rather than thinking of society as held together by collective agreement over a cohesive set of cultural standards, as do functionalists. We have several conflict theorists in this book: Max Weber (Chapter 4), Lewis Coser (Chapter 9), Ralf Dahrendorf (Chapter 9), Randall Collins (Chapter 9), William Julius Wilson (Chapter 10), and Janet Saltzman Chafetz (Chapter 10). There are others that might be classified as a conflict theorist, but they are sufficiently different to be considered independently. Conflict theory is generally oriented toward a structural analysis of social inequality. This perspective assumes that structures are objective entities that operate according to their own laws. The goal of conflict theory, then, is to discover those laws and principles. Additionally, conflict theorists argue that modern society is structured around the unequal distribution of scarce resources and that patterned competition and social conflict are ubiquitous and are the primary mechanisms of social change. Social change, then, comes as a result of upheaval rather than slow evolution.

Critical theory, on the other hand, is indebted to the philosophical Marx. It focuses on the ways in which human consciousness is formed and influenced. Critical theory gives us an opportunity to see the importance of the values or purposes of sociological work. The key assumption is that many of the factors are hidden, especially in capitalist societies. Rather than focusing on social structures as conflict theory does, critical theory looks to culture and the production of and indoctrination in knowledge. Of particular importance are such cultural systems as art, mass media, advertising, science, and the human disciplines (sociology included). In critical theory, all knowledge/culture is tied to history and social position and is more a reflection of a society's power relations than a pure reflection of reality. These main ideas originated with Marx and were initially developed by the Frankfurt School (Chapter 13). In the latter part of the twentieth century, critical theory—especially when linked to literary criticism, race, gender, or sex—has dramatically impacted almost every discipline in the social sciences and humanities. Generally speaking, there are five characteristics of critical theory: a critique of positivism and the idea that knowledge can be value-free; an emphasis on the relationship between history and society on the one hand, and social position and knowledge on the other; the need for praxis or emancipatory practices; and a desire for participatory democracy. We'll explicitly consider critical theory in Chapter 13. But the approach is more widespread than the Frankfurt School, and we'll consider different sorts of critical theorizing in most of the theories after Chapter 13.

BUILDING YOUR THEORY TOOLBOX

Learning More—Primary and Secondary Sources

- For a primary source for Marx, it is best to start off with a reader. Here's my favorite:
  - Tucker, R. C. (Ed.). (1978). *The Marx–Engels Reader.* New York: W.W. Norton.
- There are many good secondary sources for Marx. The following are a few of the good ones to start with:
  - Appelbaum, R. P. (1988). *Karl Marx.* Newbury Park, CA: Sage. (Part of the *Masters of Social Theory* series; short, book-length introduction to Marx's life and work)
  - Bottomore, T., Harris, L., & Miliband, R. (Eds.). (1992). *The Dictionary of Marxist Thought* (2nd ed.). Cambridge, MA: Blackwell. (Excellent dictionary reference to Marxist thought)
  - Fromm, E. (1961). *Marx's Concept of Man.* New York: Continuum. (Insightful explanation of Marx's idea of human nature)
  - McClellan, D. (1973). *Karl Marx: His Life and Thought.* New York: Harper & Row. (Good intellectual biography)

Seeing the Social World (knowing the theory)

- Write a 250-word synopsis of the conflict perspective.
- After reading and understanding this chapter, you should be able to define the following terms theoretically and explain their theoretical importance to Marx's theory: *species-being, idealism, materialism, dualisms, material dialectic, use-value, exchange-value, labor theory of value, industrialization, markets, commodification, the means and relations of production, class bipolarization, exploitation, surplus value, commodification, overproduction, alienation, private property, commodity fetish, ideology, false consciousness, religion, Humanistic Marxism, class consciousness.*
- After reading and understanding this chapter, you should be able to answer the following questions (remember to answer them *theoretically*):
  - Explain human nature through the idea of species-being and how it affects Marx's theory.
  - Define dialectical processes and analyze the structural dialectics of capitalism.

(Continued)

(Continued)

- o Describe Marx and Engel's theory of gender inequality.
- o Explain how overproduction occurs and its effects on capitalism.
- o Explain Marx's theory of religion and ideology.
- o Explain how class consciousness develops.

Engaging the Social World (using the theory)

- Apply the idea of exploitation to current economic relations. What has been happening to this nation's industrial base? What do you suppose this implies about global capitalism?

- Explain how industrialization, markets, and commodification are intrinsically expansive in capitalism and apply this dynamic to understanding contemporary capitalism and your or your family's buying patterns.

- Using Google or your favorite search engine, type in "job loss." Look for sites that give statistics for the number of jobs lost in the past five years or so (this can be a national or regional number). How would Marx's theory explain this?

- Get a sense about the frequency and uses of plastic surgery in this country. You can do this by watching "makeover" programs on TV, or by doing Web searches, or by reading through popular magazines, or in any number of ways. How can we understand the popularity and uses of plastic surgery using Marx's theory? (*Hint:* Think of commodification and commodity fetish.) Can you think of other areas of our life for which we can use the same analysis?

Weaving the Threads (building theory)

There are central themes in classical theory. As we proceed through our discussions of the different theorists, it is a good idea to pay attention to these themes and see how the theorists add to or modify them. In the end, we should have a clear and well-informed idea of the central dynamics in sociological theory. Thinking about Marx's theory, answer the following questions:

- What is the fundamental structure of inequality in society? How is inequality perpetuated (in other words, how is it structured)?

- How does social change occur? Under what conditions is conflict likely to take place?

- What is religion? What function does religion have in society?

- How did gender inequality begin?

- What is the purpose of the state? How is it related to other social structures? Where does power reside?

CHAPTER 4

The Irrationality of Rationality:

Max Weber

(1864–1920)

As we've seen, capitalism in modernity was intended to facilitate equality. Rather than social position being defined by birth, capitalism promised each person could progress as far as his or her talents and efforts would take them. However, Marx points out, capitalism is built upon exploitation and creates a class structure that limits, rather than facilitates, social mobility. Weber's concern is rationality. On the surface, reason and rationality appear to be the hope humankind has been looking for. Through reason and rationality we could discover the secrets of the universe and use them to better humanity. Through reason and rationality we could create social organization free of favoritism, treating all people equally. We could apply rationality to all facets of our lives, lifting them out of the dark ages of superstition and uncertainty and placing them on the sure pillar of reason. Like capitalism, the inexorable push toward rationality has brought benefits; and, like capitalism, reason and rationality have brought unanticipated and, at times, negating consequences.

Before we get into considering Weber's theory of rationalization, I want you to be aware that Weber is one of sociology's most intricate thinkers. Part of this complexity is undoubtedly due to the breadth of his knowledge. Weber was a voracious reader with an encyclopedic knowledge and a dedicated workaholic. In addition, Weber was in contact with a vast array of prominent thinkers from diverse disciplines. As Lewis Coser (2003) comments, "In leafing through Weber's pages and notes, one is impressed with the range of men with whom he engaged in intellectual exchanges and realizes the widespread net of relationships Weber established within the academy and across its various disciplinary boundaries" (p. 257). This social network of intellectuals in diverse disciplines helped create a flexible mind with the ability and tendency to take assorted points of view.

Another reason why I think Weber's writings are complex is due to the way he views the world. Weber sees that human beings are animals oriented toward meaning, and meaning, as we've seen, is subjective and not objective. Weber also understands that all humans are oriented toward the world and each other through values. Further, Weber sees the primary level of analysis to be the social action of individuals; for Weber, individual action is social action only insofar as it is meaningfully oriented toward other individuals. Weber sees these meaningful orientations as produced within a unique historical context. Weber's (1949) theoretical questions, then, are oriented toward understanding "on the one hand the relationships and the cultural significance of individual events in their contemporary manifestations and on the other hand the causes of their being historically *so* and not *otherwise*" (p. 72). What this means is that Weber contextualizes individual social action within the historically specific moment. He then asks the question, why does this cultural context exist and not another one? How is it that out of all the possible cultural worlds, this one exists right here, right now, and not a different one?

Weber's perspective, then, is a cultural one that privileges individual social action within a historically specific cultural milieu. This orientation clearly sets him apart from Spencer, Durkheim, and Marx, who were much more structural in their approaches. It also means that Weber's (1949) explanations are far more complex and tentative: "There is no absolutely 'objective' scientific analysis of culture ... [because] ... all knowledge of cultural reality . . . is always knowledge from particular points of view" (pp. 72, 81). Yet at the same time, as we will see, Weber believes that we can create objective knowledge. This knowledge is created mainly through ideal types and historical comparisons. Yet, while it is possible to create objective knowledge about how things came to be historically so and not otherwise, Weber was extremely doubtful about prediction. But I'm getting ahead of myself.

My point here is that Weber's thinking is quite complex. And, as a result, Weber probably inspired our thinking in more areas than any other person. If we are going to study religion, bureaucracy, culture, politics, conflict, war, revolution, the subjective experience of the individual, historic trends, knowledge, or the economy, then we have to incorporate Weber. He is also a founding thinker in many distinct schools of sociological thought, such as ethnomethodology, interpretive sociology, geo-political theory, the sociology of organizations, and social constructivism.

THEORIST'S DIGEST

Brief Biography

Max Weber was born on April 21, 1865, in Erfurt, Germany (Prussia). His father, Max, was a typical bourgeois politician of the time; his mother, Helene Fallenstein, was a devout Calvinist. The young Weber was exposed to many of the prominent thinkers and power brokers of the day, as well as his mother's strict Calvinist upbringing. Young Weber was a voracious reader, having extensive knowledge of the Greek classics as a young boy and being fluent in such philosophers as Kant, Goethe, and Spinoza before entering college.

In 1882, Weber entered the University of Heidelberg, where he studied law. After a year's military service in 1883, Weber returned to school at the University of Berlin, where he took his PhD.

In 1893, Weber married Marianne Schnitger. Weber continued to publish and in 1896 he returned to Heidelberg to become Professor of Economics. While at Heidelberg, Max and Marianne's home became a meeting place for the city's intellectual community. Marianne was active in these meetings, which at times became significant discussions of gender and women's rights. Georg Simmel frequently attended.

In 1897, Weber suffered a complete emotional and mental breakdown. He was unable to work and would sit staring out the window for hours on end. Weber was unable to write again until 1903; he left the university and didn't teach again for almost 20 years. After his breakdown, Weber wrote the majority of the works for which he is best known.

During World War I, Weber administered a hospital in Heidelberg. As a German nationalist, Weber initially supported the war effort but eventually became critical of it. In 1918, Weber accepted a position at the University of Vienna, where he once again began to teach. He started working on *Economy and Society,* which was to be the definitive outline of interpretive sociology. His *General Economic History* came from lectures given during this time. On June 14, 1920, Max Weber died of pneumonia.

(Continued)

(Continued)

Central Sociological Questions

It's difficult to narrow Weber down to just a few central concerns. I think however that it's safe to say that Weber wrote most about two or three subjects: religion, the state, and the economy. But it would give a false impression to simply say that he is interested in those institutions, per se. His interests are more fundamental: Weber viewed the evolution of religion, politics, and economics as a way of understanding the process of rationalization and its uneasy relationship with cultural values. Weber is also centrally concerned with how stratified systems of class, status, and power produce social change.

Simply Stated

For Weber life becomes more rational as mystery, emotion, and tradition recede—and as technical efficiency, mathematical and logical calculation, and material and social control increase. Over time, efficiency, calculation, and control have increased in tandem with technology, ethical monotheism, early Protestantism, bureaucratized government, and rational capitalism. Social change that is fueled by stratification comes as groups question the legitimacy of the existing system and meet the technical conditions of group organization (leadership, goals and ideology, and communication).

Key Ideas

ideal types, *Verstehen,* action, rationalization, magic and religion, professionalization, symbolism, traditional and rational capitalism, spirit of capitalism, bureaucracy, bureaucratic personality, instrumental-rational action, value-rational action, traditional action, affective action, credentialing, class, status, power, crosscutting stratification, legitimation, authority (charismatic, traditional, rational-legal), routinization, bureaucracy

Concepts and Theory: Cultural Sociology

Weber's approach to sociology is different than either Spencer's or Marx's. While there are many differences between the two, they both give us theories that generally speaking are scientific. Weber, however, was doubtful about the degree to which sociology could be scientific. Much of Weber's concern about social science finds its roots in the idea of culture. Weber takes seriously the notion of culture. He doesn't see it as an epiphenomenon as Marx did, nor does he see it as the most important requisite function like Durkheim, nor is he captivated by the tension between objective and subjective culture as was Simmel. Rather, Weber sees culture as a historical process that at times leads social change and at others simply reinforces it. Culture for Weber (1949) is a value concept: "Empirical reality becomes 'culture' to us because and insofar as we relate it to value ideas" (p. 76). He sees culture as creating intrinsic difficulties for a scientific sociology, as introducing complexity around the issues of stratification and oppression, and as always influencing the subjective value orientation of social actors.

Weber's view of culture is not determinative—he doesn't see culture as determining human action. According to Weber, people are very much motivated by economic and cultural interests. But culture can act like a switch on railroad tracks and actually change the course of the train: "Not ideas, but material and ideal interests directly govern men's conduct. Yet very frequently the 'world-images' that have been created by 'ideas' have, like switchmen, determined the tracks along which action has been pushed by the dynamic of interest" (Weber, 1948, p. 280).

In all his writings, Weber is interested in explaining the relationships among cultural values and beliefs (generally expressed in religion), social structure (overwhelmingly informed by the economy), and the psychological orientations of the actors. None of these elements is particularly determinative for Weber. One of the tasks, then, of Weberian sociology is to *historically explain* which factor is more critical at any given time and why, rather than predicting an outcome. So, for example, we could never have truly predicted what *African American* would mean in 2010 based on what *Negro* meant in 1950, but we can explain the historical, social, and cultural processes through which it came about. That being the case, the kind of knowledge that Weberians construct about the world is decidedly different than that proposed by the general scientific method.

Weber also sees another culture-based problem for researchers. He recognizes that to ask a question about society or humans is itself a cultural act: It requires us to place value on something. In other words, for us to even see a problem to study, we must have a value that helps us to see it. For example, it would have been almost impossible for us to study spousal abuse 300 years ago (it would have been difficult even 50 years ago). It isn't that the behaviors weren't present; it is simply that the culture would not have allowed us to define them as abusive, at least not very easily. And the same is true about everything social scientists study (and laboratory scientists, too, for that matter). Humans can ask questions only insofar as they have a culture for it, and culture is a value orientation toward the world.

So, if scientific knowledge is defined as being empirical and non-evaluative, then you can see why creating a social science might be a problem. Human reality is meaningful, not empirical; it is historical and thus concerned with unique configurations of values, and all the questions we ask are strongly informed by our culture and thus are value-laden. However, Weber is also convinced that a social science is possible, but there are certain caveats. Because human existence is a subjective one, creating an objective science about people is difficult. Knowledge about people must be based upon an interpretation of their subjective experience. And because people are self-aware free agents, the law-like principles that science wants to discover are provisional and probabilistic at best (people can always decide to act otherwise). So the kind of knowledge that we produce about people will be different than that produced in the laboratory, though Weber feels that objective knowledge is still possible. One key in creating this objective-like knowledge is that social scientists have to be reflexively and critically aware of their values in forming and researching their questions.

Creating Objective Knowledge

Weber argues that knowledge about humans in society can be made object-like through the use of ideal types. **Ideal types** are analytical constructs that don't exist anywhere in the real world. They simply provide a logical touchstone to which we can compare empirical data. Ideal types act like a yardstick against which we can measure differences in the social world. These types provide objective measurement because they exist outside the historical contingency of the data we are looking at. According to Weber, without the use of some objective measure, all we can know about humans would be subjective.

There are two main kinds of ideal types: historical and classificatory. Historical ideal types are built up from past events into a rational form. In other words, the researcher examines past examples of whatever phenomenon he or she is interested in and then deduces some logical characteristics. Weber uses this form in *The Protestant Ethic and the Spirit of Capitalism*. In that work, Weber constructs an ideal type of capitalism in order to show that the capitalism in the West is historically unique. Classificatory ideal types, on the other hand, are built up from logical speculation. Here the researcher asks himself or herself, what are the *logically possible* kinds of _____ (fill in the research interest)? As we go through this chapter you'll see Weber use ideal types repeatedly. Keep your eyes open for them, and remember that they are a theoretical method and not statements of what really exists.

In his methodology, Weber also emphasizes understanding of the subjective meanings of the actions to the actors by contextualizing it in some way. Weber advocates the use of *Verstehen*, the German word meaning "to understand." It is important to note that when Weber talks about meaning in this context, he has in mind the motivations of the actor. These motives may be intellectual in the sense that the actor has an observable and rational motive for his or her actions in terms of means and ends; or they may be emotional in the sense that the behavior may be understood in terms of being motivated by some underlying feeling like anger. So we can understand it when Sam hits John if we know that Sam is angry with John for cheating him in a business deal—the meaning of the action comes out of our knowledge of the motivation.

Weberian sociologists, then, will see the world in terms of ideal types (abstract categorical schemes), broad historical and cultural trends, or from the point of view of the situated subject (interpretive sociology). Weber's causal explanations have to do with understanding how and why a particular set of historical and cultural circumstances came together, and his general explanation is always subject to case-specific variations. There are a couple of things that this implies.

First, Weber rarely gives us highly specified relationships among his concepts:

> An "objective" analysis of cultural events, which proceeds according to the thesis that the ideal of science is the reduction of empirical reality of "laws," is meaningless. . . . It is meaningless . . . because the knowledge of social laws is not knowledge of social reality but is rather one of the various aids used by our minds for attaining this end. (Weber, 1949, p. 80)

In his work, Weber is more concerned with providing the historical preconditions for any phenomenon. Thus, it isn't as easy to create a dynamic model of Weber's theory as it is for Durkheim's, nor is it as true to the theorist's thinking to do so. What we can do is create a picture of the general historical processes that tend to produce an environment conducive to whatever issue it is we are trying to explain.

The second implication of this Weberian approach is that the general theory will hold if and only if there are no mitigating circumstances. In other words, Weber will give us a general theory, but it will only hold if nothing gets in the way. So, with religion, for example, Weber may give us a general account of how ethnical monotheism evolved from magic, but we can see histories where it didn't work the way the theory implies. That is one of the frustrating things about reading Weber's *The Sociology of Religion;* yet, it is also what makes the account more accurate than many simpler approaches.

Concepts and Theory: The Rationalization of Society—Religion

We've seen that Marx was very critical of religion. Most theories of modernity, however, see religion as an intricate part of society. For Weber (1922/1993), religion was historically the chief organizing structure and it still continues in importance today: "[T]here is no communal activity . . . without its special god. Indeed, if an association is to be permanently guaranteed, it must have such a god" (p. 14). But religion has historically changed. There are two basic approaches to explaining this movement: progressive revelation and social evolution. Progressive revelation argues that there has always been one god who is concerned with the way we behave. But because of our inability to receive the full revelation of God, he (and these gods are always male) had to progressively reveal himself to us. This perspective also posits a god who is bound to human history. In traditional Christianity, for example, humankind had to reach bottom through the revelation of the law before it was possible for God to reveal grace. Social evolution, on the other hand, posits a link between religion and society.

Weber links changes in religion to shifts in society; he thus gives us a social model of religious **evolution**. However, these two models are not necessarily exclusionary. It is possible that God works through history. And it is possible that part of humankind's preparedness to receive God's revelation is linked to society, since humans are social beings. The reason I say this is to let you know that you aren't faced with an either/or decision. If you are religious, you don't have to reject your religion in order to see value in Weber's theory. Weber is only concerned with the empirical elements of religious change. We can either believe that there are spiritual forces in back of those changes or not. In either case, our beliefs are based on assumptions we make about how the universe works. And, as is always the case, assumptions are never tested or proven.

Generally speaking Weber (1948) sees the evolution of religion changing along a path of demystification or disenchantment: "The fate of our times is characterized by rationalization and intellectualization and, above all, by the 'disenchantment of the world'" (p. 155). Specifically, an enchanted world is one filled with mystery and magic. Disenchantment, then, refers to the process of emptying the world of magical or spiritual forces. Part of this, of course, is in the religious sense of secularization. Peter Berger (1967) provides us with a good definition of *secularization:* "By secularization we mean the process by which sectors of society and culture are removed from the domination of religious institutions and symbols" (p. 107). Thus, both secularization and disenchantment refer to the narrowing of the religious or spiritual elements of the world. If we think about the world of magic or primitive religion, one filled with multiple layers of energies, spirits, demons, and gods, then in a very real way the world has been subjected to secularization from the beginning of religion. The number of spiritual entities has steadily declined from many, many gods to one; and the presence of a god has been removed from immediately available within every force (think of the gods of thunder, harvest, and so on) to completely divorced from the physical world, existing apart from time (eternal) and space (infinite). In our more recent past, secularization, and demystification and rationalization, have of course been carried further by science and capitalism.

From Magic to Religion

Weber is most interested in explaining how ethical monotheism came about. Monotheism, of course, is the belief in one god. Ethical monotheism is the belief in one god that cares about human behavior. In terms of history, such a god is a recent occurrence. For much of human history, we believed in many gods and goddesses, and we didn't feel that they much cared about how we behaved. What's more, most of the gods and goddesses were quite risqué in their own actions. The reason for his focus on ethical monotheism is that this historic shift played a powerful role in the rationalization of human behavior: A monotheistic God that is interested in such things as sin means that people need to take great care in what they say and do.

Weber first recognizes that the historical movement from magic to religion is the same as the change from naturism to symbolism. **Magic** is the direct manipulation of forces. These forces are seen as being almost synonymous with nature. So to assure a good harvest, a magician might perform a fertility ritual, because seeds and fertility are all wrapped up together. Religion, on the other hand, is more symbolic. Let's take Christian communion, for example. In Protestant churches, the bread and grape juice symbolize the body and blood of Christ. They *represent* not only the atonement but also the solidarity believers have in sharing the same body. The Catholic example is a bit more interesting. While there is quite a bit of symbolism in the Eucharist, there is also what is known as transubstantiation. In transubstantiation, the wine and bread *literally become* the blood and body of Christ. Taking the sacrament brings about union with Christ. Through it, venial sin and punishment are remitted.

The reason I compare the Protestant and Catholic versions is to bring out this point of Weber's. In Protestant communion, there are only symbolic elements present. In the Catholic Eucharist, there are actual elements present that are effectual in their own right. Weber would argue, then, that there are magical elements present in the Eucharist. To say something like this isn't meant as a slight against Catholicism (or a slight against Protestantism, depending on your perspective). It is simply meant to point out that these things work in different ways. With the Eucharist, there is a direct manipulation of forces to accomplish some purpose, which is Weber's definition of magic. We can also see the complexity of the social world in this example. Weber argues that *in general,* there is a movement from magic to religion, from physical manipulation to symbols. However, real life is more complex. Catholicism shows us that due to a religion's specific history, it may contain both symbolic and magical elements.

Generally speaking, humanity moved from magic to religion due to economic stability and professionalization. To understand these effects, we can picture a small hunter–gatherer society. In such a group, everyone lives communally, the division of labor is low, and life is uncertain. The tribe is subject to the whims of nature: Game may or may not be there and the weather may or may not have been good enough for the berries to grow. In an attempt to make their world more stable, they perform rituals before the hunt and at season changes. They perform rituals at childbirth or when they need to find water. These rituals constitute magical manipulations, and the people performing the rituals would be the same who are involved in the actual work. For example, we can imagine the men gathering before a hunt, perhaps painting themselves with animal blood or putting on masks and acting out the hunt.

Soon our tribe learns about horticulture and they plant food. They become sedentary and tied to the land, and their life becomes a bit more predictable. After some time, they learn how to use metal and how to plow the land, and they learn how to irrigate. From these small technological advances come surplus, population growth, power, and a different kind of division of labor. Rather than living communally, certain people are able to work at specialized jobs. Thus, the uncertainty of life is further diminished.

What we want to glean from this little story is how the type of economy can influence the development of religion. Early in our story, many people were involved in the practice of magic. Because people were tied to nature, their view of how things work was naturalistic and not symbolic. They were concerned with day-to-day existence: What mattered was getting food, water, and shelter. It was necessary for them to have a method of control that each person could use.

But as life became more predictable, people did not have to be as concerned with immediate sustenance, and tasks became more specialized. Some people tilled the soil; others planted the seeds. Some were in charge of the irrigation; others transported the harvested grain to the grinders. And those who had a knack for it became what Weber characterizes as the "oldest of all vocations," professional necromancers (magicians).

Three things happened as the result of the **professionalization** of magic: Individuals could devote all their time to experiencing it, they increased their knowledge surrounding the experience, and they acquired vested interests (their livelihood became dependent upon an esoteric knowledge). The experience factor is important in this case. Weber argues that ecstatic experiences are the prototypical religious experience. Religion always involves transcendence, the act of going above or outside of normal life, and ecstasy is a primal form of transcendence. Like Durkheim, Weber (1922/1993) argues that "ecstasy occurs in a social form, the orgy, which is the primordial form of communal religious association" (p. 3). For laymen, the experience is only available on occasion, but because the professional wizard is freed from daily concerns, he or she can develop practices that induce ecstatic states almost continually.

These experiences, along with increasingly available time, prompted the professional to develop complex belief systems. As a result, what had once been seen as something everyone could practice (magic) became part of secret lore and available to only a select few. Because the professional magician could afford to engage in continual transcendent experiences, he saw more behind the world than did others. The world thus became less empirical and more filled with transcendent beings, spirits that lived outside of and controlled daily life. The magician developed belief and ritual systems that reflected this growing complexity. In addition, professionals could consider their own thoughts and beliefs, and the very act of reflexive thought will tend to make ideas more abstract and complex. Reflexive thought by its nature is abstract because it isn't thinking about anything concrete. And because it isn't thinking about anything concrete, it can go anywhere it wants. Further, the connections among ideas that are "discovered" through this kind of thinking tend to be systematized around abstract ideas.

Let's think about sociology as an example of professionalization. In a very real way, everybody is a sociologist. We all have an understanding about how society works and what is involved in getting around it. That's one of the funny things about teaching an Introduction to Sociology course—most of the students have a "oh, I knew that" response to the stuff we talk about. But what do *professional* sociologists do? Well, because we get paid to do nothing but sit around and think about society, we have made things very abstract and complex. We use big words (like *dramaturgy* and *impression management*) to talk about pretty mundane things (picking out clothes to wear). And we've developed these ideas into some pretty complex theories that take years of education to understand.

Further, think about the book you are reading right now. It is the result of my thinking about other people's thinking (Weber's, for example). But it's really more than that. This chapter could not have been written right after Weber. No, what we have here is not only my reading of Weber, but my reading of other people's reading of Weber as well. And because I get paid to do this kind of thing, I can weave all this complexity into a systemic whole. More than that—and this is an important point for Weber—we have made it so that you can't understand sociology without the help of a professional. You had to pay to get this book, and you had to pay to get another professional to stand up in front of the class and explain this explanation of Weber. Thus, professionalization pushes for symbolic complexity because of practice, reflexive thinking, and vested interests (I have to make sociology complex to protect my job). This kind of process is exactly what created symbolic religion.

Figure 4.1 Evolution to Symbolism

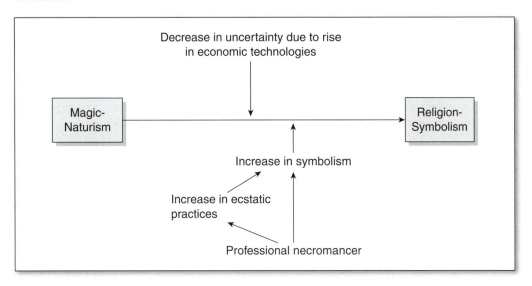

I bring the ideas of professionalization and economic changes together in Figure 4.1. As technology allows people to be less tied by direct relations to the environment, they are less dependent upon magic for manipulating nature. As the economy produces surplus and creates more complex divisions of labor, necromancers can be relieved of other duties and paid simply to practice magic—they become professionals. These two factors work together to increase the level of abstract symbolism, which in turn moves magic toward religion.

From Polytheism to Ethical Monotheism

In the beginning, religious practice was oriented around local gods and goddesses. These gods lived in specific locations and were connected to specific collectives. The next step in religious evolution was to place these local gods into organized pantheons. Organized pantheons are not simply clusters of various gods and goddeses. Rather, in a pantheon, each deity is given a specific sphere of influence, and the activities and deities are related to one another.

Professionalization and *symbolism* play important roles in the religious evolution to pantheons. Professionals affected religion primarily through increasing the level of abstraction (analogous thinking, religious stereotyping, and the use of symbols in ritual rather than actual things—Weber points out that the oldest use of paper money was to pay off the dead, not the living) and creating coherent systems of knowledge out of localized beliefs. In short, as religion became more professionalized, it tended to become more rationally and abstractly organized.

At this point in our evolution, politics has come to play a very important role as well. One of the things the idea of God does is unite different groups into a single community. A kin- or tribal-based god provides the symbolic ties that small groups need, but at some point in our history we began to bring these different collectives together through conquest or voluntary association. Different groups, each with its own god, began to form larger collectives. In order to link these groups, a more abstract and powerful god was needed, one that could be seen above all other gods, thus linking all the people. The gods that were highest on the polytheistic hierarchy began to be seen as less and less attached to the earth and more as part of the heavens. As populations with even greater diversity came together, more abstract symbols were needed to link them. These universal gods became seen as more powerful than all other gods. They became the god of gods and lord of lords.

This development toward monotheism was aided by the need of monarchs to break the hold that the priesthood had on the populace through the "multiplicity of sacerdotal gods" (sacerdotal meaning "pertaining to priests"). As long as there was a multiplicity of gods still linked to the daily needs of the people, there would be need for specific rites to approach those gods. In order to consolidate power, it was necessary for the king to eliminate those various paths, because each one represented a power that he didn't control. Monarchs thus began to monetarily and politically privilege the universal god and his priests. And the idea of the one god was thus born.

Yet one more aspect needs to be added here: morality. The gods had typically never been concerned with the behaviors of their cults. Weber argues that ethical monotheism came about in response to the increasing rationalization of the state and the social control of human behavior. Because of the changes in the way government was organized, from traditional to rational-legal authority, a culture developed that proclaimed that individual behaviors should be controlled. Of course, this was in response to the needs of a large population under a centralized state: The larger and more diverse a population, the greater the need for rational, centralized control. And, according to Weber (1922/1993), this need was reflected in religion: As the state became more interested in the actions of the populace, so did the ruling god. "[T]he personal, transcendental and ethical god is a Near-Eastern concept. It corresponds so closely to that of an all-powerful mundane king with his rational bureaucratic regime that a causal connection can scarcely be overlooked" (p. 56).

In Figure 4.2, we still see the influence of professionalization. This remains an important factor in all areas of modern life. But rather than symbolization, rationalization now plays an important role in the movement toward an ethical god. As state governments become more and more bureaucratized and rational law becomes the way in which relationships are managed, people begin to see their lives as subject to rational control. Of course, today we feel this extended to almost every area of our lives. We not only sense that our bodies, emotions, and minds *can* be rationally controlled, we believe they *should* be controlled.

Religion contributed to this belief through the role of the prophet. Weber categorizes prophecy as two kinds: exemplary and ethical. The exemplary type is found in India and other Eastern civilizations. This kind of prophet *shows* the way by being an example. The emphasis in this case is on a kind of self-actualization. There is no real sense of right and wrong, but only of a better way. And neither is there a god to whom the individual or collective owes allegiance. The Buddha is a good example of this. The ethical prophet, on the other hand, is vitally concerned with

Figure 4.2   Polytheism to Ethical Monotheism

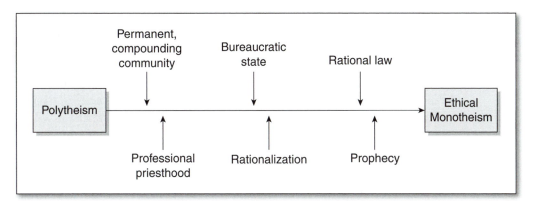

good and evil and with bringing a wayward people back to the right relationship with the dominant god. Just as a centralized state needs and creates a single national identity and story, so the ethical prophet presents the cosmos as a "meaningful, ordered totality" (Weber, 1922/1993, p. 59). Thus, God and the state come together to rationally control human behavior.

Concepts and Theory:
The Rationalization of Society—Capitalism

For Weber, there are three main factors that influenced the rise of capitalism as an economic form: religion, nation-states, and transportation and communication technologies. But, as with most of Weber's work, it is difficult to disengage their effects. There is not only quite a bit of overlap when he talks about these issues, he is also interested in explicating the pre-conditions for capitalism rather than determining a causal sequence. So, what we have are a number of social factors that overlap to create the bedrock out of which capitalism could spring, but did not necessarily cause capitalism. Picking up from our last section, we'll begin with religion.

The Religious Culture of Capitalism

The Protestant Ethic and the Spirit of Capitalism is probably Weber's best-known work. It is a clear example of his methodology. In it, he describes an ideal type of spirit of capitalism, he performs a historical-comparative analysis to determine how and when that kind of capitalism came to exist, and he uses the concept of *Verstehen* to understand the subjective orientation and motivation of the actors. Weber had three interrelated reasons for writing the book. First, he wanted to counter Marx's argument concerning the rise of capitalism—Weber characterizes Marx's historical materialism as "naïve." The second reason is very closely linked to the first: Weber wanted to argue *against* brute structural force and argue *for* the effect that cultural values could have on social action.

The third reason that Weber wrote *The Protestant Ethic* was to explain why rational capitalism had risen in the West and nowhere else. Capitalism had been practiced previously. But it was traditional, not rational capitalism. In **traditional capitalism**, traditional values and status positions still held; the elite would invest but would spend as little time and effort doing so in order to live as they were "accustomed to live." In other words, the elite invested in capitalistic ventures in order to maintain their lifestyle. It was, in fact, the existence of traditional values and status positions that prevented the rise of rational capitalism in some places. Rational capitalism, on the other hand, is practiced to increase wealth for its own sake and is based on utilitarian social relations.

Weber's argument is that there are certain features of Western culture that set it apart from any other system, thus allowing capitalism to emerge. As we talk about this culture, it is important to keep in mind that Weber is describing the culture of capitalism in its beginning stages. In many ways, the United States is now experiencing a form of late capitalism. And some of the spirit that Weber is describing has been lost to one degree or another. Also keep in mind that what he describes is an ideal type.

Weber's first task was to define the **spirit of capitalism**. The first thing I want you to notice is the word *spirit*. Weber is concerned with showing that a particular cultural milieu or mindset is required for rational capitalism to develop. This culture or mindset is morally infused: The spirit of capitalism exists as "an *ethically-oriented* maxim for the organization of life" (Weber, 1904–1905/2002, p. 16, emphasis original). This culture, then, has a sense of duty about it, and its individual components are seen as virtues.

As the above quote indicates, modern capitalism contains principles for the way in which people organize or live out their lives. For example, you woke up this morning and you will go to sleep tonight. In between waking and sleeping you will live your life, but how will you use that time? From an even broader position, you were born and you will die. What will you do with your life? Does it matter? According to Weber, under capitalism, it does matter. How you live your life is not simply a matter of individual concern; the culture of modern capitalism provides us with certain principles, values, maxims, and morals that act as guideposts telling us how to live. In my reading of Weber, I see three such prescriptions in the spirit of capitalism.

Weber begins his consideration of the spirit of capitalism with a lengthy quote from Benjamin Franklin:

> Remember, that time is money . . . that credit is money . . . that money is of the prolific, generating nature. . . . After industry and frugality, nothing contributes more to the raising of a young man in the world than punctuality and justice in all his dealings. . . . The sound of your hammer at five in the morning, or eight at night, heard by a creditor, makes him easy six months longer. . . . [Keep] an exact account for some time, both of your expenses and your income. (Franklin, as quoted in Weber, 1904–1905/2002, pp. 14–15)

From these sayings, Weber gleans the first maxim of rational capitalism: Life is to be lived with a specific goal in mind. That is, it is good and moral to be honest, trustworthy, frugal, organized, and rational because it is *useful* for a specific end: making money, which has its own end, "the acquisition of money, and more and more money." The culture of modern capitalism says that money is to be made but not to be enjoyed. Immediate gratification and spontaneous enjoyment are to be put off so that money can be "rationally used." That is, it is invested to earn more money. The making of money then becomes an end in itself and the purpose of life.

The second prescription is that each of us should have a vocational calling. Of course, another word for vocation is job, but Weber isn't simply saying that we should each have a job or career. The emphasis is on our attitude toward our vocation, or the way in which we carry out our work. There are two important demands to this attitude. First is that we are obligated to pursue work: We have a *duty* to work. In the spirit of capitalism, work is valued in and of itself. People have always worked. But generally speaking, we work to achieve an end. The spirit of capitalism, however, exalts work as a moral attribute. We talk about this in terms of a work ethic, and we characterize people as having a strong or weak work ethic. We can further see the moral underpinning when we consider that the opposite of a strong work ethic is being lazy. We still see laziness as a character flaw today. In the culture of capitalism, work becomes an end in itself, rather than a means to an end. More than that, it becomes the central feature of one's life, overshadowing other areas such as family, community, and leisure.

We not only have duty to work, we also have duty *within* work. Weber (1904–1905/2002) says that "*competence and proficiency* is the actual alpha and omega" of the spirit of capitalism (p. 18). Notice the religious reference: In the New Testament, Jesus is referred to as the "alpha and omega." Weber is again emphasizing that this way of thinking about work is a moral issue. Our duty within work is to organize our lives "according to *scientific* vantage points." That is, under the culture of capitalism, we are morally obligated to live our lives rationally.

The rationally organized life is one that is not lived spontaneously. Rather, all actions are seen as stepping stones that bring us closer to explicit and valued goals. Let me give you a contrary example to bring this home. A number of years ago, a (non-Hawaiian) friend of mine managed a condominium complex on the island of Maui. In the interest of political and cultural sensitivity, he hired an all-Hawaiian crew to do some construction. He tells of the frustrations of having a crew come to work whenever they got up, rather than at the prescribed 8 a.m. What's more, periodically during the day the crew would leave at the shout of "surf's up!" The work got done and it was quality work, but the Hawaiians that he supervised did not organize their lives rationally. They lived and valued a more spontaneous and playful life. In contrast, most of us have Outlook and Blackberrys that guide our life and tell us when every task is to be performed in order to reach our lifetime goals.

The third prescription or value of the spirit of capitalism, according to Weber, is that life and actions are legitimized "on the basis of strictly quantitative calculations." Weber makes an interesting point with regard to legitimation or **rationalization**— humans can rationalize their behaviors from a variety of ultimate vantage points. And we always do legitimize our behaviors. We can all tell stories about why our behaviors or feelings or prejudices are right. And those stories can be told from various religious, political, or personal perspectives. Weber's point here is that the culture of capitalism values quantitative legitimations. That is, capitalist behaviors are legitimized in terms of bottom-line or efficiency calculations. So, for example, *Roger and Me,* a film by Michael Moore, depicts the closing of the General Motors plants in Flint, Michigan, resulting in the loss of over 30,000 jobs and the destruction of Flint's economy. The film asks about GM's social responsibility; but from GM's position, the closing was legitimated through bottom-line, financial portfolio management.

These cultural directives find their roots in Protestant doctrine and practice. But Weber doesn't mean to imply that these tenets of capitalist culture are themselves religious—far from it. What we can see here is how culture, once born, can have unintended and independent effects from its creating group. Protestantism did not directly produce capitalism, but it did create a culture that, when cut loose from its social group, influenced the rise of capitalism.

The most important religious doctrine behind the spirit of capitalism is Luther's notion of a calling. Prior to Luther and the advent of Protestantism, a calling was seen as something peculiar to the priesthood. Men could be called out of daily life to be priests and women to be nuns, but the laity was not called. Luther, however, taught that every individual can have a personal relationship with God; people didn't need to go through a priest. Luther also taught that individuals were saved based on personal faith. Prior to this, the church taught that salvation was a property of the church—people went to heaven because they were part of the Bride of Christ, the Church. With this shift to the individual also came the notion of a calling. If each person stood before God individually, and if priests aren't called to intercede, then the ministry belongs to the laity. Each person will stand before God on Judgment Day to give an account of what he or she did in this life. That means that God cares about what each individual does and has a plan for each life. God's plan involves a calling. Luther argued that every person in the church is called to do God's will. So it is not simply the case that ministers are called to work for God— carpenters are called to work for God as well, as carpenters. One calling is not greater than another; each is a religious service. This doctrine, of course, leads to a *moral* organization of life.

This idea of a calling was elaborated upon and expanded by John Calvin. Calvin took the idea of God's omniscience seriously: If God knows something, then God has always known it. Calvin also took the "sin nature" of humanity seriously. According to the sin nature doctrine, every human being is born in sin, reckoned sinful under Adam. That being the case, there is nothing anyone can do to save himself or herself from hell. We are doomed because of our very nature. Salvation, then, is from start to finish a work of God. Taking these ideas together, we come up with the Calvinistic idea of predestination. People are born in sin, there is nothing they can do to save themselves (neither faith nor good works), salvation is utterly a work of grace, and God has always known who would be saved. We are thus predestined to heaven or hell.

This doctrine had some interesting effects. Let's pretend you're a believer living in the sixteenth century under Calvin's teaching. Heaven and hell are very real to you, and it is thus important for you know where you are headed. But there isn't anything you can do to assuage your fears. Because salvation is utterly of God, joining the church isn't going to help; neither is being baptized or evangelizing. Confessing faith isn't going to help either, because you are either predestined for heaven or you are not. And you can't go by whether or not you *feel* saved—feelings were seen as promoting "sentimental illusions and idolatrous superstition."

"*Restless work in a vocational calling* was recommended as the best possible means to *acquire* the self-confidence that one belonged among the elect" (Weber, 1904–1905/2002, p. 66, emphasis original). Good works weren't seen as a path to salvation, but they were viewed as the natural fruit: If God has saved you, then your life will be lived in the relentless pursuit of His glory. In fact, only the saved would be able to dedicate their entire lives in such a way. The emphasis was thus not on singular works, but on an entire life organized for God's glory.

Thus diligent labor became the way of life for the Calvinist. Every individual was called to a job and was to work hard at that job for the Lord. Even the rich worked hard, for time belonged to the Lord and glorifying Him was all that mattered. Everything was guarded and watched and recorded. Individuals kept journals of daily life in order to be certain that they were keeping good works. Their entire lives became rational and systematically ordered.

Further, if one was truly chosen for eternal salvation, then God would bless the individual and the fruits of one's labor would multiply. In other words, in response to your labor, you could expect God to bless you economically. Yet, aestheticism became the rule, for the world was sinful and the lusts of the flesh could only lead to damnation. The pleasures of this world were to be avoided. So the blessings of God were reinvested in the work that God had called you to.

Taken together, then, the Protestant ethic commits each individual to a worldly calling, places upon her or him the responsibility of stewardship, and simultaneously promises worldly blessings and demands abstinence. This religious doctrine proved to be fertile ground for rational capitalism: a money-generating system that values work, rational management of life, and the delay of immediate gratification for future monetary gain.

Structural Influences on Capitalism

Thus, Weber argues that rational capitalism in the West found a seedbed in a culture strongly influenced by Protestantism. Yet there are other preconditions for the emergence of capitalism. I've illustrated these preconditions in Figure 4.3. They are divided into institutional, structural, and cultural influences, but these demarcations are not clear-cut. I've pictured them as rather shapeless, overlapping preconditions, as that's how Weber talks about them. All of these processes mutually reinforce one another. With capitalism in particular, there is movement back and forth between culture and structure in terms of causal influence.

We've seen the influence of Protestantism, but in terms of institutions there also had to be a centralized, bureaucratized state, as well as significant changes in modes of transportation and communication. I will be spending far less time explaining these structural influences than I did the effects of religious culture. The structural

Figure 4.3 Preconditions of Capitalism

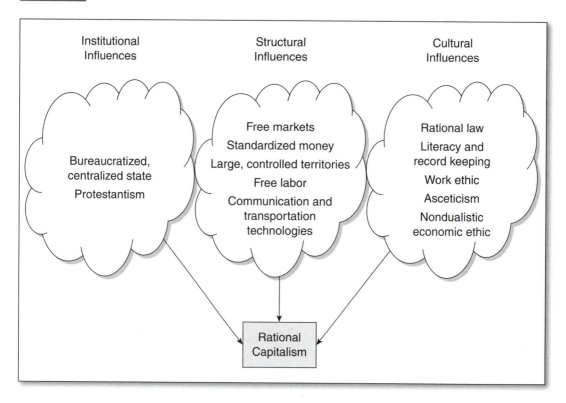

issues are more clear-cut than the cultural ones (which is generally the case). But don't let brevity fool you: These effects are equally important and you must understand how each of them works to comprehend the base for rational capitalism.

Nation-states are relatively recent inventions. Up until the nineteenth century, the world was not organized in terms of nation-states. People were generally organized ethnically, with fairly fluid territorial boundaries. They didn't have nations as we think of them today. A nation is a collective that occupies a specific territory, has a common history and identity, and sees itself as sharing a common fate. The widespread use of the idea of a nation for organizing people was necessary for capitalism. Nations were responsible for controlling large territories, standardizing money, organizing social control, and facilitating free and open markets. All of these factors allowed for easier exchanges of goods and services involving large populations of people. These kinds of exchanges are, of course, necessary for rational capitalism to exist. Labor also had to be freed from social and structural constraints. Capitalism depends on a labor force that is free to sell its labor on the open market. Workers can't be tied down to apprenticeships or guild obligations, nor can they be attached to land obligations as in feudalism.

Along with increases in communication and transportation technologies, nation-states and Protestantism helped form an objectified, rationalized culture, wherein written records were kept, people practiced a strong work ethic coupled with asceticism, and the traditional dualistic approach to economic relations would break down. This latter issue is particularly important for Weber. In traditional societies, groups usually had two different kinds of ethics when participating in exchanges. There were restrictions having to do with ritual and fairness when dealing with group members, but people not within the group could be exploited without measure. Both of these frameworks needed to be lifted in order for capitalism to flourish. All business and loans needed to be rationalized so that there could be continuity.

Concepts and Theory: The Rationalization of Society—Bureaucracy

To be human is to be social, and to be social is to be organized. Thus, organization is primary to what it means to be human. Human beings have been organized over time by different social forms, and these different organizational forms have clear consequences for us. In the not too distant past, we organized much of our lives around affective (emotionally based) systems, such as kinship. Kinship linked people through blood and marriage. In such organizations, people saw each other in terms of familial obligations and rights, which they felt as emotional ties.

But today we are organized through mostly bureaucratic means. From the time you were put in school at the age of five or six, bureaucracies have been organizing your life. You know how to stand in line, how to use time and space, and how to relate to people (the grocery clerk, the teacher, the minister, the insurance agent) as a result of spending most of your life in a bureaucracy. Even our dining experience has been strongly influenced by bureaucracy, thanks to McDonald's (Ritzer, 2004a).

Bureaucracies tend to rationalize and routinize all tasks and interactions. Tasks and interactions are rationalized in terms of means–ends efficiency, and they are routinized in the sense that they may be carried out without thought or planning or dependency on individual talents. Thus, each person and task is met in the same efficient and equal manner; personal issues and emotions do not have a place in a bureaucracy.

While bureaucracies have been around for quite awhile, for much of their history they were not the primary way in which humans organized. Certain social factors came about that simultaneously pushed out affective systems of organization (traditional) and set the stage for systems based more on reason than emotion. For Weber, these social factors are preconditions for bureaucracy, not causal forces. As these different features lined up, they created an environment ripe for rational organization.

According to Weber (1922/1968, pp. 217–226, 956–958), there are at least six preconditions for bureaucracy, and they don't necessarily occur in any specific order. These include increases in the following:

- The size and space of the population being organized
- The complexity of the task being performed
- The use of markets and the money economy

- Communication and transportation technologies
- The use of mass democracy
- The volume of complicated and rationalized culture

All these factors created needs for more objective and rational social relations and culture, thus driving a society to use rational-legal authority and bureaucracy almost exclusively. As society became larger and spread out over vast spans of geographic space, it became increasingly difficult to use personal relationships as a method of organization. However, increases in population size and geographic space aren't sufficient to make bureaucratic organization necessary. For example, China was able to primarily use an elaborate kinship system rather than bureaucracy to organize most of their behaviors for many years. Other factors are necessary to push a society toward bureaucratic organization, such as increasing complexity of the task being performed. In England and elsewhere, this occurred through the Industrial Revolution, urbanization, and high division of labor. The increasing use of money and open markets for exchange also increased the need for rationalized and speedy calculations, thus adding to rational culture.

Increasing levels of communication and transportation technologies created the demand for faster and more predictable reactions from the governing state. Insightfully, Weber (1922/1968) says that with "traditional authority it is impossible for law or administrative rule to be deliberately created by legislation" (p. 227). Remember that traditional authority is based on history and time, so the only way a new rule or law can be legitimized through tradition is to say that it is according to the wisdom of the ages. Rational-legal authority, on the other hand, can create new rules simply because it is expedient to do so. So as states came into more frequent contact with one another and dealt with more complex problems, it became necessary to respond quickly to new situations with new rules, thus pushing forward a rational-legal authority and bureaucracy.

Two additional forces created demands for rational and objective standards. The first was democracy for the masses, rather than simply the elite, which created demands for equal treatment before the law. Initially, the idea of democracy was limited to the educated and powerful. Including the masses created the demand for equal treatment regardless of power or prestige. This, of course, led to the idea that rules and laws should be blind to individual differences. The other additional social factor that pushed for bureaucratic organization was the increase in complex and rational culture. Due to the increases in knowledge that came with science and technology, a new social identity came into existence and rose to prominence—the expert, bureaucracy's manpower.

The Ideal Typology

Weber gives us an ideal type for **bureaucracy.** Remember that this ideal type is not intended to tell us what the perfect bureaucracy should look like; rather, Weber uses the ideal type as an objective yardstick against which we may measure different subjective and cultural states. Weber talks about bureaucracy in a number of different places. But if we combine his lists, we come up with six important features to the ideal type of bureaucracy: an explicit division of labor with delineated lines of authority, the presence of an office hierarchy, written rules and communication, accredited training and technical competence, management by rules that is emotionally neutral, and ownership of both the career ladder and position by the organization rather than the individual.

Each of these characteristics is a variable; organizations will thus be more or less bureaucratized. For example, the first job I ever had was with Pharmaseal Laboratories. I worked as a lead man, which meant I kept the production lines stocked with raw materials and moved the finished product to the warehouse. After about six months of working there, I was promoted to management. During my week-long orientation, I was told about AVOs (Avoid Verbal Orders) that documented in triplicate any communication or disciplinary action. I was introduced to the Human Resources department and shown the employee files and where each of those AVO copies went. I was told of my span of control, given an organizational chart of the company, and provided a complete job description for myself and every person with whom I would have business. I was also informed about the company's internal promotion policy (the career ladder)—to get past the level I was at would require additional schooling and credentialing.

On the other hand, my wife's experience at a local firm indicates a more patrimonial and less bureaucratized organization. When she first arrived at this company, she asked for the organizational chart and job descriptions. She also wanted to know exactly what her span of control was and to whom she reported. But what she found was a 70-person company that was run on personal relationships. Most of the communication was not documented, there was no organizational chart or policy defining the span of control or communication, and there were no job descriptions. Thus, there are differences in the level of bureaucratization, even in a society such as ours. However, that company has changed over the years and has become more bureaucratized. These changes are due to increasing pressures for rationalization and objectification, coming from much the same preconditions of which Weber initially spoke. (A side note: It's good to keep in mind that all the theoretical issues that Weber, and our other theorists, bring up continue to be important social variables. While we may talk about them historically, like the preconditions for bureaucracy, they continue to influence society and our lives. So, keep your eyes open.)

Effects of Bureaucratic Organization

One of the things that should become clear as we move through the different theorists is that social processes and factors are not innocuous. For example, we see from Marx that the use of money to facilitate exchanges in the end changes people. A good analogy might be putting gasoline in a car. We put gas in the car to make it run, but the accidental and almost inevitable consequence is pollution. Bureaucracies have unintended and largely unavoidable consequences as well. They influence both the people in the bureaucracies and the social system as a whole.

Because of the prominence of bureaucracy, means–ends calculation, science, secularization, and so forth, our world is emptier. Weber sees this move toward rationalization as historically unavoidable; it is above all else the defining feature of modernity. Yet it leads inexorably to an empty society. The organizational, intellectual, and cultural movements toward rationality have emptied the world of emotion, mystery, tradition, and affective human ties. We increasingly relate to our world through economic calculation, impersonal relations, and expert knowledge. Weber (1948) tells us that as a result of rationalization the "most sublime values have retreated from public life" and that the spirit "which in former times swept through the great communities like a firebrand, welding them together" is gone (p. 155). Weber sees this not only as a condition of the religious or political institutions in society, he also sees the creative arts, like music and painting, as having lost their creative spirit as well. Even our food is subject to rationalization, whether it is the McDonaldized experience (Ritzer, 2004a) or the steak dinner that is subjected to the "fact" that it contains in excess of 2,000 calories and 100 grams of fat. Thus, for Weber, the process of modernization brings with it a stark and barren world culture.

Importantly, bureaucratization and rationalization influence the kinds of actions we engage in and the kinds of relationships we have. To talk about this issue, Weber developed an ideal typology of social action with four types. *Instrumental-rational* action is behavior in which the means and ends of action are rationally related to each other. So, your action in coming to the university is instrumental-rational in that you see it as a logical means to achieve an "end," that is, a good job or career. *Value-rational* action behavior is that based upon one's values or morals. If there is no way you could get caught paying someone to write your term paper for you, then it would be instrumentally rational for you to do so. It would be the easiest way to achieve a desired end. However, if you don't do that because you think that it is dishonest, then your behavior is being guided by values or morals and is value-rational. *Traditional action* is action that is determined or motivated by habit, and *affective action* is determined by people's emotions in a given situation. All of these different types of behavior can become social action insofar as we take into account the behaviors and subjective orientations of other actors, whether present or absent.

We can tease out an important element in Weber's thinking from this ideal typology. Value-rational behavior is distinguished from affective action because Weber sees some semblance of self-aware decision-making processes in value-rationality. Values are emotional, but when we consciously decided to act because of the logic of our values, it is rational behavior. Emotion, on the other hand, is irrational and proceeds simply from the feelings that an actor may have in a given situation. According to Weber (1922/1968), both affectual and traditional behaviors lay "very close to the borderline of what can justifiably be called meaningfully oriented action" (p. 25), because they are not based on explicit decisions.

Additionally, contemporary theorists point out that living in a society that organizes through bureaucracy can produce the **bureaucratic personality**. There are at least four characteristics of this kind of temperament. One, individuals tend to live more rationally due to the presence of bureaucracy, and not just at work. People generally become less and less spontaneous and less emotionally connected to others in their lives. They understand goals, the use of time and space, and even relationships through rational criteria. Two, people who work in bureaucracies also tend to identify with the goals of the organization. Workers at levels that are less bureaucratized tend to complain about the organization; on the other hand, management who exist at more bureaucratized levels tend to support and believe in the organization. Again, this isn't something that we just put on at work—we *become* bureaucratic ourselves.

Three, because bureaucracies are based on technical knowledge, people in bureaucratic societies tend to depend on expert systems for knowledge and advice. In traditionally based societies, people would trust the advice of those they loved, or those who had extensive experience, or those who stood in a long lineage of oral discipleship. Conversely, in societies like the United States, we look to those who have credentials to help us. Honor in modern society is given to those with credentials; age and experience are of no consequence. And, lastly, bureaucracies lead to sequestration of experience. By that I mean that different life experiences are separated from one another, such as dying from living. In traditional society, life was experienced holistically. People would see birth, sickness (emotional, mental, and physical), and death as part of their normal lives. Children were conceived and grandparents died in the same home. Today, most of those experiences are put away from us and occur in bureaucratic settings where we don't see them as part of our normal and daily life; such settings include hospitals, rest homes, asylums, and so on. The world has thus become tidy, clean, and rational.

Society is affected as well by bureaucracy. There are two main effects. The first is the **iron cage of bureaucracy**. Once bureaucracies are in place, they are virtually inescapable and indestructible for several reasons: They are the most efficient form of organizing large-scale populations; they are value free; and they are based upon expert knowledge. We've just seen that individuals within a rationalized society become more and more dependent upon expert knowledge; the same is true with leaders. Whether the leaders are in charge of political, religious, or economic organizations, they become increasingly dependent upon rationally trained personnel and expert knowledge in the bureaucratic information age. As we noted under professionalization, the experts themselves engage in secrecy and mystification in order to avoid inspection and secure their position. Further, one of the definitions of a professional is self-administration, which means that bureaucratic experts become a self-recruiting and self-governing class, existing apart from any other organizational control. Thus, neither the people ruled, nor the rulers, nor the experts themselves can escape the domination of the bureaucratic form.

There is one further factor to note: Bureaucracies are value free, which means they can be used for any purpose, from spreading the gospel to the eradication of ethnic minorities. This implies that bureaucracies are quite good at co-optation. To *co-opt*, in this context, means to take something in and make it part of the group, which on the surface might sound like a good thing. But because bureaucracies are value and emotion free, there is a tendency to downplay differences and render them impotent. For example, one of the things that our society has done with race and gender movements is to give them official status in the university. One can now get a degree in race or gender relations. Inequality is something we now study, rather than the focus of social movements. In this sense, these movements have been co-opted.

Bureaucracies also accelerate the process of *credentialing*. Remember that position within a bureaucracy is achieved through diplomas and certification. It isn't supposed to be *who* you know but *what* you know that determines rank in the organization: "Bureaucratic administration means fundamentally domination through knowledge" (Weber, 1922/1968, p. 225). That being the case, society needs a legitimated process through which credentials can be conferred. The United States uses the education system. But one of the effects of that decision is that education is no longer about education. The education system is used to credential technical expertise rather than cultivate an informed citizenry. Universities are thus becoming populated by professional schools—the school of business, nursing, social work, computer technology, criminal justice, and so on—and there is mounting tension between the traditional liberal arts and these professional schools. Many students express this tension (and preference for credentialing) when they ask, "How will this course help me get a job?"

The emphasis on credentials coupled with the American view of mass education and the use of education to give credentials has created credential inflation. Every year, more and more people are going to college to get a degree so that they can be competitive in the job market. Using data from the National Center for Education Statistics, we can get a sense of how this is working. In the United States, between the mid-1980s and mid-1990s, there was a 20% increase in the number of bachelor degrees, 37% increase in master's degrees, and 44% increase in doctorates. The result is that there are too many people with advanced degrees, which, in turn, decreases the value of those degrees.

Concepts and Theory: Class, Authority, and Social Change

As we've seen with capitalism and religion, social change for Weber is a complex issue, one involving a number of variables coming together in indeterminate ways. Social change always involves culture and structure working together, and it involves complex social relations. We turn our attention now to stratification and change; here are Weber's contributions to conflict theory. Again we will see the interplay of culture and structure as well as complex social categories.

Weber's understanding of stratification is more complex than Marx's. Marx hypothesized that in capitalist countries there will be only one social category of any consequence—class. And in that category, Marx saw only two types: owners and workers. For Weber, status and power are also issues around which stratification can be based. Most importantly, class, status, and power do not necessarily co-vary. That is, a person may be high on one of those dimensions and low on another (like a Christian minister, typically high in terms of status but low in terms of class). These crosscutting life circumstances or affiliations can prevent people from forming into conflict groups and bringing about social change. For example, in the United States, a black man and a white man may both be in the poor class, but their race (status) may prevent them from seeing their life circumstances as being determined by similar factors.

Weber also argues that all systems are socially constructed and require people to believe in them. Marx did say that capitalism has a cultural component that holds it together (if not for ideology, the proletariat would immediately overthrow the system); but true communism requires no such cultural reinforcement, because it corresponds to our species-being nature. For Weber, legitimation is the glue that holds not only society together but also its systems of stratification. Thus, for Weber, issues of domination and authority go hand in hand (in fact, Weber used just one German word to denote them both—*herrschaft*). So, people must have some level of belief in the authority (culture) of those who are in charge and they must cooperate with the system to some degree in order for it to work. Though the concept may sound a bit strange, we could call this aspect of stratification cooperative oppression.

Class

But let's begin our consideration of these issues by taking a closer look at Weber's complex idea of stratification. Weber's definition of class is different than Marx's. Marx defines class around the ownership of the means of production. Weber (1922/1968), on the other hand, says that a "class situation" exists where there is a "typical probability of 1. procuring goods 2. gaining a position in life and 3. finding inner satisfaction, a probability which derives from the relative control over goods and skills and from their income-producing uses within a given economic order" (p. 302). In other words, Weber defines class based on your ability to buy or sell goods and/or services that will bring you inner satisfaction and increase your life chances (how long and healthfully you will live).

Weber also sees class as being divided along several dimensions as compared to Marx's two. Marx acknowledges that there are more than two class elements, but he also argues that the other classes (such as the lumpenproletariat or petite bourgeoisie) become less and less important due to the structural squeeze of capitalism. Weber also speaks of two main class distinctions, yet they are constructed around completely different issues, each with "positively privileged," "negatively privileged," and "middle class" positions. The property class is determined by property differences, either owning (positively privileged) or not owning (negatively privileged). *Rentiers*—people who live off property and investments—are clear examples of owners; whereas *debtors*—those who have more debt than assets—are good examples of negatively privileged. The middle property classes are those who do not acquire wealth or surplus from property, yet they are not deficient either.

The commercial class is determined by the ability to trade or manage a market position. Those positively related to commercial position are typically entrepreneurs who can monopolize and safeguard their market situation. Negatively privileged commercial classes are typically laborers. They are dependent on the whim of the labor market. The in-between or middle classes that are influenced by labor

Figure 4.4 Weber's Concept of Class

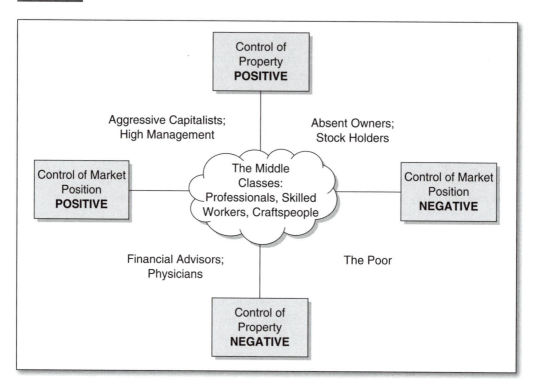

market positions are those such as self-employed farmers, craftspeople, or low-level professionals who have a viable market position yet are not able to monopolize or control it in any way.

In Figure 4.4, I've given us a picture of Weber's ideas about class. We can see that there are two axes to class: property and market position. People can have a positive, negative, or middle position with respect to each of these issues. I've conceptualized this as a typology, because Weber spoke of people holding a position on both. I have also provided some contemporary examples in this typology. Today, those in upper management, such as CEOs, are not only paid large salaries, they are also given stock options that translate into ownership, which places them high in both the property and market dimensions (they hold a monopoly with the skills they have). Weber's typology of class also allows us to conceptualize certain kinds of knowledge as a resource or market position and thus a class indicator. Those who monopolize such skills and knowledge in our society include medical doctors and other such professionals. Stock owners as well as Weber's rentiers use the control of property to attain wealth, and we find them in the upper right corner of the picture. Those who have little or no control over property and market are the poor.

Weber sees that holding a specific class position does not necessarily translate into being a member of a group. Unless and until people develop a similar identity that focuses on their class differences, they remain a statistical aggregate. In other words, the Census Bureau may know you are in the middle class, but you may not have a group identity around your class position. So, in addition to the property and commercial classes, Weber also talks about social class. His emphasis here seems to be on the social aspect—the formation of unified group identity.

Weber identifies at least three variables for the formation of social class. He argues that class-conscious organization will most easily succeed if the following criteria are met:

- *It is organized against immediate economic groups.* There must be some immediate market position or control issue, and the other group must be perceived as relatively close. Thus, in today's economy, workers are more likely to organize against management rather than ownership.

- *Large numbers of people are in the same class position.* The size of a particular group can give it the appearance, feel, and unavoidability of an object.

- *The technical conditions of organization are met.* Weber recognizes that organization doesn't simply happen; there's a technology needed to organize people. People must be able to communicate and meet with one another; there must be recognized and charismatic leadership; and there must be a clearly articulated ideology in order to organize.

Keep in mind that these are all variables. A group may have more or less of any of them. As each of these increases, there will be a greater likelihood of the formation of a social class.

Status and Party

But Weber sees stratification as more complex than class. Money isn't the only thing in which people are interested. People also care about social esteem or honor. Weber termed this issue status. **Status**, for Weber (1922/1968), entails "an effective claim to social esteem in terms of positive or negative privileges" (p. 305). Thus, status groups are hierarchically ranked by structural or cultural criteria and imply differences in honor and privilege.

Status may be based or founded on one or more of three things: a distinct lifestyle, formal education, or differences in hereditary or occupational prestige. Being a music fan may entail a distinctive lifestyle—people who listen to jazz are culturally different than those who listen to rock. And there are positive and negative privileges involved as well: You can get a degree in jazz at my university, but not in rock. Homosexuals can also be seen in terms of lifestyle status groups. One's education level can provide the basis of status as well. Being a senior at the university is better, status-wise, than being a freshman, and you have greater privileges as a senior as well. Professors are also examples of prestige by education. They are good examples because they usually rate high on occupational prestige tables but low in class and power. Race and gender are also examples of status founded on perceived heredity.

Status groups maintain their boundaries through particular practices and symbols. Boundary maintenance is particularly important for status groups because the borders are more symbolic than actual. The differences between jazz and rock, for example, are in the ear of the listener. Generally speaking, Weber argues, we maintain the boundaries around status through marriage and eating restrictions, monopolizing specific modes of acquisition, and different traditions—all of which are described in greater detail below.

The norm of marriage restriction is fairly intuitive; we can think of religious and ethnic groups who practice "endogamy" (marriage within a specific group as required by custom or law). But eating restrictions may seem counterintuitive. It may help us to realize that most religious groups have special dietary restrictions and practice ritual feasting. Feasts are always restricted to group members and are usually seen as actively uniting the group as one (the traditional Jewish Passover Seder is a good example). We can also think of special holidays that have important feast components, Thanksgiving and Christmas here in the United States. And, if you think back just a few years, I'm sure you can recall times in junior high when someone your group didn't like tried to sit at your lunch table. For humans, eating is rarely the simple ingestion of elements necessary for biological survival. It is a form of social interaction that binds people together and creates boundaries.

We also maintain the symbolic boundaries around status groups through monopolizing or abhorring certain kinds and modes of acquisition, and by having certain cultural practices or traditions. The kinds of things we buy obviously set our status group apart. That's what we mean when we say that a BMW is a status symbol. Status groups also try and guard the modes of acquisition. Guilds, trade unions, and professional groups can function in this capacity. And, of course, different status groups have different practices and traditions. Step concerts, pride marches, Fourth of July, Kwanzaa, Cinco de Mayo, and so on are all examples of status-specific traditions and cultural practices.

When sociologists talk about Weber's three issues of stratification, they typically refer to them as class, status, and **power**. However, power is not the word that Weber uses; instead he talks about party. What he has in mind, of course, is within the sphere of power, "the chance a man or a number of men to realize their own will in a social action even against the resistance of other who are participating in the action" (Weber 1922/1968, p. 926). Yet, it is important to note that power always involves social organization, or, as Weber calls it, party. Weber uses the word *party* to capture the social practice of power. The social groups that Weber would consider parties are those whose practices are oriented toward controlling an organization and its administrative staff. As Weber puts it, a party organizes "in order to attain ideal or material advantages for its active members" (1922/1968, p. 284). The Democratic and Republican parties in the United States are obvious examples of what Weber intends. Other examples include student unions or special interest groups such as the tobacco lobby, if they are oriented toward controlling and exercising power.

Crosscutting Stratification

One of Weber's enduring contributions to conflict theory is this tripartite distinction of stratification. Marx rightly argues that overt conflict is dependent upon bipolarization. The closer an issue of conflict gets to having only two defined sides, the more likely is the conflict to become overt and violent. But

Weber gives us an understanding of stratification that shows the difficulty in achieving bipolarization.

Every individual sits at a unique confluence of class, status, and party; this **cross-cutting stratification** creates various interests that sometimes contradict one another. I have a class position, but I also have a variety of status positions and political issues that concern me. While these may influence one another, they may also be somewhat different. To the degree that these issues are different, it will be difficult to achieve a unified perspective. For example, let's say you're white, gay, male, the director of human resources at one of the nation's largest firms, and Catholic. Some of these social categories come together, like being white, male, and in upper management. But some don't. If this is true of you as an individual, then it is even more so in your association with other people. You'll find very few white, gay, male, Catholic upper managers to hang around with. And if you add in other important status identities, such as Southern Democrat, it becomes even more complex. Thus, Weber is arguing that the kind of conflict that produces social change is a very complex issue. Different factors have to come together in unique ways in order for us to begin to formulate groups and identities capable of bringing about social change.

Authority and Social Change

At the heart of the issue of stratification and social change is legitimacy, and here we see Weber's emphasis on culture. When you see things through a cultural lens, as does Weber, you realize that for society or a social structure to work, people have to *believe* in it. **Legitimation** refers to the process by which power is not only institutionalized but more importantly is given moral grounding. Legitimations contain discourses or stories that we tell ourselves that make a social structure appear valid and acceptable. The strongest legitimations will make social structure appear inevitable and beyond human control (for example, the essentialist arguments surrounding gender—women cannot think logically and men cannot nurture children because of the nature of their sex). Weber argues that all oppressive structures, and, in fact, all uses of power, must exist within a legitimated order.

A legitimated order creates a unified worldview and is based on a complex mixture of two kinds of legitimations: subjective (internalized ethical and religious norms) and objective (having the possibility of enforced sanctions from the social group [conventions] or an organizational staff [law]). Weber indicates that subjective legitimacy is assumed in the presence of the objective. Underlying both subjective and objective legitimacy are three different kinds of belief systems or authority (charismatic, traditional, and rational-legal). Legitimacy works only because people believe in the rightness of the system. So, for example, your professor tells you that you will be taking a test in two weeks. And in two weeks you show up to take the test. No one has to force you; you simply do it because you believe in the right of the professor to give tests. And that's Weber's point: Social structures can function because of belief in a cultural system.

In order for a system of domination to work, people must believe in it. Part of the reason behind this need is the cost involved in the use of power. If people don't believe in authority to some degree, they will have to be forced to comply through coercive power. The use of coercive power requires high levels of external social control mechanisms, such as monitoring (you have to be able to watch and see if people are conforming) and force (because they won't do it willingly). To maintain a system of domination not based on legitimacy costs a great deal in terms of technology and manpower. In addition, people often ultimately respond to the use of coercion by either rebelling or giving up—the end result is thus contrary to the desired goal.

Authority, on the other hand, implies the ability to require performance that is based upon the performer's belief in the rightness of the system. Because authority is based on socialization, the internalization of cultural norms and values, authority requires low levels of external social control. We can thus say that any structure of domination can exist in the long run if and only if there is a corresponding culture of authority. Weber identifies three ideal types of authority. (Keep in mind that these are ideal types and may be found in various configurations in any society.)

- *Charismatic authority:* belief in the supernatural or intrinsic gifts of the individual. People respond to this kind of authority because they believe that the individual has a special calling. (Examples of this type of authority include Susan B. Anthony, Adolf Hitler, Martin Luther King Jr., John F. Kennedy, Golda Meir, and Jesus—notice that it is people's belief in the charisma that matters; thus, we can have Hitler and Jesus on the same list.)

- *Traditional authority:* belief in time and custom. People respond to this kind of authority because they honor the past and they believe that time-proven methods are the best. (Good examples of this type of authority are your parents and grandparents, the Pope, and monarchies.)

- *Rational-legal authority:* belief in procedure. People respond to this kind of authority because they believe that the requirements or laws have been enacted in the proper manner. People see leaders as having the right to act when they obtain positions in the procedurally correct way. (A good example of this type is your professor—it does not matter who the professor is, as long as he or she fulfills the requirements of the job.)

These diverse types of authority interact differently in the process of social change. According to Weber, the only kind of authority that can instigate social change is charismatic. Traditional and rational-legal authorities bring social stability—they are each designed to maintain the system. Charismatic individuals come to bring social change, yet charismatic authority is also inherently precarious. Because charisma is based on belief in the special abilities of the individual, every instance of charismatic authority will fail within that person's lifetime—the gifts die with the person. Thus, every charismatic authority will someday have to face the **problem of routinization** (making something routine and thus predicable). Every social movement based upon charismatic authority—and Weber argues that they all are—routinizes the changes by either using traditional authority or rational-legal authority.

The case of the Christian church might give us insight. Jesus was a charismatic leader. When he died, the church was faced with the problem of continuing his leadership. Though somewhat a gloss, it can be said that the Catholic Church is based upon the traditional authority of the Pope and that Protestant churches are based upon rational-legal authority. You cannot study to become a Pope, but you can study to become a Protestant minister. As I said, this is a gloss: People do study to become priests, and ministers are perceived as charismatically ordained by God. So, these authority systems are mixed (as is always the case with ideal types). But their systems are stabilized through the use of tradition and bureaucracy.

Combining Weber's ideas of class, status, and party with his argument concerning authority and social change, we can put together a theory of conflict and social change (see Figure 4.5). Social change will occur only if the legitimacy of the system of stratification is questioned. Conflict and change are likely to occur when there are clear breaks between or limited upward mobility in one of the systems—I've depicted this in the figure as "perceived group boundary." Groups will tend to perceive their boundaries when in close proximity to another competing group or when mobility is limited. It is possible for change to occur in only one of three areas, but that change will be limited due to the crosscutting influences of the other

Figure 4.5 Weber's Theory of Social Change

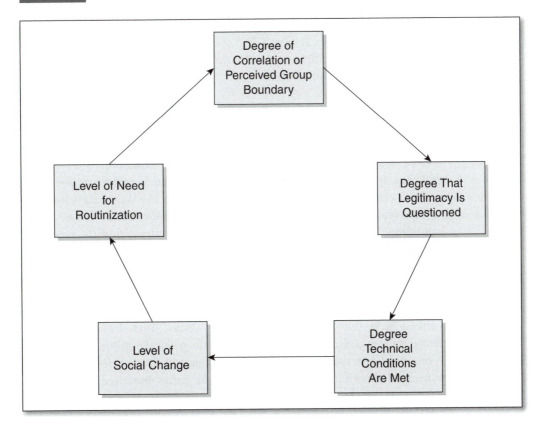

systems. In the United States, for example, many people questioned the legitimacy of the systems of race and gender during the 1960s and 1970s. These systems are primarily built around and understood through status. So, while there have been some real structural changes, it appears that *most* of the change in race and gender systems is cultural—the status of each has been improved. (Please note the "appears" in my statement: This issue needs close empirical research.)

In a Weberian sense, significant social change will occur if and when there is perceived correlation among class, status, and power ("degree of correlation" in Figure 4.5). In other words, if people perceive that certain groups are high on all three stratification systems and certain groups are low, then they are more likely to question the legitimacy of the whole system rather than just one part. This delegitimation is particularly likely when the correlation is perceived as arbitrary. As legitimacy is questioned, the technical conditions of group conflict tend to be met. These include charismatic leadership, clearly articulated goals and ideology, and the ability to meet and communicate. Note that there is a reciprocal effect between questioning legitimacy and technical conditions: Each will tend to reinforce the other. As technical conditions are met, the group will become more effectual in bringing about social change. The degree of social change in turn will impact the need for routinization.

Weber argues that routinization will in the long run lead to a kind of stratification that again sets up the conditions for conflict and change. In this respect, Weber's model is more dialectical than Marx's, which stops with the advent of communism, but Weber sees conflict and change as ubiquitous features of every social system. For Weber, social systems will move cyclically through routinization and charismatic change. At different times, for different reasons, social groups will question the legitimacy of domination.

Summary

- To think like Weber is to take seriously the ramifications of culture. Weberians focus on the historical, cultural, and social contexts wherein the subjective orientation of the actor takes place. To think like Weber, then, means to use ideal types and *Verstehen* to explain how these contexts came to exist rather than others. To think like Weber also means paying attention to the process of rationalization and the need for legitimation.

- Religion began with the movement from naturalistic to symbolic ways of seeing the world. The movement toward symbolism and religion was influenced by increases in economic technologies and professionalization. Religion was initially practiced in kinship-based groups with local deities. These local gods became hierarchically organized into pantheons due to the political organization of kinship groups into larger collectives, and the abstracting and rationalizing effects of the professional priesthood. Eventually, these same forces produced the idea of a monotheistic god under which all the other gods were subsumed and finally disappeared. Monotheism became ethical monotheism in response to the need of polity to control behavior on a large scale.

- The cultural foundations of rational capitalism were laid by Protestantism. This religious movement (through the doctrines of predestination and abstention, and the idea of a calling) indirectly created a rationalizing, individuating culture wherein money could be made for the purpose of making *more* money, rather than for immediate enjoyment. The establishment of nation-states structurally paved the way for rational capitalism by creating a free labor force, controlling large territories, standardizing money, and protecting free global markets.

- Social stratification is a complex of three scarce resources: class, status, and power. These three systems produce crosscutting interests that make social change difficult and multifaceted. Large-scale social changes become increasingly likely only as class, status, and power are seen to correlate; the legitimacy of the system is questioned; and the technical conditions of organization are met. Since social change is led by charismatic authority, each change will need to be routinized through traditional or rational-legal authority, which, in the long run, will once again set up conditions for conflict and social change.

- Bureaucratic forms of organization became prominent as societies became larger and more democratic, as tasks and knowledge became more complex, as communication and transportation technologies increased, and as markets became more widespread through the use of money. The extent of bureaucratic organization can be measured through an ideal type consisting of six variables: explicit division of labor, office hierarchy, written rules and communication, accreditation for position, affectless (without emotion or emotional connection) management by rule, and the ownership of career ladders and position by the organization. The use of bureaucracy as the chief organizing technology of a society results in the bureaucratic personality, the iron cage of bureaucracy, and social emphasis on credentials.

TAKING THE PERSPECTIVE—
CULTURAL SOCIOLOGY AND ACTION THEORY

As I mentioned previously, Weber has had significant impact on a number of diverse sociological traditions. He of course contributed to conflict theory, which we review in Chapter 3. In Chapter 9, we'll look at Ralf Dahrendorf's conflict theory and you'll see his integration of Weber's ideas. Weber is also the primary foundation for the sociology of organizations. All studies of bureaucracy come back to Weber. One of the earliest and best-known applications is found in Peter M. Blau and Marshall W. Meyer's *Bureaucracy in Modern Society*, New York: McGraw-Hill, 1987. An interesting and popular application is George Ritzer's *The McDonaldization of Society*, Thousand Oaks, CA: Pine Forge, 2004.

(Continued)

(Continued)

Weber has also had impact on cultural sociology. The concept of culture covers a broad range of issues: ideas, recipes for action, tools, products, norms, values, beliefs, art, and so on. More simply we can say that culture is made up of symbolic and material elements that transmit meaning across time and space. While culture has been central to sociology since its inception, it has appeared generally as a topic of study. But Weber gives hints at a more general approach that has recently been gaining force through the work of Jeffrey Alexander. Rather than studying culture, per se, cultural sociology keeps meaning central in all analysis (see http://research.yale.edu/ccs/), not just when studying culture. Alexander argues that the ideas, values, and discourses of a society—its culture—are structured through binary codes of purity and impurity. Social change occurs as people, organizations, and institutions interpret the meanings of these codes and put those meanings into practice.

Another significant area that Weber has influenced is action theory. **Action theory** has been an interest of philosophy since the time of Aristotle; in sociology action theory begins with Weber. Both disciplines are concerned with theories that explain the complex process of intentional or willful action. Weber argues that action takes place when a person's behavior is meaningfully oriented toward other social actors, usually as types of instrumental or value rationality. George Herbert Mead (Chapter 6) is interested in what happens within a person that makes action possible. For Mead, action first takes place in the mind through a felt impulse to act, symbolic perception and manipulation, and finally the physical act. Talcott Parsons (Chapter 8) looks at the context within which action takes place. He argues that people are motivated to act by individual biological or personal needs, but those needs must be met socially. People, then, develop shortcuts to action by creating norms and information that outline sets of ends and means. In contemporary sociology the issue of action is central to exchange and rational choice theorists, organizational theories of decision-making, and studies of how action is achieved through taken for granted rules and stocks of knowledge.

BUILDING YOUR THEORY TOOLBOX

Learning More—Primary and Secondary Sources

- For primary sources for Weber's work, I suggest starting off with *The Protestant Ethic and the Spirit of Capitalism*. It's one of his most accessible books. After that, move on to the following:
  - Weber, M. (1948). *From Max Weber: Essays in Sociology* (H. H. Gerth & C. Wright Mills, Trans. & Eds.). London: Routledge and Kegan Paul.
  - Weber, M. (1968). *Economy and Society* (G. Roth & C. Wittich, Eds.). Berkeley: University of California Press. (Originally published 1922)
  - Weber, M. (1988). *Max Weber: A Biography* (H. Zohn, Trans.). New Brunswick: Transaction Books. (Definitive biography, written by Weber's wife)

- There are a number of very good secondary sources for Weber's work; I suggest the following:
    - Bendix, R. (1977). *Max Weber: An Intellectual Portrait.* Berkeley: University of California Press. (The standard Weber reference)
    - Collins, R. (1986). *Weberian Sociological Theory.* New York: Cambridge University Press. (Systemization of Weber's theory by a prominent contemporary theorist)
    - Turner, B. S. (1992). *Max Weber: From History to Modernity.* New York: Routledge. (Explanation of Weber's theories of modernity)
    - Turner, S. P. (2000). *The Cambridge Companion to Max Weber.* New York: Cambridge University Press. (Excellent resource concerning Weber's works and influence)

Seeing the Social World (knowing the theory)

- Write a 250-word synopsis of cultural sociology.

- After reading and understanding this chapter, you should be able to define the following terms theoretically and explain their theoretical importance to Weber's theory: *ideal types, Verstehen, action, rationalization, magic and religion, professionalization, symbolism, traditional and rational capitalism, spirit of capitalism, bureaucracy, bureaucratic personality, instrumental-rational action, value-rational action, traditional action, affective action, credentialing, class, status, power, crosscutting stratification, legitimation, authority (charismatic, traditional, rational-legal), routinization, bureaucracy*

- After reading and understanding this chapter, you should be able to answer the following questions (remember to answer them *theoretically*):
    - Explain how religion evolved to ethical monotheism.
    - Explain how capitalism came to exist.
    - Describe how bureaucracies came to be the central organizing feature of modernity. What are the elements of Weber's ideal type? How do bureaucracies impact you and society?
    - Explain Weber's theory of stratification and social change.

Engaging the Social World (using the theory)

- One of the central themes in Weberian theory is rationalization (as a contemporary example, see George Ritzer's *The McDonaldization of Society*). Take a look at your life: In what ways has rationality influenced you? Do you think your life is more or less rationalized than your parents' was at your age? Let's take this one step further. Go to a place of business, like a fast-food restaurant or mall, and observe behaviors for at least two hours. How rationalized were the actions you observed? Overall, do you think that life is becoming increasingly rationalized? What are the benefits and drawbacks to rationalization? How do you think Weber felt about this process?

(Continued)

(Continued)

- Get a sense of the kinds of jobs you can get today with a college education and the jobs available with the same education 50 years ago. You can do this by using your Internet search engine, going to http://nces.ed.gov/ and searching the data, or by asking your parents and grandparents. Explain your findings using Weber's theory. What do you think society can or should do in response to these changes? Using Weber's theory, do you think this trend will continue or abate? Do you think the purpose of education has changed in this country? To what level is education completely funded by government (that is, to what level is education free); why to that level, do you think?

- Think about Weber's ideal type of the spirit of capitalism. Are those traits more or less present in the United States today? Does this imply anything about capitalism in this country? Are we perhaps practicing a different kind of capitalism? If so, what would you call it?

- Weber gives us a robust theory concerning the rise of ethical monotheism. One of the interesting things that Weber's theory of religion tells us is that religion is clearly related to a political regime's interest in social control. Do you think there have been any changes in the structure or kind of religion practiced since Weber's time? If so, what kinds of changes? What kinds of social factors do you think are responsible for these changes (think about how Weber associated professionalism and economic changes with shifts in religion)? What, if anything, do these changes indicate about the state and social control?

- In addition to being spiritual centers, churches are social organizations. As such, Weber would argue that the type of authority and the concurrent organizational type that a church uses will influence the church and its parishioners. Using either your own experiences or by calling various churches in your area, what kind of authority and organization do you find to be most prevalent? Using Weber's theory, how do you think the church is being affected?

Weaving the Threads (building theory)

- Compare and contrast Marx and Weber on the origins of capitalism. Can these theories be reconciled in any way? Do you think one is more correct than the other? Why or why not?

- Compare and contrast Marx and Weber on structures of inequality and social change. What information does Weber give us about inequality that Marx doesn't? According to Weberian theory, what class did Marx miss entirely? Do you think that negates Marx's theory? How are Marx's and Weber's theories of social change the same and different? Can we bring them together to form a more powerful theoretical understanding of the conditions under which social change or conflict are likely to occur?

- Compare and contrast Spencer and Weber on the foundation of state power. How does Marx's theory critique both Spencer and Weber?

CHAPTER 5

The Problem With Diversity:

Émile Durkheim

(1885–1917)

Cultural diversity is a byword in modern society. It generally refers to racial or ethnic diversity. However, if we think about cultural diversity theoretically, the phrase "racial or ethnic diversity" begs the question: How is it that racial or ethnic groups come to have different cultures? Most people simply assume that different races and ethnic groups have diverse cultures. Yet there is no necessary relationship between what we think of as race and cultural diversity. In fact, race itself is a cultural designation. For example, did you know that at one time in the United States, "Irish" was considered a "black" racial group? They were referred to derogatorily as the "black Irish."

Theoretically and sociologically, then, it is much better to ask how cultural diversity is created rather than simply assuming it exists. Besides, cultural diversity is much broader than merely race and ethnicity. For example, it is quite possible that the cultural differences between the elite and the poor are greater than the differences between racial groups within the same society. So, how is cultural diversity created? More specifically, what are the general processes through which cultural differences are created, whether among racial, ethnic, class, or gender groups? Émile Durkheim provides us with answers to these kinds of questions.

Yet Durkheim is actually concerned with a more important issue, one that few people think about when considering cultural diversity. His concern is based on the insight that every society needs a certain level of cultural integration and social solidarity to exist and function. Durkheim's main concern is this: How much cultural diversity can a society have and still function? Think about an extreme situation as an example: Picture two people who speak totally different languages. How easy would it be for them to carry on a conversation? If it was necessary, they undoubtedly could find a way, but what they could talk about would be limited and it would take a great deal of time to have even the simplest of conversations.

The same is true with cultural diversity. Cultural diversity includes language, but it also encompasses nonverbal cues, dialects, values, normative behaviors, beliefs and assumptions about the world, and so on. The more different people are from one another, the more difficult it will be for them to work together and communicate, which is the basis of any society. Durkheim, then, specifically asks, how can a diverse society create social solidarity and function?

One of the reasons that Durkheim is concerned with cultural diversity and moral integration is due to his assumptions about human nature. Where Marx assumes that humans are social and naturally altruistic, Durkheim assumes that people apart from society are self-centered and driven by insatiable desires. While Durkheim gives us an answer to the question of integration in the face of cultural diversity, he also addresses the deeper problem of human egoism. If we assume, as Durkheim does, that individuals tend to go off each in his or her own direction, then how can this thing called society work? Durkheim came up with an ingenious answer: the collective consciousness. Today, sociologists usually talk about norms, values, and beliefs, but in back of those terms lies Durkheim's idea of the collective consciousness.

THEORIST'S DIGEST

Brief Biography

David Émile Durkheim was born in Epinal, France, on April 15, 1858. His mother, Melanie, was a merchant's daughter, and his father, Moïse, was a rabbi, descended from generations of rabbis. Durkheim did well in high school and attended the prestigious *École Normale Supérieure* in Paris, the training ground for the new French intellectual elite.

The first years (1882–1887) after finishing school, Durkheim taught philosophy in Paris, but felt philosophy was a poor approach to solving the social ills he was surrounded by. In 1887, Durkheim was appointed as *Chargé d'un Cours de Science Sociale et de Pédagogie* at the University of Bordeaux. Durkheim thus became the first teacher of sociology in the French system. Durkheim and his desire for a science of morality proved to be a thorn in the side of the predominantly humanist faculty. During this year, Durkheim also married Louise Dreyfus; they later had two children, Marie and André.

In 1902, Durkheim took a post at the Sorbonne and by 1906 was appointed Professor of the Science of Education, a title later changed to Professor of Science of Education and Sociology. In this position, Durkheim was responsible for training the future teachers of France and served as chief advisor to the Ministry of Education.

In December 1915, Durkheim received word that his son, André, had been declared missing in action (World War I). André had followed in his father's footsteps to *École Normale* and was seen as an exceptionally promising social linguist. Durkheim had hoped his son would complete the research he had begun in linguistic classifications. The following April, Durkheim received official notification that his son was dead. Durkheim withdrew into a "ferocious silence." After only a few months following his son's death, Durkheim suffered a stroke; he died at the age of 59 on November 15, 1917.

Central Sociological Questions

Durkheim is intensely concerned with understanding how social solidarity and integration could be preserved in modernity. He recognizes that society is built on a foundation of shared values and morals. Yet he also realizes that there are structural forces at work in modernity that relentlessly produce cultural diversity, something that could tear away this foundation of social solidarity. His project, then, is to discover and implement the necessary social processes that could create a new kind of unity in society, one that would allow the dynamics of modernity to function within a context of social integration.

Simply Stated

Durkheim sees individuals apart from society as concerned only with their own desires that, because of human nature, are insatiable. Thus, the one thing society needs above all else is a common, moral culture—a set of ideas, values, beliefs, norms, and practices that guide us to act collectively rather than individually. Given that moral culture is the basis of society, Durkheim argues that society first began in religion. Modernity, however, creates a problem

(Continued)

(Continued)

that threatens to tear apart society's moral basis: social diversity created through structural differentiation and the division of labor. The main solution to this problem is that moral culture must evolve and become more general—able to embrace greater levels of social diversity—through the formation of intermediary groups, restitutive law, the centralization and rationalization of law, and social and structural interdependency.

Key Ideas

social facts, society sui generis, collective conscious, religion, sacred and profane, ritual, effervescence, social solidarity (mechanical and organic), punitive and restitutive law, the division of labor, social differentiation, cultural generalization, intermediary groups, social pathologies, anomie, suicide (altruistic, fatalistic, egoistic, and anomic), the cult of the individual

Concepts and Theory: The Reality of Society

As we saw in Spencer, the idea of society changed with the beginning of modernity. For the first time something collective, something grander than simple association, was seen to exist. People began to wonder about and try to understand this new entity modernity had brought into existence. Most of the speculations of the time were formed in philosophical terms and began with certain assumptions about the natural state of human beings apart from society. Thomas Hobbes, for example, argued that human nature is basically warlike; on the other hand, John Locke believed that humans are naturally peaceful.

In contrast to philosophical beginnings, Charles Montesquieu argued that the study of society should begin empirically: with what we see, not with what we think. In some ways, Montesquieu's book *The Spirit of Laws* may be considered the first empirical work of sociology. In it, Montesquieu argues that society must be viewed as an empirical object. As an independent object, its properties and processes could be discovered through observation. Interestingly enough, Montesquieu also argues that the human being is really the product of society, not the other way around. It follows, then, that any attempt to understand society that begins with human nature would have to be false, since human nature is itself a creation of society.

Social Facts

Durkheim draws from Montesquieu in his thinking about society. He argues that society exists as an empirical object, almost like a physical object in the environment. Durkheim uses the concept **social fact** to argue for the objectivity of society and scientific sociology. According to Durkheim, social facts gain their **facticity** because they are external to and coercive of the individual. We can't smell, see, taste, or touch them, but we can feel their objective influence. Durkheim distinguishes between material and nonmaterial elements in social facts. Material elements are like cultural artifacts: They are what would survive if the present society no longer existed. For example, a wheelbarrow is a material social fact. Nonmaterial elements consist of symbolic meanings and collective sentiments. Often such features are attached to material objects, like the meanings behind statues and flags, but many times our most important meanings and feelings have a more abstract existence, like love and freedom.

In addition, society exists as a social fact because it exists sui generis—a Latin term meaning "of its own kind." Durkheim uses the term to say that society exists in and of itself, not as a "mere epiphenomenon of its morphological base." Society is more to Durkheim than simply the sum of all the individuals within it. Society exists as its own kind of entity, obeying its own rules and creating its own effects: "*The determining cause of a social fact should be sought among the social facts preceding it and not among the states of the individual consciousness*" (Durkheim, 1895/1938, p. 110, emphasis original).

Let me give you an example of what Durkheim means when he says that the cause of social facts is other social facts. One of Durkheim's most famous studies is *Suicide*. In it, he studied suicide rates, not individual suicides. The suicide rate ("the proportion between the total number of voluntary deaths and the population of every age and sex") is a social fact. The suicide rate measures a collective's "definite aptitude for suicide" at any given historical moment and "is itself a new fact *sui generis,* with its own unity, individuality and consequently its own nature" (Durkheim, 1897/1951, p. 46). The suicide rate of any given society can be understood through social types—egoistic, altruistic, anomic, and fatalistic suicides—and each of these types is caused by its relationship to two other social facts: group attachment and behavior regulation. In other words, the suicide rate (a social fact) is caused by other social facts (group attachment and behavior regulation).

Collective Consciousness

But society does more than exist outside of us; and it does more than simply coerce us to perform actions we don't want to. In fact, society forms our basic awareness of the world around us through the collective consciousness. For Durkheim, the **collective consciousness** is the totality of ideas, representations, beliefs, and feelings that are common to the average members of society. There does exist, of course, the individual consciousness. However, whatever unique ideas, feelings, beliefs, impressions, and so forth that an individual might have are by definition idiosyncratic. In other words, "Individual consciousnesses are actually closed to one another" (Durkheim, 1995/1912, p. 231). The collective consciousness, on the other hand, does allow us a basis for sharing our awareness of the world. Yet the function of this body of culture is not simply to express our inner states to one another; the collective consciousness contributes to the making of our individual subjective states. It is through the collective consciousness that society becomes aware of itself and we become aware of ourselves as social beings.

Durkheim divides the collective consciousness into two basic features: cognitive and emotional. Durkheim argues that the collective consciousness contains primary symbolic categories (time, space, number, cause, substance, and personality). These categories are primary because we can't think without using them. They form our basic cognitions or consciousness of the world around us. These categories are, of course, of social origin for Durkheim, originating with the physical features of society. (The way the population is dispersed in space, for example, influences the way we conceive of space.) Durkheim did some work (*Primitive Classification*) in this area of cognitive categories, especially with his pupil and nephew Marcel Mauss. His work in this area also influenced Ferdinand De Saussure, the founder of French Structuralism (which led to poststructuralism and influenced postmodernism). However, I think for Durkheim the more important aspect of the collective consciousness is emotional. Social emotions or sentiments "dominate us, they possess, so to speak, something superhuman about them. At the same time they bind us to objects that lie outside our existence in time" (Durkheim, 1893/1984, p. 56).

If, as Durkheim supposes, humans are naturally self-serving, then why will self-centered human beings act collectively and selflessly? Durkheim argues that rational exchange principles are not enough. Because our entire being is involved in action, we need to be emotionally bound to our culture. We have to have an emotional sense of something greater than ourselves. This feeling of something greater is what underlies morality. We act socially because it is moral to do so. While we can always give reasons for our actions, many of our actions—especially social actions—generally come about because of *feelings* of responsibility: "Whence, then, the feeling of obligation? It is because in fact we are not purely rational beings; we are also emotional creatures" (Durkheim, 1903/1961, p. 112). So to think like Durkheim is to always be concerned with the emotional foundations of social life.

Concepts and Theory: Religious Roots of Society

Durkheim had two major purposes in writing *The Elementary Forms of Religious Life,* his thesis on religion. Durkheim's primary aim was to understand the empirical elements present in all religions. He wanted to go behind the symbolic and spiritual to grasp what he calls "the real." Durkheim intentionally puts aside the issue of God and spirituality. He argues that no matter what religion is involved, whether Christianity or Islam, and no matter what god is proclaimed, there are certain social elements that are common to all religions. To put this issue another way, anytime a god does anything here on earth, there appear to be certain social elements always present. Durkheim is interested in discovering those empirical, social elements.

Religion and Science

Durkheim's second reason for writing his book is a bit trickier to understand. For Durkheim, *religion* is the most fundamental social institution. He argues that religion is the source of everything social. That's not to say that everything social is religious, especially today. But Durkheim is convinced that social bonds were first created through religion. We'll see that in ancient clan societies, the symbol that bound the group together and created a sense of kinship (family) was principally a religious one.

Further, Durkheim argues that our basic categories of understanding are of religious origin. Humans divide the world up using categories. We understand things in terms of animal, mineral, vegetable, edible, inedible, private property, public property, male, female, and on and on. Durkheim says that many of the categories we use are of what one might call "fashionable" origin, that is, culture that is subject to change. Durkheim argues that fashion is a recent phenomenon and that its basic social function is to distinguish the upper classes from the lower. There is a tendency for fashion to circulate. The lower classes want to be like the upper classes and thus want to use their symbols (we want to drive their cars, wear the same kinds of clothes they do, and so on). This implies, in the end, that fashionable culture is rather meaningless: "Once a fashion has been adopted by everyone, it loses all its value; it is thus doomed by its own nature to renew itself endlessly" (Durkheim, 1887/1993, p. 87).

Durkheim has little if any concern for such culture (though quite a bit of contemporary cultural theory and analysis is taken up with it). He is interested in primary "categories of understanding." He argues that these categories—time, space, number, cause, substance, and personality—are of social origin, but not the same kind of social origin that fashion has. Fashion comes about as different groups demarcate themselves through decoration, and in that sense it isn't tied to anything real. It is purely the work of imagination. The primary categories of understanding, on the other hand, are tied to objective reality. Durkheim argues that the primary categories originate *empirically and objectively in society,* in what he calls social morphology.

Merriam-Webster (2002) defines morphology as "a branch of biology that deals with the form and structure of animals and plants." So, when Durkheim talks about *social morphology,* he is using the organismic analogy to refer to the form and structure of society, in particular the way in which populations are distributed in time and space. Let's take time, for example. In order to conceive of time, we must first conceive of differentiation. Time, apart from humans, appears like a cyclical stream. There is daytime and nighttime and seasons that endlessly repeat themselves. Yet that isn't how we experience time. For us, time is chopped up. Today, for example, the day I'm writing these words, is March 31, 2010. However, that date and the divisions underlying it are not a function of the way time appears naturally. So, from where do the divisions come? "The division into days, weeks, months, years, etc., corresponds to the recurrence of rites, festivals, and public ceremonies at regular intervals. A calendar expresses the rhythm of collective activity while ensuring that regularity" (Durkheim, 1912/1995, p. 10). The same is true with space. There is no up, down, right, left, and so on apart from the orientation of human beings that is itself social.

The important thing to see here is that Durkheim makes the claim that the way in which we divide up time and space, and the way we conceive of causation and number, is not a function of the things themselves, nor is it a function of mental divisions. Rather, the way we conceive of these primary categories is a function of the objective form of society—the ways in which we distribute and organize populations and social structures. Our primary categories of understanding come into existence through the way we distribute ourselves in time and space; they reflect our gatherings and rituals. Thus, all of our thinking is founded upon social facts, and these social facts, according to Durkheim, originated in religion.

Durkheim wants to make a point beyond social epistemology. He argues that if our basic categories of understanding have their roots in religion, then all systems of thought, such as science and philosophy, have their basis in religion. Durkheim (1912/1995) extends this theme, stating that "there is no religion that is not both a cosmology and a speculation about the divine" (p. 8). Notice that there are two functions of religion in this quote. One has to do with speculations about the divine—in other words, religion provides faith and ideas about God. Also notice the other function: to provide a cosmology. A *cosmology* is a systematic understanding of the origin, structure, and space–time relationships of the universe. Durkheim is right: Every religion tells us what the universe is about—how it was created, how it works, what its purpose is, and so on. But so does science, and that's Durkheim's point. Speculations about the universe began in religion; ideas about causation began in religion. Therefore, the social world, even in its most logical of pursuits, was set in motion by religion.

Defining Religion

But how did religion begin? Here we turn back again to Durkheim's principal purpose: to explain the origins of religion. In order to get at his argument, we will consider the data Durkheim uses, his definition of religion, and, most importantly, how the sacred is produced. The data that Durkheim employs are important because of his argument and intent. He wants to get at the most general social features underlying all religions—in other words, apart from doctrine, he wants to discern what is common to all religions. To discover those commonalities, Durkheim contends that one has to look at the most primitive forms of religion.

Using contemporary religion to understand the basic forms of religion has some problems, most notably the natural effects of history and storytelling. You've probably either played or heard of the game "telephone," where people sit in a circle and take turns whispering a story to one another. What happens, as you know, is that the story changes in the telling. The same is true with religion, at least in terms of its origins. Basically what Durkheim is saying is that the further we get away from the origins of religion, the greater will be the confusion around why and how religion began in the first place. Also, because ancient religion was simpler, using the historical approach allows us to break the social phenomenon down into its constituent parts and identify the circumstances under which it was born. For Durkheim, the most ancient form of religion is *totemism*. He uses data on totemic religions from Australian Aborigines and Native American tribes for his research.

Conceptually, prior to deciding what data to use, Durkheim had to create a definition of religion. In any research, it is always of utmost importance to clearly delineate what will count and what will not count as your subject. For example, if you were going to study the institution of education, one of the things you would have to contend with is whether home schooling or Internet courses would count, or do only accredited teachers in state-supported organizations constitute the institution of education? The same kinds of issues exist with religion. Durkheim had to decide on his definition of religion before choosing his data sources—he had to know ahead of time what counts as religion and what doesn't, especially since he wanted to look at its most primitive form:

> *A religion is a unified system of beliefs and practices relative to sacred things, that is to say, things set apart and forbidden—beliefs and practices which unite into one single moral community called a Church, all those who adhere to them.* (Durkheim, 1912/1995, p. 44, emphasis original)

Note carefully what is missing from Durkheim's definition: There is no mention of the supernatural or God. Durkheim argues that before humans could think about the supernatural, they first had to have a clear idea about what was natural. The term *supernatural* assumes the division of the universe into two categories: things that can be rationally explained and those that can't. Now, think about this—when was it that people began to think that things could be rationally explained? It took quite of bit of human history for us to stop believing that there are spirits in back of everything. We had gods of thunder, forests, harvest, water, fire, fertility, and so on. Early humans saw spiritual forces behind almost everything, which means that the idea of *nature* didn't occur until much later in our history. The concept of nature—those elements of life that occur apart from spiritual influence—didn't truly begin until the advent of science. So, the idea of supernatural is a recent invention of humanity and therefore can't be included in a definition of religion, since there has never been society without religion—early societies would have had religion but no concept of supernatural.

Durkheim also argues that we cannot include the notion of God in the definition of religion. His logic here concerns the fact that there are many belief systems that are generally considered religion that do not require a god. Though he includes other religions such as Jainism, his principal example is Buddhism. The focus of Buddhist faith is the Four Noble Truths, and "salvation" occurs apart from any divine intervention. There are deities acknowledged by Buddhism, such as Indra, Agni, and Varuna, but the entire Buddhist faith can be practiced apart from them. The practicing Buddhist needs no god to thank or worship, yet we would be hard pressed to not call Buddhism a religion.

Thus, three things constitute religion in its most basic form: the sacred, beliefs and practices, and a moral community. The important thing to notice about Durkheim's definition is the centrality of the notion of the sacred. Every element of the definition revolves around it. The beliefs and practices are relative to sacred things and the moral community exists because of the beliefs and practices, which of course brings us back to sacred things. So at the heart of religion is this idea of the sacred.

Creating the Sacred

But what are sacred things? By that I mean, what makes something sacred? For most of us in the United States, we think of the cross or the Bible as sacred objects. It's easy for us to think they are sacred because of some intrinsic quality they possess. The cross is sacred because Jesus died on it. However, the idea of the intrinsic worth of the object falls apart when we consider all that humanity has thought of as sacred. Humans have used crosses, stones, kangaroos, snakes, birds, water, swastikas, flags, and yellow ribbons—almost anything—to represent the sacred. Durkheim's point is that sacredness is not a function of the object; sacredness is something that is placed *upon* the object:

> Since, in themselves, neither man nor nature is inherently sacred, both acquire sacredness elsewhere. Beyond the human individual and the natural world, then, there must be some other reality. (Durkheim, 1912/1995, pp. 84–85)

We could argue that sacredness comes through association; that's true at least in part. We think the cross is sacred because of its association with Jesus. But what makes the image of an owl sacred? It can't just be its association with the owl, so there must be something else in back of it. What, then, can make both the owl and the cross of Jesus sacred? (Remember, with a positivist like Durkheim, we are looking for *general* explanations, ones that will fit all instances.) Durkheim wouldn't accept the answer that there is some general spiritual entity in back of all sacred things. To begin with, the sacred things and their beliefs are too varied. But more importantly, Durkheim is interested in the *objective* reality behind religion. So, how can we explain the power of the sacred using objective, general terms? Durkheim begins with his consideration of totemic religion.

Totems had some interesting functions. For instance, they created a bond of kinship among people unrelated by blood. Each clan was composed of various hunting and gathering groups. These groups lived most of their lives separately, but they periodically came together for celebrations. The groups weren't related by blood, nor were they connected geographically. What held them together was that all the members of the clan carried the same name—the name of their totem—and the members of these groups acted toward one another as if they were family. They had obligations to help each other, to seek vengeance on behalf of each other, to not marry one another, and so forth based on family relations.

In addition to creating a kinship name for the clans, the totem acted as an emblem that represented the clan. It acted as a symbol both to those within the clan and those outside it. The symbol was inscribed on banners and tents and was tattooed on bodies. When the clan eventually settled in one place, the symbol was carved into doors and walls. The totem thus formed bonds, and it represented the clan.

In addition, the totem was used during religious ceremonies. In fact, Durkheim (1912/1995) tells us, "Things are classified as sacred and profane by reference to the totem. It is the very archetype of sacred things" (p. 118). Different items became sacred because of the presence of the totem. For example, the clans both in daily and sacred life would use various musical instruments; the only difference between the sacred and the mundane instruments was the presence of the totemic symbol. The totem imparted the quality of being sacred to the object.

This is an immensely important point for Durkheim: The totem represents the clan and it creates bonds of kinship. It also represents and imparts the quality of being sacred. Durkheim then used a bit of algebraic logic: If A = B and B = C, then A and C are equal. So, "if the totem is the symbol of both the god and the society, is this not because the god and the society are the same?" (Durkheim, 1912/1995, p. 208). Here Durkheim begins to discover the reality behind the sacred and thus religion. The empirical reality behind the sacred has something to do with society, but what exactly?

One of the primary features of the sacred is that it stands diametrically opposed to the profane. In fact, one cannot exist in the presence of the other. Remember the story of Moses and the burning bush? Moses had to take off his shoes because he was standing on sacred ground. These kinds of stories are repeated over and over again in every religion. The sacred either destroys the profane or the sacred becomes contaminated by the presence of the profane. So, one of Durkheim's questions is, how did humans come to conceptualize these two distinct realms? The answer to this will help us discover the reality behind sacredness.

Durkheim found that the aborigines had two cycles to their lives, one in which they carried on their daily life in small groups and the other in which they gathered in large collectives. In the small groups, they would take care of daily needs through hunting and gathering. This was the place of home and hearth. Yet each of these small groups saw themselves as part of a larger group: the clan. Periodically, the small groups would gather together for large collective celebrations.

During these celebrations, the clan members were caught up in collective **effervescence**, or high levels of emotional energy. They found that their behaviors changed; they felt "possessed by a moral force greater than" the individual. "The effervescence often becomes so intense that it leads to outlandish behavior. . . . [Behaviors] in normal times judged loathsome and harshly condemned, are contracted in the open and with impunity" (Durkheim, 1912/1995, p. 218). These clan members began to conceive of two worlds: the mundane world of daily existence where they were in control, and the world of the clan where they were controlled by an external force greater than themselves. "The first is the profane world and the second, the world of sacred things. It is in these effervescent social milieux, and indeed from the very effervescence, that the religious idea seems to have been born" (Durkheim, 1912/1995, p. 220).

In some important ways, Durkheim is describing the genesis of society. Let's assume, as Durkheim and many others do, that human beings are by nature self-serving and individualistic. How, then, is society possible? One answer is found here: In Durkheimian thought, humans are linked emotionally. Undoubtedly these emotions, once established, mediate human connections unconsciously. That is, once humans are connected emotionally, it isn't necessary for them to rationally see or understand the connections, though we will always come up with legitimations. This emotional soup that Durkheim is describing is the stuff out of which human society is built. Initially, emotions run wild and so do behaviors in these kinds of primitive societies. But with repeated interactions, the emotions become focused and specified behaviors, symbols, and morals emerge.

In general, Durkheim is arguing that human beings are able to create high levels of emotional energy whenever they gather together. We've all felt something like what Durkheim is talking about at concerts or political rallies or sporting events. We get swept up in the excitement. At those times, we feel "the thrill of victory and the agony of defeat" more poignantly than at others. It is always more fun to watch a game with other people such as at a stadium. Part of the reason is the increase in emotional energy. In this case, the whole is greater than the sum of the parts, and something emerges that is felt outside the individual. This dynamic is what is in back of mob behavior and what we call "emergent norms." People get caught up in the overwhelming emotion of the moment and do things they normally wouldn't do.

Randall Collins (1988), a contemporary theorist, has captured Durkheim's theory in abstract terms. Generally speaking, there are three principal elements to the kind of interactions that Durkheim is describing: *co-presence,* which describes the degree of physical closeness in space (we can be closer or further away from one another); *common emotional mood,* the degree to which we share the same feeling about the event; and *common focus of attention,* the degree to which participants are attending to the same object, symbol, or idea at the same time (a difficult task to achieve, as any teacher knows).

When humans gather together in intense interactions—with high levels of co-presence, common emotional mood, and common focus of attention—they produce high levels of emotional energy. People then have a tendency to symbolize the emotional energy, which produces a sacred symbol, and to create **rituals** (patterned behaviors designed to replicate the three interaction elements). The symbols not only allow people to focus their attention and recall the emotion, they also give the collective emotion stability. These kinds of rituals and sacred symbols lead a group to become morally bounded; that is, many of the behaviors, speech patterns, styles of dress, and so on associated with the group become issues of right and wrong.

Groups with high moral boundaries are difficult to get in and out of. Street gangs and the Nazis are good examples of groups with high moral boundaries. One of the first things to notice about our examples is the use of the word *moral.* Most of us probably don't agree with the ethics of street gangs. In fact, we probably think their ethics are morally wrong and reprehensible. But when sociologists use the term *moral,* we are not referring to something that we think of as being good. A group is moral if its behaviors, beliefs, feelings, speech, styles, and so forth are controlled by strong group norms and are viewed in terms of right and wrong. In fact, both the Nazis and street gangs are probably more moral, in that sense, than you are, unless you are a member of a radical fringe group.

This theory of Durkheim's is extremely important. First of all, it gives us an empirical, sociological explanation for religion and sacredness. One of the problems that we are confronted with when we look across the face of humanity is the diversity of belief systems. How can people believe in diverse realities? The Azande of Africa seek spiritual guidance by giving a chicken a magic potion brewed from tree bark and seeing if the chicken lives or dies. Christians drink wine and eat bread believing they are drinking the blood and eating the body of Christ. How can we begin to explain how people come to see such diverse things as real? Durkheim gives us a part of the puzzle.

The issues of reality and sacredness and morality aren't necessarily based on ultimate truth for humans. Our experience of reality, sacredness, and morality is based on Durkheimian rituals and collective emotion (see Allan, 1998). Let me put this another way. Let's say that the Christians are right and the Azande are wrong. How is it, then, that both the Christians and the Azande can have the same experience of faith and reality? Part of the reason is that human beings create sacredness in the same way, regardless of the correctness of any ultimate truth. One of the common basic elements of all religions, particularly during their formative times, is the performance of Durkheimian rituals. These kinds of rituals create high levels of emotional energy that come to be invested in symbols; such symbols are then seen as sacred, regardless of the meaning or truth-value of the beliefs associated with the symbol.

Another reason that this theory is so important is that it provides us with a sociological explanation for the experience that people have of transcendence— something outside of and greater than themselves. All of us have had these kinds of experiences, some more than others. Some have experienced it at a Grateful Dead concert, others at the Million Man March, others watching a parade, and still others as we conform to the expectations of society. We feel these expectations not as a cognitive dialogue, but as something that impresses itself upon us physically and emotionally. Sometimes we may even cognitively disagree, but the pressure is there nonetheless.

Concepts and Theory: Social Diversity and Morality

One of the big questions that drove Durkheim is, what holds modern industrial societies together? Up until modern times, societies stayed together because most of the people in the society believed the same, acted the same, felt the same, and saw the world in the same way. However, in modern societies people are different from each other and they are becoming more so. What makes people different? How can all these different people come together and form a single society? In order to begin to answer these questions, Durkheim created a typology of societies.

A theoretical typology is a scheme that classifies a phenomenon into different categories. We aren't able to explain things directly by using a typology, but it does make things more apparent and more easily explained. Herbert Spencer—the one to whom Durkheim compares his own theory throughout *The Division of Labor in Society*—categorized societies as either industrial or militaristic. In order to construct his typology, he focused on the state. So, for example, when a society is in a militaristic phase, the state is geared toward defense and war and social control is centralized: Information, behavior, and production are tightly controlled by government. But when the same society is in an industrial phase, the state is less centralized and the social structures are oriented toward economic productivity:

Freedom in information exchange, behaviors, and entrepreneurship is encouraged. But Durkheim focuses on something different. His typology reflects his primary theoretical concern: social solidarity.

Mechanical and Organic Solidarity

Social solidarity can be defined as the degree to which social units are integrated. According to Durkheim, the question of solidarity turns on three issues: the subjective sense of individuals that they are part of the whole, the actual constraint of individual desires for the good of the collective, and the coordination of individuals and social units. It is important for us to notice that Durkheim acknowledges three different levels of analysis here: psychological, behavioral, and structural. Each of these issues becomes itself a question for empirical analysis: How much do individuals feel part of the collective? To what degree are individual desires constrained? And, how are activities coordinated and adjusted to one another? As each of these vary, a society will experience varying levels of social solidarity.

Durkheim is not only interested in the degree of social solidarity, he is also interested in the way social solidarity comes about. He uses two analogies to talk about these issues. The first is a mechanistic analogy. Think about machines or motors. How are the different parts related to each other? The relationship is purely physical and involuntary. Machines are thus relatively simple. Most of the parts are very similar and are related to or communicate with each other mechanistically. If we think about the degree of solidarity in such a unit, it is extremely high. The sense of an absolute relationship to the whole is unquestionably there, as every piece is connected to every other piece. Each individual unit's actions is absolutely constrained by and coordinated with the whole.

The other analogy is the organismic one. Higher organisms are quite complex systems, when compared to machines. The parts are usually different from one another, fulfill distinct functions, and are related through a variety of diverse subsystems. Organismic structures provide information to one another using assorted nutrients, chemicals, electrical impulses, and so on. These structures make adjustments because of the information that is received. In addition, most organisms are open systems in that they respond to information from the environment (most machines are closed systems). The solidarity of an organism when compared to a machine is a bit more imprecise and problematic.

By their very nature, analogies can be pushed too far, so we need to be careful. Nonetheless, we get a clear picture of what Durkheim is talking about. Durkheim says that there are two "great currents" in society: similarity and difference. Society begins with the first being dominant. In these societies, which Durkheim terms *segmented,* there are very few personal differences, little competition, and high egalitarianism. These societies experience **mechanical solidarity**. Individuals are mechanically and automatically bound together. Gradually, the other current, difference, becomes stronger and similarity "becomes channeled and becomes less apparent." These social units are held together through mutual need and abstract ideas and sentiments. Durkheim refers to this as **organic solidarity**. While organic solidarity and difference tend to dominate modern society, similarity and mechanical solidarity never completely disappear.

In Table 5.1, I've listed several distinctions between mechanical and organic solidarity. In the first row, the principal defining feature is listed. In mechanical solidarity, individuals are directly related to a group and its collective consciousness. If the individual is related to more than one group, there are very few and the groups tend to overlap with one another: "Thus it is entirely mechanical causes which ensure that the individual personality is absorbed in the collective personality" (Durkheim, 1893/1984, p. 242). Remember all that we have talked about concerning culture and morality (Durkheim's Law and ritual performance). People are immediately related to the collective consciousness by being part of the group that creates the culture in highly ritualistic settings. In these groups, the members experience the collective self as immediately present. They feel its presence push against any individual thoughts or feelings. They are caught up in the collective effervescence and experience it as ultimately real. The clans that Durkheim studies in *The Elementary Forms of the Religious Life* are a good illustration.

When an individual is mechanically related to the collective, all the rest of the characteristics we see under mechanical solidarity fall into place. In Table 5.1, the common beliefs and sentiments and the collective ideas and behavioral tendencies represent the collective consciousness. The collective consciousness varies by at least four features: *the degree to which culture is shared*—how many people in the group hold the same values, believe the same things, feel the same way about things, behave the same, and see the world in the same way; *the amount of power the culture has to guide an individual's thoughts, feelings, and actions*—a culture can be

Table 5.1   Mechanical and Organic Solidarity

Mechanical Solidarity	Organic Solidarity
Individuals directly related to collective consciousness with no intermediary	Individuals related to collective consciousness through intermediaries
Joined by common beliefs and sentiments (moralistic)	Joined by relationships among special and different functions (utilitarian)
Collective ideas and behavioral tendencies are stronger than individual	Individual ideas and tendencies are strong and each individual has own sphere of action
Social horizon limited	Social horizon unlimited
Strong attachment to family and tradition	Weak attachment to family and tradition
Repressive law: crime and deviance disturb moral sentiments; punishment meted out by group; purpose is to ritually uphold moral values through righteous indignation	Restitutive law: crime and deviance disturb social order; rehabilitative, restorative action by officials; purpose is to restore status quo

shared but not very powerful (A group where the members feel they have options doesn't have a very powerful culture.); *the degree of clarity*—how clear the prescriptions and prohibitions are in the culture (For example, when a man and a woman approach a door at the same time, is it clear what behavior is expected?); and the *collective consciousness varies by its content.* Durkheim is referring here to the ratio of religious to secular and individualistic symbolism. Religiously inspired culture tends to increase the power and clarity of the collective consciousness.

As we see from Table 5.1, in mechanical solidarity, the social horizon of individuals tends to be limited. Durkheim is referring to the level of possibilities an individual has in terms of social worlds and relationships. The close relationship the individual has to the collective consciousness in mechanical solidarity limits the number of possible worlds or realities the individual may consider. In modern societies, under organic solidarity, we have almost limitless possibilities from which to choose. Media and travel expose us to uncountable religions and their permutations. Today you can be a Buddhist, Baptist, or Bahai, and you can choose any of the varied universes they present. This proliferation of possibilities, including social relationships, is severely limited under mechanical solidarity. One of the results of this limiting is that tradition appears concrete and definite. People in segmented societies don't doubt their knowledge or reality. They hold strongly to the traditions of their ancestors. And, at the same time, people express their social relationships using family or territorial terms.

But even under mechanical solidarity, not everyone conforms. Durkheim acknowledges this and tells us that there are different kinds of laws for the different types of solidarity. The function of these laws is different as well, corresponding to the type of solidarity that is being created. Under mechanical solidarity, punitive law is more important. The function of *punitive law* is not to correct, as we usually think of law today; rather, the purpose is expiation (making atonement). Satisfaction must be given to a higher power, in this case the collective consciousness. Punitive law is exercised when the act "offends the strong, well-defined states of the collective consciousness" (Durkheim, 1893/1984, p. 39). Because this is linked to morality, the punishment given is generally greater than the danger represented to society, such as cutting off an individual's hand for an act of thievery.

Punitive law satisfies moral outrage and clarifies moral boundaries. When we respond to deviance with some form of "righteous indignation," and we punish the offender, we are experiencing and creating our group moral boundaries. In punishing offenses, we are drawing a clear line that demarks those who are in the group and those who are outside. Punitive law also provides an opportunity for ritual performance. A good example of this principle is the past practice of public executions. Watching an execution of a murderer or traitor was a public ritual that allowed the participants to focus their attention on a single group moral norm and to feel the same emotion about the offense. In other words, they were able to perform a Durkheimian ritual that re-created their sacred boundaries. As a result, the group was able to feel their moral boundaries and experience a profound sense of "we-ness," which increases mechanical solidarity.

Organic solidarity, on the other hand, has a greater proportion of *restitutive law,* which is designed to restore the offender and broken social relations. Because organic social solidarity is based on something other than strong morality, the function of law is different. Here there is no sense of moral outrage and no felt need to ritualize the sacred boundaries. Organic solidarity occurs under conditions of complex social structures and relations. Modern societies are defined by high structural differentiation, with large numbers of diverse structures necessitating complex interconnections of communication, movement, and obligations. Because of the diversity of these interconnections, they tend to be more rational than moral or familial—which is why we tend to speak of "paying one's debt to society." The idea of "debt" comes from rationalized accounting practices; there is no emotional component, as there would be with moral or family connections. And the interests guarded by the laws tend to be more specialized, such as corporate or inheritance laws, rather than generally held to by all, such as "thou shalt not kill." As an important side note, we can see that restitutive and punitive laws are material social facts that help us see the nonmaterial organic and mechanical solidarity within a society.

Organic solidarity thus tends to be characterized by weak collective consciousness: fewer beliefs and sentiments, and ideas and behavioral expectations tend to be shared. There is greater individuality and people and other social units (like organizations) are connected to the whole through utilitarian necessity. In other words, we need each other to survive, just like in an organism (my heart would die without its connection to my lungs and the rest of my biological system).

The Division of Labor

Earlier I mentioned that Durkheim says that similarity and mechanical solidarity gradually become channeled and less apparent. That statement gives the impression that the change from mechanical to organic solidarity occurred without any provocation, and that's not the case. The movement from mechanical to organic solidarity, from similarity to difference, from traditional to modern was principally due to increases in the division of labor. The concept of the division of labor refers to a stable organization of tasks and roles that coordinate the behavior of individuals or groups that carry out different but related tasks. Obviously, the division of labor may vary along a continuum from simple to complex. We can build a car in our garage all by ourselves from the ground up (as the first automobiles were built), or we can farm out different manufacturing and assembly tasks to hundreds of subcontractors worldwide and simply complete the construction in our plant (as it is done today). Our illustration illustrates the poles of the continuum, but there are multiple steps in between.

What kinds of processes tend to increase the division of labor in a society? Bear with me for a moment; I'm going to put together a string of rather dry-sounding concepts and relationships. The answer to what increases the overall division of labor is competition. Durkheim sees competition not as the result of individual desires (remember they are curtailed in mechanical solidarity) or free markets, but rather as the result of what Durkheim variously calls dynamic, moral, or physical density. These terms capture the number and intensity of interactions in a collective taken as a whole. The *level* of dynamic density is a result of increasing population density, which is a function of population growth (birth rate and migration) and ecological barriers (physical restraints on the ability of a population to spread out geographically).

Durkheim's theory is based on an ecological, evolutionary kind of perspective. The environment changes and thus the organism must change in order to survive. In this case, the environment is social interaction. The environment changes due to identifiable pressures: population growth and density. As populations concentrate, people tend to interact more frequently and with greater intensity. The rate of interaction is also affected by increases in communication and transportation technologies. As the level of interaction increases, so does the level of competition. More people require more goods and services, and dense populations can create surplus workers in any given job category. The most fit survive in their present occupation and assume a higher status; the less fit create new specialties and job categories, thus creating a higher degree of division of labor.

The Problem of Modernity

Now, let me ask you a question. What kind of problem do you think that increasing the division of labor might cause for the collective consciousness? The answer to this question is Durkheim's problem of modernity. If people are interacting in different situations, with different people, to achieve different goals (as would be the case with higher levels of the division of labor), then they will produce more particularized than collective cultures. Therefore, because they contain different ideas and sentiments, the presence of particularized cultures threatens the power of the collective consciousness.

There's an old saying, "Birds of a feather flock together." Well, Durkheim is telling us just the opposite: "Birds become of a feather because they flock together." In other words, the most prominent characteristics of people come about because of the groups they interact with. As we internalize the culture of our groups, we learn how to think and feel and behave, and we become socially distinct from one another. We call this process **social differentiation**. As people become socially differentiated, they, by definition, share fewer and fewer elements of the collective consciousness. This process brings with it the problem of integration. It's a problem that we here in the United States are very familiar with: How can we combine diverse populations into a whole nation with a single identity? But there's more to this problem of modernity: As the division of labor increases, so does the level of structural differentiation—the process through which the needs of society are met through increasingly different sets of status positions, roles, and norms. Spencer made this the central issue for his social theorizing. Here we see the same concern. Durkheim argues much like Spencer—structural interdependency creates pressures for integration—but he adds a cultural component: value generalization.

Thus, we are confronted with the problem of modernity. Because groups are more closely gathered together, the division of labor has increased. In response to population pressures and the division of labor, social structures have differentiated to better meet societal needs. As structures differentiate, they are confronted with the problem of integration. In addition, as the division of labor increases, people tend to socially differentiate according to distinct cultures. As people create particularized cultures around their jobs, they are less in tune with the collective consciousness and face the problem of social integration. I've illustrated these relationships in Figure 5.1.

Figure 5.1   The Division of Labor and Problems of Integration

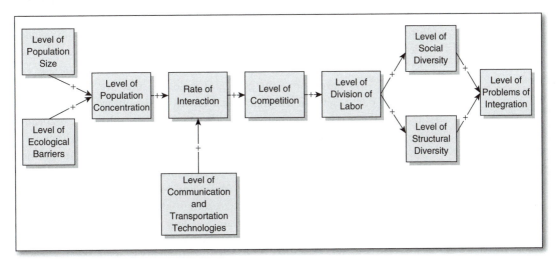

Organic Solidarity and Social Pathologies

As social and structural differentiation create problems of integration, they simultaneously produce social factors that counterbalance these problems: intermediary group formation, **culture generalization,** restitutive law and centralization of power, and structural interdependency. Together, these factors form organic solidarity. First, structures become more dependent upon one another as they differentiate (*structural interdependency*). For example, your heart can't digest food, so it needs the stomach to survive. It is the same for society as it differentiates. The different structures become dependent upon one another for survival. Further, in order to provide for the needs of other structures, they must be able to interact with one another. Thus, structural and social differentiation also create pressures for a more **generalized culture** and value system. Let's think about this in terms of communication among computers. I have a PC and my friend Jamie has an Apple. Each has a completely different platform and operating system. Yet almost every day, my computer communicates with his. How can it do this? The two different systems can communicate with one another because there is a more general system that contains values broad enough to encompass both computers (i.e., the Internet).

Societies thus produce more general culture and values in response to the need for different subsystems and groups to communicate. In contemporary structural analysis, this is an extremely important issue. Talcott Parsons termed this focus the "generalized media of exchange"—symbolic goods that are used to facilitate interactions across institutional domains. So, for example, the institutional structure of family values love, acceptance, encouragement, fidelity, and so on. The economic structure, on the other hand, values profit, greed, one-upmanship, and the like. How do these two institutions communicate? What do they exchange? How do they cooperate in order to fulfill the needs of society? These kinds of questions, and their answers, are what make for structural analysis and the most sociological of all research. They are the empirical side of Durkheim's theoretical concern.

Of course, in the United States we have successively created more generalized cultures and values. The idea of citizen, for example, has grown from white-male-Protestant-property-owner to include people of color and women. Yet generalizing culture is a continuing issue. The more diverse our society becomes, the more generalized the culture must become, according to Durkheim. For example, while we in the United States may say "In God we trust," it is now a valid question to ask "which god?" We have numerous gods and goddesses that are worshiped and respected in our society. To maintain this diversity, Durkheim would argue there has to be in the culture a concept general enough to embrace them all. According to Durkheim, if the culture doesn't generalize, we run the risk of disintegration.

The fact is that generalized culture is often too broad to invest much moral emotion, so more and more of our relations, both structural and personal, are mitigated by law. This law has to be rational and focused on relationships, not morals. For example, I don't know my neighbors. The reasons for this have a lot to do with what Durkheim is talking about: increases in transportation technologies, increasing divisions of labor, and so on. But if I don't know my neighbors, how can our relationship be managed? Obviously, if I have a problem with their dog barking or their tree limb falling on my house, there are laws and legal proceedings that manage the relationship. Increases in social and structural diversity thus create higher levels of restitutive law (in comparison to restrictive/moral law) and more centralized government to administer law and relations. Of course, one of the things we come to value is this kind of law and we come to believe in the right of a centralized government to enforce the law.

Both social and structural diversity also push for the formation of intermediary groups. Remember, Durkheim always comes back to real groups in real interaction: Culture can have independent effects but it requires interaction to be produced. Thus, the problem becomes, how do individual occupational groups create a more general value system if they don't interact with one another? Durkheim theorizes that societies will create *intermediary groups*—groups between the individual occupational groups and the collective consciousness. These groups are able to simultaneously carry the concerns of the smaller groups as well as the collective consciousness.

For example, I'm a sociology faculty member at the University of North Carolina. Because of the demands of work, I rarely interact with faculty from other disciplines (like psychology), and I only interact with medical doctors as a patient. Yet I am a member of the American Sociological Association (ASA), and the ASA interacts with the American Psychological Association and the American Medical Association, as well as many, many others. And all of them interact with the U.S. government as well as other institutional concerns. This kind of interaction amongst intermediary groups creates a higher level of value generalization, which, in turn, is passed down to the individual members. As Durkheim (1893/1984) says,

> A nation cannot be maintained unless, between the state and individuals, a whole range of secondary groups are interposed. These must be close enough to the individual to attract him strongly to their activities and, in so doing, to absorb him into the mainstream of social life. (p. liv)

As we've seen, structural interdependency, culture generalization, intermediary group formation, and restitutive law and centralization of power together create organic solidarity (see Figure 5.2). Increasing division of labor systemically pushes for these changes: "Indeed, when its functions are sufficiently linked together they tend of their own accord to achieve an equilibrium, becoming self-regulatory" (Durkheim, 1893/1984, p. xxxiv). As a side note, part of what we mean by functional analysis is this notion of system pressures creating equilibrium. Notice the dynamic mechanism: It is the system's need that brings about the change. It's kind of like pulling your car into the gas station because it needs gas. Society is a smart system, regulating its own requirements and bringing about changes to keep itself in equilibrium. However, if populations grow and/or become differentiated too quickly, the system can't keep up and these functions won't be "sufficiently linked together." Society can then become pathological or sick.

Durkheim elaborates two possible pathologies. (Actually, Durkheim mentions three—anomie, forced division of labor, and "lack of coordination"—but he clearly elaborates only the first two.) The first is anomie—social instability and personal unrest resulting from insufficient normative regulation of individual activities. Durkheim argues that social life is impossible apart from normative regulation. People are naturally driven by individual appetites, and without norms to regulate interactions, cooperation is impossible. If it were necessary to

> grope de novo for an appropriate response to every stimulus from the environing situation, threats to its integrity from many sources would promptly effect its disorganization . . . to this end, it is altogether necessary that the person be free from an incessant search for appropriate conduct." (Durkheim, 1903/1961, p. 37)

Figure 5.2 Organic Solidarity

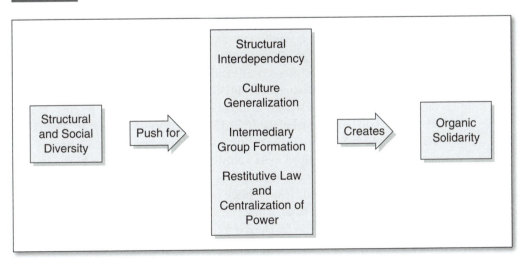

The production of norms requires interaction. However, overly rapid population growth with excessive division of labor and social diversity hinders groups from interacting. Links among and between the groups cannot be formed when growth and differentiation happen too quickly. The result is **anomie**.

The other pathology that Durkheim considers at some length involves class inequality and the forced division of labor. Durkheim argues that the division of labor must occur "spontaneously," that is, apart from external constraint. Labor should divide because of organic reasons: population growth and density. The division of labor should not occur due to a powerful elite driven by profit motivations. According to Durkheim, it is dysfunctional to force people to work in jobs for which they are ill-suited:

> We are certainly not predestined from birth to any particular form of employment, but we nevertheless possess tastes and aptitudes that limit our choice. If no account is taken of them, if they are constantly frustrated in our daily occupation, we suffer, and seek the means of bringing that suffering to an end. (Durkheim, 1893/1984, pp. 310–311)

This, of course, would represent a threat to social solidarity.

This condition is similar to what Marx talks about, but it is different as well. For Marx, alienation is a state of existence that may or may not be subjectively experienced by the individual. Alienation for Marx is defined by separation from species-being, and we only become aware of it through critical and/or class consciousness. Durkheim, on the other hand, assumes that humans are egotistical actors without an essentially good nature from which to be alienated. Durkheim's alienation comes about only as a result of a pathological form of the division of labor—forced by capitalist greed rather than organic evolution. It exists as a subjective state—we are always aware of alienation when it occurs.

Durkheim's solution for this pathological state is "justice" enforced by the state, specifically, price controls by useful labor (equal pay for equal work) and elimination of inheritance. Two of the most powerful tools in producing a structure of inequality are ascription and inheritance. Ascription assigns different status positions to us at birth, such as gender and race, and apart from legislation guaranteeing equal pay for equal work, they strongly influence inequality. For example, studies done in the United States consistently show that women earn about 70% of what a man makes for the same job with the same qualifications. Inheritance is an obvious way to maintain structural inequality; estimates are that by 2055, at least $41 trillion will be inherited in the United States (Havens & Schervish, 2003). Both ascription and inheritance make the perpetuation of class differences appear natural: Our position is ascribed to us, and we are wealthy or poor by birth. America may be the land of opportunity, but it is not the land of *equal* opportunity: It matters if you are male or female, black or white, or go to school in Harlem or Hollywood. On the other hand, if inheritance is done away with and laws are implemented that bring equal pay for equal work, structured inequality would have a difficult time surviving.

Concepts and Theory: Individualism in Modern Society

In early societies, the human self was an utterly social self. People were caught up in and saw themselves only in terms of the group. The self was an extension of the group just as certainly as your arm is an extension of your body. Yet as societies differentiated both structurally and socially, the self became more and more isolated and took on the characteristics of an individual. Thus in modern societies, the individual takes on increasing importance. We can think of many benefits from this shift. We have increased freedom of choice and individual expression under conditions of organic solidarity. Yet there are some dysfunctional consequences as well. Though Durkheim didn't phrase it in this way, in addition to the two pathologies of modern society listed above, we can include suicide.

Suicide

There are two critical issues for the individual in modern society: the levels of group attachment and behavioral regulation. People need a certain level of group attachment. We are social creatures and much of our sense of meaning, reality, and purpose comes from having interpersonal ties (both in terms of number and density) and a sense of "we-ness" or collective identity. To illustrate, imagine having something be meaningful to you apart from language and feeling—what Durkheim would call collective representations and sentiments. You might object and say, "My feelings are my own." That's true, but what do you feel? Do you feel "anger"? Do you feel "love"? Or, do you simply, purely *feel*? We rarely, if ever, simply and purely feel. What are we doing when we say we feel anger? We are labeling certain physiological responses and giving them meaning. The label is linguistic and the meaning is social.

It should be clear by now that it is extremely difficult for us to untangle personal meanings and realities from social ones. Certainly, because we are human, we can create utterly individualistic realities and meanings, although we usually see those realities and those people as either strange or crazy. Most of us are aware, and even unconsciously convinced, that our meanings and realities have to be linked in some way to the social group around us—which is why, when group attachment is too low, Durkheim argues that *egoistic suicide* is likely: Low group attachment leads to extreme individualism and the loss of a sense of reality and purpose.

However, extremely high group attachment isn't a good thing for the individual either. High attachment leads to complete fusion with the group and loss of individual identity, which can be a problem in modernity. Under conditions of high group attachment, people are more likely to commit *altruistic suicide*. The Kamikaze pilots during World War II are a good example. Some contemporary examples include religious cults, such as The People's Temple and Heaven's Gate, and the group solidarity the U.S. government fosters in military boot camps. Under conditions of high group attachment, individual life becomes meaningless and the group is the only reality.

It's important to note here that modern societies are characterized by the presence of both mechanical and organic solidarity. It is certainly true that in general the society is held together by organic means—general values, restitutive law, and dependent opposites—yet it is also true that pockets of very intense, particularized culture and mechanical solidarity exist as well. These kinds of group interactions may in fact be necessary for us. This need may explain such intense interaction groups as dedicated fans of rock music or organized sports. Both of these groups engage in the kind of periodic ritual gatherings that Durkheim explains in *The Elementary Forms of the Religious Life*. During these gatherings (shows or events), rock and sports fans experience high levels of emotional energy and create clear group symbols. Yet extremes of either organic or mechanical solidarity can be dangerous, as Durkheim notes.

The other critical issue for individuals in modern society is the regulation of their behaviors. Because in the advanced, industrialized nations we believe in individualism, the idea of someone or something regulating our behavior may be objectionable. But keep in mind Durkheim's view of human nature. Apart from regulation, our appetites would be boundless and ultimately meaningless. The individual by himself or herself "suffers from the everlasting wranglings and endless friction that occur when relations between an individual and his fellows are not subject to any regulative influence" (Durkheim, 1887/1993, p. 24). Further, our behaviors must have meaning for us with regard to time. Time, as we think of it, is a function of symbols (the past and future only exist symbolically), and, of course, symbols are a function of group membership.

Thus, there are a variety of reasons why the regulation of behaviors is necessary. Behaviors need to be organized according to the needs and goals of the collective, but the degree of regulation is important. Under conditions of rapid population growth and diversity, anomie may result if the culture is unable to keep pace with the social changes. Under these conditions, it is likely there will be an increase in the level of *anomic suicide*. The lack of regulation of behaviors leads to a complete lack of regulation of the individual's desires and thus an increase in feelings of meaninglessness. On the other hand, overregulation of behaviors leads to the loss of individual effectiveness (and thus increases hopelessness), resulting in more *fatalistic suicide*.

I've listed the suicide types in Table 5.2. It's important to keep in mind that the motivation for suicide is different in each case, corresponding to group attachment and behavior regulation. Also note that the kinds of social pathologies we are talking about here are different from the ones in the previous section. Here we are seeing how

Table 5.2 Suicide Types

	Group Attachment	Behavior Regulation
High	Altruistic Suicide	Fatalistic Suicide
Low	Egoistic Suicide	Anomic Suicide

modernity can be pathological for the *individual,* in the extremes of attachment and regulation. In the previous section, we looked at how modernity can be pathological for society as a whole and its solidarity.

The Cult of the Individual

Both egoistic and anomic suicide can be seen as a function of high levels of individuality, but individuality itself is not the problem. Individualism is in fact necessary in modernity. Before we go on, I need to make a distinction between this idea of individuality and what might be called egoistic hedonism or materialism (what most of us think of when we hear the term individualism: "I gotta be me."). From a Durkheimian view, individuals who are purely and exclusively out to fulfill their own desires can never form the basis of a group. Group life demands that there be some shared link that motivates people to work for the collective rather than individual welfare. As we've seen in our discussion of Durkheim, this kind of group life and awareness is dependent upon a certain degree of collective consciousness. The idea of the individual that we have in mind here is therefore not pure ego. Rather, what is at stake might better be understood as the idea of "individual rights" and how it has progressed historically.

To do the concept justice, we should really go back to early Greek and then Roman times. But in actuality, we need only go back to the founding of the United States. What does the following sentence mean? "We hold these truths to be self-evident, that all men are created equal, that they are endowed by their Creator with certain unalienable Rights, that among these are Life, Liberty, and the pursuit of Happiness." The history of the United States is the tale of working out the meaning of that line. Obviously, the central struggle concerns the term "all men." Initially, "all men" referred only to white, property-owning, heterosexual, Protestant males. Somewhere along the line, the U.S. government decided (often in response to fierce civil struggle, such as the fight for women's rights) that you didn't have to own property, and that you didn't have to be male, or white, or Protestant, though you still have to be heterosexual to have full access to civil rights. The reason there has been struggle over this sentence is the basis that is given for these rights. According to the quoted line, the basis for civil rights is simply being human. These rights can't be earned nor can they be taken away. They are yours not because of anything you've done or because of any group membership, but simply because of your birth into the human race. Thus, what matters isn't what group you belong to; it's you, as an *individual* human being. It is this moral idea of individualism that Durkheim has in mind and that has the potential for creating social solidarity.

Durkheim calls this new moral basis for society the "cult of the individual." The individual, as he or she is historically separated from the group, becomes the locus of social concern and solidarity. The *individual* becomes the recipient of social rights and responsibilities, rather than castes or lineages. Today we see the individual as perhaps the single most important social actor. Even our legal system here in the United States is occupied with preserving the civil rights of the perpetrator of a crime because it is the individual that is valued. The individual becomes the focus of our idea of "justice," which Durkheim sees as the "medicine" for some of the problems that come with pathological forms of the division of labor. For example, in a society such as the United States, the problems associated with labor issues, poverty, deviance, and depression (all of which can be linked to Durkheim's pathologies) are generally handled individually through the court system or counseling. Remember that Durkheim sees culture as the unifying force of society, so the importance of these kinds of cases for Durkheimian sociology has more to do with *the culture that the practices create and reproduce* than the actual legal or psychological effects. In this way, the individual becomes a ritual focus of attention, the symbol around which people can seek a kind of redress for the forced division of labor, inequality, and anomie that we noted above. Today the individual has taken on a moral life. But it is not the particular person *per se*, with all of his or her idiosyncrasies, that has value. Rather, it is the ethical and sacred *idea* of the individual that is important. As Durkheim (1957) says,

> This cult, moreover, has all that is required to take the place of the religious cultures of former times. It serves as well as they to bring about the communion of minds and wills which is a first condition of any social life. (p. 69)

Summary

- Durkheim is extremely interested in what holds society together in modern times. In order to understand this problem, he constructs a perspective that focuses on three issues: social facts, collective consciousness, and the production of culture in interaction. Durkheim argues that society is a social fact, an entity that exists in and of itself, which can have independent effects. The facticity of society is produced through the collective consciousness, which contains collective ideas and sentiments. The collective consciousness is seen as the moral basis of society. Though it may have independent effects, the collective consciousness is produced through social interaction.

- Durkheim argues that the basis of society and the collective consciousness is religion. Religion first emerged in society as small bands of hunter–gatherer groups assembled periodically. During these gatherings, high levels of emotional energy were created through intense interactions. This emotional energy, or effervescence, acted as a contagion and influenced the participants to behave in ways they normally wouldn't. So strong was the effervescent effect that participants felt as if they were in the presence of something larger than themselves as individuals, and the collective consciousness was born. The emotional energy was symbolized and the interactions ritualized so that the experience could be duplicated. The symbols and behaviors became sacred to the group and provided strong moral boundaries and group identity.

- Because of high levels of division of labor, modern society tends to work against the effects of the collective consciousness. People in work-related groups and differentiated structures create particularized cultures. As a result, society has to find a different kind of solidarity than one based on religious or traditional collective consciousness. Organic solidarity integrates a structurally and socially diverse society through interdependency, generalized ideas and sentiments, restitutive law and centralized power, and through intermediary groups. These factors take time to develop, and if a society tries to move too quickly from mechanical to organic solidarity, it will be subject to pathological states, such as anomie and the forced division of labor.

• At the center of modern society is the cult of the individual. The ideal of individuality, not the idiosyncrasies of individual people, becomes one of the most generalized values a society can have. However, the individual can also be subject to pathological states, depending on the person's level of group attachment and behavioral regulation. If a society produces the extremes of either of these, then the suicide rate will tend to go up. Suicide due to extremes in group attachment is characterized as either egoistic or altruistic. Suicide due to extremes in behavioral regulation is characterized as either anomic or fatalistic.

TAKING THE PERSPECTIVE—FUNCTIONALISM AND SOCIOLOGY OF CULTURE

In some ways, Durkheim has informed sociological theory in more profound yet diffuse ways than anyone in this book. The most obvious at the moment is that he adds to the functionalist perspective that we reviewed in Chapter 2. Durkheim specifically adds culture/collective consciousness to Spencer's three requisite functions. These four functions are brought together in Talcott Parsons' theory, which we'll look at in Chapter 8. More generally Durkheim's idea of social facts has become part of our cultural capital as sociologists. As you know, sociology is fundamentally based on the idea that there are social factors that influence human life. In that these factors are perceived as institutions or structures, chances are good that the idea comes from Durkheim's idea of the social fact. We've also seen how his study of suicide informs the kind of methodology practiced in sociology. In fact, Durkheim's concern with social order and integration is one of the primary questions in sociology today.

A more specific influence Durkheim's had is on culture: "The compelling case can be made that, more than any other classical figure, it is to Durkheim that the contemporary cultural revival . . . is most deeply in debt" (Alexander, 1988, p. 4). What Durkheim did specifically was to give culture an independent place in sociological theorizing. One of the concepts that the idea of social science is based upon is the notion of independent effects. In other words, if society can be studied scientifically, then it must contain some form of its own laws of action apart from the people who make it up and it must be able to independently act upon people. Durkheim poses this kind of question about culture and argues that culture exists independently and operates autonomously. Another way to put this is to say that culture is structured—signs,

(Continued)

(Continued)

symbols, and categories are related to one another in a way that influences how people think, feel, and act. Durkheim was really one of the first to consider such a thing, but this idea came to form an entire school of research called linguistic structuralism, which later influenced semiotics and poststructuralism (two influential contemporary schools of cultural analysis). We will consider poststructuralism in Chapter 17.

BUILDING YOUR THEORY TOOLBOX

Learning More—Primary and Secondary Sources

- Primary sources: Almost every book of Durkheim's is worth reading. The following are indispensable:
  - Durkheim, É. (1938). *The Rules of Sociological Method* (S. A. Solovay & J. H. Mueller, Trans.; G. E. G. Catlin, Ed.). Glencoe, IL: The Free Press. (Original work published 1895)
  - Durkheim, É. (1951). *Suicide: A Study in Sociology* (J. A. Spaulding & G. Simpson, Trans.). Glencoe, IL: The Free Press. (Original work published 1897)
  - Durkheim, É. (1984). *The Division of Labor in Society* (W. D. Halls, Trans.). New York: The Free Press. (Original work published 1893)
  - Durkheim, É. (1995). *The Elementary Forms of the Religious Life* (K. E. Fields, Trans.). New York: The Free Press. (Original work published 1912)
- Durkheim secondary sources:
  - Alexander, J. C. (Ed.). (1988). *Durkheimian Sociology: Cultural Studies.* Cambridge, UK: Cambridge University Press. (Excellent collection of contemporary readings concerning Durkheim's contribution to cultural sociology)
  - Giddens, A. (1978). *Émile Durkheim.* New York: Viking Press. (Brief introduction to Durkheim's work by one of contemporary sociology's leading theorists)
  - Jones, R. A. (1986). *Émile Durkheim: An Introduction to Four Major Works.* Newbury Park, CA: Sage. (Part of the *Masters of Social Theory* series; short, book-length introduction to Durkheim's life and work)
  - Lukes, S. (1972). *Émile Durkheim, His Life and Work: A Historical and Critical Study.* New York: Harper & Row. (The definitive book on Durkheim's life and work)
  - Meštrovic, S. G. (1988). *Émile Durkheim and the Reformation of Sociology.* Totawa, NJ: Rowman & Littlefield. (Unique treatment of Durkheim's work; emphasizes Durkheim's vision of sociology as a science of morality that could replace religious morals)

Seeing the Social World (knowing the theory)

- Add Durkheim's contribution to functionalist analysis that you wrote for Chapter 2.

- Compare and contrast Durkheim's approach to culture and the cultural sociology we talked about in Chapter 4.

- After reading and understanding this chapter, you should be able to define the following terms theoretically and explain their theoretical importance to Durkheim's theory: *social facts, society sui generis, collective conscious, religion, sacred and profane, ritual, effervescence, social solidarity (mechanical and organic), punitive and restitutive law, the division of labor, social differentiation, cultural generalization, intermediary groups, social pathologies, anomie, suicide (altruistic, fatalistic, egoistic, and anomic), the cult of the individual*

- After reading and understanding this chapter, you should be able to answer the following questions (remember to answer them *theoretically*):

  o Explain the organismic analogy and use it to analyze the relations among and between social structures.

  o Define social facts and explain how society exists *sui generis.*

  o Explain how society is based on religion.

  o Discuss how Durkheimian rituals create sacred symbols and group moral boundaries.

  o Define collective consciousness, social solidarity, and mechanical and organic solidarity.

  o Explain the problem of modernity and describe how organic solidarity creates social solidarity in modernity.

  o Describe how organic solidarity can produce certain social pathologies.

  o Define the cult of the individual and explain its place in producing organic solidarity.

Engaging the Social World (using the theory)

- I'd like for you to go to a sporting event—football, basketball, or hockey would be best. Analyze that experience using Durkheim's theory of rituals. What kind of symbols did you notice? What kinds of rituals? Did the rituals work as Durkheim said they would? What do you think this says about religious rituals in contemporary society? Can you think of other events that have the same characteristics?

- There are a lot of differences between gangs and medical doctors. But there might also be some similarities. Using Durkheim's theory and perspective, how are gangs and medical doctors alike?

- Explain this event and the reactions from a Durkheimian perspective: On September 11, 2001, hijacked jetliners hit the World Trade Center in New York and the Pentagon outside Washington, D.C. News headlines around the world proclaimed "America Attacked" and people in places such as San Diego, CA; Detroit, MI; and Cornville, AZ, wept openly. What Durkheimian processes must have been in place for such an event to happen? And,

(Continued)

(Continued)

how would Durkheim explain the fact that Americans had such a strong emotional reaction to the loss of people unknown to them? Also, explain the subsequent use of flags and slogans, and the "war on terrorism," using Durkheim's theory.

- Often in theory class, I will take the students on a walk. We walk through campus, through a retail business section, past a church, and through a residential area. Either think about such a walk or go on an actual walk yourself. Based on Durkheim's perspective (not necessarily his theory), what would he see? How would it be different from what Marx would see?

Weaving the Threads (building theory)

- Compare and contrast Spencer, Marx, Weber, and Durkheim on the central features of modernity. What do they say makes a society modern? What problems do they see associated with modern society and modern lives?

- Compare and contrast Spencer's and Durkheim's theories of social change and the problems of integration. How can they be integrated?

- How does Weber expand Spencer's theory on the evolution of religion? Compare and contrast Spencer, Durkheim, and Weber on the origins and functions of religion.

- Analyze Marx's position on religion using Durkheim's theory. I don't want you to argue for or against Marx; I want you to understand Marx's position using Durkheim.

CHAPTER 6

The Modern Person:

George Herbert Mead and Georg Simmel

The topics of each of the previous chapters are central to the modern project. We've talked about social structures and complex social systems, religion and the state, capitalism and bureaucracy, culture and social integration, and so on. All of these are fairly large (macro level) institutional issues that help define modernity as a historical period. In this chapter we're bringing our analysis down to the micro level and the person. In a significant way this chapter is about you. However, it is vital for you to see that the topic of this chapter is just as central to the project of modernity as those institutional forces.

Modernity was founded on a specific kind of person. Prior to the social and philosophical changes leading up to modernity, a person wasn't seen as an individual in the way we mean the term today. To help you see this, let me explain a little bit about how the modern person came about. One of the major forces in pushing modernity forward was the Protestant Reformation; it had broad based effects beyond its religious implications. For example, in Chapter 4 we saw how Luther's notion of the calling provided a cultural base for the work ethic of early capitalism. The Protestant Reformation also helped reconceptualize the person. In traditional Catholicism a person had a relationship with God based on his or her *being part of the Catholic Church*. Salvation wasn't seen individually, but, rather, collectively—a person went to heaven because he or she was part of the Church, part of the Bride of Christ.

And membership in the Church was obtained through the sacraments, such as baptism (generally at birth) and the Holy Eucharist. Further, people didn't have a direct, individual relation or experience with God; a person's connection with God was continually mediated by priests, saints, the Virgin Mary, and various other intermediaries—people weren't even deemed capable of reading the Bible on their own. This type of person was also in the political realm: Subjects of the monarchy were to be guided and cared for. The important thing I want you to see here is that none of this implied a person individually capable of making important decisions and guiding his or her life. In fact, it implies just the opposite. But with the advent of Protestantism, the person was singled out, made to stand before God on his or her own confession of faith. This is why people converting from Catholicism would be rebaptized: Being baptized as an infant did not involve personal choice. As I said, Protestantism is just one force in the redefinition of the person, but it gives us a sense of how people were viewed prior to modernity.

The Enlightenment and modernity brought with it a new kind of person, "as a fully centered, unified individual, endowed with the capacities of reason, consciousness, and action" (Hall, 1996, p. 597). Both science and citizenship are based on this idea of a new kind of person—the supreme individual with the power to use his or her own mind to determine truth and to use reason to discover the world as it exists and make rational decisions. This belief gave the Enlightenment its other name: the Age of Reason. This new idea, this reasoning person, obviously formed the basis of scientific inquiry; more importantly, for our purposes, it also formed the basis for the social project. Democracy is not only possible because of belief in the rational individual; this new person also necessitates democracy. The only way of governing a group of individuals, each of whom is capable of rational inquiry and reasonable action, is through their consent.

We will consider the modern person (you) several times throughout the book. So, keep this in mind: The person you are is not incidental to modernity. And, perhaps more importantly, the type of person that it is possible for you to be is historically specific and socially created—the possibilities of personhood, of the subject, alters with changes in social practices, structure, and culture. In this chapter we look at the modern person from two points of view. George Herbert Mead will view the modern person from the perspective of pragmatism. And he's going to give us a theory about how the modern person as a reasoning, acting individual can come to exist—he will explain how the modern person comes into being. Georg Simmel, on the other hand, is going to assume the individual. Starting there, he then considers how certain modern social processes and factors impact the person.

George Herbert Mead (1863–1931)

Theorist's Digest
Concepts and Theory: Truth, Meaning, and Action
Pragmatic Truth
Human Action
Concepts and Theory: Meaning and Interaction
Symbolic Interaction
Concepts and Theory: Making Yourself
The Mind
Three Stages of Role-Taking
Society and the Self
The I and the Me
Summary
Taking the Perspective—Symbolic Interaction

THEORIST'S DIGEST

Brief Biography

George Herbert Mead was born on February 27, 1863, in South Hadley, Massachusetts. Mead began his college education at Oberlin College when he was 16 years old and graduated in 1883. After short stints as a school teacher and surveyor, Mead did his graduate studies in philosophy at Harvard. In 1893, John Dewey asked Mead to join him to form the Department of Philosophy at the University of Chicago, the site of the first department of sociology in the United States. Mead's major influence on sociologists came through his graduate course in social psychology, which he started teaching in 1900. Among his students was Herbert Blumer (Chapter 11). Those lectures formed the basis for Mead's most famous work, *Mind, Self, and Society*, published posthumously by his students. Mead died on April 26, 1931.

Central Sociological Questions

Society as we know it came to exist in modernity. But, for Mead, society doesn't exist as macro level structures and systems. What we mean by society is actually made up of various sets of attitudes, ways of seeing and being in the world. Society is enacted and comes to exist as individuals interact one with another and take on these attitudes. Central to this social interaction, and thus to society, is a certain kind of self, one capable of taking his or her own actions as social objects and deciding to act. Mead's quest, then, is to explain how this modern person exists: "How can an individual get outside himself (experientially) in such a way as to become an object to himself? This is the essential psychological problem of selfhood or of self-consciousness" (Mead, 1934, p. 138).

Simply Stated

At the core of Mead's question is the issue of separation: The watching perspective of an individual is separate from the actions of the self. Mead wants to explain how that separation takes place. There are two chief mechanisms through which people become separated from their own actions: language acquisition and role taking. Role taking progresses through three stages as the individual develops a self that is increasingly separated from his or her own actions.

Key Concepts

pragmatism, emergence, action, meaning, natural signs and significant gestures, social objects, emergence, role-taking, perspective, self, mind, play stage, game stage, generalized other stage, I and the Me, interaction, society

Concepts and Theory: Truth, Meaning, and Action

There were many influences on Mead's thinking. In fact, his work is an early example of theoretical synthesis, bringing together several different strands of thought to create something new (for Mead's influences, see Morris, 1962). But for our purposes, we will concentrate on Mead's debt to the philosophy of pragmatism.

Pragmatism is the only indigenous and distinctively American form of philosophy, and its birth is linked to the American Civil War (Menand, 2001). The Civil War was costly in the extreme: The number of dead and wounded exceeds that of any other war that the United States has fought, and the dead on both sides were family members and fellow Americans. This extreme cost left people disillusioned and doubtful about the ideas and beliefs that provoked the war. It wasn't so much the content of the ideas that was the problem, but, rather, the fact that ideas that appeared so right, moral, and legitimate could cause such devastation. It took the United States almost 50 years to culturally recover and find a way of thinking and seeing the world that it could embrace. That philosophy was pragmatism.

Pragmatic Truth

Pragmatism rejects the notion that there are any fundamental truths and instead proposes that truth is relative to time, place, and purpose. In other words, the "truth" of any idea or moral is not found in what people believe or in any ultimate reality. Truth can only be found in the actions of people; specifically, people find ideas to be true if they result in practical benefits. Pragmatism is thus "an idea about ideas" and a way of relativizing ideology (Menand, 2001, p. xi), but this relativizing doesn't result in relativism. Pragmatism is based on common sense and the belief that the search for "truth and knowledge shifts to the social and communal circumstances under which persons can communicate and cooperate in the process of acquiring knowledge" (West, 1999, p. 151).

Understanding pragmatism helps us see the basis of Mead's concern for meaning, self, and society. As we will see, Mead argues that the self is a social entity that is a practical necessity of every interaction. We need a self to act deliberately and to interact socially; it allows us to consider alternative lines of behavior and thus enables us to act rather than react. In pragmatism, human action and decisions aren't determined or forced by society, ideology, or preexisting truths. Rather, decisions and ethics emerge out of a consensus that develops through interaction—a consensus that is based on a free and knowing subject: the self.

Pragmatism also helps us understand another important idea of Mead's: **emergence**. In general, the word *emergence* refers to the process through which new entities are created from different particulars. For Mead, then, meaning emerges out of different elements of interaction coming together. Let's take a hammer as an example. People create social objects such as hammers in order to survive, and hammers only exist as such for humans (hammers don't exist for tigers, though they might sense the physical object). But the meaning of objects isn't set in stone, once and for all. While the hammer exists in its tool context, its meaning can vary by its use, and its use is determined in specific interactions. It can be an instrument of construction or destruction depending upon how it is used. It can also symbolize an individual's occupation or hobby. Or it could be used as a weapon to kill, and it could be an instrument of murder or mercy, depending upon the circumstances under which the killing takes place. Thus, the "true" meaning of an object cannot be unconditionally known; it is negotiated in interaction. The meaning pragmatically emerges.

Human Action

Humans act—they don't react. As Mead characterizes it, the distinctly human *act* contains four distinct elements: impulse, perception, manipulation, and consumption. For most animals, the route from impulse to behavior is rather direct—they react to a stimulus using instincts or behavioristically imprinted patterns. But for humans, it is a circuitous route. The philosopher Ernst Cassirer (1944) puts it this way: "Man has . . . discovered a new method of adapting himself to his environment. Between the receptor system and the effector systems, which are found in all animal species, we find in man a third link which we may describe as the symbolic system"; this system is "the way to civilization" (pp. 24, 26).

After we feel the initial impulse to act, we perceive our environment. This perception entails the recognition of the pertinent symbolic elements—other people, absent reference groups (what Mead calls generalized others), and so on—as well as alternatives to satisfying the impulse. After we symbolically take in our environment, we manipulate the different elements in our imagination. This is the all-important pause before action; *this is where society becomes possible.* This manipulation takes place in the mind and considers the possible ramifications of using different behaviors to satisfy the impulse. We think about how others would judge our behaviors, and we consider the elements available to complete the task. After we manipulate the situation symbolically in our minds, we are in a position to consummate the act. I want you to notice something about human, social behavior: *Action requires the presence of a mind capable of symbolic, abstract thought and a self able to be the object of thought and action.* Both the mind and self, then, are intrinsically linked to society. Before considering Mead's theory of mind and self, we have to place it within the more general context of symbolic meaning.

Concepts and Theory: Meaning and Interaction

According to Mead, language came about as the chief survival mechanism for humans. We use it to pragmatically control our environment, and this sign system comes to stand in the place of physical reality. As we've seen, animals relate directly to the environment; they receive sensory input and react. Humans, on the other hand, generally need to decide what the input *means* before acting. Distinctly human action, then, is based on the world existing symbolically rather than physically. In order to talk about this issue, Mead uses the ideas of natural signs and significant gestures.

A sign is something that stands for something else, such as your GPA that can represent your cumulative work at the university. It appears that many animals can use signs as well. My dog Gypsy, for example, gets very excited and begins to salivate at the sound of her treat box being opened or the tone of my voice when I ask, "Wanna trrrreeeeet?" But the ability of animals to use signs varies. For instance, a dog and a chicken will respond differently to the presence of a feed bowl on the other side of a fence. The chicken will simply pace back and forth in front of the fence in aggravation, but the dog will seek a break in the fence, go through the break, and run back to the bowl and eat. The chicken appears to only be able to respond directly to one stimulus, where the dog is able to hold her response to the food at bay while seeking an alternative. This ability to hold responses at bay is important for higher-level thinking animals.

These signs that we've been talking about may be called **natural signs**. They are private and learned through the individual experience of each animal. So, if your dog also gets excited at the sound of the treat box, it is because of its individual experience with it—Gypsy didn't tell your dog about the treat box. There also tends to be a natural relationship between the sign and its object (sound/treat), and these signs occur apart from the agency of the animal. In other words, Gypsy did not make the association between the sound of the box and her treats; I did. So, in the absolute sense, the relationship between the sound and the treat isn't a true natural sign. Natural signs come out of the natural experiences of the animal, and the meaning of these signs is determined by a structured relationship between the sign and its object, like smoke and fire.

Humans, on the other hand, have the ability to use what Mead calls *significant gestures* or symbols. According to Mead, other animals besides humans have gestures but none have *significant* gestures. A gesture becomes significant when the idea behind the gesture arouses the same response (same idea or emotional attitude) in the self as in others. For example, if I asked about your weekend, you would use a variety of significant gestures (language) to tell me about it. So, even though I wasn't with you over the weekend, I could experience and know about your weekend because the words call out the same response in me as in you. Thus, human language is intrinsically reflexive: The meaning of any significant gesture always calls back to the individual making the gesture.

In contrast to natural signs, symbols are abstract and arbitrary. With signs, the relationship between the sign and its referent is natural (as with smoke and fire). But the meaning of symbols can be quite abstract and completely arbitrary (in terms of naturally given relations). For example, "Sunday" is completely arbitrary and is an abstract human creation. What day of the week it is depends upon what calendar is used, and the different calendars are associated with political and religious power issues, not nature. Because symbolic meaning is not tied to any object, the meaning can change over time. For example, in the United States there have been several meanings associated with the category of "people with dark skin."

According to Mead (1934), the meaning of a significant gesture, or symbol, is its "set of organized sets of responses" (p. 71)—notice the influence of pragmatism. Symbolic meaning is not the image of a thing seen at a distance, nor does it exactly correspond to the dictionary definition; rather, the meaning of a word is the action that it calls out or elicits. For example, the meaning of a chair is the different kinds of things we can do with it. Picture a wooden object with four legs, a seat, and a slatted back. If I sit down on this object, then the meaning of it is "chair." On the other hand, if I take that same object and break it into small pieces and use it to start a fire, it's no longer a chair—it's firewood. So the meaning of an object is defined in terms of its uses, or legitimated lines of behavior.

Because the meaning—legitimated actions—and objective availability (they are objects because we can point them out as foci for interaction) of symbols are produced in social interactions, they are **social object**s. Any idea or thing can be a social object. A piece of string can be a social object, as can the self or the idea of equality. There is nothing about the thing itself that makes it a social object; an entity becomes an object to us through our interactions around it. Through interaction, we call attention to it, name it, and attach legitimate lines of behavior to it.

For example, because of certain kinds of interactions, a Coke bottle here in the United States is a specific kind of social object. But to Xi, a bushman from the Kalahari Desert (in the film *The Gods Must Be Crazy*), the Coke bottle becomes something utterly different as a result of his interactions around it. For Xi, the Coke bottle dropped from the sky—an obvious gift from the gods. But when he brought it to his village, this playful gift from the gods became a curse, because there was only one and everybody wanted it. It became a scarce resource that brought conflict. Eventually, Xi had to go on a religious quest because of this gift from the gods (to us, a Coke bottle).

Symbolic Interaction

Notice in this illustration that the meaning of the Coke bottle changed as different kinds of interactions took place. In this sense, meaning is **emergent** and arises out of interaction. As Mead (1934) says, "the logical structure of meaning . . . is to be found in the threefold relationship of gesture to adjustive response and to the resultant of the given social act" (p. 80). **Interaction** is defined as the ongoing negotiation and melding together of individual actions and meanings through three distinct steps. First, there is an initial cue given. Notice that the cue itself doesn't carry any specific meaning. Let's say you see a friend crying in the halls at school. What does it mean? It could mean lots of things. In order to determine (or more properly, create or achieve) the meaning, you have to respond to that cue: "Is everything alright?" But we still don't have meaning yet. There must be a response to your response. After the three phases (cue–response–response to response), a meaning emerges: "Nothing's wrong," your friend responds, "my boyfriend just asked me to marry him."

But we probably still aren't done, because her response will become yet another cue. Imagine walking away from your friend without saying a word after she tells you she's getting married. That would be impolite (which would actually be a response to her statement). So, what does her second cue mean? We can't tell until you respond to her cue and she responds to your response.

Notice that interactions are rarely terminal or closed off. Let's suppose you told your friend who was crying in the hall that marrying this guy was a bad idea. You saw him out with another woman last Friday night. At this point, the social object—marriage—which was a cue that caused her to cry in happiness, has become an object of anger. So the meaning that emerges is now betrayal and anger. She then takes that meaning and interacts with her fiancé. In that interaction, she presents a cue (maybe she's crying again, but it has a different meaning), and he responds, and she responds to his response, and so on. Maybe she finds out that you misread the cues that Friday night and the "other woman" was just a friend. So she comes back to you and presents a cue, ad infinitum. Keep this idea of emergent meaning in mind as we see what Mead says about the self (it, too, emerges).

Concepts and Theory: Making Yourself

Have you ever watched someone doing something? Of course you have. Maybe you watched a worker planting a tree on campus, or maybe you watched a band play last Friday night. And while you watched, you understood people and their behaviors in terms of the identity they claimed and the roles they played. In short, when you watch someone, you understand the person as a social object. After watching someone, have you ever called someone else's attention to that actor? Of course you have, and it's easy to do. All you have to say is something like, "Whoa, check him/her/it out." And the other person will look and usually understand immediately what it is you are pointing out, because we understand one another in terms of being social objects.

People-watching is a pretty common experience and we all do it. We can do it because we understand the other in terms of being a social object. But let me ask you something. Have you ever watched yourself? Have you ever felt embarrassed or laughed at yourself? How is that different from watching other people? Actually, it isn't. But there is something decidedly odd about this idea of watching our self. It's easy to watch someone else, and it is easy to understand *how* we watch someone else. If I am watching a band play, I can watch the band because they are on stage and I am in the audience. We can observe the other because we are standing outside of them. We can point to them because they are *there* in the world around us. But how can we point to our self, call our own attention to our self, and understand our self as a social object? Do you see the problem? We must somehow *divorce our self from our self* so that we can call attention to our self, so that we can understand our self as meaningfully relevant as a social object. So, how is that done?

Role-taking is the key mechanism through which people develop a self and the capacity to be social, and it has a very specific definition: Role-taking is the process through which we place our self in the position (or role) of another in order to see our own self. Students often confuse role-taking with what might be called role-*making*. In every social situation, we make a role for ourselves. Erving Goffman wrote at length about this process and called it impression management (see Chapter 12). Role-taking is a precursor to effective role-making—we put ourselves in the position of the other in order to see how they want us to act. For example, when going to a job interview, you put yourself in the position or role of the interviewer in order to see how he or she will view you—you then dress or act in the "appropriate" manner. But role-taking is distinct from impression management, and it is the major mechanism through which we are able to form a perspective outside of ourselves.

A *perspective* is always a meaning-creating position. We stand in a particular point of view and attribute meaning to something. Let's take the flag of the United States, for example. To some, it means freedom and pride; to others, oppression and shame; and to still others, it signifies the devil incarnate (as for some fundamentalist sects). I want you to notice something very important here: The flag itself has no meaning. Its meaning comes from the perspective an individual takes when he or she views it. That's why something like the flag (or gender or skin color or ethnic heritage) can mean so many different things. Meaning isn't in the object; *meaning arises from the perspective we take and from our interactions.*

Here's the important point: The **self** is just such a perspective. It is a viewpoint from which to consider our behaviors and give them meaning, and by definition, a perspective is something other than the object. In this case, the self is the perspective and the object is our actions, feelings, or thoughts. Taking this perspective, the self is how all these personal qualities and behaviors become meaningful social objects. Precisely how we can get outside ourselves in this way is Mead's driving question.

The Mind

Before the self begins to form, there is a preparatory stage. While Mead does not explicitly name this stage, he implies it in several writings and talks about it more generally in this theory of the mind. For Mead, the **mind** is not something that resides in the physical brain or in the nervous system, nor is it something that is unavailable for sociological investigation. The mind is a kind of behavior, according to Mead, that involves at least five different abilities:

- To use symbols to denote objects
- To use symbols as its own stimulus (it can talk to itself)
- To read and interpret another's gestures and use them as further stimuli
- To suspend response (not act out of impulse)
- To imaginatively rehearse one's own behaviors before actually behaving

Let me give you an example that encompasses all these behaviors. A few years ago, our school paper ran a cartoon. In it was a picture of three people: a man and a woman arm-in-arm, and another man. The woman was introducing the men to one another. Both men were reaching out to shake one another's hands. But above the single man was a balloon of his thoughts. In it he was picturing himself violently punching the other man. He wanted to hit the man, but he shook his hand instead and said, "Glad to meet you."

There are a lot of things we can pull out of this cartoon, but the issue we want to focus on is the disparity between what the man felt and what the man did.

He had an impulse to hit the other man, perhaps because he was jealous. But he didn't. Why didn't he? Actually, that isn't as good a question as, *how* didn't he? He was able to not hit the other man because of his mind. His mind was able to block his initial impulse, to understand the situation symbolically, to point out to his self the symbols and possible meanings, to entertain alternative lines of behavior, and choose the behavior that best fit the situation. The man used symbols to stimulate his own behavior rather than going with his impulse or the actual world.

Mead (1934) argues that the "mind arises in the social process only when that process as a whole enters into, or is present in, the experience of any one of the given individuals involved in that process" (p. 134). Notice that Mead is arguing that the mind evolves as the social process—or, more precisely, the social interaction—comes to live inside the individual. The mind, then, is a social entity that begins to form because of infant dependency and forced interaction.

When babies are hungry or tired or wet, they can't take care of themselves. Instead, they send out what Mead would call "unconventional gestures," gestures that do not mean the same to the sender and hearer. In other words, they cry. The caregivers must figure out what the baby needs. When they do, parents tend to vocalize their behaviors ("Oh, did Susie need a ba-ba?"). Babies eventually discover that if they mimic the parents and send out a significant gesture ("ba-ba"), they will get their needs met sooner. This is the beginning of language acquisition; babies begin to understand that their environment is symbolic—the object that satisfies hunger is "ba-ba" and the object that brings it is "da-da." Eventually, a baby will understand that she has a symbol as well: "Susie." Thus, language acquisition allows the child to symbolize and eventually to symbolically manipulate her environment, including self and others. The use of reflexive language also allows the child to begin to role-take, which is the primary mechanism through which the mind and self are formed.

Three Stages of Role-Taking

After a child begins to use language, he or she is ready to begin creating a symbolic self. This happens through three stages of role-taking. The first stage is the **play stage** and here the child can take the role, or assume the perspective, of certain significant others. Significant others are those upon whom we depend for emotional and often material support. These are the people with whom we have long-term relations and intimate (self-revealing) ties. Mead calls this stage the play stage because children must literally play at being some significant other in order to see themselves. At this point, they haven't progressed much in terms of being able to think abstractly, so they must act out the role to get the perspective. This is important: *A child literally gets outside of himself or herself in order to see the self.*

Children play at being Mommy or being Teacher. The child will hold a doll or stuffed bear and talk to it as if she were the parent. Ask any parent; it's a frightening experience because what you are faced with is an almost exact imitation of your own behaviors, words, and even tone of voice. But remember the purpose of role-taking (notice this isn't role-*playing*): It is to see one's own self. So, as the child is playing Mommy or Daddy with a teddy bear, who is the bear? The child herself. She is seeing herself from the point of view of the parent, literally. This is the genesis of the self perspective: being able to get outside of the self so that we can watch the self as if on stage. As the child acts toward herself as others act, the child begins to understand self as a set of organized responses and becomes a social object to herself.

The next stage in the development of self is the **game stage**. During this stage, the child can take the perspective of several others and can take into account the rules (sets of responses that different attitudes bring out) of society. But the role-taking at this stage is still not very abstract. In the play stage, the child could only take the perspective of a single significant other; in the game stage, the child can take on the role of several others, but they all remain individuals. Mead's example is that of a baseball game. The batter can role-take with each individual player in the field and determine how to bat based on their behaviors. The batter is also aware of all the rules of the game. Children at this stage can role-take with several people and are very concerned with social rules. But they still don't have a fully formed self. That doesn't happen until they can take the perspective of the generalized other: "It is this generalized other in his experience which provides him with a self" (Mead, 1925, p. 269).

The **generalized other** refers to sets of attitudes that an individual may take toward himself or herself—it is the general attitude or perspective of a community. The generalized other allows the individual to have a less segmented self as the perspectives of many others are generalized into a single view. It is through the generalized other that the community exercises control over the conduct of its individual members.

Up until this point, the child has only been able to role-take with specific others. As the individual progresses in the ability to use abstract language and concepts, he or she is also able to think about general or abstract others. So, for example, a woman may look in the mirror and judge the reflection by the general image that has been given to her by the media about how a woman should look.

Another insightful example of how the generalized other works is given to us by George Orwell in his account of "Shooting an Elephant." Orwell was at the time a police officer in Burma. He was at odds with the job and felt that imperialism was an evil thing. At the same time, the local populace despised him precisely because he represented imperialistic control; he tells tales of being tripped and ridiculed by people in the town. One day an elephant was reported stomping through a village. Orwell was called to attend to it. On the way there, he obtained a rifle, only for scaring the animal or defending himself if need be. When he found the animal, he knew immediately that there was no longer any danger. The elephant was calmly eating grass in a field, and Orwell knew that the right thing to do was to wait until the elephant simply wandered off—but at the same time, he knew he had to shoot the animal.

As Orwell (1946) relates, "I realized that I should have to shoot the elephant after all. The people expected it of me and I had got to do it; I could feel their two thousand wills press me forward, irresistibly" (p. 152). He felt the expectations of a generalized other. Though contrary to his own will, and after much personal anguish, he shot the elephant. As Orwell puts it, at that time and in that place, the white man "wears a mask, and his face grows to fit it. . . . A sahib has got to act like a sahib" (pp. 152–153). Not shooting was impossible, for "the crowd would laugh at me. And my whole life, every white man's life in the East, was one long struggle not to be laughed at" (p. 153). We may criticize Orwell for his decision (it's always easy from a distance); still, each one of us has felt the pressure of a generalized other.

Society and the Self

For Mead (1934), there could be no society without individual selves: "Human society as we know it could not exist without minds and selves, since all its most characteristic features presuppose the possession of minds and selves by its individual members" (p. 227). We don't have a self because there is a psychological drive or need for one. We have a self because society demands it. To emphasize this point, Mead (1934) says that "the self is not something that exists first and then enters into relationship with others, but it is, so to speak, an eddy in the social current and so still a part of the current" (p. 26). Eddies are currents of air or water that run contrary to the stream. It isn't so much the contrariness that Mead wants us to see, but the fact that an eddy only exists in and because of its surrounding current. The same is true for selves: They only exist in and because of social interaction. The self doesn't have a continuous existence; it isn't something that we carry around inside of us. It's a mechanism that allows conversations to happen, whether that conversation occurs in the interaction or within the individual. So, the self isn't something that has an essential existence or meaning. Like all social objects, it must be symbolically denoted and then given meaning within interactions. And like all social-symbolic objects, the meaning of the self is flexible and emergent.

This emphasis of Mead's (1934) leads him to see society and social institutions as "nothing but an organization of attitudes which we all carry in us"; they are "organized forms of group or social activity—forms so organized that the individual members of society can act adequately and socially by taking the attitudes of others toward these activities" (pp. 211, 261–262). Society, then, doesn't exist objectively outside the concrete interactions of people, as Durkheim or Marx would have it. Rather, society exists only as sets of attitudes, symbols, and imaginations that people may or may not use and modify in an interaction. In other words, society exists only as sets of potential generalized others with which we can role-take. We'll find this emphasis on **the situation** several times during the course of this book, and it comes back to the assumption about society's existence that we addressed in Chapter 1.

The I and the Me

Thus far it would appear that the self is to be conceived of as a simple reflection of the society around it. But for Mead, the self isn't merely this social robot; the self is an active process. Part of what we mean by the self is an internalized conversation, and by necessity interactions require more than one person. Mead thus postulates the existence of two interactive facets of the self: the **I and the Me**. The Me is the self that results from the progressive stages of role-taking and is the perspective that we assume to view and analyze our own behaviors. The "I" is that part of the self that is unsocialized and spontaneous: "The self is essentially a social process going on with these two distinguishable phases. If it did not have these two phases, there could not be conscious responsibility and there would be nothing novel in experience" (Mead, 1934, p. 178).

We have all experienced the internal conversation between the I and the Me. We may want to jump for joy or shout in anger or punch someone we're angry at or kiss a stranger or run naked. But the Me opposes such behavior and points out the social ramifications of these actions. The I presents our impulses and drives; the Me presents to us the perspectives of society, the meanings and repercussions of our actions. These two elements of our self converse until we decide on a course of action. But here is the important part: The I can always act before the conversation begins or even in the middle of it. The I can thus take action that the Me would never think of; it can act differently from the community.

Summary

- There are basic elements, or tools, that go into making us human. Among the most important of these are symbolic meaning and the mind. We use symbols and social objects to denote and manipulate the environment. Each symbol or social object is understood in terms of legitimated behaviors and pragmatic motives. The mind uses symbolic-social objects in order to block initial responses and consider alternative lines of behavior. It is thus necessary in order for society to exist. The mind is formed in childhood through necessary social interaction.

- The self is a perspective from which to view our own behaviors. This perspective is formed through successive stages of role-taking and becomes a social object for our own thoughts. The self has a dynamic quality as well—it is the internalized conversation between the I and the Me. The Me is the social object, and the I is the seat of the impulses. When the self is able to role-take with generalized others, society can exist as well as an integrated self. Role-taking with generalized others also allows us to think in abstract terms.

- Society emerges through social interaction; it is not a determinative structure. In general, humans act more than react. Action is predicated on the ability of the mind to delay response and consider alternative lines of behavior with respect to the social environment and a pertinent self. Thus, mind, self, and society mutually constitute one another. Interaction is the process of knitting together different lines of action. Meaning is produced in interaction through the triadic relation of cue, response, and response to response. What we mean by society emerges from this negotiated meaning as interactants role-take within specific definitions of the situation and organized attitudes (institutions).

(Continued)

In 1914, Simmel was offered a full-time academic position at the University of Strasbourg. However, as World War I broke out, the school buildings were given over to military uses and Simmel had little lecturing to do. On September 28, 1918, Simmel died of liver cancer.

Central Sociological Questions

Many sociologists argue that people are formed through social interaction and experiences with social groups and structures. Simmel is somewhat unusual because he assumes a kind of natural state for people. In other words, people are born with certain dispositions and tendencies, and interactions and institutions affect that natural state. Simmel, then, was primarily concerned with how society and objective culture influence this more natural existence. Simmel felt that modernity brought new pressures to bear on the natural state of people; thus, theory explains how modern society creates objective rather than subjective culture and how that shift influences the individual.

Simply Stated

Simmel argues that people meet their individual needs through social encounters and that these encounters can only be carried out through identifiable forms. These forms, along with cultural generally, can become alienating (objective) and thus create difficulties for the person. Culture becomes objective and alienating in modernity through such general processes as urbanization, money, and complex social networks, as well as institutionalized religion and gender.

Key Concepts

social forms, sociability, exchange, conflict, objective culture, urbanization, the division of labor, money, web of group affiliations, normative specificity, anomie, role conflict, blasé attitude

Concepts and Theory: The Individual in Society

At the core of Simmel's thought is the individual. In contrast to Mead, Simmel assumes there is something called human nature with which we are born. For example, Simmel feels that we naturally have a religious impulse and that gender differences are intrinsic. He also assumes that in back of most of our social interactions are individual motivations. This emphasis sets up an interesting problem and perspective for Simmel. If the individual and his or her motivations and actions are paramount, then how is society possible?

In formulating his answer, Simmel follows one of his favorite philosophers, Immanuel Kant. Kant did not ask about the possibility of society. Instead, he wondered how nature could exist as the *object* "nature" to science. Basically, Kant argued that the universe could exist as "nature" to scientists only because of the *category* of nature. Objects in the universe can only *exist* as objects because the human mind orders sense perception in a particular way. But Kant didn't argue that it is all in our heads; rather, he argued for a kind of synthesis: The human mind organizes our perceptions of the world to form objects of experience. So, nature can only exist as the object "nature" because scientists are observing the world through the a priori (existing before) category of nature. In other words, a scientist can see weather as a natural phenomenon, produced through processes that we can discover, only because she assumes beforehand (a priori) that weather does *not* exist as a result of the whim of a god.

Simmel wants to discover the a priori conditions for society. This was a new way of trying to understand society, rather than using a mechanistic and organismic analogy. In understanding society, however, Simmel wants to maintain the integrity of the individual but at the same time recognize society as a true force. What Simmel argues is that society exists as **social forms** that come about through human interaction, and society continues to exist and to exert influence over the individual through these forms of interaction:

> Strictly speaking, neither hunger nor love, work nor religiosity, technology nor the functions and results of intelligence, are social. They are factors in sociation only when they transform the mere aggregation of isolated individuals into specific forms of being with and for one another, forms that are subsumed under the general concept of interaction. (Simmel, 1971, pp. 23–24)

These forms or categories of behavior, Simmel argues, are the a priori conditions of society.

Now, think about this: If Simmel is primarily concerned about the individual, what are the implications for the person if social forms take on objective existence? There is a sense in which Mead doesn't see symbols as objective. If the meaning of symbols emerges through social interaction, then they are always subjective, at least to some degree. What Simmel wants us to consider is the possibility that signs, symbols, ideas, social forms, and so forth can exist independently of the person and exert independent effects. The question then becomes, how does objective culture impact the subjectivity of the person? Guy Oakes (1984) wrote concerning Simmel, "The discovery of objectivity—the independence of things from the conditions of their subjective or psychological genesis—was the greatest achievement in the cultural history of the West" (p. 3).

Subjective and Objective Cultures

Simmel was the first social thinker to make the distinction between subjective and objective culture the focus of his research. Individual or *subjective culture* refers to the ability to embrace, use, and feel culture. Collectives can form group-specific cultures, such as the spiked Mohawk haircut of early punk culture. To wear such an item of culture immediately links the individual to certain social forms and types, and a group member would subjectively feel those links. Individuals and dyads are able to produce such culture as well. An individual could have special incense that he or she blends just for extraordinary, ritual occasions; or a couple could create a picture that would symbolize their relationship. This culture is very close to the individual and his or her psychological experience of the world.

concern in this shift is the effects it has on the individual's personal experience of the self. There are three interrelated forces in modernity that tend to increase objective culture in all three of its areas—urbanization, the division of labor, and the use of money and markets. Urbanization appears to be the principal dynamic, as it increases the level of the division of labor and the extent that money and markets are used. It also changes one's web of affiliations from a dense, primary network to a loose, secondary one. As is typical with Simmel, we will find that he believes that social processes bring some conflicting effects. Additionally, as you'll see, Simmel's argument is complex, so read the next sections carefully *by thinking through and keeping track of the theoretical connections and effects.* At the end of our discussion I'll give you a model that captures Simmel's theory.

Simmel's (1950) concern with objective culture is nowhere clearer than in his short paper "The Metropolis and Mental Life":

> The most profound reason . . . why the metropolis conduces to the urge of the most individual personal existence . . . appears to me to be the following: the development of modern culture is characterized by the preponderance of what one may call the "objective spirit" over the "subjective spirit." (p. 421)

The initial factor in back of this objective spirit is **urbanization**—the process that moves people from country to city living. This move was a major factor in creating the modern era, and in that sense urbanization is historically specific. But it's extremely important for us to keep in mind that this process didn't stop at some point. The dynamics that brought about urbanization are ongoing; thus, contemporary societies still have varying degrees of urbanization, with some areas being more or less urbanized. Thus the levels of the effects from urbanization vary as well. Urbanization created three other factors: increasing division of labor, expanding use of money and markets, and greater ratio of rational to organic group membership.

The Division of Labor

Historically, people generally moved from the country to the city because of industrialization. As a result of the Industrial Revolution, the economic base of society changed and with it the means through which people made a living. As populations became increasingly concentrated in one place, more efficient means of providing for the necessities of life and for organizing labor were needed. This increase in the *division of labor* happened so that products could be made more quickly and the workforce could be more readily controlled. Simmel (1950) argues that the division of labor also increases because of worker-entrepreneur innovation: "The concentration of individuals and their struggle for customers compel the individual to specialize in a function from which he cannot be readily displaced by another" (p. 420).

The division of labor demands an "ever more one-sided accomplishment," and we thus become specialized and concerned with smaller and smaller elements of the production process. This one-sidedness creates objective culture: We are unable to grasp the whole of the product and the production process because we are only working on a small part. The worker in a highly specialized division of labor becomes "a mere cog in an enormous organization of things and powers which tear from his hands all progress, spirituality, and value in order to transform them from their subjective form into the form of purely objective life" (Simmel, 1950, p. 422).

Simmel claims that the consumption of products thus produced has a trivializing effect. This is basically the same issue with which Marx was concerned: Commodities produced in modern economies have little if any intrinsic meaning. Before modernity most products were handmade, had very clear meanings to groups and individuals, and were usually embedded in socially reciprocal relations of gift giving, support, and lineage. While we can still accomplish this today by making a gift by hand (from start to finish) or passing down heirlooms, it isn't what characterizes our world. Both Marx and Simmel are saying that using such trivialized or empty commodities has an alienating effect on the person. Both the level of specialization and commodification that come from high divisions of labor create higher levels of objective culture.

Money and Markets

Urbanization also increases the level of exchange in a society and thus the use of money-facilitated markets. When thinking about the presence of money in society, it is important to understand it in comparison to barter. Barter is the exchange of goods or services for other goods or services. In a barter system, there is no universal value scheme. Everything is equated on an item-by-item basis and every item is equally real. Thus, the bushel of corn that I grew may be exchanged for the two chairs that you made or for the ten loaves of bread that Francis baked. The value of a product or service can vary tremendously, depending on local conditions or the subjective state of the trader.

Money creates a universal value system wherein every commodity can be understood. Of necessity, this value system is abstract; that is, it has no intrinsic worth. In order for it stand for everything, it must have no value in itself. The universal and abstract nature of money frees it from constraint and facilitates exchanges. But it also has other effects for both the individual and society at large; we will talk about four of these effects below. These effects increase the level that money (or even more abstract systems such as credit) is used.

One effect of money is that it increases individual freedom by allowing people to pursue diverse activities (paying to join a dance club or a pyramid sales organization) and by increasing the options for self-expression (we can buy the clothes and makeup to pass as a raver this week and a business professional the next; we can even buy hormones and surgery to become a different sex). Second, even though we are able to buy more things with which to express and experience our self, we are less attached to those things because of money. We tend to understand and experience our possessions less in terms of their intrinsic qualities and more in terms of their objective and abstract worth. So, I understand the value of my guitar amplifier in terms of the money it cost me and how difficult it would be to replace (in terms of money). The more money I have, the less valuable my Sunn amplifier will be, because I could afford a hand-wired, boutique amp. Thus, our connection to things becomes more tenuous and objective (rather than emotional) due to the use of money.

Third, money also discourages intimate ties with people. Part of this is due to the universal nature of money. Because of its all-inclusive character, money comes to stand in the place of almost everything, and this effect spreads. When money was first introduced, only certain goods and services were seen as equivalent to it. Today in the United States, we would be hard pressed to think of many things that cannot be purchased with or made equivalent to money, and that includes relationships. Much of this outcome is due to indirect consequences of money: The relationships we have are in large part determined by the school or neighborhood we can afford. Some of money's consequences are more direct: We buy our way into country clubs and exclusive organizations. Money further discourages intimate ties by encouraging a culture of calculation. The increasing presence of calculative and objectifying culture, even though spawned in economic exchange, tends to make us calculating and objectifying in our relationships. All exchanges require a degree of calculation, even barter, but the use of money increases the number and speed of exchanges. As we participate in an increasing number of exchanges, we calculate more and we begin to understand the world more in terms of numbers and rational calculations. Money is the universal value system in modernity, and as it is used more and more to assess the world, the world becomes increasingly quantified ("time is money" and we shouldn't "waste time just 'hanging out'").

Fourth, money also decreases moral constraints and increases anomie. Money is an amoral value system. What that means is that there are no morals implied in money. Money is simply a means of exchange, a way of making exchanges go easier. Money knows no good or evil: It can be equally used to buy a gun to kill school children as to buy food to feed the poor. So, as more and more of our lives are understood in terms of money, less and less of our lives have a moral basis. In addition, because moral constraints are produced only through group interactions, when money is used to facilitate group membership, it decreases the true social nature of the group and thus its ability to produce morality.

Thus, money has both positive and negative consequences for the individual. Money increases our options for self-expression and allows us to pursue diverse activities, but it also distances us from objects and people and it increases the possibility of anomie. In the same way, there are both positive and negative consequences for society. However, while it may seem that the negative consequences outweigh the positive for the individual, the consequences for society are mostly positive.

We will look at a total of *four effects for society* of the increasing use of money. First, the use of money creates exchange relationships that cover greater distances and last longer periods of time than would otherwise be possible. Let's think of the employment relationship as an illustration. If a person holds a regular job, he or she has entered a kind of contract. The worker agrees to work for the employer a given number of hours per week at a certain pay rate. This agreement covers an extended period of time, which should only be terminated by a two-week notice or severance pay. This relationship may cover a great deal of geographic space, as when the workplace is located on the West Coast of the United States and the corporate headquarters is on the East Coast. This kind of relationship was extremely difficult before the use of money as a generalized medium of exchange, which is why many long-term work relationships were conceptualized in terms of familial obligations, such as the serf or apprentice. And, with more generalized forms of the money principle, as with credit and credit cards, social relations can span even larger geographic expanses and longer periods of time (for example, I am obligated to my mortgage company for the next 25 years, and I just completed an eBay transaction with a man living in Japan). What this extension of relations through space and time means is that the number of social ties increases. While we may not be connected as deeply or emotionally today, we are connected to more diverse people more often. Think of society as a fabric: The greater the number and diversity of ties, the stronger is the weave.

Second, money also increases continuity among groups (level of cultural and social homogeneity). Money flattens, or generalizes, the value system by making everything equivalent to itself. It also creates more objective culture, which overshadows or colonizes subjective culture. Together these forces tend to make group-specific culture more alike than different. What differences exist are trivial and based on shifting styles. Thus, while the weave of society is more dense due to the effects of money, it is also less colorful, which tends to mitigate group conflicts.

Third, money strengthens the level of trust in a society. What is money, really? In the United States, it is nothing but green ink and nice paper. Yet we would do and give almost anything in exchange for enough of these green pieces of paper. This exchange for relatively worthless paper occurs every day without anyone so much as blinking an eye. How can this be? The answer is that in back of money is the U.S. government, and we have a certain level of trust in its stability. Without that trust, the money would be worthless. A barter system requires some level of trust, but generally speaking, you know the person you are trading with and you can inspect the goods. Money, on the other hand, demands a trust in a very abstract social form—the state—and that trust helps bind us together as a collective.

Fourth, behind this trust is the existence of a centralized state. In order for us to trust in money, we must trust in the authority of a single nation. When money was first introduced in Greek culture, its use was rather precarious. Different wealthy landowners or city-states would imprint their image on lumps or rods of metal. Because there was no central governing authority, deceit and counterfeiting were rampant. The images were easily mimicked and weights easily manipulated. Even though money helped facilitate exchanges, the lack of oversight dampened the effect. It wasn't until there was a centralized government that people could completely trust money. Thus, when markets started using money for exchanges, they were inadvertently pushing for the existence of a strong nation-state. Centralized authority is the structural component to a society's trust and it binds us together.

This factor has an effect on individual freedom of expression. While the increasing use of money and markets along with decreases in the level of normative regulation increase individual freedom of expression, there's a counter force for regulation coming from a centralized state. Modern states have increasing interest in controlling your behaviors. The list of direct and indirect regulation is almost endless, but an especially clear example is cigarette smoking. While it may still be legal to smoke tobacco, it's highly regulated in terms of where and when a person may smoke; at some firms, not smoking is a condition of employment.

Social Networks: Rational Versus Organic Group Membership

As a further result of urbanization, Simmel argues that social networks (what he calls the **web of group affiliations**) have changed. When we talk about social networks today, what we have in mind are the number and type of people with whom we associate, and the connections among and between those people. Network theory is an established part of contemporary sociology, and Simmel was one of the first to think in such terms. For his part, Simmel characterizes two types of social networks, organic and rational. We'll first consider organic social networks, which are typical of small, more rural towns and settings. Simmel uses the term *organic* to imply that these sorts of group networks come about and develop in a way that resembles the growth of a plant or animal—they occur naturally.

In small rural settings, there are relatively few groups for people to join, and most of those memberships are strongly influenced by family. We tend to join the same groups as members of our family do. In these social settings, the family is a primary structure for social organization, and families tend not to move around much. So there are likely to be multiple generations present. As a result, the associations of the family become the associations of the child. A child reared in such surroundings will generally attend the same church, school, and work as his or her parents, grandparents, cousins, and so on. Further, most of these groups will overlap. For example, it would be very likely that a worker and his or her boss attend the same church and that they will have gone to the same school.

Simmel notes that people in these settings tend to join groups because of *organic motivations*—because they are naturally or organically connected to the group. Many of the groups with which a person affiliates in this setting are primary groups. **Primary groups** are noteworthy because they are based on ties of affection and personal loyalty, endure over long periods of time, and involve multiple aspects of a person's life. Under organic conditions, a person will usually be involved with mostly primary groups, and these groups have some association with one another. This kind of community will thus contain people who are very much alike. They will draw from the same basic group influences and culture, and the groups will possess a compelling ability to sanction behavior and bring about conformity.

On the other hand, people join groups in modern, urban settings out of *rational motivations*—group membership due to freedom of choice. The interesting thing to note about this freedom is that it is forced on the individual—in other words, there are few organic connections. In large cities, people usually do not have much family around and the personal connections tend to be rather tenuous. In Southern California, for example, people move on average every five to seven years. Most only know their neighbors by sight, and the majority of interactions are work related (and people change jobs about as often as they change houses). What this means is that people join social groups out of choice (rational reasons) rather than out of some emotional and organic connectedness. These kinds of groups tend to have the characteristics of **secondary groups** (goal and utilitarian oriented, with a narrow range of activities, over limited time spans).

As a result of rational group affiliations, it is far more likely that individuals will develop unique personalities. A person in a more complex or rational web of group affiliations has multiple and diverse influences and groups' capacity to sanction is diminished. From Simmel's point of view, the group's ability to sanction is based on the individual's dependency upon the group. If there are few groups from which to choose, then individuals in a collective are more dependent upon those groups and the groups will be able to demand conformity. This power is crystal clear in traditional societies where being ostracized meant death. Of course, the inverse is also true: The greater the number of groups from which to choose and the more diverse the groups, the less the moral boundaries and **normative specificity** (the level of behaviors that are guided by norms). In turn, this decrease in sanctioning power leads to greater individual freedom of expression.

Many students, for example, are able to express themselves more freely after moving away from home to the university. This is especially true of students who move from rural to urban settings. Not only is the influence of the student's childhood groups diminished (family, peers, church), but there are also many, many more groups from which to choose. These groups often have little to do with one another. Thus, if one group becomes too demanding of time or emotion or behavior, you can simply switch groups. So, it may be the case that you experience yourself as a unique individual having choices, but it has little to do with you per se: It is a function of the structure of your network.

While decreased moral boundaries and normative specificity lead to greater freedom of expression, they can also produce *anomie*—also a concern of Durkheim's. For the individual, it speaks of a condition of confusion and meaninglessness. Unlike animals, humans are not instinctually driven or regulated. We can choose our behaviors. That also means that our emotions, thoughts, and behaviors must be ordered by group culture and social structure or they will be in chaos and will have little meaning. When group regulation is diminished or gone, it is easy for people to become confused and chaotic in their thoughts and emotions. Things in our life and life itself can become meaningless. So while we may think that personal freedom is a great idea, too much freedom can be disastrous.

Complex webs of group affiliations can have two more consequences: They can increase the level of **role conflict** a person experiences, and they contribute to the blasé attitude. Role conflict describes a situation in which the demands of two or more of the roles a person occupies clash with one another (such as when your friends want to go out on Thursday night but you have a test the next morning). The greater the number of groups with which one affiliates, the greater is the number of divergent roles and the possibility of role conflict. However, the tendency to keep groups spatially and temporally separate mitigates this potential. In other words, modern groups tend not to have the same members and they tend to gather at different times and locations. So we see the roles as separate and thus not in conflict.

Complex group structures also contribute to the **blasé attitude**, an attitude of absolute boredom and lack of concern. Every social group we belong to demands emotional work or commitment, but we only have limited emotional resources, and we can only give so much and care so much. There is, then, a kind of inverse relationship between our capacity to emotionally invest in our groups and the number of different groups of which we are members. As the number and diversity of social groups in our lives goes up, our ability to emotionally invest goes down. This contributes to a blasé attitude, but it also makes conflict among groups less likely because the members care less about the groups' goals and standards.

This blasé attitude is also produced by all that we have talked about so far, as well as overstimulation and rapid change. The city itself provides for multiple stimuli. As we walk down the street, we are faced with diverse people and circumstances that we must take in and evaluate and react to. In our pursuit of individuality, we also increase the level of stimulation in our lives. As we go from one group to another, from one concert or movie to another, from one mall to another, from one style of dress to another, or as we simply watch TV or listen to music, we are bombarding ourselves with emotional and intellectual stimulation. In the final analysis, all this stimulation proves to be too much for us and we emotionally withdraw. Further, this stimulation is in constant flux. Knowledge and culture are constantly changing. Modern knowledge constantly changes because of the basic assumptions in back of science (the modern way of knowing): Scientific knowledge is based on skepticism, testing, and the defining value of progress. The general culture of modernity is affected by changes in knowledge, yet cultural change is also fueled by ever-expanding capitalist markets and commodities and mass media.

We have covered a great deal of conceptual ground in this section. It's been made all the more complicated because each of the things we have talked about brings both functional and dysfunctional effects and the effects overlap and mutually reinforce one another. I've diagrammed Simmel's theory in Figure 6.2. Note that I've concentrated on the effects of urbanization on the individual, which is Simmel's focus. At first glance the complexity of the model may seem overwhelming. However, if you follow each of the paths, you'll find that it simply expresses what we've been talking about over the past few pages. For example, starting at the level of division of labor, we can see that increases in the division of labor create specialized cultures, which in turn increases the level of objective culture (relative to subjective) that then increases the likelihood that people will experience a blasé attitude. You can also work backwards in the model. If you want to know when it's more likely that people will have a sense of freedom in personal expression, start at that box and

Figure 6.2 Extended Effects of Urbanization

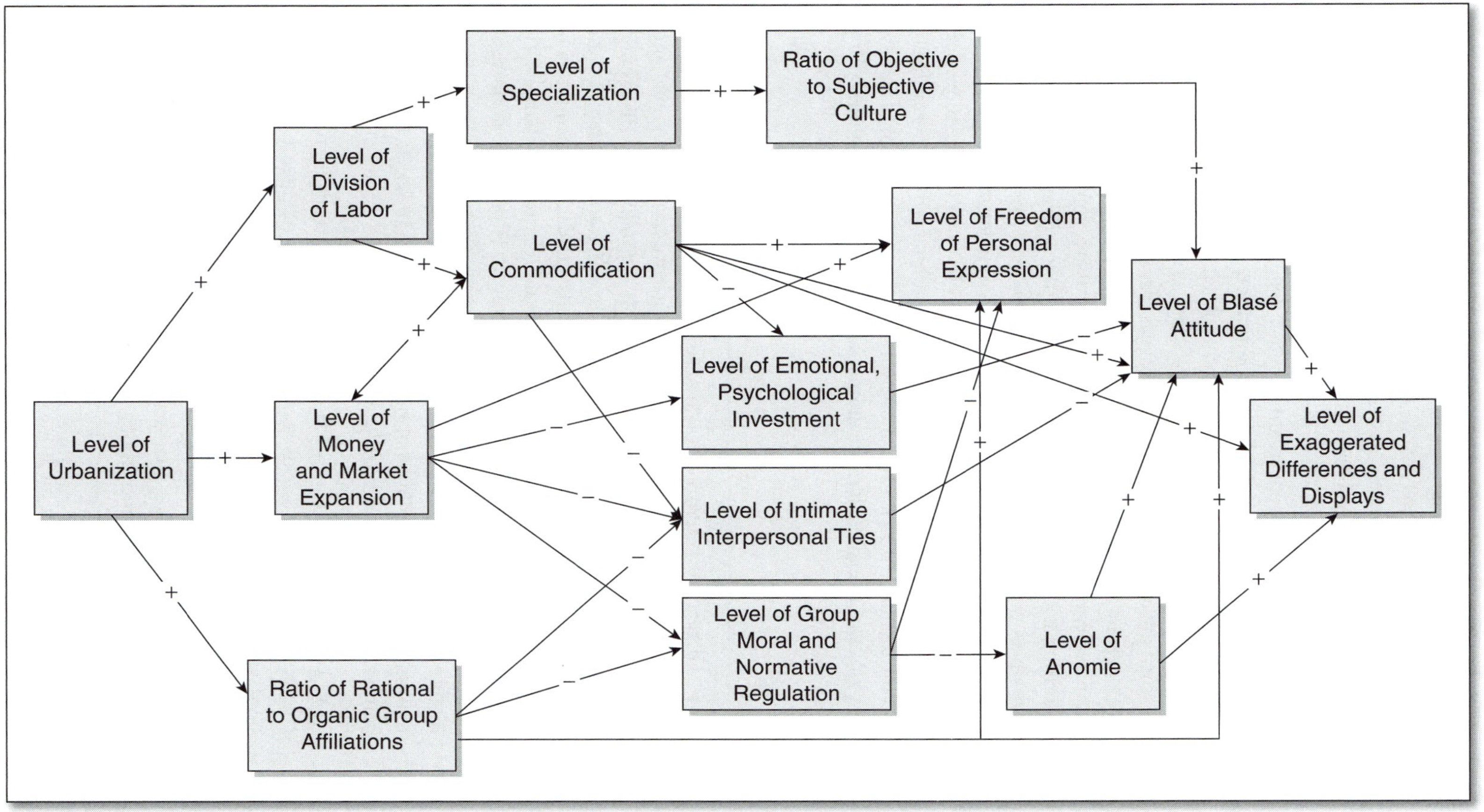

Level of Exaggerated Differences and Displays

Level of Blasé Attitude

Level of Anomie

Ratio of Objective to Subjective Culture

Level of Freedom of Personal Expression

Level of Specialization

Level of Emotional, Psychological Investment

Level of Intimate Interpersonal Ties

Level of Group Moral and Normative Regulation

Level of Commodification

Level of Division of Labor

Level of Money and Market Expansion

Ratio of Rational to Organic Group Affiliations

Level of Urbanization

work backwards from the arrows pointing to the box. Working through a model such as this is a great study aid in understanding how the theory works. Be certain you know how each concept or variable influences the others, not only in what direction but also what happens substantively.

You'll notice that there is an additional concept at the end: the level of exaggerated differences and displays. These displays of difference come about because of three issues (as you can see, there are three arrows going into the concept). Notice the long arrow coming from the level of commodification. You'll remember that modern production creates commodities void of any substantial or stable meaning. In order to sell them in mass markets, all truly personal or group-specific qualities have been bleached out of the products. Simmel argues that in the face of this we feel compelled to exaggerate any differences that do exist in the things we use in order to stand out and experience our personal selves. Two other issues contribute to this felt need: an increasing sense of a confusion and meaninglessness (blasé attitude) and a feeling of lawlessness (anomie). These too compel individuals to reach out, to be noticed, to establish themselves as a center when the modern objective culture doesn't provide it for them. As Zygmunt Bauman (1992) notes, "To catch the attention, displays must be ever more bizarre, condensed and (yes!) disturbing; perhaps ever more brutal, gory and threatening" (p. xx). Thus, modernity increases our freedom of expression, but it also forces us to express it more dramatically with trivialized culture.

Summary

- There are two central ideas that form Simmel's perspective: social forms and the relationship between the subjective experience of the individual and objective culture. Simmel always begins and ends with the individual. He assumes that the individual is born with certain ways of thinking and feeling, and most social interactions are motivated by individual needs and desires. Encounters with others are molded to social forms in order to facilitate reciprocal exchanges. These forms constitute society for Simmel. Objective culture is one that is universal yet not entirely available to the individual's subjective experience. Thus, the person is unable to fully grasp, comprehend, or intimately know objective culture. The tension between the individual on the one hand and social forms and objective culture on the other is Simmel's focus of study.

- Urbanization increases the division of labor and the use of money, and it changes the configuration of social networks. All of these have both direct and indirect influence on the level of objective culture and its effects on the individual. The use of money increases personal freedom for the individual, yet at the same time it intensifies the possibility of anomie, diminishes the individual's attachment to objects, and increases goal displacement. People join groups based on either rational or organic motivations. Rational motivations are prevalent in urban settings and imply greater personal freedom coupled with less emotional investment and possible anomie and role conflict; organic motivations imply less personal freedom and greater social conformity coupled with increased personal and social certainty.

TAKING THE PERSPECTIVE—FORMAL SOCIOLOGY

Simmel is generally seen as the founder of "Formal Sociology." Today we usually understand the word *formal* as meaning "proper" or "official." However, this isn't how Simmel intends the idea. Formal sociologists use the word *form* to refer to the shape, frame, or structure that people use to create predictable patterns of social interaction. In doing so, formal sociologists make a distinction between the content and form of an interaction. The content is what the interaction is about—the interests and purposes—such as education, marriage, business, and so forth; and most sociologists are concerned with the content. Thus the sociology of education tells us what is happening in education.

Formal sociologists, on the other hand, study the structures of social interaction that cut across such content areas. For example, a conflict in education will take the same general form as a battle in war, even though the content varies from situation to situation. Formal sociology, then, is the study of the central organizing configurations of interaction and its intention is to create a geometry of social life.

Simmel has also influenced contemporary theory in many ways. His ideas concerning culture are becoming increasingly important in the work of some postmodernists (see Weinstein & Weinstein, 1993). In this book, we will see Simmel's influence on exchange and conflict theory. Simmel was one of the first to explicate the implications of exchange on social encounters. Rather than theorizing about the structure of the economy per se, like Marx and Weber, Simmel is instead fascinated by the influence of the social form of exchange on human experience. As we'll see when we get to Chapter 12, Simmel is specifically concerned with how value is established and how it affects the use of power in social encounters.

Simmel has also had direct influence on contemporary conflict theory through Lewis Coser (Chapter 9). Before Simmel, conflict had been understood as a source of social change and disintegration. Simmel was the first to acknowledge that conflict is a natural and necessary part of society. Coser brought Simmel's idea to mainstream sociology, at least in America. From that point on, sociologists have had to acknowledge that "groups require disharmony as well as harmony" and that "a certain degree of conflict is an essential element in group formation and the persistence of group life" (Coser, 1956, p. 31).

BUILDING YOUR THEORY TOOLBOX

Learning More—Primary and Secondary Sources

- The chief source of George Mead's theory is found in a compilation of student notes:
  - Mead, G. H. (1934). *Mind, Self, and Society: From the Standpoint of a Social Behaviorist* (C. W. Morris, Ed.). Chicago: University of Chicago Press.

(Continued)

(Continued)

- Georg Simmel published quite a bit, unlike Mead. I suggest that you start off with the first two readers, and then move to his substantial work on money:
  - Simmel, G. (1959). *Essays on Sociology, Philosophy, and Aesthetics [by] Georg Simmel [and others]: Georg Simmel, 1858–1918* (K. H. Wolfe, Ed.). New York: Harper & Row.
  - Simmel, G. (1971). *Georg Simmel: On Individuality and Social Forms* (D. N. Levine, Ed.). Chicago: University of Chicago Press.
  - Simmel, G. (1978). *The Philosophy of Money* (T. Bottomore & D. Frisby, Trans.). London: Routledge and Kegan Paul.
- To read more about Mead, I would recommend the following:
  - Baldwin, J. D. (1986). *George Herbert Mead: A Unifying Theory for Sociology.* Beverly Hills, CA: Sage.
  - Blumer, H. (1969). *Symbolic Interactionism: Perspective and Method.* Englewood Cliffs, NJ: Prentice Hall.
  - Blumer, H. (2004). *George Herbert Mead and Human Conduct* (T. J. Morrione, Ed.). Walnut Creek, CA: AltaMira Press.
  - Cook, G. A. (1993). *George Herbert Mead: The Making of a Social Pragmatist.* Urbana, IL: University of Chicago Press.
- For Simmel, the following are excellent resources:
  - Featherstone, M. (Ed.). (1991). A Special Issue on George Simmel. *Theory, Culture & Society, 8*(3).
  - Frisby, D. (1984). *Georg Simmel.* New York: Tavistock.

Seeing the Social World (knowing the theory)

- Write a 250-word synopsis of the theoretical perspective of symbolic interaction.
- Write a 250-word synopsis of the theoretical perspective of formal sociology (again, don't be afraid of outside sources).
- After reading and understanding this chapter, you should be able to define the following terms theoretically and explain their theoretical importance to symbolic interaction: *pragmatism, emergence, action, meaning, natural signs and significant gestures, social objects, emergence, role-taking, perspective, self, mind, play stage, game stage, generalized other stage, I and the Me, interaction, society.*
- After reading and understanding this chapter, you should be able to define the following terms theoretically and explain their theoretical importance to Simmel's theory of the individual in modern society: social forms, sociability, exchange, conflict, subjective and objective cultures, urbanization, the division of labor, money, web of group affiliations, normative specificity, anomie, role conflict, blasé attitude.

- After reading and understanding this chapter, you should be able to answer the following questions (remember to answer them *theoretically*):
    - Define pragmatism and apply the idea to meaning, truth, and self.
    - Explain how the mind and self are effects of social interaction.
    - Demonstrate how the mind and self are necessary for the existence of society.
    - Define objective culture and be able to explain how urbanization and the use of money increase the level of objective culture.
    - Identity and describe the effects of urbanization and rational group formation on the individual.

Engaging the Social World (using the theory)

- More and more people are going to counselors or psychotherapists. Most counseling is done from a psychological point of view. Knowing what you know now about how the self is constructed, how do you think sociological counseling would be different? What things might a clinical sociologist emphasize?

- Using Google or your favorite search engine, enter "clinical sociology." What is clinical sociology? What is the current state of clinical sociology?

- Mead very clearly claims that our self is dependent upon the social groups with which we affiliate. Using Mead's theory, explain how the self of a person in a disenfranchised group might be different from one associated with a majority position. Think about the different kinds of generalized others and the relationship between interactions with generalized others and internalized Me's. (Remember, Mead himself doesn't talk about how we feel about the self.)

- How would Mead talk about and understand race and gender? According to Mead's theory, where does racial or gender inequality exist? From a Meadian point of view, where does responsibility lie for inequality? How could we understand class using Mead's theory? From Mead's perspective, how and why are things like race, class, gender, and heterosexism perpetuated (contrast Mead's point of view with that of a structuralist)?

- Remembering Simmel's definition and variables of objective culture, do you think we have been experiencing more or less objective culture in the last 25 years? In what ways? In other words, which of Simmel's concepts have higher or lower rates of variation? If there has been change, how do you think it is affecting you? Theoretically explain what the proportion of subjective to objective culture will be like for your children. Theoretically explain the effects you would expect.

- Perform a kind of network analysis on your web of group affiliations. How many of the groups of which you are a member are based on organic and rational motivations? In what kinds of groups do you spend most of your time? Over the next five years, how do you see your web of affiliations changing? Based on Simmel's theory, what effects can you expect from these changes?

(Continued)

(Continued)

Weaving the Threads (building theory)

- Mead and Simmel offer an opportunity to synthesize their theories to get a better understanding of how the self is impacted by modern factors. Think of Mead telling us about how the person is socialized, and use Simmel to explicate the social and cultural context of modern socialization. Mead talks about language acquisition and role-taking. Think of language acquisition more generally as culture, and understand role-taking occurring within urban settings, with all that implies. After you've begun to get a sense of what the modern self/person would be, think about how the self of someone growing up and living in Los Angeles, California, might be different than someone growing up and living in a small, rural town.

CHAPTER 7

The Challenges of Gender and Race:

Charlotte Perkins Gilman and W. E. B. Du Bois

As we've seen, the social project of modernity is based on the idea, value, and belief in equality, and that this belief comes from a more fundamental assumption about human beings: Every individual is capable of discerning truth, born with the capacity to reason, and not only able but required to make decisions that guide his or her life and contribute to the welfare of society at large. However, you also know that the social project fell well short of the mark—the belief in equality was in truth founded upon practices of *in*equality. Western capitalism, for example, was built on black slave labor as well as upon the free labor that women provided and continue to provide. Women were also excluded from owning property in Western societies until the middle of the nineteenth century, and they didn't have the right to vote in democratic elections until well into the twentieth century. Gender continues to be the basis for the unequal distribution of income: In 2008, the median income for women in the United States with a college degree was 26% less than for men (U.S. Bureau of Labor Statistics, 2009). Gender is also a factor in violence: Women in the United States are 6 times more likely to suffer violence from a partner than men are (Bureau of Justice Statistics, n.d.). In addition, it's estimated that 91% of rape victims are female versus 9% that are male (UCSC Rape Prevention Education, 2009).

When compared to other systems of inequality, **gender** has unique characteristics. It is the oldest system of economic and political discrimination and was quite likely the first. Gender is also ubiquitous: It's found in virtually every situation and thus crosscuts every other system of stratification. Further, gender is structured in such a way as to keep group members from connecting, sharing grief, and building solidarity—there is no neighborhood or ghetto for gender. Moreover, gender is required of every single person; thus, children are intentionally and thoroughly trained in gender, sometimes even before birth. Finally, gender is the social category that is most powerfully linked by most people to biological, genetic, and religious causes and legitimations.

Charlotte Perkins Gilman (1860–1935)

Theorist's Digest
Concepts and Theory: The Social Evolution of Gender
    Balancing Self- and Race-Preservation
    Gynaecocentric Theory
    Sexuo-Economic Relations
Summary
Taking the Perspective—Feminism

THEORIST'S DIGEST

Brief Biography

Charlotte Perkins Stetson Gilman was born Charlotte Perkins on July 3, 1860, in Hartford, Connecticut. Her father was related to the Beecher family, one of the most important American families of the nineteenth century. Gilman's great-uncle was Henry Ward Beecher, a powerful abolitionist and clergyman, and her great-aunt was Harriet Beecher Stowe, who wrote *Uncle Tom's Cabin*, which focused the nation's attention on slavery. Gilman's parents divorced early, leaving Charlotte and her mother to live as poor relations to the Beecher family, moving from house to house. Gilman grew up poor and was poorly schooled.

    Gilman's adult life was marked by tumultuous personal relationships. Her first marriage in 1884, to Charles Stetson, ended in divorce. Gilman wrote a novella about the relationship, called *The Yellow Wallpaper*, which is still being read in women's studies courses today. The book tells the story of a depressed new mother (Gilman herself) who is told by both her doctor and husband to abandon her intellectual life and avoid any writing or stimulating conversation.

The woman sinks deeper into depression and madness as she is left alone in the yellow-wallpapered nursery. Gilman's feeling of hopelessness against the tyranny of male-dominated institutions is heard in the repeated refrain of "but what is one to do?" Between her first and second marriages, a period of about 12 years, Gilman had a number of passionate affairs with women. However, her second marriage—to George Gilman, a cousin—proved to be at least a somewhat successful and important relationship for Charlotte: Some of her best work was done during the courtship and after the marriage.

In her lifetime, Gilman wrote over 2,000 works, including short stories, poems, novels, political pieces, and major sociological writings. She also founded *The Forerunner,* a monthly journal on women's rights and related issues. Among her best-known works are *Concerning Children, The Home, The Man-Made World,* and *Herland* (a feminist utopian novel). However, Gilman's most important theoretical work is *Women and Economy.* In Gilman's lifetime, the book went through nine editions and was translated into seven different languages.

Gilman was also politically active. She often spoke at political rallies and was a firm supporter of the Women's Club Movement, which was an important part of the progress toward women's rights in the United States. It initially began as a place for women to share culture and friendship. Before the development of these clubs, most women's associations were either auxiliaries of men's groups or allied with a church. In contrast, many of the clubs of the Women's Club Movement became politically involved, but others were simply public and educational service organizations. One such club became the Parent–Teacher Association (PTA).

Sick with cancer, Charlotte Gilman died by her own hand on August 17, 1935, in Pasadena, California.

Central Sociological Questions

Gilman's question is basic yet profound: How did gender inequality begin? Most theorists of gender don't theorize about the genesis of gender oppression; they are generally concerned about how it works today. Gilman, however, explains the root causes of gender inequality.

Simply Stated

Gilman uses evolutionary theory to explain gender inequity. She argues that there were twin problems humans had to overcome in order to create society (the human evolutionary advantage): the male's independent nature and the taming of the natural environment. Natural selection choose patriarchy and monogamy to solve these issues. As a result, women's bodies changed and developed exaggerated secondary sex characteristics in order to attract a mate. However, human beings have now dominated the natural environment utterly and have created complex social relations extending far past kinship. Thus, these early adaptive changes of patriarchy, monogamy, and exaggerated sexual dimorphism are now dysfunctional for human society.

Key Concepts

gender, social evolution, self-preservation, race-preservation, gynaecocentric theory, sexuo-economic relations, morbid excess in sex distinction

Concepts and Theory: The Social Evolution of Gender

Gilman is an evolutionist. Like Spencer, she generally understands the history of human society as moving from simple to complex systems, with various elements being chosen through the mechanism of survival of the fittest. Gilman argues that humans began as brute animals pursuing individual gain. Survival of the fittest at that point was based on individual strength and competition. The males would hunt for food and fight one another for sexual rights to the females. It was a day-by-day existence with no surplus or communal cooperation. Wealth was, of course, unknown, as it requires surplus and social organization. Competition among men was individual and often resulted in death. Women, as is the case with many other life forms, would choose the best fit of the men for mating. There was no family unit beyond the provision of basic necessities for the young, mostly provided by women. Life was short and brutal.

As competition between species continued, humans gradually developed social organization beyond its natural base. Very much like an organism, society began to form out of small cells of social organization that joined with other small cells. Gilman (1899/1975) says that "society is the fourth power of the cell" (p. 101). By that she means that once societies started to grow and structurally differentiate, the process continued in a multiplicative manner. The reason for this is simple: Just as in organic evolution, more complex social systems, because of the level of social cooperation and division of labor, have a greater chance of survival than do individuals or simple societies. As societies became more complex, and thus more social, structures and individuals had to rely on each other for survival. Just as the different organs in your body must depend upon other organs and processes, so every social unit (individuals and structures) must depend upon the others:

> The proposition is that Society is the whole and we are the parts: that the degree of organic development known as human life is never found in isolated individuals, and that it progresses to higher development in proportion to the evolution of the social relation. (Gilman, as cited in Lengermann & Niebrugge-Brantley, 1998, p. 142)

An interesting thing happened for humans because of the development of complex, social organization. All animals are influenced by their environment. If the environment turns cold, then the organism will either develop a way of regulating body temperature (polar bears are well-suited for the Arctic), move to a different environment, or die out. Humans at one time were equally affected by the environment. But after we organized socially, our organization and culture allowed us to live in a controlled manner with regard to the environment: Humans can now exist in almost any environment, on or off the planet. We thus distanced ourselves from the natural environment, but at the same time we created a new environment in which to live. Gilman argues that human beings have become more influenced by the social environment of culture, structure, and relations than by the natural setting—we thus have a new evolutionary environment. Keep this idea of a new environment in mind; it becomes extremely important later on in Gilman's theory of gender.

Like Marx, Gilman argues that this new environment, this social structure that improved humanity's chances of survival, is the economy. All species are defined by their relationship to the natural environment. Stated in functionalist terms, structures in an organism are formed as the organism finds specific ways to survive (structure follows function); the same is true in society. The economy is the structure that is formed in response to our particular way of surviving, and it is thus our most defining feature. We are therefore most human in our economic relations. Marx argued that we are alienated from our nature as we are removed from direct participation in the economy, as with capitalism. Gilman also argues that alienation occurs, but the source of that alienation is different. Where Marx saw class, Gilman sees gender. Gilman, in fact, is quite in favor of capitalism—in no other system has our ability to survive been so clearly manifested. Even so, there are alienating influences that originate in our gendered relationship to the economy, most specifically the limitation of women's workforce participation.

Balancing Self- and Race-Preservation

Like Marx, Gilman argues that the basic driving force in humanity is economic production: Creative production is the way that we as a species survive. In all species, survival needs push the natural laws of selection, which results in a functional balance between **self-preservation and race-preservation**. Natural selection in self-preservation develops those characteristics in the individual that are needed to succeed in the struggle for self-survival. In the evolutionary model, individuals within a species fight for food, sex, and so on. Natural selection equips the individual for that fight.

Race-preservation, on the other hand, develops those characteristics that enable the species as a whole to succeed in the struggle for existence. Gilman is using the term *race* in the same way I'm using the term *species*; that is, she's using it in the more general sense, rather than to make racial distinctions. The most important point here is that the relationship between self- and race-preservation is balanced: Individuals are selfish enough to fight for their own survival and selfless enough to fight for the good of the whole species.

Gilman's idea is interesting because most evolutionists assume that these two factors are one and the same; in other words, self-preservation is structured in such a way that it functions as species-preservation. This assumption is what allows social philosophers like Adam Smith to take for granted that severe individualism in systems like capitalism is natural and beneficial. Gilman insightfully perceives that these two functions can be at odds with one another. She thus creates an empirical research question where many people don't see any problem or make a value judgment, such as in the inherent goodness of capitalistic free markets.

Human evolution then becomes specific. Because of our overwhelming dependency on social organization for survival, we develop laws and customs that in turn support the equilibrium between self- and race-preservation, as noted by the feedback arrow. With the idea of "accumulation of precedent," Gilman has in mind art, religion, habit, and institutions other than the economy that tend to reinforce and legitimate our laws and customs. There is a reinforcing cycle among the race-self-preservation proportion; social laws and customs; and the institutions, culture, and habits of a society. This social loop becomes humankind's unique environment. Of course, we still relate to and are affected by the natural world, but the social environment becomes much more important for the human evolutionary progress (or lack thereof). This entire process works together to increase the likelihood of the survival of the human race.

That's the model of how things are supposed to and did work for quite some time. But a threshold was reached and patriarch and monogamy became dysfunctional (we can see the same thing with technological control of the environment creating toxic waste and lack of sustainability). The same central dynamics are present: Economic necessity pushes the laws of selection, which in turn produce the proportion of self- to race-preservation characteristics, which then create laws and customs that reinforce those characteristics and produce social behaviors, culture, and institutions that strengthen and justify the laws and customs. This time, however, the social loop doesn't result in greater species survivability, but, rather, in gender, sex, and economic dysfunctions.

Gynaecocentric Theory

Gilman argues that human sexuality and the kinship structure were evolutionarily selected. In the predawn history of humankind, it became advantageous for us to have two sexes that joined together in monogamy. From an evolutionary perspective, the methods of reproducing the species are endless. They run from the extremes of hermaphroditism (both sexes contained in a single organism) to multiple-partnered egg hatcheries. Because human beings need high levels of culture and social organization to survive, the two-sex model was naturally selected along with monogamy. Thus, having two sexes that are distinct from one another is natural for us. In this model, the physical distinctions between the sexes produce attraction and competition for mates, just as in other species. Eventually, however, because of the need for social organization among humans, the brutal competition for mates was mitigated and the social bond extended past mother–child through monogamy.

This process, however, became tainted by patriarchy. Gilman presents a unique and fascinating argument as to why patriarchy came about. According to Gilman, there are distinct, natural male and female energies. The basic masculine characteristics are "desire, combat, self-expression; all legitimate and right in proper use" (1911/2001, p. 41). Female energy, on the other hand, is more conservative and is characterized by maternal instincts—the love and care of little ones. In this, Gilman sees us as no different from most other species—these energies are true of many male and female creatures.

Yet the natural level of these energies posed a problem for human evolution. To survive as humans, we required a higher degree of social organization than simple male and female energy could provide. The male energy in particular was at odds with this need. As long as "the male savage was still a mere hunter and fighter, expressing masculine energy . . . along its essential line, expanding, scattering"

(Gilman, 1899/1975, p. 126), social organization of any complexity was impossible. Men were aggressive and individualistic and thus had to be "maternalized" for social organization to grow.

In this argument, Gilman is using and expanding a theory from Lester F. Ward. Gilman acknowledged her debt by dedicating her book *The Man-Made World* to "Lester F. Ward, Sociologist and Humanitarian, one of the world's great men . . . and to whom all women are especially bound in honor and gratitude for his Gynaecocentric Theory of Life." In **gynaecocentric theory**—the word *gynaeco-centric* means "woman-centered"—the female is the general race type while male is a sex type. The argument begins with the assumption that kinship is the basis of social organization. All species, including humans, are related to one another biologically through descent. In our case, we used those biological relations to build social connections. The basic kin relationship is found between mother and child. This is the one relationship that has always been clear: It's obvious from whom the child comes. In order to build social relations on that basic tie, fathers had to be included through some mechanism. Of all the possible forms of marriage, monogamy provides the clearest connection between father and child, and thus the strongest, most basic social relationship.

What Ward and Gilman add is the idea of intrinsic male and female energy. Male energy is at odds with family and social ties. The "giant force of masculine energy" had to be modified in order to add and extend the social tie between father and child. This was accomplished through the subjugation of women. When men created patriarchy and dominated women, they also made women and children dependent upon men. In natural arrangements, both men and women produce economically, but as men dominated women, they also removed them from the world of economic production. Women could no longer provide for themselves, let alone their children. Men had to take on this responsibility, and as they did, they took on "the instincts and habits of the female, to his immense improvement" (Gilman, 1899/1975, p. 128). Therefore, men became more social as a result of patriarchy.

This functional need was a two-way affair. Not only did men need to take on some of the women's traits, the natural environment could be more thoroughly tamed by men rather than women. By taking women out of the productive sphere, and therefore forcing men to be more productive, "male energy . . . brought our industries to their present development" (Gilman, 1899/1975, pp. 132–133). Both men and human survival in general benefited from patriarchal arrangements.

Gilman draws two conclusions from gynaecocentric theory. First, women should not resent the past domination by men. Great harm to individuals and society has come through this system, but necessary and great good has come as well,

> In the extension of female function through the male; in the blending of facilities which have resulted in the possibility of our civilization; in the superior fighting power developed in the male, and its effects in race-conquest, military and commercial; in the increased productivity developed by his assumption of maternal function; and by the sex-relation becoming mainly proportioned to his power to pay for it. (Gilman, 1899/1975, pp. 136–137)

The second thing Gilman draws from this theory is that the women's movements, and all the changes that they bring, are part of the evolutionary path for humanity. While women's economic dependence upon men was functional for a time, its usefulness is over. In fact, Gilman tells us, the women's and labor movements are misnamed—they ought more accurately to be called human movements. The reason that we've become aware of the atrocities associated with male dominance at this time in our history is that the dysfunctions are now greater than the functions. The behaviors and problems of patriarchy have always existed, but the benefits outweighed the costs and it therefore remained functional. Now, because of the level of social and economic progress, it is time to cast off this archaic form.

Sexuo-Economic Relations

Gilman characterizes the overall system and its effects as sexuo-economic. In **sexuo-economic relations**, two structures overlap, one personal and the other public. The social structure is the economy and the private sphere is our sexual relationships. The basic issue here is that women are dependent upon men economically; as a result, two structures that ought to be somewhat separate intertwine. Historically, as women became more and more dependent upon men for their sustenance, they were removed further and further from economic participation.

As we've noted, the economy is the most basic of all our institutions: It defines our humanness. A species is defined by its mode of survival; survival modes, then, determine the most basic features of a species. In our case, that basic feature is the economy. The economy is where we as a species compete for evolutionary survival. It is where we as a species come in contact with the environment and where the natural laws of selection are at work. Thus, when workforce participation is denied to women, they are denied interaction with the natural environment of the species. That natural environment, with all of its laws and effects, is replaced with another one. Man (meaning males) becomes woman's economic environment, and, just as any organism responds to its environment, woman changed, modified, and adapted to her new environment (form and function).

Gilman talks about several effects from living in this new environment, but the most important are those that contribute to **morbid excess in sex distinction**. All animals that have two sexes also have sex distinctions. These distinctions are called secondary sex characteristics: those traits in animals that are used to attract mates. In humans, according to Gilman, those distinctions have become accentuated so much that they are morbid or gruesome. In societies where they are denied equal workforce participation, the primary drive in women is to attract men: "From the odalisque with the most bracelets to the débutante with the most bouquets, the relation still holds good—women's economic profit comes through the power of sex-attraction" (Gilman, 1899/1975, p. 63). Rather than improving her skills in economic pursuits, she must improve her skills at attracting a man. In fact, expertise in attraction skills *constitutes her basic economic skills,* which means that the secondary sex characteristics of women become exaggerated. She devotes herself to cosmetics, clothes, primping, subtle body-language techniques, and so on. Most of these are artificial, yet there are also natural, physical effects. Because women are pulled out from interacting with the natural environment, their bodies change: They become smaller, softer, more feeble, and clumsy.

The increase in sex distinctions leads to greater emphasis on sex for both men and women. The importance given to sex far exceeds the natural function of procreation and comes to represent a threat to both self- and race-preservation. The natural ordering of the sexes becomes perverted as well. In most animals, it is the male that is flamboyant and attractive; this order is reversed in humans. To orient women toward this inversion, the sexual socialization of girls begins early: "It is what she is born for, what she is trained for, what she is exhibited for. It is, moreover, her means of honorable livelihood and advancement. But—she must not even look as if she wanted it!" (Gilman, 1899/1975, p. 87).

In our time, young girls are taught that women should be beautiful and sexy, and they are given toys (such as Barbie) that demonstrate the accentuated sex distinctions, toy versions of makeup kits used to create the illusion of flamboyancy in women, and games that emphasize the role of women in dating and marriage. Another result of this kind of gender structure and socialization is that women develop an overwhelming passion for attachment to men at any cost; Gilman points to women who stay in abusive relationships as evidence. In the end, because of the excess in sex distinction brought on by the economic dependence of women, marriage becomes mercenary.

Obviously, the economic dependency of women will have economic results as well. Women are affected most profoundly as they become "nonproductive consumers." According to Gilman, in the natural order of things, productivity and consumption go hand in hand, and production comes first. Like Marx, Gilman sees economic production as the natural expression of human energy, "not sex-energy at all but race-energy." It's part of what we do as a species and there is a natural balance to it when everybody contributes and everybody consumes.

The balance shifts, however, as women are denied workforce participation. The consumption process is severed from the production process and the whole system is therefore subject to unnatural kinds of pressures. Noneconomic women are focused on noneconomic needs. In the duties of her roles of wife, homemaker, and mother, she creates a market that focuses on "devotion to individuals and their personal needs" and "sensuous decoration and personal ornament" (Gilman, 1899/1975, pp. 119–120).

The economy, of course, responds to this market demand. Contemporary examples of this kind of "feminized" market might include such things as fashion items (such as jewelry, chic clothing, alluring scents, sophisticated makeup, and so forth); body image products (such as exercise tapes, health clubs, day spas, dietary products, and the like); fashionable baby care products (such as heirloom baby carriages, designer nursery décor, and special infant fashions by the Gap, Gymboree, Baby B'Gosh, Tommy, Nike, Old Navy, ad infinitum); and decorative products for the home (such as specialized paints, wallpaper, trendy furnishings, and so on).

> As the priestess of the temple of consumption, as the limitless demander of things to use up, her economic influence is reactionary and injurious. . . . Woman, in her false economic position, reacts injuriously upon industry, upon art, upon science, discovery, and progress. (Gilman, 1899/1975, pp. 120–121)

Gilman argues that the creative efforts of men, which should be directed to durable commodities for the common good, are subject to the creation and maintenance of a "false market." Women are thus alienated from the commodities they purchase because they don't participate in the production process nor are their needs naturally produced, and men are alienated because they are producing goods and services driven by a false market.

The morbid excess in sex distinction disables the laws of natural selection and puts self- and race-preservation out of balance. As a result, the customs and laws of society respond, as do the social institutions and practices (accumulation of precedent). Institutions and practices that properly belong to humankind become gendered. For example, the governing of society is a "race-function," but in societies that limit women's workforce participation, it is seen as the duty and prerogative of men. Decorating is also distinctly human; it is a function of our species, but it is perceived as the domain of women. Religion, an obvious human function, is dominated by men and has been used to justify the unequal treatment of women, as have law, government, science, and so forth.

Yet Gilman does tell us that things are changing. She sees the women's movements as part of our evolutionary path of progress. Implied in this conclusion is the idea that equality is a luxury. Under primitive circumstances, only the strong survive. The weak, the feeble, and the old are left behind or killed. As social relationships come into existence, cooperation is possible, and as people cooperate, a surplus develops. For the most part, the powerful control the surplus and turn it into wealth, yet at the same time, it is then feasible to support some who had once been cut off. These people are integrated into society and society continues to grow. It becomes more complex and technically better able to control the environment and produce surplus. In turn, other groups are brought into the fold, and increasing numbers of disenfranchised groups are able to live and prosper. It is Gilman's position that just as technical progress is our heritage, so is ever-expanding equality. Evolution of the species not only involves economic advancement but increasing compassion as well; ethical and technical evolutions are inexorably linked.

At the present evolutionary moment, we are only hindered by our own blindness. We can afford the luxury of complete equality, but we fail to see the problem. Gilman says that this is due to a desire for consistency: We don't notice what we are used to. Even evil can become comfortable for us and we will miss it when it's gone. This is one of the reasons why slavery wasn't seen as evil for so many years of our history. We also have a tendency to think in individual terms rather than general terms. It's easier for us to attribute reasons for what we see to individuals rather than to broad social factors.

> Being used to them, we do not notice them, or, forced to notice them, we attribute the pain we feel to the evil behavior of some individual, and never think of it as being the result of a condition common to us all. (Gilman, 1899/1975, p. 84)

Summary

- Gilman is a critical evolutionist. All species fight for survival and create organic structures to help them survive in their environment. In this case, the function produces the structure. For humans, the primary evolutionary structure is the economy. It is through the economy that we as a species survive.

- When women were removed from the economy through male domination, several things happened. First, women were taken out of the natural environment of economic production and given a false environment—men, and indirectly the home and family, became women's environment. Gilman is a social evolutionist and argues that, as every species will, woman changed in response to changes in her environment. This change in environment made the distinctions between the sexes more pronounced. Rather than being equipped to economically produce, women became equipped to pursue a husband (their survival depended upon it). Their bodies became smaller and softer from disconnection with the natural world, and women augmented these changes through artificial means (such as makeup, clothing, etc.). Human beings now have a morbid excess in sex distinction, and as a result, the natural order has been reversed. In most animals, it is the male that is marked for attraction; in humans, it is the female. In order to produce this artificial order, girls have to be socialized from birth to want to be attractive and to value having a husband over all else. Further, in societies where women's workforce participation is limited, women become unnatural consumers. The natural relationship is production followed by consumption. Women are simply consumers without production. As such, their perceived needs are radically changed and they produce a market focused on beauty, decoration, and private relationships. This market makes men produce dysfunctional goods, and they are thus alienated from the work of their hands; women, on the other hand, purchase goods that are not a natural part of their essential nature, thus alienating them from the commodity. Further, to support and legitimate this economy, the other institutions, laws, and customs in society have become gendered, and those things that are properly human (such as government, religion, and education) are now seen as the domain of one sex.

- This evolutionary path has also had functional consequences. The natural energy of men is aggressive, individualistic, and dominating. The male is, then, ill suited for social life. However, in making women and children dependent upon him, he also obligated himself to provide for them (to be socially involved and committed). Thus, through gender oppression, the natural energy of men has been modified: They now have maternal feelings and higher social abilities. Further, large societies require highly developed systems that can control the environment and extract resources. Gilman argues that men and women together could not have achieved the needed level of economic and technological development. In Gilman's evolutionary scheme, men are naturally more aggressive and objectifying. Thus, having men solely responsible for the economic sphere meant that society produced more and achieved higher levels of technological control. Thus, pulling women out of the workforce functioned to allow the economy to develop fully.

• Humans have, however, reached the point where the suppression of women is more dysfunctional than functional. The women's movements are sure signs that evolution is pushing us toward higher levels of equality.

TAKING THE PERSPECTIVE—FEMINISM

The term *feminism* was first used to refer to feminine traits in general. It wasn't until the First International Women's Conference of 1892 that the term took on its critical, political bent. Since then it has been associated with two principle ideas. The first is a set of ideas and beliefs about knowledge and ways of governing that are defined as distinctly feminist and are set against the masculinist ways of exercising power and knowing about the world. The second refers to a variety of perspectives that are used to understand gender inequality. These two main ideas can blend together in various ways for different theorists, but Gilman clearly falls in the latter, as she adopts positivism.

In Western European societies inequalities of gender have been addressed through three waves of feminism. Inklings of the first wave began when ideas about the equal rights of women emerged during the Enlightenment. The first significant expression of these concerns was Mary Wollstonecraft's book *A Vindication of the Rights of Woman* (1792). But the first wave of feminism didn't become organized until the 1848 Seneca Falls Convention, which called for equal rights to vote and own property, full access to educational opportunities, and equal compensation for equal work.

The second wave of feminism grew out of the civil rights movements of the 1960s. Publication of Simone de Beauvoir's *The Second Sex* (1949) and Betty Friedan's *The Feminine Mystique* (1963) were particularly important for this second wave of feminists, as was the founding in 1966 of the National Organization for Women (NOW). Central issues for this movement were pay equity; equal access to jobs and higher education; and women's control over their own bodies, including but not limited to sexuality, reproduction, and the eradication of physical abuse and rape.

In the early 1970s, two clear divisions began to appear among second-wave feminists. One camp emphasized the more traditional concerns of women's rights groups and generally focused on the similarities between men and women. Their primary concern was structural inequality. The other group moved to more radical issues. Rather than emphasizing similarities, they focused on fundamental differences between men and women. In some ways, the concerns of this group, described in the paragraph below, are more radical than equal opportunity. This more critical group is often described as a "third wave" of feminism.

The idea of third-wave feminism began to take hold around the intersection between race and gender—there are marked distinctions between the experiences of black and white women.

But more recently, it has gained currency with reference to age. It appears that the experiences of young, contemporary feminists are different from those of second-wave feminists.

Young feminists grew up in a social world where feminism was part of common culture. These young women are also playing out some of the postmodern ideas of fluid identities. The result is that many young feminists can best be described through contradiction and ambiguity. As Jennifer Drake (1997) says in a review essay, "What unites the Third Wave is our negotiation of contradiction, our rejection of dogma, our need to say 'both/and'" (p. 104). For example, third wavers might claim their right to dress sexy for fun while simultaneously criticizing patriarchy for objectifying women.

In this book, there are five theorists featured who specifically address gender. Our next feminist is in Chapter 10: Janet Saltzman Chafetz. Like Gilman, Chafetz uses positivistic science to understand gender inequality. Her concerns are in keeping with second-wave feminists: political and economic rights. The other three feminists generally take the most critical approach and question the foundations of social scientific knowledge. For them, the life experiences and perspectives of men and women are different, and gender equality is more fundamental than structural equality—thus, while affirming the concerns of second wavers, their interests more closely coincide with third-wave feminists. Dorothy E. Smith (Chapter 17) focuses on the unique consciousness and lived experience of women. Smith argues that women have a bifurcated awareness of the world, split between the objective world of men and their own lived experiences. Patricia Hill Collins (Chapter 17) offers a clear critique of positivistic social science and argues for the power and insight of feminist ways of knowing. Collins is also interested in the ways race and gender come together for women.

W. E. B. Du Bois (1868–1963)

Theorist's Digest
Concepts and Theory: Cultural Oppression
  History as Ideology
  Representation
  Stereotypes and Slippery Slopes
  The Impact of Culture on the Person
Concepts and Theory: The Dark Nations and World Capitalism
  The Need for Color
Summary
Taking the Perspective—Race Theory

While gender is more universal, the use of race as a category of distinction has historically been more destructive. Though women have been seen as less than men, in general their essential humanity hasn't been denied. The modern category of race, however, is based on such a distinction. While people have obviously always been aware of differences of skin tone and facial features, in premodern societies race wasn't an important way that people used to mark difference. Religion, territory, and eventually being civilized versus uncivilized were much more important categories for most of human history. Race, as such, only became important with the dawn of modernity and specifically capitalism. Capitalism provided the motivation (accruing profit at the least possible expense) and the means (commodification) to make race the primary marker of difference in modern nations. While slavery had always existed, it wasn't until the advent of capitalism that *chattel* slavery—people seen as property—could exist. It was also modernity that brought to the forefront the issue of human nature as a political concern. You'll recall that political rights in modernity exist for the individual simply because of his or her humanity. Thus, one's standing as a human became an issue of concern and definition.

We are without a doubt at a significant moment of change in U.S. race relations. In 2008, the country elected its first black president. But are we now in a "postracial" society, one in which race no longer makes a difference? Current statistics appear to say no. The 2008 median income for white families was $55,530, while black family median income was $34,281 ("Income, Poverty, and Health Insurance Coverage in the United States: 2008"). The U.S. Department of Justice (2008) reports that at midyear 2008, there were 4,777 black male inmates per 100,000 U.S. residents being held in state or federal prison and local jails, compared to just 727 white male inmates per 100,000 U.S. residents. The National Urban League (2009) has an overall statistical measure of African American equality as compared to whites: The 2009 Equality Index is 71.1 %.

THEORIST'S DIGEST

Brief Biography

As I mentioned earlier, W. E. B. Du Bois' life is at least as important as his theoretical writings. In keeping with that idea, I'm giving Du Bois an extended biographical treatment. William Edward Burghardt Du Bois was born in Great Barrington, Massachusetts, on February 23, 1868. His mother was Dutch African and his father French Huguenot-African. Du Bois' father, who committed bigamy in marrying Du Bois' mother, left the family when the boy was just two years old, but Du Bois grew up without experiencing the depth of suffering blacks felt at that time. Du Bois' education in the abject realities of blackness in America came during his college years at Fisk, in Tennessee; it was his first visit to the southern United States during "Jim Crow." In addition, he taught children for two summers at a rural Tennessee school and saw firsthand the legacy of slavery in the South. As a result, Du Bois became an ardent advocate of social change through protest. His belief in confrontation and dissent put Du Bois at odds with Booker T. Washington, a prominent black leader who favored accommodation. This disagreement with Washington influenced the early part of Du Bois' political life; he founded the Niagara Movement in large part to counter Washington's arguments.

Through most of his life, Du Bois generally favored integration, but toward the end he became discouraged at the lack of progress and increasingly turned toward Black Nationalism: He encouraged blacks to work together to create their own culture, art, and literature, and to create their own group economy of black producers and consumers. The cultural stand was directed at creating black pride and identity; the formation of a black economic community was the weapon to fight discrimination and black poverty. Du Bois was also a principal force in the Pan-African movement, which was founded on the belief that all black people share a common descent and should therefore work collectively around the globe for equality. In the latter part of his life, Du Bois became disheartened at the lack of change regarding the color line in the United States. In the end, he renounced his citizenship, joined the Communist Party, and moved to Ghana, Africa.

More than any other single person, Du Bois was responsible for black consciousness in America and probably the world during the twentieth century. His book, *The Souls of Black Folk*, defined the problem of the color line. He was a founding member of the National Association for the Advancement of Colored People (NAACP) and its chief spokesperson during its most formative years. Du Bois also produced the first scientific studies of the black condition in America.

Central Sociological Questions

In his work, Du Bois was passionate about one thing: the obliteration of the color line.

Simply Stated

A good deal of Du Bois' writings were deeply spiritual. I don't intend that in any specifically religious way; rather, his writings were appeals to the human spirit. Some of his writings were directed at articulating what it is like to live in a society where one's human existence is made a problem; and some were directed to rousing the black community to become coworkers in the cultural field along with whites—these writings also exhorted the white community and exposed ways that whites excluded black America. Du Bois' theoretical work focused on how culture was used to oppress—through ideological history, cultural representations, and double consciousness—and how capitalism and the white middle class were dependent upon the exploitation of blacks around the world.

Key Concepts

Centered subject, seventh son, veil, grand narrative, history as ideology, representation, denotation, connotation, stereotypes, default assumptions, looking-glass self, double consciousness, exploitation, dark nations, personal whiteness

There are a couple of things that strike the thinking reader as he or she spends time with Du Bois' texts. The first is that Du Bois centers the subject in his writing. One of the things most of us are taught in college English is that we should write from a de-centered point of view. We are supposed to avoid using "I" and "me" and should always write from an objective perspective. Yet Du Bois begins one of his most famous works, *The Souls of Black Folk,* with the phrase "Between me and the other world . . ." In another place he wonders, "Who and what is this I . . . ?" Du Bois isn't being self-centered nor is he unaware of the rules of composition. Du Bois is being quite deliberate in his use of personal pronouns and the centered subject. I believe one of the things he is telling us is that race is not something that can be understood through the cold, disassociated stance of the researcher. Race and all marginal positions must be experienced to be understood. Du Bois uses his life as the canvas upon which he paints the struggles of the black race in America and in the world.

The other thing that impresses the reader is that much of Du Bois' writing is a multimedia presentation. Du Bois moves back and forth among intellectual argumentation, song, prayer, poetry, irony, parable, data, riddles, analogy, and declaration. He weaves a tapestry for the reader, one that touches every part of the reader's being. He wants us to be able to understand the objective state of blackness as well as experience its soul. In this he reminds me of a colleague of mine. My colleague is a black man who has done some amazing work with Los Angeles gang members. One time I asked him to present a guest lecture to one of my classes. You know what a lecture looks like, right? Imagine my surprise when he asked us all to close our eyes and lay our heads down on the desks. His lecture consisted of a dramatic reading of a poem—complete with gunshots and cries—that left the class stunned and some in tears.

It might well be coincidence that both Du Bois, who is one of the few writers I've seen use such varied venues in writing, and the only professor I've seen break the mold of lecture so soundly are African American. Yet it does give us pause and it provides me with a transition into one of Du Bois' important points. Though Du Bois undoubtedly sees the color line as something that is socially created, he also acknowledges and honors the unique characteristics of and contributions from the "souls of black folk." He maintains that American music and folklore, faith and reverence, light-hearted humility, literature and poetry, speech and styles of interaction, practices of sport, and our political fabric are all strongly influenced by African American culture. Yet it isn't a simple listing of accomplishments or influences alone that Du Bois has in mind; it is the soul of a particular kind of lived experience: "that men may listen to the striving *in the souls of* black folk" (Du Bois, 1903/1996a, p. 107, emphasis added).

There are two things I think this subjective stance implies: The first is my own comment, the other is something I think Du Bois has in mind. First, any secondary reading of Du Bois, such as the book you have in your hands, falls short of the mark. This is generally true of any of the thinkers in this book—you would be much richer reading Durkheim than reading what somebody *says* about Durkheim—but it is particularly true of Du Bois. Part of what you can acquire from reading Du Bois is an experience, and that experience is a piece of what Du Bois wants to communicate.

The second implication of Du Bois' multidimensional, subjective approach is theoretical. Du Bois (1903/1996a) says that "the Negro is a sort of seventh son, born with a veil, and gifted with second-sight in this American World—a world which yields him no true self-consciousness, but only lets him see himself through the revelation of the other world" (p. 102). Du Bois employs spiritual language here. The veil of which he speaks is the birth caul. In some births, the inner fetal membrane tissue doesn't rupture and it covers the head at delivery. This "caul" appears in about 1 in 1,000 births. Due to its rarity, some traditional cultures consider such a birth spiritually significant and the caul is kept for good luck. The same is true of the seventh son reference. The seventh son is considered to have special powers, and references to such are to be found in many folk and blues songs as well as in the Bible. The "second-sight" is a reference to clairvoyant or prophetic vision.

Thus, Du Bois is saying that because of their experiential position, African Americans are gifted with special insight—a prophetic vision—into the "American World." They see themselves not simply as they are; they also see their position from the perspective of the "other world"—the white social world around them. In other words, blacks and other oppressed groups have a particular point of view of society that allows them to see certain truths about the social system that escape others. This idea of critical consciousness goes back to Marx. Marxian philosophy argues that only those on the outside of an oppressive system can understand its true workings; it is difficult to critically and reflexively understand a system if you accept its legitimation. In other words, capitalists and those who benefit from capitalism by definition believe in capitalism. It is difficult for a capitalist to understand the oppressive workings of capitalism because in doing so the person would be condemning himself or herself.

Generally, Du Bois' perspective is more in keeping with contemporary theories of difference than others of his time. One of the things that oppression in modernity has done is deny the voice of the other. In the Durkheim chapter, we saw that one of the necessities for social solidarity is a collective consciousness—or what some contemporary theorists refer to as a *grand narrative*. Modern nation-states provide all-encompassing stories about history and national identity through a grand narrative. The purpose of these narratives is to offer a kind of Durkheimian rallying point for social solidarity. This sort of solidarity is necessary for nations to carry out large-scale programs, especially such things as colonization and war. The problem with such a narrative is that it hides inequities. For example, the grand narrative of equality in the United States was actually a story about white Anglo-Saxon Protestant males. Hidden in the national narrative and history was (and still is) the subjugation of Native Americans, African Americans, women, Mexican Americans, homosexuals, and so forth.

Contemporary theories of difference, then, focus on the subjective experience of the disenfranchised in contrast to this grand narrative. One of the things that is important in the fight for equality is allowing multiple voices to be heard; thus, we have recently moved in the United States from the cultural picture of the "melting pot" to that of the "salad bowl" (with each ingredient maintaining its own unique character). Du Bois' perspective is quite in keeping with this emphasis. In his own work, he uses the subjective mode to express the experience of the oppressed. He becomes a representative figure through which we might understand the plight of black people in America. Part of what this multiple-voice approach entails is valuing the outsider's point of view. Interestingly, Du Bois is much more in tune with the feminist idea of standpoint theory than either Martineau or Gilman, neither of whom privileges outsider knowledge. In that sense, Du Bois' work contains a more critical edge, again in keeping with much of contemporary analysis.

In my opinion, I think that Du Bois' lasting contribution to social theory is his understanding of *cultural oppression*. In the section we will see that it is just as necessary as structural oppression in the suppression of a social group. Du Bois' understanding of this process is quite good. He argues that cultural oppression involves exclusion from history, specific kinds of symbolic representations, and the use of stereotypes and their cultural logic of default assumptions. This cultural work results in a kind of **double consciousness** wherein the disenfranchised see themselves from two contradictory points of view. However, Du Bois isn't only interested in cultural oppression; he also gives us a race-based theory of world capitalism. We will see that it isn't only the elite capitalists that benefit from the exploitation of blacks and other people of color; the middle class benefits as well.

Concepts and Theory: Cultural Oppression

History as Ideology

If we can get a sense of the subjectivity that Du Bois is trying to convey, we might also get a sense of what horrid weight comes with cultural oppression. Undergirding every oppressive structure is cultural exclusion. While the relative importance of structure and culture in social change can be argued, it is generally the case that structural oppression is legitimated and facilitated by specific cultural moves—historical cultural exclusion in particular. In this case, African Americans have been systematically excluded from American history, and they have been deprived of their own African history.

History plays an important part in legitimating our social structures; this is known as *history as ideology*. No one living has a personal memory of why we created the institutions that we have. So, for example, why does the government function the way it does in the United States? No one personally knows; instead, we have a historical account or story of how and why it came about. Because we weren't there, this history takes on objective qualities and feels like a fact, and this facticity legitimates our institutions and social arrangements unquestionably. But, Du Bois tells us, the current history is written from a politicized point of view: Because women and people of color were not seen as having the same status and rights as white men, our history did not see them. We have been blind to their contributions and place in society. The fact that we now have Black and Women's History Months underscores this historical blindness. Du Bois calls this kind of ideological history "lies agreed upon."

Du Bois, however, holds out the possibility of a *scientific history*. This kind of history would be guided by ethical standards in research and interpretation, and the record of human action would be written with accuracy and faithfulness of detail. Du Bois envisions this history acting as a guidepost and measuring rod for national conduct. Du Bois (1935/1996c) presents this formulation of history as a choice. We can either use history "for our pleasure and amusement, for inflating our national ego," or we can use it as a moral guide and handbook for future generations (p. 440).

It is important for us to note here that Du Bois is foreshadowing the contemporary emphasis on culture in studies of inequality. Marx argued that it is class and class alone that matters. Weber noted that cultural groups—i.e., status positions—add a complexity to issues of stratification and inequality. But it was not until the work of the Frankfurt School (see Chapter 1 on Marx) during the 1930s that a critical view of culture itself became important, and it was not until the work of postmodernists and the Birmingham School in the 1970s and 1980s that representation became a focus of attention. Yet Du Bois is explicating the role of culture and representation in oppression in his 1903 book, *The Souls of Black Folk*.

Representation

Representation is a term that has become extremely important in contemporary cultural analysis. Stuart Hall, for example, argues that images and objects by themselves don't mean anything. We see this idea in Mead's theory as well. The meaning has to be constructed, and we use representational systems of concepts and ideas to do so. *Representation*, then, is the symbolic practice through which meaning is given to the world around us. It involves the production and consumption of cultural items and is a major site of conflict, negotiation, and potential oppression.

Let me give you an illustration from Du Bois. Cultural domination through representation implies that the predominantly white media do not truly represent people of color. As Du Bois (1920/1996d) says, "The whites obviously seldom picture brown and yellow folk, but for five hundred centuries they have exhausted every ingenuity of trick, of ridicule and caricature on black folk" (pp. 59–60). The effect of such representation is cultural and psychological: The disenfranchised read the representations and may become ashamed of their own image. Du Bois gives an example from his own work at *The Crisis* (the official publication of the NAACP). *The Crisis* put a picture of a black person on the cover of the magazine. When the readers saw the representation, they perceived it (or consumed it) as "the caricature that white folks intend when they make a black face." Du Bois queried some of his office staff about the reaction. They said the problem wasn't that the person was black; the problem was that the person was *too black*. To this Du Bois replied, "Nonsense! Do white people complain because their pictures are too white?" (Du Bois 1920/1996d, p. 60).

While Du Bois never phrased it quite this way, Roland Barthes (1964/1967), a contemporary semiologist (someone who studies signs), explains that cultural signs, symbols, and images can have both denotative and connotative functions. Denotative functions are the direct meanings that can be looked up in an ordinary dictionary. Cultural signs and images can also have secondary, or connotative, meanings. These meanings get attached to the original word and create other, wider fields of meaning.

At times these wider fields of meaning can act like myths, creating hidden meanings behind the apparent. Thus, systems of connotation can link ideological messages to more primary, denotative meanings. In cultural oppression, then, the dominant group represents those who are subjugated in such a way that negative connotative meanings and myths are produced. This complex layering of ideological meanings is why members of a disenfranchised group can simultaneously be proud and ashamed of their heritage. Case in point: The black office colleagues to whom Du Bois refers can be proud of being black but at the same time feel that an image is *too black*.

Stereotypes and Slippery Slopes

In addition to history and misrepresentation, the cultural representation of oppression consists of being defined as a problem: "Between me and the other world this is ever an unasked question. . . . How does it feel to be a problem?" (Du Bois, 1903/1996a, p. 101). Representations of the group thus focus on its shortcomings, and these images come to dominate the general culture as stereotypes:

> While sociologists gleefully count his bastards and his prostitutes, the very soul of the toiling, sweating black man is darkened by the shadow of a vast despair. Men call the shadow prejudice, and learnedly explain it as the natural defense of culture against barbarism, learning against ignorance, purity against crime, the "higher" against the "lower" races. To which the Negro cries Amen! (Du Bois, 1903/1996a, p. 105)

I want to point out that last bit of the quote from Du Bois. He is saying that the black person *agrees* with this cultural justification of oppression. Here we can see one of the insidious ways in which cultural justifications can work. It presents us with an apparent truth that once we agree to can reflexively destroy us. Here's how this bit of cultural logic works: The learned person says that discrimination and prejudice are necessary. Why? They are needed to demarcate the boundaries between civilized and uncivilized, knowledge and ignorance, morality and sin, right and wrong. We agree that we should be prejudiced against sin and evil, and against uncivilized and barbarous behavior, and we do so in a very concrete manner. For example, we are prejudiced against allowing a criminal into our home. We thus agree that prejudice is a good thing. Once we agree with the general thesis, it can then be more easily turned specifically against us.

In this movement from general to specific, Du Bois hints at another piece of cultural logic that is used in oppression. Douglas R. Hofstadter (1985), in reference to gender issues, calls this the "slippery slope of sexism." Hofstadter argues that there can be a relationship between the general and specific use of a term, and therefore some of the connotations of each will rub off on the other. You are aware of examples of this process in gender, such as in the statements "all men are created equal" and "there was a four-man crew on board." Is the use of the masculine pronoun meant in its specific or its general meaning? Are we referring to men specifically or to mankind? When such slippery slopes of language occur, it is easy for society to obliterate or oppress a cultural identity, which is one reason why feminist scholars talk about the invisible woman in history.

Du Bois has a similar slope in mind, but obviously one that entails race. In the section from *The Souls of Black Folk* from which I have been quoting, Du Bois (1903/1996a) says that the Negro stands "helpless, dismayed, and well-nigh speechless" before the "nameless prejudice" that becomes expressed in "the all-pervading desire to inculcate disdain for everything black" (p. 103). In *Darkwater*, Du Bois (1920/1996b) refers to this slippery slope as a "theory of human culture" (p. 505) that has "worked itself through [the] warp and woof of our daily thought" (p. 505). We use the term "white" to analogously refer to everything that is good, pure, and decent. The term "black" is likewise reserved for things or people that are despicable, ignorant, and that instill fear. There is thus a moral, default assumption in back of these terms that automatically includes the cultural identities of white and black.

In our cultural language, we also perceive these two categories as mutually exclusive. For example, we will use the phrase "this issue isn't black or white" to refer to something that is undecided, that can't fit in simple, clear, and mutually exclusive categories. The area in between is a gray, no-person's land. It is culturally logical, then, to perceive unchangeable differences between the black and white races, which is the cultural logic behind the "one drop rule" (an historical slang term used to capture the idea that a person is considered black if he or she has any black ancestor). Again, keep in mind that this movement between the specific and the general is unconsciously applied. People don't have to intentionally use these terms as ways to racially discriminate. The cultural default is simply there, waiting to swallow up the identities and individuals that lie in its path.

The Impact of Culture on the Person

Du Bois attunes us to yet another insidious cultural mechanism of oppression: the internalization of the double consciousness. With this idea, Du Bois again demonstrates how far ahead of his time he was. Racial oppression doesn't simply affect the life chances of blacks; it has a significant impact on the psyche of the individual. We see this emphasis clearly in the work of a number of postcolonial theorists, such as Frantz Fanon (1967; 2004), and in Cornel West's work (Chapter 17). To conceptualize this effect, Du Bois draws on his knowledge of early pragmatic theories of self (see Chapter 6). He knew William James and undoubtedly came in contact with the work of both Mead and Charles Horton Cooley (1998). We can think of Mead's theory of role-taking and Cooley's looking-glass self (see below) and see how the double consciousness is formed. According to Du Bois, African Americans have another subjective awareness that comes from their particular group status (being black and all that that entails), and they have an awareness

constructed. Again, Du Bois beat contemporary social theory to the punch: We didn't begin to seriously think of "white" as a construct until the 1970s, and it didn't become an important piece in our theorizing until the late 1980s.

Du Bois argues that the idea of "personal whiteness" is a very modern thing, coming into being only in the nineteenth and twentieth centuries. Humans have apparently always made distinctions, but not along racial lines. Prior to modernity, people created group boundaries of exclusion by marking civilized and uncivilized cultures, religions, and territorial identity. As William Roy (2001) notes, these boundaries lack the essential features of race—they were not seen as biologically rooted or immutable and people could thus change. Race, on the other hand, is perceived as immutable and is thus a much more powerful way of oppressing people.

As capitalism grew in power and its need for cheap labor increased, indentured and captive slavery moved to chattel slavery. Slavery has existed for much of human history, but it was used primarily as a tool for controlling and punishing a conquered people or criminal behavior, or as a method of paying off debt or getting ahead. The latter is referred to as indentured servitude. People would contract themselves into slavery, typically for seven years, in return for a specific service, like passage to America, or to pay off debt. In most of these forms of slavery, there were obligations that the master had to the slave, but not so with chattel slavery. Under capitalism, people could be defined as property—the word *chattel* itself means property—and there are no obligations of owner to property. In this move to chattel slavery, black became not simply *a* race but *the* race of distinction. The existence of race, then, immutably determined who could be owned and who was free, who had rights and who did not.

Summary

- Du Bois' perspective is that of a black man, and his subjective experience of race is central in his work. He often uses himself as a representational character, and he is vastly interested in drawing the reader into the experience of race. Du Bois also believes that being a member of a disenfranchised group, specifically African American, gives one a privileged point of view. People who benefit from the system cannot truly see the system. Most of the effects of active social oppression are simply taken for granted by the majority. They cannot see them.

- All structural oppression must be accompanied by cultural oppression. There are several mechanisms of cultural suppression: denial of history, controlling representation, and the use of stereotypes and default assumptions. As a result of cultural suppression, minorities have a double consciousness. They are aware of themselves from their group's point of view, which is positive, and they are conscious of their identity from the oppressor's position, which is negative. They are aware of themselves as black (in the case of African Americans), and they are aware of themselves as American—two potentially opposing viewpoints.

- Capitalism is based on exploitation: Owners pay workers less than the value of their work. Therefore, capitalism must always have a group to exploit. In global capitalism, where the capitalist economy overreaches the boundaries of the state, it is the same: There must be a group to exploit. Global capitalism finds such a group in the "dark nations." Capitalists thus export their exploitation, and both capitalists and white workers in the core nations benefit, primarily because goods produced on the backs of sweatshop labor are cheaper.

TAKING THE PERSPECTIVE—RACE THEORY*

I've found that the writings of people who study and think about race tend to be distinct and different from people writing about other sociological issues. Probably the best known of "classic" race theorists in the United States is W. E. B. Du Bois, who wrote from the 1890s through the early 1960s. Du Bois gave us a number of significant theoretical ideas, such as double consciousness, and produced some of the first social scientific studies of black Americans. Yet, reading Du Bois is more than reading theory and data, it is an *experience.* In his writing Du Bois moves back and forth among intellectual argumentation, song, prayer, poetry, irony, parable, data, riddles, analogy, and declaration. He weaves a tapestry for the reader, one that touches every part of the reader's being. He wants us to be able to understand the objective state of blackness as well as experience its soul.

This dual approach of blending theory and experience seems fairly common among African American writers. A colleague of mine who teaches African American Social Thought in our department said it this way: "When these folks write...they are presenting a lens of dual reality, blackness in America, America on blackness: 'How do I feel about my country and how does my country feel about me?'" (S. Cureton, personal communication, October 9, 2009). A good contemporary example of this approach is Cornel West, who we'll consider in Chapter 17. However, this issue isn't limited to sociologists—it runs deeper. Quite a few African American authors writing about race in fiction, essay, poetry, and the like, tend to include what we see as social and sociological theory, because "challenging race legacy touches on everything we know to be sociological!" (S. Cureton, personal communication, October 9, 2009).

I think that a good part of the reason for this twofold nature of black writing is due to the fact that to write about blackness is to write about humanness. Frantz Fanon (1961/2004) writing about colonialism and race said, "The *ruling species* is first and foremost the outsider from elsewhere, different from the indigenous population, 'the others'" (p. 5, emphasis added). He wrote this in comparison to Marx's idea of the "ruling class." For Fanon "ruling class" does not adequately capture how this type of ruling takes place. It's not a class issue, *it is a species issue.* Racial oppression squarely stands on denying or limiting the humanness of blacks. Thus centering race in writing, either creative or scientific, can always evoke the existential cry "How does it feel to be a problem?" in response to "measuring one's soul by the tape of a world that looks on in amused contempt and pity" (Du Bois, 1903/1996, pp. 101–102).

(Continued)

(Continued)

Additionally, this approach to doing sociology and writing chronicles and puts in the public record the very human experiences of blacks living under inhuman circumstances. This record serves two purposes. It first preserves a truer history of black experience for the African American community. The writings, both disciplinary and otherwise, contain generational knowledge that provides the building stones for a black identity that "speaks to the existential issues of what it means to be a degraded African" and "involves self-respect and self-regard, realms inseparable from, yet not identical to, political power and economic status" (West, 2001, p. 97). The second purpose is that these writings offer for "public consumption the 'soul of blackness' . . . in a society that addresses blackness as deviant" (S. Cureton, personal communication, November 20, 2009). They proclaim the strength of a people proven in a cauldron of suffering. This was undoubtedly the intent that Du Bois had when he penned the above words for the beginning lines of *The Souls of Black Folk*.

*My thanks to Dr. Steven R. Cureton, Associate Professor, UNCG Department of Sociology for enlightening conversations and priceless insights into the writings of black Americans. All the mistakes are mine; all the pearls of wisdom are his.

BUILDING YOUR THEORY TOOLBOX

Learning More—Primary and Secondary Sources

- For Du Bois, I recommend that you pick up *The Oxford W. E. B. Du Bois Reader*, edited by Eric Sundquist. It contains two of Du Bois' books in their entirety (*The Souls of Black Folk* and *Darkwater*) as well as myriad other important writings.

- For Gilman, start with *The Yellow Wallpaper*, and then move on to *Women and Economics, The Home, Human Work*, and *The Man-Made World*, or *Our Androcentric Culture*.

- Each of these thinkers also published autobiographies (in fact, Du Bois wrote two, at different points of his life): For Du Bois, *The Autobiography of W. E. B. Du Bois: A Soliloquy on Viewing My Life From the Last Decade of Its First Century*, and *Dusk of Dawn: An Essay Toward an Autobiography of a Race Concept*; and for Gilman, *The Living of Charlotte Perkins Gilman: An Autobiography*.

- In terms of introductions to other neglected theorists, I recommend Howard Brotz's reader, *Negro Social and Political Thought, 1850–1920*; and *The Women Founders: Sociology and Social Theory, 1830–1930*, by Patricia Madoo Lengermann and Jill Niebrugge-Brantley.

Seeing the Social World (knowing the theory)

- Write a 250-word synopsis of the theoretical perspective of feminism.

- Write a 250-word synopsis of the theoretical perspective of race theory.

- After reading and understanding this chapter, you should be able to define the following terms theoretically and explain their theoretical importance to Gilman's theory of the origins of gender inequality: *gender, social evolution, self-preservation, race-preservation, gynaecocentric theory, sexuo-economic relations, morbid excess in sex distinction.*

- After reading and understanding this chapter, you should be able to define the following terms theoretically and explain their theoretical importance to Du Bois' theory of racial oppression: *centered subject, seventh son, veil, grand narrative, history as ideology, representation, denotation, connotation, stereotypes, default assumptions, looking-glass self, double consciousness, exploitation, dark nations, personal whiteness.*

- After reading and understanding this chapter, you should be able to answer the following questions (remember to answer them *theoretically*):

    ○ Explain the unique characteristics of gender as a system of inequality.

    ○ Explain the differences between self- and race-preservation and discuss their implications for gender.

    ○ Explain the sexuo-economic theory of evolution and its effects on the economy and gender.

    ○ Discuss the reasons why the perspectives of oppressed groups are able to give the kinds of critical insights necessary for social change.

    ○ Describe how history and representation can be used as tools in oppression and in silencing the voices of disenfranchised groups.

    ○ Explain how race is used in capitalism.

Engaging the Social World (using the theory)

- Go home and watch TV. Intentionally watch programs that focus on African Americans and pay particular attention to commercials that feature people of color. Using Du Bois' understanding of representation and Barthes' ideas of denotation and connotation, analyze the images that you've seen. What are some of the underlying connotations of the representations of blacks, Chicanos, Asians, and other minorities? How do you think this influences the consciousness of members of these groups?

- Evaluate the idea of critical knowledge. If we accept the idea that knowledge is a function of a group's social, historical, and cultural position, then is this idea of critical knowledge correct? If so, what are the implications for the way in which we carry on the study of society? If you disagree with the idea of standpoint theory, from what position is true or correct knowledge formed?

(Continued)

(Continued)

- According to Du Bois, one of the ways cultural oppression works is by excluding the voices and contributions of a specific group in the history of a society. The Anti-Defamation League has a group exercise called "name five." The challenge is to name five prominent individuals in each category: Americans; male Americans; female Americans; African Americans; Hispanic Americans; Asian or Pacific Islander Americans; Native Americans; Jewish Americans; Catholic Americans; pagan Americans; self-identified gay, lesbian, or bisexual Americans; Americans with disabilities; and Americans over the age of 65. For which categories can you name five prominent people? For which can't you name the five? What does this imply about the way we have constructed history in this country? In addition to trying this activity on yourself or a friend, go to the Biography Channel's Web page (www.biography.com). There you will find a searchable database of over 25,000 people whose lives are deemed important. Try each of the categories that we mentioned. What did you find?

Weaving the Threads (building theory)

- Gilman gives us a very specific theory of gender oppression. Compare her theory with what Marx said about gender oppression. How are these thinkers similar and different on the issue of gender? Which do you think is more accurate? Why? How do the different theories create different ideas about how to bring about gender equality?

- One of Weber's factors in social stratification is status. Race and gender are both status groups. Compare and contrast Gilman's and Du Bois' theories to Weber's theory of status and social change. What do Gilman and Du Bois add? How significant are their additions? Justify your answer.

Part II

Mid-Twentieth Century Sociological Theory

CHAPTER 8

Structural Functionalism:

Talcott Parsons and Robert K. Merton

I n Chapter 1, we saw that understanding modernity is vital for understanding contemporary theory and sociology. It's equally important for us to also understand a couple of the developments in the mid-twentieth century that formed contemporary theory, especially in the United States. For our purpose the two most significant are Talcott Parsons and the Frankfurt School. In many ways these two forces took the social disciplines in opposite directions: Parsons saw himself building on the ideals of modern knowledge—the Frankfurt School did just the opposite and argued that rather than leading to social justice, social science destroys the possibility of freedom and equality. Both were centrally concerned with culture: Parsons saw culture as the most important factor leading to social cohesion and harmony—the Frankfurt School saw culture, especially popular culture, as producing false consciousness. And both have influenced contemporary theory beyond their specific ideas.

Historically, the Frankfurt School developed first. However, I'm going to start with Parsons because he extends and systematizes the things we learned about modern knowledge and society in Chapter 1. Additionally, as you'll see through this book, Parsons' influence is more central as many contemporary theorists continue to see themselves arguing for or against his work. There are good reasons for giving this much influence to Parsons, but there's also a sense in which I'm making him an ideal type, similar to what I did with modernity. Both Parsons and modernity exist and are clearly important; but I'm not presenting a well-reasoned and documented case for either. I'm using them as heuristics for our discussion throughout the book—they represent ways for us to discover questions, ideas, and theories that come with each of our theorists. And because the influence of the Frankfurt School actually becomes increasingly important toward the end of the twentieth century, rather than mid-century, I'll be saving our consideration of that perspective for the last chapter in this section. The ideas of critical theory set the stage well for Part III: Contemporary New Visions and Critiques.

In this chapter, I will be introducing the work of two functionalists, Talcott Parsons and Robert K. Merton. In preparation for reading Parsons, I recommend that you first review the synopsis for functionalism that you wrote for Chapter 2—notice how Parsons draws on the functionalism of both Spencer and Durkheim. Parsons sets the overall parameters of functionalist thinking in the twentieth century and gives us a very abstract, analytical model of functionalism. Merton was a student of Parsons, yet he also was critical of certain elements of his mentor's approach. As we'll see, Merton wanted to more firmly ground functionalist analysis in the empirical world, and he wanted to open the perspective up to alternative possibilities.

Analytical Functionalism:
Talcott Parsons (1902–1979)

Theorist's Digest
Concepts and Theory: Making the Social System
  Voluntaristic Action
  Constraining and Patterning Social Action
Concepts and Theory: System Functions and Control
  System Relations
  Cybernetic Hierarchy of Control
Concepts and Theory: Social Change
  Cultural Strain
  Revolution
Summary

Parsons was a man with a grand vision. He wanted to unite the social and behavioral disciplines into a single social science and to create a single theoretical perspective. Parsons worked at this not only theoretically but also organizationally. In 1942, Parsons became department chair of sociology at Harvard University. One of the first things he did was to combine sociology, anthropology, and psychology into one department, the Department of Social Relations. The reason he did this was to break down the barriers between disciplines in order to create a general science of human action. His desire, then, wasn't simply to understand a portion of human action (as in sociology); he wanted, rather, to comprehend the totality of the human context and to offer a full and complete explanation of social action. The department existed from 1945 to 1972 and formed the basis of other interdisciplinary programs across the United States.

After 10 years of work, Parsons' first book was published in 1937: *The Structure of Social Action*. This book is characterized by Lewis Coser (1977) as a "watershed in the development of American sociology in general and sociological theory in particular . . . [which] set a new course—the course of functional analysis—that was to dominate theoretical developments from the early 1940s until the middle of the 1960s" (p. 562). More than any other single book, it introduced European thinkers to American sociologists and gave birth to structural functionalism. His other prominent works include *The Social System, Toward a General Theory of Action, Economy and Society, Structure and Process in Modern Societies,* and *The American University*. For much of the twentieth century, Parsons was "the major theoretical figure in English-speaking sociology, if not in world sociology" (Marshall, 1998, p. 480). The "question of what the field of sociology is and how it should be done . . . was more or less settled in the post-war period by the dominance of Parsons' functionalism" (Calhoun, Gerteis, Moody, Pfaff, & Virk, 2002, pp. 221–222). As Victor Lidz (2000) notes, "Talcott Parsons . . . was, and remains, the pre-eminent American sociologist" (p. 388).

There are at least three ways in which Parsons helped shape the center of sociological discourse in the twentieth century: the way he theorized, the problem he addressed, and the theory itself. We'll start with his theorizing. Recall that science is built upon positivism and empiricism. As such, science assumes that the universe is empirical, it operates according to law-like principles, and humans can discover those laws through rigorous investigation. Science also has very specific goals, as do most knowledge systems. Through discovery, scientists want to explain, predict, and control phenomena. Additionally there are two other important issues in positivistic theory, which we find in the following quotes from prominent contemporary theorists:

> The essence of science is precisely theory . . . as a *generalized* and coherent body of ideas, which explain the range of variations in the empirical world in terms of general principles. . . . [I]t is explicitly *cumulative and integrating.* (Collins, 1986, p. 1345, emphasis added)

> A true science *incorporates the ideas* of its early founders in introductory texts and moves on, giving over the analysis of its founders to history and philosophy. (Turner, 1993, p. ix, emphasis added)

The first thing I want us to glean from the above quotes is that scientific theory is *generalized*. To make an idea or concept general means to make it applicable to an entire group of similar things. As you'll see when we consider Parsons' theory, his concepts are very general (and thus fairly dry—but, then, all scientific theory is that way). Scientific knowledge also involves both theory synthesis and cumulation. Synthesis involves bringing together two or more elements in order to form a new whole. For example, water is the synthesis of hydrogen and oxygen. *Theoretical synthesis,* then, involves bringing together elements from diverse theorists so as to form a theory that robustly explains a broader range of phenomena. Cumulation refers to the gradual building up of something, such as the cumulative effects of drinking alcohol. *Theory cumulation* specifically involves the building up of explanations over time. This incremental building is captured by Isaac Newton's famous dictum, "If I have seen further it is by standing on the shoulders of giants." Yet, what isn't clear in Newton's quote is that the ultimate goal of theory cumulation is to forget its predecessors.

To make this clear, let's compare the writings of two authors, Edgar Allan Poe and Albert Einstein. Here's one of Poe's famous stanzas:

> Once upon a midnight dreary, while I pondered, weak and weary,
>
> over many a quaint and curious volume of forgotten lore,
>
> While I nodded, nearly napping, suddenly there came a tapping,
>
> As of someone gently rapping, rapping at my chamber door.
>
> "'Tis some visitor," I muttered, "tapping at my chamber door;
>
> Only this, and nothing more."

Here's one of Einstein's famous quotes:

$E = mc^2$

There are some obvious differences between these two quotes: One is poetry and the other a mathematical equation. But I want you to see a bit more. Does it matter who wrote "Once upon a midnight dreary"? Yes, it does. A large part of understanding poetry is knowing who wrote it—who they were, how they lived, what their other works are like, what style they wrote in, and so on. These issues are part of what makes reading Poe different from reading Emily Dickinson. Now, does it matter who wrote $E = mc^2$? Not really. You can understand everything you need to know about $E = mc^2$ simply by understanding the equation. The author in this sense is immaterial.

One of the above quotes is from Jonathan H. Turner's book *Classical Sociological Theory: A Positivist's Perspective.* Turner's (1993) goal in that book is "to codify the wisdom of the masters so that we can move on and *make books on classical theory unnecessary*" (p. ix, emphasis added). That last highlighted section is the heart of theory cumulation: Cumulating theory implies that we do away with the individual authors and historic contexts and keep only the theoretical ideas that explain, predict, and control the social world. In that spirit, here's a theoretical statement from Turner's (1993) book:

> The degree of differentiation among a population of actors is a gradual s-function of the level of competition among these actors, with the latter variable being an additive function of:
>
> A. the size of this population of actors,
>
> B. the rate of growth in this population,
>
> C. the extent of economical concentration of this population, and
>
> D. the rate of mobility of actors in this population. (p. 80)

First, notice how general the statement is; it can be applied to any group of people, living anywhere, at any time. Notice also that there's no mention of from whom these ideas originally came. Now, you and I might know from whom this proposition comes (Durkheim), but does it matter? No. Like Einstein's formula, it's immaterial. If we are doing social science, what matters is whether or not we can show this statement to be false through scientific testing. If we can't, then we can have a certain level of confidence that the proposition accurately reflects a general process in the social world. In science, authorship is superfluous; *it's the explanatory power of the theory that matters*. The cumulation of these general statements is one of the main goals of scientific theory.

Of his groundbreaking work, Parsons (1949) says, "*The Structure of Social Action* was intended to be primarily a contribution to systematic social science and not to history" (pp. A–B). His work is actually a synthesis of three theorists. Parsons (1961) notes how he used each one:

> for the conception of the social system and the bases of its integration, the work of Durkheim; for the comparative analysis of social structure and for the analysis of the borderline between social systems and culture, that of Max Weber; and for the articulation between social systems and personality, that of Freud. (p. 31)

Yet Parsons clearly wants us to forget the historical and personal origins of the theories—for science, it's the power of the synthesized theory to illuminate and delineate social factors and processes that matters. This approach to theory is also what led to the three sociological perspectives or paradigms you were taught in your introduction to sociology courses: structural-functionalism, conflict theory, and interactionism. To say that someone is a functionalist, for example, is to pay more attention to the general features of the theory than what he or she contributes originally.

THEORIST'S DIGEST

Brief Biography

Talcott Parsons was born December 13, 1902, in Colorado Springs, Colorado. As a young man, Parsons began his university studies at Amherst. He planned on becoming a physician but later changed his major to economics. Parsons received his BA in 1924. Beginning in that year, Parsons studied political economy abroad, first at the London School of Economics. There he came in contact with the anthropologist Bronislaw Malinowski, who was teaching a modified Spencerian functionalism. Parsons also met his wife-to-be, Helen Walker, while in London. Parsons then studied at the University of Heidelberg, where Max Weber had attended and taught. At Heidelberg, Parsons studied with Karl Jaspers, who had been a personal friend of Weber's.

(Continued)

(Continued)

After teaching a short while at Amherst, Parsons obtained a lecturing position at Harvard. He was one of the first instructors (along with Carle Zimmerman and Pitirim Sorokin) in Harvard's new sociology department in 1931. Parsons became department chair in 1942 and began work on the Department of Social Relations—formed by combining sociology, anthropology, and psychology. It was Parsons' vision to create a general science of human behavior. The department was in existence from 1945 to 1972 and formed the basis of other interdisciplinary programs across the United States.

After 10 years of work, Parsons' first book was published in 1937: *The Structure of Social Action*. More than any other single book, it introduced European thinkers to American sociologists and created the first list of "classical" theorists. Parsons was particularly responsible for bringing Max Weber to the attention of U.S. sociologists; Parsons translated several of Weber's works, including *The Protestant Ethic and the Spirit of Capitalism*.

Parsons died on May 8, 1979, while touring Germany on the 50th anniversary of his graduation from Heidelberg.

Central Sociological Questions

Parsons was a man with a grand vision. He wanted to unite the social and behavioral disciplines into a single social science and to create a single theoretical perspective. His desire, then, wasn't simply to understand a portion of human behavior; he wanted, rather, to comprehend the totality of the human context and to offer a full and complete explanation of social action. His central concern was with social order: If humans are basically self-motivated, how is social order achieved? (Notice that Parsons' assumption about human nature is basically the same as Durkheim's, in Chapter 5).

Simply Stated

People are motivated to action because of biological and personal needs, but in achieving those needs people also build up a system that is governed primarily by culture and information. The context, then, of human action is what Parsons calls the "unit act": a situation where the means and ends of action are outlined by cultural norms. These norms are explicitly found in social institutions that manage what Parsons calls latent pattern maintenance, institutions that socialize us into the norms, values, and beliefs of society (like family and religion). Society also has three other needs around which institutions are built: needs for adaptation, goal attainment, and integration. These form the larger context for latent pattern maintenance and action. Social change occurs as a result of cultural strain, moments where cultural expectations don't meet what the other three institutions are able to provide.

Key Concepts

the problem of social order, voluntaristic action, action theory, the unit act, modes of orientation, adaptation, goal attainment, integration, latent pattern maintenance, generalized media of exchange, values, motives, cultural patterns, action types, institutionalization, AGIL, socialization, cybernetic hierarchy of control, equilibrium, cultural strain, alienative motivational elements

Concepts and Theory: Making the Social System

Parsons saw himself responding to *the problem of social order* posed by the philosopher Thomas Hobbes (1588–1679). Parsons' understanding of this Hobbesian problem of social order begins with the fact that all humans are ruled by passions. And, all people are motivated to fulfill these passions; and, more importantly, they have the right to fulfill them because "there is 'no common rule of good and evil to be taken from the nature of the objects themselves'" (Hobbes, as quoted in Parsons, 1949, p. 89). In other words, things aren't good or bad in themselves and people have different desires for diverse things—thus there is no basis for rule. In the absence of any rule, people will use the most efficient means possible to acquire their goals. "These means are found in the last analysis to be force and fraud" (Parsons, 1949, p. 90). Thus the most natural state of humanity is war of all against all. The question, then, is how is social order achieved? Parsons' basic response is the normative order—social order achieved through norms. While some of the language might be new to you, most of Parsons' response will probably feel familiar. The reason that's probably the case is that Parsons' answer to the problem of social order has become for many sociologists the basic answer given in introduction to sociology classes. Parsons begins with what he considers to be the basic element of society: voluntaristic action.

Voluntaristic Action

Parsons credits Max Weber with his beginning point for theory. This area of theorizing is referred to as action theory. Action theory references a group of theories that focus on human action rather than structure. Within this group are theories that center on meaning and interpretation (like Mead), and theories that are concerned with the nature of human action (like exchange theory, Chapter 11). Weber was concerned with both, but he explicitly developed a typology of social action.

According to Weber, simple behavior is distinguished from social action by the subjective orientation of the actor. If, in the action, the person takes into consideration the meaning of the act for others, then it is social action. Weber argued that there are four distinct types of social action: traditional, affective, value-rational, and instrumental-rational. The focus of Weberian action theory is on the latter two types, and it is concerned with the degree of rationality in human behavior. Exchange and rational choice theories take up these issues in particular, and argue that action is best understood in terms of people making rational choices in which they maximize their utilities (hence the name "utilitarianism"). In other words, people have clear preferences and try to get the most out of every encounter with other people by weighing costs and benefits. The question here becomes, how rational can people be in exchanges?

Parsons specifically names his approach "voluntaristic action theory." He isn't so much concerned about how meanings are negotiated in interaction, like Mead, but he wants to understand the context of human action. Like rational choice theories, **voluntaristic action** draws from utilitarianism in that it sees humans as making choices between means and ends. But it modifies utilitarianism by seeing these choices as circumscribed by the physical and cultural environments.

An example of voluntaristic action is your behavior right now. In order to read this book, you had to enroll in class, pick up the syllabus, buy the book, schedule time to read, and actually sit down and read it. All of this may be seen as voluntaristic action: You voluntarily acted, choosing among various ends and means—you could be drinking a beer and watching TV right now, but you selected this behavior. "But," you say, "I didn't volunteer to do this class work!" Yes, you did; nobody physically forced you. However, you volunteered under certain influences from the environment. The same with shaving or not shaving this morning, or the clothes you are wearing right now. They are all aspects of voluntaristic action; the questions have to do with how much freedom you have in making choices in action, and what goes into the decisions that you make in order to act.

Parsons' first theoretical work, *The Structure of Social Action*, explains this by giving us an analytical model of action. It's a framework or scheme through which we can view and understand human action. Parsons' scheme doesn't predict the kinds of actions in which people will engage; his thinking is more fundamental than that. He gives us an analytical model that we can take into any situation and begin to understand the myriad elements that go into human action.

The Unit Act

This analytical model in its completion is termed the **unit act**. Parsons argues that every act entails two essential ingredients: an agent or actor and a set of goals toward which the action is directed. We can see here Weber's notion of social action (in particular, instrumental rationality) and its influence on Parsons' theory. The initial state within which the actor chooses goals and directs his or her process of action has two important elements: the conditions of action and the means of action. The actor has little immediate agency or choice over the conditions under which action takes place. Parsons has in mind such things as the presence of social institutions or organizations, as well as elements that might be specific to the situation, such as the social influence of particular people or physical constraints of the environment. For example, being at a fraternity party (physical setting) will influence your action, but so will the presence of your parents (social influence) at the same party.

When it comes to the means, on the other hand, the actor does potentially have choice. Some situations allow quite a bit of freedom, but others, such as being in a jail, do not. However, notice that even in those situations where there is freedom of choice about the means and goals, the normative orientation of the action limits or defines the choices made. For Parsons, this is an extremely important point. Parsons says that the concept of human action demands that there be normative influence. In other words, Parsons is arguing that human action is distinctly *cultural* action. Remember that *norms* are behaviors that have sanctions attached to them, be they positive or negative. Such behaviors necessarily have social meaning attached to them, have a position on a **value** hierarchy, and are directly or indirectly related to some social group. Most of the rest of Parsons' work may be seen as an explication of the environment, particularly the cultural one, wherein social action takes place.

Constraining and Patterning Social Action

Having understood that human action is circumscribed by various conditions, Parsons sets out to understand those circumstances. In explaining the conditions, Parsons in the end creates an abstract theory of the social system. Let's begin by thinking about the situation. Remember, Parsons is thinking abstractly, so we don't want to be too specific. So, what do you bring with you to a social interaction, whether you are meeting to practice for a play or to study for a test? Parson argues that you bring two things: motivations and values. He refers to these as **modes of orientation** because they orient or position us within the situation, whatever it might be. **Motives**, of course, refer to something within a person (such as a need, idea, or emotion) that stimulates her or him to action. Motives are the energy for action: A person without motivation is like a car without gas—nothing happens. Value refers to a thing's worth and it is always a position on a hierarchy—some things are valued more highly than others. Thus, in every situation we are motivated to do something and we have certain ideas about what will be valued in the encounter with regard to the action.

According to Parsons (1990), all social action is understood in terms of some form of relation between means and ends: "This appears to be one of the ultimate facts of human life we cannot get behind or think away" (p. 320). The relationship between means and ends is formed through shared value systems. In this sense, cultural value systems function basically as a scale of priorities that contains the fundamental alternatives of selective orientations. This shared value system prioritizes means and ends, and, because it is shared, value hierarchies stabilize interactions across time and situations. Action and interaction would be disorganized without the presence of a value system that organizes and prioritizes goals and means. The evaluative aspect of culture is particularly important in this respect because it defines the patterns of role expectations and sanctions, and the standards of cognitive as well as appreciative judgments for any interaction. In other words, the values that we hold tell us the kinds of behaviors we can expect from others and how to judge those behaviors and other social objects.

Let me give you an example. I had coffee with a colleague the other day. We are in the planning stages of a book on sociological social psychology. There are a number of ways to look at social psychology from a sociological position, and in my department there are several people who hold these various views. I am not planning on writing a book with them, nor did I invite them to go to coffee. It's not that I don't like them; I do, but I have a particular perspective about social psychology based on valuing certain aspects of the literature more than others. My colleague shares those views. Because of that shared value system, we know what to expect from each other and how to value and appraise what is said and done, both intellectually and aesthetically.

Parsons sees value systems as having multiple levels that correspond to various degrees of commitment. Action may be stabilized through a shared system of meanings and priorities, but for a society to be integrated, people need to be committed to paying the costs necessary to preserve the system. In any functional interaction, we can name and prioritize the things that are important, but this discursive or cognitive accounting isn't enough. We must also be committed to some things more than others in terms of willingness to sacrifice. People are compelled to sacrifice when the collective *means* something to them, that is, when they have a significant level of emotional investment in the group; the more meaningful is the collective, the more willing people are to make sacrifices. Thus, the value system of any group varies by degree of commitment, with orientations and preferences at the most basic level and ultimate meanings and values at the highest level.

Like Durkheim, Parsons recognizes the basic human need for "ultimate" meanings, yet his argument concerning the need for ultimate significance is more tied to group identification and Weber's concern with legitimacy. Parsons argues that interaction requires individual actions to have meanings that are definable with reference to a common set of normative conceptions. In other words, our behaviors become meaningful because they are related to a group and its expectations.

Group identity is, of course, symbolic. In general, humans are not tied together by blood or instinct but by *meaningful* issues, such as the ideas of freedom and democracy in a national identity. By their very nature, symbols require legitimacy, grounds for believing in the meanings and system. No symbolic or normative systems are ever self-legitimating, nor are they legitimated by appeal to simple utilitarian issues. For example, we rarely hear someone justify the institution of American education by saying that it is necessary to the survival of the American system (unless you're in a sociology class). Legitimating stories always appeal to a higher source. Thus, Parsons (1966) argues that legitimation is always "meaningfully dependent" (p. 11) upon issues of ultimate meaning and therefore is always in some sense religious.

According to Parsons, we hold three general kinds of values: cognitive, appreciative, and moral. In other words, in any situation, we will place importance on empirical, factual knowledge (cognitive); standards of beauty and art (appreciative); or ultimate standards of right and wrong (moral). There are also three kinds of motives: cognitive, cathectic, and evaluative. *Cognitive motivation* refers to a need for information. You might be motivated to meet with your advisor because you need information about which courses to take. *Cathectic motivation* is the need for emotional attachment. You might feel the need to call home some weekend in order to experience emotional attachment to your family. With *evaluative motivation,* we are prompted to act because we feel the need for assessment, such as talking with your boss halfway to your year-end evaluation to find out where you stand.

There are also three types of **cultural patterns**. Culture acts as a resource for both our motivations and our values in action, so it shouldn't surprise us to find that Parsons' types of culture correspond to his types of motivations and values. Culture, then, contains a *belief system.* While we might think of beliefs in a religious sense, Parsons has in mind belief as cognitive significance. It's interesting that he would phrase cognitions in terms of belief. He's acknowledging that the ideas we hold in our head, through which we see and know the world around us, are in fact beliefs about the way things are. Culture also contains *expressive symbols.* Thus, culture not only provides the things we know, it also patterns the way we feel. These feelings are captured, understood, and expressed through symbols such as wedding rings to express love, or gang colors to symbolize aggression. Culture also contains systems of *value-orientation standards*. It is culture that tells us what to value and how to value it.

These different kinds of motives, values, and cultural patterns combine to produce three distinct types of social action. These function much like Weber's ideal types in that they are ways of understanding action, and none of them usually appears in its pure form. I've pictured how these ideal types are formed in Figure 8.1. Each type of action—strategic, expressive, and moral—is formed by combining a motivation with a value. Each of the specific culture systems provides information and meaning for each of the **action types** as well as the corresponding needs and values. As you can see, the ideal type of instrumental action is composed of the need for information and evaluation by objective criteria. Expressive action is motivated by the need for emotional attachment and the desire to be evaluated by artistic standards. Moral action is motivated by the need for assessment by ultimate notions of right and wrong.

In any social encounter, then, we will be oriented toward it with varying degrees of motivation and values. There are three different kinds of motivations and three types of value systems. The motivations and values will combine to create three different types of action. Any social action will have varying degrees of each type, depending on the specific combination of motives and values, and can be understood in terms of being closer to or further from any of the ideal types of action. However, the importance of this scheme of social action is not simply its potential for measurement. Parsons goes beyond Weber in proposing a typology of social action, and he uses it to form a broader theory of institutionalization.

What Parsons is doing is building from the ground floor to the top of the system, from the actor in the unit act to society. He starts with one small action and then argues that actors have discernable orientations toward their behavior. As a result, actions tend to fall into specific types. In brief, we have come this far: voluntaristic action → unit act → modes of orientation → types of action. From this point, Parsons argues that people tend to interact with others who share similar orientations and actors. So, if I want to engage in strategic, instrumental action, with whom will I be most likely to interact? For instance, if I'm interested in buying a guitar that has been advertised in the paper (strategic), then I'm not interested in interacting with someone who wants to talk about the evils of rock music (moral) or the beauty of a Vivaldi concerto (expressive).

Obviously, I will seek out others who want the same kind of thing out of the interaction. As we interact over time with people who are likewise oriented, we produce patterns of interaction and a corresponding system of status positions, roles, and norms. *Status positions* tell us where we fit in the social hierarchy of esteem or honor; *roles* are sets of expected behaviors that generally correspond to a given status position (for example, a professor is expected to teach); and *norms* are expected behaviors that have positive and/or negative sanctions attached to them. Together, these form a social system—an organization of interrelated parts that function together for the good of the whole. Society is composed of various social systems like these.

Figure 8.1 Types of Action

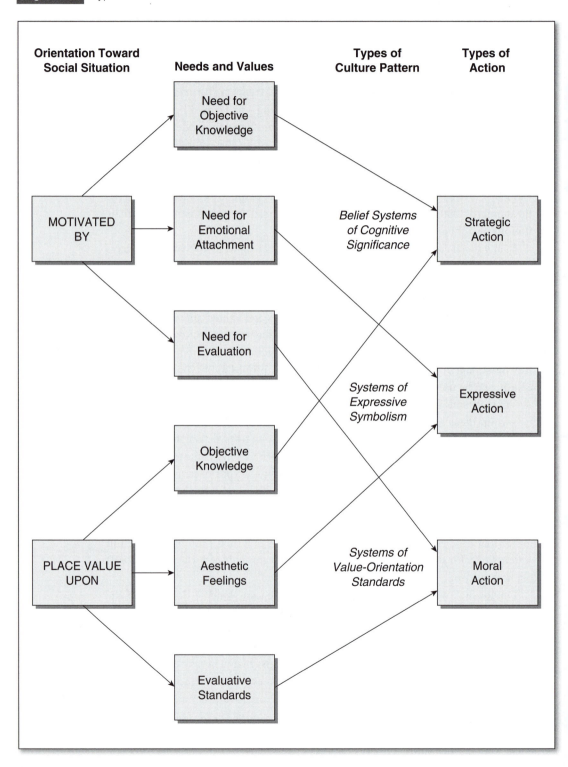

For this, Parsons gives us a theory of institutionalization. The notion of **institutionalization** is very important in sociology. Generally speaking, institutionalization is the way through which we create institutions. For functionalists such as Parsons, institutions are enduring sets of roles, norms, status positions, and value patterns that are recognized as collectively meeting some societal need. In this context, then, *institutionalization* refers to the process through which behaviors, cognitions, and emotions become part of the taken-for-granted way of doing things in a society ("the way things are").

I've diagrammed Parsons' notion of institutionalization in Figure 8.2. Notice that we move from voluntaristic action within a unit act and modes of orientation to social systems. In this way, Parsons gives us an aggregation theory of macro-level social structures. One of the classic problems in sociological theory is the link between the micro and macro levels of society. In other words, how are the levels of face-to-face interaction and large-scale institutions related? How do we get from one to the other? Most sociologists simply ignore the question and focus on one level or another for analysis. Here Parsons gives us the link through the process of institutionalization. Large-scale institutions are built up over time as individuals with particular motivations and values interact with like-minded people, thus creating patterns of interaction with corresponding roles, norms, and status positions.

There's a follow-up question to the micro–macro problem: Once created, how do institutions relate back to the interaction? For Durkheim, the collective consciousness becomes an entity that can act independently upon the individual and the interaction. It does this through moral force: People feel the presence and pressure of something greater than themselves and conform. For Parsons, it's a bit different, even though he does acknowledge moral force. According to

Figure 8.2   The Process of Institutionalization

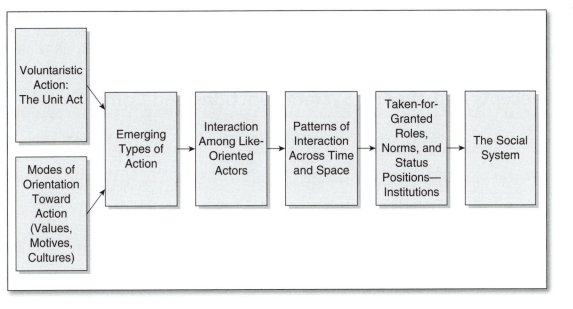

Parsons, all social arrangements, whether micro or macro, are subject to system pressures. Thus, institutions influence interactions not so much because of their independent moral force, but rather because interactions function better when they are systematically embedded in known and accepted ways of doing things. In addition, rather than being dependent upon individual people or interactions, or having its own whimsical nature as Durkheim would have it, society is subject to self-regulating pressures because it is a system.

Getting back to the actual process of institutionalization, Parsons argues that it has two levels: the structuring of patterned behaviors over time (this is the level we've been looking at) and individual internalization or socialization. Parsons understands internalization in Freudian terms. Freud's theory works like this: People are motivated by internal energies surrounding different need dispositions. As these different psychic motives encounter the social world, they have to conform in order to be satisfied. Conformity may be successful (well-adjusted) or unsuccessful (repressed), but the point to notice here is that the structure of the individual's personality changes as a result of this encounter between psychic energy and the social world. The superego is formed through these encounters.

For Parsons, the important point is that cultural traditions become meaningful to and part of the need disposition of individuals. The way we sense and fulfill our needs is structured internally by culture. For Parsons, then, the motivation to conform comes principally from within the individual through Freudian internalization patterns of value orientation and meaning. As the same set of value patterns and role expectations is internalized by others, that cultural standard is said to be, from the point of view of the individual, institutionalized.

It is worth pointing out that Parsons argues that the content of the institutional solutions to societal needs doesn't matter. So, for example, it doesn't matter if a collective perpetuates itself biologically through the institution of family (however it is defined) or through an institutionalized hatchery such as a chicken farm. What is important is that the perceived solutions are a set of highly ritualized behaviors that are seen as typical, belonging to particular settings (such as church rather than school), and are believed to solve collective problems.

Concepts and Theory: System Functions and Control

We came across the idea of requisite needs in Chapter 2. You'll remember that functionalism argues that all societies have certain needs that must be met in order to function, just like the human body. With Durkheim we saw that society needs a certain level of solidarity, which is provided through the collective consciousness. Parsons not only gives us additional needs, he talks about them more abstractly than did Durkheim. Parsons argues that society is a system and that it functions like any other system. In other words, he contends that all systems have the same needs, whether social, biological, physical, cultural, or any other system. There are four such needs: adaptation, goal attainment, integration, and latent pattern maintenance.

To get us thinking, let me ask you a question: Are you hungry? Maybe you aren't now, but sooner or later you will be, because every body needs food to live. Yet it isn't really food per se that you need. You need the nutrients that are *in* the food to survive. When you eat something, your body has a system that extracts the necessary resources from the food and converts it into usable things (like protein). So, your body doesn't really need a steak; it needs what is in it. Parsons calls this function **adaptation** because it adapts resources and converts them into usable elements.

Let's use a larger illustration. Every organism, society, or system exists within and because of an environment. For example, ducks are not found at the South Pole but penguins are. Each of these organic systems has adapted to a given environment and extracts from the surroundings what it needs to exist. It is the same with society. In order to exist, each and every society must *adapt* to its environment by inventing ways of taking what is needed for survival (such as soil, water, seeds, trees, animals) and converting them into usable products (food, shelter, and clothing). Society must also move those products around so that they are available to every member (or at least most members). In society, we call this subsystem the economy. The economy extracts raw resources from the environment, converts them into usable commodities, and moves the commodities from place to place.

Be aware that the economy and adaptation are not the same thing. The economy is *the subsystem in society that fulfills the adaptation need*. In the body, it's the digestive subsystem. Yet the digestive system and the economy are obviously not the same things. They fulfill the same function but in different systems. The reason I'm taking such pains here is that it is important to see that Parsons' scheme is very abstract and can be used to analyze any system, so I want you to be clear on how to apply it. (In addition, if your professor asks you to explain the adaptation function and you say that it is the economy, you'll be wrong.)

Every system also needs a way of making certain that every part is energized and moving in the same direction or toward the same goal. Parsons refers to this subsystem as goal attainment. In the human body, the part of us that activates and guides all the parts toward a specific goal is the mind. The mind puts before us certain goals, things that we need or want to do. We feel motivated to action because our mind invests emotion into these goals.

Let's say that you have the goal of becoming the next Jimi Hendrix. So you set about listening to all of the legendary rock guitarist's CDs, you read all the books about Hendrix's style, and you practice six hours a day. You also work a job and save your money in order to buy the same kind of guitar and equipment that Hendrix used so you can sound just like him. You are motivated. Your mind has caught the image of yourself playing guitar and has controlled and coordinated your fingers, arms, and legs—in short, all your actions—to move you toward that goal. On the other hand, perhaps you aren't as motivated about school. After all, you're going to be a big rock star, so who needs school? So the different parts of your body are not energized and coordinated to meet the goal of doing well in school. In the body, it's the mind that coordinates all the different actions and subsystems to achieve a goal. In the social system, the institution that meets this need for goal attainment is government, or polity (same meaning, different word).

Systems also need to be integrated. By definition, systems do not contain a single part, but many different parts, and these parts have to be brought together to form a whole. Have you ever watched a flock of geese in flight? Rather than flying singularly in a haphazard manner, their actions are coordinated and integrated. The dictionary defines "integration" as meaning to form, coordinate, or blend into a functioning or unified whole; to unite with something else; and to incorporate into a larger unit. The geese are able to form into a larger unit mostly because of instincts. For human beings, it is a bit more complex.

Humans generally use norms, folkways, and mores to integrate their behavior. Norms can be informal (such as the norms surrounding our behavior in an elevator) or they can be formal and written down. Formal and written norms are called laws. Laws help to integrate our behaviors so that, rather than millions of individual units, we can function as larger units. Parsons refers to this function as integration, and in society that function is performed by the legal system. The legal system links the various components together and unites them as a whole. When, for example, Apple Computer crosses the boundaries of IBM, it is the legal system that makes them work together, even though they probably don't want to.

As should be apparent, polity and the legal system are intimately connected, because these two functions are closely related. In our bodies, for instance, the mind functions as the goal-attainment system and it uses the central nervous system to actually move the different parts of the body. But the mind and the central nervous system are two different things. A person can be completely paralyzed and still have full access to his or her mind, or the body can be in perfect working order with the mind completely gone. In the same way, polity and law are related but separate.

The final requisite function that Parsons proposes is latent pattern maintenance. Every system requires not only direct management, such as that performed by a government, but also indirect management, which Parsons terms **latent pattern maintenance**. Not everything that goes on in our body is directed through cognitive functions. Rather, some of these functions, like breathing, are managed and maintained through the autonomic nervous system, a subsystem that maintains patterns with little effort. Society is the same way. It is too costly to make people conform to social expectations through government and law; there has to be a method of making them *willing* to conform. For this task, society uses the processes of *socialization* (the internalization of society's norms, values, beliefs, cognitions, sentiments, etc.). The principal socializing agents in society are the structures that meet the requirement of latent pattern maintenance—structures such as religion, education, and family. (By the way, the word *latent*, from which Parsons gets his term, means not visible, dormant, or concealed.)

Parsons argues that these four requirements can be used as a kind of scheme to understand any system. When beginning a study of a system, one of the first things that must be done is to identify the various parts and how they function. Parsons' scheme allows us to categorize any part of a system in terms of its function for the whole. In Figure 8.3, I have diagrammed the way this analytical scheme looks. The four functions are noted by the initials **AGIL**. The larger box represents that system as a whole, which, of course, needs the four functions. Because they function as systems themselves, each of the four subsystems can be analyzed in terms of the same scheme. I've used adaptation in this case, but the same can be done with each of them.

Figure 8.3   AGIL—Functional Requisites

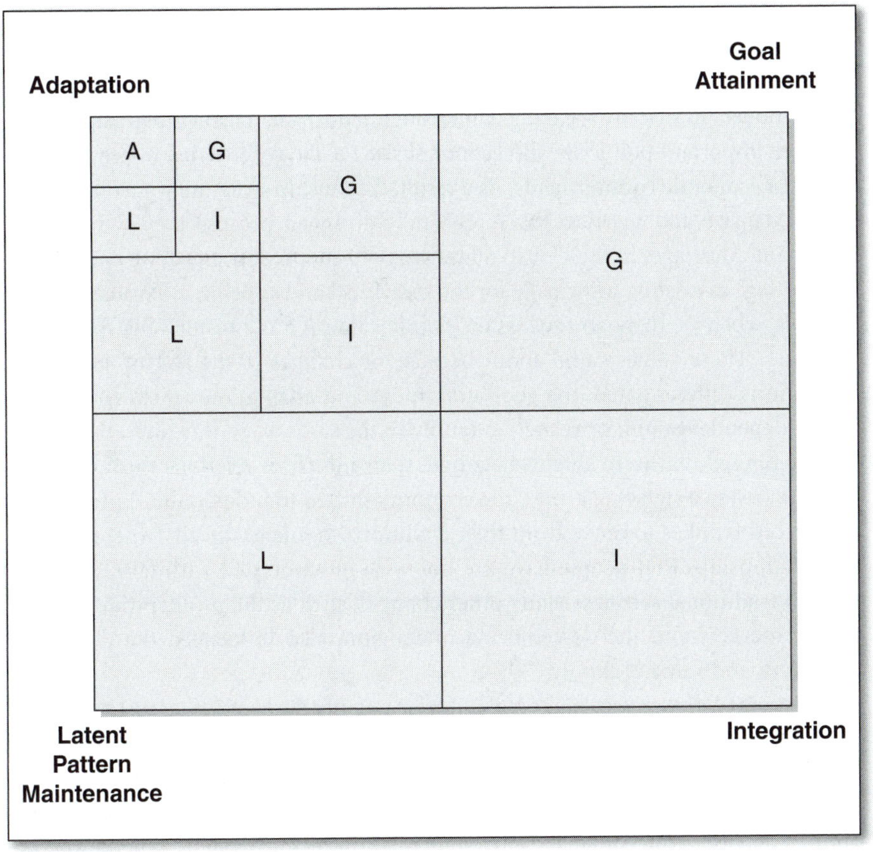

System Relations

Further, Parsons gives us a way of understanding interinstitutional relations. This is important but little explored ground. What usually passes as institutional analysis is *within* an institutional sphere rather than between. For example, we might look at the institution of family in the United States and see that changes are occurring. Some of these changes are society-wide (such as the increase in single-parent families), some are the subject of much moral debate (such as whether or not to define gay couples as family), and some are present but not part of the public discourse (like an acquaintance of mine who introduced me to his wife, the mother of his children, and his girlfriend—three different women—who were all four living happily together in this arrangement). We can also look at marriage and divorce rates, birth and death rates, proportions of families under the poverty line, and so on.

These kinds of research agendas can be enlightening, but they are also quite limited. Studying the phenomenon of "latchkey kids" is important, but it only explains one small part of the institution of family and by itself says nothing about the instructional relations between the family and government. As we've noted, each subsystem is part of a whole and, as such, each is related to the other. If, for illustration, I put dirt in the fuel system of an automobile, it will affect the rest of the car, not just the fuel system itself. The same is true for society. If there are changes in one subsystem, those changes will ripple their way through all of society.

Family, in our society, is usually thought of as a married couple with 2.5 kids. Yet this model, called the nuclear family, has not always been the norm. In fact, it is a pretty recent model, historically speaking. Up through feudalism, marriage and family were far more important politically and economically. People got married to prevent wars or to seal economic commitments. As a result, the kinship structure was considerably more extensive and marriages were generally arranged because they were *socially* important. Marriages in the United States are not generally arranged; we conceptualize marriage as existing principally for the individual and as being motivated by love.

Thus, when we bemoan the loss of "family values," it is a historically specific set of values. These values came about because of changes in the rest of society. As institutions differentiated, the goal-attainment and adaptation functions were no longer dependent upon or related to family in the same ways. Bureaucratic nation-states emerged that were able to negotiate their interstate relations through treaty and war (using a standing army); the economy shifted to industrialized production and forced families to move from their traditional home to the city where most of the relationships that people have are not with or associated with family, as they were in traditional settings. Many other changes, such as the proliferation of capitalistic markets and the de-centering of religion, also influenced the definition, functions, and value of family.

The point I'm trying to make is that for us to truly understand an institution, we must see it in its institutional context, in its relationships to other institutions. From a systems or functionalist point of view, the environment for any institution is created by other institutions (subsystems); they mutually affect and sustain one another. Parsons conceptualizes subsystem relations using his AGIL scheme and the actual paths of influence as boundary exchanges. Just as the digestive subsystem in our bodies provides nutrients for the circulatory subsystem, and the circulatory system in exchange provides blood to the digestive system, so every social institution is locked in a mutual exchange. I've listed these boundary exchanges in Table 8.1. What you will see is that each relationship is defined in terms of what one subsystem gives to another. Both Spencer and Durkheim argued that as institutions differentiate, they become mutually dependent, but neither of them explicated the dependency. Here Parsons does that for us.

As you can see, the table outlines what each subsystem or institution gives to the other three. Let's look at family as the originating subsystem for a moment in the table. You can read the list of its outputs in the center column and the receiving institutions on the right. The list shows the functions that family provides for the other subsystems. Through proper socialization, family provides political loyalty to the government; it provides a compliant pool of labor for the economy; and it influences the moral content of socialized patterns of norms that become law. I don't want to take us through each of these relations; you can do that on your own. The most important thing to glean is the idea of interinstitutional relations. In addition, while we may at some point become more sophisticated in our analysis of the associations, the place to begin is right where Parsons does: the functional dependencies.

Table 8.1   Interinstitutional Relations

Originating Subsystem	Output ⟶	Receiving Subsystem
Economy (A)	Productivity	Polity (G)
	New output combinations	Law (I)
	Consumer goods and services	Family (L)
Polity (G)	Imperative coordination	Law (I)
	Allocation of power	Family (L)
	Capital	Economy (A)
Law (I)	Motivation to pattern conformity	Family (L)
	Organization	Economy (A)
	Contingent support	Polity (G)
Family (L)	Labor	Economy (A)
	Political loyalty	Polity (G)
	Pattern content	Law (I)

Cybernetic Hierarchy of Control

Parsons develops an overall model of how the systems surrounding human life integrate. The model is called the general system of action or the **cybernetic hierarchy of control**. Cybernetics is the study of the automatic control system in the human body. The system is formed by the brain and nervous system and control is created through mechanical-electrical communication systems and devices. In using the term "cybernetic," Parsons tells us that control and thus integration are achieved primarily through information. Also note that in cybernetics, control is achieved automatically, through what Parsons calls latent patterned maintenance.

I've outlined the control system in Figure 8.4. As you can see, the cybernetic hierarchy of control is understood through Parsons' AGIL system. (In the model, I have also expanded the social system to indicate what we have already seen: The social system is understood in terms of AGIL as well.) There are thus four systems that influence our lives: the culture, social, personality, and organic systems. The culture system is at the top, indicating that control of human behavior and life is achieved through cultural information. This emphasis on culture would obviously not be true for most animals. Regardless of the recent news and debates about apes being able to use and possibly share sign language, culture is not the primary information system for any animal other than humans. For most animals, information comes generally through sensory data, instinctual predispositions, and habitual patterns of action.

Figure 8.4 Cybernetic Hierarchy of Control

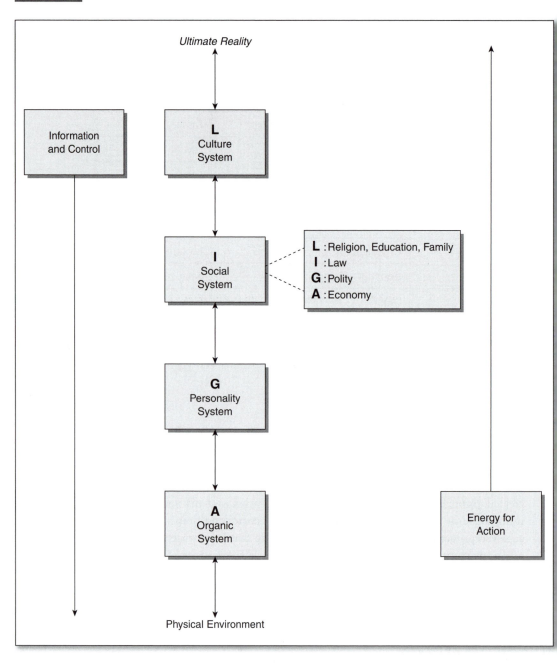

The position of culture at the top also indicates that it requires the most energy to sustain. As information flows from the top down, energy moves from the bottom up. Culture has no intrinsic energy. It is ultimately dependent upon the systems that are lower in the hierarchy for its existence. Without such energy, culture will cease to exist. For example, anthropologists and archaeologists know that a Babylonian culture existed at one time. That knowledge of past existence is itself part of our culture, but the Babylonian culture has long since died because its support mechanisms have passed away.

Culture is most immediately dependent on the social system for its existence. It is also dependent upon the personality system, because it is individual humans who internalize and enact culture. Since the personality system is dependent upon the organic system (the human mind needs the human body), culture is indirectly dependent upon it as well. I'd like to pause here and mention one thing: Recent theorizing argues that culture is also directly reliant on the organic body. Pierre Bourdieu (1979/1984), for instance, argues that culture becomes embodied. There are not simply cognitive and emotional elements in culture. Culture also contains practices that form part of the way our bodies exist. Through our culture we develop tastes, dispositions, and automatic behaviors. For example, our taste in food is dependent upon our culture. Moreover, not only is our language cultural, but so is the way we speak it, as in regional accents.

Notice also that human life is contextualized by conditions of ultimate reality and the physical environment. Parsons never makes any comment about what ultimate reality is, but its understood existence is extremely important for the culture system. Remember that our most important values are framed in terms of ultimate truths, and these truths are religious in nature. Parsons, then, sees religion as an important influence on the culture system in general.

Overall, information moves down and energy moves up. Each system is embedded in and dependent upon the other—systems are reciprocally related to one another. One of the things that Parsons wants to point out with this kind of model is that differentiated, complex systems are dependent upon **generalized media of exchange** for facilitating communication and cooperation among and between the diversified parts. For example, in a complex society, each of the major structures has distinct goals, values, norms, and so forth. The capitalist economy has the goal of producing profit, while the education system has the goal of producing critical thinking. These value-oriented goals may at times clash, but a generalized medium of exchange will tend to keep the system in **equilibrium**. Parsons offers language as the prototype of such generalized media of communication and explicitly identifies money (from the adaptive subsystem), power (from goal attainment), and influence (integration) as other such media.

Concepts and Theory: Social Change

One of the critiques often leveled against Parsons is that he only sees systems in equilibrium and his theorizing thus maintains the status quo. The criticism is not entirely correct. Parsons does assume that systems are in a state of equilibrium; that is, the forces of integration and disintegration are balanced. He feels that any social system worth studying would have a fair degree of permanence, and thus, "there must be a tendency to maintenance of order except under exceptional circumstances" (Parsons & Shils, 1951, p. 107). Parsons (1951) calls this tendency toward equilibrium the "first law of social process" (p. 205) and the "law of inertia" (p. 482). However, it is not the case that Parsons ignores social change. He actually has a notion of revolutionary change in addition to slow evolutionary change.

Like Durkheim, Parsons argues that the principal dynamic of evolutionary change is differentiation, and he sees that structural differentiation brings about problems of integration and coordination. Parsons argues that these problems would create pressures for the production of an integrative, generalized value-culture and a generalized medium of exchange. Thus, like Durkheim, Parsons argues that culture is the most important facet of a complex social system. It is culture that provides the norms, values, and beliefs that allow us to interact, and it is culture that provides the general information that the social system needs in order to operate.

Cultural Strain

However, the process of culture generalization, Parsons (1966) notes, may also bring about severe **cultural strain**: "To the fundamentalist, the demand for greater generality in evaluative standards appears to be a demand to abandon the 'real' commitments" (p. 23). For example, in U.S. society, the call to return to "family values" is just such an issue. Societies that are able to resolve these conflicts move ahead to new levels of adaptive capacity through innovation. Others may "be so beset with internal conflicts or other handicaps that they can barely maintain themselves, or will even deteriorate" (Parsons, 1966, p. 23).

It is at this point that revolutionary change becomes more likely. Culture generally allows people and other social units (like organizations) to interact. It provides us with a language and value system. When people or organizations begin to value different kinds of things or to speak different languages, the situation is ripe for conflict. Parsons sees this kind of problem as a type of strain; *strain* is defined as a disturbance of the cultural expectation system. When we have different values, we do not know what to expect in an encounter. Strain always sets up re-equilibrating processes, but these processes may take a long time to reach balance and the system may be substantially different as a result. Change due to revolution occurs in two phases: (1) the ascendancy of the movement; and (2) the adoption of the movement as "setting the tone" for the society—the re-equilibrating process (this latter is the part that Marx and critical theorists leave out of their theories of revolutionary change).

Revolution

Four conditions must be met for a revolutionary movement to be successful. First, the potential for change must exist; Parsons refers to this potential as the alienative motivational elements. People become motivated to change the system as the result of value inconsistencies. These inconsistencies are inevitable and continually present in an empirical system of action, particularly one that has been generalized to incorporate a number of diverse groups, such as in the United States. For example, the term *equality* has been stretched to include groups not intended by the founding documents (blacks weren't originally included in "all men are created equal"). The term has become more general, yet at the same time, the generality of the term sets up conflicts as more and more groups see themselves as disenfranchised, and others—the fundamentalists—see the generalization as movement away from traditional or received truth.

Second, dissatisfaction with the system is not enough to begin a revolutionary movement; the subgroup must also become organized. The organization of a group around a subculture enables members to evade sanctions of the main group, create solidarity, create an alternative set of normative expectations and sanctions, and it enables expressive leadership to arise.

Third, the organized group must develop an ideology that incorporates symbols of wide appeal and can successfully put forward a claim to legitimacy. The ability to develop an alternative claim to legitimacy is facilitated by two factors. One is that the central value system of large societies is often very general and is therefore susceptible to appropriation by deviant movements. The other factor is that serious strains and inconsistencies in the implementation of societal values create legitimacy gaps that can be exploited by the revolutionary group.

The fourth condition that must be met is that a revolutionary subgroup must eventually be connected to the social system. It is this connection that institutionalizes the movement and brings back a state of equilibrium. There are three issues involved: (1) The utopian ideology that was necessary to create group solidarity must bend in order to make concessions to the adaptive structures of society (e.g., kinship, education)—in other words, the revolutionary group must meet the reality of governing a social system; (2) the unstructured motivational component of the movement must be structured toward its central values—the movement must institutionalize its values both in terms of organizations and individuals; and (3) out groups must be disciplined vis-à-vis the revolutionary values that are now the new values of society.

Summary

- Parsons is usually the one credited with having clearly articulated a systems approach in sociology. This kind of theoretical method encourages us to see society in terms of system pressures and needs. Two issues in particular are important: the boundary between the system and its environment and the internal processes of integration. Parsons divides each of these into two distinct functions. External boundaries are maintained through adaptation and goal attainment; internal-process functions are fulfilled by integration and latent pattern maintenance. Systems theory also encourages us to pay attention to the boundaries between subsystems, in terms of their exchanges and communication. Because relatively smart or open systems have goal states, take in information, and contain control mechanisms, they tend toward equilibrium. Parsons conceptualizes society as just such a system. In addition, because Parsons sees everything as operating systemically, his theory is cast at a very abstract level and is intended to be applied to any and all systems.

- Parsons builds his theory of the social system from the ground up. He begins with voluntaristic action occurring within the unit act. Humans exercise a great deal of agency in their decisions; however, their decisions are also circumscribed by the situation and normative expectations. The normative expectations in particular are where human agency is most expressed and where culturally informed motives and values hold sway. These different motives and values orient the actor to the situation and combine to create three general types of action: strategic, expressive, and moral. People tend to interact socially with those who share their general types of action. As a result, interactions become patterned in specific ways, which in turn tends to create sets of status positions, roles, and norms. We may say that status positions, roles, and norms are institutionalized to the degree that people pattern their behaviors according to such sets and internalize the motives, values, and cultures associated with them.

- Different sets of institutionalized status positions, roles, and norms are clustered around different societal needs. Because society functions as a system, there are four general needs that must be met: adaptation, goal attainment, integration, and latent pattern maintenance. In complex, differentiated societies, these functions are met by separate institutional spheres. The different institutions are integrated through the system pressures of mutual dependency and generalized media of exchange. The social system itself is only one of four systems that surround human behavior. There are the cultural, social, personality, and physical systems, each corresponding to AGIL functional requisites. Because systems are dependent upon information, the culture system is at the top. Information flows from the top down, and the energy upon which culture is dependent flows from the bottom up. Parsons refers to this scheme as the cybernetic hierarchy of control.

- Systems tend toward equilibrium. They can, however, run amiss if the subsystems are not properly integrated. In the social system, this happens through cultural strain. As societies become more differentiated, the media of exchange must become more general. In this process, it is possible that some groups will seek to hold onto the dysfunctional culture. This case sets up a strain within the system, with some subsystems or groups refusing to change and other subsystems moving ahead. Motivation for social revolution is possible under these conditions. After people are motivated to change society, they must then create a subculture that can function to unite their group and create an alternative set of norms and values. This culture must eventually have wide enough appeal to successfully make a claim to legitimacy. In a revolution, either side could win (the reformers or the fundamentalists), but in either case, certain steps are systemically required to reintegrate the system. After the revolution, the subgroup must produce a culture that can unite the system. Institutionalization occurs at this point as it does at any other time: through behaviors patterned and people socialized around a set of status positions, roles, and norms.

Empirical Functionalism:
Robert K. Merton (1910–2003)

Theorist's Digest
Concepts and Theory: Critiquing Parsons' Functionalism
　　Functionalism's Assumptions
Concepts and Theory: Dynamic Functionalism
　　Emergent Social Change
Summary

As you undoubtedly noticed, Parsons' work is very abstract. His desire was to create a scheme that could be used to analyze almost any social phenomenon in its broader context. We can call this kind of approach a grand theory. A *grand theory* is one that explains all phenomena through a single set of concepts. Grand theorists like Parsons generally assume that everything in the universe operates in system-like ways, and that all systems are built on the same principles and are subject to the same dynamics. For example, biology, psychology, sociology, and physics are all similar systems and can be ultimately explained using the same theory. Thinking as a grand theorist implies that you tend to see things working in very abstract and mechanistic terms. The theory has to be abstract in order to embrace all the phenomena in the universe. For instance, in a grand theory you couldn't use simple psychological terms to explain psychology because they wouldn't apply in sociology or biology—the terms of a grand theory must be more abstract than any one discipline.

THEORIST'S DIGEST

Brief Biography

Robert K. Merton was born on July 4, 1910, in Philadelphia to Jewish immigrant parents. Merton's given name was Meyer R. Schkolnick, which he initially changed to better suit his amateur magician show. As a young man, Merton spent many hours at the Andrew Carnegie Library reading and studying history, science, and biographies. Merton studied

(Continued)

(Continued)

and worked with Pitirim Sorokin, Talcott Parsons, and Paul Lazarsfeld, all significant names in sociology. He finished his PhD from Harvard in 1936 and soon became a part of the faculty there. Merton moved to Tulane University (New Orleans) in 1939, and in 1941 took a position at Columbia University in New York, where he remained for the rest of his career.

Merton served as president of the American Sociological Association, the Eastern Sociological Society, and the Society for Social Studies of Science. His honors include more than 20 honorary doctoral degrees and membership in the National Academy of Sciences. In 1994, the president of the United States awarded Merton the National Medal of Science. In addition, Robert K. Merton was the father of Robert Cox Merton who won the Nobel Prize in economics (1997). Many of the concepts that Merton coined have made their way into popular culture, such as "self-fulfilling prophecy," "role model," "manifest and latent functions," and "unintended consequences."

Merton passed away on February 23, 2003.

Central Sociological Questions

As a student of Parsons,' Merton was unhappy with the analytical level that Parsons' theory is cast. He argued that sociology hadn't done enough empirical research to make the kinds of statements Parsons did. Merton's concern, then, was to bring functionalism down to the empirical level where it could be tested.

Simply Stated

In place of Parsons' abstract theory, Merton grounds functionalism using functional alternatives, manifest and latent functions, dysfunctions, and unanticipated consequences. All four of these issues can move a society in a direction that simple functionalism wouldn't foresee or be able to explain. Merton also argues that other factors can bring social change rather than equilibrium: unanticipated consequences of social action, deviance, and sociological ambivalence.

Key Concepts

middle-range theory, functional alternatives, manifest and latent functions, dysfunctions, unanticipated consequences, structural theory of deviance, sociological ambivalence

Concepts and Theory: Critiquing Parsons' Functionalism

Although his focus was ultimately on theory, Merton worked relentlessly to ground functionalism in the empirical world first, before making grand, abstract statements. His alternative approach is to work with **middle-range theories.** Middle-range theories "lie between the minor but necessary working hypotheses . . . and the all-inclusive systematic efforts to develop a unified theory that will explain all the observed uniformities of social behavior, social organization and social change" (Merton, 1967, p. 39). Merton argues that sociology is too young a discipline to be concerned with grand theories, and his intent with the concept is to ground socio-logical theory in "theoretically oriented empirical research" (p. 56).

There are five attributes to *middle-range theories:* (1) They consist of a limited set of assumptions that lead to specific hypotheses, which in turn are empirically confirmed; (2) they are capable of being brought together with other middle-range theories to form wider networks of theory; (3) middle-range theories can be generalized and applied to different situations (so the theory is not merely organized descriptive data); (4) because they don't address the more abstract assumptions of grand theory, middle-range theories can fit easily into different systems of theory, like Parsons' social systems or Marx's historical materialism; and (5) middle-range theories will typically be in harmony with the method of classical theorists.

Parsons' and Merton's approaches represent two methods of theory building: Parsons privileges reason and argues that theories should be logically deduced, and Merton's tactic privileges empirical data and induction. Of course, middle-range theories contain abstractions, "but they are close enough to observed data to be incorporated in propositions that permit empirical testing" (Merton, 1967, p. 39). Middle-range theories usually come in the "theories of" form, such as theories of gender inequality, role conflict, deviance, and so forth. These middle-range theories don't try to explain society at large; rather, they explicate some small portion of it without necessarily connecting it to any other aspect of society. Merton's idea is that, as these mid-level theories are proposed and tested, they will be brought together to form a more comprehensive and empirically grounded general theory. For example, after sufficient empirical testing, we could take Lemert's labeling theory of deviance and Merton's structural strain theory and blend them together to form a more general theory of deviance, rather than bringing them together at the abstract level as Parsons does.

Functionalism's Assumptions

Merton also raises questions about three of functionalism's major claims. Up until Merton, these assumptions seemed to be the defining features of functional-ism. First, functionalism posits a *functional unity of society.* This postulate states that the social activities and cultural items that are patterned and standardized across society are functionally related. In other words, all working societies have a functional unity in which all parts of the system work together with a fairly high level of accord and consistency. For example, the functional unity of society princi-ple would assume that the education, government, and religious sectors all work together harmoniously and without fail as parts of the same system. This assump-tion is what underlies the idea of system equilibrium.

The second assumption that Merton questions is the idea of *universal function-alism.* This supposition postulates that all social activities or cultural items have positive sociological functions. In other words, if there is a patterned feature in society, then it must be functional by the very fact that it exists. For example, find-ing a society such as the United States where male aggression has high value, the functionalist assumes that it must have positive benefits for the whole.

The last postulate of functionalism that Merton challenges is that of *indispensability:* Every patterned part of society and culture fulfills a vital function within the society and is therefore indispensable. This postulate not only assumes there are certain functions that a society cannot do without, it also assumes that those functions must be fulfilled by certain cultural or social forms and those forms are therefore indispensable. For example, a functionalist may decide that every society needs a system of ultimate meanings that gives relevance to all other meanings. The functionalist may then assume that it is only religion that can provide those meanings. By such reasoning, religion itself becomes necessary for society, when in fact the function may be met through other institutions.

Merton sees these assumptions as potentially obscuring true research. Generally speaking, if we assume that something is true, we can usually find evidence for it. The first thing Merton wants to do, then, is change each of these assumptions into empirical questions. Rather than assuming that government and religion are positively integrated, make it a research question: In what ways are government and religion related to one another? Or, might not male aggression have effects that are other than positive? As you can probably tell, to ask such questions implies some ideas that Parsonian functionalism does not contain.

Concepts and Theory: Dynamic Functionalism

In order to help us think more clearly about functional relations in society, Merton gives us several new concepts: functional alternatives, manifest and latent functions, dysfunctions, and unanticipated consequences. The idea of *functional alternatives* conceptualizes the possibility that other kinds of structures may meet societal needs. For example, the function of biological reproduction doesn't necessarily have to be met through family. Or, for another example, could the meanings that religion provides be supplied through other institutions, such as a "civil religion"?

The concepts of *manifest and latent functions* specifically refer to the positive contributions that a social structure has for society, but the concepts allow us to see functions in a more complex light. Manifest functions are the known contributions and latent functions are the hidden or unacknowledged contributions of social structures. A good example is education: A manifest function of education is to pass on the cultural knowledge of a society; a latent function of education is to provide a marriage market that pairs people on several important dimensions (such as class).

Merton also wants us to be able to see that social structures or institutions may have negative effects, when seen from a functionalist position. A *dysfunction,* then, is a consequence of a social structure that leads to less adaptation and integration. The idea of a dysfunctional family is a micro-level phenomenon that comes from Merton's concept (here the dysfunctional consequences come from the performance of a social role, such as father or mother). In addition, dysfunctions may be manifest or latent.

Latent functions and dysfunctions are concepts that describe the outcomes of social structures. The idea of **unanticipated consequences,** on the other hand, generally refers to the effects of social acts of individuals. Unanticipated consequences, then, are those outcomes of social action that are not intended by the actor. Merton (1976) gives us several sources of unanticipated consequences. Among them are *ignorance* (at times, there is such a wide range of possible consequences that they can't all be known); *chance consequences* ("those occasioned by the interplay of forces and circumstance that are so numerous and complex that prediction of them is quite beyond our reach" [p. 151]); *error* (the most common source of which is habitual action); *imperious immediacy of interest* (concern for immediate consequences blocks out consideration of long-term effects); and *basic values* (the actor is concerned with subjective rightness rather than objective consequences: "Here is the essential paradox of social action—the 'realization' of values may lead to their renunciation" [p. 154]).

Emergent Social Change

With the idea of unanticipated consequences, Merton is opening up the social system for unpredictable change. Functionalism has usually seen social change in evolutionary terms—slow change over long periods of time that in the long run leads to increased complexity and thus survivability. As we've seen, Parsons opens this idea up a bit by giving us a functional theory of social revolution. The reasons it's a functional theory are that revolutions are only possible because of system strain, such as value inconsistency, and that all revolutions must reintegrate or equilibrate the system. Merton takes us a step further.

Not only are large systems susceptible to strain, as Parsons has it, but the behaviors of individual actors within the system are also susceptible to unanticipated consequences, because of ignorance, mistakes, values, failure to take the long run into account, and chance consequences. Unanticipated consequences, then, function as a wild card in the social system. Both the idea of dysfunctions and that of unintended consequences are particularly important for Merton's (1976) theory because they both lead to structural change. Structures change through "cumulatively patterned choices in behavior and the amplification of dysfunctional consequences resulting from certain kinds of strains, conflicts, and contradictions in the differentiated social structure" (p. 125), and through "unanticipated consequences of purposive social action" (p. 146).

There are two more issues that are important in structural change, according to Merton: deviance and ambivalence. Merton's structural theory of deviance argues that society values certain *goals* and the *means* to achieve those goals. In the United States, for example, we value economic success and believe that education and hard work are the proper means to achieve that goal. However, in any social system there are disenfranchised people who do not have equal access to the legitimate means to achieve success, yet are nonetheless socialized to value the same goals as the majority. This structural location puts these people in a position of tension or strain. Generally speaking, most people accept the goals and means of society; Merton calls this type of response *conformity* (acceptance of both goals and means). But for those in structural strain, there are four other possibilities: *innovation* (accept the goals but use innovative means, such as robbery), *ritualism* (abandon the goals and perform the means without any hope of success), *retreatism* (deny both the goals and the means and retreat through such things as alcoholism or drug abuse), or *rebellion* (the individual creates his or her own goals and means). As with unintended consequences, deviant behaviors may accumulate to the point where they influence the social structure.

We can think of this idea of accumulation within a system in terms of the heat thermostat in your home. If it's cold outside and you have your thermostat set at 65 degrees, the internal temperature of your house will trip the thermostat, which will turn your heat on. If you come into your house while the heat is on, chances are good that it will stay on—your body will have very little influence on the internal temperature. However, if you bring several of your friends and keep adding more people, the total mass of bodies within the house will eventually generate enough heat to trip the thermostat in the opposite direction and turn the heat off. If you keep adding people to your house, you will eventually create enough heat that the thermostat will probably turn the air-conditioner on. It's not a perfect analogy, but you can see where we are heading. Relatively few acts of deviance or unintended consequences will have little effect, but as they accumulate, the social system will respond and change just as your thermostat would.

Ambivalence generally refers to emotional or psychological attitudes that conflict with one another. **Sociological ambivalence,** on the other hand, refers to *"opposing normative tendencies in the social definition of a role"* (Merton, 1976, p. 12, emphasis original). It is important for us to see that the ambivalence here is structural, not individual—the ambivalence exists within the social structure. For example, medical doctors experience contradictory role expectations: They are expected to be emotionally detached in their professional relations with their patients, and at the same time they are expected to display compassion and concern for their patients. There is a way in which sociological ambivalence is an effect of modern social change: Ambivalence has "evolved to provide the flexibility of normatively acceptable behavior required dealing with changing states of a social relation" (Merton, 1976, p. 31).

Thus, in Merton's scheme of functionalism, social structures and systems are robust and complex. Merton argues that systems are not simply subject to functional consequences; rather, systems regularly experience dysfunctions, manifest and latent functions, and functional alternatives. With these ideas, Merton is proposing that functional analysis be open to the possibility of multiple consequences and focus on the net balance of outcomes. Merton also presents us with a picture of the individual social actor, with culture on one side and social structure on the other. These two structures form the salient environment for the person. That is, individuals set about doing their tasks within this environment that both restrains and enables. The different structural environments that individuals find themselves within produce differing rates and kinds of deviance and social ambivalence. Together, ambivalence, deviance, unanticipated consequences, and dysfunctions—all of which are intrinsic to social structure—accumulate to create social change.

Summary

- Merton critiques Parsons' analytical approach to theory, arguing that scientific theory must accumulate over time and begin with testable middle-range theories. Once tested, these mid-range theories, in turn, can be brought together to form more general theories of social structure and action.

- Merton also wants to ground functionalism in the empirical world by getting rid of some of the more abstract assumptions underlying functional theorizing. In particular, Merton questions the functional unity of society, universal functionalism, and indispensability.

- Merton further establishes an empirical base for functionalism by arguing that there may be alternative outcomes to structural arrangements and individual social action. Merton proposes four concepts to help us think about different outcomes: functional alternatives, manifest and latent functions, dysfunctions, and unanticipated consequences.

- Merton also sensitizes us to more subtle and continuous social change. Merton sees quite a bit of social change building up through unanticipated consequences of social action, deviance, and sociological ambivalence. People rarely have full knowledge of the possible outcomes of their behaviors. If enough of the unanticipated consequences of behavior are similar, they will in the long run accrue enough presence or force to bring social change. Deviance also builds up over time; however, deviant behavior is more structurally based than unanticipated consequences. People have structured relations with the goals and means of any society. These relations result in four different types of deviance: innovation, ritualism, retreatism, and rebellion. As similar forms of deviance accumulate, they too will push for social change. Like deviance, sociological ambivalence is structured. If the behaviors that emerge from these structured positions become patterned, they will also create pressures within the social system for change.

BUILDING YOUR THEORY TOOLBOX

Learning More—Primary and Secondary Sources

- Primary readings for Talcott Parsons:
  - Parsons, T. (1937). *The Structure of Social Action.* New York: McGraw-Hill. (Parsons' magnum opus)
  - Parsons, T. (1964). *Social Structure and Personality.* New York: Free Press.
  - Parsons, T. (1966). *Societies.* Englewood Cliffs, NJ: Prentice Hall. (Perhaps the most easily understood of Parsons' writings)

(Continued)

(Continued)

- Primary readings for Robert K. Merton:

    ○ Merton, R. K. (1949). *On Theoretical Sociology*. New York: Free Press.

    ○ Merton, R. K. (1957). *Social Theory and Social Structure* (Rev. ed.). New York: Free Press.

    ○ Merton, R. K. (1976). *Sociological Ambivalence and Other Essays*. New York: Free Press.

- To read more about Parsons, I would recommend the following:

    ○ Holton, R. J., & Turner, B. S. (1989). *Talcott Parsons (Key Sociologists)*. Chichester, UK: Ellis Horwood.

    ○ Lidz, V. (2000). Talcott Parsons. In G. Ritzer (Ed.), *The Blackwell Companion to Major Social Theorists*. Oxford, UK: Blackwell.

    ○ Robertson, R., & Turner, B. S. (Eds.). (1991). *Talcott Parsons: Theorist of Modernity*. London: Sage.

- For Merton, read the following:

    ○ Sztompka, P. (1986). *Robert K. Merton: An Intellectual Profile*. New York: St. Martin's Press.

Seeing the Social World (knowing the theory)

- Write a 250-word synopsis of Parsons' analytical functionalism.

- Write a 250-word synopsis of Merton's empirical functionalism.

- After reading and understanding this chapter, you should be able to define the following terms theoretically and explain their theoretical importance to Parsons' theory of social order: *the problem of social order, voluntaristic action, action theory, the unit act, modes or orientation, adaptation, goal attainment, integration, latent pattern maintenance, generalized media of exchange, values, motives, cultural patterns, action types, institutionalization, AGIL, socialization, cybernetic hierarchy of control, equilibrium, cultural strain, alienative motivational elements.*

- After reading and understanding this chapter, you should be able to define the following terms theoretically and explain their theoretical importance to Merton's empirical functionalism: *middle-range theory, functional alternatives, manifest and latent functions, dysfunctions, unanticipated consequences, structural theory of deviance, sociological ambivalence.*

- After reading and understanding this chapter, you should be able to answer the following questions (remember to answer them *theoretically*):

    ○ Explain how social systems are formed through modes of orientation and types of action, and through roles, norms, and status positions and how these social systems solve the problem of social order.

    ○ Describe a system's functional requisites and interstructural relations using Parsons' AGIL analytical scheme.

    ○ Explain how the cybernetic hierarchy of control works and its importance for understanding how society functions.

o Discuss the process of social change from the beginnings of a social movement to the ordering of the new social system (equilibrium).

o Explain what middle-range theories are and how they fit into the overall enterprise of theory building.

o Discuss Merton's critiques of functionalism and his proposed alternatives.

o Use Merton's structural theory of deviance to discuss how deviance occurs in a society.

Engaging the Social World (using the theory)

- Parsons' primary point of view is that he sees things as a system. Recall what makes a system a system and analyze this society in terms of a system. Is this society a system? If so, in what ways? If not, in what ways does it not meet the criteria? Let's take it down a level: Analyze the university you attend in terms of system qualities. Is it a system? What about your classroom? Is it a system in Parsonian terms? Can you analyze your friendship network in terms of systems? What about you as a person? Do you exist as a system? If all these are systems, how are they linked together?

- Do you think that we can understand globalization from a systems perspective? If so, name at least five different ways that Parsons' theory could be used on a global basis.

- Remembering Parsons' idea of cultural strain, take a look at the society in which you live. Is it ripe for cultural strain? If so, why? What kinds of cultural strain can you identify? From a Parsonian approach, what are the effects we might expect?

- Use Parsons' unit act analytical scheme to explain your behaviors at school today. Take the scheme and use it in at least five different settings (such as school, home, shopping mall, crosswalk, beach, and so on). How does his scheme hold up? Were you able to analyze all of the behaviors equally well?

- Recalling Parsons' idea of generalized media of exchange, I'd like for you to choose two institutions. What generalized media of exchange do you think exist between these two institutions? How would you go about determining if the media you propose are actually at work?

- Pick two different social institutions, such as religion and the economy. Analyze each institution using Merton's ideas of functional alternatives, manifest and latent functions, dysfunctions, and unanticipated consequences.

- Using a copy of today's newspaper (local or national), find all the articles that cover some form of deviance. Use Merton's theory of deviance to categorize and understand what is going on.

Weaving the Threads (building theory)

- How did Parsons set the theoretical landscape for much of the twentieth century?

- Compare and contrast the synopsis of functionalism you wrote for Spencer with those of Parsons and Merton. Combine these into a robust definition of functionalism.

(Continued)

(Continued)

- One of sociology's abiding concerns revolves around the issue of social change. In the chapter on Durkheim, I asked you to consider Spencer and Durkheim's theories of social change and the problems of integration. In the chapter on Weber, I asked you to compare and contrast Marx and Weber on the issues of inequality and social change. How does Parsons' theory of revolution and change include the issues from the Spencer/Durkheim synthesis and the Marx/Weber synthesis? In other words, to what extent does Parsons' theory include both conflict and functional issues of social change? What does Parsons' theory leave out?

- Spencer and Durkheim both propose requisite functions. Compare and contrast both Spencer's and Durkheim's lists with Parsons'. Where do Spencer's functions fit? Where does Durkheim's function fit? Does Parsons leave anything out?

- Compare and contrast Mead's theory of action with that of Parsons. Do you see any way these two apparently discrepant theories can be brought together to form fuller understanding of human action?

- Another of sociology's abiding concerns is the relationship between the individual and society. Sometimes this problem is phrased in terms of agency (free will) versus structure (determination), and other times it is talked about as the micro–macro link. How are the individual and society related? How do the actions of people in face-to-face encounters get translated to macro-level structures? How do structures influence actors? Parsons doesn't answer all these questions, but he gives us one of our first detailed theoretical explanations of the micro–macro link. According to Parsons, how do the actions of people in face-to-face encounters get translated to macro-level structures? Does his theory seem reasonable to you?

CHAPTER 9

Conflict Theory:

Lewis Coser, Ralf Dahrendorf, and Randall Collins

Conflict theory has a long history in sociology. Without question, Karl Marx's work in the early to mid-1800s formed the initial statements of this perspective. As you know, Marx was centrally concerned with class and the dialectics of capitalism. He argued that capitalism would produce its own gravediggers by creating the conditions under which class consciousness and a failing economy would come into existence. In this juncture between structure and class-based group experience, the working class revolution would take place.

In the early twentieth century, Max Weber formulated a response to Marx's theory. Weber saw that conflict didn't overwhelmingly involve the economy, but that the state and economy together set up conditions for conflict. Of central importance to Weber's scheme is the notion of legitimation. All systems of oppression must be legitimated in order to function. Thus, legitimation is one of the critical issues in the idea of conflict. Weber also saw that class is more complex than Marx initially supposed, and that there are other factors that contribute to social inequality, most notably status and party (or power).

Since that time, a number of efforts have combined different elements from one or both of these theorists to understand conflict. In this chapter, we will consider three of those efforts. Our first theorist is Lewis Coser. Coser's work is interesting for two reasons. First, he intentionally draws the majority of his theoretical ideas from Georg Simmel rather than Marx or Weber. Coser uses Marx and Weber now and then to frame or elaborate upon what Simmel has to say, but by and large Coser (1956) presents "a number of basic propositions which have been distilled from theories of social conflict, in particular from the theories of Georg Simmel" (p. 8). Keep this in mind as we talk about Coser's theory: We could easily substitute Simmel's name for Coser's.

The second reason Coser is remarkable is that he is the first to consider the functional consequences of conflict—other than Simmel, that is. Before Simmel, conflict had been understood as a source of social change and disintegration. Simmel was the first to acknowledge that conflict is a natural and necessary part of society; Coser brought Simmel's idea to mainstream sociology, at least in America. From that point on, sociologists have had to acknowledge that

> groups require disharmony as well as harmony, dissociation as well as association; and conflicts within them are by no means altogether disruptive factors. . . . Far from being necessarily dysfunctional, a certain degree of conflict is an essential element in group formation and the persistence of group life. (Coser, 1956, p. 31)

In terms of the history of social thought and the layout of this book, it is interesting to note that Coser (1956) was motivated to consider the functional consequences of conflict to address a deficiency in Talcott Parsons' theory: "Parsons considers conflict primarily a 'disease'" (p. 21). There's a way in which conflict theorists are interested in the same question as Parsons: the problem of social order. Conflict theorists argue that conflict is normal for society and provides a good portion of its organizing features. Social order is achieved and built around issues of conflict.

Our second theorist is Ralf Dahrendorf. He clearly blends elements from Marx and Weber and he sprinkles in elements from Coser to present a new understanding of conflict in society. From Marx he takes the idea of dialectical change: "Social structures . . . are capable of producing within themselves the elements of their supersession and change" (Dahrendorf, 1957/1959, p. viii). If you don't recall Marx's use of the dialectic, I encourage you to look back at Chapter 3.

Dahrendorf also uses Marx's notion of political interests stemming from bipolarized social positions. Remember that Marx argued that capitalism contains only two classes that really matter: the owners and the workers. These two positions are inherently antagonistic and by their nature dictate different political interests; that is, all workers have the same political interests as do all owners. From Weber, Dahrendorf takes the idea of power and authority. Rather than seeing class as the central characteristic of modern society, Dahrendorf claims that *power* is the one unavoidable feature of all social relations. In light of the theorists covered in the previous chapter, it's worth noting that Dahrendorf (1957/1959) regards Merton's theories of the middle range as "the immediate task of sociological research" (p. x), and he sees his own theory as a necessary corrective of Parsons' "equilibrium approach."

On the other hand, our third conflict theorist, Randall Collins, is much less concerned with orienting his work around Parsons' project. Rather, Collins (1975) draws on the work of Weber, Durkheim, and Goffman to argue that symbolic goods and emotional solidarity are among the "main weapons used in conflict" (p. 59). This micro-level orientation is a unique and powerful addition to the conflict perspective. Most other conflict theories are oriented toward the macro level. Stratification is generally understood as operating through oppressive structures that limit access and choices (the idea of the "glass ceiling" is a good example), and power is conceived of as working coercively through the control of material resources and methods of social control. Collins also attunes us to a different level of analysis than either Coser or Dahrendorf—the global level of geopolitics where political conflicts are analyzed within the context of history and geography.

The Functional Consequences of Conflict:
Lewis Coser (1913–2003)

Theorist's Digest
Concepts and Theory: Variation in Conflict
  Basic Sources of Conflict
  Predicting the Level of Violence
Concepts and Theory: The Integrating Forces of Conflict
  Internal Conflict
  External Conflict
Summary

THEORIST'S DIGEST

Brief Biography

Lewis Coser was born in Berlin, Germany, in 1913. His family moved to Paris in 1933 where he studied literature and sociology at the Sorbonne. Because of his German heritage, Coser was arrested and interned by the French government near the beginning of World War II. He later was able to get political asylum in the United States and arrived in New York in 1941. Coser did his PhD work at Columbia University, where he studied under Robert K. Merton. His dissertation, *The Functions of Social Conflict,* took conflict theory in a new direction and was later named as one of the best-selling sociology books of the twentieth century by the journal *Contemporary Sociology.* Coser also authored *Masters of Sociological Thought,* which became one of the most

(Continued)

(Continued)

influential sociological theory books in the English language. In addition, Coser established the Department of Sociology at Brandeis University; founded *Dissent* magazine; served as president of the American Sociological Association (1975), the Society for the Study of Social Problems, and the Easter Sociological Association (1983); and is honored annually through the American Sociological Association's Lewis A. Coser Award for Theoretical Agenda-Setting. Coser died in July 2003.

Central Sociological Questions

Coser sought to explain the place conflict has in the lives of humans generally. Specifically, what functional consequences does conflict have for society? James B. Rule (2003), writing in memoriam for *Dissent* magazine, said of Coser, he always considered himself an intellectual first and a sociologist second. His aim was always to make some sort of comprehensive sense of the human condition—a sense of the best that social life could offer and a hardheaded look at the worst things human beings could do to one another, a vision of possibilities of change for the better and an assessment of the forces weighing for and against those possibilities.

Simply Stated

Conflict can have functional consequences for the groups involved. Conflict internal to the group will serve to release pent-up hostilities, create norms regulating conflict, and develop clear lines of authority and jurisdiction. Conflict that is directed at the group from an external source will create stronger group boundaries, higher social solidarity, and more efficient use of power and authority.

Key Concepts

crosscutting influences, absolute deprivation, relative deprivation, rational and transcendent goals, functional consequences of conflict, internal and external conflict, types of internal conflict, network density, group boundaries, internal solidarity, coalitions

Concepts and Theory: Variation in Conflict

Coser argues that conflict is instinctual for us, so we find it everywhere in human society. There is the conflict of war, but there is also the conflict that we find in our daily lives and relationships. But Coser also argues that conflict is different for humans than for other animals in that our conflicts can be goal related. There is generally something that we are trying to achieve through conflict, and there are different possible ways of reaching our goal. The existence of the possibility of different paths opens up opportunities for negotiation and different types and levels of conflict. Because Coser sees conflict as a normal and functional part of human life, he can talk about its variation in ways that others missed, such as the level of violence and functional consequences.

Basic Sources of Conflict

First, we want to consider what brings on social conflict in the first place. Most social conflict is based on the unequal distribution of scarce resources, which Weber identified as class, status, and power. Weber, as well as Simmel, also pointed out the importance of the *crosscutting influences* that originate with the different structures of inequality. For example, a working class black person may not share the same political interests as a working class white person. The different status positions of these two people may cut across their similar class interests. Thus, what becomes important as a source of social conflict is the covariance of these three systems of stratification. If the public perceives that the same group controls access to all three resources, it is likely that the legitimacy of the system will be questioned because people perceive that their social mobility is hampered.

The other general source of conflict comes from Marx. Marx's concern was with a group's sense of deprivation caused by class. This sense of deprivation is what leads a group to class consciousness and produces conflict and social change. Marx was primarily concerned with explaining the structural changes or processes that would bring the working class to this realization, such things as rising levels of education and worker concentration that are both structurally demanded by capitalism.

Contemporary conflict theory has modified the idea of deprivation by noting that it is the shift from absolute to relative deprivation that is significant in producing this kind of critical awareness. *Absolute deprivation* refers to the condition of being destitute, living well below the poverty line where life is dictated by uncertainty over the essentials of life (food, shelter, and clothing). People in such a condition have neither the resources nor the willpower to become involved in conflict and social change.

Relative deprivation, however, refers to a sense of being underprivileged relative to some other person or group. The basics of life aren't in question here; it's simply the sense that others are doing better and that we are losing out on something. These people and groups have the emotional and material resources to become involved in conflict and social change. But it isn't relative deprivation itself that motivates people; it is the shift from absolute to relative deprivation that may spark a powder keg of revolt. People who are upwardly mobile in this way have the available resources, and they may experience a sense of loss or deprivation if the economic structural changes can't keep pace with their rising expectations.

Predicting the Level of Violence

Coser moves us past these basic premises to consider the ways in which conflict can fluctuate. One of the more important ways that conflict can vary is by its level of violence. If people perceive conflict as a means to achieving clearly expressed *rational goals*, then conflict will tend to be less violent. A simple exchange is a good example. Because of the tension present in exchanges, conflict is likely, but it is a low-level conflict in terms of violence. People engage in exchange in order to achieve a goal, and that desired end directs most other factors. Another example is a worker strike. Workers generally go on strike to achieve clearly articulated goals and the strikers usually do not want the struggle to become violent—the violence can detract from achieving their goals (though strikes will become violent under certain conditions). The passive resistance movements of the 1960s and early 1970s are other examples. We can think of these kinds of encounters as the strategic use of conflict.

However, conflict can be violent, and Coser gives us two factors that can produce violent conflict: *emotional involvement* and *transcendent goals*. In order to become violent, people must be emotionally engaged. Durkheim saw that group interaction could increase emotional involvements and create moral boundaries around group values and goals. He didn't apply this to conflict, but Coser does. The more involved we are with a group, the greater is our emotional involvement and the greater the likelihood of violent conflict if our group is threatened.

Conflict will also tend to have greater levels of violence when the goals of a group are seen to be transcendent. As long as the efforts of a group are understood to be directed toward everyday concerns, people will tend to moderate their emotional involvement and thus keep conflict at a rational level. If, on the other hand, we see the goals of our group as being greater than the group and the concerns of daily life, then conflict is more likely to be violent. For example, when the United States goes to war, the reasons are never expressed by our government in mundane terms. We did not say that we fought the First Gulf War in order to protect our oil interests; we fought the war in order to defeat oppression, preserve freedom, and protect human rights. Anytime violence is deemed necessary by a government, the reasons are couched in moral terms (capitalists might say they fight for individual freedoms; communists would say they fight for social responsibility and the dignity of the collective). The existence of transcendent goals is why the Right to Life side of the abortion conflict tends to exhibit more violence than advocates of choice—their goals are more easily linked to transcendent issues and can thus be seen as God-ordained.

Concepts and Theory: The Integrating Forces of Conflict

Coser makes the case for two kinds of *functional consequences of conflict:* conflict that occurs within a group and conflict that occurs outside the group. An example of internal conflict is the tension that can exist between indigenous populations or first nations and the national government. Notice that this internal conflict is actually between or among groups that function within the same social system. Examples of external group conflicts are the wars in which a nation may involve itself. When considering the consequences for internal group conflict, Coser is concerned with low-level and more frequent conflict. When explaining the consequences for external conflict, he is thinking about more violent conflict.

Internal Conflict

Internal conflict in the larger social system, as between different groups within the United States, releases hostilities, creates norms for dealing with conflict, and develops lines of authority and judiciary systems. Remember that Coser sees conflict as instinctual for humans. Thus, a society must always contend with the psychological need of individuals to engage in conflict. Coser appears to argue that this need can build up over time and become explosive. Low-level, frequent conflict tends to *release hostilities* and thus keep conflict from building and becoming disintegrative for the system.

This kind of conflict also creates pressures for society to produce *norms governing conflict*. For example, most of the formal norms (laws) governing labor in Western capitalist countries came about because of the conflict between labor and management. We can see this same dynamic operating at the dyad level as well. For example, when a couple in a long-term relationship experiences repeated episodes of conflict, such as arguing, they will attempt to come up with norms for handling the tension in a way that preserves the integrity of the relationship. The same is true for the social system, but the social system will go a step further and develop formal authorities and systems of judgment to handle conflict. Thus, frequent, low-level conflict creates moral and social structures that facilitate social integration.

Coser also notes that not every internal conflict will be functional. It depends on the types of conflict and social structure that are involved. In Coser's theory, there are two basic *types of internal conflict:* those that threaten or contradict the fundamental assumptions of the group relationship and those that don't. Every group is based on certain beliefs regarding what the group is about. Let's take marriage as an example of a group. For many people, a basic assumption undergirding marriage is sexual fidelity. A husband and wife may argue about many things—such as finances, chores, toilet seats, and tubes of toothpaste—but chances are good that none of these will be a threat to the stability of the "group" (dyad) because they don't contradict a basic assumption that provides the basis of the group in the first place. Adultery, on the other hand, may very well put the marriage in jeopardy because it goes against one of the primary defining features of the group. Conflict over such things as household chores may prove to be functional in the long run for the marriage, while adultery may be dysfunctional and lead to the breakup of the group.

However, I want you to notice something very important here: In Coser's way of thinking about things, adultery won't break a marriage up because it is morally wrong. Whether the relationship will survive depends on the couple's basic assumptions as to its reasons for existence. A couple may have an "open marriage" based on the assumption that people are naturally attracted to other people and sexual flings are to be expected. In such a case, outside sexual relations will probably not break the group apart. Couples within such marriages may experience tension or fight about one another's sexual exploits—and research indicates that they often do—but such conflict will tend to be functional for the marriage because of its basic assumptions. Note also that conflict over household chores may indeed be dysfunctional if the underlying assumption of the marriage is egalitarianism, but the actual division of labor in the house occurs along stereotypical gender lines.

The *group structure* will also help determine whether or not a conflict is functional. As Coser (1956) explains, "social structures differ in the way in which they allow expression to antagonistic claims" (p. 152). To talk about this issue, let's make a distinction based on network density. *Network density* speaks of how often a group gets together, the longevity of the group, and the demands of the group in terms of personal involvement. Groups whose members interact frequently over long periods of time and have high levels of personal and personality involvement have *high network density*. Such groups will tend to suppress or discourage conflict. If conflict does erupt in such a group, it will tend to be very intense for two reasons. First, the group will likely have built up unresolved grievances and unreleased hostilities. Once unfettered, these pent-up issues and emotions will tend to push the original conflict over the top. Second, the kind of total personal involvement these groups have makes the mobilization of all emotions that much easier. On the other hand, groups whose members interact less frequently and that demand less involvement—those with *low network density*—will be more likely to experience the functional benefits of conflict.

External Conflict

The different groups involved in conflict also experience functional results, especially when the conflict is more violent. As a group experiences external conflict, the boundaries surrounding the group become stronger, the members of the group experience greater solidarity, power is exercised more efficiently, and the group tends to form coalitions with other groups (the more violent the conflict is, the more intensified are these effects). In order for any group to exist, it must include some people and exclude others. This inclusion/exclusion process involves producing and regulating different behaviors, ways of feeling and thinking, cultural symbols, and so forth. These differences constitute a *group boundary* that clearly demarcates those who belong from those who do not.

As a group experiences conflict, the boundaries surrounding the group become stronger and better guarded. For example, during World War II the United States incarcerated those Americans of Japanese descent. Today we may look back at that incident with shame, but at the time it made the United States stronger as a collective; it more clearly demarcated "us" from "them," which is a necessary function for any group to exist. Conflict makes this function more robust: "Conflict sets boundaries between groups within a social system by strengthening group consciousness and awareness of separateness, thus establishing the identity of groups within the system" (Coser, 1956, p. 34).

Along with stronger external boundaries, conflict enables the group to also experience higher levels of *internal solidarity*. When a group engages in conflict, the members will tend to feel a greater sense of camaraderie than during peaceful times. They will see themselves as more alike, more part of the same family, existing for the same reason. Group-specific behaviors and symbols will be more closely guarded and celebrated. Group rituals will be engaged in more often and with greater fervency, thus producing greater emotional ties between members and creating a sense of sacredness about the group.

In addition, a group experiencing conflict will tend to produce a more *centralized power structure*. A centralized government is more efficient in terms of response time to danger, regulating internal stresses and needs, negotiating external relations, and so on. Violent conflict also tends to produce *coalitions* with previously neutral parties. Again, World War II is a clear example. The story of World War II is one of increasing violence with more and more parties being drawn in. Violent conflict produces alliances that would have previously been thought unlikely, such as the United States being allied with Russia.

> Coalition . . . permits the coming together of elements that . . . would resist other forms of unification. Although it is the most unstable form of socialization, it has the distinct advantage of providing some unification where unification might otherwise not be possible. (Coser, 1956, p. 143)

Summary

- Contrary to the claims of most previous theorists, Coser argues that conflict can have integrating as well as disintegrating effects. Conflict functions differently whether it is between unrelated groups (external) or inside a group, between factions (internal).

- For internal conflict, the question of functionality hinges on the conflict being less violent and more frequent, not threatening the basic assumptions of the group at large, and the group having low interactional network density. Under these conditions, internal conflict will produce the following functional consequences: conflicts will serve to release pent-up hostilities, create norms regulating conflict, and develop clear lines of authority and jurisdiction (especially around the issues that conflict develops).

- External conflict that is more violent will tend to have the following functional consequences: stronger group boundaries, higher social solidarity, and more efficient use of power and authority. Conflict violence will tend to increase in the presence of high levels of emotional involvement and transcendent goals.

Power and Dialectical Change:
Ralf Dahrendorf (1929–)

Theorist's Digest
Concepts and Theory: Power and Group Interests
 Latent and Manifest Interests
Concepts and Theory: Conditions of Conflict and Social Change
 Social Change
Summary

We move now to Ralf Dahrendorf's theory of power and dialectical change. Like Coser, Dahrendorf sees conflict as universally present in all human relations. But Dahrendorf doesn't see the inevitability of conflict as part of human nature; he sees it, rather, as a normal part of how we structure society and create social order. In this sense, Dahrendorf is concerned with the same issue as Talcott Parsons: How is social order achieved? However, rather than assuming collective agreement about norms, values, and social positions, as Parsons does, Dahrendorf argues that it is *power* that both defines and enforces the guiding principles of society. Dahrendorf also follows Coser in talking about the level of violence and its effects, but Dahrendorf adds a further variable: conflict intensity.

THEORIST'S DIGEST

Brief Biography

Ralf Dahrendorf was born in Hamburg, Germany, on May 1, 1929. His father was a Social Democratic politician and member of the German Parliament who was arrested and imprisoned by the Nazis during World War II. The younger Dahrendorf was arrested as well, fortuitously escaping death by only a few days. His father continued in politics after World War II in the Soviet-held portion of Germany, but was again arrested, this time by the Soviets. He eventually escaped and fled with Ralf to England. Young Dahrendorf later returned to Germany to study at the University of Hamburg, where he received his first PhD in philosophy; he earned his second PhD (sociology) in England at the London School of Economics. Dahrendorf taught sociology at the universities of Hamburg, Tübingen, and Konstanz between 1957 and 1969. In 1969, Dahrendorf turned to politics and became a member of the German Parliament. In 1970, he was appointed a commissioner in the European Commission in Brussels. From 1974 to 1984, Dahrendorf was the director of the London School of Economics. In 1988, Dahrendorf became a British citizen, and in 1993 he was given life peerage and was named Baron Dahrendorf of Clare Market in the City of Westminster by Queen Elizabeth II. Sir Dahrendorf is currently a member of the House of Lords.

Central Sociological Questions

In describing his own intellectual search, Dahrendorf (1989) says that it is

> my firm belief that the regulation of conflict is the secret of liberty in liberal democracy. That if we don't manage to regulate conflict, if we try to ignore it, or if we try to create a world of ultimate harmony, we are quite likely to end up with worse conflicts than if we accept the fact that people have different interests and different aspirations, and devise institutions in which it is possible for people to express these differences, which is what democracy, in my view, is about. Democracy, in other words, is not about the emergence of some unified view from "the people," but it's about organizing conflict and living with conflict.

Simply Stated

Conflict is a normal part of social organization. The issue is whether or not a group acts on power inequities. For a group to act it must meet the technical, political, and social conditions of group organization. When conflict does erupt it can vary by intensity and violence. If a group is successful in its bid for power, it will, like the group it deposed, create social order around its interests.

Key Concepts

power, authority, imperatively coordinated associations, constraint approach, class, quasi-groups, interest groups, technical conditions, political conditions, social conditions, conflict violence and intensity

Concepts and Theory: Power and Group Interests

Who has power, where is it located, and how is it exercised? Those questions have proven themselves to be quite difficult for social scientists to answer. Some theorists see power as an element of social structure—something attached to a position within the structure, such as the power that comes with being the president of the United States. In this scheme, power is something that a person can possess and use. Other theorists define power as an element of exchange (see Chapter 10). Others see power more in terms of influence. This is a more general way in which to think of power, because many types of social relationships and people can exercise influence. Still other thinkers, as we will see when we get to Michel Foucault (Chapter 16), define power as insidiously invested in text, knowledge, and discourse (see also Dorothy E. Smith, Chapter 17). I want to encourage you to pay close attention to the way our theorists speak of power and how it is used in society and social relations. It's an extremely important social factor and one that is multifaceted in the ways it is used.

For his part, Dahrendorf (1957/1959), here quoting Weber, defines **power** as "the probability that one actor within a social relationship will be in a position to carry out his own will despite resistance, regardless of the basis on which this probability rests" (p. 166). Dahrendorf also makes the distinction, along with Weber, between power and authority. Power is something that can be exercised at any moment in all social relations and depends mostly on the personalities of the individuals involved. Because of its universal characteristic, Dahrendorf calls power "factual": It is a fact of human life.

Power can be based on such different sources as persuasion and brute force. If someone has a gun pointed at your head, chances are good that the person has the power in the encounter; that is, if he or she is willing to use it and you're afraid of dying, then chances are good you'll do what the person says—those individual features are where personality comes in. Persuasion works subtly as we are drawn in by the personal magnetism of the other person. Persuasion can also be based on skills: If someone knows how interactions work and knows social psychology, then he or she can manipulate those factors and achieve power in the interaction. Again, a specific personality is involved—knowing how to manipulate people and actually doing it are two different things.

However, like Weber, Dahrendorf is more interested in authority than this kind of factual power. Authority is a form of power, of course, but it is legitimate power. It is power that is "always associated with social positions or roles" (Dahrendorf, 1957/1959, p. 166). *Authority* is part of social organization, not individual personality. Please note where Dahrendorf locates authority—the legitimated use of power is found in the status positions, roles, and norms of organizations. Obvious examples are your professors, the police, your boss at work, and so on. Because of its organizational embeddedness, Dahrendorf refers to authoritative social relations as **imperatively coordinated associations** (ICAs). I know that sounds like a complex idea, but it actually isn't. If something is imperative, it is binding and compulsory; you must do it. So the term simply says that social relations are managed through legitimated power (authority). While the term is straightforward, it is also important.

As I mentioned before, like Parsons, Dahrendorf is concerned with the problem of social order but positions himself against Parsons. Dahrendorf (1968) makes the distinction between the "equilibrium approach" to social order and the "constraint approach" (pp. 139–140). Dahrendorf (1968) recognizes that "continuity is without a doubt one of the fundamental puzzles of social life" but argues that social order is the result of constraint rather than some consensus around social beliefs (pp. 139–140). In the *constraint approach,* the norms and values of society are established and imposed through authoritative power. Be careful to see the distinction that's being made. In the equilibrium model, the actions of individuals are organized through a collectively held and agreed-upon set of values, roles or types of action, expressive symbols, and so on. In this Durkheim–Parsons model, these cultural elements hold sway because they are functional and/or they have moral force. These elements produce an equilibrium or balance between individual desires and social needs.

Dahrendorf, however, points out that there is an assumed element of power in the equilibrium model. By definition, "a norm is a cultural rule that associates people's behavior or appearance with rewards or punishments" (Johnson, 2000, p. 209). Not all behaviors are *normative*—that is, not all are governed by a norm or standard. To bring out this point, let's compare normal (in the usual sense) and normative. Some behaviors can be normal (or not) and yet not be guided by a norm. For example, I usually wear jeans, T-shirts, and Chuck Taylor shoes to teach in. That's not normal attire for a professor at my school, but I'm not breaking a norm in dressing like that. There are no sanctions involved—I don't get rewarded or punished. I'm sure you see Dahrendorf's point: Norms always presume an element of power in that they are negatively or positively enforced.

Dahrendorf agrees with Durkheim and Parsons that society is created through roles, norms, and values, but he argues that they work through power rather than collective consensus. Here is where we can see the primary distinction between the functional and conflict theory approaches: Functionalists assume some kind of cultural agreement and don't see power as a central social factor; in contrast, conflict theorists argue that power is the central feature of society. Further, as a conflict theorist, Dahrendorf (1968) sees that the substance of social roles, norms, status positions, values, and so forth "may well be explained in terms of the interests of the powerful" (p. 140). Like Marx, Dahrendorf argues that the culture of any society reflects the interests of the powerful elite and not the political interests of the middle or lower classes.

It is also important to note that Dahrendorf sees class as related more to power than to money or occupation. Both of those might be important, but the reason for this is that they contribute to an individual's power within an ICA. Thus, for Dahrendorf (1957/1959), classes "are social conflict groups the determinant . . . of which can be found in the participation in or exclusion from the exercise of authority within any imperatively coordinated association" (p. 138). Keep this distinction in mind. It implies that Dahrendorf's concern with conflict is more narrowly defined than is Coser's. Coser is interested in explaining *any* internal and external conflict, while Dahrendorf's main interest is internal *class* conflict.

Latent and Manifest Interests

Like Marx, Dahrendorf sees the interests of power and class in dichotomous terms: You either can wield legitimated power or you can't. Now that I've said that, I need to qualify it. Remember that Dahrendorf calls the social relationships organized around legitimated power imperatively coordinated associations. One of the ideas implied in the term is that social relations are embedded within a hierarchy of authority. What this means is that most people are sandwiched in between power relations. That is, they exercise power over some and are themselves subject to the authority of those above them. However, this idea also points out that embedded within this hierarchy of power are dichotomous sets of interests.

For example, let's say you are a manager at a local eatery that is part of a restaurant chain. As manager, you will have a number of employees over whom you have authority and exercise power. You will share that power with other shift or section managers. In the restaurant, then, there are two groups with different power interests: a group of managers and a group of employees. At the same time, you have regional and corporate managers over you. This part of the organizational structure sets up additional dichotomous power interests. In this case, you are the underling and your bosses exercise power over you and others. If you stop and think about it, you'll see what Dahrendorf wants us to see: Society is set up and managed through imperatively coordinated associations. Society is a tapestry that is woven together by different sets of power interests.

Okay, social relationships are coordinated through authority and power is everywhere. What's the big deal? What else does Dahrendorf want us to see? There's an important distinction and significant question that Dahrendorf wants us to become aware of. Using two terms from Merton, Dahrendorf argues that everyone is involved in positions and groups with latent power interests. People with these similar interests are called quasi-groups. *Quasi-groups* "consist of incumbents of roles endowed with like expectations of interests" and represent "recruiting fields" for the formation of real *interest groups*. Interest groups, Dahrendorf tells us, "are the real agents of group conflict" (Dahrendorf, 1957/1959, p. 180). Everybody is part of various quasi-groups. For example, you and your fellow students form a loose aggregate of interests opposed to the professors at your university. Here's the significant question that Dahrendorf wants us to consider: How do latent interests become manifest interests? In other words, what are the social factors that move an aggregate from a quasi-group to an interest group?

Concepts and Theory:
Conditions of Conflict and Social Change

Before we get into the conditions of conflict, let me reemphasize an important sociological point. Every one of us maintains different positions within social aggregates. An aggregate is simply "a mass or body of units or parts somewhat loosely associated with one another" (Merriam-Webster, 2002). For example, you have an economic class position; perhaps you're working or middle class. Yet, while you share that position with a vast number of others, you may not experience any sense of group identity or shared interests. When, why, and how these aggregates actually form into social groups is a significant sociological question. As an illustration, ask yourself what would have to happen for you and your fellow students to become an active social group that would rise up against the authority of your professors or campus administrators. More significantly, what are the conditions under which disenfranchised groups such as gays and lesbians (in the United States) would challenge the existing power arrangements?

Dahrendorf gives us three sets of conditions that must be met for a group to become active in conflict: technical, political, and social conditions. The *technical conditions* are those things without which a group simply can't function. They are the things that actually define a social group as compared to an aggregate. The technical conditions include members, ideas or ideologies (what Dahrendorf calls a "charter"), and norms. The members that Dahrendorf has in mind are the people who are active in the organization of the group. For an illustration, we can think of a Christian church. As any pastor knows, within a congregation there are active and inactive members. There are the people who actually make the church work by teaching Sunday school or organizing bake sales; and then there are the people who show up once or twice a week and simply attend. We can see the same thing in political parties: There are those who are active year in and year out and there are those who simply vote. It's the workers or "leading group" that Dahrendorf has in mind as members.

For a collective to function as a group, there also has to be a defining set of ideas, or an ideology. These ideas must be distinct enough from the ruling party to set the conflict group apart. For example, for the students at your school to become an interest group, there would have to be a set of ideas and values that are different from the ones the administration and faculty hold. Just such an ideology was present during the free speech movement at the University of California at Berkeley during the 1960s. A friend of mine taught his first introduction to sociology class at Berkeley during this time. He walked in on the first day of class and handed out his syllabus. In response, the students, all 300 of them, got up and walked out. Why?

The students believed that they should have had input in making up the syllabus—a value that most professors don't hold. (My friend, by the way, invited them back to collectively negotiate a syllabus.)

A group also requires norms. Groups are unruly things. Without norms, people tend to go off in their own direction either by mistake or intention. There must be some social mechanism that acts like a shepherd dog, nipping at the heels of the sheep to bring them back to the flock. So important are norms to human existence, Durkheim argued that people would commit suicide if there were no clear norms to guide behavior (anomic suicide). Norms are particularly important for interest groups involved in conflict. Conflict demands a united stand from the interest group, and norms help preserve that solidarity. Note also that the existence of norms implies a power hierarchy within the interest group itself—a leadership cadre.

The *political conditions* refer specifically to the ability to meet and organize. This is fairly obvious but is nonetheless important. Using our student revolt example, let's say that your university administration got wind of student unrest. Now, where is the most logical and the easiest place for a group of students to meet? The college campus would be the best place; many students live there and perhaps have limited transportation, and the campus is also the place that every student knows. However, the administration controls access to all campus facilities and could forbid students to gather, especially if they knew that the students were fomenting a revolt.

The administration could further hamper meetings through the way the campus is built. I attended a school that was building a student center while I was there. Everybody was excited, and we students were looking forward to having all the amenities that come with such a facility, such as greater choices in food (we would be getting Burger King, Kentucky Fried Chicken, Pizza Hut, and assorted other options) and a movie theater. What most of us didn't realize at the time was that the university had had plans long before to build a student center, but those plans got scrapped. Why? The original center was supposed to be built in 1964, right in the middle of the civil rights and free speech movements. The university didn't build the center then because they didn't want to provide the students with an opportunity to gather together. The center was eventually built during the latter part of the 1980s, when students seemed most content with capitalist enterprise. Now, move this illustration out to general society and you'll see the importance of these political conditions: Governments can clearly either hamper or allow interest groups to develop.

Social conditions of organization must also be met. There are two elements here: communication and structural patterns of recruitment. Obviously, the more people (quasi-groups) are able to communicate, the more likely they will form a social group (interest group). A group's ability to communicate is of course central to Marx's view of class consciousness. Dahrendorf (1957/1959) brings it into his theory with updates: "In advanced industrial societies this condition may be assumed to be generally given" (p. 187).

Marx of course was aware of some communication technologies, such as printing and newspapers, but still saw that bringing people together in physical proximity was necessary for communication. Dahrendorf, writing in the 1950s, saw even more technological development than did Marx, and you and I have seen this condition fully blossom with the advent of computer technologies and the Internet. Communication is thus a given in modern society. But hold onto this idea of non–face-to-face communication until we get to Randall Collins; he's going to give us a caveat to Dahrendorf's assumed level of communication.

The second part of Dahrendorf's social conditions also sets a limit on communication. The social connections that people make must be structurally predictable for an interest group to develop. Let's use Internet communication as an example. When email and the Internet first began, there were few mechanisms that patterned the way people got in touch with one another. People would email their friends or business acquaintances, and in that sense computer technologies only enhanced already established social connections. But with the advent of search engines like Google and Web sites like Yahoo, there are now structural features of the Internet that can more predictably bring people together.

For instance, I just opened the Yahoo homepage. Under "Groups" is listed "From Trash to Treasure; React locally, impact globally." If I'm concerned about ecological issues, then my communication with other like-minded people is now facilitated by the structure of the Internet. However, my accessing the Yahoo homepage is not structured. Whether or not you or I use Yahoo and see the discussion group is based on "peculiar, structurally random personal circumstances," which "appear generally unsuited for the organization of conflict groups" (Dahrendorf, 1957/1959, p. 187). Thus, while parts of these social conditions appear to be structured, others are not. The thing I want you to see here is that this condition is highly variable, even though we are living in a technologically advanced society.

Social Change

According to Dahrendorf, conflict will vary by its level of intensity and violence. *Conflict intensity* refers to the amount of costs and involvement. The cost of conflict is rather intuitive; it refers to the money, life, material, and infrastructure that are lost due to conflict. Involvement refers to the level of importance the people in the conflict attach to the group and its issues. We can think of this involvement as varying on a continuum from the level that a game of checkers requires to that of a frontline soldier. Checkers only requires a small portion of a person's personality and energy, while participating in a war where life and death are at stake will engulf an individual's entire psyche. For Dahrendorf, *conflict violence* refers to how conflict is manifested and is basically measured by the kinds of weapons used. Peaceful demonstrations are conflictual but exhibit an extremely low level of violence, while riots are far more violent.

Often class conflict, especially over longer periods of time, involves both intensity and violence and thus they are difficult to empirically disengage from one another. A good example of these factors is the civil rights movement in the United States. I invite you to check out a civil rights timeline by using your favorite Internet search engine; be sure to use a timeline that goes back at least to 1954. Think about the types of conflict, whether intense or violent, and the kinds of social changes occurring.

Level of Violence

Within a society, the violence of class conflict, as defined by Dahrendorf, is related to three distinct groups of social factors: (1) the technical, political, and social conditions of organization; (2) the effective regulation of conflict within a society; and (3) the level of relative deprivation. Violence is negatively related to the three conditions of organization. In other words, the more a group has met the technical, political, and social conditions of organization, the less likely it is that the conflict will be violent. Remember, we saw this idea in a more basic form with Coser. While some level of organization is necessary for a group to move from quasi- to interest group, the better organized a group is, the more likely it is to have rational goals and to seek reasonable means to achieve those goals.

The violence of a conflict is also negatively related to the presence of legitimate ways of regulating conflict. In other words, the greater the level of formal or informal norms regulating conflict, the greater the probability that both parties will use the norms or judicial paths to resolve the conflict. However, this factor is influenced by two others. In order for the two interested parties to use legitimate roads of conflict resolution, they must recognize the fundamental justice of the cause involved (even if they don't agree on the outcome), and both parties need to be well-organized. In addition, the possibility of violent conflict is positively related to a sense of *relative deprivation*. We reviewed this idea with Coser, but here Dahrendorf is specifying the concept more and linking it explicitly to the level of violence.

Level of Intensity

Within a social system, the level of *conflict intensity* is related to the technical, political, and social conditions of organization; the level of social mobility; and to the way in which power and other scarce resources are distributed in society. Notice that both violence and intensity are related to group organization and the relationship in both cases is negative. The violence and intensity of conflict will tend to go down as groups are better organized—again, for the same reason: Better organization means more rational action.

With Coser, we saw that people will begin to question the legitimacy of the distribution of scarce resources as the desired goods and social positions tend to all go to the same class. Here, Dahrendorf is being more specific and is linking this issue with conflict intensity. The relationship is positive: The more society's scarce resources are bestowed upon a single social category, the greater will be the intensity of the conflict. In this case, the interest groups will see the goals of conflict as more significant and worth more involvement and cost. Finally, the intensity of a conflict is negatively related to social mobility. If an ICA (imperatively coordinated association) sees its ability to achieve society's highly valued goods and positions systematically hampered, then chances are good the group members will see the conflict as worth investing more of themselves in and possibly sustaining greater costs.

In Table 9.1, I've listed the various propositions that Coser and Dahrendorf give us concerning the varying levels of conflict violence and intensity. As you can see, the level of violence tends to go up with increasing levels of emotional involvement, the presence of transcendent goals, and a sense of change from absolute to relative

Table 9.1 Coser and Dahrendorf's Propositions of Conflict Violence and Intensity

Propositions Concerning the Level of Conflict Violence	
↑ Emotional Involvement	↑ Violence
↑ Transcendent Goals	↑ Violence
↑ Sense of Absolute to Relative Deprivation	↑ Violence
↑ Class Organization	↓ Violence
↑ Explicitly Stated Rational Goals	↓ Violence
↑ Normative Regulation of Conflict	↓ Violence
Possible functional effects: greater rapidness of change; stronger group boundaries; greater group solidarity; centralization of power	
Propositions Concerning the Level of Conflict Intensity	
↓ Class Organization	↑ Intensity
↓ Social Mobility	↑ Intensity
↑ Association of Authority and Rewards	↑ Intensity
Possible effects: more profound structural changes	

deprivation. Conversely, the likelihood of violence in conflict tends to go down when the interest groups meet the technical, social, and political conditions of organization (class organization); when they have explicitly stated rational goals; and when there are norms and legal channels available for resolving conflict. As the violence of conflict increases, we can expect social changes to come rapidly and we can anticipate groups to experience stronger boundaries, solidarity, and more efficient control and authority. Only Dahrendorf comments on conflict intensity, and he argues that decreasing class organization and social mobility and increasing covariance of authority and rewards will tend to produce higher levels of intensity, which in turn will produce more profound structural changes.

Regardless of how fast or how dramatically societies change, the changes must be institutionalized. We saw this idea with Parsons. For Dahrendorf (1957/1959), institutionalization occurs within structural changes "involving the personnel of positions of domination in imperatively coordinated associations" (p. 231). What you should notice about this statement is that social change involves changing personnel in ICAs. Remember that ICAs are how Dahrendorf characterizes the basic structure of society. The roles, norms, and values of any social group are enforced through the legitimated power relations found in ICAs. Every ICA contains quasi-groups that are differentiated around the issue of power. ICAs move from quasi-group status to interest groups, and concerns of power move from latent to manifest, as these groups meet the technical, political, and social conditions of group organization. This conflict then brings different levels and rates of change based on its intensity and violence. These changes occur in the structure of ICAs, with different people enforcing different sets of roles, norms, and values, which, in turn, sets up new configurations of power and ICAs. Then this power dialectic starts all over again.

Summary

- Dahrendorf argues that underlying all social order are imperatively coordinated associations (ICA). ICAs are organizational groups based on differential power relations. These ICAs set up latent power interests between those who have it and those who don't. These interests will tend to become manifest when a group meets the technical, political, and social conditions of group organization. Conflict generated between interest groups varies by intensity and violence.

- The intensity of conflict is a negative function of group organization and social mobility, and a positive function of association among the scarce resources within a society. The more intense conflicts are, the more profound are the structural changes.

- The violence of conflict is a negative function of the conditions of group organization and already existing legitimate ways of resolving conflict, and a positive function of relative deprivation. The more violent is the conflict, the quicker structural change occurs.

- Social change involves shifts in the personnel of ICAs. The new personnel impose their own hierarchy of status positions, roles, norms, and values, which sets up another grouping of ICAs and latent power interests.

Emotion and the World in Conflict:
Randall Collins (1941–)

Theorist's Digest
Concepts and Theory: Four Main Points in Conflict
    Sociology
        Scarce Resources and Mobilization
        The Propagation and End of Conflict
Concepts and Theory: Geopolitics
        The Role of the State
        Geopolitical Dynamics
        The Demise of Soviet Russia
Summary

Randall Collins takes us in a different direction from either Coser or Dahrendorf. First, Collins' work of synthesis is broader and more robust. As I've already mentioned, Collins draws not only from the classical conflict theorists, he also uses Durkheim and Erving Goffman (Chapter 12). The inclusion of Durkheim is extremely important. Using Durkheim allows Collins to consider the use of emotion and ritual in conflict. As you'll see, these are important contributions to our understanding of conflict. In talking about Collins' theory, I'm not going to review what Durkheim said about rituals and emotion. So, be sure to bring the information you learned in Chapter 3 into your thinking here. If you need to, please review Durkheim's theory of ritual.

But more than adding new ideas, the scope of Collins' project is much wider. In 1975, Collins published *Conflict Sociology*. His goal in the book was to draw together all that sociologists had learned about conflict and to scientifically state the theories in formal propositions and hypotheses. The end result is a book that contains hundreds of such statements.

Without a doubt, his book represents the most systematic effort ever undertaken to scientifically explain conflict, even to this day. Then, in 1993, Collins reduced the hundreds of theoretical statements from his 1975 work to just "four main points of conflict theory" (1993a, p. 289). Anytime a theorist does something like this, the end statement is theoretically powerful. In essence, what Collins is saying is that most of what we know about conflict can be boiled down to these four points. Collins also takes us further because he considers more macro-level, long-range issues of conflict in a new theoretical domain called "geopolitical theory."

THEORIST'S DIGEST

Brief Biography

Randall Collins was born in Knoxville, Tennessee, on July 29, 1941. His father was part of military intelligence during World War II and then a member of the state department. Collins thus spent a good deal of his early years in Europe. As a teenager, Collins was sent to a New England prep school, afterward studying at Harvard and the University of California, Berkeley, where he encountered the work of Herbert Blumer and Erving Goffman, both professors at Berkeley at the time. Collins completed his PhD at Berkeley in 1969. He has spent time teaching at a number of universities, such as the University of Virginia and the Universities of California at Riverside and San Diego, and has held a number of visiting professorships at Chicago, Harvard, Cambridge, and at various universities in Europe, Japan, and China. He is currently at the University of Pennsylvania.

Central Sociological Questions

Collins has enormous breadth but seems focused on understanding how conflict and stratification work through face-to-face ritualized interactions. Specifically, his passion is to understand how societies are produced, held together, and destroyed through emotionally rather than rationally motivated behaviors.

Simply Stated

In order for conflict to erupt, continue, and be violent or intense, people need to be emotionally and materially invested. As emotional and material resources are exhausted or not renewed, conflict will subside. Collins is specifically concerned with modern nations. Two factors are important: legitimacy and territory. Legitimacy is maintained through Durkheimian rituals, and nations will create or respond to threat in order to achieve and keep legitimacy. Territory limits the geographic reach of a state. When heartland and/or marchland advantages are exceeded, the scope of a nation's power will decrease.

Key Concepts

conflict mobilization, material and emotional resources, resource mobilization, ritualized exchange of atrocities, bureaucratization of conflict, ritual solidarity, geopolitical theory, the state, state legitimacy, heartland advantage, marchland advantage, overexpansion

Concepts and Theory: Four Main Points in Conflict Sociology

Scarce Resources and Mobilization

Point 1: The unequal distribution of each scarce resource produces potential conflict between those who control it and those who don't. Dahrendorf argues that there is one primary resource in society: power. Randall Collins, on the other hand, follows the basic outline that Weber gave us of the three different types of scarce resources: *economic resources,* which may be broadly understood as all material conditions; *power resources,* which are best understood as social positions within control or organizational networks; and status or *cultural resources,* which Collins understands as control over the rituals that produce solidarity and group symbols.

Notice that Collins expands and generalizes two of these resources. Both Marx and Weber saw economic resources in terms of class position; Collins, however, argues that economic resources ought to be seen as encompassing a much broader spectrum of issues—control over any material resources. These may come to us as a consequence of class, but they also may accrue to a person working in an underground social movement through thievery or other illegal means.

Point 2: Potential conflicts become actual conflicts to the degree that opposing groups become mobilized. There are at least two main areas of *resource mobilization:* The first area involves emotional, moral, and symbolic mobilization. The prime ingredient here is collective rituals. This is one of Collins' main contributions to conflict theory. Groups don't simply need material goods to wage a battle; there are also clear emotional and symbolic goods used in conflict. As Durkheim (1912/1995) says, "We become capable to feelings and conduct of which we are incapable when left to our individual resources" (p. 212). Collins uses Durkheim's theory of ritual performance to explain symbolic mobilization. In general, the more a group is able to physically gather together, create boundaries for ritual practice, share a common focus of attention, and have a common emotional mood, the more group members will:

1. Have a strong and explicit sense of group identity

2. Have a worldview that polarizes the world into two camps (in-group and out-group)

3. Be able to perceive their beliefs as morally right

4. Be charged up with the necessary emotional energy to make sacrifices for the group and cause

The second main area for mobilization concerns the material resources for organizing. Material mobilization includes such things as communication and transportation technologies, material and monetary supplies to sustain the members while in conflict, weapons (if the conflict is military), and sheer numbers of people. While this area is pretty obvious, the ability to *mobilize* material resources is a key issue in geopolitical theory.

There are a couple of corollaries or consequences that follow these propositions. If there are two areas of mobilization, then there are two ways in which a party can win or lose a conflict. The first has to do with material resources, which get used up during conflicts. People die; weapons are spent; communication and transportation technologies are used up, break down, or are destroyed; and so on. A conflict outcome, then, is dependent not only upon who has the greatest resources at the beginning of a war, but also upon who can replenish those supplies.

A group can also win by generating higher levels of ritual solidarity as compared to their enemies. Collins gives the example of Martin Luther King Jr. King obviously had fewer material resources than the ruling establishment, but the civil rights movement was able to create higher levels of ritualized energy and was able to generate broad-based symbolic, moral appeal. Of course, a group can also lose the conflict if its members are unable to renew the necessary emotional energies. Emotional energy and all the things that go with it—motivation, feelings of morality, righteous indignation, willingness to sacrifice, group identity, and so on—thus have a decay factor.

Symbols and ideas aren't themselves sacred or moral, nor do they actually "carry" sacredness or morality; they only act as prompts to evoke these emotions in people. It is necessary, then, to renew the collective effervescence associated with the symbol, moral, or group identity. If collective rituals aren't continually performed, people will become discouraged, lose their motivation, entertain alternatives views of meaning and reality, and become incapable of making the necessary sacrifices.

The Propagation and End of Conflict

Point 3: Conflict engenders subsequent conflict. In order to activate a potential conflict, parties must have some sense of moral rightness. Groups have a difficult time waging war simply on utilitarian grounds. They have to have some sense of moral superiority, some reason that extends beyond the control of oil or other material good. As a result, conflicts that are highly mobilized tend to have parties that engage in the *ritualized exchange of atrocities*. Collins calls this the negative face of social solidarity. This is a somewhat difficult subject to illustrate, because if you hold to or believe in one side in a conflict, its definition of atrocities or terrorism will seem morally right. The trick is to see and understand that there has never been a group that has entered into a conflict knowing or feeling that they are wrong. For instance, the people who flew the airplanes into the World Trade Center felt morally justified in doing so.

We can think of many, many examples from around the world, such as the Croats and Serbs and the Irish Catholics and Protestants. And the history of the United States is filled with such illustrations. For example, there is still a debate concerning the reasons and justifiability of the use of nuclear weapons during World War II. Whatever side of the debate people take, it is undeniable that retribution was and is part of the justification. As President Truman (1945a, 1945b) said,

> The Japanese began the war from the air at Pearl Harbor. They have been repaid many fold. And the end is not yet. With this bomb we have now added a new and revolutionary increase in destruction. . . . Having found the bomb we have used it. We have used it against those who attacked us without warning at Pearl Harbor, against those who have starved and beaten and executed American prisoners of war, against those who have abandoned all pretense of obeying international laws of warfare.

In addition to satiating righteous indignation and affirming social solidarity, ritualized retributions are used to garner support. We can see this clearly in the United States' use of the attacks of September 11, Israel's use of the Holocaust, the anti-abortionists' conceptualization of abortion as murder, and various civil rights groups' use of past atrocities. Atrocities thus become a symbolic resource that can be used to sway public opinion and create coalitions.

Point 4: Conflicts diminish as resources for mobilization are used up. Just as there are two main areas of conflict mobilization, there are two fronts where demobilization occurs. For intense conflicts, emotional resources tend to be important in the short run, but in the long run, material resources are the key factors. Many times, the outcome of a war is determined by the relative balance of resources. Randall Collins gives us two corollaries. The first is that milder or sporadic forms of conflict tend to go on for longer periods of time than more intense ones. Fewer resources are used and they are more easily renewed. This is one reason why terrorism and guerilla warfare tend to go on almost indefinitely. Civil rights and relatively peaceful political movements can be carried out for extended periods as well.

The second corollary Collins gives us is that relatively mild forms of conflict tend to deescalate due to the *bureaucratization of conflict*. Bureaucracies are quite good at co-optation. To co-opt means to take something in and make it one's own or make it part of the group, which on the surface might sound like a good thing. But because bureaucracies are value and emotion free, there is a tendency to downplay differences and render them impotent. For example, one of the things that our society has done with race and gender movements is to give them official status in the university. One can now get a degree in race or gender relations. Inequality is something we now study, rather than it being the focus of social movements. In this sense, these movements have been co-opted. "This is one of the unwelcome lessons of the sociology of conflict. The result of conflict is never the utopia envisioned in the moments of intense ideological mobilization; there are hard-won gains, usually embedded in an expanded bureaucratic shell" (Collins, 1993a, p. 296).

The second front where conflicts may be lost is *deescalation of ritual solidarity*. A conflict group must periodically gather to renew or create the emotional energy necessary to sustain a fight. One of the interesting things this implies is that the intensity of conflicts will vary by focus of attention. Conflict that is multifocused will tend not to be able to generate high levels of emotional energy. The conflict over civil rights in the United States is just such a case. The civil rights movement today has splintered because the idea of civil rights isn't held as a universal moral by everyone involved. That is, the groups involved don't focus on civil rights per se; they focus on civil rights for their group. For example, there are those working for the equal rights of African Americans who would deny those same rights to homosexuals.

Concepts and Theory: Geopolitics

There are two things that I want to point out before we consider geopolitical theory. The first is that geopolitical processes happen over the long run. These forces take time to build up and aren't readily apparent, especially to most of us living in the United States. In this country, we have difficulty thinking in the long term. We are focused on the individual and immediate gratification, and even the economic planning that is done is oriented toward short-term portfolio management. Geopolitical theory is sociology over the long term. It explains how nations grow and die. The processes and dynamics can't be seen by just looking at our daily concerns. We have to rise above ourselves and look historically.

The second thing I want to point out is that geopolitical theory focuses on the state rather than the economy. Generally speaking, world-systems theory, like that of Immanuel Wallerstein (Chapter 15), focuses on the economy. Collins understands the world system in more Weberian terms, where the nation-state is the key actor on the world stage. As mentioned earlier, nation-states are relatively recent inventions. Up until the sixteenth century, the world was not organized in terms of nation-states. People were generally organized ethnically with fairly fluid territorial limits, as with feudalism. Feudalistic states were based on land stewardship established through the relation of lord to vassal. Its chief characteristics were homage, the service of tenants under arms and in court, wardship, and forfeiture. A nation-state, on the other hand, is a collective that occupies a specific territory, shares a common history and identity, is based on free labor, and sees its members as sharing a common fate.

The Role of the State

In Weberian terms, *the state* is defined as an entity that exercises a monopoly over the legitimate use of force within and because of a specific geographic territory. First and foremost, nation-states have a monopoly on force. In fact, one of the main impetuses behind the nation is the ability to regularly tax people for the purpose of creating a standing army. Previously, armies were occasional things that were gathered to fight specific wars. A standing army is one that is continually on standby; it is ready to fight at a moment's notice.

Notice that nation-states are organized around the legitimate use of power. Thinking about power in terms of legitimacy brings in cultural and ritual elements. If power is defined as the ability to get people to do what you want, then legitimacy is defined in terms of the *willingness* of people to do what you want. In order for any system of domination to work, people must believe in it. As we saw in Weber's theory, to maintain a system of domination not based on legitimacy costs a great deal in terms of technology, money, and peoplepower. In addition, people generally respond in the long run to the use of coercion by either rebelling or giving up—the end result is thus contrary to the desired goal. Authority and legitimacy, on the other hand, imply the ability to require performance that is based upon the performer's belief in the rightness of the system.

With nation-states, there is an interesting relationship between force and legitimacy. According to Randall Collins (1986c), this legitimacy is a special kind of emotion: It's "the emotion that individuals feel when facing the threat of death in the company of others" (p. 156). Legitimacy isn't something that is the direct result of socialization, though it plays a part. Rather, legitimacy is active; it ebbs and flows and is stronger at some times than at others—people feel more or less patriotic depending on a number of factors, most notably ritual performance.

The governments of nation-states are painfully aware of the active nature of legitimacy. Legitimacy provides the government's right to rule. Though also associated with economic prosperity and mass education, nationalism—the nation-state's particular kind of legitimacy—is dependent upon a common feeling that is most strongly associated with ritualized interactions performed in response to perceived threat. This threat can be internal, as in the case of minority group uprisings, crime, and deviance, but it is most strongly associated with externally produced threat and shock. You will notice that *state legitimacy* comes up again in the next section on critical theory, but from a different perspective.

The other defining feature of the nation-state is the control of a specific geographic territory. One of the reasons that a standing army originally came about was to defend a specific territory. As humans first became settled due to agriculture, it became increasingly necessary to defend the territory and internally organize a population that was growing in both size and diversity. The geographic contours of this territory are extremely important for Collins. Collins (1987) argues that the idea of property "upholds the macroworld as a social structure" (p. 204). The reason behind this is that property is the fundamental backdrop against which all interaction rituals are produced. Further, geographic space is not simply the arena in which interactions take place; it is one of the fundamental elements over which people struggle for control, thus making space a strong ritual focus of attention. Thus, on one level, the explicitness and increased size of the territories associated with nation-states have important implications for the production of interaction ritual chains and macro-level phenomena in general.

Geopolitical Dynamics

Territory is also important because specific geopolitical issues are linked to it. All forms of political organization come and go, including nation-states. Nations are born and nations die. A sociological study in the long run ought to explain—and predict, if it is scientific—the life course of a nation. The geopolitical factors that predict and explain the rise and fall of nations are linked to territory. There are two territorial factors: heartland and marchland advantages. *Heartland advantage* is defined in terms of the size of the territory, which is linked to the level of natural resources and population size. The logic here is simple. Larger and wealthier territories can sustain larger populations that in turn provide the necessary tax base and manpower for a large military. Larger nations can have larger armies and will defeat smaller nations and armies. *Marchland advantage* is defined in terms of a nation's borders: Nation-states with fewer enemies on their immediate borders will be stronger than other nations with more enemies nearby but a similar heartland advantage. Marchland nations are geographically peripheral; they are not centered in the midst of other nations.

Taken together, we can see that larger, more powerful states have a cumulative resource advantage: Nations with both heartland and marchland advantage will tend to grow cumulatively over time, and the neighbors of such nations will tend to diminish. Eventually, as smaller nations are annexed, larger nations confront one another in a "showdown" war, unless a natural barrier exists (such as an ocean). Natural barriers form a buffer between powerful states and will bring a stable balance of power. On the other hand, nations that are geographically central and have multisided borders will tend to experience internal political schisms and conflict that can lead to long-term fragmentation.

The key to geopolitical theory and the demise of heartland/marchland nations is *overexpansion*. A nation can overextend itself materially and culturally. One of the important features of warfare is the cost involved with keeping an army supplied. The further away an army has to go to fight, the greater are the costs involved in transporting goods and services to it. This issue becomes important as the size of the army increases past the point where it can forage or live off the land. A critical point is reached when a nation tries to support an army that is more than one heartland away (if there is another nation or more in between the two warring factions). A nation-state can also overextend itself culturally. Remember that legitimacy is a cultural good. The legitimacy of a nation is strained the farther away it moves from its ethnic base. In other words, there is an increase in the number and extent of tension points the more a nation increases its social diversity. There are more areas of potential disagreement within a diverse population than among a homogeneous population, especially if the other ethnic groups are brought into society through warfare or other measures of forced annexation.

The Demise of Soviet Russia

Randall Collins gives us an example of these geopolitical forces in the case of the USSR. On Christmas day in 1991, the Union of Soviet Socialist Republics officially collapsed. Five years prior, Collins (1986c, pp. 186–209) published a book with a chapter titled "The Future Decline of the Russian Empire." Collins' prediction of the fall of the USSR was based on geopolitical theory. The historical expansion of Russia illustrates these principles of geopolitical theory.

The expansion began with Moscow in the late fourteenth century, a small state with a marchland advantage. Fighting fragmented rivals, Moscow made slow cumulative growth. By 1520, Moscow had annexed all of ethnic Russia. By the late 1700s, Russia had expanded across Siberia and the Southern Steppes and was a strong military power in Europe. Russia further expanded by taking advantage of Napoleon's wars, the fall of the Ottoman Empire, and China's prolonged civil wars—this further expansion was based on geopolitical factors. In the end, the USSR was the largest country on the globe, consisting of 15 soviet socialist republics whose territories reached from the Baltic and Black Seas to the Pacific Ocean, an area of 8,649,512 square miles, 11 time zones, and, most importantly, common boundaries with six European and six Asian countries.

Thinking in terms of geopolitical issues, the problems that faced the USSR are obvious. The nation was overextended both culturally and economically. It no longer held heartland advantage: In terms of total population, the enemies of the USSR outnumbered them 3.5 to 1; and in terms of economic resources, it was 4.6 to 1. In addition, because of its successful expansion, the USSR no longer had a marchland advantage. It had done away with all weak buffer states and only faced powerful enemy nations in all directions. Further, the USSR had to exert military control over its Eastern European satellites, which were two and three times removed from the heartland. All told, it had to defend borders totaling 58,000 kilometers, or over 36,000 miles. What's more, the USSR contained at least 120 different ethnic groups. As Collins (1986c) projected, "If Russia has shifted from a marchland to an interior position, it may be expected that in the long-term future Russia will fragment into successively smaller states" (p. 196).

Summary

- According to Collins, in order for conflict to become overt, people must become mobilized through the material resources for organizing, and they must be emotionally motivated and sustained, feel moral justification, and be symbolically focused and united. Once conflict begins, it tends to reproduce itself through a ritualized exchange of atrocities. The back-and-forth exchange of atrocities reproduces and boosts emotional motivation and moral justification, and it creates further representative symbols for additional ritual performances. After a time, conflicts are won or lost primarily as the two different kinds of resources are gained or lost.

- Nation-states are based on the legitimate use of force and territorial boundaries. Legitimacy is a product of ritual performance. The rituals that produce nationalism, the nation-state's specific form of legitimacy, occur most frequently in response to the perception of threat. Threat can come from outside, as from other nations, or inside, as from social movements. Because nationalism, as with all forms of emotional energy, has a natural decay factor, it is in the government's best interest to keep the perception of threat somewhat high.

- The other defining feature of nation-states is territory, and territory, like legitimacy, carries its own set of influences, specifically heartland and marchland advantages. Heartland advantages concern material resources: natural resources, population size, and tax base. Marchland advantage is an effect of national boundaries and the number and distance from enemy territories. The key variable in geopolitical theory is overexpansion, a condition where a nation overextends its reach materially (supporting armies too far from the heartland) and culturally (controlling too diverse a population).

BUILDING YOUR THEORY TOOLBOX

Learning More—Primary Sources

- Primary source for Lewis Coser:
  - Coser, L. (1956). *The Functions of Social Conflict.* New York: Free Press.
- Primary source for Ralf Dahrendorf:
  - Dahrendorf, R. (1959). *Class and Class Conflict in Industrial Society.* Palo Alto, CA: Stanford University Press.
- Primary sources for Randall Collins:
  - Collins, R. (1975). *Conflict Sociology.* New York: Academic Press.
  - Collins, R. (1993). What Does Conflict Theory Predict About America's Future? *Sociological Perspectives, 36,* 289–313.

Seeing the Social World (knowing the theory)

- Write a 250-word synopsis of the theoretical perspective of postmodernism.
- After reading and understanding this chapter, you should be able to define the following terms theoretically and explain their theoretical importance to conflict theory: *cross-cutting influences; absolute deprivation; relative deprivation; rational and transcendent goals; functional consequences of conflict; internal and external conflict; types of internal conflict; network density; group boundaries; internal solidarity; coalitions; power and authority; imperatively coordinated associations; Hobbesian problem of social order; class; quasi-groups; interest groups; technical conditions; political conditions; social conditions; conflict violence and intensity; conflict mobilization; material and emotional resources; resource mobilization; ritualized exchange of atrocities; bureaucratization of conflict; ritual solidarity; geopolitical theory; state legitimacy; heartland advantage; marchland advantage; overexpansion.*

- After reading and understanding this chapter, you should be able to answer the following questions (remember to answer them *theoretically*):
  - Explain the two basic sources of conflict.
  - Identify the factors that predict the level of violence in conflict and how the level of violence affects the results of conflict.
  - Explain the social factors that influence the level of conflict intensity and how the level of intensity affects the results of conflict.
  - Describe the functional consequences for groups experiencing internal and external conflict.
  - Discuss the social factors that influence the functionality of conflict for internal conflict.
  - Explain the social factors that move an aggregate of people from quasi-group to interest group status.
  - Describe the place that resource mobilization and depletion play in determining the outcome of a conflict.
  - Analyze how conflict engenders further conflict, paying special attention to the place that the ritualized exchange of atrocities has in the process.
  - Evaluate how bureaucracies influence conflict.
  - Explain the role the state plays in geopolitical theory, giving specific attention to heartland and marchland advantages and overexpansion.
  - Analyze the downfall of the Soviet Union in geopolitical terms.

Engaging the Social World (using the theory)

- Consult a daily national newspaper for one week. How many of the reported events would you say qualify as conflictual? Pick two of the most interesting and analyze each using the various ideas we covered with Coser, Dahrendorf, and Collins. Which ideas seem most important? Why? Based on what you've been able to glean from the news, can you make any predictions about the intensity, violence, or consequences of the conflicts? Explain how you used theory to predict the results.

- For a larger project, analyze the U.S. civil rights movement, from the late 1950s through to present times, using our three conflict theorists. Which theories seem to explain the most?

- Choose an on-campus activist group. Find out what their goals and methods are. Using the three theories in this chapter, write a proposal that would help the group achieve its goals.

Weaving the Threads (building theory)

- Compare and contrast the theories in this chapter and their statements of social order with that of Parsons. How can these theories fit together to give a more complete picture about how society is organized?

CHAPTER 10

Structures of Racial and Gender Inequality:

William Julius Wilson and Janet Saltzman Chafetz

I n Chapter 7, we considered some early theories of gender and racial inequalities. You recall that Gilman used evolutionary theory to explain how gender inequality first came to exist, and that Du Bois was centrally concerned with cultural oppression and how it impacts a person's psyche. For the most part, evolutionary theories are rarely used today to understand gender. Most of our theorists have moved to consider how gender inequality is currently working. If we accept Gilman's explanation of its origin, one way to think of Janet Saltzman Chafetz's theory is in response to the question of why and how gender inequality continues. Chafetz's argument is structural: There are structures working at every level of human action and organization that keep women socially disadvantaged. This structural approach implies something very important that I'd like you to keep in mind: In these kinds of theories, *individuals aren't as important as structures.* You'll see this specifically when we get to Chafetz's theory about how gender inequality can change.

While the issue of race and culture is still very much alive (Cornel West's theory is a good illustration), William Julius Wilson approaches race as Chafetz does gender, from a structural point of view, but he gives us a unique and complex way of seeing racial inequality. Obviously, his concern is the oppression of black people in the United States, but to simply see this inequality as a product of racism is too simplistic. There are two components to *racism:* beliefs and practices. A racist belief system assumes that physical, mental, emotional, and behavioral characteristics are genetically inherited, attributes these characteristics to race, and believes that these characteristics are hierarchically valued, privileging one race over another. Racist practices are those that in fact privilege one race over another. It's important to know that these two issues don't necessarily go together. A person may believe racist ideology but never act it out. And actions that privilege one race over another don't necessarily have to be based on racist beliefs. We'll see this distinction with Wilson.

Wilson argues that racism as such, entailing both beliefs and practices, requires a particular kind of structural configuration among the state, the economy, and social relations. Conceptually, this triangle of relations comes from Marx. But Wilson recognizes that the relationship between business and government changes depending on the circumstances, which Marx never saw. Wilson's approach is to first understand the state as a relatively independent actor that can limit capitalism as well as support it. Wilson also questions whether racism is always the causal force in the oppression of blacks. In order to answer that question, Wilson analyzes black inequality in the United States from slavery to the current system.

In the end, Wilson argues that racism (entailing both beliefs and practices) as a causal factor in determining the overall condition of blacks in the United States has been declining in significance since the Civil War. To document the causal force of racism, Wilson tracks the changing relationships between the economy and the state. We'll see that to be effective, racism needs a particular kind of institutional configuration. In its absence, other factors become important for influencing the position of blacks in the United States—in particular, a split labor market and class. As we discuss Wilson's theory, keep in mind that he is not arguing that racism is no longer present or important. Racism is still a problem, but Wilson is pointing out that because of shifts in the relationship between the economy and the state, the *relative importance* of race has declined over time and has been replaced by class-based issues.

Both Wilson and Chafetz are structural theorists and use Karl Marx's theory of the economy as their beginning point. So, if you need review about structures or Marx's theory, please review Chapter 2 for the idea of social structures and Chapter 3 for Marx's explanation of capitalism. Additionally, we covered the perspectives of race and gender in Chapter 7. So, again, review those perspectives so that you can read these theories with the overall perspectives in mind.

The Declining Significance of Race:
William Julius Wilson (1935–)

Theorist's Digest
Concepts and Theory: American Racial History
    The Plantation Economy
    Post–Civil War to New Deal Politics
    World War II and Beyond
Concepts and Theory: Policy Implications
Summary

THEORIST'S DIGEST

Brief Biography

William Julius Wilson was born on December 20, 1935, in Derry Township, Pennsylvania. Wilson attended Wilberforce and Bowling Green Universities before completing his PhD in sociology at Washington State University in 1966. His first professorship was at the University of Massachusetts at Amherst, and he joined the faculty of the University of Chicago in 1972. There he held the position of professor and was the director of the Center for the Study of Urban Inequality. He moved to Harvard in 1996, where he currently holds the Lewis P. and Linda L. Geyser University Professorship. Wilson has received many top honors in his career, including the 1998 National Medal of Science (the highest such honor given in the United States), and he was named by *Time* magazine as one of America's 25 Most Influential People in 1996. He has authored several groundbreaking and significant books including *The Declining Significance of Race, The Truly Disadvantaged,* and *When Work Disappears: The World of the New Urban Poor.*

Central Sociological Questions

Wilson is driven to discover the structural causes of poverty that exist in the United States for African Americans. His interest is fueled by the question of policy—He wants to know how racial inequality works so it can be eradicated. So, his central question is, "What social policies need to be in place to improve the lives of African Americans?"

Simply Stated

Race relations in the United States have gone through three distinct phases: the plantation economy, post–Civil War to late 1930s, and World War II to present day. Because of changes in the relationships among government, capitalists, and workers, each of these phases needs to be understood using different theories: classic Marxian analysis, split labor market theory, and class-based analysis. Wilson (1980) concludes that "economic class is now a more important factor than race in determining job placement for blacks" (p. 120).

Key Ideas

racism, exploitation, split labor market, Jim Crow, postindustrial economy

Concepts and Theory: American Racial History

Wilson divides U.S. history into three economic phases and demonstrates that different theories are best at explaining different kinds of economic, race relations. There's an important insight into theory that we can glean from Wilson's approach. Most theories contain scope conditions; there are very few claims to be a "theory of everything." Scope conditions limit the applicability of any theory, and understanding the scope conditions of a theory is a part of evaluation in critical thinking. Most students understand that scope conditions can be set by topic. So, for example,

Blumer's social psychological theory may not be the best bet for explaining global-ization. But scope conditions can also include issues of time or historical change. In Wilson's case, he uses three different theories—Marx's state-capitalist collusion, split labor market theory, and his own class-state theory—to explain race relations for the three different time periods: pre–Civil War, post–Civil War through the 1930s, and post–World War II.

The Plantation Economy

Marx's theory argues that capitalists as the dominant class use their power to exploit workers and to enlist the state's active support. Modern capitalism is defined by the endless pursuit of capital for its own sake. People have always produced and sold goods, but the purpose of such selling was to earn money to live on. The goal of modern capitalism, however, isn't enough money to live on; nor is it really mak-ing enough money to be rich. Both of those goals can be achieved. But modern cap-italism is insidious in the sense that its goal can never be achieved. The goal is to acquire capital in order to invest; profit from the investment is reinvested in order to make more capital. This is why modern capitalism is restless, always creating new products and markets.

The fundamental source of profit and capital is exploitation. **Exploitation** is the difference between what a worker produces and what a worker is paid. Capitalists must pay workers less than they earn, and they will always gravitate to the lowest possible wage. The key here is for you to see that the very nature of modern capi-talism drives exploitation; and because the drive for capital has no natural limit, the drive for exploitation is just as limitless. Using race as a key in exploitation gave cap-italists a group of workers they could exploit without limit, a group that had no power: "There is a chance for exploitation on an immense scale for inordinate profit . . . This chance lies in the exploitation of darker peoples" (Du Bois, 1920/1996, pp. 504–505). With the invention of chattel slavery, capitalism changed blacks into commodities, and commodities have no power over their owners what-soever. But notice that this type of exploitation is based on cooperation with the state. The state must support the capitalists' claim that certain racial groups have no civil rights.

In this model the state and economy are in collusion to exploit the worker. Wilson argues that Marx's theory is best for explaining the racial-caste system that worked under the American plantation economy, at least in the South. This type of non-manufacturing agrarian society is characterized by a simple division of labor and a small aristocracy. In such a society, there is very little if any job market com-petition. During this period in the southern United States, working whites were either craftsmen or serfs, and blacks were generally held as slaves. Additionally, in a plantation economy there is a vast distance between the upper and lower classes. Because of this distance, there is little contact between classes, and what contact does happen is highly ritualized and subject to strong social norms of manners and etiquette. These conditions result in little to no class conflict, with the white work-ers having "little opportunity to challenge the control of the aristocracy" (Wilson, 1980, p. 13).

In such systems of production, the aristocracy dominates both economic and political life. In the United States, the white, landed elite were able to secure laws and policies extremely favorable to their economic interests, and they were able to propagate a ruling ideology concerning the differences between the races. As in classic Marxian thought, the system of production and the state formed a mutually reinforcing cycle. As a result, "the system of slavery severely restricted black vertical and horizontal mobility" (Wilson, 1980, p. 24) and race relations with elite whites took the form of paternalism (the care and control of subordinates as a father). An important issue to notice is *who benefits from the system:* In this case, it's the capitalist class.

Post–Civil War to New Deal Politics

After the U. S. Civil War, the industrialization of the economy grew quickly and the southern economy in particular expanded rapidly. In addition, the Thirteenth and Fourteenth Amendments to the Constitution abolished slavery and granted civil rights to the black population. As a result, from the latter part of the nineteenth century through the 1930s, there were massive changes in the system of production and race relations. This period marks a shift from race relations based on a paternal racial-caste system to a more class-based labor market. In the South, economic expansion greatly increased the political power of the white working class. Blacks were freed but had very little economic or political power. White workers, then, attempted to control the newly available skilled and unskilled positions. The outcome was an elaborate system of *Jim Crow* segregation that was reinforced with a strong ideology of biological racism. The name "Jim Crow" doesn't refer to an actual person but to the stereotypical characterization of blacks in minstrel shows at the time. The idea of Jim Crow segregation references the laws that many states enacted after the Civil War in order to control blacks and preserve white privilege. Jim Crow segregation generally benefited the higher-paid white working class by keeping blacks out of the competition for jobs, especially in the South.

The North experienced a different configuration. Due to high levels of migration of blacks from the South and high immigration rates of European whites, blacks most often entered the job market as strikebreakers. White workers would strike for better wages or working conditions and management would bring in black workers to keep production going. In some cases, management would preempt a strike by hiring black workers on permanently. This move obviously created high tension between black and white workers, which culminated in a number of race riots in 1917 and 1919. The Great Depression of the 1930s shifted things considerably for both black and white workers in the North. During the Depression, there was a strong movement toward unionizing. The unions themselves began to recruit black workers. As a result, black antagonism toward the unions was reduced; black and white workers saw themselves as united in their stand for economic reforms; and the practice of employers using blacks as strikebreakers was eliminated.

Wilson argues that race relations in this time period are best explained using *split labor market theory.* This theory assumes that after slavery business would support a free and open market where all laborers compete against one another regardless of race. This kind of competition would result in an overall higher level of exploitation because capitalists could pit blacks against whites. In addition, split labor theory proposes three key classes, rather than the two of orthodox Marxian theory: the capital business class, higher-paid labor, and cheaper labor. Understanding that there is another interest in the labor market besides capitalists, and knowing that capitalists would benefit from an open rather than restricted job market, we see that segregation benefited the white working class rather than capitalists.

The emphasis in this theory is on how the market for labor splits and who benefits. The labor market refers to any collective of workers vying for the same or similar positions within a capitalistic economy. A labor market splits when there are two or more social groups whose price for the same work is different, one being cheaper than the other. The price difference is primarily based on dissimilar resource levels, determined by economic and political resources and the availability of information. That is, if there is an ethnic or racial group within a labor market whose standard of living is significantly lower, who lacks the ability to politically organize, and who is less informed about labor market conditions, then the labor market will split. The important thing to see here is that when a market splits, it is more beneficial to higher-paid workers than to business owners. According to this theory, free and open competition would displace the higher-paid workforce and result in lower wages and higher exploitation generally.

Race, then, became a tool of the higher-paid working class to preserve their own economic interests. The white higher-paid working class promoted racist ideologies and discriminatory practices in order to monopolize skilled labor and management positions, prevent blacks from obtaining necessary skills and education, and deny blacks political resources. Thus, while race was still an issue, it originated with white workers rather than collusion between capitalists and the state. Also notice that class became increasingly important during this time. Labor markets are primarily split over class, not race. Race, then, became a marker for class antagonisms rather than for racism itself.

World War II and Beyond

Before describing this time period, I want us to be clear about Wilson's theoretical argument. It's a structural argument, which means that structural arrangements determine social relations. For Marx, the driving structure is the economy: The means of production determine the relations of production. As we've seen, Wilson adds an independent state to this theory. What this implies about Marx's notion of the means and relations of production is that it isn't just the economy that structures social relationships: The interrelations between the state and economy will structure our social relationships, in this case race relations and black inequality. Wilson argues that the role of the state is continuing to change from the classic Marxian model. World War II brought a ban on discrimination in defense and government agencies. This move also provided for on-the-job training for blacks. Black workforce participation continued to expand under the equal employment legislation of the 1950s and 1960s and growing affirmative action programs.

These changes obviously didn't come as a result of the government's desire for equality, but in response to civil rights movements, which also boosted black political involvement. But regardless of the source, the state took successive steps to address black inequality.

In addition, the trend toward industrialization that began in the North prior to the Civil War expanded geographically and exponentially from the 1940s onward. This facilitated a shift in the black population toward urbanization, away from rural, agricultural settings and low-paying farm jobs and to cities and industries with better-paying jobs. A large black population thus began to develop in urban centers which, in turn, prompted the growth of black business owners and black professionals oriented toward serving the needs of the growing black community. As a result of affirmative action and these economic and population shifts, more and more businesses were seeking black employees. For example, during the 10-year period between 1960 and 1970, the average number of corporate recruitment visits to traditionally black colleges jumped from 4 to 297; in some southern colleges, the number rose from zero to 600 corporate visits. During this time, there was also a jump in the percentage of blacks working in government jobs, rising from 13% to almost 22%, and the overall percentage of black males in white-collar positions rose from 16% to 24% (Wilson, 1980, pp. 88–109).

However, the United States began to noticeably shift toward a *postindustrial economy* beginning in the 1970s. This move away from manufacturing and toward service- and knowledge-based goods brought the decentralization of U.S. businesses, further expansion in government and corporate sectors, and demographic shifts from urban to suburban settings (sometimes referred to as "white flight"). These economic and population changes created a situation in which city tax resources either declined or increased at slower than necessary rates. At the same time, and due to the same social factors, cities experienced a sharp increase in expenditures. This situation obviously creates problems for municipal services, such as public assistance and urban schools.

The picture that Wilson gives us of the time following World War II involves two push–pull forces. On the one hand, political and economic opportunities for blacks increased dramatically. Through the 1930s, 1940s, and 1950s, the black working class experienced increasing opportunities and urbanization, which at the time was a positive move. On the other hand, from the 1970s on, there was the decentralization of American business, decreases in manufacturing and increases in government and corporate jobs, and white flight from urban to suburban settings. These overlapping yet opposing forces fragmented the black labor force and resulted in "vastly different mobility opportunities for different groups in the black population" (Wilson, 1980, p. 121).

Those African Americans who were already moving toward the middle class were poised to take advantage of the economic and political shifts. They continued to experience upward mobility and "unprecedented job opportunities in the corporate and government sectors" (Wilson, 1980, p. 121). These middle-class blacks, like their white counterparts, have been able to move to more affluent neighborhoods. The other segment of the black labor force, however, has become locked into the cycle of inner-city problems: declining city revenues in the face of increasing social needs. These are "the relatively poorly trained blacks of the inner city, including the growing number of younger blacks emerging from inferior ghetto schools" (Wilson, 1980, p. 121) who are locked into low-paying jobs with high turnover rates and little hope of advancement.

Wilson wants us to see that race, as it was used in previous times, is a declining factor in predicting the economic and political success of blacks in the United States. Again, this is a proportional evaluation. Race still matters, but class distinctions within the black population have greater impact on black opportunities than does race itself. Prior to the mid-1960s, studies indicated that "race was so much of a dominant factor that very little of black economic achievement was determined by class background" (Wilson, 1980, p. 167). Since that time, those blacks already "in the system" have continued to experience occupational and salary gains. "For those blacks who are not in the system, however, who have not entered the mainstream of the American labor market, the severe problems of low income, unemployment, underemployment, and the decline in labor-force participation remain" (Wilson, 1980, p. 171). It is thus the class positions prior to the 1960s and 1970s that currently oppress poor and working-class blacks rather than race itself.

In addition, Wilson argues that the character of racial strife has changed. Previous to this time period, racial tensions focused on the economy. From the Civil War through the civil rights era, racial tensions revolved around granting blacks equal access to economic opportunities. Since the segmentation of the black labor pool, racial tensions have shifted to the sociopolitical order. The actors are the same—blacks and the white working class—"but the issues now have more to do with racial control of residential areas, schools, municipal political systems, and recreational areas than with the control of jobs" (Wilson, 1980, p. 121).

Concepts and Theory: Policy Implications

Wilson's basic conclusion is that concern for racial equality needs to move from a focus on race to a focus on class. In other words, policies pointed at creating a tight labor market will go further toward improving the overall condition of blacks in the United States today than will laws aimed at ending racial discrimination. The differences between a tight and a slack labor market basically revolve around the level of employment. In a tight labor market, there are a high number of job openings relative to the labor pool. In other words, those who want to work can work. High employment/low unemployment rates mean that it is a worker's market: Workers have choices of positions; wages are high; and unemployment, when it does occur, is relatively short. On the other hand, a slack labor market means that there are more workers than positions (unemployment is high). This is a capitalist's market: Business owners have their choice of workers, wages are low, and unemployment is chronic.

Unfortunately, in recent times the United States has moved away from "using public policy as a means to fight social inequality" and instead has placed emphasis "on personal responsibility, not inequalities in the larger society" (Wilson, 1996–1997, pp. 569–570). For example, in the year 2000, low-income programs made up 21% of the federal budget but constituted 67% of the spending cuts.

In order to combat this trend, Wilson is acting to galvanize both private and public support for creating national performance standards for schools. Wilson specifically cites other capitalist democracies that have national policies that emphasize critical and higher-order thinking skills. Along with this emphasis on national standards, Wilson argues that national policy should provide the kind of support needed by inner-city and disadvantaged neighborhood schools to meet such standards. Currently, the unequal funding of schools produces what Jonathon Kozol (1991) refers to as "savage inequalities."

Wilson also advocates improving the family support system in the United States. Currently, the United States is the only modernized country that does not provide universal preschool, child support, and parental leave programs—much-needed support structures in the face of changes in the family and the social structures surrounding it. Along with this support for the changing family structure, Wilson argues that the United States needs to do a better job at linking families, schools, and work. Currently, U.S. firms take five years longer than other developed nations to hire high school graduates. Where in Germany and Japan students are hired directly out of high school, typically the larger firms in the United States don't hire high school graduates until they have reached their mid-twenties.

Unfortunately, we don't have the space to review all of Wilson's proposals. Wilson has fully documented his policy concerns in *When Work Disappears: The World of the New Urban Poor* (1997), and I encourage you to read it. But from what was just discussed, you can see that Wilson has shifted the discourse concerning the plight of black Americans from one that focuses specifically on race to one that emphasizes class. I want to point out that Wilson's conclusions are based on his ability to use different theories in diverse contexts. Explanations of social injustice aren't as simple as most of us think, and this is becoming truer the more our society and economy become globalized. Having a number of theories at our disposal and possessing the flexibility of mind to use them creatively will go a long way in enabling us to see, explain, and impact the social world around us.

Wilson shows us that our very best efforts at ending racial inequality should be vitally concerned with and aimed at improving the class opportunities of Americans as a whole, especially as we move into a postindustrial, globalized economy. While these efforts would alleviate the economic suffering of many people,

> Their most important contribution would be their effect on the children of the ghetto, who would be able to anticipate a future of economic mobility and share the hopes and aspirations that so many of their fellow citizens experience as part of the American way of life. (Wilson, 1997, p. 238)

Summary

- Wilson considers three different theories in explaining race relations in the United States: Marxist elite theory, which sees complicity between elite capitalists and the state; split labor market theory, which calls attention to the different resource levels of diverse class positions; and Wilson's own class–state theory.

Wilson's theory argues that economic and race relations are based on changing configurations among the state, economy, and class relations. Further, Wilson argues that racism requires a specific kind of relationship between economic elite and polity that was most purely found in the plantation South.

- Using these three different theories, Wilson examines three periods of American race relations: pre– and early post–Civil War, the latter 1800s to the 1930s, and the period from World War II on. Race relations within each of these periods is best explained by different theories: Marxist elite theory best explains the racism prevalent in pre– and post–Civil War America; split labor market theory explains the class growth period up until the Great Depression of the 1930s; and Wilson's class-state theory describes current race relations. Wilson's conclusion is that over time there has been a declining significance of race in explaining the position of African Americans.

- Based on his analysis, Wilson proposes a number of policy changes aimed at improving the overall welfare of the American worker, which, in turn, will improve the conditions of African Americans.

Structures of Gender Inequality:
Janet Saltzman Chafetz (1942–2006)

Theorist's Digest
Concepts and Theory: Coercive Structures of Gender
    Inequality
        Macro-Level Coercive Structures
        Meso-Level Coercive Structures
        Micro- and Personal-Level Coercive Structures
        The Structure of Gender Inequality
Concepts and Theory: Changing Gender Inequality
        Unintentional Change
        Intentional Change
Summary

While Gilman is interested in explaining how gender inequality came about, Chafetz is interested in explaining how social structures maintain gender inequality in modern societies. Her theory is particularly powerful because she theorizes at four structural levels, and she brings her theory full circle. Sociologists tend to think about society on four levels: macro, meso, micro, and individual. Macro level analysis is of the institutions and structures that form the largest factors and processes that make up society; meso phenomena are at the level of the organization; micro level phenomena are those that occur in face-to-face interactions; and individual analysis is of the person. In addition to hitting all four levels, Chafetz explains how gender inequality works—how gender stratification is patterned over time—and uses the same theoretical elements to explain how gender disparity can be changed. Thus Chafetz' is perhaps the most comprehensive structural explanation of gender stratification.

THEORIST'S DIGEST

Brief Biography

Janet Saltzman Chafetz was born in Montclair, New Jersey, in 1942. She received her BA in history from Cornell University and her MA in history from the University of Connecticut. While at the University of Connecticut, she began graduate studies in sociology and completed her PhD at the University of Texas at Austin. Chafetz served as president of Sociologists for Women in Society (SWS), 1984–1986, and as chairperson of the American Sociological Association (ASA) Theory Section, 1998–1999. Chafetz was also honored as the first invited lecturer for the Cheryl Allyn Miller Endowed Lectureship Series, sponsored by SWS; her book *Gender Equity* won the American Educational Studies Association Critic's Choice Panel Award (1990) and was selected by *Choice Magazine* for their list, Outstanding Academic Books (1990–1991). Chafetz was Professor of Sociology at the University of Houston and had recently been working on immigrant and transnational religion. Professor Chafetz passed away July 6, 2006, after a seven-year struggle with cancer.

Central Sociological Questions

Chafetz is a positivist seeking to understand and facilitate change in the system of gender inequality. She approaches gender inequality like a scientist would approach disease. In order to eradicate a disease the laboratory researcher must first understand how it works. Understanding how it works can lead to targeted methods of cure rather than trial-and-error shots in the dark. As Chafetz (1990) says, "in practical terms, a better understanding of how change occurs…could contribute to the development by activists of better strategies to produce change" (p. 100).

Simply Stated

Gender inequality is replicated by four different levels of structure: macro, meso, micro, and individual. The chief structuring agent is the gendered division of labor in the economy—proportionately there are fewer women than men in the economy, and women who do work have significantly less power, prestige, and pay associated with their jobs than do men who do the same work. This pattern of workforce participation creates organizational structures that reduce women's opportunities for advancement and their relative numbers, as well as ghettoizing women in positions with little power. These three issues work collectively to create a sense of learned helplessness, which in turn produce practices that affirm gender stereotypes. Because women have fewer economic resources, when they marry they are in an unequal exchange relation. In order to balance the exchange, women offer compliance and

(Continued)

(Continued)

deference to men; men use this power to control women's access to work and to gender the household division of labor. Boys and girls raised in such a home learn that they are rewarded when they perform according to gender stereotypes and punished when they do not. Additionally, the fact that the man is little involved in the home and parenting sets up dynamics that form gendered intrapsychic structures, which then provide the basis for women continuing to "choose" to be oppressed by believing in and replicating the very actions that produce gender inequality, most notably the choices associated with workforce participation.

Key Ideas

feminism, social structure, levels of analysis, women's workforce participation, organizational variables (career path, organizational power, relative numbers), social exchange, micro-power, gender definitions, legitimation, intrapsychic structures, social learning, gendered impression management, unintentional and intentional forces of change

Concepts and Theory: Coercive Structures of Gender Inequality

Macro-Level Coercive Structures

Chafetz's primary orientation for the macro-level structural features of gender stratification comes from Marxian feminist theory. The basic orientation here is that patriarchy and capitalism work together to maintain the oppression of women. And the central dynamic in the theory is *women's workforce participation*. Marx argued that social structure sets the conditions of social intercourse. In this sense, society itself has an objective existence and it thus strongly influences human behavior. More than that, social change occurs because of structural change. In Marx's theory, the economic structure itself contains dynamics that push history along. In general, Chafetz draws from Marx's emphasis on the economy as the most important site for social stability and change. She also explores his ideas about the way capitalism works.

Capitalism requires a group who controls the means of production as well as a group that is exploited. This basic social relationship is what allows capitalists to create profit. Patriarchy provides both: men who control the means of production and profit and women who provide cheap and often free labor. That latter part is particularly important. Much of what women do in our society is done for free. No wages are paid for the wife's domestic labor—this work constitutes the unpaid labor force of capitalism. Without this labor, capitalism would crumble. Paying women for caring for children and domestic work would significantly reduce profit margins and the capitalists' ability to accumulate capital. In addition, the man's ability to fully work is dependent upon the woman's exploitation as a woman as well. When women are allowed in the workforce, they tend to be kept in menial positions or given lower wages for the same work as men. Please notice: Chafetz is arguing that gender inequality is driven by the structural need of capitalism.

Because of the importance of women's cheap and free labor to the capitalist system, elite males formulate and preach a patriarchic ideology that gives society a basis for believing in the rightness of women's primary call to childrearing and domestic labor. Elite men also use their structural power to disadvantage women's workforce participation. For example, in the United States, elite males have been able to systematically block most attempts at passing national comparable worth amendments or laws that would guarantee equal pay for equal work.

In brief, Chafetz argues that the greater the workforce participation of women, particularly in high-paying jobs, the less the structure of inequality is able to be maintained. The inverse is true as well: The less workforce involvement on the part of women, the greater the inequality on all levels. Thus, the type and level of their involvement in the workforce (macro) play out at both the meso and micro levels. Though we've framed our discussion in terms of capitalism, Chafetz notes that since humans began to farm and herd animals, men have disproportionately controlled the means of production and its surplus. Throughout time, men have been slow to give up their economic positions.

Meso-Level Coercive Structures

To explicate the dynamics that sustain gender inequality at the meso level, Chafetz cites Rosabeth Kanter's (1977) work on organizations. Kanter gives us a social-psychological argument where the structural position of the person influences her or his psychological states and behaviors. Kanter points to three factors related to occupational position that influence work and gender in this way: the possibility of advancement, the power to achieve goals, and the relative number of a specific type of person within the position. Each of these factors in turn influences the individual's attitudes and work performance—or what we could call his or her organizational personality.

The Possibility of Advancement

Most positions in an organization fall within a specific career path for advancement. The path for a professor, for example, goes from assistant, to associate, to full professor. The position of dean doesn't fall within that path. A professor could aspire to become dean, but she would have to change her career trajectory. Kanter argues that women typically occupy positions within an organization that have limited paths for advancement. We can think of the occupational path for women as constricted in two ways: (1) The opportunities for advancement in feminized occupations, such as administrative assistant or secretary, are limited by the nature of the position, and (2) women who are on a professional career path more often than not run into a glass ceiling that hinders their progress.

The Power to Achieve Goals

Positions also have different levels of power associated with them. Again, this is a feature of the location within the organization, not of the individual. For example, if you were in my theory class, I would have you write theory journals. Most of my students do the journals because I tell them to. But my authority to assign work doesn't have anything to do with me; it's a quality of the position. If there were another person in my position, the students would do what he or she told them. Please note that this power is different than the power that comes out of exchanges between men and women in long-term relations (see below). Again, women typically hold positions with less power attached to them than do men. Clearly, there are some women who transcend this situation. But women who are in positions of power are typically seen as "tokens," because there are no similar others in those positions within the company (Kanter's third organizational variable).

Relative Numbers

One of the things within organizations that facilitates upward mobility is the relative number of a social type within a position. Imagine being a white male and reporting to work on your first day. You're given a tour of the facilities. As you are introduced to different people in the company, you notice that almost all the positions of power are held by black men. Most of the offices are occupied by black men, and most of the important decisions are made by black men. There are whites at this place of employment, but they almost all hold menial jobs. By and large they are the secretaries and assistants and frontline workers. Being white, how would you gauge your chances for advancement at such a firm? Further, imagine that after the end of your first week, you notice that there are two or three whites who seem to hold important positions. Would the presence of a few whites in management change your perception? It isn't likely. Though we like to talk as if individuals are the only things that matter, in fact, humans respond more readily to social types than to individual figures. That's why the few minorities that do make it up the corporate ladder are seen as tokens—exceptions to the rule—rather than as any real hope that things are changing.

As I've pointed out, these qualities are attributes of the position more than the person. This issue is important for Kanter's argument because social contexts influence individuals and their attitudes and behaviors. Positions that are similar in the organization produce similar contexts for people that most importantly include power and opportunity. These contexts influence the way the incumbents—the people that occupy the position—think and act. In situations where power is available and the gates in the organizational flow lines are open, people develop a sense of efficacy. They feel empowered to control their destiny within the organization, and they behave in a "take charge" manner. The reverse is true as well. People in positions where there are few opportunities and where power is limited are much less certain about showing positively aggressive behaviors. They feel ineffectual and limited in what they can achieve within the organization.

These issues are true for any who occupy these different positions. Humans are intimately connected to their context. Our social environment always influences who we are and how we act. The problem in organizations is that women are systematically excluded from positions of power and opportunity. As a result, they experience and manifest a self that corresponds to the position, one that feels and behaves ineffectual and limited. Though these differences in behavior and attitude are linked to organizational position, people generally attribute them to the person. Thus, women who occupy positions that have little power or hope of advancement demonstrate powerlessness and passivity. These attitudes and behaviors are then used to reinforce negative stereotypes of gender and work, which, in turn, are used to reinforce gender inequality within the organization.

I've modeled the relationships we've talked about so far in Figure 10.1. Follow the arrows and think through the relationships—remember, these are theoretical relationships and speak of the direction of the relationships. So, signs on the arrows (paths of effects) may not mean what you think at first. The negative sign (−) means that the relationship is inverse. That is, if one variable goes up, the other will go down (and the inverse is true as well). The positive sign (+) means that the relationship is positive and both variables move in the same direction, either up or down. To get you started, let's look at part of one of the paths. The path from the level of capitalist exploitation to women's workforce participation is marked with a negative sign. This means as exploitation goes up, women's presence in the job market goes down. As women's workforce participation goes down, the three organizational variables (career path, power, relative numbers) all go down as well. Keep working through the model until you understand the relationships.

Micro- and Personal-Level Coercive Structures

Before we begin this section, I want to point out that even though we are talking about the micro level, Chafetz is talking about structures that have the power of coercion. This is important to keep in mind because many micro-level theories are oriented toward choice and agency. Chafetz talks about those issues in the section on voluntaristic gender inequality, but for now we are considering how gender inequality is a structural force at the micro level. Chafetz uses exchange theory to begin to explicate coercive processes at the micro level (see Chapter 6).

Gendered Social Exchanges

Exchange theory argues that people gravitate toward equal exchanges. Both partners in an exchange need to feel they are getting as much as they are giving. If an exchange isn't balanced, if one of the participants has more resources than the other, the person who has less will balance the exchange by offering compliance and deference. Because everyone has access to his or her own behaviors and abilities, compliance and deference are generalized goods. What that means is that they can be offered in exchange for almost anything else (because they are the one thing that everyone has). According to exchange theory, this is the source of power in social relationships.

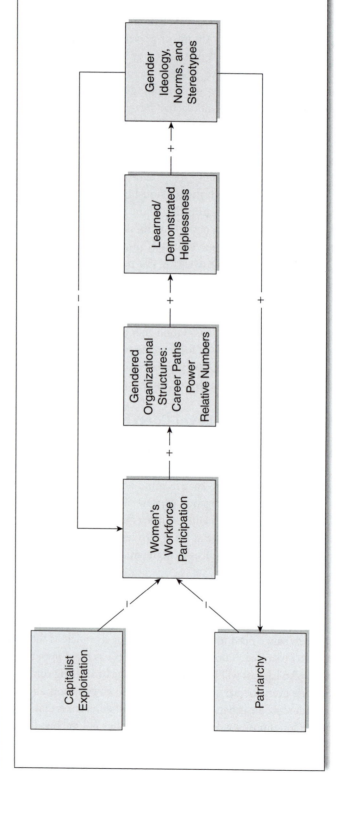

Figure 10.1 Macro–Meso Dynamics of Gender Inequality

Exchange theory also makes a distinction between economic and **social exchanges**. Economic exchanges are governed by explicit agreements, often in the form of contracts. The particulars of the exchange are well known in advance, and there is a discernable end to the exchange. For example, if you are buying a car on credit, you know exactly how much you have to pay every month and when the payments will stop. You know when your debt is paid off. However, in social exchanges the terms of the exchange cannot be clearly stated or given in advance. Imagine a situation where a friend of yours invites you over for dinner and tells you when and how you will be expected to repay. Chances are you wouldn't go to dinner because the other individual broke the norms that make an exchange social. Thus, social exchange is implicit rather than explicit and it is never clear when a debt has been paid in full.

Chafetz argues that these two issues together create a coercive micro structure that perpetuates gender inequality for women. Because of their systematic exclusion from specific workforce participation, women typically come into intimate relationships with fewer resources than men in terms of power, status, and class. The imbalance is offset by the woman offering deference and compliance to the man. This arrangement gives the man *micro-power* within the relationship. The man's power in this exchange relationship is insidious precisely because it is based on social exchange. As we've seen, social exchanges are characterized by implicit agreements rather than explicit ones, with no clear payoff date or marker. While insidious, this micro power is variable. Generally speaking, the more the economic structure favors men in the division of labor, the greater will be a man's material resources relative to the woman's, and the greater will be his micro-level power. The inverse is also true: "The higher the ratio of women's material resource contribution to men's, the less the deference/compliance of wives to their husbands" (Chafetz, 1990, p. 48).

The greater power that men typically have is used in a variety of ways. One common way is in relation to household work. Much of the work around the home, especially in caring for the young, is dull, repetitive, and dirty. Men typically choose the kinds of tasks that they will do around the home, as well as the level of work they contribute. Thus, men usually do more of the occasional work rather than repetitive work, such as mowing the lawn or fixing the car rather than the daily tasks of doing dishes or changing diapers. Men can also use their power to decide whether or not women work out of the home and to influence what kinds of occupations their wives take. Because women in unbalanced resource relations bear the greater workload responsibility for the children and home, they are restricted to jobs that can provide flexible hours and close proximity to home and school.

I've modeled the micro level variables in Figure 10.2. Notice that I've also taken the liberty of placing the different issues in voluntaristic gender inequality in the model as well. As you can see from the model, the micro level variables are all driven by the level of women's workforce participation and their subsequent ability to participate in equal exchanges with their life partner. This is precisely what you would expect from a theory that begins with Marx's idea that economic relations are the things that ultimately drive everything else in society. Again, follow the direction of the relationships. The relationship between equality in exchange and

Figure 10.2   Micro-Level Dynamics of Gender Inequality

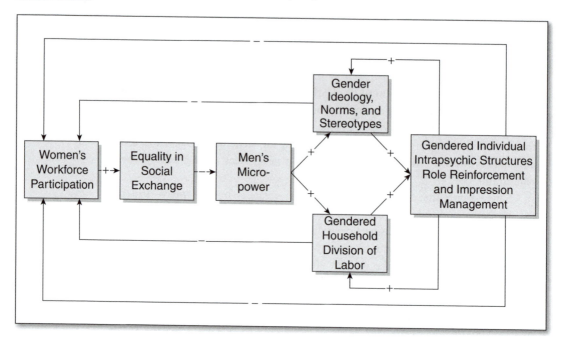

men's micro power is negative, which means the more the exchange is equal, the less micro power men will have. And, obviously, the reverse is true. In an unequal exchange relation, women offer deference and compliance and men use their micro power to control gender ideologies, norms, and stereotypes, as well as the gendered household division of labor. Controlling those decreases women's workforce participation (shown by the feedback arrows) and increases the level that individuals are socialized into gender specific practices and tend to see and experience themselves as gendered individuals.

Voluntaristic Gender Inequality

As we noted before, gender inequality usually functions without coercion. This implies that women cooperate in their own oppression. More exactly, "people of both genders tend to make choices that conform to the dictates of the gender system status quo" (Chafetz, 1990, p. 64). Chafetz refers to this as voluntaristic action; but, as we'll see, some of these behaviors and attitudes are unthinkingly expressed and so aren't "voluntary" in the sense of chosen. The patterns that support gender inequality are latently maintained; they are quiet and hidden.

The reason for this kind of maintenance is simple, and it is how society works in general: We simply believe in the culture that supports our social structures. Max Weber pointed this out many years ago. Every structural system is sustained through legitimation, whether it is a system of inequality or the most egalitarian organization imaginable, and legitimation provides the moral basis for power—it gives us reasons to believe in the right to rule. Part of the way legitimation works has to do with the place culture has in human existence: Culture works for humans as instinct does for animals. Another important reason for the significance of legitimation is that coercive power is simply too expensive, in terms of costs of surveillance and enforcement, to use on anything but an occasional basis.

Thus, Chafetz argues that much of what sustains the system of gender inequality is voluntarism. Both men and women continue to freely make choices and display behaviors that are stereotypically gendered. There are three types of *gender definitions* that go into creating gendered voluntaristic action: gender ideology, norms, and stereotypes. These three types vary by the level of social consensus and the extent to which gender differences are assumed. Chafetz draws on three theoretical traditions to explain these issues: Freudian psychodynamic theory; social learning theory; and theories of everyday life, including symbolic interactionism, ethnomethodology, and dramaturgy.

Intrapsychic Structures

Nancy Chodorow's work (1978) forms the basis of Chafetz's psychodynamic theory. Chodorow argues that men's and women's psyches are structured differently due to dissimilar childhood experiences. The principle difference is that the majority of parenting is given by the mother with an absent father. Before we talk too much about Chodorow's theory, we need to make sure we understand the idea of psychic structure, or, more specifically, *intrapsychic structure*. The idea comes from Freud who argues that the psychic energy of an individual gets divided up into three parts: the id, the ego, and the superego. These three areas exist as structures in the obdurate sense. They are hard and inflexible and produce boundaries between the different internal elements of the person. Thus, when we are talking about intrapsychic structures, we mean the parts of the inner person that are fixed and divided off from one another. It's almost like we're talking about the structure of the brain. The "intra" part of intrapsychic structures refers to how these three parts are internally related to each other. Thus, Chodorow's, and Chafetz's, argument is that the internal workings of boys and girls are structurally different—their intrapsychic structures are gendered.

Both boys and girls grow up with their chief emotional attachment being with their mother. Girls are able to learn their gender identity from their mothers, but boys have to sever their emotional attachment to their mother in order to learn their gender identity. The problem, of course, is that the father has historically been absent. His principle orientation is to work, a situation that was exacerbated through industrialization and the shift of work from the agricultural home to the factory. Girls' intrapsychic structure, then, is one that is built around consistency and relatedness—they don't have to break away to learn gender and their social network is organically based in their mother. Women, then, value relationships and are intrapyschically oriented toward feelings, caring, and nurturing. Boys have to separate from their mother in order to learn gender, but there isn't a clear model for them to attach to and emulate. More exactly, the model they have is "absence."

The male psyche, then, is one that is disconnected from others, values and understands individuality, is more comfortable with objective things than relational emotions, and has and values strong ego boundaries. According to Freud, this male psyche also develops a fear and hatred of women (misogyny)—as the boy tries to break away from his mother, she continues to parent because of the absent father. The boy unconsciously perceives her continued efforts to "mother" as attempts to smother his masculinity under an avalanche of femininity. He thus feels threatened and fights back against all that is feminine.

Remember, these differences between males and females are dissimilarities in the structure of their psyches. This is a much stronger statement than saying that boys and girls are socialized differently. Intrapsychic structures are at the core of each person, according to Freudian theory, and much of what happens at this level is unconscious. Chafetz isn't necessarily saying that men consciously fear or hate women—it's much deeper than that. It is at the core of their being. But also keep in mind that these structures vary according to the kind of parenting configuration a child has. It's very possible today for a boy to be raised principally by the father while the mother works (though our economic structure makes this unlikely), or for a single father to raise a child. The intrapsychic structure of such a boy would be dramatically different than those raised in a situation where maleness is defined by absence and separation.

These intrapsychic differences play themselves out not only in male/female relationship but also in the kinds of jobs men and women are drawn to. Generally, then, men are drawn to the kinds of positions that demand individualism, objectification, and control. Women, on the other hand, are drawn to helping occupations where they can nurture and support. While there have certainly been changes in occupational distribution over the past 30 years, most of the stereotypically gendered fields continue to have disproportionate representation. Thus, for example, while there are more male primary school teachers and nurses today than 30 years ago, the majority continue to be women, and while there are more women who are CEOs, construction workers, and politicians today, those fields continue to be dominated by men. The important point that Chafetz is bringing out here is that the "personal preference" individuals feel to be in one kind of occupation rather than another is strongly informed by gendered intrapsychic structures. These personal choices, then, "voluntarily" perpetuate gender structures of inequality.

Gendered Social Learning

Chafetz also draws on socialization theories such as social learning to explain the voluntaristic choices men and women make. The important components of *social learning theory* come to us from Albert Bandura (1977). Bandura argues that learning through experimentation is costly and therefore people tend to learn through modeling. For example, it's much easier to learn that fire is hot by the way others act around it than by sticking your hand in it. Social learning occurs through four stages: attention, retention, motor reproduction, and motivation.

Children pay attention to those models of behavior that seem to be the most distinctive, prevalent, or emotionally invested or have functional value. And they retain those models through symbolic encoding and cognitive organization, as well as rehearsing the behaviors symbolically and physically. Motor reproduction refers to acting out the behaviors in front of others. Further motivation to repeat behaviors comes through rewards and positive reinforcement. Children are discouraged from repeating inappropriate behaviors through punishment and negative reinforcement. Eventually, children negatively or positively reinforce their own behaviors—as adults we thus self-sanction most of our gendered behaviors.

Gendered Impression Management

Theories of everyday life look at how people produce social order at the level of the interaction and manage their self-identities. Chafetz specifically draws on Erving Goffman's (1977) work on gender. Goffman argues that selves are hidden and the only way others know the kind of self we are claiming is by the cues we send out. Others read these cues, attribute the kind of self that is claimed, and then form righteously imputed expectations. People expect us to live up to the social self we claim. If we don't, that part of our self will be discredited and stigmatized.

Because gender is arguably the very first categorization that we make of people—one of the first things we "see" about someone is whether the person claims to be male or female—gender is thus an extremely important part of impression management and self-validation. As such, Goffman (1959) would see gender as a form of idealized performance in that we "incorporate and exemplify the officially accredited values of the society" (p. 35). In other words, social norms, ideologies, and stereotypes are used more strongly in gendered performances than in most others. Goffman also sees idealization as referencing a part of the "sacred center of the common values of the society" (p. 36) and this kind of performance as a ritual.

Thus, gender is an especially meaningful and risky performance that is produced in almost every situation. We tend to pay particular attention to the cues we give out about our gender and the cues others present. Goffman further points out that we look to the opposite gender to affirm our managed impression. Our gendered performances then are specifically targeted to the opposite sex and tend to be highly stereotypical. According to Chafetz (1990), "For men, this quest [for affirmation] entails demonstrations of strength and competence. However, for women it entails demonstrations of weakness, vulnerability, and ineptitude" (p. 26).

The Structure of Gender Inequality

In Figure 10.3, I've placed our two models together to give us a complete picture of how gender inequality is structured. It's extremely important that you think through each of the relationships keeping in mind two things. First, notice the direction of the relationship. The reason this is important is that Chafetz is going to tell us how to change gender inequality. Good theories explain how something works and in doing so they also explain how to change something. If this model depicts a good theory of gender stratification, then changing it involves working within the theoretical relationships that it gives us. The second thing I want you to

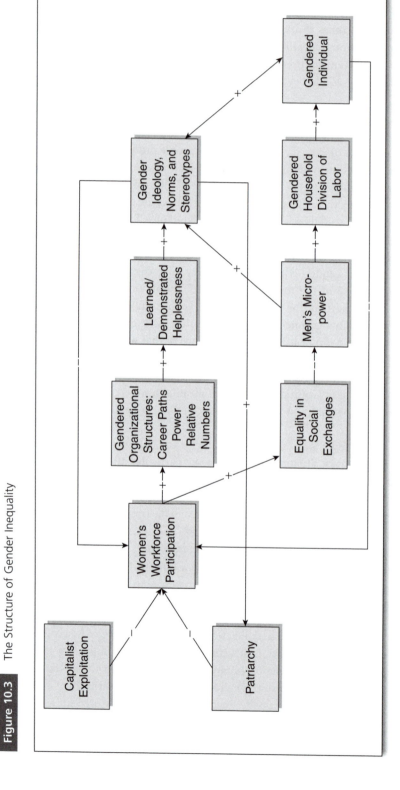

Figure 10.3   The Structure of Gender Inequality

think through is why or how each of the variables influences the others. Knowing that the gendered division of labor in the household has a positive relationship to gendered individuals is good, but it isn't enough. What is it about gendered household chores that impacts intrapsychic structures, role reinforcement, and impression management? So, a good, theorist will know both the direction and the reasons for the relationship.

Concepts and Theory: Changing Gender Inequality

To begin this section, we should note that Chafetz argues that structural rather than cultural changes are necessary to bring about gender equality. As we will see throughout this book, sociologists give different weights to culture and structure. Some argue that culture is an extremely important and independent variable within society; others claim that culture simply reinforces structure and that structure is the most important feature of society. Chafetz falls into the latter camp. While voluntaristic processes, which are associated in one way or another with culture, are the key way gender inequality is sustained, "substantial and lasting change must flow 'downward' from the macro to the micro levels" (Chafetz, 1990, p. 108).

Unintentional Change

Like her understanding of gender stability, Chafetz divides her theory of gender change into unintentional and intentional processes. Quite a bit of the change regarding the roles of women in society has been the result of unintended consequences. Another way to put this is that the bulk of changes in the gender system of inequality happen for structural reasons, not because people willingly and intentionally want to change things. For example, the moves from hunter-gather to horticulture to agrarian economies were motivated by advances in knowledge and technology. But these moves also produced the first forms of gender inequality, as men came to protect the land (which gave them weapons and power) and to control economic surplus through inheritance and the control of sexual reproduction (women's bodies). The intent behind technological advancement wasn't gender inequality; the intent was first survival and then to make life less burdensome. But in the end, economic developments produced gender inequality.

In explicating the unintended change processes, Chafetz is interested in what she terms the demand side. She argues that quite a bit of work on gender focuses on the supply side, which concentrates on the general attributes of women. For example, contemporary women tend to have fewer children, to be better educated, and to marry later than in previous generations. These supply side attributes may influence what kinds of women become involved in the economy, but they "do not determine the rate of women's participation" (Chafetz, 1990, p. 122). For example, a woman may have a master's level education, but unless there is a structural demand for this quality, she will remain unemployed. In addition, Chafetz assumes gender stability in theorizing about change. This means that males are the default to occupy a given position in the economy. The bottom line here is that "*as long as there are a sufficient number of working-age men available to meet the demand for the work they traditionally perform, no change in the gender division of labor will occur"* (p. 125, emphasis original). Thus, what we are looking for are structural demands that outrun the supply of male labor.

Chafetz identifies four different kinds of processes that can unintentionally produce changes in the structure of gender inequality: population growth or decline, changes in the sex ratio of the population, and technological innovations and changes in the economic structure. The processes and their effects are listed here:

- *Population changes:* If the number of jobs that need to be filled remains constant, then the greater the growth in the working age population, the lower will be women's workforce participation. The inverse is true as well: As the size of the working population declines, women will gain greater access to traditionally male jobs, if the number of jobs remains constant.
- *Sex ratio changes:* The sex ratio of a population, the number of males relative to the number of females, tends to change under conditions of war and migration. If in the long run there is a reduction in the sex ratio (more women than men) of a population, women will gain access to higher paying and more prestigious work roles. Conversely, if there is an increase in the sex ratio, the restrictions on women's workforce participation will tend to increase.
- *Economic and technological changes:* There are two general features of men's and women's bodies that can influence women's workforce participation: Men on average tend to be stronger than women, and women carry, deliver, and nurse babies. When technological innovations alter strength, mobility, and length of employment requirements, then there are possibilities for gender change in those jobs. Women will tend to gain employment if new technologies reduce strength, mobility, and time requirements. In addition to work requirements, technology can also change the structure of the job market. As the economy expands due to technological innovations, women will tend to achieve greater workforce participation (holding population growth constant). On the other hand, if the economy contracts for whatever reason, women will tend to lose resource-generating work roles.

Intentional Change

In addition to unintentional change processes, Chafetz argues that there are specific ways in which people can act that help to address gender inequality. But before we get into those processes, we need to note that Chafetz maintains that gender change is particularly difficult for two reasons. First, women have more cross-cutting influences than any other group. Think about it this way: Almost every social group is gendered. This means that women are black, white, Chicano, Baptist, Buddhist, Jewish, pagan, homosexual, bisexual, heterosexual, homeless, professional, and so on. Women thus "differ extensively on all social variables except gender" (Chafetz, 1990, p. 170). These cross-cutting group affiliations make it extremely difficult to form a woman's ideology that doesn't cut across or offend some of the women the ideology is trying to embrace. The second issue is that women, unlike many disenfranchised groups, do not live in segregated neighborhoods. Chafetz argues that this reduces women's political clout because they are "dispersed throughout all electoral districts" (p. 171). Because of these difficulties, gender change may occur more slowly or diffusely than other types of change.

I've placed Chafetz's addition intentional change factors into the model we've developed thus far (see Figure 10.4). Again, I want you to think through the relationships both in terms of direction and influence (What specifically does this factor accomplish?). You'll notice that the initial variables (capitalism and patriarchy) have been replaced with macro level variables. Chafetz's approach to gender is similar to the way Karl Marx saw the production of class consciousness. According to Marxian theory, structure leads social change. Class consciousness is necessary for social change but it is produced as dialectical elements of the economic structure, such as increasingly disruptive business cycles and overproduction, play themselves out. For Marx, it is the structure that pushes people together and gives them the ability to see their oppression, communicate with one another, and mount the resistance that will lead to the demise of capitalism.

The macro-structural changes that Chafetz focuses on are *industrialization, urbanization,* and *the size of the middle class.* Chafetz claims that historically almost all women's movements have been led by middle-class women. These women are among the first to experience gender consciousness due to the effects of industrialization and urbanization. Industrialization initiates a large number of social changes such as increases in urbanization, commodification, the use of money and markets, worker education, transportation and communication technologies, and so forth. These all work together to expand the size of the middle class. The importance of this expansion isn't simply that there are more middle-class people; it also means that there are more middle-class jobs available. Many of these are nondomestic jobs that may be filled by women.

Industrialization thus structurally creates workforce demands that women can fill. Women are more likely to be called upon to fill these roles when the number of males is kept fairly constant or at least the number doesn't increase at the same rate as the demand for labor. The more rapid the growth of industrialization and urbanization, the more likely the demand for labor will outpace the supply of men. As women increase their workforce participation, they increase their level of material and political resources as well, thus decreasing males' relative micro power and the level of gender differentiation, as well as weakening gender stereotypes, ideologies, and normative expectations (gender social definitions). In addition, as women's resources and thus their micro power increase, they are more able to influence the household division of labor and men's contribution to familial and domestic work; and, as men contribute more to domestic and familial work, women are more able to gain resources through workforce participation. So far what we've talked about all fits with the model in Figure 10.4. It's the structural changes that put into motion the possibility of successful social movements.

In addition to influencing these micro-level issues, industrialization, urbanization, and women's increased workforce participation do two other things: They

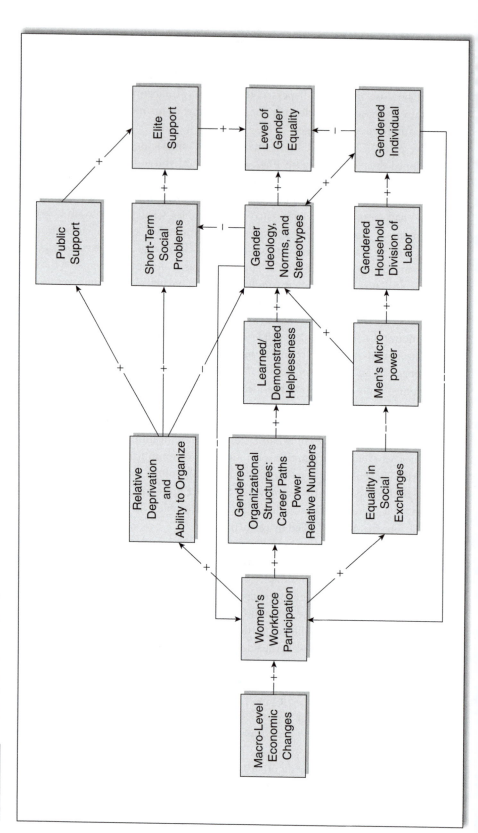

Figure 10.4 Reducing Gender Inequality

increase women's experience of relative deprivation and the number of women's social contacts. While absolute deprivation implies uncertain survival, relative deprivation is a subjective, comparative sense of being disadvantaged. Social movements are extremely unlikely with groups that experience absolute deprivation. They have neither the will nor the resources to organize political movements. *Relative deprivation,* on the other hand, implies a group that has resources and experiences rising expectations. Thus, women who are newly moving into the workforce will tend to experience relative deprivation. They will begin to see that their salaries are not comparable to men's, and they will begin to accumulate resources that can potentially be used to become politically active.

Urbanization and industrialization also increase a group's ability to organize. Ralf Dahrendorf (1957/1959) talked about this ability to organize as the principal difference between quasi-groups and interest groups. Quasi-groups are those collectives that have latent identical role interests; they are people that hold the same structural position and thus have similar interests but do not experience a sense of "belongingness." Interest groups, on the other hand, "have a structure, a form of organization, a program or goal, and a personnel of members" (p. 180).

The interest group's identity and sense of belonging are produced when people have the ability to communicate, recruit members, form leadership, and create a unifying ideology. Urbanization and industrialization structurally increase the probability that these conditions of interest group membership will be met. Women living and working in technically advanced urban settings are more likely to come into contact with like others who are experiencing relative deprivation and the status and role dilemmas that come from women working a *double workday.*

As women begin to organize and as traditional gender definitions become weakened, public support for change is likely to arise. Chafetz argues that a significant portion of what women's movements have been able to achieve is related to articulated critical gender ideologies and radical feminist goals. While the public may not buy into a radical ideology or its set of goals, the ideologies and goals of women's movements will tend to justify gender change more broadly. This support, along with pressure from short-term social problems and a direct effect from women's workforce participation, place pressure upon elites to create laws, policies, and programs to help alleviate the unequal distribution of scarce resources by gender.

Let's pause a moment and talk about *short-term social problems.* Chafetz argues that as a result of women having and using greater levels of resources, short-term social problems are likely to arise. Chafetz uses the term "social problem" in a general sense to indicate the challenges that society at large have to overcome anytime significant change occurs. In other words, change to the social system brings a kind of disequilibrium that has to be solved so that actions and interactions can once again be patterned. Such social problems tend to accompany any type of social change as a society adjusts culturally and socially. In the case of gender, the short-term problems are related to women having greater levels of resources and thus higher levels of independence and power. Examples of these kinds of problems include increases in the divorce rate and women's demands for control over their own bodies. Social disruptions such as these tend to motivate elite support of women's rights in order to restore social order.

Sociologists have learned that every social movement eventually requires support from the elite. *The elite* not only pass laws and oversee their enforcement, they can also lend other material or political support, such as money and social capital (networks of people in powerful positions). The first way elites show up is in the way we have been talking about so far. Elites create new or support already established laws that help bring social order. In this case, the support comes mostly because elites perceive some form of social disorder. In other words, "they may perceive that basic problems faced by their society, which negatively affect large numbers of people and may possibly jeopardize their incumbency in elite roles, are exacerbated by a gender system that devalues and disadvantages women" (Chafetz, 1990, p. 152). This kind of change may be incremental and not specifically associated with women's movements. Elite may also support women's movements as women are perceived as a political resource.

Summary

- In general, Chafetz argues that workforce participation and control over material resources both stabilize and change a system of gender inequality. Gender inequality is perpetuated when women's participation in the workforce is restricted and reduced when women are allowed to work and control material resources.

- Chafetz argues that gender is stabilized more through voluntaristic actions rather than the use of coercive power. When men control the division of labor in society, they are able to exercise authority at the meso level through assuring male incumbency in elite positions and at the micro level through women's exchange of deference and compliance for material resources. Men thus control gender social definitions that set up engenderment processes: psychodynamic structuring, gender socialization, and the idealized expression of gender through impression management and interaction. Engenderment and wifely compliance work in turn to solidify women's exclusion from the workforce, to impose double duty upon those women who do work, to stabilize the unequal distribution of opportunities and resources, and to define negative worker attributes for women but positive ones for men.

- Gender inequality is reduced as women are allowed greater participation in the workforce and increased control over material resources. These factors decrease women's reliance upon men and men's authority over women. Men then contribute more to domestic and familial work, which further frees women to participate in the workforce and weakens gender stereotypes, norms, and ideologies. In addition, women's access to resource-generating work roles increases the probability of women's political movements, which along with weakened gender definitions positively impacts public opinion and elite support for women. Short-term social issues that come about because of women's increased workforce participation also impact elite support, as well as the elite's desire to consolidate or gain political power. Gender stratification is reduced as women move into the workforce and control more material resources, as elites support women's rights and legislation, and as men's micro resource power is reduced and their domestic contribution increased.

BUILDING YOUR THEORY TOOLBOX

Learning More—Primary and Secondary Sources

- Primary sources for William Julius Wilson:
  - Wilson, W. J. (1980). *The Declining Significance of Race* (2nd ed.). Chicago: University of Chicago Press.
  - Wilson, W. J. (1987). *The Truly Disadvantaged.* Chicago: University of Chicago Press.
  - Wilson, W. J. (1997). *When Work Disappears.* New York: Vintage.

- Primary sources for Janet Saltzman Chafetz:
  - Chafetz, J. (1990). *Gender Equity: An Integrated Theory of Stability and Change.* Newbury Park, CA: Sage.
  - Chafetz is also the editor of the excellent *Handbook of the Sociology of Gender,* Kluwer/Plenum, 1999.
  - In 1993, Chafetz joined Rae Lesser Blumberg, Scott Coltrane, Randall Collins, and Jonathan Turner to produce a synthesized theory of gender stratification. This is their rare and powerful effort: "Toward an Integrated Theory of Gender Stratification," *Sociological Perspectives, 36,* 185–216.

Seeing the Social World (knowing the theory)

- Write a 250-word synopsis of the exchange theory perspective.
- After reading and understanding this chapter, you should be able to define the following terms theoretically and explain their theoretical importance to Wilson's theory of racial and class inequality: *social structure, racism, exploitation, split labor market, Jim Crow, postindustrial economy.*
- After reading and understanding this chapter, you should be able to define the following terms theoretically and explain their theoretical importance to Chafetz's theory of gender inequality: *feminism, social structure, levels of analysis, women's workforce participation, organizational variables (career path, organizational power, relative numbers), social exchange, micro-power, gender definitions, legitimation, intrapsychic structures, social learning, gendered impression management, unintentional and intentional forces of change.*
- After reading and understanding this chapter, you should be able to answer the following questions (remember to answer them *theoretically*):
  - Compare and contrast Marxian elite theory, split labor market theory, and Wilson's class–state theory.
  - Explain Wilson's three periods of American race relations and use Marxian elite theory, split labor market theory, and Wilson's class–state theory to analyze the different periods. In other words, you should be able to demonstrate, using Wilson's theory, that class is becoming more important in race relations than race itself.

(Continued)

(Continued)

- Explain why the workforce of women is so important to Chafetz's theory.
- Explain how exchange processes work to produce gender inequalities. How do men use their micro power to their gendered advantage?.
- Explain the differences between the intrapsychic structures of boys and girls. Explain how they are created and how they influence gender inequality.
- Explain how social learning theory and dramaturgy contribute to our understanding of how gender inequality is voluntaristically reproduced.
- Explain how gender inequality unintentionally changes.
- Tell which two characteristics of gender, according to Chafetz, make change difficult. (Be sure to explain them fully.)
- Explain how women's movements form and how they influence changes in gender inequality. What does this tell us about social movements in general?.

Engaging the Social World (using the theory)

- Using your favorite Internet search engine, type in "African American policy." Thoroughly review at least three sites. Would you say that the information and thrust of the sites are in keeping with Wilson's analysis and policy implications? In not, why do you think that is? If so, which policies do you think will have the greatest impact on structural inequality? How can you get involved in promoting this or other policy changes?

- Consult at least four reliable Internet sources to learn about the "separation of spheres." What is it and how does it figure into Chafetz's theory? List at least six ways that this historical, structural issue influences your life.

- Using your favorite search engine, type in "global gender inequality." Based on information from at least three different societies, prepare a report on the state of gender inequality in these diverse countries. Also, compare and contrast these societies with the one you live in. How applicable do you think Chafetz's theory would be in those other three societies?

- Volunteer at a local women's shelter or resource center.

CHAPTER 11

Exchange Theory:

George Homans, Peter Blau, and Randall Collins

O ne of the social domains that we are most familiar with is the one that we experience every time we talk to or encounter another person. So far we've seen that we symbolically interact (Chapter 6) and we've seen that social action is surrounded by norms, values, and beliefs that both enable and constrain what we do (Chapter 8). In this chapter we'll see that there's even more going on: We're involved in exchanges. This idea of social exchange was always implied in modernity. It began with *utilitarianism,* an eighteenth-century philosophy that came out of the Age of Enlightenment's concern with human happiness and scientific calculation. The principles of utilitarianism were most clearly stated by Jeremy Bentham (1789/1996, pp. 11–16), who argued that happiness and unhappiness are based on the two sovereign masters of nature: pleasure and pain. The "utility" in utilitarianism refers to those things that are useful for bringing pleasure and thus happiness. Bentham developed the *felicific* or *utility calculus,* a way of calculating the amount of happiness that any specific action is likely to bring. The calculus had seven variables: intensity, duration, certainty/uncertainty, propinquity/ remoteness, fecundity, purity, and extent. Exchange theory, then, is naturally part of the shift from traditional to modern society. It specifically addresses the idea of the reasoning actor, and it takes seriously the process of rationalization that Weber explains (Chapter 4).

This chapter is important for a couple of other reasons as well. First, it gives us a way of thinking about what's called the micro-macro link. This issue is one that is obvious in contemporary theory yet virtually unknown in classical theory. For some time, sociologists have thought about macro-level phenomena and micro-level interactions separately. In some ways, the two different domains seemed to discount one another. Micro-level theorists such as George Herbert Mead saw social institutions more in terms of symbols and ways of thinking and behaving, with their importance and influence emerging out of interactions. On the other hand, structuralists such as Émile Durkheim saw social facts as being created by other social facts or institutions. Eventually, sociologists began to see a theoretical issue here. If there are two separate fields—face-to-face interactions and social structures—then how are they related? Parsons gave us one answer through the idea of institutionalization. In this chapter, we will get two other answers to this problem, one from Blau and the other from Collins.

The second reason it's important is that it gives us another theoretical explanation about how power develops in social relations. Weber thought about power, especially in its relationship to authority. And power is obviously a concern with conflict theory (Chapter 9). But there it's more of an issue of inequality and is by and large seen as existing in the structures and organizations of society. Here we'll see how power evolves as an outcome of the exchanges we make between one another on a daily basis. This idea, especially as it is explained by Blau, forms a basis on which Janet Saltzman Chafetz explains gender inequality (Chapter 10).

Elementary Forms of Social Behavior:
George Homans (1910–1989)

Theorist's Digest
Concepts and Theory: Basic Principles of Behavioral
    Psychology
       Secondary Propositions
Summary

George Homans very clearly sees his theory as a corrective to Parsons. In his Presidential Address to the 1964 annual meeting of the American Sociological Association he characterizes the question of Parsons' theory as "the most general intellectual issue in sociology" (Homans, 1964, p. 809). He characterizes structural-functionalism as making its beginning point the study of norms, its empirical interest the interrelationships of roles and institutions, and being more concerned with the consequences (functions) rather than the causes of institutions. Homans' first point is, perhaps, the most obvious and in his mind the most detrimental; it is captured in the title of his address: "Bringing men back in" (today we would say "bringing people back in"). If you look at the characterizations of Parsons' theory, you'll see his point—there are no people in structural-functionalism.

Homans' (1964) second point is that Parsons' theory isn't theoretical in the scientific sense: "If sociology is to be a science, it must take seriously [the job] of providing explanations for the empirical relations it discovers" (p. 818). You'll remember from Chapter 1 that positivistic theory is to explain how something works or came into existence. In order to do that, it must contain relationships between concepts. As Homans (1961) puts it, "No explanation without propositions!" (p. 10). I invite you to go back and quickly look over Parsons' theory in Chapter 8. If you do, you'll see Homans' point. Parsons gives us an analytical scheme, a set of concepts that can be used as a perspective to describe what is happening. You won't find any statements of relationship.

Homans' interest and intent, however, is very similar to Parsons. He wants to explain how social behaviors are patterned over time. To do this he starts in a similar way as Parsons. You recall that Parsons got down to what in his mind at least was the most basic piece of society: action. And he proceeded to describe how action takes place within a unit of voluntaristic action. Homans wants to bring people back in and so he looks at what happens between two people in social encounters. What Homans sees is that behaviors that are rewarded are the ones that are repeated; repeated, patterned behaviors are what we're concerned with in the problem of social order. Then, in order to explain how rewards work to pattern behaviors, he turns to psychological behaviorism, which provides him with a set of propositions that explain the conditions under which a person is likely to repeat behaviors. Before we consider the theory, I want to point out one thing. Homans is usually categorized as an exchange theorist, and that isn't quite accurate. While there is a back and forth exchange-like movement between two people, the focus of the theory and the dynamic that produces patterns is more on the individual than the relationship. It's important in any theory to see where the driving force is located, and for Homans it's the individual. This becomes clear when Homans talks about a situation becoming a stimulus for behavior, rather than the exchange relation.

THEORIST'S DIGEST

Brief Biography

George Homans was born August 11, 1910, in Boston, Massachusetts, and was a true Bostonian, as his mother was a descendant of President John Adams. Homans graduated from Harvard University in 1932 with a degree in English Literature. Homans never earned a doctorate and came to sociology by accident, having collaborated on a sociological paper.

(Continued)

(Continued)

Homans taught at Harvard between 1939 and 1971, when he retired; he served in the navy during World War II. His two most important books are the *Human Group* (1950) and *Social Behavior: Its Elementary Forms* (1961). Homans served as president of the American Sociological Association in 1964. Of Homans' work, Jonathan Turner (1991) says he was "one of the most prominent theorists of this century" (p. 303). Homans died on May 29, 1989.

Central Sociological Questions

Homans (1961) was interested in what he called *elementary social behavior,* which "occurs at all times and never lacks form" (p. 4). The form that he was interested in wasn't located in social structures or rules but, rather, in the person. He was interested in social order, like Parsons, yet did not look to either institutions or even situations for understanding how it comes about. Homans defined social behavior in terms of specific relationships of one person to another; specifically, when a person acts toward another he or she must be rewarded or punished by that person and not by a third party. So, in a manner similar to Parsons and Blumer, Homans reduced action down to what he felt were its basic elements. To phrase it as a question: What are the fundamental elements of social behavior?

Simply Stated

The basic social relationship is one through which people learn how to socially behave toward another. The drive behind this relationship is the desire to receive rewards and avoid punishments. Social behavior will tend to be patterned when it is repeatedly reinforced with high value rewards. The situations where the behaviors and rewards occur can themselves become valuable to people, thus allowing for long chains of patterned actions. However, if a reward is given too often, it will lose value; and if an expectation of reward isn't forthcoming, the person will become angry and aggressive.

Key Ideas

elementary social behavior, respondent behaviors, respondent conditioning, law of effect, reinforcement, matching law, stimulus proposition, value, success proposition, value proposition, deprivation-satiation proposition, frustration-aggression proposition

Concepts and Theory: Basic Principles of Behavioral Psychology

The basic tenets of behavioral psychology that Homans (1987) lays out are, first, the *law of effect.* Behavioral psychology makes a distinction between respondent and operant behaviors. *Respondent behaviors* are those that are automatic and occur by simple application of a stimulus; we often talk about these as knee-jerk reactions. The source of such behaviors is genetic and the result of natural selection. These, then, are fixed action patterns. The classic example is Pavlov's dogs. Dogs salivating when presented with food is a natural association between stimulus (food) and response (salivation)—this is respondent behavior. Pavlov created an unnatural association between the presenting of food and a ringing bell, paired stimuli. After Pavlov repeated this association enough times, the dogs would salivate in response to the bell alone. The dog's response to the bell was conditioned—the process through which the connection was made is called *respondent conditioning* (or sometimes classical conditioning). I've diagramed these relationships in Figure 11.1.

Operant behaviors, on the other hand, are those where a connection is made between stimulus and behavior that isn't there naturally. Rather than some part of the environment acting as a stimulus for behavior, as with the natural association between food and salivation, the behaviors first *operate on the environment,* hence the name operant conditioning. All animals, including people, have general drives or needs, such as the drive for sex or food. The strength of these drives differs by species and individuals. So, for example, one person's sex drive may be stronger than another. When one of these drives is unfulfilled, the animal/person becomes

Figure 11.1   Respondent Conditioning

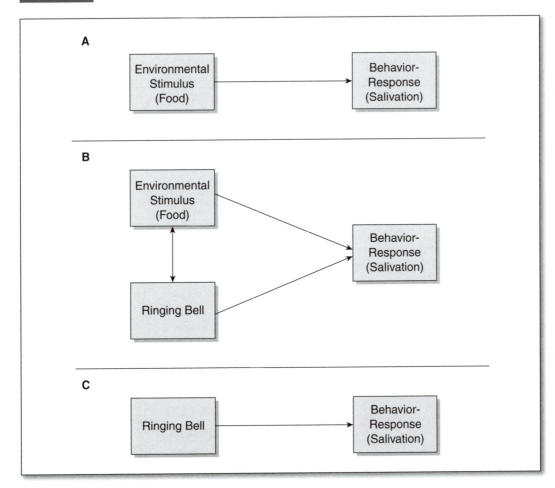

agitated and moves about "exploring and investigating its environment" (Homans, 1987, p. 59). Eventually this directionless activity hits upon something that satisfies a drive. The behavior has provoked a response in the environment. *Reinforcement* occurs, then, as the link between behavior and stimulus is strengthened in such a way as to increase the probability of the behavior occurring again. Homans calls this the *stimulus proposition*.

As just described this reinforcement of the behavior is happenstance. However, the association can also be intentional. The fundamental idea behind operant conditioning is that learning is based on consequences. Animals and people learn things that they associate with positive rewards. The goal is to either increase or decrease the frequency of the behavior. Positive responses increase the frequency and negative responses decrease the frequency; to be effective, the response or reinforcer must follow the response quickly and be clearly contingent on the response. So a professor may want you to contribute to class discussion. He or she could figure out a reward (positive reinforcement) that would be given the first time you spoke up. The more frequently this association is made, the more likely you are to contribute. The trick here of course is that the reward has to offset whatever negative reinforcement you may associate with speaking up in class, like embarrassment or peer sanctions. This relationship is depicted in "A" of Figure 11.2.

Figure 11.2   Operant Conditioning

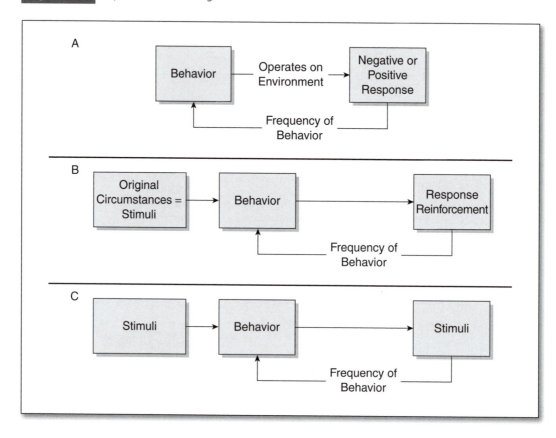

Further, the original circumstances (the "environment" in Figure 11.2 A) may become a stimulus to behavior. This is what you see in Figure 11.2 "B." Thus in our above example as you speak up in class and get rewarded repeatedly, simply being in class will act as a stimulus and prompt your behavior. The next step is that the stimulus itself can become its own reward. It our example simply being in class becomes rewarding in and of itself. This is depicted in "C" of Figure 11.2.

Homans (1987) talks about this as the *matching law* and is "of the greatest importance for the understanding of human behavior" (p. 61). There are two reasons for this importance. First, humans are able to link together long chains of stimuli → response patterns. If you think about this for a moment, you'll probably see that this is yet another answer to Parsons' problem of social order. These long chains create patterns of behavior, all based on operant conditioning. The second reason this law is important for understanding people is that it allows Homans to introduce a new variable: value. *Value* here is understood as the degrees of reward a stimulus provides. Adding this variable allows Homans to describe two factors that determine how often a person will perform one action over others when confronted with choices.

The first factor is the *success proposition* and is based on relative frequency of reward. If you're faced with five different sets of behaviors you have to choose from and one of them has been more consistent in giving rewards than the others, you will more likely choose the consistently rewarded behavior. The second factor that determines choice is value, and Homans naturally calls this the *value proposition*. The more highly valued a particular result, the more likely a person is to perform that action. Using our class example for both of these, if I give you a choice between working in small groups verses a class discussion and you have consistently received rewards in class discussion but not small group work, you will tend to choose class discussion more consistently. If, on the other hand, you still get embarrassed in class despite my best efforts and you don't in small group work, then avoiding embarrassment has greater value for you and you will tend to choose small group work more frequently. Note that I just introduced a new idea: cost. Homans (1958) calls this "adverse stimulation"—avoiding adverse stimulation is its own reward (p. 589).

Taking these together, Homans comes up with a rationality principle. In choosing between alternate actions, people take into account the probability of obtaining a particular reward times the value of the reward (Value X Probability = Action). Notice that the relationship is multiplicative, which basically means they reinforce one another. However, and this is a point Homans specifically wants to make, this rationality principle only holds in the moment. What this means is that you may make a decision today that in two years looks really dumb. So, Homans (1987) holds this idea of rationality lightly and actually sees *the idea* of rational behavior working in a way we might not expect: "'Rational' is a normative term, used to persuade people to behave in a certain way" (p. 62).

Secondary Propositions

Homans (1987) maintains that there are two secondary propositions that "a sociologist ought to keep with the main ones in his intellectual kit if he is to understand human social behavior" (p. 62). These are derived from the above and are the deprivation-satiation proposition and the frustration-aggression proposition. *Deprivation-satiation proposition* says that people have thresholds of value. Thus, if a person's action is rewarded past this threshold, subsequent rewards become less and less valuable and the frequency of behavior goes down as a result. For example, on a whim a man may bring his wife flowers Friday evening after work. She is so surprised and delighted that her face beams, she jumps in his arms and gives him a long kiss, she excitedly brings out the best vase, and then calls her best friend to brag on him. A light bulb goes on in the guy's head: Friday night flowers = happy wife (stimulus proposition). So, he of course repeats the behavior next Friday (success proposition), brings his wife flowers and get the same response. He figures it's a gold mine and does this weekly. Soon he notices that his wife isn't nearly as happy, he gets a slight kiss on the cheek, the flowers laid on the table, and no phone calls to the best friend (satiation). The reverse is true as well: If deprived of a thing of value, its value goes up. Homans says this principle may not hold for generalized reinforcers like money, because these may be used to obtain other more specific rewards.

The *frustration-aggression proposition* is based on expectations. It says that if a person doesn't receive the response he or she expects or receives punishment when expecting a reward, the person will become angry and tend to act out aggressively. This emotionally driven behavior can then function in the place of the reward as a way of satisfying the initial desire: A person may learn to use aggressive action like any operant that is followed by a reward.

Summary

- The basic behavioral exchange propositions are (1) the success proposition: people will repeat behaviors for which they are rewarded; (2) the value proposition: the more highly valued a reward or result is to a person, the more likely he or she is to repeat behaviors associated with that reward/response; (3) the stimulus proposition: if a particular situation has been the occasion where a person's behaviors have been rewarded, then the more closely a situation mirrors the first, the more likely the person is to repeat those behaviors; (4) the rationality proposition: given alternative choices among behaviors, a person will most likely choose the behavior that is seen to be the most rational, determined by the value of the reward times the probability of receiving it.

- From these are derived two secondary propositions: (1) the satiation proposition: the more frequently in the recent past a person has received a reward, the less valued the reward becomes and the less likely the person is to perform the behaviors associated with it; (2) the aggression proposition: when a person does not receive an expected reward (either less than expected or punishment), the more likely is the person to be angry and act aggressively, the responses to such behavior become valued.

Social Exchanges and Power:
Peter Blau (1918–2002)

Theorist's Digest
Concepts and Theory: Social Exchanges
>   *Basic Exchange Principles*
Concepts and Theory: Creating Power and Social Structures
>   *Building Social Structures*
Summary

Blau and Homans have an interesting intellectual relationship. Homans, for his part, uses the empirical data from Blau's book, *The Dynamics of Bureaucracy,* in forming his theory of the elementary forms of social behavior. Blau singles out Homans' book, *Social Behavior: Its Elementary Forms,* as an important influence on his thinking, "despite some fundamental differences in approach" (Blau & Meyer, 2003, p. xix). And I think you'll pick up on these differences right away. The most fundamental one is that while Homans is more focused on the behavioral dynamics of the individual, Blau is concerned with the social exchange relation itself. As I mentioned in the Homans' section, it's important and informative to clearly understand where a theorist is focused.

Broadly speaking, Blau recognizes two main influences on human behavior: (1) the situational and personal factors that influence the preferences people have and the choices they make and (2) those external conditions that restrict or enable those choices and preferences. Blau recognizes three factors that influence choices and preferences. There are the psychological or personality aspects (individual likes and dislikes), the social-psychological factors (how social position/class and experience influence choice and preference), and the actual properties of exchange. Blau argues that exchange is an emergent property of interaction that cannot be reduced to the psychological attributes of individuals. And, so, that's where he starts.

For Blau, exchange is an elementary process of human life and the prototype of social phenomena. By definition, exchange can only take place in social settings between two or more people. Social exchange focuses on the actions of the participants and how they are influenced by both the anticipated and past actions of others. The influence, then, is decidedly social and not based on personal achievements, such as education, or individual attitudes. However, Blau claims, not all face-to-face interactions are exchanges. This is a rather unique position among exchange theorists, many of whom see exchange or rational choice as universal to all human action. Blau (1968), on the other hand, sees that "the concept of exchange loses its distinctive meaning and becomes tautological if all behavior in interpersonal relations is subsumed under it" (p. 453). Other factors he sees as influencing people in interactions are morals in the form of internalized norms, irrationality (purely emotional responses), and coercion.

THEORIST'S DIGEST

Brief Biography

Peter M. Blau was born on February 7, 1918, in Vienna, Austria, the year the Austro-Hungarian Empire fell. The son of secular Jews, he watched the rise of fascism in postwar Austria with growing concern. Blau became a U.S. citizen in 1943, and he served in the U.S. Army during World War II, earning the Bronze Star for valor. After the war, Blau attended school and was awarded his PhD from Columbia University in 1952; Robert K. Merton was his dissertation chair. His dissertation was subsequently published as *The Dynamics of Bureaucracy* and has since become a classic in organizational literature. Peter Blau held professorships at Chicago, Columbia, the State University of New York at Albany, and the University of North Carolina at Chapel Hill. He also taught at the Academy of Social Sciences in Tianjin, China, and he was president of the American Sociological Association in 1973. Blau published hundreds of articles and 11 books, and he received numerous awards for his contributions to sociology and to society at large. Peter Blau passed away March 12, 2002.

Central Sociological Questions

Not all relationships are equal. But what makes them equal or unequal? How is power created in social relationships? How do these sorts of relationships provide the basis for larger social structures? These are the questions that occupy Blau.

Simply Stated

Blau uses two basic factors to understand how power and structures are created: reciprocity and imbalance. All social encounters happen because each actor hopes to gain something from it. Reciprocity, then, the give and take of some elements of value, is the fundamental element of social relations and is intimately related to balance. People will always try to balance out exchanges. If they are unable to, or if they can't find alternatives, then deference and compliance will be offered to balance the relationship. In the relation between a group and single supplier, which by definition involves power, power will be legitimated if the norms of reciprocity and fair exchange are adhered to and will be opposed if not.

Key Ideas

social exchanges, rationally motivation, power, alternatives, marginal utilities, norm of reciprocity, norm of fair exchange, secondary exchange relations

Concepts and Theory: Social Exchanges

Social exchanges are distinct from economic exchanges in at least four ways. First, they lack specificity. All economic exchanges take place under the contract model. In other words, almost all of the elements of the exchange are laid out and understood in advance, even the simple exchanges that occur at the grocery store. Social exchanges, on the other hand, cannot be stipulated in advance; to do so would be a breach of etiquette. Imagine receiving an invitation for dinner that also stipulated exactly how you would repay the person for such a dinner ("I'll give you one dinner for two lunches"). Social exchanges, then, cannot be bargained and repayment must be left to the discretion of the indebted.

This first difference implies the second: Social exchanges necessarily build trust, while economic exchanges do not. Since social exchanges suffer from lack of specificity, we must of necessity trust the other to reciprocate. This implies that relationships that include social exchange—and almost all do—build up slowly over time. We begin with small exchanges, like calling people on the phone, and see if they will reciprocate. If they do, then we perceive them as worthy of trust for exchanges that require longer periods of time for reciprocation, such as friendship.

The third difference between social and economic exchanges is that social exchanges are meaningful. The way we are using it here, meaning implies signification. In other words, an object or action has meaning if it signifies something beyond itself. What we are saying about exchange is that a purely economic exchange doesn't mean anything beyond itself; it is simply what it is: the exchange of money for some good or service. Social exchanges, on the other hand, always have meaning. For an example, let's take what might appear as a simple economic exchange: prostitution. If a married man gives a woman who is not his wife money for sex, it is a social exchange because it has meaning beyond itself: In this case, the meaning is adultery.

Finally, the fourth difference between social and economic exchanges is that social benefits are less detached from the source. We use money in economic exchanges, but the value of money is completely detached from the person using it. I may use money every time I go to the music store, but the value of that money for exchange is a function of the U.S. government and has nothing to do with me—the value of money is completely detached from me. However, the value in all social exchanges is dependent upon the participants in some way. For example, the social exchange between you and your professor requires you to fulfill the requirements of the course to get a grade. Someone else can't do the work and you can't legitimately buy the grade.

Taken together, these four unique features of social exchange create diffuse social obligations. For example, let's say you and your partner invite another couple over for dinner. You expect that the invitation will be reciprocated in some way, but exactly how the other couple is to reciprocate isn't clear—nor can it be clear; to make it clear would reduce it to an economic exchange. So you have a general, unspecified expectation that the other couple will reciprocate in some way. The reciprocation has to be in the indefinite future (the other couple can't initially respond to your invitation by scheduling their "repayment" dinner—then it would really look like a repayment in economic terms), yet it has to be repaid specifically by the couple (the other couple can't have a different couple invite you for dinner and have it count for them). The dinner is meaningful, but the meaning isn't clear as of yet (Are you all going to be friends? If so, what kind of friends?). Thus, you have to trust the other couple to provide the future unspecified meaning and reciprocation. The other couple is obligated to you, but in a very diffuse manner.

Basic Exchange Principles

There are three basic exchange principles that Blau gives us; they concern motivations, alternatives, and marginal utilities. The first principle is that people are *rationally motivated* in exchanges to weigh out costs and benefits. In this respect, the ideal type of exchange is economic, where the calculations are specific and known. As we've seen, Blau argues that social exchanges are different from economic ones, and one implication of this is that our calculations will be different. They are not as specific or concrete as economic calculations. Thus, we have to view social exchange "rationality" in limited terms. It's a general motivation in back of our actions. We don't specifically think, "If I invite Bob to the barbeque, then I can borrow his truck next Thursday." It's more of a general and diffuse motivation—a broad desire for social profits and a sense of how we stand in our exchanges.

Alternatives are extremely important in exchange relations. We'll talk more about alternatives when we get to the section on power, but for now we should simply be aware that when alternatives are present, people will gravitate toward exchanges among equals. We tend to look for someone with whom we can balance out costs and benefits in the long run. These balanced exchange relations tend to reduce uncertainty and to lessen power differences. Blau also notes that balanced relationships tend to create unbalanced relations elsewhere. In this, Blau is positing that we have limited resources and to invest resources in one relationship is to deny it to another.

Let's use the example of dating and marriage. When we get married, one of the things we are doing is committing a large amount of our personal resources to one relationship. We do so because of the anticipation of rewards, both intrinsic and extrinsic, but when we do so we simultaneously take away the possibility of using those resources in an alternative relationship. In these circumstances, friendships can only go so far. If you are married, and if one of your friends wants to exchange more than you are able due to the commitment of resources to your marriage partner, then that friendship will become an unbalanced exchange relation. Unbalanced or unequal exchange relations tend to be less strained if the differences are known, clear, and marked. We can see this easily in our marriage example: Your unbalanced relationship with your friend who wants more will be very strained if you are unclear about what you are willing and unwilling to exchange. However, the strain is lessened as the trade boundaries become clear and marked—the other person will be less likely to entertain unreal exchange expectations.

The principle of *marginal utilities* posits that people have satiation points regarding goods and services. In other words, too much of a good thing may not be a good thing. When we first enter into an exchange relationship, the profits that we glean have high value. However, repeated profits of the same kind have declining value. As in the example of the man who gives flowers to his partner, the first time it has high value. And it probably has high value the second and third times it happens. But if the man brings flowers to his partner every Friday after work, the value of the gift declines as the partner becomes satiated. Thus, the value of any good or service is higher if there is some degree of uncertainty or a sporadic quality associated with it.

Concepts and Theory: Creating Power and Social Structures

There are two norms associated with social exchange: the *norm of reciprocity* and the norm of fair exchange. Blau sees exchange as the starting mechanism for social interaction and group structure. Before group identities and boundaries, and before status positions, roles, and norms are created, interaction is initiated in the hopes of gaining something from exchange. That we are dependent upon others for reaction implies that the idea of reciprocation is central in exchange. The word *reciprocate* comes from Latin and literally means to move back and forth. Exchange, then, always entails the give and take of some elements of value, such as money, emotion, favors, and so forth. As such, one of the first behaviors to receive normative power is reciprocity. The norm of reciprocity implies another basic feature of society, that of trust. As we've seen, social exchange requires that the reciprocated good or service be unspecified and that reciprocation is delayed to some undisclosed future. This lack of specificity obviously demands trust, which forms the basis of society and our initial social contact. Exchanges are also guided by *the norm of fair exchange*. Something is fair, of course, if it is characterized by honesty and free from fraud or favoritism. The expectation of fairness increases over the length of the exchange relation.

Because of the lack of specificity in social exchange and the norm of reciprocity, exchange creates bonds of friendship and establishes power relations. The basic difference between friendship and power relationships concerns the equity of exchange and is expressed in the amount of repayment discretion. Friendship is based on an equal exchange relationship: All parties feel that they give about as much as they take in the relationship. This equal reciprocity among friends leads to a social bond built on trust and a high level of discretion in repayment. On the other hand, inequality in exchange leads to unfulfilled obligations that, in turn, grant power over repayment to the other.

According to Blau, four conditions affect the level of social power. I've diagramed these conditions in Figure 11.3. In the diagram, we have a social exchange relation between A and B. In thinking through the way the model works, you can visualize yourself as either person and get a sense of the way the power flows in the relationship. Social capital refers to the ability to participate in an exchange with goods or services that the other desires. As you can see, there is a negative relationship between social capital and power. In other words, the less ability Actor A has to control goods and services (exchange capital) that Actor B desires, the greater will be B's power over A. Alternatives are important for power as well. If I have a large number of alternatives through which I can obtain the social good or service

Figure 11.3 Exchange Principles of Power

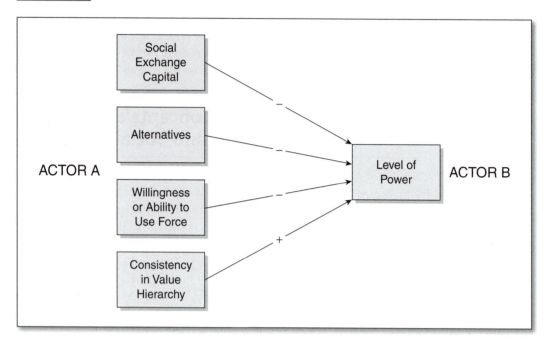

that I desire, then others will have little power over me. However, the fewer the number of alternatives, the greater will be the power of others who control the social good. This inverse relationship is noted by the negative sign.

There are two other important factors in establishing social power: the actor's willingness to use force and the consistency of the value hierarchy. If Actor A has the ability and willingness to use force, then by definition there is no exchange relation and, thus, social power is impossible. This somewhat obvious condition tells us something important about social power: There is always a choice involved. With social power, "There is an element of voluntarism . . . the punishment could be chosen in preference to compliance" (Blau, 2003, p. 117). The relationship between Actor A's willingness to use force and Actor B's power is negative: The less likely Actor A is to use force to obtain social goods, the greater is the potential for social power for Actor B.

The last condition implies a consistent value hierarchy. If the value system of Actor A changes and he or she no longer values the social goods B controls, then there can be no power. If, on the other hand, Actor A consistently values the goods B has to offer, then social power will increase, if the other conditions hold as well. Try this thinking exercise: Think about the relationships that you have with various professors as exchange relations. Use each of these four variables—social capital, alternative, willingness to use force, and consistent value hierarchy—and ask the following: Who has more power and why? I believe you'll find that your professors have varying levels of power because of the different ways these factors align. At minimum, this implies that social power is not a simple function of bureaucratic position.

There are five possible responses to power. Four of the responses correspond to the four conditions of power and constitute attempts to change the balance of power. In other words, if you want to change the amount of power someone has over you, you could

- Increase your exchange capital by obtaining a good or service that the other person desires
- Find alternative sources to what you receive from the other person
- Get along without the good or service the other person controls
- Attempt to force the other person to give you what you need

The only other possible response is subordination and compliance. Compliance, unlike most features of social exchange, can be specified and functions like money: "Willingness to comply with another's demands is a generic social reward, since the power it gives him is a generalized means, parallel to money, which can be used to attain a variety of ends" (Blau, 2003, p. 22). The power to command is like a credit, an I.O.U. in social exchange. It is what we give to others when we can't participate in an equal exchange yet we desire the goods they control.

Building Social Structures

Secondary exchange relations result from power and occur at the group level among those who are collectively indebted to someone or to another group. In order for secondary exchange relations to come into play, people who are individually indebted to a person or group must have physical proximity and be able to communicate with one another. For example, let's say you are tutoring a number of students in sociology without charging them money. Each of those individuals would be socially indebted to you, and each individual relationship would be subject to the dynamics of exchange (alternatives, marginal utilities, and norms). As long as you only met with each person individually and they were unaware of each other, the exchange relations would remain individual. On the other hand, if you decide that your time would be better spent tutoring them as a group, then secondary exchange relations could come into play. You've provided them with the ability to become a group through physical proximity and communication. When a group like this is brought together physically and able to communicate, two possibilities exist with regards to power: The group may either legitimate or oppose your power as the tutor.

Blau gives us a very basic process through which power is either legitimated or de-legitimated. Both possibilities are in response to the group's perception of how those in power perform with regard to the norms of fair exchange and reciprocity. If the norms of reciprocity and fair exchange are adhered to, then social power will be legitimated. Blau posits that the path looks something like this: reciprocity and fair exchange with those in power → common feelings of loyalty → norm of compliance → legitimation and authority → organization → institutionalized system of exchange values. As the group communicates with one another about the level of adherence of those in power to the norms of fair exchange and reciprocity, they collectively develop feelings of loyalty and indebtedness. Out of these feelings comes the norm of compliance: The group begins to sanction itself in terms of its relationship to those in power. This process varies in the sense that the more those in power are seen as consistently generous, that is, exceeding the norms of fairness and reciprocity, the more the group will feel loyal and the stronger will be the norm of compliance and sense of legitimation. Out of legitimation come organization and an institutionalized system of values regarding authority (see Blau & Meyer, 1987, for Blau's treatment of bureaucracy).

In his theory of secondary exchange relations, Blau is giving us an explanation of the micro–macro link. We can see this move from individual exchanges to institutions in the path of secondary relations noted above. The "glue" that holds this path together consists of generalized trust and the norm of reciprocity. As we've already seen, all social exchanges are built on trust; the element of time and lack of specificity in social exchanges demand trust. Organizations and institutions are, in Blau's scheme, long chains of indirect exchanges of rewards and costs. And, as we've seen, exchange intrinsically entails reciprocation. Every step, then, along the chain of exchanges is held together by the norm of reciprocity.

Secondary exchange relations can thus lead to legitimated authority, but they can also lead to opposition and conflict. If those in power do not meet the norms of fair exchange and reciprocity, and if those indebted are brought together physically and are able to communicate with one another, then feelings of resentment will tend to develop. These feelings of resentment obviously lead to de-legitimation of authority. This path of secondary exchange relations looks like this: lack of reciprocity and fairness from those in power → feelings of resentment → communication (a function of physical proximity and communication technologies) → de-legitimation of authority → ideology → solidarity → opposition → probability of change.

Groups experiencing a lack of fairness and reciprocity that are in close physical proximity and are able to communicate with one another will tend to develop a set of beliefs and ideas that both justify their resentment and their de-legitimation of authority. This ideology, in turn, enables group solidarity and overt opposition, thus increasing the probability of change. The last part of this path comes from the conflict theories of Marx and Weber. To this general theory of conflict and change, Blau adds the micro dimension of exchange: the beginning part of the path. Keep in mind that all of these factors function as variables and are therefore changeable.

Summary

• Social exchanges are different from economic exchanges because they lack specificity, they require and build trust, they are meaningful, and social benefits are detached from the source. These differences imply that social exchanges create diffuse obligations, which in turn form the basis of society—social relations must be maintained in order to guarantee repayment of these obligations. Population structures are made up from the distributions of a population along various continuums of difference or social position. These continuums of difference create or hinder opportunities for social contact, social mobility, and social conflict.

• There are three basic principles and two norms of exchange. The contours of all social exchanges are set by the principles of rational motivation, the presence of alternatives, and satiation. Because of the peculiar properties of social exchanges, rationality within them is limited, as compared to economic exchanges. People are rational in social exchanges to the extent that they tend to repeat those actions that they received rewards from in the past. People are also rational in the sense that they will gravitate toward exchanges that are equal, the equality of exchanges being determined by the presence of alternatives. And all social exchanges are subject to the principle of marginal utilities—a social good loses its value in exchange as people become satiated; in other words, value in exchange is determined to some extent by scarcity and uncertainty. All social exchanges are subject to the norms of reciprocity and fair exchange.

• Social actors achieve power through unequal exchanges, with inequality in exchange determined by four factors: the level of exchange capital, the number of potential source alternatives, the willingness and ability to use force, and consistency in value hierarchy. The first three are negatively related to power. That is, in an exchange relationship between Actor A and Actor B, as Actor A's capital, alternatives, and ability to use force go down, Actor B's power over Actor A increases. Consistency is a positive or at least steady relationship—continuing to value the goods that Actor B controls places Actor A in a possible subordinate position.

Ritualized Exchanges:
Randall Collins (1941–)

Theorist's Digest
Concepts and Theory: Emotion—The Generalized Media of
    Exchange
Concepts and Theory: Interaction Ritual Chains (IRCs)
    Ritualized Social Structures
Concepts and Theory: The Ritualized Production of
    Stratification
    The Vertical Dimension of Power
    The Horizontal Dimension of Networks
    Reproducing Class and Power
Summary

Collins (1993) brings us yet another way of seeing exchanges. Like Homans, Collins has a strong individual component to his theory. But Collins isn't interested in the psychological processes of the individual. In fact, he's doubtful about the existence of what is usually implied by the "individual." He points out that what we mean by the individual varies by the social and cultural context and is thus a poor focus for social science research. There are two ways to understand his point. The first is to understand that what we mean by "the individual" is really the social point at which various social identities meet. For example, if I were to ask you to tell me who you are, most of your answers would be in the form of social categories and would involve such things as age, gender, sexuality, friendship, marital status, and so on. The individual, from this point of view, is *a reflection of sociopolitical organization rather than essential characteristics.*

The other way to see that the individual varies by social context is much more profound. From this perspective, the entire idea of "the individual" is the product of political, religious, and social changes that have occurred in the past few centuries. More specifically, the idea of the individual came about as Western society defined civil rights (as a result of the rise of democracy) and moral responsibilities (as a result of the Protestant Reformation). The idea of the individual also became more pronounced through capitalism (consumerism) and social diversity. About the individual, Collins (2004) says,

> The human individual is a quasi-enduring, quasi-transient flux in time and space. . . . It is an ideology of how we regard it proper to think about ourselves and others . . . not the most useful analytical starting point for microsociology. (p. 4)

Like Blau, Collins is more interested in what happens between people than within the individual, but Collins focuses on broader elements of the situation than simply the exchange relation per se. Collins also has a different way of seeing how "society" comes about. In the end, Blau, like Parsons, falls back on the power of norms. For Collins, social structures and systems are *heuristics*—that is, they are aids to discovery. Collins (1987) is arguing that we can use the ideas of structure and social systems to "make generalizations about the workings of the world system, formal organizations, or the class structure by making the appropriate comparisons and analyses of its own data" (pp. 194–195). But the reality behind these heuristics is the pure number of face-to-face situations strung together through time and space. In other words, *social structures are built up by the aggregation of many interactions over long periods of time and large portions of geographic space.* The primary way in which they are linked together is emotion.

THEORIST'S DIGEST

Brief Biography

Randall Collins was born in Knoxville, Tennessee, on July 29, 1941. His father was part of military intelligence during World War II and then a member of the state department. Collins thus spent a good deal of his early years in Europe. As a teenager, Collins was sent to a New England prep school, afterward studying at Harvard and the University of California, Berkeley, where he encountered the work of Herbert Blumer and Erving Goffman, both professors at Berkeley at the time. Collins completed his PhD in 1969. He has spent time teaching at a number of universities, such as the University of Virginia, the Universities of California at Riverside and San Diego, and has held a number of visiting professorships at Chicago, Harvard, Cambridge, and at various universities in Europe, Japan, and China. He is currently at the University of Pennsylvania.

Central Sociological Questions

Collins has enormous breadth. Overall his passion is to understand how societies are produced, held together, and destroyed through emotionally rather than rationally motivated behaviors. In terms of social exchange, then, his interest is to understand how emotion forms the basic motivation and outcome of an exchange. And, like Blau, he's interested in how each individual situated exchange is linked together to form macro level structures of inequality.

Simply Stated

Collins argues that the most general goods that are exchanged among people are emotional energy and cultural capital, and that the basic social unit is the interaction ritual. The level of ritualized activities varies by co-presence, common emotional mood and focus of attention, and barrier to outsiders. As these variables go up, the group involved will create higher levels of emotion, which then creates group solidarity and group symbols; these, in turn, are carried within the individual and provide the motivation to re-create rituals. Collins argues that this process is how stratified power and class are reproduced.

Key Ideas

emotional energy, rituals, co-presence, shared focus of attention, rhythmic entrainment, common emotional mood, barrier to outsiders, group symbols, group solidarity, standards of morality, generalized and particularized cultural capital, market opportunities, stratification, deference and demeanor, principle of order giving, principle of ritual coercion, principle of anticipatory socialization, principle of bureaucratic personality, social network, authoritarian, cosmopolitan

Concepts and Theory: Emotion—The Generalized Media of Exchange

Collins' use of emotion is based on three long-standing critiques of exchange theory. First, exchange theory has a difficult time accounting for altruistic behavior. Merriam-Webster (2002) defines altruism as "uncalculated consideration of, regard for, or devotion to others' interests." If most or all of our interactions are exchange-based and if all our exchanges are based on self-motivated actors making rational calculations for profit, how can altruism be possible? Collins claims that exchange theorists are left arguing that the actor is actually selfish in altruistic behavior—he or she gains some profit from being altruistic. However, just what that profit is has generally been left unspecified.

Second, there is evidence that suggests that people in interactions are rarely rational or calculative. In support of this, Collins cites Goffman's and Garfinkel's work (Chapter 12), the idea of bounded rationality in organizational analysis, as well as psychological experiments that indicate that when people are faced with problems that should prompt them to be rational, they use non-optimizing heuristics instead. These heuristics function like approximate or sufficient answers to problems rather than the most rational or best answer. The third criticism of exchange theory is that there is no common metric or medium of exchange. Money, of course, is the metric and medium of trade for exchanges involving economically produced goods and services; however, money isn't general enough to embrace all exchanges, all goods, and all services.

Collins sees each of these problems solved through the idea that **emotional energy** is the common denominator of rational action. Let's note from the beginning that this approach is rather adventuresome in that it combines two things that have usually been thought of as oil and water—emotion and rationality just don't mix. At least, they didn't before Collins came along. Emotional energy does not refer to any specific emotion; it is, rather, a very general feeling of emotion and motivation that an individual senses. It is the "amount of emotional power that flows through one's actions" (Collins, 1988, p. 362). Collins (2004) conceptualizes emotional energy as running on a continuum from high levels of confidence, enthusiasm, and good self-feelings to the low end of depression, lack of ambition, and negative self-feelings (p. 108). The idea of emotional energy is like that of psychological drive, but emotional energy is based in social activity.

Collins is arguing that emotional energy is general enough to embrace all exchanges. In fact, emotional energy is the underlying resource in back of every exchanged good and service, whether it's a guitar, a pet, a conversation, a car, a friend, your attendance at a show or sporting event, and so on. *More basic than money, emotional energy is the motivation behind all exchanges.* Emotional energy can also be seen in back of social exchanges that might seem counterintuitive. Why would I exchange my free time to work at a soup kitchen on Sunday mornings? This, of course, is an example of altruistic behavior. Exchange theory, apart from the idea of emotional energy, is hard pressed to explain such behaviors in terms of exchange. Collins gives us a more general property of exchange in the form of emotional energy. People engage in altruistic behaviors because of the emotional energy they receive in exchange.

The idea of emotional energy also solves the problem of the lack of rational calculations. As Collins notes, people aren't generally observed making rational calculations during interactions. Rather than being rationally calculative, "Human behavior may be characterized as emotional tropism" (Collins, 1993, p. 223). A tropism is an involuntary movement by an organism that is a negative or positive response to a stimulus. An example of tropism is the response of a plant to sunlight. The stems and leaves react positively to the sun by reaching toward it, and the roots react negatively by moving away from it and deeper in the ground. Collins is telling us that people aren't cognitively calculative in normal encounters. Instead, people emotionally feel their way to and through most interactions, much like the leaves of a plant reach toward the sun.

Concepts and Theory: Interaction Ritual Chains (IRCs)

For Collins, **rituals** are patterned sequences of behavior that bring four elements together: bodily co-presence, barrier to outsiders, mutual focus of attention, and shared emotional mood. These elements are variables—as they increase, so also will the effects of ritualized behavior. There are five main effects of interaction rituals:

group solidarity, group symbols, standards and feelings of morality, individual emotional energy, and individual cultural capital. Collins' theory is diagrammed in Figure 11.4.

One of the first things that the model in Figure 11.4 calls our attention to is physical *co-presence,* which describes the degree of physical closeness. Even in the same room, we can be closer or farther away from one another. The closer we get, the more we can sense the other person. As Durkheim (1912/1995) says, "The very act of congregating is an exceptionally powerful stimulant. Once the individuals are gathered together, a sort of electricity is generated from their closeness and quickly launches them to an extraordinary height of exaltation" (pp. 217–218). Bodily presence appears theoretically necessary because the closer people are, the more easily they can monitor one another's behaviors.

Part of what we monitor is the level of involvement or *shared focus of attention,* the degree to which participants are attending to the same behavior, event, object, symbol, or idea at the same time (a difficult task, as any teacher knows). We watch bodily cues and eye movements, and we monitor how emotions are expressed and how easily others are drawn away from an interaction. Members of similar groups have the ability to pace an interaction in terms of conversation, gestures, and cues in a like manner. Part of the success or intensity of an interaction is a function of this kind of rhythm or timing.

The key to successful rituals "is that human nervous systems become mutually attuned" (Collins, 2004, p. 64). Collins means that in intense interactions or ritual performance, we physically mimic one another's body rhythms; we become physically "entrained." *Rhythmic entrainment* refers to recurrent bodily patterns that become enmeshed during successful rituals. These bodily patterns may be large

Figure 11.4   The Interaction Ritual

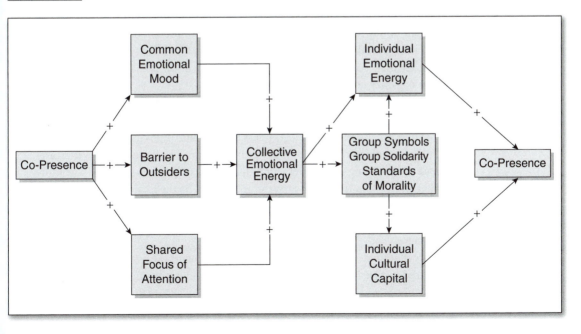

and noticeable as in hand or arm expressions, or they may be so quick and minute that they occur below the level of human consciousness.

It is estimated that human beings can perceive things down to about 0.2 second in duration. Much of this entrainment occurs below that threshold, or below the level of consciousness—which indicates that people literally feel their way through intense ritualized interactions. Collins (2004, pp. 65–78) cites evidence from conversational analysis and audience–speaker behavior to show that humans become rhythmically coordinated with one another in interactions. Some research has shown that conversations not only become rhythmic in terms of turn-taking, but the acoustical voice frequencies become entrained as well. EEG (electroencephalogram) recordings have indicated that even the brain waves of interactants can become synchronized. In a study of body motion and speech using 16mm film, Condon and Ogston (1971) discovered that in interaction, "A hearer's body was found to 'dance' in precise harmony with the speaker" (p. 158).

A shared focus of attention and common emotional mood tend to reinforce one another though rhythmic entrainment. *Common emotional mood* refers to the degree to which participants are emotionally oriented toward the interaction in the same way. In ritual terms, it doesn't really matter what kind of emotion we're talking about. What is important is that the emotion be commonly held. Having said that, I want to point out that there is an upper and lower limit to ritual intensity. One of the things that tends to become entrained in an interaction is turn-taking. The rule for turn-taking is simple: One person speaks at a time. The speed at which turns are taken is vitally important for a ritual. The time between statements in a successful conversation will hover around 0.1 second. If the time between turns is too great, at say 1.0 second, the interaction will be experienced as dull and lifeless and no solidarity will be produced. If, on the other hand, conversational statements go in the other direction and overlap or interrupt one another, then the "conversation" breaks down and no feeling of solidarity results. These latter kinds of conversations are typically arguments, which can be brought about by a hostile common emotional mood. Collins (2004) points out that it is generally the case at the micro level that "solidarity processes are easier to enact than conflict processes. . . . The implication is that conflict is much easier to organize at a distance" (p. 74).

Being physically co-present tends to bring about the other variables, particularly, as we've seen, the shared focus of attention. Co-presence also aids in the production of ritual barriers. *Barrier to outsiders* refers to symbolic or physical obstacles we put up to other people attempting to join our interaction. The use of barriers increases the sense of belonging to the interaction that the participants experience. The more apparent and certain that boundary, the greater will be the level of ritualized interaction and production of group emotional energy. Sporting events and rock concerts are good illustrations of using physical boundaries to help create intense ritual performance.

Notice that there is a total of five effects coming out of the emotional energy that is produced in rituals. Let's talk about the interrelated group effects first: solidarity, group symbols, and standards of morality. *Group symbols* are those symbols we use to anchor social emotions. The greater the level of collective effervescence that's created in rituals, the greater will be the level of emotion that the symbol comes to represent. It's this investment of group emotion that makes the symbol a collective symbol. The symbol comes to embody and represent the group. If the invested emotion is high enough, these symbols take on sacred qualities. We can think of the U.S. flag, gang insignia, and sport team emblems and colors as examples, in addition to the obvious religious ones. The symbols help to create group boundaries and identities. Group symbols have an important ritual function: They are used to facilitate ritual enactment by focusing attention and creating a common emotional mood.

Group solidarity is the sense of oneness a collective can experience. This concern originated with Durkheim (1893/1984, pp. 11–29) and meant the level of integration in a society, measured by the subjective sense of "we-ness" individuals have, the constraint of individual behaviors for the group good, and the organization of social units. Collins appears to mean it in a more general way. Group solidarity is the feeling of membership with the group that an individual experiences. It's seeing oneself as part of a larger whole. One of the important things to see here is that the sense of membership is emotional. It is derived from creating high levels of collective effervescence. Of course, the higher the level of effervescence, the higher will be the sense of belonging to the group that an individual can have.

Standards of morality refer to group-specific behaviors that are important to group membership and are morally enforced. Feelings of group solidarity lead people to want to control the behaviors that denote or create that solidarity. That is, many of the behaviors, speech patterns, styles of dress, and so on that are associated with the group become issues of right and wrong. Groups with high moral boundaries have stringent entrance and exit rules (they are difficult to get in and out of). Today's street gangs and the Nazi Party of World War II are good examples of groups with high moral boundaries.

One of the things to notice about our example is the use of "moral." Most of us probably don't agree with the ethics of street gangs. In fact, we probably think their ethics are morally wrong and reprehensible. But when sociologists use the term *moral*, we are not referring to something that we think of as being good. A group is moral if its behaviors, beliefs, feelings, speech, styles, and so forth are controlled by strong group norms and are viewed by the members in terms of right and wrong. Because the level of standards of morality any group may have is a function of their level of interaction rituals, we could safely say that, by this definition, both gangs and Nazis are probably more "moral" than we are, in this sense, unless one of us is a member of a radical fringe group.

Ritualized Social Structures

Notice the arrows coming out of individual cultural capital and emotional energy in Figure 11.4. They feed into and create another co-presence—this is how interaction rituals become linked or chained together. In Collins' theory of interaction ritual chains, the individual is the carrier of the micro–macro link. There are two components to this linkage: emotional energy and cultural capital. Emotional energy is the emotional charge that people can take away with them from an interaction. And as such, emotional energy predicts the likelihood of repeated interactions: If the individual comes away from an interaction with as high or higher emotional energy than he or she went in with, then the person will be more likely to seek out further rituals of the same kind. Emotional energy also sets the person's initial involvement within the interaction. People entering an interaction who are charged up with emotional energy will tend to be fully involved and more readily able to experience rhythmic entrainment and collective effervescence.

Cultural capital is a shorthand way of talking about the different resources we have to culturally engage with other people. The idea of cultural capital covers a full range of cultural items: It references the way we talk; what we have to talk about; how we dress, walk, and act—in short, anything that culturally references us to others. Collins lists three different kinds of cultural capitals. *Generalized cultural capital* is the individual's stock of symbols that are associated with group identity. As Figure 11.4 notes, a great deal of this generalized cultural capital comes from interaction rituals. This kind of cultural capital is group specific and can be used with strangers, somewhat the way money can. For example, the other day I was in the airport standing next to a man wearing a handmade tie-dye T-shirt with a dancing bear on it. Another fellow who was coming off a different flight saw him and said, "Hey, man, where ya from?" These two strangers were able to strike up a conversation because the one man recognized the group symbols of Deadheads—fans of the band The Grateful Dead. They were able to engage one another in an interaction ritual because of this generalized cultural capital.

Particularized cultural capital refers to cultural items we have in common with specific people. For example, my wife and I share a number of words, terms, songs, and so forth that are specifically meaningful to us. Hearing Louis Armstrong, for instance, instantly orients us toward one another, references shared experiences and meanings, and sets us up for an interaction ritual. But if I hear an Armstrong song around my friend Steve, it will have no social effect—there are no shared experiences (past ritual performances) that will prompt us to connect. From these two examples, you get a good sense of what cultural capital does: It orients people toward one another, gives them a shared focus or attention, and creates a common focus of attention, which are most of the ingredients of an interaction ritual.

The last kind of cultural capital that Collins talks about is *reputational capital.* If somebody knows something about you, he or she is more likely to engage you in conversation than if you are a complete stranger. That makes sense, of course, but remember that this is a variable. Mel Gibson, for example, has a great deal of cultural capital. If he were seen in a public space, many people would feel almost compelled to engage him in an interaction ritual.

Thus every person comes into an interaction with stocks of emotional energy (EE) and cultural capital (CC) that have been gleaned from previous interactions. The likelihood of an individual seeking out an interaction ritual is based on his or her levels of emotional energy and cultural capital; the likelihood of two people interacting with one another is based on both the similarity of their stocks and the perceived probability that they might gain either emotional energy or cultural capital from the encounter. The micro–macro link for Collins, then, is created as individual carriers who are charged up with emotional energy and cultural capital seek out other interaction rituals in which to revitalize or increase their stocks.

One further point before we leave this idea: People have a good idea of their *market opportunities*, which are directly linked to cultural capital and indirectly to emotional energy. As we noted earlier, we exchange cultural capital in the hopes of receiving more cultural capital back. Part of our opportunity in the cultural capital market is structured: Our daily rounds keep us within our class, status, and power groups. However, our interpersonal markets are far more open in modern societies than they were in traditional ones. In these open markets, we are "rational" in the sense that we avoid those interactions where we will spend more cultural capital than we gain, and we will pursue those interactions where we have a good chance of increasing our level of cultural capital. We also tend to avoid those interactions where our lack of CC will be apparent. As a result, we tend to separate ourselves into symbolic or status groups.

Concepts and Theory: The Ritualized Production of Stratification

Using the idea of status from Weber, the notion of deference and demeanor from Goffman (Chapter 12), and his theory of interaction rituals, Collins forms a theory of stratification that has important cultural, social-psychological elements. *Stratification* is always an issue of replication: How is the unequal distribution of scarce resources perpetuated generationally by social groups? Collins' theory looks at how stratification is enacted empirically in the situation and how people subjectively experience their lives differently based on social stratification; in particular, he looks at deference and demeanor rituals. *Deference* refers to respect given and *demeanor* to the cues that indicate the level of respect anticipated. In that these are ritualized, Collins is telling us that these behaviors produce emotional energy and cultural capital and that they are generally part of our regular routine in interaction. For example, you probably don't even notice when you call your instructor "Professor" or "Doctor," but in doing so, you are performing a deference ritual that creates and perpetuates status inequalities.

The Vertical Dimension of Power

In the main, Collins argues that there are two dimensions of stratification: the vertical dimension of power and the horizontal dimension of social networks. As we make our way through Collins' ideas about power, notice that power is not so much seen as a property of social structure as it is enacted in ritual performance. On the vertical power dimension, there are four variables or principles: the principles of order giving, ritual coercion, anticipatory socialization, and bureaucratic personality. The *principle of order giving* says that the occupational position of people runs on a continuum of order giving and taking. At the high end are those who do not take orders from anyone but give orders to many; at the low end are those that only take orders and do not give them; and in the middle are those who take orders from some and give orders to others.

We can understand order giving and taking as types of Goffmanian front- and backstage rituals. Order givers dominate the front stage and give off cues through their demeanor that they are worthy of respect. They make themselves appear dominant and in control, and they internally link their organizational position with their own sense of self. We can also understand order givers as a type of sacred object in the rituals where power is at issue. They are the focus of the interaction and set the emotional mood. In some sense, "It is no longer a mere individual who speaks but a group incarnated and personified" (Durkheim, 1912/1995, p. 212). Order givers dominate the front stage and develop a front stage personality; they idealize their jobs and see them as more than simple occupations. Order takers, on the other hand, are passive in the front stage and find their rewards in the backstage of organizational life, in such activities as being a sports fan, playing games, or watching television.

The *principle of ritual coercion* says that the more coercion and threat are used in order giving rituals, the greater will be the level of deference demanded and given, and the greater will be the effects of the principle of order giving. Two obvious examples are medieval aristocracies and the U.S. military; both demand high levels of deference, noted by such terms as "your highness" and "sir" and "ma'am." The *principle of anticipatory socialization* explains that individuals who look forward to occupying an order giving position sometime in the future tend to identity with that culture even if they are presently order takers. Thus, those in middle and non-management positions who expect promotion will begin to perform the deference and demeanor ritual in keeping with their anticipated position.

Finally, the *principle of bureaucratic personality* addresses the people in the middle, those that take orders from some and give orders to others. These people will have a rather unique cultural outlook and practice. Their place is in between: They stand between upper management and workers or between the organization and the public. As such, they tend to exhibit personal tendencies of both positions: They identify outwardly with the rules and regulations of the organization rather than inwardly believing in the overall mission of the group, and they tend to strictly enforce the rules and regulations on the front stage (in performance for the public or workers) because it is the only stage that they can control.

The Horizontal Dimension of Networks

The second dimension of stratification is the social network aspect of occupational cultures. Every one of us has a *social network*—a string or chain of interactions that form a pattern. The way in which that pattern is put together is vitally important. Social networks are particularly important because they form the way a person thinks and sees the world. Let's use the analogy of cloth to get a grasp on what we are talking about.

Cloth is made out of a network of threads. Two things about this network are especially important for the kind of cloth with which we will end up: the diversity of threads and the density of the weave. The diversity of threads is a vital issue. If the threads that are used are all of one color, what will be the result? A cloth of one color. The same is true of social networks. If the diversity of a person's network is low, if she doesn't interact with different kinds of people in different kinds of situations, then her fabric will only be of one color. This kind of individual will tend to see things concretely, with very little overlap. Her point of view will be very narrow and her number of lifestyle alternatives few. The inverse is true as well: If an individual's social network reveals diversity, then her ideas and perspectives will be more abstract and encompassing. She will tend to be more accepting of others and a diversity of lifestyles.

In cloth, the density of the weave helps determine how durable it is. With social networks, this function is fulfilled by network density. Network density varies by frequency and longevity of interactions. The more frequently a person interacts with the same people and the greater the length of time over which these interactions take place, the denser will be his or her network. Both network diversity and density correspond to elements in interaction rituals. The diversity of the network gets at the degree to which we share a common focus of attention. If the groups that you interact with share a common focus of attention, if there is little variety in what you are paying attention to, then the social objects that occupy your attention become reified.

Social density brings in another ritual element—physical co-presence. Let's think about our cloth again. If the threads of a piece of cloth are tightly wound and densely packed together, what kind of cloth is the result? The cloth would be tough, inflexible, and resilient. Dense interaction networks where people spend a great deal of time in one another's presence tend to yield people who tend to have reified ideas; that is, their ideas are seen as the only possible reality.

There's an old saying: "Birds of a feather flock together." What Collins is telling us is just the opposite: "Birds become of a feather *because* they flock together." In other words, the most prominent characteristics of people come about because of the pattern of their interactions. People tend to be narrow-minded if their interaction pattern is not diverse; people tend to be more accepting and to hold abstract rather than particularized beliefs if their interaction pattern is diverse. And socially constructed ideas tend to be seen as objectively real when the interaction network is dense. These two variables don't necessarily have to go together, but when they do, the results are impressive. Interaction rituals that take place within homogeneous, dense networks produce high levels of social conformity. Some contemporary examples where the network is both dense and uniform include religious cults such as the People's Temple and Heaven's Gate, and the group solidarity the U.S. government fosters in military boot camps.

Reproducing Class and Power

When power and network variables come together, they form predictable patterns of personalities. Remember that for Collins there isn't a self that people are born with; nor is the self a particularly individual entity—the self is social in both creation and function. Like Blumer, Collins sees the self as emerging from patterns of interaction. George Herbert Mead (1934), the philosopher from whom Blumer draws, explains that "the self is not something that exists first and then enters into relationship with others, but it is, so to speak, an eddy in the social current and so still a part of the current" (p. 26). Eddies are currents of air or water that run contrary to the stream. It isn't so much the contrariness that Mead wants us to see, but the fact that an eddy only exists in and because of its surrounding current. The same is true for selves: They only exist in and because of social interaction. The self doesn't have a continuous existence; it isn't something that we carry around inside of us. It's a mechanism that allows social interactions and action to happen.

With Collins we may find the analogy of a "junction" useful. A junction is a place or point where two or more elements are joined. Here the elements are the dimensions of power and network—the person is where these two social factors meet and are expressed. Someone who is high on both network density and power will have an *authoritarian*, upper-class-type personality, and he or she will display all the front stage work that comes with it. They generally interact only with those with whom they share similar interests—they attend the same schools, parties, country clubs, and so forth—and they interact frequently with those people. As a result, they are quite rigid in their sense of what is right and wrong. They are authoritarian and attempt to impose their values on society at large.

An individual who is high on the power dimension but low on network/ritual density will have and display a *cosmopolitan*, upper-class personality. Merriam-Webster (2002) defines *cosmopolitan* as "marked by interest in, familiarity with, or knowledge and appreciation of many parts of the world: not provincial, local, limited, or restricted by the attitudes, interests, or loyalties of a single region, section, or sphere of activity." The cosmopolitan upper classes, then, are those that have a broad view of the world and are very accommodating in terms of accepting people. Because their ritual density is low, they associate with many, many different kinds of groups and thus give credence to a variety of viewpoints. These are the kind of upper-class people that tend to use their influence and money to help others through political and humanitarian efforts, such as Band-Aid and the international AIDS foundations.

The same sort of personality type is located in the working class as well, but with different practices. Someone who is low on the order giver/taker dimensions and high on the social network dimension will conform to local, working-class culture. The stereotype of "redneck" is a good example. On the other hand, someone low on the power dimension and low on the network dimension will be part of the working-class party crowd. It isn't important for you to know these types, but it is important for you to see what Collins is arguing. Collins is showing us that class isn't simply an economic structure: It's a power structure that is modified by complex networks of ritual density. Collins takes us beyond Marx and Weber in our understanding of stratification by including Durkheim and Goffman.

Summary

- Rituals are patterned sequences of behavior that entail four elements: bodily co-presence, barrier to outsiders, mutual focus of attention, and shared emotional mood. Each of these is a variable, with increasing levels of each leading to increasing ritual performance and effects. Rituals result in group solidarity, group symbols, feelings of morality, individual emotional energy, and individual cultural capital. The greater the level of ritual performance, the greater will be the levels of each of these outcomes. Emotional energy and cultural capital are particularly important because they create the links among chains of interaction rituals. As individuals move from one interaction to another, they carry differing levels of emotional energy and cultural capital. These differing levels strongly influence the likelihood and subsequent effects of further rituals.

- Drawing on Weber, Durkheim, and Goffman, Collins argues that there are two dimensions of class stratification: power and social networks. Collins conceptualizes power in terms of order taking and order giving. In their jobs, people regularly experience a given proportion of order giving and taking. These relatively stable positions result in predictable and repeated ritual performances around deference and demeanor. Order givers are the focus of attention in such rituals; thus, the greater the level of power a person has, the more he will be the ritual focus of attention, the more his identity will take on sacred qualities, and the more he will develop a front stage personality. Social networks vary by their level of diversity and density. Network diversity and density are both associated with authoritarian or cosmopolitan orientations—higher density and lower diversity create an authoritarian outlook, and lower density and higher diversity produce the more flexible, cosmopolitan perspective. The two features of social networks tend to vary inversely, with low levels of diversity being associated with high levels of density, and high levels of diversity being associated with low levels of density. However, they don't necessarily vary in this way, and this feature adds a great deal of complexity to the class stratification system.

TAKING THE PERSPECTIVE—EXCHANGE THEORY

The idea of exchange as a social dynamic began with utilitarianism, an eighteenth-century philosophy that came out of the Age of Enlightenment's concern with human happiness and scientific calculation. The principles of utilitarianism were most clearly stated by Jeremy Bentham (1789/1996, pp. 11–16), who argued that happiness and unhappiness are based on the

(Continued)

(Continued)

two sovereign masters of nature: pleasure and pain. The "utility" in utilitarianism refers to those things that are useful for bringing pleasure and thus happiness. Bentham developed the felicific or utility calculus, a way of calculating the amount of happiness that any specific action is likely to bring. The calculus had seven variables: intensity, duration, certainty/uncertainty, propinquity/remoteness, fecundity, purity, and extent. Thus Bentham introduced the idea of rational calculation being used to decide human behavior and the moral status of any act.

Georg Simmel (1858–1919) was probably the first sociologist to specifically consider exchange. He argued that most relationships for people are governed by exchange principles. The primary evidence that Simmel has for this claim is that the majority of our relationships are reciprocal. That is, most of our activities are at least a two-way give-and-take. It's important for us to see this definition of exchange because many exchange theorists insist that it is governed by rationality, the evaluation of costs and benefits. This issue has opened exchange theory up to criticism, for there are other theories that insist humans are usually not rational in their behaviors—humans minimize their cognitive efforts and often behave through routine or emotion. While Simmel sees pure economic exchange as governed by cost and benefit analysis, it isn't necessarily true for social exchange generally. Exchange, then, as understood through *reciprocation*, is the basic form of society: "Value and exchange constitute the foundation of our practical life" (Simmel, 1971, p. 47).

In addition to the theories covered here, contemporary exchange theory has by and large gone in two different directions. First is an approach initially developed by Richard Emerson (1972) and his colleague Karen Cook (1978). In contrast to Blau, who focuses on the exchange between two people (dyad) as the archetype of exchange, Emerson and Cook focus more on the network of exchange rather than the exchange itself. Social networks are defined by the patterns and positions of a group's interaction. For a quick example, think about an organizational chart. A person's position on that chart determines his or her general pattern of interaction. The same is true for any social group of which you are a member. Within a group there are specific patterns of interaction: Some members of the group interact more than others, and some members don't interact together at all, even though they are in the same group. Social networks, then, are another kind of structure that produces effects that don't originate with the individual, that don't come from social group membership or identity, and about which the individual may or may not be aware.

The second major approach is rational choice theory, which shifts focus back to the individual and the outcomes of his or her rational choices. One of the problems posed is that what may be rational for a group may not be rational for the individual. For example, if a group of six people were to move a piano upstairs, it's rational for the group to work together but not rational for the individual. People rationally seek to avoid cost and pain; moving a piano involves one and perhaps both. From the point of view of the individual, then, it's rational to appear as if he or she is contributing but in fact allow the others to do the actual work. This is called the problem of the "free rider." Because of this tendency of rationality and because there are certain goods that can only be created by a group, people rationally develop norms that limit or require action. These norms are rights given to some individuals to control the actions of others, and members agree to these obligations in exchange for comparable limitations and obligations being placed on others. (See James S. Coleman's [1990] *Foundations of Social Theory* for a systematic argument from this perspective.)

BUILDING YOUR THEORY TOOLBOX

Learning More—Primary and Secondary Sources

- Primary sources for George Homans:
  - Homans' two most important works are the *Human Group,* Harcourt Brace Jovanovich, 1950, and *Social Behavior: Its Elementary Forms,* Harcourt, Brace & World, 1961.
  - For a very good, brief introduction to his work, see "Behaviourism and After," in A. Giddens & J. H. Turner (Eds.), *Social Theory Today,* Stanford University Press, 1987.
- Primary sources for Peter Blau:
  - Blau's most significant work in exchange theory is *Exchange and Power in Social Life,* Transaction, 2003. Blau moved on from exchange theory and became concerned with population structures. That work can be found in *Structural Contexts of Opportunities,* University of Chicago Press, 1994.
- Blau has also written two short pieces that provide an excellent overview of his ideas:
  - "Social Exchange." In David L. Sills (Ed.), *International Encyclopedia of the Social Sciences,* Macmillan, 1968.
  - "Macrostructural Theory." In Jonathan H. Turner (Ed.), *Handbook of Sociological Theory,* Kluwer Academic/Plenum, 2002.
- Primary sources for Randall Collins:
  - For an introduction to Collins' central idea of interaction ritual chains, read pages 188 to 203 in his *Theoretical Sociology,* Harcourt Brace Jovanovich, 1988. For a complete exposition of this idea, read *Interaction Ritual Chains,* Princeton University Press, 2004.
  - Collins integrates a number of exchange principles in his theory. For his basic ideas on this subject, read "Emotional Energy as the Common Denominator of Rational Action," *Rationality and Society,* 5, 203–230, 1993; for an interesting look at markets, see "Market Dynamics as the Engine of Historical Change," *Sociological Theory,* 8, 111–135, 1990.
- Secondary sources for Collins:
  - *George C. Homans: History, Theory, and Method,* by A. Javier Trevino, Paradigm Publishers, 2007.
  - *Structures of Power and Constraint: Papers in Honor of Peter M. Blau,* edited by Craig J. Calhoun, Marshall W. Meyer, and W. Richard Scott, Cambridge University Press, 1990.

Seeing the Social World (knowing the theory)

- Write a 250-word synopsis of the exchange theory perspective.

(Continued)

(Continued)

- After reading and understanding this chapter, you should be able to define the following terms theoretically and explain their theoretical importance to Homans' theory of the elementary forms of social behavior: *elementary social behavior, respondent behaviors, respondent conditioning, law of effect, reinforcement, matching law, stimulus proposition, value, success proposition, value proposition, deprivation-satiation proposition, frustration-aggression proposition.*

- After reading and understanding this chapter, you should be able to define the following terms theoretically and explain their theoretical importance to Blau's exchange theory: *social exchanges, rationally motivation, power, alternatives, marginal utilities, norm of reciprocity, norm of fair exchange, secondary exchange relations.*

- After reading and understanding this chapter, you should be able to define the following terms theoretically and explain their theoretical importance to Collins' theory of ritual exchanges: *emotional energy, rituals, co-presence, shared focus of attention, rhythmic entrainment, common emotional mood, barrier to outsiders, group symbols, group solidarity, standards of morality, generalized and particularized cultural capital, market opportunities, stratification, deference and demeanor, principle of order giving, principle of ritual coercion, principle of anticipatory socialization, principle of bureaucratic personality, social network, authoritarian and cosmopolitan personalities.*

- After reading and understanding this chapter, you should be able to answer the following questions (remember to answer them *theoretically*):

  ○ Explain how behaviors are patterned (social order is achieved) using Homans' theory of elementary behaviors.

  ○ Explain how power is achieved through social exchanges.

  ○ What are the five possible responses to power?

  ○ How are social structures created through social exchange?

  ○ Explicate the dynamics and effects of interaction rituals.

  ○ How do interaction rituals produce a micro–macro link?

  ○ How are power and status produced and reproduced through interaction rituals?

  ○ One of the enlightening aspects of exchange theory is that it helps us understand our relationships in terms of exchange. For example, what kinds of exchange dynamics are at work in your family or significant relationships? How can you understand your relationship with your professor using exchange theory? Specifically, how is power achieved and how could you reduce the level of power?

  ○ What does Collins' theory add to understanding race, class, gender, and sexual inequalities?

  ○ How does emotion solve the three long-standing critiques of exchange theory?

Engaging the Social World (using the theory)

- Explain your relationship with the professor of this class using Blau's and Collins' theories. Focus explicitly on the issue of power. In other words, how does exchange theory explain the power differences between you and your professor? If you wanted to change that inequity, how would you do so (explain theoretically)?

- Using at least one element from each of the three theorists in this chapter, use exchange theory to explain how to maintain happiness in a significant relationship.

Weaving the Threads (building theory)

- Compare and contrast Blau's and Collins' ideas of power. What is power and how does it work in these two theories? Now, compare those findings with Dahrendorf. How can these three theories be brought together?

- Compare and contrast Blau's and Collins' theories of the micro–macro link. Put them together in such a way as to begin to form a single theory. What do you think is still missing?

- Compare and contrast Mead's theory of the self with Collins' idea of the individual. In this analysis be certain to explore and give examples of situations where the symbolic interactionist's idea of the self is more appropriate or functional and situations where Collins' notion of the person as carriers of ritual elements makes more sense. Which do you find more theoretically persuasive and why?

- You've now been exposed to three different perspectives about how social order is achieved: Parsons' structural functionalism, conflict theory (mostly Coser and Dahrendorf), and now exchange theory. Write a detailed paragraph for each that describes the approach and most important points.

CHAPTER 12

The Late Modern Person and the Situation:

Erving Goffman, Harold Garfinkel, and R. S. Perinbanayagam

The title of this chapter is meant to play off the title of Chapter 6: The Modern Person. As I've mentioned several times, modernity was founded on a unique idea of the person, *naturally endowed* with reason and the ability to make rational decisions. One of the important features of this idea was the part I have in italics. This idea of the person went along with the one "endowed by their Creator with certain unalienable rights." Both the rights and the reason were part of human nature by birth.

In Chapter 6, Mead gave us a way to understand how people can make reasoned decisions. Through various stages of role-taking people develop a self that is able to take one's own actions as social objects, to consider various potential lines of action, and to choose one to fit into the actions of others (thus, inter-action). But Mead did something else. He opened a Pandora's Box. He wasn't alone in this; certainly the work of Sigmund Freud took us further. But what both Mead and Freud did was to question the naturalness of the human self or subject; "whose 'center' consisted of an inner core which first emerged when the subject was born, and unfolded with it, while remaining essentially the same . . . throughout the individual's existence" (Hall, 1996, p. 597). In both Freud and Mead's schemes the person is *formed by social encounters;* no longer natural, it is a socially created reality. As we'll see later in the book, this reality of a natural self or subject is deeply questioned by some contemporary theorists. Here Goffman is going to attune us to the idea that the reality of the self is comprised of multiple images that we put together for the sake of social encounters. Goffman's emphasis on image begins to help us think about the influence that mass media might have on the self. And R. S. Perinbanayagam, our final theorist in this chapter, will play out some of the ramifications of the self being based in language, something Mead saw but didn't expand.

But there's more going on in this chapter than just the late modern person. Like Mead's symbolic interactionism, there's a challenge in these theories for what is generally meant by society. You remember from Chapter 1 that one of the primary assumptions a social researcher makes is about society: Of what kind of "stuff" is society made? Most of the people that we met in the first seven chapters of this book saw society as a macro level entity, built from social structures that guide and constrain human behavior. Weber and Mead dissented, but by and large that was the model of early modern sociology (and of course of Parsons' defining work).

Each of the theorists in this chapter challenges the idea that society exists as its own kind of entity, obeying its own rules and creating its own effects. This critique is then used to give different answers to the problem of social order. As we'll find out, the theorists in this chapter see people at the micro level (the level of face-to-face social encounters) producing social order without the influence of social norms or macro level structures. Erving Goffman will show us that order is produced simply because we have to present a self in every situation, and doing so places certain demands on the encounter that incidentally create order. Harold Garfinkel will tells us that we achieve social order in social situations; but then we hide the fact that social order is created right here, right now, in just this way. And R. S. Perinbanayagam's theory implies the textual nature of society, an idea that gets expanded later in our book.

Finally, two of the theorists in this chapter present us with new perspectives. Erving Goffman uses a dramaturgical analogy to understand what is happening in social situations, and Harold Garfinkel introduces us to ethnomethodology. R. S. Perinbanayagam, on the other hand, is by and large a symbolic interactionist and builds on Mead's theory. Thus, while there will be Taking the Perspective boxes for Goffman and Garfinkel, I refer you back to Chapter 6 for symbolic interactionism.

Performing the Self:
Erving Goffman (1922–1982)

Theorist's Digest
Concepts and Theory: Impression Management
  Putting Up a Front
  Role Performance
  Entertaining Stigma
  The Interaction Order
Concepts and Theory: Frames and Keys
Summary
Taking the Perspective—Dramaturgy

The significance of Goffman's work lies in his emphasis on the presentation of self or what we would today call image. Goffman's work was published from the 1950s through the early 1980s. This period of time is culturally marked by the emergence and then dominance of television. Prior to this period, words, whether written (books and newspapers) or spoken (radio), defined mass media. Words give importance to story, and story emphasizes coherence and meaning. Television, however, shifted the power of mass media from word to image. What became important in news, for example, is not whether the story was complete and meaningful, but, rather, whether or not there was film or video. This emphasis on image that television conveyed was bolstered by technical advances in movie and magazine production. Movies became spectacles and magazines filled with glossy pictures. These shifts in the cultural context impacted the way people understood themselves. Self-image became increasingly important and at the same time became less tied to real social groups and more informed by images seen in television, commercials, movies, and advertisement. The importance of meaning and coherence gave way to the power of an image to gain attention, to be attractive. What Goffman gives us, then, is a theory that explains how we manage our images and the impression we make on others.

THEORIST'S DIGEST

Brief Biography

Goffman was born on June 11, 1922, in Alberta, Canada. He earned his PhD from the University of Chicago. For his dissertation, he studied daily life on one of the Scottish islands (Unst). The dissertation from this study became his first book, *The Presentation of Self in Everyday Life*, which is now available in 10 different languages. In 1958, Herbert Blumer invited Goffman to teach at the University of California, Berkeley. He stayed there for 10 years, moving to the University of Pennsylvania in 1968, where he taught for the remainder of his career. Goffman also served as president of the American Sociological Association in 1981 and 1982. Goffman died of cancer on November 19, 1982.

Central Sociological Questions

Goffman (1983) was inquisitive about everything people did in face-to-face interactions: "For myself I believe that human social life is ours to study naturalistically. . . . From the perspective of the physical and biological sciences, human social life is only a small irregular scab on the face of nature, not particularly amenable to deep systematic analysis. And so it is. But it's ours" (p. 17). Goffman probed this social life incessantly. He watched people continually and asked, what are people doing? What's going on just beneath the surface of what we see? What is required for a social encounter to occur? How do these requirements influence everything that people do when they meet? Specifically, how do the constraints of presenting a self create social order?

(Continued)

(Continued)

Simply Stated

Goffman argues that for any social encounter to take place people need to present a self. This presentation, however, isn't something that people take for granted. Impression management is serious business and people manipulate specific cues in the setting and in their appearance and manner in order to present a specific kind of self to others. These cues are prepared in the backstage and presented in a front stage wherein the audience reads the cues and in response demands a certain kind of performance from the actor. This performance may be team based, and it entails deference and demeanor rituals, face-work, and may result in stigma, if not properly executed. This fundamental need to present a self for an encounter to occur results in social order, though that is not the intent of the actors.

Key Ideas

dramaturgy, social identities, personal identities, ego identities, impression management, front, setting, appearance, manner, ritual states, backstage, performance teams, roles, role distance, stigma, face, deference and demeanor rituals, face-work, frames, keys, interaction order, biographies, cognitive relations

Concepts and Theory: Impression Management

Goffman uses a **dramaturgical analogy** to help us see the social world differently. As it probably sounds, dramaturgical analysis relies on the *analogy of the dramatic stage.* In this perspective, people are seen as performers who are vitally concerned with the presentation of their character (the self) to an audience. Where Mead and Simmel in Chapter 6 were concerned with the social context of the self and how the self is socialized, Goffman focuses on how the self is presented and perceived outside the individual. Another difference is that for Mead the self is a social object that may or may not become the focus of an interaction. Goffman, however, argues that the self is more basic to the interaction than a topic. The self isn't one of many possible social objects; the self is *the central organizing feature* of all social encounters. For Goffman it's the presentation of a self that creates and maintains social order. The central, driving force in this social organization is embarrassment, or what Goffman (1967) refers to as face: "His aim is to save face; his effect is to save the situation" (p. 39).

Putting Up a Front

The basic concept Goffman uses to explain the presentation of self is that of a front. A **front** is the expression of a particular self or identity that is formed by the individual and read by others. The front is like a building façade.

Merriam-Webster's (2002) first definition of façade is remarkably like Goffman's idea of a front: A façade is "a face (as a flank or rear facing on a street or court) of a building that is given emphasis by special architectural treatment." Like a façade, a front is constructed by emphasizing and deemphasizing certain sign vehicles. In every interaction, we hold things back, things that aren't appropriate for the situation or that we don't want those in the situation to attribute to our self; we accentuate other aspects in order to present a particular kind of self with respect to the social role. A social front is constructed using three main elements: the setting, appearance, and manner.

The idea of the **setting** is taken directly from the theater: It consists of all the physical scenery and props that we use to create the stage and background within which we present our performance. The clearest example for us is probably the classroom. The chalkboard, the room layout with all the desks facing the front, the media equipment, and so on are all used by the professor to make claim to the role of teacher. All this is obvious, but notice that the way the setting is used cues different kinds of professorial performances. I may choose to "de-center" the role of teacher and instead claim the role of facilitator by simply rearranging the desks in a circle and using multiple, mobile chalkboards placed all around the room.

Settings tend to ground roles by making definitions of the situation consistent. For example, it would be more difficult (but not impossible) for me to use the classroom as a setting for the definition of "bar." This grounding of settings is part of what makes us think that roles, identities, and selves are consistent across time and space. There is a taken-for-grantedness about the **definition of the situation** when we are in a geographic location that becomes more pronounced the more institutionalized the location is. When I say that a location is institutionalized, I mean that the use of a specific place appears restricted: The front of the classroom looks as if students are restricted, yet it is available to many professors; the office of the CEO of Microsoft, on the other hand, is even more institutionalized and restricted. However, there is still a great deal of flexibility and creativity available to those that use the space.

In addition to the physical setting, a front is produced by using appearance and manner. *Appearance* cues consist of clothing, hair style, makeup, jewelry, cologne, backpacks, attaché cases, piercings, tattoos, and so on—in short, anything that we can place upon our bodies. While appearance refers to those things that we do to our bodies, manner refers to what we do with our bodies. *Manner* consists of the way we walk, our posture, our voice inflection, how we use our eyes, what we do with our hands, what we do with our arms, our stride, the way we sit, how we physically respond to stimuli, and so on. Both appearance and manner function to signify the performer's social statuses and temporary ritual state. What we mean by social statuses should be fairly clear. Bankers and bikers have different social statuses, and they dress differently. They don't dress differently because they have dissimilar tastes; they dress differently because different appearance cues are associated with different status positions.

Ritual states refer to at least two things. The most apparent is the ritual state associated with different life phases. We have fewer of these than do traditional societies, but we still mark some life transitions with rituals, like birthdays, grad-uations, promotions, and retirement. The second idea that the notion of ritual state conveys is our readiness to perform a particular role. Our appearance tells others how serious we are about the role we claim. For example, if you see two people riding bicycles and they are dressed differently, one in normal street clothes and the other in matching nylon/lycra jersey and shorts along with cycling shoes and helmet, then you can surmise that one is really serious about riding and the other is less so.

As in the theater, fronts are prepared backstage and presented on the front stage. Most of what is implied in these concepts is fairly intuitive. For example, every day before you go to school you prepare your student-self in the *backstage*. You pick clothes, shower, do your hair, put on makeup, or whatever it is that corresponds to the self that you want others to see and respond to. Your work in the backstage for school is different from your work in the backstage of a date (unless someone you're dating will see your performance at school). You then present the student-self that you've prepared in the *front stages* of class, lunchroom, hallway, and so forth. But the backstage of school extends further back than your morning preparations. All students will study, read, and write to a certain degree in preparation for class. This too is part of the backstage for class. Even if you don't read or study, you are prepar-ing to perform as a certain kind of student. As I said, most of this is intuitive. However, we need to realize that there are multiple front and back stages and that they can occur at almost any time and place.

There is another way that we can use the ideas of front and back stages. There are certain roles and thus encounters that are particular to different kinds of stages. For example, the role of company CEO is more on the front stage than the role of line worker. The CEO represents the company as a whole, while the factory worker is rarely involved in representing the company directly. These sorts of front and back stage differences significantly impact the person. People who play front stage roles tend to be identified with the role, by both others and the person himself or herself. These roles are sort of like ritual centers: Images and practices around which encounters are organized—they are the focus of attention. Front stage people tend to emotionally connect with and value their performances in these roles, thus creating a consistent and protected face.

Role Performance

Every definition of a social situation contains roles that are normal and regu-larly expected. Goffman considers *roles* as bundles of activities that are effectively laced together into a situated activity system. Some of these role-specific activi-ties we will be pleased to perform and others we perhaps will not. We can thus distance ourselves from a role or we can fully embrace it. *Role distancing* is a way of enacting the role that simultaneously allows the actor to lay claim to the role and to say that he or she is so much more than the role. Let's take the role of student, for example. There are certain kinds of behaviors that are expected of students: They should read the material through several times before class, they should sit in the front row and diligently take notes, they should ask questions in class and consistently make eye contact with the professor, they should systematize and rewrite their notes at least every week, they should make it a point to introduce themselves to the professor and stop by during office hours to go over the material, and so forth. You already know the list, though you probably haven't taken the time to write it out.

But how many of you actually perform the role in its entirety? Why don't you? It isn't a matter of ignorance or ability; you know and can perform everything we've listed and more. So, why don't you? You don't perform the role to its fullest because you want to express to people, mostly your peers, that there is more to you than simply being a student. When presenting the role of student, it is difficult to simultaneously perform another role. Thus, in order to convey to others that you might be more than a student, you leave gaps in the presentation. These gaps leave possibilities and questions in the minds of others—who else is this person? Sometimes we fill the gaps with hints of other selves (like "athletic female" or "sensitive male") that aren't necessarily part of the definition of the situation.

Contained within the idea of role distance is role embracement. In *role embracement,* we adhere to all that the role demands. We effectively become one with the role; the role becomes our self. We see and judge our self mainly through this role. We tend to embrace a role when we are new to a situation or when we feel ourselves to be institutional representatives (like a parent or teacher). When we do embrace a role like this, we *idealize* the situation and its roles. That is, we "incorporate and exemplify the officially accredited values of the society" (Goffman, 1959, p. 35). When we manage our front in such a way, we place claims upon the audience—first, to recognize the self that we are presenting as one that embodies society, and second, to present our self in such a way as to represent society as well.

Some of the decision to distance or embrace a role is personal, but most of it is situational. For example, we expect university students to experiment and try out different things. It's a time between highly institutionalized spaces. You are no longer a child fully under the demands of your parents, nor are you working at a job that fully demands your time, effort, and impression management. However, when you do become a full member of the economy, you won't have the time or occasion to experience different situations and the selves they entail. Your daily rounds will be more restricted and managed by others. And you will be expected to more fully embrace the self that work requires. Of course, role distancing is still possible, but we have to work harder at it and it is circumscribed by our situations.

Entertaining Stigma

However, it's not true that we are free to present any type of self—every presented front is an attempt to pass as an identifiable and meaningful person; if we fail to pass, we run the risk of stigma. In every situation we make claim to be a certain type of person. These claims constitute the individual's *virtual self* in the situation. Participants compare the virtual self to the *actual self,* the actual role-related behaviors. The differences between the virtual and actual selves—and there are always differences—create the possibility of *stigma*. The word *stigma* comes from the Greek and originally meant a brand or tattoo. Today, stigma is used to denote a mark of shame or discredit. There are well-known and apparent stigmas; among the ones that Goffman mentions are disabilities and deformities. People with such apparent stigmas are *discredited* by those that Goffman calls "normals." Having someone with an obvious stigma creates tension in encounters. Normals practice careful "disattention" and the discredited use various devices to manage the tension, such as joking or downplaying.

There are also well-known but not so apparent stigmas. People in this category are *discreditable:* They live daily and in every situation with the potential of being stigmatized. One such category that is prominent today in the United States is that of homosexuals. Being homosexual in this society is a stigmatized identity—the homosexual is viewed as having failed to live up to the expectations associated with being a sexual person. Many homosexuals practice information management (as compared to tension management); they work to pass as a normal. *Passing* is a concerted and well-organized effort to appear normal based on the knowledge of possible discrediting; this impression management entails a directedness that isn't usual for normals.

The deeper truth that Goffman wants us to see is that all of us pass, because we all engage in information management. We know what cues to avoid in order to successfully pull off a performance. Remember when we listed the cues associated with the perfect student? Well, we could just as easily record the signals associated with being a poor student. If we think back to the issue of role distance, we can see that role distancing requires a delicate balance between claiming enough cues to still be considered a student without being discredited as a poor student. Since we all pass, we are constantly in danger of being stigmatized: "The issue becomes not whether a person has experience with a stigma of his own, because he has, but rather how many varieties he has had his own experience with" (Goffman, 1963, p. 129).

The reason that stigmas can exist and are an issue is that *identities* belong to and represent society's values and beliefs. The representational, symbolic character of identities and the way in which we interact around those identities indicate that identities and selves are sacred objects. Sacred things represent society, are reserved for special use, and are protected from misuse by clear symbolic boundaries. The sacred self, like all sacred objects, has boundaries that are guarded against encroachment. The sacred quality of identities and selves is the source of shame: "As sacred objects, men are subject to slights and profanation" (Goffman, 1967, p. 31). The flip side of stigma and shame is equally related to this collective feature of identities: a sense of pride in the sacred self.

Goffman uses the idea of face to express the dynamics of the sacred self. *Face* refers to the positive social value that a person claims in an interaction. As we've seen, when we present cues and we lay claim to a social identity, others grant us the identity and attribute to us a host of internal characteristics. Through role distancing we can negotiate some of these attributions, but in order to make an effective claim on the situated self, we must keep our performance within a given set of parameters—otherwise we could not be identified. Every established identity has positive social values attached to it, and over time we can become emotionally involved with those values. As individuals, we experience these emotions as our ego identity. And every time we present an identity we expose our face, our ego identity, to risk. We risk embarrassment, but the risk is necessary in order to feel pride and a strong sense of self.

The Interaction Order

This idea of putting our face at risk implies that the encounter or interaction is of a ritual order. Goffman (1967) argues that interactions are ritualized insofar as they represent "a way in which the individual must guard and design the symbolic implications of his acts while in the immediate presence of an object that has a special value to him" (p. 57). Encounters, then, are highly ritualized social interactions. It's this need to present and preserve a self-image that creates social order, according to Goffman. It is an order that is produced out of the simple demand that a self is needed to interact. It is ritualized—patterned in unthinking ways—because what occurs is for the express purpose of presentation, the first and primary step in a social encounter.

The content of the interaction, its meanings and motivations, isn't Goffman's concern. For us to interact there are certain rules, ways of behaving, and effects that are demanded and come about simply because a presentation is required. These have little if anything to do with our personal motives, but have significant power over the effects of the interaction. For example, when we enter an interaction, we find out what people are talking about, what kinds of roles are important, what statuses are claimed, how involved people are in the interaction, and so on. Then, once we've checked out the terrain, we gradually introduce our talk and self into the flow of interaction. The motive behind such care, Goffman tells us, is to save our self from embarrassment. The effect, however, is that the organization of the interaction is preserved: "His aim is to save face; his effect is to save the situation" (Goffman, 1967, p. 39).

Goffman, however, is quick to tell us that he is not proposing a situational reductionism, where the only thing that exists is face-to-face interactions. Goffman doesn't talk in terms of structures or institutions, but he names at least three things that exist outside of the immediate interaction. First, *settings* strongly inform the definition of the situation. The definition of the situation is important because it tells us what kind of selves to present, what to expect from others, how to interpret meaning, and so forth. For example, the selves, meanings, and others available in a university classroom are different than at a local bar.

Another element that exists outside the encounter is *biographies*. People come into interactions with biographies. These biographies are previously established stories about our self and others. There are two kinds of biographical stories that we use, individual and categoric. If we see someone with whom we have interacted previously, then we have an individual biography of that person and he or she of us.

As we will see, these biographies or story lines are the result of impression management. Yet, once established, you and I are both committed to maintaining that
story. When a personal biography isn't available, as when you first meet someone,
then categoric biographies are used—stories that go along with the type of person
you are meeting. For example, when you first meet a professor, there's a categoric
biography that you access, a story about that person even though you've never met
before. Both individual and categoric biographies structure the encounter.

The third extra-interactional element that Goffman (1983) explicitly talks about is
cognitive relations: "At the very center of interaction life is the cognitive relation we
have with those present before us" (p. 4). As members of categoric groups, each of us
has identifiable knowledge bases, and these islands of knowledge are related to other
specific categoric groups. For example, let's say it's Friday after work and you've just
stopped by a local bar to unwind. As you sit down at the bar, the person next to you
strikes up a conversation. The small talk continues as you chat about work, the poker
tournament on the television, and other bits and pieces of social life. Then one of you
mentions music and you find out that one plays guitar and the other drums.
Suddenly an entire horizon of shared knowledge opens up. You can almost feel the
expansion from a narrow sliver of shared reality to a world of cognitive relations.

Thus, Goffman isn't arguing that more macro level entities don't exist, or that
they are any less an abstraction than the interaction order (though you might
notice that the way he talks about such large-scale things is distinctly different from
most structural sociologists). It's Goffman's (1983) perspective that "in all these
cases [of both the macro and micro phenomena] what we get is somebody's crudely
edited summaries" (p. 9). Yet Goffman is also arguing that interactions are unique
in that they, more than any other social site, are "worn smooth" through constant
use. People interact more in face-to-face encounters than they do in other social
units, such as formal organizations (for example, Wal-Mart and Target) or nations
(like the United States and England). The interaction order achieved through
encounters, then, is our most stable and routine social entity, and it seems "more
open to systematic analysis than are the internal or external workings of many
macroscopic entities" (Goffman, 1983, p. 9).

Concepts and Theory: Frames and Keys

In one of his last works, Goffman took on the social construction of reality, but with
a twist. Generally, concern has focused on human reality itself. In contrast,
Goffman begins with the individual and asks the question, "Under what conditions
do we think things are real?" As such, Goffman (1974) is interested in the internal
organization of individual experience: "I am not addressing the structure of social
life but the structure of experience individuals have at any moment of their social
lives" (p. 13). Specifically, this means that Goffman is not interested in the reality or
ontological status of the world itself, but, rather, in the process through which an
individual might experience a portion of the world as being more real than another.

In taking this perspective, Goffman is intentionally distancing himself from
Garfinkel's ethnomethodology. Garfinkel is similarly concerned with the reality

status of the world, but he approaches it more in terms of the rules and methods people use in interactions to create a sense of taken-for-grantedness about a shared reality. In other words, Garfinkel is interested in the folk methods people use in social interaction to gloss over the subjective and reflexive nature of reality. To present his answer to the reality question, Goffman shifts his analytical focus and changes his analogy. Up to this point, Goffman has been focused on the encounter. However, to analyze the reality experience, Goffman focuses on the individual, not the situation. Goffman also changes his analogy from the stage to photography. Goffman uses the notion of a film strip (this was before digital photography) to talk about the stream of human activity: Apart from the categories, or in this case, frames, that we use, our experience of the world through time is an undifferentiated stream of intimately linked events—it's like a film strip that never ends.

If we look closely at a strip of film, what we see are individual frames wherein activity is stopped or freeze-framed. This notion of "frame" is Goffman's chief concept for understanding how people have real or less real experiences. **Frames** are principles of organization that govern social events and our subjective involvement in them. We use frames to pick out certain elements of a situation to pay attention to and others to ignore. Just like literal picture or film-strip frames, frames of organization include and exclude certain things from the picture. For example, picture frames tell us where art ends and the mundane wall begins.

One of the things that Goffman does with his notion of frames is to expand the idea of the definition of the situation. The various definitions that a situation may have are built up from the principles of organization that are found in frames. Frames thus tell us not only what to see but also how to be involved actively and emotionally in any occasion. Notice that we are now talking about many definitions of a situation rather than the definition. Goffman argues that multiple frames can be used in any setting. They can be built up and layered in almost endless ways. Thus, the human experience can be complex and layered. And since roles and selves are attached to definitions of the situation, we can play multiple roles in any location.

Structuring the experience of multiple realities are two primary frames. Primary frames are seen by the people using them as not based upon or requiring a previous interpretation; primary frames initially organize activity into something that is meaningful. Primary frames divide the world into two spheres: natural and social. A natural frame tells people that whatever is occurring is not due to some intentional act or human agency; it is simply and purely physical. The rising of the sun is generally understood as a natural event. Social frames, on the other hand, imply that a human agent or willful intention is involved or necessary. Economic or political activities are two clear examples.

Primary frames can be keyed. Goffman has in mind the keying of music, where music written in one key may be transposed into a different key: The music is basically the same, but it sounds different. Keying thus refers to sets of conventions through which a strip of activity that has already been given meaning by a primary frame is experienced by the participants as something else. That definition sounds pretty academic, but I think it will become clear once we consider the various ways we key things.

Goffman lists five basic keys employed in our society: make-believe, contests, ceremonies, technical redoings, and regroupings. Make-believe is activity that looks real but the participants don't expect any real outcomes. One of the things that Goffman finds interesting about make-believe is that it requires our full attention and we tend to become engrossed in the process, even though everyone acknowledges that what is happening isn't real. Play, fantasy, and dramatic scripting are three examples of make-believe keying. One of the most common examples of play is when we "joke around." The very label we use—joking around—is designed to bracket off some behaviors from reality and key them into a different meaning. Make-believe fantasy keys are very common today, particularly with the widespread use of computers and the Internet. Obviously, a lot of what we do with computers is seen as real, but the territory itself—virtual reality—leads us to key action strips to the fantastic: We can maintain multiple virtual identities associated with a variety of avatars (or incarnations) interacting with manifold groups in imaginary rooms of our choosing.

In addition to make-believe, we also use the contest key. For example, the army regularly participates in war games. These are contests that look like the real thing and that demand full attention, yet aren't really wars, though there are always winners. Sports are another example of contest keying. Sports like boxing, football and soccer, lacrosse, hockey, and especially the Olympic Games can be seen as ritualized violence. Another interesting type of keying is ceremonial. A ceremonial key references an event, such as the opening ceremony of the Olympic Games, wherein the event and people represent some significant social meaning. Ceremonies thus take events and social positions and idealize them and link them to a symbolic meaning that transcends the activity strip itself.

We have two more kinds of keys to consider: technical redoings and regroupings. Regroupings are, as Goffman (1974) notes, "the most troublesome of the lot" (p. 74). The idea of regrouping references the participants' motives—some motives in performing a strip of activity are in keeping with those that are normally expected and others are outside the normal expectations. An example of regrouping is an upper-class woman working as a salesperson at a church yard sale. In technical redoings, we take ordinary activities out of their context and perform them for reasons completely different from those that are normally understood. A male might, for example, practice different pickup lines with a close female friend; a music group might rehearse the show they will perform in a week; we watch demonstrations of laying carpet at the local Home Depot; or in therapy we might be asked to act out our feelings or talk to a dead father. Goffman notes that people can conceptualize (key) almost anything as an experiment.

By now it should be clear that our experience of life can be pretty complex. That is part of Goffman's point. People are playing with and moving in and out of keys almost continually. To top things off, keys and frames can be fabricated. There is an assumption of authenticity with any of the keyings that we've looked at. Even with such things as make-believe, we assume that it is authentically make-believe, that there is no other hidden agenda behind the play or fantasy. But sometimes there is something else going on and the keyed frame that we are asked to accept is a fabrication. Under a keyed frame, all the participants have the same point of view. But under a keyed frame that is fabricated, there are different perspectives. All con games work using fabricated frames. A less dramatic example might be a high school girl who joins the school production of a play in order to be close to someone she is interested in. At rehearsal, the play is keyed (note that the play itself is the result of a keying), and everybody at rehearsal understands the key, including the young woman. However, she has a different perspective than the rest: For her, the key enables her to meet and interact with her love interest.

This multi-contextual game is probably more prominent today, in technically advanced societies, than in previous ages. The reasons for this change are extensive and complex, but they are not our concern at the moment. Our cultural life is extremely complex and will probably become more so. Goffman's point is that no matter how complex the keys and fabrications might become, they are generally built up from two primary frames. We can think of our experience, particularly in the beginnings of the twenty-first century, as layered from the most basic to the most abstract. We might play with virtual selves and abstract ideas like hyperreality, but the scaffolding of keys and fabrications can and will fall apart like a house of cards when reality asserts itself, as it tends to do.

Summary

• In an interaction, participants depend upon cues to attribute an identity and its attendant attitudes to the individual. The identity and its attitudinal and behavioral expectations form righteously imputed expectations. Sensing this, most people are careful in the way they manage the impression they give others. This work can be seen to vary on a continuum from role distance to role embracement. In role distance, one manages impression in such a way as to simultaneously lay effective claim to the role, its virtual self, and a yet unseen self. The purpose of such work is to claim a self that is more than the role communicates. In role embracement, the individual disappears within the virtual self. Such work idealizes the situation and its roles.

• The longer we perform a particular role or the closer we come to role embracement, the greater is the possibility of embarrassment. Goffman refers to this emotional attachment to roles as face. Every interaction represents a risk to self: We can either lose or maintain face. As such, most interactions are ritualized around face-work.

• Settings and encounters obtain meaning through the use of frames. Frames are interpretive schemes that individuals use to section off parts of the endless stream of activities and events. There are two primary frames: natural and social. The natural frame sections off elements from the stream of life and interprets them as normal and natural—rather than due to some intentional act or human agency. The social frame interprets activities and events in terms of a human agent or willful intention. The use of these two primary frames is how individuals experience things as real. The frames, however, may be keyed through make-believe, contests, ceremonies, technical redoings, and regroupings, and those keys may be authentic or fabricated. Keys and fabrications allow for the possibility of multiple and abstract levels of meaning, yet they are all tied to one of the two primary frames.

TAKING THE PERSPECTIVE—DRAMATURGY

As Fine and Manning (2003) note, "It is difficult to trace precisely the intellectual forces that influenced Goffman's distinct creativity" (p. 41). Goffman rarely, if ever, engaged in the scholastic practice of citing sources in order to substantiate his position or to build on the work of predecessors (a distinct practice of science). What he did was to describe in minute detail the social happenings he explored. "Though Goffman was surely the sociologist he professed to be, he was every bit as much, simply, a writer" (Lemert, 1997, p. xiii). Though there's little in Goffman's writings to link him to any theoretical tradition, it is undoubtedly the case that his graduate student days at the University of Chicago affected his perspective. According to Fine and Manning, his cohort took a "skeptical stance toward the dominant functionalist and quantitative perspective of mid-century American sociology, postulating an alternative . . . of interpretive sociology" (p. 41). We also know that Goffman was invited to Berkeley by Herbert Blumer, an invitation he accepted, and both *Forms of Talk* (1981) and *Frame Analysis* (1974) were written in response to ethnomethodology.

Briefly, dramaturgy is a theoretical perspective and methodology that uses the analogy of the stage to understand and illuminate social life. In this perspective people are seen as actors who constantly manage the impression others have of self. Importantly, the need for and emphasis upon the presentation of self in every social encounter creates an underlying structuring process that produces social order. Dramaturgists are interested in the continual production of a social self, which places moral imperatives on the interaction order.

For example, Arlie Hochschild (1983) extends Goffman's interests in impression management and demonstrates how we manage emotions as part of our front. According to Hochschild there are a variety of ways we do this kind of emotion work. One method is cognitive: We can try and change our ideas or thoughts in order to change the way we feel about something. Another approach involves the body. We can use the body to try and lead our emotions in a desirable direction. For example, we will breathe deeply in order to calm our nerves when speaking in front of a crowd. A third way of managing emotion involves using expressive gestures. Sometimes we'll smile in order to make ourselves feel happy. But the most important way that we manage our emotions is through deep acting. Like method acting, where the performer *becomes* the character to such an extent that the audience is almost secondary, in deep acting the person creates a real emotional response within in order to express it to others.

Theoretically, perhaps Goffman's biggest impact is with frame analysis and interaction ritual theory. Frames are basic cognitive structures that guide perception and attention; frames thus tell us what is real. Frame analysis extends Goffman's theory to social movements (Benford & Snow, 2000). The argument is that before a social movement can begin, certain frames must exist that call attention to specific details in society. This can be done intentionally through frame alignment, linking new frames to existing ones.

Organizing Ordinary Life:
Harold Garfinkel (1917–)

Theorist's Digest
Concepts and Theory: Everyday Social Order as an
      Accomplishment
            Understanding Ethnomethodology
            Accounting
            Documentary Method
Concepts and Theory: Doing Society—Reflexively
            Situationally Constructing Reality
Summary
Taking the Perspective—Ethnomethodology

Harold Garfinkel was a student of Parsons and like Parsons is concerned with human action. However, like symbolic interactionism, Garfinkel has problems with the discrepancy between what Parsons' voluntaristic action proposes and what is empirically available. Following Freud, Parsons (1951) argued that the "need disposition in the actor's own personality structure" operates unconsciously so that people don't really know why they are doing what they're doing (p. 37). Yet empirically people can give an explanation of what they are doing and why they are doing it. A potential problem then "arises between the . . . analyses of action developed by sociologists and the accounts of action developed . . . by the participants" (Heritage, 1984, pp. 22–23). Thus, Garfinkel argues that standard sociological methods miss the mark of empirical science: True sociological knowledge is provided in the immediate experiences of our day-to-day life.

Garfinkel draws inspiration from the work of Alfred Schutz. More than any other, Schutz (1967) is responsible for bringing phenomenology into the social disciplines. As a philosophy, **phenomenology** is concerned with consciousness and seeks to discover it in its purest form, apart from language and any preconceptions. The idea is to get at the essential structures of the human experience. Arguing that humans are defined socially, Schutz takes this basic idea of primary experience and argues that it is found in social things rather than the individual consciousness. Schutz tells us that the purest form of human experience is found in the natural attitude that people have in their lifeworlds. The **lifeworld** refers to the world as it is immediately experienced by each person. This lifeworld is by definition shared with others. Within this lifeworld people have a natural attitude. The natural attitude is characterized by being wide awake, suspending doubt, being engaged in work, and assuming intersubjectivity (a shared inner world). Using Schutz's work, Garfinkel is telling us that *everything we need to understand the social order can be* *found in the lifeworld and people's natural attitude toward it.* Sounds pretty simple, doesn't it? In principle it may be, but I think in practice and understanding it might be one of the more difficult sociological perspectives. If you get lost in our discussion of Garfinkel's theory, come back to this tenant of phenomenology.

THEORIST'S DIGEST

Brief Biography

Harold Garfinkel was born on October 29, 1917, in Newark, New Jersey. He grew up during the depression and was discouraged from attending the university. While attending business classes at a local school, Garfinkel was exposed to the idea of "accounting practices," which he later saw as the primary feature of interaction, as well as a group of sociology students. Those experiences, along with a summer spent at a work camp building a dam, prompted Garfinkel to hitchhike to the University of North Carolina, Chapel Hill (UNCCH), where he was admitted to graduate school. He completed his master's at UNCCH, after which he was drafted into the army during World War II. After the war, Garfinkel went to Harvard to study for his PhD under Talcott Parsons. In 1954, Garfinkel joined the faculty at the University of California, Los Angeles, where he stayed until his retirement in 1987. Garfinkel's most important work is *Studies in Ethnomethodology*, which was published in 1967.

Central Sociological Questions

Social order and meaning are age-old questions for sociologists. But Garfinkel's gaze penetrates beneath the usual sociological answers. For one, he isn't so much interested in whether or not social order and meaning are actually present. That kind of concern about order and meaning always implies questions of reality, which for Garfinkel are philosophic concerns. He's interested in how we *achieve a sense* that there is order and meaning. This phrases the question empirically because whether or not there is really such a thing as society or meaning, it is empirically true that people have a sense that social order exists. He is also disturbed by how quickly sociologists explain order and meaning by referring to outside forces, like norms and social structures. This critique is also driven by an emphasis on what empirically exists: Garfinkel wants to know how a sense of social order and meaning are produced in just this way and at just this time.

Simply Stated

Social orders are identical to the commonsense methods fully aware actors use to render the situation accountable and sensible. Social situations are thus reflexive and ordered by the accounts offered and enacted by participants. Accounts are indexical; that is, they reference what is commonly understood by participants; and accounts proceed using a documentary method.

Key Ideas

lifeworld, phenomenology, ethnomethodology, accounts, documentary method, reciprocity of perspectives, reflexivity, indexical expressions, incorrigible assumptions, secondary elaborations of belief

Concepts and Theory: Everyday Social Order as an Accomplishment

I think that one of the reasons that ethnomethodology can seem difficult is that it relies on what we do in unremarkable interactions to explain social order. Rather than looking for big issues like norms and structures, Garfinkel calls our attention to such small things we do unthinkingly in every social situation. The taken-for-grantedness of these behaviors is both the power and problem of the ethnomethodological account. It's powerful because it helps us see what else is going on just beneath the surface—it lets us see that you and I are more responsible for social reality than we might imagine; the ethnomethodological account is problematic for us precisely because we do these things without thinking and they seem so mundane.

Understanding Ethnomethodology

My initial exposure to Garfinkel's work came in my first semester of graduate school. I was a teaching assistant in an introduction to sociology class. The teacher was a visiting professor by the name of Eric Livingston. As is customary, on the first day of class the professor explained what the course was about. He told us that we were taking an ethnomethodological approach to sociology. At the time, nobody knew what that meant, but he did tell us one thing that struck us all as odd: We had a textbook and we were going to read it, but not in the usual fashion. You know, we usually read textbooks to understand the topic. We approach the text as an authoritative source: Geography books teach us about the earth and sociology texts teach us about society. It sounds pretty straightforward, right? Well, not in this case. Dr. Livingston told us that we were going to use the textbook as an example of how sociology organizes itself to be sociology. We were to read the book not to learn about society, but, rather, we were to study the text to see how members of sociology render situations knowable as sociology. If you're like me, that last part was really confusing when Dr. Livingston said it. Except when you realize what we've been talking about since Chapter 1: In order to study society *one must first assume that society exists as some separate entity.*

If we don't assume that society exists as a separate entity, what are we left with? The simple answer is the one that Garfinkel wants us to see: We're simply left with what people do in the situation. Garfinkel's interest, then, is in the everyday procedures or methods people use to create a sense of social order. In fact, the term *ethnomethodology* means the study of folk methods. Garfinkel (1974) began using the term as a result of a study he did on jury deliberations. He noticed that there were distinct methods used to render the conversations, deliberations, decisions, and judgments "jury-like," rather than sounding like the mundane opinions of the person on the street. In the process of "becoming a juror," these people drew on multiple sources for information, but the people themselves did not change much. In fact, according to Garfinkel (1967), "a person is 95 percent juror before he comes near the court" (p. 110). The process of becoming a juror didn't change the people that Garfinkel observed. They basically acquired knowledge and made decisions in the same way they always did. What did change were the accounts that the jurors offered for the way in which they came to their decisions. Juries and jury decisions are *produced by the accounts that people tell about what they did.*

Accounting

Social order, then, isn't the result of institutionalized types of social action; rather, Garfinkel argues, social order is the result of members making settings **account-able**. Garfinkel is using the term *account* in the sense of to regard or classify, such as "she was accounted to be a powerful senator." To make something account-able, then, is to make it capable of being regarded or classified as a certain kind of object or event. As we render a situation accountable, we simultaneously produce social order and reality. For example, a few years ago I was visiting my sister in San Diego and we went to Balboa Park, a gorgeous recreational area with museums, fountains, restaurants, street musicians, art exhibits, and so forth. While we were walking through some of the gardens, my sister said, "Oh, look, a wedding." How could my sister recognize what was happening as a wedding? That sounds like a simple and maybe silly question, but the implications are important for Garfinkel. We were all able to recognize the event before us as a wedding because the people who organized the setting did it in such a way that it would appear as a wedding, not only to others but specifically to themselves.

When we as a group organize ourselves to do something, whether it is forming a queue or waging war, there are "requirements of recognizability" (Rawls, 2003, p. 129) that must be met. In meeting those requirements, the situation is rendered accountable as a recognizable social achievement. This work of accounting is the primary job of the members. For example, if we had gone up to the people at the wedding at any time during the event (while preparing, setting up, performing, or celebrating) and asked them, "What are you doing?" their response would be something like, "We're having a wedding." This is Garfinkel's point: The members of any situation are cognitively aware of what they are doing—they are knowingly organizing their actions in just such a way as to create a sense of social order (a wedding). Because members are knowingly producing social order within a scene, and because answerability is the simplest explanation, it follows that accounting is the primary force behind social organization.

Garfinkel thus sees social order as the result of members' practical actions that are oriented toward making the setting accountable. Notice that social order is the result of members' practical actions—not the result of people conforming to external norms, values, and beliefs that guide and guard behaviors; and not the result of social structures determining people's behaviors; and not the result of self-centered actors who cooperate only to obtain gain in a battle of profit and loss. We can see accountability practices in the story of jury selection mentioned earlier. Though the way in which they actually made decisions didn't change much, the way in which the jurors accounted for their decision making did change—the accounting practices rendered them jurors doing the business of the jury.

Garfinkel (1967, pp. 18–24) tells a story of a research project he worked on at the UCLA Outpatient Clinic. The research was to determine the criteria by which applicants were selected for treatment. Two graduate students examined 1,582 clinic files. As is usually the case, the student coders were provided with a coding sheet and instructions for its use. And, as is usually the case, the findings were subjected to inter-coder reliability tests, which are used to determine the extent to which the coders agree with one another. It's generally thought that the higher the statistic, the greater the reliability. In other words, if I'm doing a study of television commercials and I have five different coders working from the same coding sheet and their inter-coder reliability is 85%, then I can be fairly certain that what they are coding actually exists in the commercials.

However, Garfinkel found that in order to code the contents of the folders, the coders actually assumed knowledge of the way in which the clinic was organized. This assumed knowledge base "was most deliberately consulted whenever, for whatever reasons, the coders needed to be satisfied that they had coded 'what really happened'" (Garfinkel, 1967, p. 20). Notice something important here: The coders were to find out how the clinic was organized, yet in order to fill out the coding sheet, the coders assumed knowledge about the way the clinic was organized—they assumed what they were supposed to find out. Thus, the coders' reliability rate wasn't due to their reliable use of the coding sheet to document what happened in the clinic; the reliability rate was due to something the coders themselves were doing, apart from the coding sheet or the folders.

Most researchers in Garfinkel's position would regard such issues as problems with the measurement instrument and as threats to the research. Garfinkel (1967) likens these responses to "complaining that if the walls of a building were only gotten out of the way one could see better what was keeping the roof on" (p. 22). Garfinkel is saying that most social scientists miss the boat: They don't see what's really going on because they are preoccupied in producing "sociology" or "psychology" rather than seeing the social world as it is. For Garfinkel, the graduate students' task as they saw it was to "follow the coding instructions." What the graduate students produced, then, was just that: a setting or scene that could be understood and accountable as "following the coding instructions." Garfinkel's (1967) ethnomethodological question in this case became, "What actual activities made up those coders' practices called 'following coding instruction'?" (p. 20).

Getting back to my experience with Eric Livingston, while he didn't use the textbook to teach us about social things, he did teach us about "society." Professor Livingston used everyday occurrences—he pointed us to the simple ways we make something social. One of the students' assignments was to learn how to dance; another assignment involved standing in a line; another was going out to lunch. On one occasion, he didn't come to class until 15 minutes after the period started. He had me come in and set a boom box on a stool in the center of the stage. I had been instructed to turn the tape player on at the beginning of class. I didn't know what was on the tape and I wasn't to give any sort of preamble—just walk over and turn it on. I expected a taped lecture; what I got was a ringing telephone. The boom box played the sound of a ringing phone to 300 students for 15 minutes.

But, you say, dancing, lunch, lining up, and a ringing phone are no way to teach sociology! It is, if what you mean by sociology is the study of the methods people use in everyday life to render situations accountably organized as specific kinds of social events. How is it that we organize our behaviors in just such a way as to make them understandable as a dance? How do we in just this way and at just this time organize our behaviors to make the situation appear as lunch? What are the methods we use to produce a queue? Livingston's point, and Garfinkel's too, is that this kind of methodology—the methods used by the actual people in the actual situation—is found in every setting, large or small. The powerful implication of this point is that *everything we need to understand how society works is present in the observable situation.*

Documentary Method

To understand the practices through which we claim to be competent to offer accounts, Garfinkel (1967) uses the idea of **documentary method:** "The method consists of treating an actual appearance as 'the document of,' as 'pointing to,' as 'standing on behalf of' a presupposed underlying pattern" (p. 78). Anytime we interpret something, we make a kind of identity statement—"this is that." We do this when we interpret conversations or when we recognize the person standing outside our door as the mail carrier. Thus, the documentary method is the work we do when we take an object or event and set it in correspondence with a structure of meaning. We do this all the time, but how do we do it?

In order to put the documentary method in sharp relief, Garfinkel did an experiment. He brought in 10 undergraduates and told them that they were part of an experiment to explore a new, alternative method of psychotherapy. The students were given the opportunity to ask the "therapist" about anything they desired. The students needed to first provide the background to the problem and then phrase their questions in such a way that they could be answered yes or no. The therapist and students were in different rooms and communicated via an intercom. The students were instructed to give the background to the problem, ask their question, listen to the therapist's answer (yes or no), and then turn the intercom off and give their reactions. The procedure was repeated for as many questions as the students wanted to ask. Of course, the hitch in the experiment was that there was no new therapy and the "therapist's" answers were given randomly. Thus, there was no real "sense" to the answers; the issue then was exactly how (using what methods) the students made sense out of the answers—how the students understood the answers as "standing on behalf of a presupposed underlying pattern."

Garfinkel (1967) gleaned several insights from this experiment; I'll list but a few:

The students perceived the experimenter's responses as "answers-to-questions."

After the first question, the questions the students asked were motivated by the experimenter's response—in other words, the students framed their questions by looking back at "answers" and anticipated future "helpful answers."

When the meaning of the experimenter's response wasn't apparent, the student "waited for clarification" or engaged in an "active search" for the meaning.

Incongruent answers were interpreted by imputing knowledge and motivation to the therapist.

Contradictory answers prompted an "active search" for meaning in order to rid the answer of disagreement or meaninglessness.

There was a constant search for a pattern.

The subjects made specific references to normatively valued social structures that were treated as if shared by both and as setting the conditions of meaningful decisions—for example, what "everyone knows" about family (pp. 89–94).

Garfinkel's point is that the students rendered meaningful something that was not. The work of documenting—searching for and assigning a pattern—is performed by us all in every situation. A common culture or cognitive scheme isn't so much shared as the sense of commonality in documenting is achieved. The students give us a clear case where there were no cultures or cognitive schemes shared. Nonetheless, in most cases a correspondence was achieved between the event and a meaningful structure. The students' descriptions of the events were given in such a way as to assure their "rights to manage and communicate decisions of meaning" (Garfinkel, 1967, p. 77). Further, notice that even though the individual students were doing all the work, it was perceived and reported by the students as group work, as work between the student and therapist.

Concepts and Theory: Doing Society—Reflexively

I hope you're beginning to see what Garfinkel wants us to notice: A sense of social order is reflexively constructed in each and every situation. The notion of *reflexivity* is at the heart of Garfinkel's work and ethnomethodology in general. Something is reflexive if it can turn back on itself. Ethnomethodology's "central recommendation is that the activities whereby members produce and manage settings of organized everyday affairs are identical with members' procedures for making those settings 'account-able.' The 'reflexive,' or 'incarnate' character of accounting practices and accounts makes up the crux of that recommendation" (Garfinkel, 1967, p. 1).

One of the primary ways in which scenes are reflexively organized is through **indexical expressions**. To index something is to make reference to it or to point to it. Think of your index finger: It's the finger you use to point with. This book has an index. In this case, the index points to all the important issues that may be found in the book. This last example is very important. An indexical expression is like an index entry in a book: It points to itself. The only way a book index makes any sense at all is within the context of the book. Sometime try using the index from one book to find important items in a different book; it won't work. Indexical expressions, then, are situated verbal utterances that point to and are understood within the situation.

This is a very different notion than what is commonly held. Most of us, including many social scientists, believe that language, including verbal language, is representative. If I say "tree," then I am using that word to point to the physical object. One of the difficulties associated with this idea is that language doesn't represent very well. This problem is exemplified by color (Heritage, 1984, pp. 144–145): The human eye can distinguish about 7,500,000 colors. Yet the language with the most color names (English) only has 4,500 words that denote color, and of those 4,500 words, just 8 are commonly used.

It's plain, then, that in our everyday language we are not very concerned with representation. Part of what Garfinkel is talking about with indexical expressions is similar to symbolic interaction (Chapter 6), except what Garfinkel notes isn't the emergent quality of meaning; it is the reflexive character of meaning. For Garfinkel, the meanings of such phrases as "How's it going?" "That's a nice one," "He's a novice," and "What's up?" aren't negotiated through interaction. The meanings of indexical expressions don't emerge; they are found in the context itself. In fact, if you try to explicitly negotiate the meanings of indexical expressions, the chances are good that you'll be sanctioned or the setting will break up. To demonstrate this Garfinkel engaged in a number of breaching experiments; you can try it too. Next time someone says "How's it going?" stop and ask them what he or she means: "How's what going?" Meanings for phrases such as "That's a nice one" are assumed to be contextually given, as is the meaning of "nice." For example, if I am showing you the new guitar I just bought and you say "That's a nice one," we both assume the meaning is given in the context or situation. Thus, indexical expressions are reflexive because they appear in and reference the unique context in which they occur.

Situationally Constructing Reality

However, indexical expressions are reflexive for another reason. They not only appear in and reference the situation; they also bring the situation into existence. Mehan and Wood (1975) give us the example of "hello." Let's say you see me in the hall at school. You say, "Hello." What have you done? You have initiated or created a social situation through the use of a greeting. When you said "Hello," you immediately drew a circle around the two of us, identifying us as a social group distinct from the other people around us. That social situation, which we can call an encounter, interaction, or situated activity system, didn't exist until you said "Hello." But notice something very important about "hello": It can only exist as a social greeting within social situations. Every time "hello" is used, a social situation is created. Yet "hello" is only found in social situations, either real ones or imaginary ones (like with our example). Thus, "hello" is utterly reflexive: It simultaneously creates, exists, and finds meaning within the social situation.

It isn't just "hello" that exists reflexively. Let's take the phase, "you're beautiful." Its meaning is obviously contextual. You might say "you're beautiful" to a queen, to your partner after making love, to your friend who just made a particularly ironic comment, or to your friend dressed up to go to a Halloween party. But notice also that saying "you're beautiful" also creates the situation wherein beautiful is understood. The beauty of the ironic comment didn't exist until you said it; once said, it can be understood within the context that it created. Further, indexical expressions aren't limited to these sorts of catch phrases. At one point, Garfinkel asked his students to go home and record a conversation. They were to also report on the complete meaning of what was said. The following is a small snippet of one such report (Garfinkel, 1967, pp. 25–26).

	What was said:	*What was meant:*
Husband:	Dana succeeded in putting a penny in a parking meter today without being picked up.	This afternoon as I was bringing Dana, our four-year-old son, home from the nursery school, he succeeded in reaching high enough to put a penny in a parking meter when we parked in a metered parking zone, whereas before he has always had to be picked up to reach that high.
Wife:	Did you take him to the record store?	Since he put a penny in a meter, that means that you stopped while he was with you. I know that you stopped at the record store either on the way to get him or on the way back. Was it on the way back, so that he was with you, or did you stop there on the way to get him and somewhere else on the way back?

The first thing to point out, of course, is that what was actually said is incomprehensible apart from what the members could assume the other knew. There is an entire world of experience that the husband and wife share in the first statement about Dana that gives the statement a meaning that any observer would not be able to access. So, the first point is apparent: Vocal utterances reference or index presumed shared worlds.

The second point may not be quite so obvious. The students had a difficult time filling out the far right column. It was hard to put down in print what was actually being said and indexically understood. However, it became a whole lot tougher when Garfinkel asked them to indexically explain what was said in the far right column. Garfinkel wanted them to explain the explanation because the explanation itself assumed indexical worlds of meaning. Garfinkel (1967) reports that "they gave up with the complaint that the task was impossible" (p. 26). The task of explaining every explanation is impossible because all our talk is indexical. Many of us come up against this issue in the course of raising a 2-year-old. All 2-year-olds are infamous for asking the same insistent question: "Why?" And every parent knows that once started, that line of questioning never ends—every answer is just another reason to ask why. It never ends because our culture is indexical and reflexive.

Mehan and Wood (1975) further point out just how fundamentally reflexive our world really is. Every social world is founded upon incorrigible assumptions and secondary elaborations of belief. **Incorrigible assumptions** are things that we believe to be true but never question. These assumptions are incorrigible because they are incapable of being changed or amended. And these assumptions form the base of our social world. **Secondary elaborations of belief** are pre-scribed legitimating accounts that function to protect the incorrigible assump-tions. In other words, secondary elaborations of belief are ready-made stories that we use to explain why some empirical finding doesn't line up with our incorrigi-ble assumptions. The really interesting thing about incorrigible assumptions is that the empirical world doesn't always line up with the cultural assumptions that guide and create our reality.

Mehan and Wood (1975) give us the illustration of a lost pen. Our search for the lost pen is based on the assumption of object consistency—physical objects main-tain their consistency through time and space. "Say, for example, you find your missing pen in a place you know you searched before. Although the evidence indi-cates that the pen was first absent and then present, that conclusion is not reached" (p. 12). To do so would challenge the incorrigible assumption upon which that real-ity system is based—we never consider the possibility that a poltergeist took the pen or that a black hole swallowed it up. Our assumption of object consistency is pro-tected through secondary elaborations of belief. When we find the pen where we had already looked, we say, "I must have missed it."

I want us to take one further step into this issue of reflexivity. Not only are cul-tures reflexively created and protected, evidence for any reality system is always reflexively provided as well. Let us take the incident of two automobiles colliding. What would you call it? Most of us would call it an "accident." But what is implied in calling this collision an accident? Accidents can only exist if humans assume that there are no other, outside forces in back of events. But what if one of the drivers is a fundamentalist Christian? Then the episode, from the point of view of that driver, may well be defined as "God's will."

Let's ask the obvious question first: What is the incident really? According to ethnomethodology, it isn't anything really; it becomes something meaningful as we make assumptions about the world and how it works. But once we make our assumptions, what can happen to the events around us? Think about the two cars colliding. In this example, the event becomes either an accident or God's will. Then, through a neat little trick, the event becomes proof of the system that defined it in the first place. The person who has had an "accident" is confirmed in her belief that "shit happens." The person who has experienced "God's will" is confirmed in her belief in an omnipotent and merciful God. Either way, the collision is used to legitimate an existing reality system—proof of the event's definition is provided by the self-same meaning system. The same is true for science (and sociology): What counts as "proof" for the validity of science is defined by science.

Summary

- Garfinkel's perspective is unique among sociologists. He sees social order and meaning as achievements that are produced in situ. That is, Garfinkel sees social order and meaning as achieved within its natural setting—face-to-face interactions—and not through such things as institutions that exist outside the natural setting.

- The principal way this is done is through accounting. A basic requirement of every social setting is that it be recognizable or accountable as a specific kind of setting. Thus, the practical behaviors that create a setting just as it is are seen but not noticed for what they are; they are the very behaviors that achieve the setting in the first place.

- All settings and talk are therefore indexical; they index or reference themselves. The actions that create the situation of a wedding or a class are simultaneously understood as meaningful, social activities within the situation. Human activity always references itself; it is thoroughly reflexive, based upon incorrigible assumptions, discovered through the documentary method, proven through indexical methods, and protected by secondary elaborations of belief.

TAKING THE PERSPECTIVE—ETHNOMETHODOLOGY

Generally speaking ethnomethodology came into existence as Harold Garfinkel worked through Parsons' action theory and his answer to the Hobbesian problem of social order. Garfinkel was particularly bothered by the way Parsons discounted actors' knowledge of the situation (see Heritage, 1984, p. 9). Garfinkel saw that the simple empirical truth is that people are aware of what they're doing and why they are doing it, and that any empirically based social discipline must begin there. Garfinkel drew on Alfred Schutz's (1967) understanding of phenomenology as a way to bracket preconceptions and take the social world of empirically situated actors at face value. Simply said, "Ethnomethodology ... is the study of the methods people use for producing recognizable social orders" (Rawls, 2003, p. 123). It's based on the theoretical ideas that everything needed to understand social things is located in the situation and that "to be human is to know, virtually all of the time ... both what one is doing and why one is doing it" (Giddens, 1991, p. 35).

In brief, ethnomethodology is a theoretical perspective that studies the commonsense procedures people use to reflexively achieve social order and render it sensible. Ethnomethodology assumes that social orders and the methods through which they are created are identical; in every situation people are aware of what they are doing and why they are doing it; and that social order is an ongoing endogenous achievement in which the procedures used are recognizable and commonsensical. While general sociology takes facticity (the existence of facts) for granted, ethnomethodology takes the way people develop a sense of facticity as a subject of study. The implication of this is that ethnomethodology literally opens up every aspect of human doings and situations for study. The general form of an ethnomethodological question is: What are the local methods used whereby people organize and make sensible _____?

(Continued)

(Continued)

Because the ethnomethodological question is open-ended, there are innumerable applications and extensions of Garfinkel's work. Perhaps the most explored and/or well known applications are in the areas of conversation analysis and science studies. Probably more than any other, Harvey Sacks (1995) is responsible for the ethnomethodological study of conversation. Sacks basically asked what else, besides words, is being communicated when people talk with each other. He discovered people that use certain conversational devices to accomplish specific social orders. Candace West and Don Zimmerman (1987) show us an example of Sacks' approach in studying gender. West and Zimmerman ask, what conversational mechanisms are used to order gender inequality?

Ethnomethodological studies of science look at the ways scientists create a sense of doing science and producing scientific data (see Lynch, 1997). In a recent and fascinating study Linda Derksen (2010) looks at DNA measurement. While there are some distinctions from ethnomethodology, her approach is clearly ethnomethodological. In the article she details the moment when what were subjective decisions of the operator became invisible and were rendered objective.

However, generally speaking, Garfinkel's work has also been hotly contested because it offers such a unique approach, one that can and does take general sociology as a topic of study. Yet Garfinkel's influence extends to many prominent general theories in sociology. One example found in this book is the work of Anthony Giddens, especially in his work on self-identity. Another interesting example where Garfinkel's influence may be seen is in Jonathan H. Turner's *A Theory of Social Interaction* (1988, Stanford University Press). Turner's goal in the book, like Garfinkel, is to critique Parsons' analysis of the act, yet Turner's work itself could not be classified as ethnomethodological. Turner weaves Garfinkel's theory into a more positivistic and comprehensive explanation of the motivations and actions within social interaction.

The Language and Reality of the Self:
R. S. Perinbanayagam (1934–)

Theorist's Digest
Concepts and Theory: Dialogic Acts and Agency
   Putting the Self Into Play
Concepts and Theory: Language of Identity
   Artful Ethics
Summary

Like Goffman, Perinbanayagam is interested in how the self is presented; and like Mead he's interested in the self's involvement in interaction. He moves our understanding of the self and action beyond Mead by incorporating more current cultural and social shifts, the most important of which is the *linguistic turn*. Though the roots go further back, the linguistic turn occurred between the 1960s and 1980s and refers to a sea-change in philosophy, the humanities, and the social and behavioral sciences that continues to this day. This dramatic shift was a move away from the idea that language could represent reality to the conviction that language constitutes reality. One of the founding tenets of the Enlightenment was the belief that people could discover how the physical and social worlds work and then use that knowledge to better the human condition. Behind this belief was the assumption that scientific language could truly and accurately correspond to these worlds: Language thus expresses reality.

The linguistic turn assumes just the opposite: *Language is reality for human beings.* According to this view, there isn't a relationship between some physical reality and the language (and culture) we use. Rather than being a window through which we can see the universe, language is a kind of mirror that only reflects our own image back to us. In other words, language only refers to itself. To help us see this issue let's think about magic and science. Today we "know" that the people who practiced magic were wrong. But magic being "wrong" didn't matter to those people. They thought it was real and that it worked. Today we think that science is real and that it works. But notice that with both magic and science being truly right or wrong doesn't matter to people—both science and magic are simply language games.

The idea of *language games* is simple but profound: The rules of the game constitute the game. For example, what makes a game "baseball"? Isn't it the rules of baseball that make it what it is? The rules tell us what kinds of objects to use (bases, bats, gloves, and so on), how to relate the objects one to another (like the distance between home plate and first base), what we're supposed to do with the objects (hit the ball), the division of play (innings), and so forth. It's only when we play by the rules that baseball exists. By analogy that's what the linguistic turn shows us about everything we humans do—language is our reality and it makes us what and who we are.

THEORIST'S DIGEST

Brief Biography

R. S. Perinbanayagam earned his bachelor's degree in Sri Lanka (the University of Ceylon) and completed his doctorate in the United States (the University of Minnesota). He is currently department head of sociology at Hunter College, City University of New York. Among his more important works are *The Karmic Theater: Self, Society and Astrology in Jaffna, Sri Lanka; Signifying Acts: Structure and Meaning in Everyday Life; Discursive Acts;* and *The Presence of Self* (for which he won The Charles Horton Cooley Award). Perinbanayagam was also awarded

(Continued)

(Continued)

The George Herbert Mead Award for Lifetime Achievement in 1998. His newest book, *Games and Sport in Everyday Life: Dialogues and Narratives of the Self*, investigates the myth building narratives that not only create and present the athlete's identity and self but also promote and sustain some of society's most cherished values.

Central Sociological Questions

George Herbert Mead characterized the self as based in symbolic interaction. Perinbanayagam takes the recent interest in language and asks, What are the implications in saying that the self exists because of and within language? How do people "manage" their self linguistically? Are there certain things that people do regularly in presenting the self in dialog?

Simply Stated

Perinbanayagam's theory is an extension of Mead's theory of the self using the recent emphasis on language. He also draws on ideas from Goffman to argue that people put a self into play linguistically just as certainly as through impression management. Among the most important rhetorical devices people use are ways that we tell others how we want our self to be addressed and answered, as a particular kind of person. Identities tend to be more stable and certain because they are more directly tied to specific languages. These linguistic structures of identity provide continuity among people and situations.

Key Concepts

linguistic turn, language games, dialogic acts, interactional others, significant others, generalized others, rhetorical devices, addressive processes, answerability processes, identity, the linguistic structures of identity, artful ethics

Concepts and Theory: Dialogic Acts and Agency

Perinbanayagam builds on the idea that language constitutes reality but gives it a base in pragmatism and Mead's symbolic interaction (Chapter 6). Following Mead, Perinbanayagam argues that any time we act, we are actually interacting. Remember human action is always meaningful and nothing has intrinsic meaning; through social interactions we place meaning on everything. These meanings create relationships and are like symbolic bridges of meaning within which people act and have their being. Because we are situated within a context of meaning, Perinbanayagam characterizes human behavior as *dialogic acts*. Dialogic actions are simply *actions that are based on conversation;* but the implications of this simple definition are profound. This quality of action is clear when we're talking about actions that are directed toward people—it's plain that we're talking to one another—but it is also true when we act toward things. Remember the internal dialog in Mead's theory of the act. While things may not intentionally speak to us, we understand everything in terms of meaning and these meanings speak to us, even if the objects are physical and can't deliberately speak. The meanings of objects and actions are results of that conversation you have with yourself.

From all this Perinbanayagam (2003) concludes that "[t]he individual, then, is not so much an agent as an *interactive agent*. . . . Being is always understood concretely in terms of actions and roles, in doings and becomings" (p. 70). Perinbanayagam is saying we exist in interactions. It's kind of like a fish: If you take a fish out of water, it will die. Everything about a fish is determined by its existence in water. The same sort of thing is true about you and me—we only exist in conversations; take us out of conversation and the self no longer exists. The reality of the self is language and dialog. People, then, are never truly individual and they don't exist in and of themselves. Because of the matrix of relationships within which every act occurs, there is always an element of other in self. I exist in "the paradox of being simultaneously an individual and an other" (Perinbanayagam, 2000, p. 10). But this is only a paradox if we don't understand emergence and interaction; self and other mutually constitute one another, and the self is forever in process—it exists in ongoing, never-ending streams of dialogic acts. As the philosopher Heraclitus implied, you can't step twice in the same river. Every dialogic act is new and alive with potential for human beings. As we'll see, there are ethical implications from understanding dialogic acts.

Putting the Self Into Play

Generally speaking, when we communicate either verbally or nonverbally (dialogic acts), we are addressing not only the others present but also our self. And we can respond to our self, such as when we laugh at our own joke or become embarrassed. In addition to the self, there are three different kinds of others that may be addressed in the dialogic act, each with its own particular influence. The *interactional other* is immediately present in the interaction and provides situational control through immediate feedback to the self. The *significant other* speaks for the people the individual cares for the most and provides an emotional basis for the act; significant others may be distant from or present in the dialogic act. And *generalized others* are clusters of attitudes and perspectives and provide the individual the standards of the community in the dialogic act.

Perinbanayagam also builds upon Goffman's idea of the presentation of self. As we've seen, Goffman argues that social encounters can't take place without selves being presented. Because of the nature of the self, Perinbanayagam adds that selves can't exist apart from dialogic acts. Thus in every act we put the self into play. As an analogy, let's again think of a baseball game. At the beginning of every game the ball is "put into play." Sometimes it is significant, as when the president or vice president of the United States throws in the first ball of the first game of the season; other times its significance is mundane, as when the umpire throws the ball into play. But in every case, there is a specific method or ritual and meaning that follows how the ball is put into play. The same is true when the different players are put into the game, especially if there is a substitution. There are specific ways in which players are "put into play" and each method conveys meaning.

The conversational or discursive nature of the self implies that people use *rhetorical devices* in interactions to be seen and noticed. Webster's (1983) defines rhetoric as "the art or science of using words effectively in speaking or writing, so as to influence or persuade" (p. 1555). The use of rhetorical devices with self, then, implies that people use particular ways of communicating in order to make the self felt, present, known, and in some ways indisputable to others. Perinbanayagam gives us four rhetorical modes the self uses: the reflexive process, addressive process, answerability process, and the referential process. The *reflexive process* is basic to the self and communication in general. Every act of the self is reflexive in that it involves an internalized conversation between the I and the Me. People are also reflexive in the sense that they track the acts of others "as *expressions* and *indices* of the other's attitudes in order to organize one's own self" (Perinbanayagam, 2000, p. 55, emphasis original).

The addressive and answerability processes are the specific ways in which we present a self in the dialogic act. *Addressive processes* are ways of addressing someone, such as Mrs., Mr., Professor, Sam, Samuel, buddy, wife, friend, best friend, loser, and so on. And in addressing others we also address our self. Each form of address denotes a different kind of self and has a dialog or discourse that goes along with it. For example, I once gave a presentation at another university and in a particular part of that talk I referred to my wife. But I didn't address her as "wife"; I called her "my partner." My wife wasn't at the talk, but because I addressed her, she was a significant other present in the act for the other people. After the talk, a lesbian graduate student came up and asked if I was married. I said, "Yes," and she replied, "You called your wife the right thing. I'm impressed." So in addressing my partner, I also addressed myself and created a specific image in the minds of the people listening.

Once addressed, selves may be answered or unanswered. It is impossible to have an interaction without such addressive acts, yet it is a risky endeavor. When we put a particular kind of self or other into play, we risk not being answered as such. Using my talk example: If I had addressed my spouse as "wife" instead of "partner," I (my self) would not have been answered by that specific woman and I wouldn't have been able to work on a very exciting dissertation. How the self is answered or not answered is important. In their study of the homeless, David Snow and Leon Anderson (1992) quite clearly point out the power involved in answered and unanswered selves. The homeless are constantly putting a self into play that is unanswered. As a result, "to be homeless in America is not only to have fallen to the bottom of the status system; it is also to be confronted with gnawing doubts about self-worth and the meaning of existence" (p. 199).

This point concerning the answered and unanswered selves is, perhaps, even more important than what it might seem. Perinbanayagam (2000) says that one of the principal reasons for conversation is it "*enables the individual to objectify himself or herself as well as enables the other to objectify himself or herself*" (p. 189, emphasis original). In fact, as Jonathan H. Turner (1988) claims, "The most central of these [motivations in interaction] is the need to sustain a self-concept" (p. 61). In other words, one of the most important reasons we engage in conversation is because we need to present a self that is answered and thus confirmed by others. In an interesting analysis of a conversation at a book club, Perinbanayagam notes that "it really didn't matter what novel they talked about, so long as they . . . gathered and discussed something and *gave presence to their selves*" (p. 195, emphasis added).

In addition to addressive processes, the self is involved in *answerability processes*. We've just talked about the answered and unanswered self, but Perinbanayagam has something else in mind with answerability processes, so be certain to keep them separate. While the concept of the answered and unanswered self is the response others give to the presented self, answerability processes are part of the way an individual puts a self in play. Answerability refers to the obligation we have to the self we present. For example, if I present myself as a professor, I am answerable or obligated to the expectations that go along with such a self. Perinbanayagam's point is that we choose the way in which we present a self—in some ways of self-presentation the answerability is clear but in others it is not. A good example of the lack of clarity in answerability is when people dress androgynously and don't make a clear claim to a gender identity. This ambiguous answerability makes others uncomfortable because they don't know how to "answer" that person's gender. Because of this reciprocal link between selves that are put into play, Perinbanayagam concludes that making a self clearly answerable "confers a 'gift' on the other, making it an act of grace; the other can thereby understand what has been put forward and resolve—however tentatively—the mystery of the other, appreciate it, and answer it" (p. 67).

Concepts and Theory: Language of Identity

Up to this point of Perinbanayagam's theory we have a picture of a self that is only present in conversations (both internal and external), emerges out of the interaction process, and is dependent upon the reaction of others for its objective existence. Turner's comments let us see that the emergent and incidental qualities of the self create high levels of anxiety in the individual, to the degree that sustaining the story of the self becomes a chief motivation in interaction. This position is indeed where interactionism leaves us. However, Perinbanayagam includes a structural component to his theory with the idea of identity. The self uses signs and words to make itself present. Those signs, words, and language constitute *identity*.

Situations and interactions are negotiated and emergent. They may or may not happen and they may proceed in almost any direction. Situations are also insular. That is, they are not naturally connected one to another. Your day is filled with isolated dialogic acts with people at school, home, work, the grocery store, gift shop, and so on. What connects all these acts? Well, you do, but as we've seen the self is situational not trans-situational (it doesn't span situations). There is, however, something that is intrinsic to dialogic acts that is trans-situational and structured: language. In order to carry on a conversation we must use language and there is a particular language that is relevant to the self: the discourse or language of identity. While the self is emergent, we can think of identity as "a *regulated way* of 'speaking' about persons" (Barker, 2008, p. 224, emphasis added). In fact, the word *identity* comes from the Latin root *idem*, which implies "sameness and continuity" (Marshall, 1998, p. 293).

We've already noted that people use rhetorical devices in the act to be seen and noticed. The way in which this occurs is through *the linguistic structures of identity*. There are three ideas that accompany this way of seeing identity. First, identities differ by range and depth. *Range* speaks of the number of people who can claim an identity, and *depth* captures the complexity of an identity. For example, the depth of the Christian identity is far more profound than the identity of student. If we picture depth as a web of identity, the Christian is situated in a many stranded web of mythic and linguistic structures that span all of time and creation, and the strands of this web reach into every facet of the Christian's life. The identity of student, as important as it might be, does not have near the depth as the Christian: The myths and stories associated with student are far less in number and complexity, and the strands of the identity web only connect to certain portions of the student's life.

The second effect of the linguistic structure of identity *provides continuity* among people and situations. As we've noted, in and of themselves situations are insular. But the language of identity links them together. Yesterday, as I put myself into play at work, I claimed the identity and was answered as professor; tomorrow I will do the same thing. Though both days and situations are separated by many hours and many other interactions, the language of "professor" remains relatively unchanged. Thus, when I claimed and will again claim the identity of professor, the language and discourse used in such claims and their addressive and answerability processes link those emergent selves and their situations together. Further, the language of identity, in this case professor, links the claimed identity to the interactional, significant, and generalized others. That is, the word "professor" is part of an entire way of talking that includes other terms such as student, dean, chancellor, full, associate, and assistant professor, and so on.

In contrast, the third idea that follows from the notion that language is the basis of identity is *differentiation*. Linguistically, identities work like categories, and the basic function of categories is to include and exclude. The strongest kind of categorical distinction is dichotomous, as with gender: To be male simultaneously means to not be female. This kind of bifurcation indicates a powerful element of social control around gender that is structured into our language. Other identities aren't as strongly differentiated but are nonetheless always formed over and against another: "Differentiation of identity, with whatever cultural vocabulary that is available, is not something that a functioning human consciousness can avoid; rather it is an ontological condition of the beingness of itself and of the others it encounters" (Perinbanayagam, 2000, p. 107).

Artful Ethics

We've seen that there are various tensions or paradoxes at work in formulating a self. On the one hand, you have a self that is an emergent property of interactions; on the other, you claim and use identities that are structured by language and push toward sameness and continuity. You are also individual and other at the same time. You are also simultaneously a being and a performance. These tensions imply that "human agents bring both *artistry* (the intentional use of form and shape, order, and discipline) and *artfulness* (connecting method to purpose) to their perfor-mances" (Perinbanayagam, 2003, p. 78, emphasis original). As Goffman noted, we manage the impressions we give to others. This is because we are principally ori-ented toward meaning. And because meaning isn't intrinsic, we have freedom to paint the canvas of life and reality any way we choose. Yet that absolute freedom of agency is tempered by the demands of dialog and sensibility. Our art must make sense to those who view it; it must communicate to and enter into a dialog with others. The way in which we do that becomes our style, our individuated self. "For one's life to become a work of art, for it to develop 'style,' an individual must be able to take control and fashion a self that conformed to the exacting demands of an artistry and an aesthetic" (Perinbanayagam, 2000, p. 33).

Yet the purpose of this expression isn't simply individualistic. Symbols, language, and dialogic acts are ways through which we persuade others to cooperate in our expression of self in the world. The art of selfhood thus inevitably asks others, both people and physical things, to bend to and support our expression in the world. And because of these intrinsic connections, a dialogic act is "capable of inducing an ethical dimension into it" (Perinbanayagam, 2000, p. 5). When we act, when we make our self present, we invariably insert our values and realities into the social and physical worlds around us. And because of the time period in which we live, this ethical dimension of action falls more squarely upon us as individuals than ever before. In traditional societies, and even early modern societies, there were fewer choices and fewer realities from which to choose. There were more and clearer guidelines and people knew less of the consequences of choice. The politics of choice are more real today than every before. The question Perinbanayagam leaves us with, then, is what kind of artists will we be? What type of values and realities will we ask the world to conform?

Summary

• Perinbanayagam works with the symbolic interactionist's idea of the self and interaction being emergent, but more specifically characterizes them both as dialogic acts. The self, then, is a mechanism that allows conversations to occur, whether internal or external to the individual. The conversational nature of the self indicates that people use rhetorical devices, such as the addressive process, to be seen and noticed.

• As with all rhetorical devices and speech, the self can be answered or unanswered. Others in the interaction can choose to acknowledge the self that one puts into play, in which case the addressive process (how we tell others to address us) is answered. In different cases, people may ignore the particular self put into play and the individual will probably put a "spin" on the self and try again. For Perinbanayagam, then, the self doesn't exist per se, but is something that is used to facilitate conversation.

• Perinbanayagam adds a structural element to this brand of symbolic interaction. People not only have selves, they have identities too. Identities are used in conversation but they don't exist there. Identities exist in language and language is structured. Using the same language to talk about the self in various situations makes the self appear trans-situational, but it is the language or discourse of identity that links the various situations, not the self. Identity languages create continuity and differentiation among people and they vary by their range and depth.

BUILDING YOUR THEORY TOOLBOX

Learning More—Primary and Secondary Sources

- Primary sources for Erving Goffman:

  - I would suggest that you begin with Goffman's last publication, "The Interaction Order" (1983), in the *American Sociological Review, 48.* Then move to his classic, *The Presentation of Self in Everyday Life* (1959). There is also a good reader: *The Goffman Reader,* edited by Charles Lemert and Ann Branaman (Eds.), Blackwell, 1997.

- Secondary sources for Goffman:

  - There are two good secondary sources for Goffman: Gary Alan Fine and Philip Manning's chapter on Goffman in *The Blackwell Companion to Major Contemporary Social Theorists,* edited by George Ritzer (Blackwell, 2000), and *Goffman's Legacy,* edited by A. Javier Treviño (Rowman & Littlefield, 2003), contain good chapters on Goffman's impact on or connections with other ideas and schools of thought.

- Primary sources for Harold Garfinkel:

  - For Garfinkel, I suggest *Studies in Ethnomethodology,* Prentice Hall, 1967; and *Ethnomethodology's Program: Working Out Durkheim's Aphorism,* edited and introduced by Anne Warfield Rawls, Rowman & Littlefield, 2002.

- Secondary sources for Garfinkel:

  - Secondary sources for Garfinkel include the standard text for ethnomethodology, John Heritage's *Garfinkel and Ethnomethodology,* Polity Press, 1984; and Eric Livingston's *Making Sense of Ethnomethodology,* Routledge & Kegan Paul Books, 1987.

- Primary sources for R. S. Perinbanayagam:

  - For Perinbanayagam, I suggest you start with *The Presence of Self,* Rowman & Littlefield, 2000; and then move to his newest work, *Games and Sport in Everyday Life: Dialogues and Narratives of the Self,* Paradigm, 2007.

Seeing the Social World (knowing the theory)

- Write a 250-word synopsis of the dramaturgical analogy and ethnomethodology. For Perinbanayagam add to the synopsis you wrote for symbolic interaction in Chapter 6.

- After reading and understanding this chapter, you should be able to define the following terms theoretically and explain their theoretical importance to the analysis of impression management: *dramaturgy, social, personal, and ego identities, impression management, front, setting, appearance, manner, ritual states, backstage, performance teams, roles, role distance, stigma, face, deference and demeanor rituals, face-work, frames, keys, interaction order, biographies, cognitive relations.*

- After reading and understanding this chapter, you should be able to define the following terms theoretically and explain their theoretical importance to ethnomethodology: *life-world, phenomenology, ethnomethodology, accounts, documentary method, reciprocity of perspectives, reflexivity, indexical expressions, incorrigible assumptions, secondary elaborations of belief.*

- After reading and understanding this chapter, you should be able to define the following terms theoretically and explain their theoretical importance to dialogic acts: *linguistic turn, language games, dialogic acts, interactional others, significant others, generalized others, rhetorical devices, addressive processes, answerability processes, identity, the linguistic structures of identity, artful ethics.*

- After reading and understanding this chapter, you should be able to answer the following questions (remember to answer them *theoretically*):

  o What produces the interaction order?

  o What is a front and how is it managed?

  o What are the different ways in which we can relate to social roles? What are the effects of these different ways?

  o How are frames related to social reality and how do they work?

  o What does it mean that Garfinkel is interesting in analyzing events "in just this way and at just this time"? What does his approach imply about social order and social structures?

  o How are situations reflexively organized? Specifically, how do accountability, indexicality, and the documentary method function to reflexively organize social events?

  o What are incorrigible assumptions and secondary elaborations of belief? How do they work to produce a sense of reality? Use an example from the newspaper to illustrate your answer.

  o How is the self put into play linguistically?

  o How are identities structured through language?

Engaging the Social World (using the theory)

- Compare and contrast at least two of your professors using Goffman's idea of impression management. How are their offices different? How about the way they dress and talk? How do they use the setting differently? How do their demeanors communicate different levels of expected deference?

- How would flirting and video games be understood as forms of keying? What other examples of keying can you think of?

(Continued)

(Continued)

- Using Goffman's theory, explain Internet interactions. How are they both different from and similar to face-to-face interactions?

- Perform an ethnomethodological analysis of a common, ordinary practice, such as riding the elevator or crossing a street on campus. Precisely how was that social order achieved without reference to extra situational structures?

- The next time you're at a social gathering use Perinbanayagam's theory of dialogic acts to analyze what's happening. How are selves presented (addressability) in such a way that they may be answered in a specific way? How can these presentations be understood as artful ethics?

Weaving the Threads (building theory)

- Garfinkel gives us a theory of how social order is achieved at the micro level. Blau gives us a theory of how power is achieved and maintained at the micro level. How can these two theories be joined? Is power a part of social order? If so, how?

- Compare and contrast Goffman's approach to understanding the social construction of reality and that of ethnomethodology. Evaluate the strengths and weaknesses of each.

- We have now examined four different ways that we can conceptualize what happens when social actors get together: symbolic interaction, ethnomethodology, dramaturgy, and exchange. Come up with a one- or two-word description for what each perspective tells us is happening. Now, under each of the descriptors, list at least five points that make that perspective unique and five insights you would get using that theory (in other words, what is the theory good for?).

- You've now been exposed to four different perspectives about how social order is achieved: Parsons' structural functionalism, conflict theory (mostly Coser and Dahrendorf), exchange theory, and now Goffman and Garfinkel. Write a detailed paragraph for each that describes the approach and most important points.

- What do the theories in this chapter imply about the self that modernity was founded upon? What do they imply about how identities such as race and gender are oppressed?

CHAPTER 13

Critical Theory:

Jürgen Habermas

(1929–)

As I pointed out in Chapter 8, there are two major factors that helped define contemporary social and sociological theory. We first considered the work of Talcott Parsons. Parsons very clearly worked within the modern idea of social science and he addressed the most basic of all modern social issues: the problem of social order. Many of the theorists we've considered since have responded to Parsons in one way or another, and most are empirical positivists. Even the theorists in our last chapter are empiricists, especially Garfinkel, though they present a critique of the idea that society exists as a system of macro level social structures.

The second factor that dramatically impacted contemporary theory is the Frankfurt School of critical theory. In general, *critical theory* "aims to dig beneath the surface of social life and uncover the assumptions and masks that keep us from a full and true understanding of how the world works" (Johnson, 2000, p. 67). Critical theory isn't interested in simply explaining how society operates. Rather, the purpose of critical theory is to uncover the unseen or misrecognized ways in which society operates to oppress certain groups while maintaining the interests of others. Compare that to the goals of scientific theory we discussed in Chapter 1: explain, predict, and control. Thus, critical theory has a very clear agenda that stands in opposition to scientific sociology. And as you'll see in the rest of our book, a good many of the theorists from this point on take a similar critical stand, through not all are related to the Frankfurt School. I'm going to start this chapter off with a short introduction to the Frankfurt School and the work of two of its founding members: Theodore Adorno and Max Horkheimer. The rest of the chapter will be taken up with the critical theory of Jürgen Habermas.

Historical Roots of the Frankfurt School

Briefly, the Frankfurt School (also known as the Institute of Social Research) began in the early 1920s at the University of Frankfurt in Germany. It was formed by a tight group of radical intellectuals and, ironically, financed by Felix Weil, the son of a wealthy German merchant. Weil's goal was to create "an institutionalization of Marxist discussion beyond the confines both of middle-class academia and the ideological narrow-mindedness of the Communist Party" (Wiggershaus, 1986/1995, p. 16). As the Nazis gained control in Germany, the Frankfurt School was forced into exile in 1933, first to Switzerland, then New York, and eventually California. In 1953, the school was able to move back to its home university in Frankfurt. The various leaders and scholars associated with the school include Theodore Adorno, Max Horkheimer, Herbert Marcuse, Eric Fromm, and Jürgen Habermas.

Though there were many reasons why the School and its critical theory approach came into existence, one of the early problems that these theorists dealt with was the influence of Nazism in Germany. The two decades surrounding World War II were watershed moments for many disciplines. The propaganda machine in back of Nazism and the subsequent human atrocities left a world stunned at the capacity of humanity's inhumanity. The actions of the holocaust and the beliefs that lay at their foundation spurred a large cross-disciplinary movement to understand human behavior and beliefs. One of the best known attempts at understanding these issues is Stanley Milgram's (1974) psychological experiments in authority.

The sociological attempt at understanding this horror demanded that culture be studied as an independent entity, something Marx didn't do. It was clear that what happened in Germany was rooted in culture that was used to intentionally control people's attitudes and actions—this use of culture was formalized in 1933 with the Reich Ministry for Popular Enlightenment and Propaganda. Additionally, ideology became seen as something different, something more insidious, than perhaps Marx first suspected. The Frankfurt School asks us to see ideology as more diffuse, as not simply a direct tool of the elite, but, rather, as a part of the cultural atmosphere that we breathe.

In general, the Frankfurt School elaborates and synthesizes ideas from Karl Marx, Max Weber, and Sigmund Freud, and focuses on the social production of knowledge and its relationship to human consciousness. This kind of Marxism focuses on Marx's indebtedness to Georg Wilhelm Hegel. Marx basically inverted Hegel's argument from an emphasis on ideas to material relations in the economy. The Frankfurt School reintroduced Hegel's concern with ideas and culture but kept Marx's critical evaluation of capitalism and the state. Thus, like Marx, the Frankfurt School focuses on ideology; but, unlike Marx, critical theory sees ideological production as linked to culture and knowledge rather than simply class and the material relations of production. Ideology, according to critical theorists, is more broadly based and insidious than Marx supposed.

The Problem With Positivism: Max Horkheimer and Theodor Adorno

The clearest expression of early critical theory is found in Max Horkheimer's and Theodor Adorno's (1972) book, *Dialectic of Enlightenment*, first published in 1944. Adorno was born in Germany September 11, 1903. His father was a well to do wine merchant and musician. Adorno himself studied music composition in Vienna for three years beginning in 1925, after studying sociology and philosophy at the University of Frankfurt. He finished his advanced degree in philosophy under Paul Tillich (Christian socialist) in 1931, and started an informal association with the Institute. In two short years Adorno was removed by the Nazis due to his Jewish heritage. He moved to Merton College, Oxford, in 1934 and to New York City in 1938, where he fully affiliated with the Frankfurt School in exile. When the school returned to Germany, Adorno became assistant director under Max Horkheimer, who had served as director since 1930. Horkheimer was German, also Jewish, and born into a wealthy family on February 14, 1895. After World War I, Horkheimer studied psychology and philosophy, finishing his doctorate in philosophy in 1925 at Frankfurt University, where he became a lecturer and eventually met Adorno. Horkheimer became the second director of the Institute of Social Research in 1930 and continued in that position until 1958, when Adorno took the directorship.

In the *Dialectic of Enlightenment* Horkheimer and Adorno argue that the contradictions Marx saw in capitalism are eclipsed by the ones found in the Enlightenment.

The Enlightenment promises freedom through the use of reason, rationality, and scientific method. But in the end it brings a new kind of oppression, not one that is linked to the externalities of life (such as class) but one that extinguishes the spirit and breath of human nature. As we've seen, positivism is based on reason and assumes the universe is empirical. Reason is employed to discover the laws of nature in order to predict and control it. Horkheimer and Adorno argue that the very definition of scientific knowledge devalues the human questions of ethics, aesthetics, beauty, emotion, and the good life, all of which are written off by science as concerns only for literature, which under positivism isn't valued as knowledge at all.

Science is based on the Cartesian dichotomy of subject and object, but the human sciences (sociology, psychology, psychiatry, anthropology, history, and the like) have in applying the scientific method objectified the human being through and through. In objectifying, controlling, and opposing nature, the scientific method opposes human nature—human nature is treated like physical nature, objectified and controlled. It results in such things as seeing all human sensualities and sensibilities as evil forces that must be controlled (the Freudian id); and the human psyche, emotions, sensualities, and body must all be managed and brought under the regime of science. People in positivistic social sciences become statistics in a population that must be controlled for the interests of the state (current examples include sexual practices, emotion management, bodily weight, child rearing, smoking, drinking, and so on—all of which are seen as weakness or problems within the individual).

Through the Enlightenment and science, rationality has been enthroned as the supreme human trait. Yet Horkheimer and Adorno trace this ascendency back to fear of the unknown. Rationality began in religion, as magicians, shamans, and priests began to organize and write doctrine, and this impetus toward safety and control accelerated as society relieved such people from the burden of daily work; spirit guides became professional. Their work systematized and provided control over rituals and capricious spirits. Eventually God was rendered predictable through the ideas of sin and ritualized redemption, and the idea of direct cause and effect was established. Religious issues became universal, with one version of reality, one explanation of the cosmos and humankind's place in it. The hierarchy of gods and individual responses were thus replaced by instrumental reason. The same fear of uncertainty was the motive behind science as well. The technical control of the physical world promised to relieve threats from disease, hunger, and pestilence. And to one degree or another it has done that. Yet science, like religion before it, takes on myth form and reifies its own method: There is only one form of knowledge, only one way of knowing that is valid.

This unstoppable engine of rationality also extends to the control of everyday life (and we can see how much we've "progressed" in this since the time of Horkheimer and Adorno). The modern life is an *administered life*. Every aspect is open to experts and analysis and is cut off from real social contact and dependency. People are isolated through technology, whether it's the technologies of travel (cars and planes), technologies of communication (such as phones and computers), or the technology of management (bureaucracies). People rationally manage time, space, and relationships, as well as their own self. Self-help is the prescription of the day, guided by experts of every kind. But what's lost is self-actualization—there are only remnants of a self that hasn't been administered, only small portions to self-actualize, and even those are squashed in the name of the administered life.

Originally, the Enlightenment had an element of critical thought, where the process of thinking was examined. But it soon became as mechanical as the technologies that it creates, and it denies other ways of knowing and being. Horkheimer and Adorno's story of the Enlightenment is, then, "an account of how humankind, it its efforts to free itself from subjugation to nature, has created new and more all-encompassing forms of domination and repression" (Alway, 1995, p. 33).

The irony and problem is that the Enlightenment was to free humankind. Yet it has created a new kind of *unfreedom,* a binding of the mind that prevents it from perceiving its own chains of bondage. This of course is what Marx meant when he spoke of **false consciousness**, but to Horkheimer and Adorno the blindness is ever more insidious. The very tools of thought that were to bring enlightenment instead bring the administered life. How is it possible to get out of this conundrum? This is precisely where critical theory comes in.

First, it's important to understand that there isn't a specific goal or program. Gone are the lofty goals of the Enlightenment and the method of reason and rationality are useless as well. In back of this negation is a caution and realization. The caution is about being derailed again by believing that we've found *the way*—unlike the capitalists in Marx's scheme, the philosophers of the Enlightenment may be seen as having the best of intentions. We should then be cautious of any single answer. The realization is that human beings are social beings; we reflect and express the spirit of the age and the position we hold in society. Knowledge is therefore never pure.

Knowing this implies a second feature of critical theory: The way to freedom is through continual process and critical thinking, the goal of which is to unearth. In his introduction to Adorno's *Culture Industry,* Bernstein (1991) notes,

> In reading Adorno, especially his writings on the culture industry, it is important to keep firmly in mind the thought that he is not attempting an objective, sociological analysis of the phenomena in question. Rather, the *question* of the culture industry is raised from the perspective of its relation to the possibilities for social transformation. The culture industry is to be understood from the perspective of it potentialities for promoting or blocking "integral freedom." (p. 2, emphasis original)

Notice that Adorno's reading of the culture industry is not intended as a systematic, objective, sociological study. Rather, it is an act of interrogation. But it is questioning with a purpose: in Adorno's case, to assess the potentials for integral freedom that pop culture provides. The image of integral freedom calls up many images, but among the most important are that freedom must be understood with reference to the whole being of human—including social relations, economic achievement, spirituality, sensuality, aesthetics, and so on—and that its chief value is the dignity of the person. "Reason can realize its reasonableness only through reflecting on the disease of the world as produced and reproduced by man" (Horkheimer, 2004, p. 120).

Jürgen Habermas: Modernity and Reason

Habermas picks up this critique of positivism and argues that there are three kinds of knowledge and interests: empirical, analytic knowledge that is interested in the technical control of the environment (science); hermeneutic or interpretive knowledge that is interested in human understanding and cooperation; and critical knowledge that is interested in emancipation. Because scientific knowledge seeks to explain the dynamic processes found within a given phenomenon, social science is historically bound. That is, it only sees things as they currently exist. That being the case, scientific knowledge of human institutions and behaviors can only describe and thus reinforce existing political arrangements (since society is taken "as is").

Further, positivistic social science is blind to its own conditions of knowledge: It uncritically places itself fully within the political and economic framework of modernity, and then proclaims to express objective truth or knowledge. The main problem is that the social science model has bought into the wrong part of the discourse of modernity. Remember the first assumption of science: The universe is empirical and objective. It's out there and we can observe it objectively and discover how it works. By definition, human beings aren't objective; they are subjectively oriented toward meaning. Nor is society "out there" in the same way the moon is. We can study the moon objectively because it truly exists apart from us; if human beings had never existed, the moon would be exactly the same. But this can't be said about society. Human beings make up society; it exists only because of us. Therefore we can't stand outside of it to create objective knowledge.

Critical theory, on the other hand, purposefully stands within the social world where the dramas of oppression and social justice are played out. Rather than aligning itself with the assumption of objectivity, as social science has done, critical knowledge embraces the democratic project as its foundation. Its values, then, are known, questioned, and at the center of the production of critical knowledge, rather than hidden and denied as in social science. The intent of critical knowledge is to further the democratic project and social justice by exposing the distortions, misrepresentations, and political values found in our knowledge and speech.

This critique of positivism forms the foundation for Habermas's theory of reason and modernity. The interesting thing about Habermas is that he is just as hopeful about the social project of modernity as were the earlier philosophers. However, besides the problem with a positivistic approach to human ethics, there are structural problems that have disabled the social features that were to have led us to freedom and equality. Habermas's theory about how this has happened and what can be done fill the rest of this chapter.

THEORIST'S DIGEST

Brief Biography

Jürgen Habermas was born on June 18, 1929, in Düsseldorf, Germany. His teen years were spent under Nazi control, which undoubtedly gave Habermas his drive for freedom and democracy. His educational background is primarily in philosophy but also includes German literature, history, and psychology. In 1956, Habermas took a position as Theodor Adorno's assistant at the Institute of Social Research in Frankfurt, which began his formal association with the Frankfurt School of critical thought. In 1961, Habermas took a professorship at the University of Heidelberg, but returned to Frankfurt in 1964 as a professor of philosophy and sociology. From 1971 to 1981, he worked as the director of the Max Planck Institute, where he began to formalize his theory of communicative action. In 1982, Habermas returned to the institute in Frankfurt, where he remained until his retirement in 1994.

Central Sociological Questions

Born out of the political oppression of Nazi Germany, Habermas is driven to produce a social theory of ethics that would not be based on political or economic power and would be universally inclusive. He is a critical theorist who sees humankind's hope of rational existence within the inherent processes of communication. Specifically he asks, how can the civil sphere of democracy be revitalized so that participatory democracy can move forward?

Simply Stated

As a result of organized capitalism, the commodification of mass media, and the scientific study of society and human relations, democracy has been disabled through the colonization of the lifeworld and public sphere. However, the qualities inherent in critical theory and communication could form the base for the revitalization of civil society and participatory democracy as they are enacted in speech communities.

Key Ideas

administered life, false consciousness, legitimacy, authority, lifeworld, liberal capitalism, depoliticized class, public sphere, pragmatic consensus, organized capitalism, legitimation crisis, colonization of the lifeworld, steering, generalized media of exchange, colonization of the public sphere, public opinion, analytic knowledge, interpretive knowledge, critical theory, speech communities, communicative action, civil society

Concepts and Theory: Capitalism and Legitimation

Drawing on Karl Marx's theory of capitalism, Max Weber's ideas of the state and legitimation, Edmund Husserl's notion of the lifeworld, and Talcott Parsons' view of social systems, Habermas gives us a model of social evolution and modernity (our current historical context). By now, you should be familiar enough with

Marx's, Weber's, and Parsons' ideas. And, though we covered the lifeworld in Chapter 12, I want to mention it again because it is an important feature of Habermas' theory. The concept of **lifeworld** originally came from the philosopher Edmund Husserl. Habermas uses the idea to refer to the individual's everyday life—the world as it is experienced immediately by the person, a world built upon culture and social relations, and thus filled with historically and socially specific meanings. The purpose of the lifeworld is to facilitate communication: to provide a common set of goals, practices, values, languages, and so on that allow people to interact, to continually weave their meanings, practices, and goals into a shared fabric of life. Hold onto this idea of the lifeworld; it's important and we will come back to it shortly.

Liberal Capitalism and the Hope of Modernity

Drawing from Marx and Weber, Habermas argues that there have been two phases of capitalism: liberal capitalism and organized capitalism. Each phase is defined by the changing relationship between capitalism and the state. In *liberal capitalism,* the state has little involvement with the economy. Capitalism is thus able to function without constraint. Liberal capitalism occurred during the beginning phases of Western capitalism and the nation-state.

Capitalism and the nation-state came into existence as part of sweeping changes that redefined Western Europe and eventually the world. Though beginning much earlier, these changes coalesced in the seventeenth and eighteenth centuries. Prior to this time, the primary form of government in Europe was feudalism, brought to Europe by the Normans in 1066. Feudalism is based on land tenure and personal relationships. These relationships, and thus the land, were organized around the monarchy with a clear social division between royalty and peasants. Thus, the lifeworld of the everyday person in feudal Europe was one where personal obligations and one's relationship to the land were paramount. The everyday person was keenly aware of her or his obligations to the lord of the land (the origin of the word "landlord"). This was seen as a kind of familial relationship, and fidelity was its chief goal. Notice something important here: People under feudalism were subjects of the monarchy, not citizens.

Capitalism came about out of an institutional field that included the state, Protestantism, and the Industrial Revolution. The nation-state was needed to provide the necessary uniform money system and strong legal codes concerning private property; the Protestant Reformation created a culture with strong values centered on individualism and the work ethic; and the Industrial Revolution gave to capitalism the level of exploitation it needed.

Habermas argues that together the nation-state and capitalism depoliticized class relations, proposed equality based on market competition, and contributed strongly to the emergence of the public sphere. In contrast to Dahrendorf, Habermas uses the term *class* in its traditional Marxian sense. This use of the term class came into existence between 1770 and 1840—a time period that corresponds to the Industrial Revolution as well as the French and American political revolutions. Almost everything about society changed during this time, in particular the ideas of individual rights and accountability and the primacy of the economic system. The modern word class, then, carries with it the ideas that the individual's position is a product of the social system and that social position is made rather than inherited.

> What was changing consciousness was not only increased individual mobility, which could be largely contained within the older terms, but the new sense of a society or a particular social system which actually created social division, including new kinds of divisions. (Williams, 1985, p. 62)

Thus, according to Habermas, class is no longer a *political* issue, it is an *economic* one—class relations are no longer seen in terms of personal relations and family connections, but rather as the result of free market competition. Under capitalism and the civil liberties brought by the nation-state, all members of society are seen equally as citizens and economic competitors. Any differences among members in society are thus believed to come from economic competition and market forces, rather than birthright and personal relationships. Clearly, liberal capitalism brought momentous changes to the lifeworld: It became a world defined by democratic freedoms and responsibilities. Social relationships were no longer familial but rather legal and rational. The chief goal for the person in this lifeworld was full democratic participation. According to Habermas, the mechanism for this full participation is the public sphere.

The combination of the ideals of the Enlightenment, the transformation of government from feudalism to nation-state democracy, and the rise of capitalism created something that had never before existed: the public sphere. The public sphere is a space for democratic, public debate. Under feudalism, subjects could obviously complain about the monarchy and their way of life, and no doubt they did. But grumbling about a situation over which one has no control is vastly different from debating political points over which one is expected to exercise control. Remember, this was the first time Europe or the Americas had citizens, with rights and civic responsibilities; there was robust belief and hope in this new person, the citizen. The ideals of the Enlightenment indicated that this citizenry would be informed and completely engaged in the democratic process, and the public sphere is the place where this strong democracy could take place.

Habermas sees the public sphere as existing between a set of cultural institutions and practices on the one hand and state power on the other. The function of the public sphere is to mediate the concerns of private citizens and state interests. There are two principles of this public sphere: access to unlimited information and equal participation. The public sphere thus consists of cultural organizations such as journals and newspapers that distribute information to the people, and it contains both political and commercial organizations where public discussion can take place, such as public assemblies, coffee shops, pubs, political clubs, and so forth. The goal of this public sphere is pragmatic consensus.

Thus, during liberal capitalism, the relationship between the state and capitalism can best be characterized as *laissez-faire*, which is French for "allow to do." The assumption undergirding this policy was that the individual will contribute most successfully to the good of the whole if left to her or his own aspirations. The place of government, then, should be as far away from capitalism as possible. In this way of thinking, capitalism represents the mechanism of equality, the place where the best are defined through successful competition rather than by family ties. During liberal capitalism, then, it was felt that the marketplace of capitalism had to be completely free from any interference so that the most successful could rise to the top. In this sense, faith in the "invisible hand" of market dynamics corresponded to the evolutionist belief in survival of the fittest and natural selection.

Organized Capitalism and the Legitimation Crisis

Such was the ideal world of capitalism and democracy coming out of the Enlightenment. The central orienting belief was progress; humankind was set free from the feudalistic bonds of monarchical government and each individual would stand or fall based on his or her own efforts. In addition to economic pursuit, these efforts were to be focused on full democratic participation. Each citizen was to be fully and constantly immersed in education—education that came not only from schools but also through the public sphere. The hope of modernity was thus invested in each citizen and that person's full participation—people believed that rational discourse would lead to decisions made by reason and guided by egalitarianism.

Two economic issues changed the relationship between the economy and the state, which, in turn, had dramatic impacts on the lifeworld and public sphere. First, rather than producing equal competitors on an even playing field, free markets tend to create monopolies. Thus, by the end of the nineteenth and beginning of the twentieth century, the United States' economy was essentially run by an elite group of businessmen who came to be called "robber barons." Perhaps the attitude of these capitalists is best captured by the phrase attributed to William H. Vanderbilt, a railroad tycoon: "The public be damned."

These men emphasized efficiency through "Taylorism" (named after Frederick Taylor, the creator of scientific management) and economies of scale. The result was large-scale domination of markets. These monopolies weren't restricted to the market; they extended to "vertical integration" as well. With vertical integration, a company controls before-and-after manufacture supply lines. One example is Standard Oil, who at this time dominated the market, owned wells and refineries, and controlled the railroad system that moved its product to market.

The response of the U.S. government to widespread monopolization was to enact antitrust laws. The first legislation of this type in the United States was the Sherman Antitrust Act of 1890. In part the act reads,

> Every contract, combination in the form of trust or otherwise, or conspiracy, in restraint of trade or commerce among the several States, or with foreign nations, is declared to be illegal. . . . Every person who shall monopolize, or attempt to monopolize, or combine or conspire with any other person or persons, to monopolize any part of the trade or commerce among the several States, or with foreign nations, shall be deemed guilty of a felony.

However, capitalists fought the act on constitutional grounds and the Supreme Court prevented the government from applying the law for a number of years. Eventually the Court decided for the government in 1904, and the Antitrust Act was used powerfully by both Presidents Theodore Roosevelt and William Taft. This regulatory power of the U.S. government was further extended under Woodrow Wilson's administration and the passing of the Clayton Antitrust Act in 1914.

The second economic issue that modified the economy's relationship with the state was economic fluctuations. As Karl Marx had indicated, capitalist economies are subject to periodic oscillations, with downturns becoming more and more harsh. By the late 1920s, the capitalist economic system went into severe decline, creating worldwide depression in the 1930s. What came to be called "classic economics" fell out of favor and a myriad of competitors clamored to take its place. Eventually the ideas of John Maynard Keynes took hold and were explicated in his 1936 book, *The General Theory of Employment, Interest and Money.* His main idea was simple, and reminiscent of Marx: Capitalism tends toward overproduction—the capacity of the system to produce and transport products is greater than the demand. Keynes' theory countered the then-popular belief in the invisible hand of the market and argued that active government spending and management of the economy would reduce the power and magnitude of the business cycle.

Keynes' ideas initially influenced Franklin D. Roosevelt's belief that insufficient demand produced the depression, and after World War II Keynes' ideas were generally accepted. Governments began to keep statistics about the economy, expanded their control of capitalism, and increased spending in order to keep demand up. This new approach continued through the 1950s and 1960s. While the economic problems of the 1970s cast doubt upon Keynesian economics, new economic policies have continued to include some level of government spending and economic manipulation.

Thus, due to the tendency of completely free markets to produce monopolies and periodic fluctuations, the state became much more involved in the control of the economy. *Organized capitalism,* then, is a kind of capitalism where economic practices are controlled, governed, or organized by the state. According to Habermas, the change from liberal to organized capitalism, along with the general dynamics of capitalism (such as commodification, market expansion, advertising, and so on), have had three major effects.

First, there has been a shift in the kind and arena of crises. As we've seen, liberal capitalism suffered from economic crises. Under organized capitalism, however, the economy is managed by the state to one degree or another. This shift means that the crisis, when it hits, is a crisis for the state rather than the economy. It is specifically a legitimation crisis for the state and for people's belief in rationality.

There are two things going on here in the relationship between the state and the economy: The state is attempting to organize capitalism and it is employing scientific knowledge to do so. Together, these issues create *crises of legitimation and rationality* rather than simply economic disasters. Nevertheless, Habermas argues that the economy is the core problem: Capitalism has an intrinsic set of issues that continually create economic crises. However, due to the state's attempts to govern the economy, what the population experiences are ineffectual and disjointed responses from the state rather than economic crises. More significantly, in attempting to solve economic and social problems, the state increasingly depends upon scientific knowledge and technical control. This reliance on technical control changes the character of the problems from social or economic issues to technical ones (recall Habermas' three types of knowledge).

Concepts and Theory: The Colonization of Democracy

The other two important effects concern the lifeworld and the public sphere. In our discussion of legitimation and rationality crises, we can begin to see the changes in the lifeworld. The lifeworld of liberal capitalism was constructed out of a culture that believed in progress through science and reason. In this lifeworld, the person was expected to be actively involved in the democratic process. However, the general malaise that grows out of the crisis of legitimation reduces people's motivation and the meaning they attach to social life.

Colonization of the Lifeworld

In addition, according to Habermas, the lifeworld is becoming increasingly colonized by the political and economic systems. To understand what Habermas means, we have to step back a little. As I've already noted, Habermas gives us a theory that involves social evolution. In general, social evolutionists argue that society progresses by becoming more complex: Structures and systems differentiate and become more specialized. The evolutionary argument is that this specialization and complexity produce a system that is more adaptable and better able to survive in a changing environment.

One of the problems that comes up in differentiated systems concerns coordination and control, or what Habermas refers to as "steering." This is one of the problems that Talcott Parsons identified. The issue is trying to guide social structures that have different values, roles, status positions, languages, and so forth. Differentiated social structures tend to go off in their own direction. We have seen that Parsons felt this problem was solved through generalized media of exchange. The idea of media is important, so let's consider it again for a minute. Merriam-Webster (2002) defines *medium* (*media* is plural) as "something through or by which something is accomplished, conveyed, or carried on." For example, language is a form of media: It's the principal medium through which communication is organized and carried out. Different social institutions or structures use different media. In education, for instance, it's knowledge, and in government, it's power. These are the instruments or media through which education and government are able to perform their functions.

For Parsons, the solution to the problem of social integration and steering is for the different social subsystems to create media that are general or abstract enough that all other institutions could use them as means of exchange. We can think about this like boundary crossings. Visualize a boundary between different social structures or subsystems, such as the economy and education. How can the boundary between economy and education be crossed? Or, using a different analogy, how can the economy and education talk to each other when they have different languages and values?

Habermas is specifically concerned with the boundaries between the lifeworld and the state and economy. In Habermas' terms, Parsons basically argues that the state and economy use power and money respectively as media of exchange with the lifeworld. If you think about this for a moment, it seems to make sense: You exist in your lifeworld, so what does the economy have that you want? You might start a list of all the cars, houses, and other commodities that you want, but what do they all boil down to? Money. And how does the economy entice you to leave your lifeworld and go to work? Money. So, money is the medium of exchange between the lifeworld and the economy. The same logic holds for the boundary between the lifeworld and the state: Power is what the state has and what induces us to interact with the state. However, Habermas (1981/1987) sees a problem:

> I want to argue against this—that in the areas of life that primarily fulfill functions of cultural reproduction, social integration, and socialization, mutual understanding cannot be replaced by media as the mechanism for coordinating action—that is, it *cannot be technicized*—though it can be expanded by technologies of communication and organizationally mediated—that is, it can be *rationalized*. (p. 267, emphasis original)

Habermas (1981/1987) is arguing that there is something intrinsic about the lifeworld that cannot be reduced to media, such as money and power, "without sociopathological consequences" (p. 267). Let me give you an easy example from a different issue: the sex act. Most people would agree that you cannot "technicize" this behavior using the medium of money without fundamentally changing the nature of it; there is a clear distinction between making love with your significant partner and having sex with a prostitute. Habermas is making the same kind of argument about humanity and communication in general. For him, the sphere of mutual understanding—the lifeworld—cannot be reduced to power and money without essentially changing it.

Yet Habermas isn't arguing that Parsons made a theoretical mistake. Parsons saw himself as an empiricist and merely sought to describe the social world. So in this sense, Parsons was right: There is something going on in modernity that tries to mediate the lifeworld. Habermas takes this idea from Parsons and argues that in imposing their media on the lifeworld, the state and economy are fundamentally changing it. The lifeworld, by definition, cannot be mediated through money or power without deeply altering it.

According to Habermas, the lifeworld is naturally achieved through consensus. This is basically the same thing that Mead and the symbolic interactionists argue. Remember, interactions emerge and are achieved by individuals consciously and unconsciously negotiating meaning and action in face-to-face encounters. This negotiation, or consensus building, occurs chiefly through speech. Thus, using money or power fundamentally changes the lifeworld. In Habermas' (1981/1987) words, it is colonized: "The *mediatization* of the lifeworld assumes the form of a *colonization*" (p. 196, emphasis original).

This idea of the **colonization of the lifeworld** is perhaps one of Habermas' best-known and most provocative concepts. Using Merriam-Webster (2002) again, a colony is "a body of people settled in a new territory, foreign and often distant, retaining ties with their motherland or parent state . . . as a means of facilitating established occupation and [governance] by the parent state." Habermas is arguing that the modern state and economic system (capitalism) have imposed their media upon the lifeworld. In this sense, money and power act just like a colony—they are means through which these distant social structures seek to occupy and dominate the local lifeworld of people.

Habermas (1981/1987, p. 356) argues that four factors in organized capitalism set the stage for the colonization of the lifeworld. First, the lifeworld is differentiated from the social systems. Historically, there was a closer association between the lifeworld and society; in fact, in the earliest societies they were *coextensive;* in other words, they overlapped to the degree that they were synonymous. As society increases in differentiation and complexity, the lifeworld becomes "decoupled" from institutional spheres.

Second, the boundaries between the lifeworld and the different social subsystems become regulated through differentiated roles. Keep in mind that social roles are scripts for behavior. In traditional societies, most social roles were related to the family. So, for example, the eldest male would be the high priest—the family and religious positions would be filled and scripted by the same role. This kind of role homogeneity made the relationship between the lifeworld and society relatively nonproblematic, and, more importantly, it served to connect the two spheres.

Third, the rewards for workers in organized capitalism in terms of leisure time and expendable cash offset the demands of bureaucratic domination. "Wherever bourgeois law visibly underwrites the demands of the lifeworld against bureaucratic domination, it loses the ambivalence of realizing freedom at the cost of destructive side effects" (Habermas, 1981/1987, p. 361). And fourth, the state provides comprehensive welfare. Worker protection laws, social security, and so forth reduce the impact of exploitation and create a culture of entitlement where legal subjects pursue their individual interests and the "privatized hopes for self-actualization and self-determination are primarily located . . . in the roles of consumer and client" (Habermas, 1981/1987, p. 350).

For simplicity's sake, we can group the first two and last two items together. The first two factors are generally concerned with the effects of complex social environments. The more complex the social environment, due to structural differentiation, the greater will be the number and diversity of cultures and roles with which any individual will have to contend. This in turn dismantles the connections among the elements that comprise the lifeworld: culture, society, and personality.

The second two factors concern the effects of the state's position under organized capitalism. Under organized capitalism, the state protects the capitalist system, the capitalists, and the workers. In doing so, the state mitigates some of the issues that would otherwise produce social conflict and change. But perhaps more importantly, the state further individualizes the person. The roles of consumer and client, both associated with a climate of entitlement, overshadow the role of democratic citizen.

As a result of these factors, everything in organized capitalism that informs the life-world, such as culture and social positions, comes to be defined or at least influenced by money and power. Money and power have a certain logic or rationality to them. Weber (Chapter 4) talked about four distinct forms of rationality, two of which are pertinent here: instrumental and value rationality. As a reminder, *instrumental-rational action* is related to means-and-ends calculation and *value-rational action* is defined as behavior that is motivated by a person's values or morals.

Value rationality is specifically tied to the lifeworld and instrumental rationality to the state and economy. Thus, a good deal of what happens when the life-world is colonized is the ever-increasing intrusion of instrumental rationality and the emptying of value rationality from the social system. The result is that "systemic mechanisms—for example, money—steer a social intercourse that has been largely disconnected from norms and values. . . . [And] norm-conformative attitudes and identity-forming social memberships are neither necessary nor possible" (Habermas, 1981/1987, p. 154).

In turn, people in this kind of modern social system come to value money and power, which are seen as the principal means of success and happiness. Money is used to purchase commodities that are in turn used to construct identities and impress other people. Rather than being a humanistic value, respect becomes something demanded rather than given—a ploy of power rather than a place of honor.

To see the significance of this, let's recall the ideal of the lifeworld of modernity. When the lifeworld changed in the move from traditional to modern society, it took on new priorities and importance. The lifeworld was ideally to be dominated by democratic freedoms and responsibilities and occupied by citizens fully engaged in reasoning out the ways to fulfill the goals of the Enlightenment—progress and equality—through communication and consensus building. As Habermas (1981/1987) says, "The burden of social integration [shifts] more and more from religiously anchored consensus to processes of consensus formation in language" (p. 180).

As you can see, using money or power as steering media in the lifeworld is the antithesis of open communication and consensus building. One of the results of this situation is that the lifeworld decouples from or becomes incidental to the social system, in terms of its integrative capacities. A lifeworld colonized by money and power cannot build consensus through reasoning and communication, and people in this kind of lifeworld lose their sense of responsibility to the democratic ideals of the Enlightenment.

Colonization of the Public Sphere

This process is further aggravated by developments in the **public sphere**. As we've seen, the public sphere and its citizens came into existence with the advent of modernity. Citizens "are endowed by their Creator with certain unalienable Rights." This phrasing in the U.S. Declaration of Independence is interesting because it implies that these rights are moral rather than simply legal. There is a moral obligation to these rights that expresses itself in certain responsibilities:

> [W]henever any Form of Government becomes destructive of these ends, it is the Right of the People to alter or to abolish it, and to institute new Government, laying its foundation on such principles and organizing its powers in such form, as to them shall seem most likely to effect their Safety and Happiness.

Thus, the most immediate place for involvement of citizens is the public sphere. In that space between power on the one hand and free information on the other, citizens are meant to engage in communication and consensus formation. It is in that space that discussion and decisions about any "form of government" are to be made. However, the public sphere has been colonized in much the same way as the lifeworld. Specifically, the public sphere, which began in the eighteenth century with the growth of independent news sources and active places of public debate, transformed into something quite different in the twentieth century. It became the place of public opinion—something that is measured through polls, used by politicians, and influenced by a mass media of entertainment.

There are two keys here. First, public opinion is something that is manufactured through social science. It's a statistic, not a public forum or debate that results in consensus. Recall what we saw earlier about how Habermas views the knowledge of science, even social science: Its specific purpose is to control. Transforming consensus in the public sphere into a statistic makes controlling public sentiment much easier for politicians, both subjectively and objectively.

The second key issue I want us to see is the shift in news sources. Most of the venues through which we obtain our news and information today are motivated by profit. In other words, public news sources aren't primarily concerned with creating a democratic citizenry or with making available information that is socially significant. As such, information that is given out is packaged as entertainment most of the time. In a society like the United States, the consumers of mass media are more infatuated with "wicked weather" than they are concerned about the state of the homeless.

Concepts and Theory: Communicative Action and Civil Society

When we began this discussion, I mentioned that Habermas still holds out the promise of modernity. This hope is anchored in two arenas: speech communities and civil society. Both of these are rather straightforward proposals, though achieving them is difficult under the conditions created by organized capitalism, where the possibility and horizon of moral discourse is stunted.

Ideal Speech Communities

Let's talk first about ideal speech communities. These communities or situations are the basis for ethical reasoning and occur under certain guidelines to communication. Before we get to those guidelines, we need to consider what Habermas calls *communicative action:* action with the intent to communicate. Habermas makes the point that all social action is based on communication. However, to understand Habermas's intent, it might be beneficial to consider something that looks like social communication but isn't. We can call this "strategic speech." Strategic speech is associated with instrumental rationality and it is thus endemic within the lifeworld of organized capitalism as well as the social system.

In this kind of talk, the goal is not to reach consensus or understanding, but rather for the speaker to achieve his or her own personal ends. For example, the stereotypical salesperson or "closer" of a deal isn't trying to reach consensus; he or she is trying to sell something (a more immediate example is the student explaining why he or she missed the test). In strategic talk, speech isn't being practiced simply as communication; communication is being *used* to achieve egocentric ends, which is contrary to the function of communication: "Reaching understanding is the inherent telos [ultimate end] of human speech. Naturally, speech and understanding are not related to one another as means to end" (Habermas, 1981/1984, p. 287).

Communicative action within an ideal speech situation is based upon some important assumptions. As we are reviewing these assumptions, keep in mind that Habermas is making the argument that communication itself holds the key and power to reasoned existence and emancipatory politics. Communication has intrinsic properties that form the basis of human connection and understanding. Habermas points out that every time we simply talk with someone, in every natural speech act, we assume that communication is possible. We also assume that it is possible to share intersubjective states. These two assumptions sound similar but are a bit different. Communication simply involves your assuming that your friend can understand the words you are saying. Sharing intersubjective states is deeper than this. With *intersubjectivity,* we assume that others can share a significant part of our inner world—our feelings, thoughts, convictions, and experiences.

A third assumption we make in speech acts is that there is a truth that exists apart from the individual speaker. In this part of speech, we are making *validity claims.* We claim that what we are saying has the strength of truth or rightness. This is an extremely important point for Habermas and forms the basis of discourse ethics and universal norms. All true communication is built upon and contains claims to validity, which inherently call for reason and reflection. Further, these claims assume validity is possible; that truth or rightness can exist independent of the individual, which implies the possibility of universal norms or morals; and that validity claims can be criticized, which implies that they are in some sense active and accountable to reason. Validity claims also facilitate intersubjectivity in that they create expectations in both parties. The speaker is expected to be responsible for the reasonableness of her or his statement, and the hearer is expected to accept or reject the validity of the statement and provide a reasonable basis for either.

These assumptions are basic to speech: We assume that we can communicate; we assume we can share intersubjective worlds; and we assume that valid statements are possible. What Habermas draws out from these basic assumptions of speech is that it is feasible to reasonably decide on collective action. This is a simple but profound point: Intrinsic to the way humans communicate is the hope of decisive collective action. It is possible for humanity to use talk in order to build consensus and make reasoned decisions about social action. This is both the promise and hope of modernity and the Enlightenment.

Ethical reason and substantive rationality are thus intrinsic to speech, but it isn't enough in terms of making a difference in organized capitalism. As with all critical theorists, Habermas has a praxis component. Praxis for Habermas is centered in communication and the creation of ideal speech situations. Here, communication is a skill, one that as democratic citizens we need to cultivate in order to participate in the civil society. As we consider these points of the ideal speech community, notice how many of them have to do more with listening than with speaking. In an ideal speech situation,

- Every person who is competent to speak and act is allowed to partake in the conversation—full equality is granted and each person is seen as an equal source of legitimate or valid statements.
- There is no sense of coercion; consensus is not forced; and there is no recourse to objective standings such as status, money, or power.
- Anyone can introduce any topic; anyone can disagree with or question any topic; everyone is allowed to express opinions and feelings about all topics.
- Each person strives to keep his or her speech free from ideology.

Let me point out that this is an ideal against which all speech acts can be compared, and toward which all democratic communication must strive. The closer a community's speech comes to this ideal, the greater is the possibility of consensus and reasoned action.

> If we assume that the human species maintains itself through the socially coordinated activities of its members and that this coordination has to be established through communication. . . . then the reproduction of the species also requires satisfying the conditions of a rationality that is inherent in communicative action. (Habermas, 1981/1984, p. 397)

Civil Society

Ideal speech communities are based upon and give rise to civil society. Civil society for Habermas is made up of voluntary associations, organizations, and social movements that are in touch with issues that evolve out of communicative action in the public sphere. In principle, civil society is independent of any social system, such as the state, the market, capitalism in general, family, or religion. Civil society, then, functions as a midpoint between the public sphere and social interactions. The elements of civil society provide a way through which the concerns developed in a robust speech community get expressed to society at large. One of the more important things civil society does is continually challenge political and cultural organizations in order to keep intact the freedoms of speech, assembly, and press that are constitutionally guaranteed. Examples of elements of civil society include professional organizations, unions, charities, women's organizations, advocacy groups, and so on.

Habermas gives us several conditions that must be met for a robust civil society to evolve and exist.

- It must develop within the context of liberal political culture, one that emphasizes equality for all, and an active and integrated lifeworld.
- Within the boundaries of the public sphere, men and women may obtain influence based on persuasion but cannot obtain political power.
- A civil society can exist only within a social system where the state's power is limited. The state in no way occupies the position of the social actor designed to bring all society under control. The state's power must be limited and political steering must be indirect and leave intact the internal operations of the institution or subsystem.

Overall, Habermas rekindles the social vision that was at the heart of modernity's birth. Modernity began in the fervor of the Enlightenment and held the hope that humanity could be the master of its own fate. There were two primary branches of this movement, one contained in science and the other in democratic society. In many ways, science has proven its worth through the massive technological developments that have occurred over the past 200 years or so.

However, Habermas argues that the hope of democracy has run aground on the rocks of organized capitalism. In communicative action and civil society, he points the way to a fully involved citizenry reasoning out and charting their own course. But what Habermas gives us is an ideal—not in the sense of fantasy, but in the sense of an exemplar vision. In his theory, it is the goal toward which societies and citizens must strive if they are to fulfill the promise of modernity. Habermas, then, lays before us a challenge, "the big question of whether we could have had, or can now have, modernity without the less attractive features of capitalism and the bureaucratic nation-state" (Outhwaite, 2003, p. 231).

Summary

- Habermas' theory of modernity is in the tradition of the Frankfurt School of critical theory. His intent is to critique the current arrangements of capitalism and the state, while at the same time reestablishing the hope of the Enlightenment, that it is possible for human beings to guide their collective life through reason.

- Habermas argues that modernity has thus far been characterized by two forms of capitalism: liberal and organized. The principal difference between these two forms is the degree of state involvement. Under liberal capitalism, the relationship between the state and capitalism was one of *laissez-faire*. The state practiced a hands-off policy in the belief that the invisible hand of market competition would draw out the best in people and would result in true equality based on individual effort. However, *laissez-faire* capitalism produced two counter-results: the tendency toward monopolization and significant economic fluctuations due to overproduction. Both unanticipated results prompted greater state involvement and oversight of the capitalist system.

• Organized capitalism is characterized by active government spending and management of the economy. This involvement of the state in capitalism facilitates three distinct results, all of which weaken the possibility of achieving the social promise of modernity:

1. *A crisis of legitimation and rationality.* Because the state is now involved in managing the economy, fluctuations, downturns, and other economic ills are perceived as problems with the state rather than the economy. When they occur, these problems threaten the legitimacy of the state in general. In addition, because the state uses social scientific methods to forecast and control economies, belief in rationality is put in jeopardy. These crises in turn reduce the levels of meaning and motivation felt by the citizenry.

2. *The colonization of the lifeworld.* The lifeworld is colonized by the state and economy, as the media of power and money replace communication and consensus as the chief values of the lifeworld.

3. *The reduction of the public sphere to one of public opinion.* This occurs principally as the media have shifted from information to entertainment value and as the state makes use of social scientific methods to measure and then control public opinion.

• However, Habermas argues that the hope of social progress and equality can be embraced once again through communicative action and a robust civil society. Communication is based upon several assumptions, the most important of which concern validity claims—these inherently call for reason and reflection. Together, such assumptions lead Habermas to conclude that the process of communication itself gives us warrant to believe it is possible to reach consensus and rationally guide our collective lives.

• Communicative action is also a practice. True communicative action occurs when full equality is granted and each person is seen as an equal source of legitimate or valid statements; objective standings such as status, money, or power are not used in any way to persuade members; all topics may be introduced; and each person strives to keep her or his speech free from ideology.

• Communicative action results in and is based upon a robust civil society. Civil society is made up of midlevel voluntary associations, organizations, and social movements. Such organizations grow out of educated, rational, and critical communicative actions and become the medium through which the public sphere is revitalized. A civil society is most likely to develop under the following conditions: A liberal political culture is present that emphasizes education, communication, and equality; men and women are prevented from obtaining or using power in the public sphere; the state's power is limited.

TAKING THE PERSPECTIVE—CRITICAL THEORY

As we've seen, critical theory took its cue and impetus from the inhumanity of Nazism and the Holocaust. And these forces of destruction only became more widespread through World War II and its aftermath: the American destruction of Hiroshima and the continued threat of nuclear annihilation, and the atrocities of Stalinism and the subsequent Cold War. These were forces of destruction not just of human life but of human spirit as well. The hope with which the twentieth century began lay in ashes by the end. Even the student "revolutions" of 1968 were smothered under the weight of state sponsored capitalism, incessant commodification and advertising, and the spread of lifeless, homogeneous popular culture through the mass media. To continue to hope in participatory democracy and social justice seemed naive at best; and more generally the hope was swept under the rug of political apathy and the unceasing hunger for cultural stimulation with which the twenty-first century began. The face of humanity revealed during the twentieth century was as different as the one hoped for in the eighteenth as the darkness of Hades is from the splendor of paradise.

That was critical theory's defining moment. The skepticism and critique born out of those historical moments are the weight that it bears, not as a burden (though burdensome it is) but as that which gives it presence and propels it forward. Having said that, there are questions about "whether it has any coherence as a 'school' of thought at all" (Ray, 1990, p. x). There have been at least three and maybe four phases that the Frankfurt School has gone through. And there are many works that have a sense of critical theory about them but owe little to the actual School itself. However, I think there are four issues around which most critical theory gathers.

First there is an emphasis on the relationship between history and society on the one hand and social position and knowledge on the other. To understand any society, you must first understand its historical path and the structural arrangements within it. The knowledge and political interests that people hold within any society are based upon a person's social position within a historically specific social and cultural context.

Second, critical theory specifically critiques positivism and the idea that knowledge can be value-free. With humans, all knowledge is based on and reflects values. Positivistic knowledge through social science is simply blinded to its own biases and is but a reification of method. The supreme use of reason is emancipation, bringing equality and freedom to all humankind. The purpose then of theory and sociology is not understanding, not control, but emancipation. Critical theory, then, is always applied to the human condition.

Third, the work of critical theory is open-ended and is simply and only dependent upon and guiding by critical thinking. Overall the work of the Frankfurt School and those who have followed indicate that it isn't possible to clearly, truthfully, and accurately plan out the right path for humanity; there is no right society, no goal toward which we strive. The idea that there is lays at the base of why "social science" is an oxymoron—control in order to bring freedom, objectification to understand the subject. But not only is the idea wrongheaded, humans living in rationalized, commodified, mediated culture are too entwined with the spirit of the age to

(Continued)

(Continued)

see clearly. We can but see dimly at best. Critical theory and critical thinking are meant to help us examine and deconstruct our thoughts and thinking. The goal of critical theory is subversion: "The project of Critical Theory has been to develop ways of thinking so subversive of dominant legitimations, that to understand them was to resist them" (Ray, 1990, p. xviii).

This leads to the fourth quality, which is found particularly in Habermas: The vehicle for social change is participatory democracy guided by critical theory and thought. Most of what passes as "democracy" is nothing but oligarchy by the powerful elite. This rule by few produces a false totality, which, in truth, is antagonistic and held together by oppressive power. In contrast, the intent of social democracy is the intellectual and practical involvement of all its citizens.

BUILDING YOUR THEORY TOOLBOX

Learning More—Primary and Secondary Sources

- See the following works by Jürgen Habermas:

  o *The Theory of Communicative Action, Vol. 1: Reason and the Rationalization of Society*, Beacon Press, 1984; *Vol. 2: Lifeworld and System: A Critique of Functionalist Reason*, Beacon Press, 1987.

  o *The Philosophical Discourse of Modernity: Twelve Lectures*, MIT Press, 1990.

  o *The Structural Transformation of the Public Sphere: An Inquiry Into a Category of Bourgeois Society*, MIT Press, 1991.

- For secondary resources see:

  o *Habermas's Critical Theory of Society*, by Jane Braaten, SUNY Press, 1991.

  o *Habermas and the Public Sphere*, edited by Craig Calhoun, MIT Press, 1993.

  o *Habermas: A Critical Introduction*, by William Outhwaite, Stanford University Press, 1995.

Seeing the Social World (knowing the theory)

- Write a 250-word synopsis of critical theory.

- After reading and understanding this chapter, you should be able to define the following terms theoretically and explain their theoretical importance for Habermas' theory: *legitimacy, authority, lifeworld, liberal capitalism, depoliticized class, public sphere, pragmatic consensus, organized capitalism, legitimation crisis, colonization of the lifeworld, steering, generalized media of exchange, colonization of the public sphere, public opinion, analytic knowledge, interpretive knowledge, critical theory, speech communities, communicative action, civil society*

- After reading and understanding this chapter, you should be able to answer the following questions (remember to answer them *theoretically*):

  ○ How does scientific knowledge devalue the human questions of ethics, aesthetics, beauty, and emotion?

  ○ Explain the path of freedom offered by critical theory (Horkheimer and Adorno).

  ○ Explain the differences between liberal and organized capitalism. Pay particular attention to the changing relations between the state and economy.

  ○ Define the lifeworld and its purpose, and explain how it became colonized.

  ○ Define the public sphere and explain how it came about, its purpose, and its colonization.

  ○ What is communicative action and how does it form the basis of value-rational action?

  ○ Define ideal speech situations (or communities) and explain how they give rise to civil society.

  ○ What is civil society? What are the conditions under which it can survive? How is it important to a democratic society?

Engaging the Social World (using the theory)

- Using your favorite Internet search engine, look up "participatory democracy." How would Habermas' ideal speech community fit this model? Does the Internet provide greater possibilities for ideal speech situations to develop? How could Internet communities be linked to civil society?

- Racial, ethnic, gender, sexual identity, and religious groups have all been and are being disenfranchised in modern society. How does the ideal speech situation "enfranchise" these groups? In other words, how does the ideal speech situation do away with the possibility of disenfranchised groups?

- What social group do you belong to that most nearly approximates the ideal speech community?

Weaving the Threads (building theory)

- Write a two-page analysis of the modern project of democracy using Habermas' theory. As a reference for the modern project, use the material presented in Chapter 1.

Part III

Contemporary New Visions and Critiques

Throughout this book we have, in a very general way, considered the influence of historical changes on theory. Sociological theory as we know it today began as a result of the massive changes that Western society experienced during the eighteenth and nineteenth centuries. These were times of upheaval that were both transformative and energizing. Clearly there were problems in the move from traditional to modern society, and one of the chief motivations of our classical theorists was to identify these problems and speculate about how they might affect society. Marx focused on capitalism, Weber looked at rationality and bureaucracy, Durkheim was concerned with social diversity and decreasing cultural consensus, Simmel saw the problems associated with urbanization and increasing levels of objective culture, and Gilman and Du Bois pointed to the inconsistencies of inequality in a democratic society.

Yet, on the whole, these critiques were based on the hopes of modernity as well. Modernity is not simply a period of time; it is an attitude of mind—the belief that through reason human beings can control their world, and use that control to make progress to a better life, both socially and technically (for example, in medicine). Society thus was moving upward. As we moved into early twentieth-century theorizing, we saw this confidence continue to be reflected in the way sociological theory was proceeding. Sociology busied itself with theory testing and cumulation. Knowledge of social things was valued on its own merit, much as pure research is valued in the hard sciences. Schools of thought were organized and research agendas launched.

But the twentieth century also brought doubt and despair and, with these, critical theory. The "war to end all wars" (World War I) didn't. World War II came and brought with it the Holocaust, a haunting testimony to the depths the human soul can sink. The twentieth century also initiated the atomic age and catastrophic risk—risk due not only to nuclear escalation but also to the ever-expanding potential of global ecological destruction. In addition, after World War II the last remnants of the British Empire fell, and with it came the end of colonialism: "For the peoples of most of the earth, much of the twentieth century involved the long struggle and eventual triumph against colonial rule" (Young, 2003, p. 3). Yet this one rule was replaced by another—the United States became hegemonic, and global dominion moved from colonialism to a triadic combination of capitalism, culture, and militarism. To keep and expand that rule, the United States has entered into a succession of never-ending and rarely "won" police actions. In this century of doubt, the 1960s perhaps stands central. The contradictions of democracy and the failure of the projects of modernity, both social and technical, became clearer than ever before, and the decade brought worldwide upheaval. There were student movements not only in the United States but also around the globe, including in China, West Germany, Poland, Italy, Japan, Vietnam, Czechoslovakia, and Mexico. This period of time marks what has been called the first "world revolution."

Contemporary theory, then, is more and more characterized by criticism than hope (or, perhaps, a guarded, different hope than first launched modernity). As we've seen, modernist theory is based on the twin beliefs in technical progress and secular salvation. The events of the twentieth century cast deep doubts on these ideas of the Enlightenment. In the West, we became increasingly aware that modern democracy is built on inequality—it became painfully obvious that not all "men" are created equal. We also awakened to the destructive side of capitalism and science—the exploitation of people and land can have long-term and initially hidden effects. Contemporary theory is characterized by this same awareness. Just as criticism and doubt gradually dawned on people in the twentieth century, and just as these twin themes weave themselves in and out of the twenty-first-century consciousness, so it is with contemporary theory.

There are four chapters in this section, each with a specific theme. In Chapter 14, we'll be considering how societies are constructed. By and large, most of the theories we've looked at so far have taken society for granted or have reduced the idea of society to the micro-level situation. But neither Giddens nor Bourdieu takes society for granted nor do they retreat to the social situation. They want to first understand how society comes into existence. Their basic premise is that knowing how society exists will have a significant impact on what we pay attention to in our theorizing; for Giddens the focus is late modernity and for Bourdieu the central question is class. Both work with some of Marx's ideas but both also push Marx to incredibly new visions.

The theorists in Chapter 15 want us to change the way we look at society as well. But rather than looking at the essence of society, Wallerstein and Castells want to change the level of analysis, because the level at which the social exists now transcends national boundaries (the modernist defining lines of society). In Chapter 16, we come to poststructuralism and postmodernity. If we know nothing else about these theories, we know that they come after structuralism and modernity simply by their names. These theories have changed the way we look at social reality forever. And in Chapter 17, we will again consider the political person; but, as we'll see, the late or postmodern person is significantly different than the modern subject. And with these changes, there are also changes in the politics of democracy.

CHAPTER 14

Toward a New Vision of Society:

Anthony Giddens and Pierre Bourdieu

I n the social sciences, there is a central dichotomy that sets up some of the basic parameters of our discipline, such as the distinction between quantitative and qualitative methods and the divergence between structuralism and interactionism. This dichotomy also sets up one of the thorniest issues sociologists address: the dilemma of structure (objective) versus agency (subjective). The question that accompanies this dilemma is, how much agency or free will do individuals have in the face of social structures? We saw this issue in a different form in Chapters 11 and 12. Through different versions of exchange theory Blau and Collins attempt to bridge the gap by explaining how the two different domains are linked together through either exchange processes or elements of ritual. And in Chapter 12, Goffman and Garfinkel argue that the true acting unit of "society" is the social encounter.

Our two theorists in this chapter take different approaches. Pierre Bourdieu (1985) characterizes the dichotomy between structure and agency as one of the most harmful in the social sciences, and sees working to overcome this dichotomy as the most steadfast and important goal in the social disciplines (p. 15). As we'll see, Bourdieu's theory seeks to solve this dilemma by pointing out the creative tension that exists between structure and agency. Anthony Giddens agrees with Bourdieu's assessment but solves the problem by doing away with both structure and agency, at least in the usual meanings of the words. In addition, both Giddens and Bourdieu have specific social issues to which they apply their theories. For Giddens, the issue is modernity; for Bourdieu, the topic is social class.

Structuration and Modernity:
Anthony Giddens (1938–)

As we've seen, modernity began as a time when human beings believed they could control the physical and social worlds in order to live human existence. We've also seen, and are aware from simply living in this age, that there are problems. Yet Anthony Giddens takes us on another path, not pointing to the issues that have come up along the way but, rather, the idea of modernity contains intrinsic contradictions that make it impossible to fulfill its own reason for existence. According to Giddens (1990), modernity is a juggernaut, "a runaway engine of enormous power which, collectively as human beings, we can drive to some extent but which also threatens to rush out of our control and which could rend itself asunder" (p. 139). The word *juggernaut* comes from the Hindi word *Jagannātha*, which refers to a representation of the god Vishnu or Krishna—the lord of the universe. Every year the god's image would be paraded down the streets amid crowds of the faithful dancing and playing drums and cymbals. It's thought that at times believers would throw themselves under the wheels of the massive cart, to be crushed to death in a bid for early salvation. A juggernaut, then, is an irresistible force that demands blind devotion and sacrifice.

This image of an irresistible force conjures up the thrilling ride of the rollercoaster, with its twin sensations of trust and danger, but the juggernaut of modernity isn't as controllable or predictable as a rollercoaster. Here we can see a chief difference between Giddens and Habermas: For Habermas, rational control is central to modernity and imminently possible, inherent in the very act of communication; but for Giddens, modernity is almost by definition out of control. The intent of modernity is progress—but the effect of modernity is the creation of mechanisms and processes that become a runaway engine of change. And we, like the devotees of Jagannātha, are drawn to modernity's power and promise.

> The ride is by no means wholly unpleasant or unrewarding; it can often be exhilarating and charged with hopeful anticipation. But, so long as the institutions of modernity endure, we shall never be able to control completely either the path or the pace of the journey. In turn, we shall never be able to feel entirely secure, because the terrain across which it runs is fraught with risks of high consequence. (Giddens, 1990, p. 139)

THEORIST'S DIGEST

Brief Biography

Anthony Giddens was born January 18, 1938, in Edmonton, England. He received his undergraduate degree with honors from Hull University in 1959, studying sociology and psychology. Giddens did his master's work at the London School of Economics, finishing his thesis on the sociology of sport in 1961. From then until the early 1970s, Giddens lectured at various universities including the University of Leicester, Simon Fraser University, the University of California at Los Angeles, and Cambridge. Giddens finished his doctoral work at Cambridge in 1976. He remained at Cambridge through 1996, during which time he served as dean of Social and Political Sciences. In 1997, Giddens was appointed director of the London School of Economics and Political Science. Giddens is the author of some 34 books that have been translated into well over 20 languages. Giddens is also a member of the Advisory Council of the Institute for Public Policy Research (London, England) and served as advisor to British prime minister Tony Blair.

Central Sociological Questions

Giddens is a political sociologist, driven by both political questions and political involvement. While his early work certainly contained a typical Marxian interest in class, his later work is much more concerned with the political ramifications of globalization and what he characterizes as the juggernaut of modernity or the runaway world. Given the juggernaut of modernity, he asks, how are interactions and behaviors patterned over time? How can people become politically involved? In order to answer those questions, Giddens must first understand the essence of society. In this, Giddens seeks an ontology of the social world: What kinds of things go into the making of society? Precisely how does it exist?

Simply Stated

Society is not made up of objective structures that determine and pattern action across time and space. Rather, because the human world is a constructed world, people are psychologically motivated to routinize their behaviors and to see them as belonging in specific social places. In traditional society, these were assured through kinship, community, and religion. But modern society has rendered those ineffectual through radical reflexivity, the emptying of time and space,

(Continued)

(Continued)

disembedding of social relationships, and globalization. The result is that the certitude of traditional society has been replaced with tenuous social relations, individualized and uncertain projects of self-actualization, and lifestyle politics rather than the politics of emancipation.

Key Ideas

structuration theory, duality of structure, social structures, normative rules, signification codes, authoritative resources, allocative resources, time–space distanciation, modalities of structuration, domination, institutional orders, reflexive monitoring, rationalization of action, discursive consciousness, practical consciousness, routinization, regionalization, ontological security, radical reflexivity, separation of time and space, disembedding mechanisms, symbolic tokens, expert systems, reflexive project of the self, bodily regimes, organization of sensuality, pure relationships, emancipatory politics, life politics, mediated experiences

Concepts and Theory: The Reality of Society and Its People

I usually address the perspective of the theorist latter in the chapter. But with Giddens, I need to put it first. In order to understand the power of what Giddens says about modernity, we have to understand his perspective first. We've seen that the social project of modernity is based on the existence of two factors: society and free agents. In order to use science to understand and guide society, society must exist as an object capable of being studied and discovered. And in order to guide society through democracy, citizens had to have the power of reason and the ability to make free choices. We have come across critiques of this already. But Giddens proceeds in a different direction. His understanding of modernity is based on a distinct understanding of what society is and how people can affect it. He also reformulates the problem of social order. And we have to grasp these issues before we can appreciate his theory of modernity. His understanding of society and social actors is called **structuration theory**.

The Way Society Exists

Here's the simple version: Society doesn't exist as objective structures; rather, it is continually built or structured by reflexive social actors (people). That might sound familiar, and it should. Giddens uses insights from the material we covered in Chapters 3, 8, and 12: Marx, Parsons, symbolic interaction, ethnomethodology, and dramaturgy. It might also sound simple, but be careful. In using and explaining these insights he explains their ontology. The word **ontology** means the study of existence. So Giddens explains the fundamental reality in back of symbolic interaction, ethnomethodology, and dramaturgy. He does so because it's important for us to understand the way society exists to truly grasp what is going on in modernity.

Step 1: Understanding Two Things at Once

Giddens draws on ethnomethodology for this idea, and it simply says that social things exist together, not apart. Like Garfinkel, Giddens argues that the subject–object divide (or agent–structure) is a false dichotomy, created to explain away the complexity of human practice. Giddens (1986) says, "Human social activities, like some self-reproducing items in nature, are recursive" (p. 2). It's like the chicken and egg question, which in some ways is a silly one. When you have the egg, you have the chicken. They are one and the same, just in different phases. So, to follow the analogy, it's like this: Social actors produce social reality, but the mere fact that you have "social actors" presumes an already existing social world.

The primary insight of Giddens' structuration theory is that social structures and agency are recursively and reflexively produced: They are continuously brought into existence at the same moment through the same behaviors. Rather than seeing structure and agency as a dualism, as two mutually exclusive elements, Giddens proposes a duality—two analytically distinguishable parts of the same thing. The *duality of structure* indicates that structure is both the medium and the outcome of the social activity or conduct that it reflexively organizes.

"This is a difficult concept to understand, so let me give you an example." And I just did. I put the first sentence of this paragraph in quotation marks because it is our example. Anytime we write or speak a sentence, we do a couple of things. First, and most obviously, we create the sentence. The second and less obvious thing we do is re-create the rules through which the sentence was made in the first place. This is a little tricky, so pay close attention. In order to put together a sentence, we have to follow the rules. If we don't, the sentence won't make any sense and it won't really be a sentence. Thus, in order to exist as a sentence, the line of words must be formed according to the rules. Yet, at the same moment we create the sentence, we also re-create the rules through which the sentence was made in the first place.

You might say, "Wait a minute, the rules existed before the sentence." Did they? You learned the rules in school and those rules are found in English grammar texts, right? In fact, we often refer to the grades between the primary levels and high school as "grammar school" because that's where you learn the rules of grammar. But is that really where you learned the rules? If it was, it would imply that you couldn't form a sentence before reaching that point in school. But the fact is you could form sentences well before you "learned the rules"; further, studies have shown that five- and six-year-olds make use of very complex grammars. In truth-, the rules you learned in school are the rules you already knew. The difference is that the rules found in grammar texts are formalized interpretations of the rules that already exist in the language itself; grammars and dictionaries are produced by academics based on the study of language. Note that grammarians study the language to discover the rules—the rules are already there in the language. The rules for making the sentence are in the sentence itself—the expression and the structure are created in the same moment. According to Giddens, the same is true about social agents and structures.

Step 2: The Stuff of Social Structures

Here Giddens simply says that social structures aren't things that exist apart from people, *social structures* exist in the ways that people use rules and resources. There are two kinds of rules: normative rules and codes of signification. Keep in mind that in both cases these "rules" are fluidly embedded in social practices. They don't exist abstractly or independently. Giddens also notes that rules may be consistently or rarely invoked, tacit or discursive, informal or formal, and weakly or strongly sanctioned. You should be familiar with *normative rules*—they are rules that govern behavior, such as the norm against littering. But signification codes require a bit of explanation.

Signification codes are rules through which meaning is produced. In our sentence illustration above, the signification code is lodged in the practices of speaking and writing. One example of the consequence of these codes or rules is the rhetoric of political spin-doctors. Spin-doctors want to guide us so that we interpret events in a specific manner; but in doing so they must abide by generally accepted rules of interpretation. If they don't, then chances are good that we won't buy their "spin." It's important to mention that these rules are historically and culturally specific. That's why interpretations can change over time. There are also two kinds of resources: authoritative and allocative. *Authoritative resources* are made up of such things as techniques or technologies of management, organizational position, and expert knowledge. *Allocative resources* come from the control of material goods or the material world. Resources, then, involve the control of people and supplies.

I've pictured the duality of structure in Figure 14.1. As we've seen, Giddens argues that structure and agency are mutually formed in the same act. Just as in our sentence example, the rules and resources that are used in social encounters both create and are found in the interaction and structure. The act of social co-presence is possible only through the use of social rules and resources—and the rules and resources only exist in the act of social co-presence. Thus, structure and agency are mutually constructed through the use of the exact same rules and resources, as noted by all the two-headed arrows in the figure.

Step 3: Expressing Structure and Creating Social Order

We want to see two things in this step. First, Giddens talks about the problem of social order that Parsons and Garfinkel were concerned about as really just a problem of time and space. If we're all together at once in one place, it's easy to see how we make sure everybody acts together. The problem of order comes about when different interactions are separate either through geographic space or time. Notice the large arrow linking the two sets of interactions in Figure 14.1. The arrow indicates how behaviors and encounters are patterned over time. Giddens (1986) rephrases the problem of patterning action in terms of **time–space distanciation**: "*The fundamental question of social theory* . . . is to explicate how the limitations of individual 'presence' are transcended by the 'stretching' of social relations across time and space" (p. 35, emphasis added). The idea of time–space distanciation refers to the ways in which physical co-presence is stretched through time and

Figure 14.1 Duality of Structure

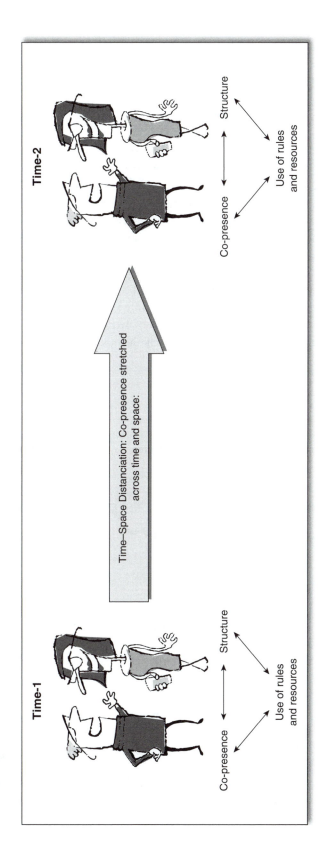

space. This is a fairly unique and graphic way of thinking about patterning behaviors. We can think of Giddens' idea as an analogy: If you've ever played with Silly Putty or bubble gum by stretching it out, then you can see what he is talking about. What this analogy implies is that the interactions at Time-1 and Time-2 appear patterned because they are made out of the same materials that are stretched out over time and space.

The second thing Giddens wants us to see here is his answer to the question in the quote above: How does it happen? His answer is found in his idea of **modalities of structuration**. The word *modality* is related to the word *mode*, which refers to a form or pattern of expression, as in someone's mode of dress or behavior. For example, in writing this book, I'm currently in my academic mode. Modalities of structuration, then, are simply ways in which rules and resources are knowingly used by people in interactions.

I've pictured a bit of what Giddens is getting at in Figure 14.2. Notice that there are three elements in the circle: social practices, modalities, and structures. Modalities of structuration are ways in which structure and practice (or agency) are expressed. I've indicated that relationship by the use of overlapping diamonds. In a loose way, we can think of structures as the music itself; the modalities as the mode of reproduction, as

Figure 14.2 Modalities of Structuration

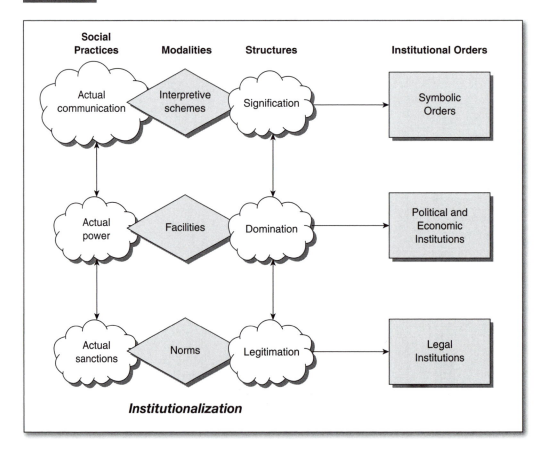

in analog or digital; and the social practices as the musician. As you can see, Giddens gives us three modalities or modes of expression (interpretive schemes, facilities, and norms), corresponding on the one hand to three social practices (communication, power, and sanctions), and on the other to structures (signification, domination, and legitimation).

This isn't as complicated as it might seem. Let's use the example of you talking to your professor in class. Let's say that in this conversation you refuse to take the test that he or she has scheduled. The professor reacts by telling you that you will fail the course if you don't take the test. What just happened? You can break it down using Giddens' modalities of structuration, following the model in Figure 14.2. First, there were actual social practices that involved communication and sanctions. Your communication was interpreted using a scheme that both you and your professor know. For convenience sake, let's call this scheme "meanings in educational settings." You know this interpretive scheme because it is part of the general signification structure of this society at the beginning of the twenty-first century. Second, the professor invoked sanctions based on norms of classroom behavior. Again, you both know these norms because they are part of the legitimation structure of this society.

I'm sure you were able to follow this discussion through the model without any difficulty. And I'm also sure that you didn't have any trouble with any of the phrases I used in the above explanation. Things like "society at the beginning of the twenty-first century" sound reasonable and familiar. But remember, the first principle of structuration theory is duality, not dualism. So when we use the terms *society* or *structure* we are not talking about something separate from social practices. Like our sentence illustration, the actual conversation between you and the professor, and the interpretive schemes and the structure of signification, all come into existence at the same moment. Apart from signification and interpretation, communication can't exist; likewise, without actual communication, interpretation and communication can't exist. Obviously, the same is true for the sanctions that the professor invoked.

In terms of Giddens' definition of structure as rules and resources, signification and legitimation are more closely tied to rules and domination is more linked to resources (facilities). *Domination* is expressed as actual power through the facilities of authoritative and allocative resources. For example, part of the way the actual power of the university over me as a professor is expressed is through the facilities of classroom space, computer and Internet access, and so forth. By encircling all these elements together and by using two-headed arrows, I'm indicating that all these processes—the social practices, modalities, and structures—are reflexive and recursive. That is, they mutually and continuously influence one another.

Part of what I want you to see in Figure 14.2 is the connectedness of all social practices, modalities, and structures. They are all tied up together and expressed and produced in the same moment. Further, the recursive and interpenetrated nature of these facets of social life are what Giddens means by institutionalization, or the stretching out of co-presence across time and space. Remember, human life is ongoing. The process that I've placed a circle around in Figure 14.2 works cyclically in that it keeps repeating. It is this continuity of recursive practices and structures that stretches interactions across time and space. Comparing Figure 14.1 and Figure 14.2, we can think of the two men talking as moments in which we stopped the ball and looked inside. The arrow between the two sets of interactions depicts the movement of the ball between those two moments.

There's one other thing that we need to notice from Figure 14.2. All of this action of institutionalization results in different *institutional orders*. While there are some terms in there that look familiar, like "economic institutions," they aren't the same as we usually think of them. Many sociologists think of institutions as substantive and distinct (or "differentiated," in functionalist terms). In other words, most sociologists treat institutions as if they are real, separate objects with independent effects. However, Giddens is saying that institutions don't exist as substantive things or objects and they aren't truly separate and distinct. Notice that the different institutional orders are all made from the same fabric; it's just cut or put together differently in each case. They all draw from the same structures (rules and resources) of signification (S), domination (D), and legitimation (L), but emphasizing one of the elements over the others produces different kinds of institutional orders.

Making Society and Hiding It: How Much Do We Really Know?

Mead, Garfinkel, and Goffman all agree that we actually create society in face-to-face interactions. So, that's not news for us. What Giddens is going to do is go deeper, behind the scenes to see what's going on inside us as we achieve social order and reality. Some of it we're aware of, but probably not in the way you think. And some of it works below the level of our awareness. Giddens argues that there are three important things going on in interactions: reflexive monitoring of action, rationalization of action, and motivation for action. Giddens thinks of these tasks as being "stratified," or as having different levels of awareness. The behavior that we're most aware of is *reflexive monitoring*. In order to interact with one another, people must watch the behaviors of other people, monitor the flow of the conversation, and keep track of their own actions. As part of this routine accomplishment, we can also provide reasons for what we do; that is, we can provide a rationalization of our own actions.

In talking about *rationalization of action*, Giddens makes a distinction between discursive and practical consciousness. The word *discursive* is related to discourse or conversation. But it has a deeper meaning as well: It's a discourse marked by analytical reasoning. So **discursive consciousness** refers to the ability to give a reasoned verbal account of our actions. It's what we know and can express about social practices and situations. This consciousness is clearly linked to reflexive monitoring of the encounter and the rationalization of action—discursive consciousness is our awareness of these two.

Practical consciousness refers to the knowledge that we have about how to exist and behave socially. However, people can't verbally express this knowledge. Social situations and practices are extremely complex, according to Giddens, and they thus require a vast and nuanced base of knowledge, and we have to act more by intuition than by rational thought. This idea isn't as difficult as it might seem. We can think of the ability to perform an opening ritual ("Hey, how's it going?") as part of this practical consciousness. People know *how* to perform an opening ritual, but most people can't rationally explain *why* they do it.

There's an important point to note about discursive and practical consciousnesses: They aren't necessarily linked. At first glance, it might appear that discursive consciousness is our ability to explain what practical consciousness tells us to do. But notice what I said above about practical consciousness: "People can't verbally express this knowledge." So discursive consciousness (the explanation) isn't necessarily associated in any real way with practical consciousness (the actions). We know how to act and we know how to explain our action, but both of these issues are part of the social interaction, not part of the unconscious motivations of the actor.

The All-Important Unconscious Motivation

Practical consciousness is bound up with the production of routine. It's like driving a car or riding a bicycle; most of what is involved is done out of habit or practical consciousness. In the same way, most of what we do socially on a daily basis is routine. Routinization "is a fundamental concept in structuration theory" (Giddens 1986, p. xxii) and refers to the process through which the activities of day-to-day life become habitual and taken-for-granted. *Routinization,* then, is a primary way in which face-to-face interactions are stretched across time and space (Figure 14.1). Or put another way, routinization is one of the main ways through which the modalities of structuration are institutionalized (Figure 14.2). Part of the way we routinize activities is through *regionalization,* which is the zoning of time and space in relation to routinized social practices. In other words, because we divide physical space up, we can more easily routinize our behaviors. Thus, certain kinds of social practices occur in specific places and times. Regionalization varies by form, character, duration, and span.

The form of the region is given in terms of the kinds of barriers or boundaries that are used to section it off from other regions. The form allows greater or lesser possible levels of co-presence. When you stop and talk with someone in the hallway, there is a symbolic boundary around the two of you that is fairly permeable; it is very possible that others could join in. However, when you go into the men's or women's restroom, there is a physical and symbolic barrier that explicitly limits the possibility of co-presence.

The character of the region references the kind of social practices that can typically take place within a region. For example, people have lived in houses for centuries, but the character of the house has changed over time. In agrarian societies, the home was the center of the economy, government, and family; but in modern capitalist societies, the home is the exclusive domain of family and is thus private rather than public.

The duration and span of the region refer to the amount of geographic space and to the length or kind of time. Certain regions are usually available for social practices only during certain parts of the day or for specific lengths of time; the bedroom is an example in the sense that it is usually associated with "sleep time." Regions also span across space in varying degrees. So, a coliseum gives unique opportunities for co-presence and social activities when compared to an airplane.

We come now to what actually patterns structuration and time–space distanciation—Giddens calls it **ontological security**. As we've seen, the word *ontology* refers to existence, so ontological security is simply being secure in the reality we've created. But even though that sounds simple, it's pretty amazing. We create reality then we make ourselves feel secure that the created reality is actually real. The truth of the matter is that the reality of the human world is existentially moored in meaning, which is fallible, mutable, and uncertain. As the philosopher Ernst Cassirer (1944) puts it,

> No longer can man confront reality immediately; he cannot see it, as it were, face to face. Physical reality seems to recede in proportion as man's symbolic activity advances. Instead of dealing with the things themselves man is in a sense constantly conversing with himself. (p. 42)

According to Giddens, if people ever notice this about their reality, they will suffer deep psychological angst. We are motivated, then, as a result of this unconscious psychological insecurity about the socially created world, *to make the world routine and thus taken-for-granted*. Note that this anxiety is unconscious—it isn't usually experienced; but when it is, it is felt as a diffuse, general sense of unease.

According to Giddens (1990), ontological security refers to the feelings of "confidence that most humans [sic] beings have in the continuity of their self-identity and in the constancy of the surrounding social and material environments of action" (p. 92). Giddens argues that the fundamental trust of ontological security is generally produced in early childhood and maintained through adult routines. Because most of the social practices in our lives are carried out by routine, we experience trust in the world, due to its routine character, and we can take for granted the ontological status of the world. In premodern societies, trust and routine in traditional institutions covered up the contingency of the world. Kinship and community created bonds that reliably structured actions through time and space. Religion provided a cosmology that reliably ordered experience. And tradition itself structured social and natural events, because tradition by definition is routine.

Now we're about to take our final step in our journey to understand society and its people. Remember the fundamental problem of social order? It's time–space distanciation. And remember why it's a problem? Because according to Giddens there are no such things as objective social structures that coerce us to act in certain ways. So, how and why do we do it? The how is structuration but the why is extremely important. The ultimate force behind us solving the problem of time–space distanciation is our deep-seated need for ontological security. That need drives us to routinize and regionalize behaviors.

Traditional societies provided routinization and regionalization without fail through kinship, community, and religion. However, in modern societies *none of these institutional settings produces a strong sense of trust and ontological security*. According to Giddens, those needs are met differently: Routine is integrated into abstract systems, pure relationships substitute for the connectedness of community and kin, and reflexively constructed knowledge systems replace religious cosmologies—but not with the certainty or the psychological rewards of pre-modern institutions. The result is that ontological insecurity—anxiety regarding the "existential anchoring of reality" (Giddens, 1991, p. 38)—is a greater possibility in modern rather than traditional societies.

Concepts and Theory: The Contours of Modernity

We have now laid the groundwork for Giddens' understanding of how society works in general: Actors are motivated to routinize social actions and interactions by the psychological need for ontological security. These routines serve to stretch out face-to-face encounters through time and space as actors use different modalities to express the social structures of signification, domination, and legitimation through their social practices. This constant structuration produces different institutional orders that, along with regionalization, work to stabilize routine. Routinization and the institutional orders that it generates stabilize time–space distanciation and thus give the individual a continual basis of trust in her or his social environment, which, in turn, provides the individual with ontological security.

Thus, in Giddens' scheme, society isn't structured—it doesn't exist as an obdurate object with an independent existence. The important point here is that society by its nature is continually susceptible to disruption or change. This constant possibility is, of course, what creates the diffuse and unconscious sense of insecurity that people have about the reality of society. However, this possibility is also what makes modernity an important issue, for both the process of structuration and for the person. In the next section, I will ask you to think about how living in modernity influences your experience of yourself and others. But for now, simply think about how the dynamic quality of modernity radically changes structuration and time–space distanciation. There are four analytically distinct factors that produce the dynamism of modernity: radical reflexivity, the separation of time and space, disembedding mechanisms, and globalization. As we'll see, though we can separate these areas analytically, they empirically reinforce one another.

Radical Reflexivity

Giddens sees reflexivity as a variable, rather than a static condition. He argues that modernity dramatically increases the level of reflexivity. Previous to this time, people didn't think much about society. In fact, the entire idea of society as an entity unto itself wasn't really conceived of until the work of people such as Montesquieu and Durkheim. Today, we are quite aware of society and we think deliberatively about our nation and the organizations and institutions in which we participate.

Progress and reflexivity are thus intrinsically related. It only takes a moment's reflection to see that progress demands reflexivity. It is endemic in modernity because every social unit must constantly evaluate itself in terms of its mission, goals, and practices. However, the hope of progress never materializes—the ideal of progress means that we never truly arrive. Every step in our progressive march forward is examined in the hopes of improving what we have achieved. Progress becomes a motivating value and a discursive feature of modernity, rather than a goal that is never reached.

Here's a real-life example: Chances are good that you are attending an accredited college or university. Schools of higher education are certified by regional accrediting organizations. Being accredited allows you as a student to qualify for federal financial aid and to transfer credits from one college to another, and it allows professors to apply for federal grants for research. At my university, we just finished our reaccreditation self-study, which took two years to complete. Even though this seems like a long time, we actually began preparing for the self-study the two years previous by evaluating our mission statement in light of the new criteria for accreditation.

Out of the earlier study came a new mission statement that was then used during the following study to reevaluate every aspect of the university (notice the reflexive element). The self-study produced recommendations for the next 10 years, and the study and its recommendations were scrutinized by a committee of academics and administrators sent by our regional affiliation. Changes were and will be implemented as a result of the study. The interesting thing to me is that 80% to 90% of the study deals with things that are only tangentially related to actual learning, which is what we think the university is about. Most of the study addresses symbolic or political issues that have little to do with what happens in the classroom or in your learning experience. The greater proportion of the changes, then, would not have come about except for their symbolic or political values and reflexive organization.

As Weber pointed out, modern organizations are bureaucratic in nature and are thus bound up with rational goal setting, recursive practices, and continual reflexivity. For example, the reaccreditation study I just mentioned will be repeated in 10 years and every 10 years thereafter. This year, my department is doing its self-study, and it gets repeated every five years. When I worked for Denny's restaurants as a manager, we had corporate plans that helped form the regional plans that helped create the unit plans, which strongly influenced my personal plans as a manager. Depending on the level, those plans were systematically evaluated every one to five years. Modern organizations, institutions, and society at large are thus defined through the continued use of reflexive evaluation.

One further point about radical reflexivity: It forms part of our basic understanding of knowledge and rational life. Modern knowledge is equivalent to scientific knowledge, and part of what makes knowledge scientific is continual scrutiny and systematic doubt. This understanding of knowledge is woven into the fabric of our culture. Every child in the United States receives training in what is called "scientific literacy." According to the National Academy of Sciences (1995),

> This nation has established as a goal that all students should achieve scientific literacy. The *National Science Education Standards* are designed to enable the nation to achieve that goal. They spell out a vision of science education that will make scientific literacy for all a reality in the 21st century.

Thus, children in the United States are systematically trained to be reflexive about knowledge in general.

Emptying Time and Space

In this section, it is very important for you to keep in mind what Giddens means by time–space distanciation—it's his way of talking about how our behaviors and actions are patterned and are thus somewhat predictable. Therefore, whatever happens to time and space in modernity influences the patterns of interaction that make up society. With that in mind, Giddens argues that the *separation of time and space* is crucial to the dynamic quality of modernity.

In order to understand how time and space can be emptied and separated, we have to begin by thinking about how humans have related to time and space for most of our existence. Up until the beginnings of modernity, time and space were closely linked to natural settings and cycles. People have always marked time, but it was originally associated with natural places and cycles. The cycle of the sun set the boundaries of the day, the cycle of the moon marked the month, and the year was noted by the cycles of the seasons. But the week, which is the primary tool we use to organize ourselves today, exists nowhere in nature—it's utterly abstract in terms of the natural world. Something similar may be said about the mechanical clock. Previous to the invention and widespread use of the mechanical clock, people regulated their behaviors around the moving of the sun (see McCready, 2001; Roy, 2001, pp. 40–45).

Thus, in modern societies, time and space have become abstract entities that have been emptied of any natural connections. Further, the concept of place itself has become stretched out and more symbolic than physical. As I mentioned, modernity is distinguished by the belief in progress. Progress implies change, and the emptying of time and space "serves to open up manifold possibilities of change by breaking free from the restraints of local habits and practices" (Giddens, 1990, p. 20). Making time and place abstract has also aided in another distinctive feature of modernity, the bureaucratic organization. Our lives are subject to rational organization precisely because time and place are emptied of natural and social relations. My students and I can all meet at 9:45 a.m. in the Graham building, Room 308, for class because time and place have been emptied. Similarly, Boeing airplane manufacturing in California can order parts from a steel plant in China to be ready for assembly beginning in January because time and place are abstract.

The emptying of time and place means that time–space distanciation can be increased almost without limit, which is one of the defining characteristics of modernity. Traditional societies are defined by close-knit social networks that create high levels of morality, and an emphasis on long-established social practices and relationships. Any social form that could break with the importance of tradition would have to be built upon something other than close-knit social groups. Modernity, then, is defined as the time during which greater and greater distances are placed between people and their social relations. As we'll see, increasing time–space distanciation and escalating reflexivity mutually reinforce one another, and together they create the dynamism of modernity—the tendency for continual change.

Institutions and Disembedding Mechanisms

In discussing the transition from traditional to modern society, many sociologists talk about structural differentiation, especially functionalists. The problem that Giddens sees in institutional differentiation is that it can't give a reasoned account of a central feature of modernity: radical time–space distanciation. However, thinking about institutions in terms of disembedding mechanisms can do so. Thus, Giddens claims that the distinction between traditional and modern institutions isn't differentiation so much as it is embedding versus disembedding. **Disembedding mechanisms** are those practices that lift out social relations and interactions from local contexts. Again, let's picture a kind of ideal type of traditional society where most social relationships and interactions take place in encounters that are firmly entrenched in local situations. People would live in places where they knew everybody and would depend upon people they knew for help. Distant situations, along with distant others, were kept truly distant. There are two principal mechanisms that lifted life out of its local context: symbolic tokens and expert systems.

Symbolic tokens are understood in terms of media of exchange that can be passed around without any regard for a specific person or group. There are a few of these kinds of tokens around, but the example par excellence is money. Money creates a universal value system wherein every commodity can be understood according to the same value system. Of necessity, this value system is abstract; that is, it has no intrinsic worth. In order for it to stand for everything, it must have no value in itself. The universal and abstract nature of money frees it from constraint and facilitates exchanges over long distances and time periods. Thus, by its very nature, money increases time–space distanciation. The greater the level of abstraction of money, such as through credit and soft currencies, the greater will be this effect.

The other disembedding mechanism that Giddens talks about is *expert systems*. Let's again think about a traditional community. If you were a woman who lived in a traditional community and were going to have a baby, to whom would you go? If in the same group you experienced marital problems, where would you go for advice? If you wanted to know how to grow better crops or appease the gods or construct a building or do anything that required some form of social cooperation, where would you go? The answer to all these questions, and all the rest of the details of living life, would be your social network. If you wanted to grow better crops, you might go to your friend Paul whose fields always seem to thrive and produce abundantly. For marital advice, you would probably go to your grandparents; for childbirth help, you'd go to the neighbor's wife who had been practicing midwifery for as long as you can remember.

Where do we go for these things today? We go to experts—people that we don't personally know, who have been trained academically in abstract knowledge. But we don't really have to "go to" an expert to be dependent upon expert systems of knowledge. For instance, I have no idea how to construct a building that has many levels and can house a myriad of classrooms and offices, yet I'm dependent upon that expert knowledge every time I go to my office or teach in a classroom. Every time we turn on a computer or flick a light switch or start our car or go to buy food at the grocery store—in short, every time we do anything that is associated with living in modernity—we are dependent upon abstract, expert systems of knowledge. Systems of expert knowledge are disembedding because they shift the center of our life away from local contexts and toward dependence on abstract knowledge and distant others, who sometimes never even appear.

Globalization

Giddens argues that four institutions in particular form the dynamic and the time period of modernity: capitalism, industrialism, monopoly of violence, and surveillance. In terms of the dynamic of modernity, capitalism stands out. Capitalism is intrinsically expansive. It is driven by the perceived need for profit, which in turn drives the expansion of markets, technologies, and commodification.

Industrialization is of course linked to capitalism, but it has its own dynamics and relationships with the other institutional spheres. Industrialism, the monopoly of coercive power, and surveillance feed one another and create what is generally referred to as the industrial-military complex. A military complex is formed by a standing army and the parts of the economy that are oriented toward military production. Once a coercive force begins to use technology, it not only becomes dependent upon industrialism, but it also provides a constant impetus for more and better technologies of force and surveillance. A military complex by its very existence is not only available for protection, it is also in its best interests to instigate aggression whenever possible in order to expand its own base and the interests of its institutional partners.

Thus, the institutional dimensions of modernity are explicitly tied up with globalization. *Globalization* is a term that was coined in the early 1990s to describe

> the closer integration of the countries and peoples of the world which has been brought about by the enormous reduction of costs of transportation and communication, and the breaking down of the ratification barriers to the flows of goods, services, capital, knowledge, and (to a lesser extent) people across borders. (Stiglitz, 2003, p. 9)

While the boundaries of what is to be included in the definition of globalization are unclear, it is most commonly seen as an economic phenomenon, one that is focused on free trade. In this economy, as in most economists' models, market forces and invisible hands operate like devices of natural selection to control prices and the behaviors of firms.

That last part is important for understanding what sociologists do with the term. Rather than assuming market forces, sociologists generally define globalization more precisely around explicit social factors. Three theorists in this book talk about globalization: Giddens, Immanuel Wallerstein, and Manuel Castells. As you'll see, each of these theorists defines the term somewhat differently. Because globalization is possibly one of the most important social processes that will influence your life through the twenty-first century, I encourage you to keep track of the different elements of this idea as we consider Giddens, Wallerstein, and Castells. Synthesizing these theories will give you a fuller understanding of how globalization works.

Giddens (1990) defines globalization as "the intensification of worldwide social relations which link distant localities in such a way that local happenings are shaped by events occurring many miles away and vice versa" (p. 64). Globalization is thus defined in terms of a dialectic relation between the local and the distant that *further stretch out co-presence through time and space.* The four dimensions of globalization, according to Giddens, are the world capitalist economy, the world military order, the international division of labor, and the nation-state system.

In order to help us get a handle on what Giddens is arguing, I've drawn out the chief processes that we've been talking about in Figure 14.3. Most all of the factors on the far left of the model are interrelated in some way. For example, the use of bureaucratic, rational management increases in the presence of world capitalism and expert systems. But to draw out all the relationships at that level would defeat the purpose of the model as a heuristic device. I have indicated the mutual effects at the next level. All of these dynamics—radical reflexivity, separation of time and place, disembedding, globalization—mutually imply and affect one another. For example, as time and place are separated from the actual, institutions can further remove the social from the local, which in turn allows more abstract connections at the global level. These all mutually reinforce one another and build the dynamism of modernity. Collectively, this figure and all that it implies answers the question, "Why are change and discontinuity endemic in modernity?" Use Figure 14.3 to think through that question and Giddens' theory of modernity.

Concepts and Theory: The Experience of Modernity

It is extremely difficult to see the effects of modernity in our own lives. We live our lives as if they are essential, as if there were nothing more to us than our inner personality and experiences. Yet sociology teaches us that we are social beings created for and out of social relations, and the sociological imagination encourages us to see the intersections of biography, history, and society. Giddens paints a portrait of the modern individual and asks us to look behind (or in front of) our own subjective experiences and understand them as finding their roots in a particular social organization called modernity. Modernity is characterized by endemic reflexivity and time–space distanciation. What this implies for the person is that the individual and her or his subjective experiences have been lifted out of densely packed social networks and required to do increasing amounts of work on their own. Quite a bit of this personal work centers on the reflexive project of the self, life politics, and intimate relations.

Figure 14.3   Dynamism of Modernity

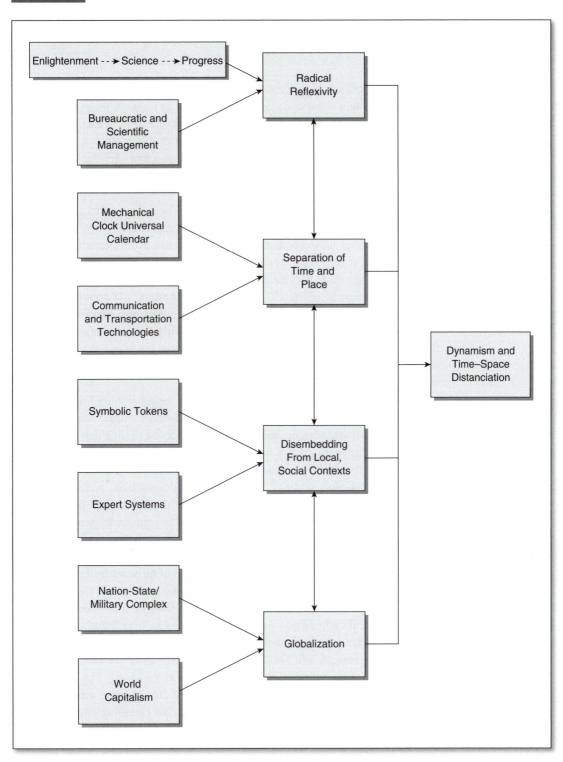

The Reflexive Project of the Self

Recall that in Chapter 6, Mead argued that reflexivity is a necessary state of existence for the self. In his understanding of reflexivity, Giddens defines it as a variable: While some level of reflexivity is essential, humans can be more or less reflexive.

In times previous to modernity, the self was deeply embedded in the social. People were caught up in and saw themselves only in terms of the group. The self was an extension of the group just as certainly as your arm is an extension of your body. The individual life was not only seen as part of the group, but its trajectory was also plotted and marked socially. So, for example, a boy knew for certain when he had changed from a boy to a man—he went through a rite of passage. Such is not the case today.

In late modernity, the individual stands alone. The individual is "free." You, for example, are free to express yourself in any number of ways. You have a plethora of potential identities and experiences open to you. But at the same time, you no longer have any institutional markers to guide you or to define your "progress," and there are no institutions that are directly responsible for you. In the *reflexive project of the self,* you have to reflexively define your own options and opportunities with regard to social and personal change. The self is no longer an entity embedded in known and firm social and institutional relationships and expectations. This shift from the traditional, social self with clear institutional guidelines to the individual reflexive project was brought about because of the dynamics of modernity that we reviewed in the previous section.

The body is drawn into this reflexive project as well. Before radical modernity, the body was, for the most part, seen as either the medium through which work was performed or a vehicle for the soul. In either case, it was of little consequence and received little attention unless it became an obstacle to work or salvation. In radical modernity, on the other hand, the body becomes part of self-expression and helps to sustain "a coherent sense of self-identity" (Giddens, 1991, p. 99). The body becomes wrapped up with the reflexive project of the self in four possible ways: appearance, demeanor, sensuality, and through bodily regimes. We covered the first two ways in the chapter on Goffman, so here we will just review the last two.

The body is involved in the self-project through *bodily regimes*. In radical modernity, "we become responsible for the design of our own bodies" (Giddens, 1991, p. 102). The body is no longer a simple reflection of one's work but can become a canvas for a self-portrait. Capitalism, mass media, advertising, fashion, and medical expert knowledge have produced an overabundance of information about how the body works and what kinds of behaviors result in what kinds of body images. We are called upon to constantly review the look and condition of our body and to make adjustments as necessary. The adjustments are carried out through various body regimens of diet, exercise, stress-reducing activities (yoga, meditation), vitamin therapies, skin cleansing and repair, hair treatments, and so forth.

With the *organization of sensuality,* Giddens has in mind the entire spectrum of sensual feeling of the body, but the idea is particularly salient for sexuality. Together, mass education, contraceptive technologies, decreasing family size, and women's political and workforce participation created the situation where "today, for the first time in human history, women claim equality with men" (Giddens, 1992, p. 1). Giddens links women's freedom with the creation of an "emotional order" that contains "an exploration of the potentialities of the 'pure relationship'" and "plastic sexuality" (pp. 1–2). The idea of *plastic sexuality* captures a kind of sexuality that came into existence as sex was separated from the demands of reproduction. Plastic sexuality is an explicit characteristic of modernity. For the first time in history, sexuality could become part of self-identity. We should also note that since sexuality is part of the reflexive project of the self, it is subject to reflexive scrutiny and intentional exploration.

Pure Relationships

To begin our discussion of pure relationships, let's think about friendship. Giddens points out that early Greeks didn't even have a word for friend in the way we use it today. The Greeks used the word *philos* to talk about those who were the most near and dear, but this term was used for people who were in or near to family. And the Greek *philos* network was pretty well set by the person's status position; there was little in the way of friends as we think of them, as personal choices.

In traditional societies in which languages did have a word for friend, these friends were seen within the context of group survival. Friends were the in-group and others were the out-group. The distinction was between friend and enemy, or, at best, stranger. Keep in mind that groups were far more important then than they are now because individual survival was closely tied to group affiliations and resources. A friend was someone you turned to in time of need; thus, the values associated with friendship were honor and sincerity. Today, however, because of disembedding mechanisms and increased time–space distanciation, not all friends are understood in terms of in-group membership and actual assistance. The individual can have distant friends and is enabled and expected to take care of himself or herself (the reflexive project).

A fundamental change has thus occurred in friendships: from friendship with honor based on group identity and survival, to friendship with authenticity based on a mutual process of self-disclosure. Rather than trust being embedded in social networks and rituals, trust in modernity has to be won, and the means through which this is done is self-evident warmth and openness. By implication, this authenticity and self-regulation provide the personal, emotional component missing in trust in the abstract systems of modernity.

Intimate relations in modernity are thus characterized by *pure relationships*— friendships and intimate ties that are entered into simply for what the relationship can bring to each person. Remember that traditional relationships were first set by existing networks and institutions and the motivation behind them was usually social, not personal. For example, most marriages were motivated by politics or economics (not by love) and were arranged for the couple by those most responsible for the social issues in question (not by the couple themselves). This is the way in which modern relationships are pure: They occur purely for the sake of the relationship.

Most of our relationships today are not anchored in external conditions, like the politically or economically motivated marriage. Rather, they are "free-floating." The only structural condition for a friendship or marriage is proximity: We have to be near enough to make contact. But with modern transportation and communication technologies, our physical space is almost constantly in motion and can be quite far-ranging, and we have "virtual" space at our fingertips.

In addition to the free-floating and pure nature of these relations, they are also reflexively organized, based on commitment and mutual trust, and focus on intimacy and "self"-growth. Like the reflexive project of the self, relationships are reflexively organized; that is, they are continually worked at by the individuals, who tend to consult an array of sources of information. The number of possible sources for telling us how to act and be in our friendships and sexual relations is almost endless. Daytime television is filled with programming that explores every facet of relationships; the magazine rack at the local supermarket is a cornucopia of surveys and advice on how to have the best communication/sex life/romance, or any other aspect of an intimate relationship; it's estimated that over 2,000 new self-help book titles are published every year in the United States; and the Internet resources available for improving relationships are innumerable. Most of us have taken a relationship quiz with our partner at some point (if you haven't, just wait—it's coming), and all of us have asked of someone the essential question for relationships that are reflexively organized: "Is everything all right?" This kind of communication is a moral obligation in pure relationships; the gamut of communication covers everything from the mundane ("How was your day at work?") to the serious ("Do you want to break up with me?").

Choice and Life Politics

Along with the accelerating changes in modernity, there has been a shift from emancipatory politics to life politics. *Emancipatory politics* is concerned with liberating individuals and groups from the constraints that adversely affect their lives. In some ways, this type of political activity has been the theme of modernity—it was the hope that democratic nation-states could bring equality and justice for all. And, in some respects, this theme of modernity has failed. We are more than ever painfully aware of how many groups are disenfranchised.

Life politics, by way of contrast, is the politics of choice and lifestyle. It is not based on group membership and characteristics, as is emancipatory politics; rather, it is based on personal lifestyle choices. We have come to think of choice as a freedom we have in the United States. But it is more than that—it has become an obligation, a fundamental element in contemporary living. This principality of choice is based on disembedding mechanisms and time–space distanciation, and results in, as we've seen, the reflexive project of the self. Part of that project comes to be centered on the politics of choice.

Mass media also play a role in creating choice by facilitating mediated experiences. *Mediated experiences* are a contrast to social experiences that take place in face-to-face encounters and are created as people are exposed to multiple accounts of situations and others with whom they have no direct association through time and space. Every time you watch television or read a newspaper, you have experiences that are "mediated." You are exposed to lives to which you have absolutely no real connection, and like so many other features of modernity, this stretches out co-presence but it also creates a collage effect. The pictures and stories that we receive via the media do not reflect any essential or social elements. Instead, stories and images are juxtaposed that have nothing to do with one another. The picture we get of the world, then, is a collage of diverse lifestyles and cultures, not a direct representation.

As a result of being faced with this collage, what happens to us as individuals? One implication is that the plurality of lifestyles presented to us not only *allows* for choice, it *necessitates* it. In other words, what becomes important is not the issue of group equality, but rather, the insistence on *personal* choice. What is at issue in this milieu is not so much political equality (as with emancipatory politics) as inner authenticity. In a world that is perceived as constantly changing and uprooted, it becomes important to be grounded in one's self. Life politics creates such grounding. It creates "a framework of basic trust by means of which the lifespan can be understood as a unity against the backdrop of shifting social events" (Giddens, 1991, p. 215). Life politics, then, helps to diminish the possibility and effects of ontological insecurity.

A good example of life politics is veganism—the practice of not eating any meat or meat byproducts. Not only is eating flesh avoided, but also any products with dairy, eggs, fur, leather, feathers, or any goods involving animal testing. One vegan I know summed it up nicely when she said, veganism "is an integral component of a cruelty-free lifestyle." It is a political statement against the exploitation of animals, and for some it is clearly a condemnation of capitalism—capitalism is particularly responsible for the unnatural mass production of animal flesh as well as commercial animal testing. Yet, for most vegans, it is a lifestyle, one that brings harmony between the outside world and inner beliefs, and not necessarily part of a collective movement.

However, it would be wrong to conclude that life politics are powerless because they do not result in a social movement. Quite the opposite is true. Life politics springs from and focuses attention on some of the very issues that modernity represses. What life politics does is to "place a question mark against the internally referential systems of modernity" (Giddens, 1991, p. 223). Life politics asks, "Seeing that these things are so, what manner of men and women ought we to be?" In traditional society, morality was provided by the institutions, especially religion. Modernity has wiped away the social ground upon which this kind of morality was based. Life politics "remoralizes" social life and demands "renewed sensitivity to questions that the institutions of modernity systematically dissolve" (p. 224). Rather than asking for group participation, as does emancipatory politics, life politics asks for self-realization, a moral commitment to a specific way of living. Rather than being impotent in comparison to emancipatory politics, life politics "presage[s] future changes of a far-reaching sort: essentially, the development of forms of social order 'on the other side' of modernity itself" (p. 214).

Summary

- According to Giddens, the central issue for social theory is to explain how actions and interactions are patterned over time and space; or, to use Giddens' terms, social theory needs to explain how the limitations inherent within physical presence are transcended through time–space distanciation. There are two primary ways through which this occurs: the dynamics of structuration and of routinization.

- Structuration occurs when people use specific modalities to produce both structure (rules and resources of signification, domination, and legitimation) and practice (physical co-presence). Thus, the very method of structuration reflexively and repeatedly links structure and person and facilitates time–space distanciation.

- Routinization is psychologically motivated by a diffuse need for ontological security. The reality of society is precarious because it depends on structuration, which is reflexive and recursive. In other words, the process of structuration doesn't reference anything other than itself and it depends on ceaseless interactional work. This precariousness is unconsciously sensed by people, which, in turn, motivates them to routinize their actions and interactions and to link their routines to physical regions and institutional orders, which further adds stability.

- Routinization was unproblematically achieved in traditional societies. People rarely left their regions and the institutional orders were slow to change. Modernity, however, is characterized by dynamism and increasing time–space distanciation. Dynamism and time–space distanciation are both directly related to radical reflexivity, extreme separation of time and place, the disembedding work of modern institutions, and globalization. These factors are related to the proliferation of science and progress, bureaucratic management, the mechanical clock and universal calendar, communication and transportation technologies, symbolic tokens and expert systems of knowledge, the military complex, and world capitalism.

- As a result of radical modernity, the individual is lifted out of the social networks and institutions that socially situated the self by acquiring certain identities, knowledge, and life-course markers. The modern individual is given the reflexive project of the self that is only internally referential. As part of the reflexive project of the self, the individual involves himself or herself in strategic life planning using expert systems of knowledge and mediated experiences, all of which are permeated with doubt. The reflexive project of the self involves constant evaluation and reevaluation based on possible new information (ever revised by experts and available through mass media) and self-reflection (How am I doing? Should I be feeling this way?). The reflexive project includes lifestyle politics in which the individual must reflexively work her or his way through continuously presented and expanding arenas of social existence. Individuals, then, become hubs for social change as they reflexively order their life in response to a constantly changing political landscape.

Constructivist Structuralism and Class:
Pierre Bourdieu (1930–2002)

Theorist's Digest
Concepts and Theory: Constructivist Structuralism
    Overcoming Dichotomies
Concepts and Theory: Structuring Class
    Habitus
    Fields
Concepts and Theory: Replicating Class
    Linguistic Markets
    Symbolic Struggle
Summary

One of the wonderful things about working in academia is that it is part of my job to new learn things. In preparing to write this chapter, I read Craig Calhoun's (2003) chapter on Bourdieu. The first section is titled "Taking Games Seriously." In it, Professor Calhoun talks about Bourdieu's life as a former rugby player and how it influenced his theory. Throughout Bourdieu's writing, he uses such terms as "field," "game," and "practice," and he talks about the bodily inculcation of culture. I had read Bourdieu and approached such terms and ideas as theoretical concepts. For some reason, it never occurred to me to understand their use as a kind of analogy—the analogy of the game. But as I read Calhoun's three pages about Bourdieu's fascination with rugby, his ideas and terms all came alive for me in a new way.

So, thanks to Craig Calhoun, the first thing we will talk about in introducing Bourdieu is his analogy of the game. It's important to keep in mind that Bourdieu's use of the analogy doesn't come from a background in playing cards. Bourdieu was a rugby player. Rugby is a European game somewhat like American football, but it is considered by most to be much more grueling. In rugby, the play is continuous with no substitutions or time-outs (even for injury). The game can take anywhere from 60 to 90 minutes, with two halves separated by a 5-minute halftime. An important part of the game is the scrum. In a *scrum*, eight players from each side form a kind of inverted triangle by wrapping their arms around each other. The ball is placed in the middle and the two bound groups of players struggle head to head against each other until the ball is freed. To see the struggle of the scrum gives a whole new perspective on Bourdieu's idea of social struggle.

Rugby matches take place on a field, involve strategic plays and intense struggles, and are played by individuals who have a clear physical sense of the game. Matches are of course structured by the rules of the game and the field. The field not only delineates the parameters of the play, but each field is also different and thus knowledge of each field of play is important for success. The rules are there and, like in all games, come into play when they are broken, but a good player embodies the rules and the methods of the game. The best plays are those that come when the player is in the "zone," or playing without thinking.

Trained musicians can also experience this zone by jamming with other musicians. Often when in such a state, the musician can play things that he or she normally would not be able to, and might have a difficult time explaining after the fact. The same is true for athletes. There is more to a good game than the rules and the field; the game is embodied in the performer. And, finally, there is the struggle, not only against the other team, but also the limitations of the field, rules, and one's own abilities.

You may not know it, but I just gave you a brief overview of Bourdieu's theory through the use of analogy. I will occasionally mention the game analogy as we work our way through the material, but I think if you keep it consistently in mind, you'll find it much easier to grasp the intent of Bourdieu's thinking.

THEORIST'S DIGEST

Brief Biography

Pierre Bourdieu was born August 1, 1930, in Denquin, France. Bourdieu studied philosophy under Louis Althusser at the École Normale Supérieure in Paris. After his studies, he taught for 3 years, 1955–1958, at Moulins. From 1958 to 1960, Bourdieu did empirical research in Algeria (*The Algerians*, 1962) that laid the groundwork for his sociology. In his career, he published over 25 books, one of which, *Distinction: A Social Critique of the Judgment of Taste*, was named one of the twentieth century's 10 most important works of sociology (International Sociological Association). He was the founder and director of the Centre for European Sociology, and he held the French senior chair in sociology at Collège de France (the same chair held by sociologist and anthropologist Marcel Mauss). Craig Calhoun (2003) writes that Bourdieu was "the most influential and original French sociologist since Durkheim" (p. 274). Bourdieu died in Paris January 23, 2002.

Central Sociological Questions

Bourdieu's passion was intellectual honesty and rigor. He of course was concerned with class, and particularly the way class is created and re-created in subtle, non-conscious ways. But above and beyond these empirical concerns was a driving intellect bent on refining critical thinking and never settling on an answer: "An invitation to think with Bourdieu is of necessity an invitation to think beyond Bourdieu, and against him whenever required" (Wacquant, 1992, p. xiv).

Simply Stated

Bourdieu tells us that class is structured in the body through cultural capital, which is made up of tastes, habits, social and linguistic skills, and so on. People thus display their class position in an unthinking ongoing manner, simply in the way they walk, sit, talk, and so forth. Every social encounter becomes then a market. In interactions where class positions are comparable, people will feel comfortable because everybody's tastes are similar. The disadvantage of such encounters is that no one can gain higher levels of cultural capital. In encounters where the class positions are different, people with lower cultural capital will tend to feel uncomfortable and will be likely to not participate or participate poorly. Thus when in a position to increase cultural capital, and thus class position, most people withdraw and are unable to gain profit. Class is thus structured in the body where it insidiously restricts and replicates a person's class position in all social interactions.

Key Ideas

economic capital, social capital, symbolic capital, cultural capital, taste, habitus, distance from necessity, education, field, linguistic market, symbolic violence, constructivist structuralism, dialectic

Concepts and Theory: Constructivist Structuralism

Like Giddens, Bourdieu's perspective is unique and is important to understand in advance of his theory. So, we start with constructivist structuralism, a theory like Giddens' in that Bourdieu is redefining what we mean by society, yet quite different in how he explains how society is constructed. While Bourdieu's work covers a diverse landscape, I think it is fair to say that his focus is on the replication of class. In this, his work is Marxist, and there is a sense in which Bourdieu's theory may be seen as the mirror image of Marx. According to Marx, the economy and class are two of the most important structures in society. Bourdieu's theory begins with material class, but he clearly moves the reproduction of class structures into the symbolic realm. In the reproduction of class, it is the symbolic field and the relations expressed by and through what he calls habitus that have the greater causal force. Both the symbolic field and habitus are unique kinds of structures that are in tension one with another, and this tension is generative—it not only creates and reproduces class, it also allows for new and unexpected behaviors. But I'm getting ahead of myself. What I want to point out here is that Bourdieu uses a new theoretical approach to understand how class positions are reproduced: constructivist structuralism.

Overcoming Dichotomies

Bourdieu brings the two sides of the structure–agent dichotomy together in **constructivist structuralism** (or structuralist constructivism—Bourdieu uses the term both ways). In this scheme, both structure and agency are given equal weight. Concerning social structures, Bourdieu (1989) says that within the social world there are "objective structures independent of the consciousness and will of agents, which are capable of guiding and constraining their practices or their representations" (p. 14). Yet, at the same time, Bourdieu emphasizes the agent and subjective side. In Bourdieu's (1989) scheme, the subjective side is also structured in terms of "schemes of perception, thought, and action" (p. 14), which he calls habitus. Part of what Bourdieu does is to detail the ways through which both kinds of structures are constructed; thus, there is a kind of double structuring in Bourdieu's theory and research. But Bourdieu doesn't simply give us a historical account of how structures are produced. His theory also offers an explanation of how these two structures are dialectically related and how the individual uses them strategically in linguistic markets.

In preserving both sides of the dichotomy, Bourdieu has created a unique theoretical problem. He doesn't want to conflate the two sides as Giddens does, nor does he want to link them up in the way that Collins and Blau do. He wants to preserve the integrity of both domains and yet he characterizes the dichotomy as harmful. He is thus left with a sticky problem: How can Bourdieu keep and yet change the dichotomy between the objective and subjective moments without linking them or blending them together?

Let's take this issue out of the realm of theory and state it in terms that are a bit more approachable. The problem that Bourdieu is left with is the relationship between the individual and society. Do we have free choice? Bourdieu would say yes. Does society determine what we do? Again, Bourdieu would say yes. How can something be determined and yet the product of free choice? I've stated the issue a bit too simplistically for Bourdieu's theory, but I want you to see the problem clearly. Structure and agency, or the objective and subjective moments, create tension because they stand in opposition to one another. And that tension is exactly how Bourdieu solves his theoretical problem.

Bourdieu argues that the objective and constructive moments stand in a dialectical relationship. Understanding dialectical processes is extremely important here. Therefore, if you're at all hazy about how it works, please go back and review the sections where we've talked about it previously (see Chapter 3). Bourdieu's dialectic occurs between what he calls the field and the habitus. Both are structures; *habitus* is "incorporated history" and the field is "objectified history" (Bourdieu, 1980/1990, p. 66). We will go into more depth later on, but for now think of habitus as that part of society that lives in the individual as a result of socialization, and think of the field as social structures. They are both much more, but what I want us to see now is Bourdieu's dialectic. The tension of the dialectic is between the subjective and objective structures. The dialectic itself is found in the individual and collective struggles or practices that transform or preserve these structures through specific practices and linguistic markets.

In other words, Bourdieu is arguing that a number of different elements in our lives are structured, and among them are the habitus of the individual (schemes of thought, feeling, and action) and the social field (structured social positions and the distribution of resources). These different structures dialectically exert force upon one another through the strategic actions and practices of people in interaction. And, as with most dialectics, the tension can produce something new and different out of the struggle; these differences can then influence the structures of habitus and field.

Concepts and Theory: Structuring Class

The basic fact of capitalism is capital. Capital is different from either wealth or income. Income is generally measured by annual salary and wealth by the relationship between one's assets and debt. Both income and wealth are in a sense static; they are measurable facts about a person or group. Capital, on the other hand, is active: It's defined as accumulated goods devoted to the production of other goods. The entire purpose of capital is to produce more capital.

Bourdieu actually talks about four forms of capital—economic, social, symbolic, and cultural—all of which are invested and used in the production of class. Bourdieu uses *economic capital* in its usual sense. It is generally determined by one's wealth and income. As with Marx, Bourdieu sees economic capital as fundamental. However, unlike Marx, Bourdieu argues that the importance of economic capital is that it strongly influences an individual's level of the other capitals, which, in turn, have their own independent effects. In other words, economic capital starts the ball rolling; but once things are in motion, other issues may have stronger influences on the perpetuation of class inequalities.

Social capital refers to the kind of social network an individual is set within. It refers to the people you know and how they are situated in society. The idea of social capital can be captured in the saying, "It isn't what you know but who you know that counts." The distribution of social capital is clearly associated with class. For example, if you are a member of an elite class, you will attend elite schools such as Phillips Andover Academy, Yale, and Harvard. At those schools, you would be afforded the opportunity to make social connections with powerful people—for example, in elections over the past 30 years, there has been at least one Yale graduate running for the office of president of the United States. But economic capital doesn't exclusively determine social capital. We can build our social networks intentionally, or sometimes through happenstance. For example, if you attended Hot Springs High School in Arkansas during the early 1960s, you would have had a chance to become friends with Bill Clinton.

Symbolic capital is the capacity to use symbols to create or solidify physical and social realities. With this idea, Bourdieu begins to open our eyes to the symbolic nature of class divisions. Social groups don't exist simply because people decide to gather together. Max Weber recognized that there are technical conditions that must be met for a loose collection of people to form a social group: People must be able to communicate and meet with one another; there must be recognized leadership; and a group needs clearly articulated goals to organize. Yet, even meeting those conditions doesn't alone create a social group. Groups must be symbolically recognized as well.

With the idea of symbolic capital, Bourdieu pushes us past analyzing the use of symbols in interaction. Symbolic interactionism argues that human beings are oriented toward meaning, and meaning is the emergent result of ongoing symbolic interactions. We're symbolic creatures, but meaning doesn't reside within the symbol itself; it must be pragmatically negotiated in face-to-face situations. We've learned a great deal about how people create meaning in different situations because of symbolic interactionism's insights. But Bourdieu's use of symbolic capital is quite different.

Bourdieu recognizes that all human relationships are created symbolically and not all people have equal symbolic power. For example, I write a good number of letters of recommendation for students each year. Every form I fill out asks the same question: "Relationship to applicant?" And I always put "professor." Now, the *meaning* of the professor–student relationship emerges out of my interactions with my students, and my professor–student relationships are probably somewhat different from some of my colleagues as a result. However, neither my students nor I *created* the professor–student relationship.

Recall our earlier discussion about Bourdieu's critique of sociology's dichotomy. Here we can see both Bourdieu's critique and his answer: Social phenomenology can't account for the creation of the categories it uses, and social physics reifies the categories—Bourdieu (1991) tells us that objective categories and structures, such as class, race, and gender, are generated through the use of symbolic capital: "Symbolic power is a power of constructing reality" (p. 166).

Bourdieu (1989) characterizes the use of symbolic capital as both the power of constitution and the power of revelation—it is the power of "world-making . . . the power to make groups. . . . The power to impose and to inculcate a vision of divisions, that is, the power to make visible and explicit social divisions that are implicit, is political power par excellence" (p. 23). This power of world-making is based on two elements. First, there must be sufficient recognition in order to impose recognition. The group must be recognized and symbolically labeled by a person or group that is officially recognized as having the ability to symbolically impart identity, such as scientists, legislators, or sociologists in our society. Institutional accreditation, particularly in the form of an educational credential (school in this sense operates as a representative of the state), "frees its holder from the symbolic struggle of all against all by imposing the universally approved perspective" (p. 22).

The second element needed to world-make is some relation to a reality—"symbolic efficacy depends on the degree to which the vision proposed is founded in reality" (Bourdieu, 1989, p. 23). I think it's best to see this as a variable. The more social or physical reality is already present, the greater will be the effectiveness of symbolic capital. This is the sense in which symbolic capital is the power to consecrate or reveal. Symbolic power is the power to reveal the substance of an already occupied social space. But note that granting a group symbolic life "brings into existence in an instituted, constituted form . . . what existed up until then only as . . . a collection of varied persons, a purely additive series of merely juxtaposed individuals" (p. 23). Thus, because legitimated existence is dependent upon symbolic capacity, an extremely important conflict in society is the struggle over symbols and classifications. The heated debate over race classification in the U.S. 2000 census is a good example.

There is a clear relationship between symbolic and cultural capital. The use of symbolic capital creates the symbolic field wherein cultural capital exists. In general, cultural capital refers to the informal social skills, habits, linguistic styles, and tastes that a person garners as a result of his or her economic resources. It is the different ways we talk, act, and make distinctions that are the result of our class. Bourdieu identifies three different kinds of cultural capital: objectified, institutionalized, and embodied. *Objectified cultural capital* refers to the material goods (such as books, computers, and paintings) that are associated with cultural capital. *Institutionalized cultural capital* alludes to the certifications (like degrees and diplomas) that give official acknowledgment to the possession of knowledge and abilities. *Embodied cultural capital* is the most important in Bourdieu's scheme. It is part of what makes up an individual's habitus, and it refers to the cultural capital that lives in and is expressed through the body. This function of cultural capital manifests itself as taste.

Taste refers to an individual preference or fondness for something, such as "she has developed a taste for expensive wine." What Bourdieu is telling us is that our tastes aren't really individual; they are strongly influenced by our social class—our tastes are embodied cultural capital. Here a particular taste is legitimated, exhibited, and recognized by only those who have the proper cultural code, which is class specific. To hear a piece of music and classify it as baroque rather than elevator music implies an entire world of understandings and classification. Thus, when individuals express a preference for something or classify an object in a particular way, they are simultaneously classifying themselves. Taste may appear as an innocent and natural phenomenon, but it is an insidious revealer of position. As Bourdieu (1979/1984) says, "Taste classifies, and it classifies the classifier" (p. 6). The issue of taste is "one of the most vital stakes in the struggles fought in the field of the dominant class and the field of cultural production" (p. 11).

Habitus

Taste is part of habitus, and habitus is embodied cultural capital. Class isn't simply an economic classification (one that exists because of symbolic capital), nor is it merely a set of life circumstances of which people may become aware (class consciousness)—class is inscribed in our bodies. **Habitus** is the durable organization of one's body and its deployment in the world. It is found in our posture, and our way of walking, speaking, eating, and laughing; it is found in every way we use our body. Habitus is both a system whereby people organize their own behavior and a system through which people perceive and appreciate the behavior of others.

Pay close attention: This system of organization and appreciation is felt in our bodies. We physically feel how we should act; we physically sense what the actions of others mean, and we approve of or censure them physically (we are comfortable or uncomfortable); we physically respond to different foods (we can become voracious or disgusted); we physically respond to certain sexual prompts and not others—the list can go on almost indefinitely. Our humanity, including our class position, is not just found in our cognitions and mental capacity; it is in our very bodies.

One way to see what Bourdieu is talking about is to recall the rugby analogy. I love to play sand volleyball, and I only get to play it about once every five years, which means I'm not very good at it. I have to constantly think about where the ball and other players are situated. I have to watch to see if the player next to me is going for the ball or if I can do so. All this watching and mental activity means that my timing is way off. I typically dive for the ball 1.5 seconds too late, and I end up with a mouthful of sand (but the other bunglers on my team are usually impressed with my effort). Professional volleyball players compete in a different world. They rarely have to think. They sense the ball and their teammates, and they make their moves faster than they could cognitively work through all the particulars. Volleyball is inscribed in their bodies.

Explicating what he calls the Dreyfus model, Bent Flyvbjerg (2001) gives us a detailed way of seeing what is going on here. The Dreyfus model indicates that there are five levels to learning: novice, advanced beginner, competent performer, proficient performer, and expert. Novices know the rules and the objective facts of a situation; advanced beginners have concrete knowledge but see it contextually; and the competent performer employs hierarchical decision-making skills and feels responsible for outcomes. With proficient performers and experts, we enter another level of knowledge. The first three levels are all based on cognitions, but in the final two levels, knowledge becomes embodied. Here situations and problems are understood "intuitively" and require skills that go beyond analytical rationality. With experts, "their skills have become so much a part of themselves that they are not more aware of them than they are of their own bodies" (p. 19).

Habitus thus works below the level of conscious thought and outside the control of the will. It is the embodied, non-conscious enactment of cultural capital that gives habitus its specific power,

> beyond the reach of introspective scrutiny or control by the will . . . in the most automatic gestures or the apparently most insignificant techniques of the body . . . [it engages] the most fundamental principles of construction and evaluation of the social world, those which most directly express the division of labour . . . or the division of the work of domination. (Bourdieu, 1979/1984, p. 466)

Bourdieu's point is that we are all, each one, experts in our own class position. Our mannerisms, speech, tastes, and so on are written on our bodies beginning the day we are born.

There are two factors important in the production of habitus: education and distance from necessity. In *distance from necessity,* necessity speaks of sustenance—the things necessary for biological existence. Distance from the necessities of life enables the upper classes to experience a world that is free from urgency. In contrast, the poor must always worry about their daily existence. As humans move away from that essential existence, they are freed from that constant worry, and they are free to practice activities that constitute an end in themselves. For example, you probably have hobbies. Perhaps you like to paint, act, or play guitar as I do. There is a sense of intrinsic enjoyment that comes with those kinds of activities; they are ends in themselves. The poorer classes don't have that luxury. Daily life for them is a grind, a struggle just to make ends meet. This struggle for survival and the emotional toll it brings are paramount in their lives, leaving no time or resources for pursuing hobbies and "getting the most out of life."

Think of distance from necessity as a continuum, with you and I probably falling somewhere in the middle. We have to be somewhat concerned about our livelihood, but we also have time and energy to enjoy leisure activities. The elite are on the uppermost part of the continuum, and it shows in their every activity. For example, why do homeless people eat? They eat to survive. And if they are hungry enough, they might eat anything, as long as it isn't poisonous. Why do members of the working classes or nearly poor people eat? For the same basic reason: The working classes are much better off than the homeless, but they still by and large live hand to mouth. However, because they are further removed from necessity, they can be more particular about what they eat, though the focus will still be on the basics of life, a "meat and potatoes" menu. Now, why do the elite eat? You could say they eat to survive, but they are never aware of that motivation. Food doesn't translate into the basics of survival. Eating for the elite classes is an aesthetic experience. For them, plate presentation is more important than getting enough calories.

Thus, the further removed we are from necessity, the more we can be concerned with abstract rather than essential issues. This ability to conceive of form rather than function—aesthetics—is dependent upon "a generalized capacity to neutralize ordinary urgencies and to bracket off practical ends, a durable inclination and aptitude for practice without a practical function" (Bourdieu, 1979/1984, p. 54). This aesthetic works itself out in every area. In art, for example, the upper class aesthetic of luxury prefers art that is abstract while the popular taste wants art to represent reality. In addition, distance from economic necessity implies that all natural and physical desires and responses are to be sublimated and dematerialized. People in the working class, because it is immersed in physical reality and economic necessity, interact in more physical ways through touching, yelling, embracing, and so forth than do the distanced elite. A lifetime of exposure to worlds so constructed confers cultural pedigrees, manners of applying aesthetic competences that differ by class position.

This embodied tendency to see the world in abstract or concrete terms is reinforced and elaborated through *education*. One obvious difference between the education of the elite and the working classes is the kind of social position in which education places us. The education system channels individuals toward prestigious or devalued positions. In doing so, education manipulates subjective aspirations (self-image) and demands (self-esteem). Another essential difference in educational experience has to do with the amount of rudimentary scholastics required—the simple knowing and recognizing of facts versus more sophisticated knowledge. This factor varies by number of years of education, which in turn varies by class position. At the lower levels, the simple recitation of facts is required. At the higher levels of education, emphasis is placed on critical and creative thought. At the highest levels, even the idea of "fact" is understood critically and held in doubt.

Education also influences the kind of language we use to think and through which we see the world. We can conceive of language as varying from complex to simple. More complex language forms have more extensive and intricate syntactical elements. Language is made up of more than words; it also has structure. Think about the sentences that you read in a romance novel and then compare them to those in an advanced textbook. In the textbook, they are longer and more complex, and that complexity increases as you move into more scholarly books. These more complex syntactical elements allow us to construct sentences that correspond to multileveled thinking—this is true because both writing and thinking are functions of language. The more formal education we receive, the more complex are the words and syntactical elements of our language. Because we don't just think *with* language, we think *in* language, the complexity of our language affects the complexity of our thinking. And our thinking influences the way in which we see the world.

Here's a simple example: Let's say you go to the zoo, first with my dog and then with three different people. You'd have to blindfold and muzzle my dog, but if you could get her to one of the cages and then remove the blinders, she would start barking hysterically. She would be responding to the content of the beasts in front of her. All she would know is that those things in front of her smell funny, look dangerous, and are undoubtedly capable of killing her, but she's going to go down fighting. Now picture yourself going with three different people, each from a different social class and thus education level. The first person has a high school education. As you stand in front of the same cage that you showed to my dog, he says, "Man, look at all those apes." The second person you go with has had some college education. She stands in front of the cage and says, "Gorillas are so amazing." The third person has a master's level education and says, "Wow, I've never seen *gorilla gorilla, gorilla graueri,* and *gorilla berengei* all in the same cage."

Part of our class habitus, then, is determined by education and its relationship to language. Individuals with a complex language system will tend to see objects in terms of multiple levels of meaning and to classify them abstractly. This type of linguistic system brings sensitivity to the structure of an object; it is the learned ability to respond to an object in terms of its matrix of relationships. Conversely, the less complex an individual's classification system, the more likely are the organizing syntactical elements to be of limited range. The simple classification system is characterized by a low order of abstractedness and creates more sensitivity to the *content* of an object, rather than its structure.

Bourdieu uses the idea of habitus to talk about the replication of class. Class, as I mentioned earlier, isn't simply a part of the social structure; it is part of our body. We are not only categorized as middle class (or working class or elite), we also *act* middle class. Differing experiences in distance from necessity and education determine one's tastes, ways of seeing and experiencing the world, and "the most automatic gestures or apparently most insignificant techniques of the body—ways of walking or blowing one's nose, ways of eating or talking" (Bourdieu, 1979/1984, p. 466). We don't choose to act or not act according to class; it's the result of lifelong socialization. And, as we act in accordance with our class, we replicate our class. Thus, Bourdieu's notion of how class is replicated is much more fundamental and insidious than Marx and more complex than Weber.

However, we would fall short of the mark if we simply saw habitus as a structuring agent. Bourdieu intentionally uses the concept (the idea originated with Aristotle) in order to talk about the creative, active, and inventive powers of the agent. He uses the concept to get out of the structuralist paradigm without falling back into issues of consciousness and unconsciousness. In habitus, class is structured but it isn't completely objective—it doesn't merely exist outside of the individual because it's a significant part of her or his subjective experience. In habitus, class is *structured but not structuring*—because, as with high-caliber athletes and experts, habitus is intuitive. The idea of habitus, then, shows us how class is replicated subjectively and in daily life, and it introduces the potential for inspired behaviors above and beyond one's class position. Indeed, the potential for exceeding one's class is much more powerful with Bourdieu's habitus than with conscious decisions—most athletes, musicians, and other experts will tell you that their highest achievements come under the inspiration of visceral intuition rather than rational processes. It is through habitus that the practices of the dialectic are performed.

Fields

As we talk about Bourdieu's notion of the **field**, keep the rugby analogy in mind. Just like in rugby, fields are delineated spaces wherein "the game" is played. Obviously, in Bourdieu's theoretical use of field, the parameters are not laid out using fences or lines on the ground. The parameters of the theoretical field are delineated by networks or sets of connections among objective positions. The positions within a field may be filled by individuals, groups, or organizations. However, Bourdieu is adamant that we focus on the relationships among the actors and not on the agents themselves. It's not the people, groups, or even interactions that are important; it's the relationships among and between the positions that set the parameters of a field. For example, while the different culture groups (such as theater groups, reading clubs, and choirs) within a region may have a lot in common, they probably do not form a field because there are no explicit objective relationships among them. On the other hand, most all the universities in the United States do form a field. They are objectively linked through accreditation, professional associations, federal guidelines, and so forth. These relationships are sites of active practices; thus, the parameters of a field are always at stake within the field itself. In other words, because fields are defined mostly through relationships and relationships are active, which positions and relationships go into making up the field is constantly changing. Therefore, what constitutes a field is always an empirical question.

Fields are directly related to capitals. The people, groups, and organizations that fill the different objective positions are hierarchically distributed in the field, initially through the overall volume of all the capitals they possess and secondly by the relative weight of the two particular kinds of capital, symbolic and cultural. More than that, each field is different because the various cultures can have dissimilar weights. For example, cultural capital is much more important in academic rather than economic fields; conversely, economic capital is more important in economic fields than in academic ones. All four capitals or powers are present in each, but they aren't all given the same weight. It is the different weightings of the cultures that define the field, and it is the field that gives validity and function to the capitals.

While the parameters of any field cannot be determined prior to empirical investigation, the important consideration for Bourdieu is the correspondence between the empirical field and its symbolic representation. The objective field corresponds to a symbolic field, which is given legitimation and reality by those with symbolic capital. Here symbolic capital works to both construct and recognize empirical, social positions; it creates and legitimates the relations between and among positions within the field. In this sense, the empirical and symbolic fields are both constitutive of class and of social affairs in general. It is the symbolic field that people use to view, understand, and reproduce the objective.

I've pictured Bourdieu's basic theory of class structuring in Figure 14.4. When reading the model, keep in mind Bourdieu's intent with open concepts. This model is simply a heuristic device—something we can use to help us see the world. The figure starts on the far left with the objective field and the distribution of capitals. But for Bourdieu, the objective field isn't enough to account for class reality and replication, and that is where many sociologists stop. Bourdieu takes it further in that the objective field becomes real and potentially replicable through the use of symbolic capital. The use of symbolic capital creates the symbolic field, which in turn orders and makes real the objective field. The exercise of symbolic capital, along with the initial distribution of capitals, creates cultural capital that varies by distance from necessity and by education. Cultural capital produces the internal

Figure 14.4 Habitus and the Replication of Class

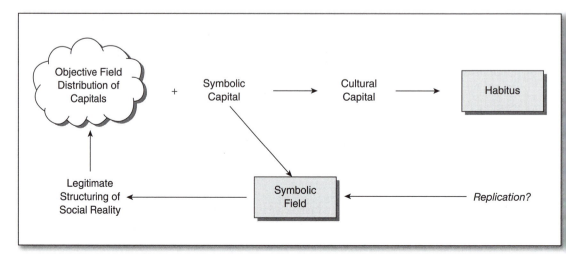

structuring of class: habitus. But notice that the model indicates that the potential of habitus to replicate is held in question—it is habitus exercised in linguistic markets and symbolic struggles that decides the question.

Concepts and Theory: Replicating Class

Linguistic Markets

Bourdieu (1991) says that "every speech act and, more generally, every action" is an encounter between two independent forces (p. 37). One of those forces is habitus, particularly in our tendency to speak and say things that reveal our level of cultural capital. The other force comes from the structures of the linguistic market. A linguistic market is "a system of relations of force which impose themselves as a system of specific sanctions and specific censorship, and thereby help fashion linguistic production by determining the 'price' of linguistic products" (Bourdieu & Wacquant, 1992, p. 145).

The **linguistic market** is like any other market: It's a place of exchange and a place to seek profit. Here exchange and profit are sought through linguistic elements such as symbols and discourses. The notion of a free market is like an ideal type: It's an idea against which empirical instances can be measured. All markets are structured to one degree or another, and linguistic markets have a fairly high degree of structuring. One of the principal ways they are structured is through formal language.

Every society has formalized its language. Even in the case where the nation might be bilingual, such as Canada, the languages are still formalized. Standard language comes as a result of the unification of the state, economy, and culture. The education system is used to impose restrictions on popular modes of speech and to propagate the standard language. We all remember times in grammar school when teachers would correct our speech ("There is no such word as *ain't*."). In the university, this still happens, but mostly through the application of stringent criteria for writing.

Linguistic markets are also structured through various configurations of the capitals and the empirical field. As we've seen, empirical fields are defined by the relative weights of the capitals—so, for example, religious fields give more weight to symbolic capital and artistic fields more import to cultural capital, but they both need and use economic capital. The same is true with linguistic markets. Linguistic markets are defined through the relative weights of the capitals and by the different discourses that are valued. For example, the linguistic market of sociology is heavily based on cultural capital. In order to do well in that market, you would have to know a fair amount about Karl Marx, Émile Durkheim, Michel Foucault, Pierre Bourdieu, Dorothy Smith, and so forth. Linguistic markets are also structured by the empirical field, in particular by the gaps and asymmetries that exist between positions in the field (by their placement and position of capitals, some positions in a field are more powerful than others). These empirical inequalities help structure the exchanges that take place within a linguistic market.

When people interact with one another, they perform speech acts—meaningful kinds of behaviors that are related to language. In a speech act, habitus and linguistic markets come together. In other words, the person's embodied class position and cultural capital are given a certain standing or evaluation within the linguistic market. The linguistic market contains the requirements of formal language; the salient contour of capitals; and the objective, unequal distribution of power within the empirical field.

Let me give you three examples from my own life. When I go to a professional conference, I present papers to and meet with other academics. My habitus has a number of different sources, among them training in etiquette by a British mother and many years spent studying scholarly texts and engaging in academic discourse. The linguistic market in academia is formed by the emphasis on cultural and symbolic capital, and by the positions in the empirical field held by academics such as those at the conference; some people have more powerful positions and others less so. Each encounter, each speech act, is informed by these issues. In such circumstances, I tend to "feel at home" (habitus), and I interact freely, bantering and arguing with other academics in a kind of "one-upmanship" tournament.

This weekend, I will be going to the annual Christmas party at my wife's work. Here the linguistic market is different. Economic capital and the cultural capital that goes along with it are much more highly prized, and the empirical field is made up of differing positions and relationships achieved in the struggle of American business. Because of these differences, my market position is quite different here from what it was at the professional conference. In fact, I have no market position. Worse, my habitus remains the same. The way I talk—the words I use and the way I phrase my sentences—is very different from the other people at this event. The tempo of my speech is different (it's much slower) as is the way I walk and hold myself. In this kind of situation, I try to avoid speech acts. When encounters are unavoidable, I say as little as possible because I know that what I have to say, the way I say it, and even the tempo of my speech won't fit in.

These two different examples illustrate an extremely important point in Bourdieu's theory: Individuals in a given market recognize their institutional position, have a sense of how their habitus relates to the present market, and anticipate differing profits of distinction. In my professional conference example, I anticipate high rewards and distinction, but in the office party example, I anticipate low distinction and few rewards. In situations like the office example, anticipation acts as a *self-sanctioning mechanism* through which individuals participate in their own domination. Perhaps "domination" sounds silly with reference to an office party, but it isn't silly when it comes to job interviews, promotions, legal confrontations, encounters with government officials, and so forth. I gave you an example that we can relate to so that we can more clearly understand what happens in other, more important speech acts.

These kinds of speech acts are the arena of symbolic violence. Symbolic violence is the exercise of violence and oppression that is not recognized as such. More specifically, "Symbolic power is that invisible power which can be exercised only with the complicity of those who do not want to know that they are subject to it or even that they themselves exercise it" (Bourdieu, 1991, p. 164). For example, for quite some time, patriarchy had been seen as part of the natural order of things. Yet, in believing in her husband's right to rule, a woman participated in and blinded herself to her own oppression. Here's another example: In believing that schools should be locally controlled and funded and that education is the legitimate path to upward social mobility, we actively participate in the perpetuation of the class system in the United States.

More insidious for Bourdieu is the way language is used to inflict **symbolic violence**. Have you ever been around someone of higher social status that you wanted to talk to but didn't? Why didn't you? If you're like me, you didn't because you were afraid of making a fool out of yourself. I had a professor in graduate school that I so admired, but I never talked to him unless it was absolutely necessary. I just knew that I would misspeak and say something foolish. Every social group has specific languages. It is easily seen with such pop culture groups as hip-hop, skaters, and graffiti taggers. But it is also true with experts and people in high-status positions, including the elite class. They typically have specialized languages. And, while we don't know the language, we *know* that we don't know the language, "which condemns [us] to a more or less desperate attempt to be correct, or to *silence*" (Bourdieu, 1991, p. 97, emphasis original).

In society, power is seldom used as coercive force but is translated into symbolic form and thereby endowed with a type of legitimacy. Symbolic power is an invisible power and is generally misrecognized: We don't see it as power; we see it as legitimate. In recognizing as legitimate the hierarchical relations of power in which they are embedded, the oppressed are participating in their own domination:

> All symbolic domination presupposes, on the part of those who submit to it, a form of complicity which is neither passive submission to external constraint nor a free adherence to values. . . . It is inscribed, in a practical state, in dispositions which are impalpably inculcated, through a long and slow process of acquisition, by the sanctions of the linguistic market. (Bourdieu, 1991, pp. 50–51)

My third example is from a conversation with a friend. In most conversations among equals, formal linguistic markets have little if any power. We talk and joke around, paying no attention to the demands of proper speech. I'm certain that you can think of multitudes of such speech acts: talking with friends at a café or at the gym or in your apartment. Those kinds of speech acts will always stay that way, unless one of you has a higher education or a greater distance from necessity—that is, unless your habitus is different from that of your friends. Even in such cases, however, linguistic markets usually won't come into play. But they can. "Every linguistic exchange contains the *potentiality* of an act of power, and all the more so when it involves agents who occupy asymmetric positions in the distribution of the relevant capital" (Bourdieu & Wacquant, 1992, p. 145, emphasis original). Bourdieu tells us that in such situations, where the market position is different or the habitus is different, the potential for power and symbolic violence is only set aside for the moment.

Symbolic Struggle

Social change for Bourdieu is rooted in *symbolic struggle,* which makes sense given Bourdieu's emphasis on symbolic capital and power. Part of that struggle occurs within the speech act or encounter. As we've seen, encounters are structured by markets of differing distinction, and habitus expresses itself naturally within those markets. We will feel at home or foreign in an encounter; we will speak up or silence ourselves, all without thought. However, we also have to keep in mind that habitus is embodied and expresses itself through intuitive feelings. And sometimes our intuitions can lead us to brilliant moves, whether on the sports field, the game board, the music stage, or in the speech act. Just so, our habitus at times can lead us to speech acts that defy our cultural, symbolic, economic, or social standings.

This kind of symbolic struggle can bring some incremental change. Bourdieu gives us hints about how more dynamic change can occur, but keep in mind that his isn't a theory of social change or revolution. Bourdieu allows that there are two methods by which a symbolic struggle may be carried out, one objectively and the other subjectively. In both cases, symbolic disruption is the key. Objectively, individuals or groups may act in such a way as to display certain counter-realities. His example of this method is group demonstrations held to manifest the size, strength, and cohesiveness of the disenfranchised. This type of symbolic action disrupts the taken-for-grantedness that all systems of oppression must work within—it offers an objective case that things are not what they seem.

Subjectively, individuals or groups may try and transform the categories constructed by symbolic capital through which the social world is perceived. On the individual level, this may be accomplished through insults, rumors, questions, and the like. A good example of this approach is found in bell hooks' (1989) book *Talking Back:* "It is that act of speech, of 'talking back,' that is no mere gesture of empty words, that is the expression of moving from object to subject—the liberated voice" (p. 9).

Groups may also operate in this way by employing more political strategies. The most typical of these strategies is the redefinition of history—that is, "retrospectively reconstructing a past fitted to the needs of the present" (Bourdieu, 1989, p. 21). But notice with each of these kinds of struggle, a response from those with symbolic capital would be required. These disruptions could bring attention to the cause, but symbolic power would be necessary to give it life and substance within the symbolic field first and then the objective field.

Summary

- Bourdieu's basic approach is constructivist structuralism. With this idea, Bourdieu is attempting to give us a point of view that gives full weight to structure and agency. There is tension between constructivism and structuralism, between agency and structure, and it is that tension that Bourdieu uses to understand how both can coexist. The tension is a dialectic and is played out in symbolic markets and social practices.

• Bourdieu is specifically concerned with the reproduction of class. In contrast to Marx, Bourdieu sees class replicated through symbolic violence rather than overt oppression. Bourdieu argues that there are four types of capital: economic, social, cultural, and symbolic. The latter two are his greatest concern. Symbolic capital has the power to create positions within the symbolic and objective fields. The objective field refers to social positions that are determined through the distributions of the four capitals. But these positions don't become real or meaningful for us unless and until someone with symbolic capital names them. This naming gives the position, and the individuals and groups that occupy it, social viability. The symbolic field has independent effects in that it can be manipulated by those with symbolic capital. Also, people use the symbolic field to view, understand, and reproduce the objective field.

• Cultural capital refers to the social skills, habits, linguistic abilities, and tastes that individuals have as a result of their position in the symbolic and objective fields. Cultural capital is particularly important because it becomes embodied. This embodiment of cultural capital becomes the individual's habitus: the way the body exists and is used in society. Distance from necessity and level of education are two of the most important ways in which habitus is structured, both of which are related to economic capital. Class position, then, is replicated through the embodied, non-conscious behaviors and speech acts of individuals.

• Habitus is expressed in linguistic markets. Linguistic markets are structured by different weightings of the various capitals. One's position within the market is determined by different rankings on the capitals and the embodied ability to perform within the market. Linguistic markets are played out in speech acts where individuals sense how their habitus relates to the market and thus anticipate differing profits of distinction. This non-conscious sense provides the basis for symbolic violence: Anticipating few rewards in acts where they are "outclassed," individuals simultaneously sanction themselves and legitimate the hierarchical relations of class and power.

• There is, however, the possibility of symbolic struggle. The struggle involves symbolic disruption. First, individuals or groups can act in such a way as to objectively picture alternative possibilities. This is what we normally think of as social movements or demonstrations. But because Bourdieu sees the importance of symbolic power in the replication of class, he understands these demonstrations as pictures—they are objective images of symbolic issues that disrupt the taken-for-grantedness in which oppression must operate. Second, individuals and groups can challenge the subjective meanings intrinsic within the symbolic field. In daily speech acts, the individual can disrupt the normality of the symbolic field through insults, jokes, questions, rumors, and so on. Groups can also challenge "the way things are" by redefining history.

BUILDING YOUR THEORY TOOLBOX

Learning More—Primary and Secondary Sources

- Primary sources for Anthony Giddens:

  - To learn more about Giddens' theory of structuration, you should read *The Constitution of Society,* University of California Press, 1986. For Giddens' theory of modernity, I recommend *Modernity and Self-Identity: Self and Society in the Late Modern Age,* Stanford University Press, 1991.

- Giddens secondary sources:

  - An excellent encounter with Giddens' theory (not just a review) is Stjepan Gabriel Mestrovic's *Anthony Giddens: The Last Modernist,* Routledge, 1998.

- Primary sources for Pierre Bourdieu:

  - *Distinction: A Social Critique of the Judgment of Taste,* Harvard University Press, 1984; "Social Space and Symbolic Power," *Sociological Theory,* 7, 14–25, 1989; *Language and Symbolic Power,* Harvard University Press, 1991; *An Invitation to Reflexive Sociology,* University of Chicago Press, 1992.

- Bourdieu secondary sources:

  - David Swartz, *Culture and Power: The Sociology of Pierre Bourdieu,* University of Chicago Press, 1998; Richard Jenkins: *Pierre Bourdieu (Key Sociologists),* *Routledge,* 2002.

Seeing the Social World (knowing the theory)

- Write a 250-word synopsis of Giddens' structuration theory.

- Write a 250-word synopsis of Bourdieu's constructivist structuralism.

- After reading and understanding this chapter, you should be able to define the following terms theoretically and explain their theoretical importance to Giddens' ontology of society and theory of modernity: *structuration theory, duality of structure, social structures, normative rules, signification codes, authoritative resources, allocative resources, time–space distanciation, modalities of structuration, domination, institutional orders, reflexive monitoring, rationalization of action, discursive consciousness, practical consciousness, routinization, regionalization, ontological security, radical reflexivity, separation of time and space, disembedding mechanisms, symbolic tokens, expert systems, reflexive project of the self, bodily regimes, organization of sensuality, pure relationships, emancipatory politics, life politics, mediated experiences.*

- After reading and understanding this chapter, you should be able to define the following terms theoretically and explain their theoretical importance to Bourdieu's theory: *economic capital, social capital, symbolic capital, cultural capital, taste, habitus, distance from necessity, education, field, linguistic market, symbolic violence, constructivist structuralism, dialectic.*

- After reading and understanding this chapter, you should be able to answer the following questions (remember to answer them *theoretically*):
    - What is time–space distanciation, and why is it the central question for Giddens? How does modernity affect time–space distanciation?
    - What are social structures, in Giddens' scheme? How do they exist, and what do they do?
    - What are modalities of structuration? What are the three modalities? What is the function of modalities of structuration?
    - What are the three institutional orders, and how are they created?
    - What are practical and discursive consciousnesses, and how do they fit in with reflexive monitoring?
    - What is the unconscious motivation in human interaction? What specific processes come about due to this motivation? How does each process vary? What are their effects?
    - What are the main processes that produce the dynamic of modernity? There are at least four. Define each process and explain how it contributes to the dynamic character of modernity.
    - What is the reflexive project of the self? How did it become individualized? How is the body involved, and why do you think the body is important in this project?
    - Explain the differences between emancipatory and lifestyle politics. Why is lifestyle politics more prevalent than emancipatory today?
- After reading and understanding this chapter, you should be able to answer the following questions (remember to answer them *theoretically*):
    - Explain Bourdieu's constructivist structuralism approach.
    - How are symbolic fields produced?
    - What is habitus and how is it produced?
    - How are class inequalities replicated, and how is class contingent? In your answer, be certain to explain linguistic markets, symbolic violence, and the role that habitus plays.

Engaging the Social World (using the theory)

- Giddens is one of the architects and proponents of what is known as the "third way" in politics. Using your favorite Internet search engine, look up "third way." What is the third way, and how is Giddens involved? How can you see it related to his theory?

- Use Bourdieu's theory to describe and explain the differences between the way you talk with your best friend versus the way you talk with your theory professor.

- Choose the structure of inequality that you know best (race, gender, sexuality, religion). Using what you already know, analyze that structure using Figure 14.4. How would approaching the study of inequality change using Bourdieu?

(Continued)

(Continued)

Weaving the Threads (building theory)

- Compare and contrast Giddens' theory of structuration with Bourdieu's constructivist-structuralism approach. Specifically, how are patterns of behavior replicated in the long run? How does each one overcome the object–subject dichotomy? Do you find one approach to be more persuasive? Why or why not?

- Compare and contrast Habermas' and Giddens' views of modernity. I recommend you start with their defining characteristics of modernity and review the issues that are implied in the definitions. After you've worked your way through these comparisons, define modernity and its chief problems.

- In Chapter 13 I asked you to write a two-page analysis of democracy using Habermas' theory. Do the same now for Giddens (remember that modernity and democracy are tied up together).

- Check the index in this book and look up the different definitions and explanations of "social structures." Evaluate each of these approaches and create what you feel to be a clear, robust, and correct definition-explanation of social structures. Justify your theory.

- What does Bourdieu's theory of linguistic markets add to our understanding of symbolic interaction (Chapters 6 and 12)?

- How could you specifically integrate Goffman's (Chapter 12) theory of impression management with Bourdieu's theory of habitus and linguistic markets?

- Can you think of ways in which you could use Bourdieu's theory to make Chafetz's (Chapter 10) theory of gender inequality more robust, especially in her ideas of what happens at the micro level?

CHAPTER 15

Globalizing Systems:

Immanuel Wallerstein and Manuel Castells

We started our journey in Chapter 1 with a specific definition of society: a macro-level entity made up of interdependent social structures marked out by the geographic boundaries and legitimated power of the nation-state. This is the idea of society on which democracy was built, which is why your rights and obligations as a citizen are defined by national boundaries. We also saw in Chapter 1 that democracy within a nation was enabled by an active *civil society*: "Civil society refers to all the places where individuals gather together to have conversations, pursue common interests and, occasionally, try to influence public opinion or public policy" (Jacobs, 2006, p. 27). There were a number of institutional supports for this civil society, including capitalism, but one of the most important was the "press," organizations that collected and disseminated ideas and knowledge necessary for participatory democracy, which is why freedom of the press is so important.

Of course we've seen different versions of society. Both Giddens and Bourdieu work to overcome the dichotomy that is inherent in the structural view in modernity's initial formulation. And we've seen theories that argue that the only empirically available site for "society" is the social encounter. However, the theories in this chapter do something different and in the long run their implications are much more profound. In some ways our theorists in this chapter suppose the modern view of society defined by the nation-state (where Giddens, Bourdieu, and the micro level theorists argue that that version was never how society existed or operated). I think we should see both Wallerstein and Castells as not questioning the version of national society upon which modernity was founded. Rather, what they argue is that society can no longer be contained within those boundaries because of globalizing processes. "The term globalization applies to a set of social processes that appear to transform our present social condition of weakening nationality into one of globality. At its core, then, globalization is about shifting forms of human contact" (Steger, 2009, p. 9). Globalization by definition, then, challenges our concepts of modern society (weakening nationality) and by extension democracy (human contact and agency).

Global Capitalism:
Immanuel Wallerstein (1930–)

THEORIST'S DIGEST

Brief Biography

Immanuel Wallerstein was born in New York City on September 30, 1930. He attended Columbia University where he received his bachelor's (1951), master's (1954), and PhD (1959) degrees. Wallerstein has also formally studied at various universities around the globe, including the Université Paris 7–Denis-Diderot, Université Libre de Bruxelles, and Universidad Nacional Autónoma de México. His primary teaching post was at Binghamton University (SUNY), where he taught from 1976 to his retirement in 1999. However, he has also held visiting professor posts in Amsterdam, British Columbia, and the Chinese University of Hong Kong, as well as several other locations. In addition to many professional posts, he has served as president of the International Sociological Association and director of the Fernand Braudel Center for the Study of Economies, Historical Systems, and Civilizations.

Central Sociological Questions

Wallerstein is driven to first critically understand (through a Marxian perspective) how the nations of the world are joined together in a global system of capitalism, and second to find ways to politically act to change that system.

Simply Stated

Because of exploitation and overproduction, global capitalist economy goes through cycles of expansion and depression. Each cycle is deeper than the previous, and the cycles eventually reach a point where the economy can't rebound. During that last depression the global system will go through a chaotic period out of which a new system will be born.

Key Ideas

modern capitalism, globalization, systems, exploitation, dialectical materialism, division of labor, externalized costs, quasi-monopolies, overproduction, world-empires, world-economies, core states, periphery states, semi-periphery states, Kondratieff waves, world-systems theory

Concepts and Theory: The Dialectics of Capitalism

Wallerstein's critique is essentially a Marxist one. Marx did what Wallerstein says needs to be done: He focused on structures moving through dialectic or cyclical time. He was particularly interested in capitalism—and, according to Wallerstein, the elements of capitalism are in fact the only features that can truly create a world-system today. Certain of Marx's concepts, then, have special importance in explaining and critiquing the world-system. Among them are the division of labor, exploitation, accumulation, and overproduction.

The Division of Labor and Exploitation

For Wallerstein, the importance of the *division of labor* is that it is the defining characteristic of an economic world-system. Labor, of course, is an essential form of human behavior; without it we would cease to exist. By extension, the division of labor creates some of the most basic kinds of social relationships, and these relationships are, by definition, relations of dependency. In our division of labor, we depend upon each other to perform the work that we do not. I depend upon the farmer for food production, and the farmer depends upon teachers to educate his or her children. These relations of dependency connect different people and other social units into a structured whole or system. Wallerstein argues that the world-system is connected by the current capitalist division of labor: World-systems are defined "quite simply as a unit with a single division of labor and multiple cultural systems" (Wallerstein, 2000, p. 75). Multiple cultural systems are included because world-systems connect different societies and cultures.

The important feature of this division of labor is that it is based on exploitation. I've already gone into some detail defining exploitation, so I won't do it again now (see Chapter 3). But as we go through the next section, keep in mind two things: First, exploitation is a measurable entity: It is the difference between what a worker gets paid and what he or she produces. Different societies can have different levels of exploitation. For example, if we compare the situation of automobile workers in the United States with those in Mexico, we will see that the level of exploitation is higher in Mexico. The second thing to keep in mind is that exploitation is fundamental to capitalism. Surplus labor and exploitation are the places from which profit comes and are thus necessary for capitalism.

What is important to see here is that profit is based on exploitation and there are limitations to exploitation. Yet the drive for exploitation doesn't let up; capitalists by definition are driven to increase profits. The search for new means of exploitation, then, eventually transcends national boundaries: Capitalists *export exploitation.* Because of the limitations on the exploitation of workers in advanced capitalist countries—due primarily to the effects of worker movements, state legislation, and the natural limitations of technological innovation—firms seek other labor markets where the level of exploitation is higher. Marx had a vague notion of this, but Wallerstein's theory is based upon it. It is the exportation of exploitation that structures the division of labor upon which the world economy is based.

Accumulation and Overproduction

We all know what modern capitalism is: It is the investment of money in order to make more money (profit). As Wallerstein (2004) says, "We are in a capitalist system only when the system gives priority to the *endless* accumulation of capital" (p. 24, emphasis original). We see the drive to make money in order to make more money all around us, but most people only think about the personal effects this kind of capitalism has (like the fact that Bill Gates is worth $46.6 billion). But what are the effects on the economy? Most Americans would probably say that the effect on the economy is a good one: continually expanding profits and higher standards of living. Perhaps, but Wallerstein wants us to see that something else is going on as well. In order to fully understand what he has in mind, we need to think about the role of government in the endless pursuit of the accumulation of capital.

It's obvious that for capitalism to work, it needs a strong state system. The state provides the centralized production and control of money; creates and enforces laws that grant private property rights; supplies the regulation of markets, national borders, inter-organizational relations; and so forth. But there is something else that the state does in a capitalist system. We generally assume that the firm that pays the cost enjoys the benefits, as in the capitalist invests the money so he or she can enjoy the profit. However, the state actually decides what proportion of the costs of production will be paid by the firm. In this sense, capitalists are subsidized by the state.

There are three kinds of costs that the state subsidizes: the costs associated with transportation, toxicity, and the exhaustion of raw materials. Firms rarely if ever pay the full cost of transporting their goods; the bulk of the cost for this infrastructure is borne by the state, for such things as road systems. Almost all production produces toxicity, whether noxious gases, waste, or some kind of change to the environment. How and when these costs are incurred and who pays for them is always an issue. The least expensive methods are short-term and evasive (dumping the waste, pretending there isn't a problem), but the costs are eventually paid and usually by the state. Capitalist production also uses up raw materials, but again firms rarely pay these costs. When resources are depleted, the state steps in to restore or re-create the materials. Economists refer to the expenses of capitalist production that are paid by the state as *externalized costs,* and we will see that in this matter not all states are created equal.

However helpful these externalized costs are to the pursuit of accumulation, states that contain the most successful capitalist enterprises do more: They provide a structure for *quasi-monopolies.* A monopoly is defined as the exclusive control of a market or the means of production. Quasi-monopolies don't have exclusive control but they do have considerable control.

Wallerstein argues that totally free markets would make the endless accumulation of capital impossible. Totally free markets imply that all factors influencing the means of production are free and available to all firms, that goods and services flow without restriction, that there is a very large number of sellers and a very large number of buyers, and that all participants have complete and full knowledge. "In such a perfect market, it would always be possible for the buyers to bargain down the sellers to an absolutely minuscule level of profit," which would destroy the basic underpinnings of capitalism (Wallerstein, 2004, pp. 25–26). The converse of a totally free market is a monopoly, and monopolized processes are far more lucrative than those of the free market. Thus, the perfect situation for a capitalist firm is to have monopolistic control; it would then be able to pursue the endless accumulation of capital with the greatest efficiency and success.

The most important way in which states facilitate quasi-monopolies is through patent laws that grant exclusive production rights for an invention for a certain number of years. This state guarantee allows companies to gain high levels of profit in a monopolistic market for long enough to obtain considerable accumulation of capital. The practice of granting patents also results in a cycle of leading products. The largest and most successful firms actively market a patented product as long as the profit margin is high. As soon as the product becomes less profitable through more open competition, the product is given over to less profitable companies, with the original firm creating new leading products. Producers of the unpatented product engage in freer competition but with less profit.

You'll recall from Chapter 3 that capitalism is subject to *overproduction.* Because capitalists are driven to accumulate ever-increasing levels of capital, and because, unlike other animals, human beings can create new needs, capitalists will continue to create new and produce existing commodities until the market will no longer bear it. The cycles of overproduction and exploitation work in tandem, both of them driven by accumulation. Accumulation increases the demand for labor and product innovation. State protection through patent rights, tax incentives, and the like creates a state-sanctioned quasi-monopoly that in and of itself increases accumulation, better enabling the firm to engage in product innovation and increasing the demand for labor.

Over time, the demand for labor decreases the size of the labor pool, which drives wages up and profits down, which, in turn, precipitates an economic slowdown, the collapse of small businesses, and the search for new methods of exploitation through technological innovation in the work process or exporting exploitation. In the medium run, exporting exploitation is the more efficient of the two because technologies become diffused throughout the business sector. Exporting exploitation implies the movement of specific goods outside the national boundaries, and product movement from most profitable to less profitable firms explicitly entails such a shift. Both processes, then, move goods and labor from advanced capitalist countries to rising capitalist countries. And both processes lead to the collapse of small businesses and the centralization of accumulation—that is, capital held in fewer and fewer hands.

Concepts and Theory: The End of the World as We Know It

World-Empires and World-Economies

Very few people think about their world ending, but all worlds do. The great Mesopotamian, Greek, and Roman empires are gone; the sun has set on the British Empire; and even more recently, the USSR crumbled and is no more. Of course, just like the Phoenix, new worlds arise out of the ashes and history moves on. But what of our world? History tells us all worlds fail—when will our world fail?

Wallerstein asks us to consider the possibility that our world is failing and that we are in a chaotic period between historical moments. Perhaps shockingly for some of us, Wallerstein argues that this shift in historical epochs will lead to the demise of the United States as we know it. So, let's take these questions seriously: In what historical epoch do we live, and how is it affecting our world?

Wallerstein argues that there have been two types of world-systems throughout history, one with a common political system and one without. Systems with a common political entity are called world-empires. *World-empires* exist through military dominance and economic tribute (money paid from one country to another as acknowledgment of submission). The political influence of one government is spread and held in place through a strong military, but this sets up a cycle that eventually leads to the demise of the empire. Maintaining a standing army that is geographically extended costs quite a bit of money. This money is raised through tribute and taxation. Heavy taxes make the system less efficient, in terms of economic production, and this increases the resistance of the populace as well. Increasing resistance means that the military presence must be increased, which, in turn, increases the cost, taxation, and resistance, and it further lowers economic efficiency. These cycles continue to worsen through structural time (see historicity above) until the empire falls. Examples of such world-empires include Rome, China, and India.

These world-empire cycles continued until about 1450, when a world-economy began to develop. Rather than a common political system, *world-economies* are defined through a common division of labor and through the endless accumulation of capital. As we saw earlier, in the absence of a political structure or common culture, the world-system is created through the structures intrinsic to capitalism. The worldwide division of labor created through the movement of products and labor from advanced capitalist nations to rising capitalist nations creates relationships of economic dependency and exploitation. These capitalist relationships are expressed through three basic types of economic states: core, semi-periphery, and periphery.

Briefly, *core states* are those that export exploitation; enjoy relatively light taxation; have a free, well-paid labor force; and constitute a large consumer market. The state systems within core states are the most powerful and are thus able to provide the strongest protection (such as trade restrictions) and capitalist inducements, such as externalizing costs, patent protection, tax incentives, and so on. *Periphery states* are those whose labor is forced (very little occupational choice or worker protections) and underpaid. In terms of a capitalist economy and the world-system, these states are also the weakest—they are able to provide little in the way of tax and cost incentives and they are the weakest players in the world-system. The periphery states are those to which capitalists in core states shift worker exploitation and more competitive, less profitable products. These shifts result in "a constant flow of surplus-value from the producers of peripheral products to the producers of core-like products" (Wallerstein, 2004, p. 28).

The relationship, then, between the core and the periphery is one of production processes and profitability. There is a continual shift of products and exploitation from core to periphery countries. Furthermore, there are cycles in both directions: Periphery countries are continually developing their own capitalist-state base. As we've seen, profitability is highest in quasi-monopolies and these, in turn, are dependent upon powerful states. Thus, changing positions in the capitalist world-economy is dependent upon the power of the state.

Over time, periphery economies become more robust and periphery states more powerful: Worker protection laws are passed, wages increase, and product innovation begins to occur. The states can then begin to perform much like the states in core countries—they create tax incentives and externalize costs for firms, they grant product protection, and they become a more powerful player in the world-system economy. These nations move into the semi-periphery. *Semi-periphery states* are those that are in transition from being a land of exploitation to being a core player, and they both export exploitation and continue to exploit within their own country.

A good illustration of this process is the textile industry. In the 1800s, textiles were produced in very few countries and it was one of the most important core industries; by the beginning of the twenty-first century, textiles had all but moved out of the core nations. A clear and recent example of this process is Nike. Nike is the world's largest manufacturer of athletic shoes, with about $10 billion in annual revenue. In 1976, Nike began moving its manufacturing concerns from the United States to Korea and Taiwan, which at the time were considered periphery states. Within four years, 90% of Nike's production was located in Korea and Taiwan.

However, both Korea and Taiwan were on the cusp, and within a relatively short period of time they had moved into the semi-periphery. Other periphery states had opened up, most notably Bangladesh, China, Indonesia, and Vietnam. So, beginning in the early 1990s, Nike began moving its operations once again.

Currently, Indonesia contains Nike's largest production centers, with 17 factories and 90,000 employees. But that status could change. Just a few years ago, in 1997, the Indonesian government announced a change in the minimum wage, from $2.26 per day to $2.47 per day. Nike refused to pay the increase and in response, 10,000 workers went on strike. In answer to the strike, a company spokesperson, Jim Small, said, "Indonesia could be reaching a point where it is pricing itself out of the market" (Global Exchange, 1998).

Yet the existence of the semi-periphery doesn't simply serve as a conversion point—it has a structural role in the world-system. Because the core, periphery, and semi-periphery share similar economic, political, and ideological interests, the semi-periphery acts as a buffer that lessens tension and conflict between the core and periphery nations. "The existence of the third category means precisely that the upper stratum is not faced with the *unified* opposition of all the others because the *middle* stratum is both exploited and exploiter" (Wallerstein, 2000, p. 91, emphasis original).

Kondratieff Waves

Since 1450, world-economies have moved through four distinct phases. These phases occur in what are called Kondratieff waves (K-waves), named after Nikolai Kondratieff, a Russian economist writing during the early twentieth century. Kondratieff noticed patterns of regular, structural change in the world-economy. These waves last 50 to 60 years and consist of two phases: a growth phase (the A-cycle) and a stagnation phase (the B-cycle).

Much of what drives these phases in modern economic world-systems comes from the cycles of exploitation and accumulation that we've already talked about. During the A-cycle, new products are created, markets are expanded, labor is employed, and the political and economic influence of core states moves into previously external areas—new geographic areas are brought into the periphery for labor and materials (imperialism). At 25 to 30 years into the A-cycle, profits begin to fall due to overproduction, decreasing commodity prices, and increasing labor costs. In this B-cycle, the economy enters a deep recession. Eventually, the recession bottoms out and small businesses collapse, which leaves fewer firms and greater centralization of capital accumulation (quasi-monopolistic conditions), which, in turn, sets the stage for the next upswing in the cycle (A_2-cycle) and the next recession (B_2-cycle). Historically, these waves reach a crisis point approximately every 150 years. Each wave has its own configuration of core and periphery states, with generally one dominant state, at least initially.

Wallerstein sees these waves as phases in the development of the world-system. Within each phase, three things occur: The dominant form of capitalism changes (agricultural → mercantilism → industrial →consolidation), there is a geographic expansion as the division of labor expands into external areas, and a particular configuration of core and periphery states emerges. There have been four such phases thus far in the world-system. In Figure 15.1, I've outlined the different phases and their movement through time. I've also noted some of the major issues and the

Figure 15.1   Wallerstein's World-Systems Phases

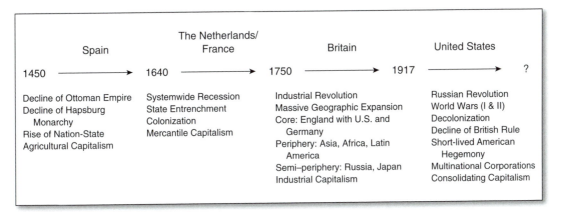

hegemonic core nations for easy comparison. Wallerstein (2004) uses the term *hegemonic* to denote nations that for a certain period of time

> were able to establish the rules of the game in the interstate system, to domi-
> nate the world-economy (in production, commerce, and finance), to get their
> way politically with a minimal use of military force (which however they had
> in goodly strength), and to formulate the cultural language with which one
> discussed the world. (p. 58)

I'm not going to go into much historic detail here. You can read Wallerstein's (1974, 1980, 1989) three-volume work for the specifics. But briefly, Phase 1 occurred roughly between 1450 and 1640, which marks the transition from feudalism and world-empires to the nation-state. Both the Ottoman Empire and the Hapsburg dynasty began their decline in the sixteenth century. As the world-empires weakened, Western Europe and the nation-state emerged as the core, Spain and the Mediterranean declined into the semi-periphery, and northeastern Europe and the Americas became the periphery. During this time, the major form of capitalism was agricultural, which came about as an effect of technological development and ecological conditions in Europe.

The second phase lasted from 1640–1750 and was precipitated by a systemwide recession that lasted approximately 80 years. During this time, nations drew in, centralized, and attempted to control all facets of the market through mercantilism, the dominant form of capitalism in this phase. Mercantilism was designed to increase the power and wealth of the emerging nations through the accumulation of gold, favorable trade balances, and foreign trading monopolies. These goals were achieved primarily through colonization (geographic expansion). As with the previous period, there was a great deal of struggle among the core nations, with a three-way conflict among the Netherlands, France, and England.

The third phase began with the Industrial Revolution. England quickly took the lead in this area. The last attempt by France to stop the spread of English power was

Napoleon's continental blockade, which failed. Here capitalism was driven by industry and it expanded geographically to cover the entire globe. Wallerstein places the end of the third phase at the beginning of World War I and the beginning of the fourth phase at 1917 with the Russian Revolution.

The Russian Revolution was driven by the lack of indigenous capital, continued resistance to industrializing from the agricultural sector, and the decay of military power and national status. Together these meant that "the Russian Revolution was essentially that of a semi-peripheral country whose internal balance of forces had been such that as of the late nineteenth century it began on a decline towards a peripheral status" (Wallerstein, 2000, p. 97). During this time, the British Empire receded, due to a number of factors including decolonization, and two states in particular vied for the core position: Germany and the United States. After World War II, the United States became the leading core nation, a position it enjoyed for two decades.

Hegemonic or leading states always have a limited life span. Becoming a core nation requires a state to focus on improving the conditions of production for capitalists, but staying hegemonic requires a state to invest in political and military might. Over time, other states become economically competitive and the leading state's economic power diminishes. In attempts to maintain its powerful position in the world-system, the hegemonic state will resort first to military threats and then to exercising its military power (note the increasing U.S. military intervention over the past 25 years). The "use of military power is not only the first sign of weakness but the source of further decline," as the capricious use of force creates resentment first in the world community and then in the state's home population as the cost of war increases taxation (Wallerstein, 2004, pp. 58–59).

Thus, the cost of hegemony is always high and it inevitably leads to the end of a state's position of power within the world-system. For the United States, the costs came from the Cold War with the USSR; competition with rising core nations, such as Japan, China, and an economically united and resurgent Western Europe; and such displays of military might as the Korean, Vietnam, Gulf, and Iraqi Wars. The decline of U.S. hegemony since the late 1960s has meant that capitalist freedom has actually increased, due to the relative size and power of global corporations. There are many multinational corporations now that are larger and more powerful than many nations. These new types of corporation "are able to maneuver against state bureaucracies whenever the national politicians become too responsive to internal worker pressures" (Wallerstein, 2000, p. 99). The overall health of world capitalism has also meant that the semi-periphery has increased in strength, facilitating growth into the core.

The Modern Crisis

There are several key points in time for the world-system, such as the Ottoman defeat in 1571, the Industrial Revolution around 1750, and the Russian Revolution in 1917. Each of these events signaled a transition from one capitalist regime to another. Wallerstein argues that one such event occurred in 1968, when revolutionary movements raged across the globe, involving China, West Germany, Poland, Italy, Japan, Vietnam, Czechoslovakia, Mexico, and the United States. So many nations were caught up in the mostly student-driven social movements that, collectively, they have been called the "first world revolution."

As you'll recall from the introduction to this section, part of what defines the period of time in which we live is a critique of the projects of modernity, both social and technical. Wallerstein tells us that the upheavals of 1968 were directed at the contradictions and failures of society to fulfill the hope of modernity: liberation for all. Students by and large rejected much of the benefits of technological develop-ment and proclaimed society had failed at the one thing that truly mattered: human freedom. The material benefits of technology and capitalism were seen as traps, things that had blinded people to the oppression of blacks, women, and all minori-ties. And this critique wasn't limited to technologically advanced societies:

> In country after country of the so-called Third World, the populaces turned against the movements of the Old Left and charged fraud. . . . [The people of the world] had lost faith in their states as the agents of a modernity of liber-ation. (Wallerstein, 1995, p. 484)

The 1968 movements in particular rejected American hegemony because of its emphasis on material wealth and hypocrisy in liberation.

In Wallerstein's (1995) scheme, the collapse of Communism was simply an exten-sion of this revolt, one that most clearly pointed out the failure of state government to produce equality for all: "Even the most radical rhetoric was no guarantor of the modernity of liberation, and probably a poor guarantor of the modernity of tech-nology" (p. 484). Interestingly, Wallerstein sees the collapse of Leninism as a disaster for world capitalism. Leninism had constrained the "dangerous classes," those groups oppressed through capitalist ideology and practice. Communism repre-sented an alternative hope to the contradictions found in capitalist states. With the alternative hope gone, "the dangerous classes may now become truly dangerous once again. Politically, the world-system has become unstable" (p. 484).

Structurally, the upheavals of 1968 occurred at the beginning of a K-wave B-cycle. In other words, the world was standing at the brink of an economic downturn or stagnation, which lasted through the 1970s and 1980s. As we've seen, such B-cycles occur throughout the Kondratieff wave, but this one was particularly severe. The 20-year economic stagnation became an important political issue because of the prosperity of the preceding A-cycle. From 1945 to 1970, the world experienced more economic growth and prosperity than ever before. Thus, the economic downturn gave continued credence and extra political clout to worldwide social movements. Economically, the world-system responded to the downturn by attempting to roll back production costs by reducing pay scales, lowering taxes associated with the wel-fare state (education, medical benefits, retirement payments), and re-externalizing input costs (infrastructure, toxicity, raw materials). There was also a shift from the idea of developmentalism to globalization, which calls for the free flow of goods and capital through all nations.

However, while the world-system is putting effort into regaining the A-cycle, there are at least three structural problems hindering economic rebound. First, as we've noted, there are limits to exporting exploitation. Four hundred years of capitalism have depleted the world's supply of cheap labor. Every K-wave has brought continued geographic expansion, and it appears that we have reached the limit of that expansion. More and more of the world's workforce is using its political power to increase the share of surplus labor or profit it receives (see Chapter 1 for discussion of surplus labor). Inevitably, this will lead to a sharp increase in the costs of labor and production and a corresponding decrease in profit margins. Remember, capitalism is defined by continual accumulation. This worldwide shift, then, represents a critical point in the continuation of the current capitalist system.

Second, there is a squeeze on the middle classes. Typically, the middle classes are seen as the market base of a capitalist economy. And, as we've seen, a standard method of pulling out of a downturn is to increase the available spending money for the middle classes, either through tax breaks or through salary increases. This additional money spurs an increase in commodity purchases and subsequently in production and capital accumulation. However, this continual expanding of middle class wages eventually becomes too much for firms and states to bear. One of two things must happen: Either these costs will be rolled back, or they will not. If they are not reduced, "both states and enterprises will be in grave trouble and frequent bankruptcy" (Wallerstein, 1995, p. 485). If they are rolled back, "there will be significant political disaffection among precisely the strata that have provided the strongest support for the present world-system" (p. 485).

In the United States, indications are that the costs are being rolled back. Between 1967 and 2001, the income of the middle 20% of the population dropped from 17.3% to 14.6% of the total, while the upper 20% increased from 43.8% to 50.0%. Further, between 1981 and 1999, there was a 340% increase in middle class bankruptcies. And, in 2001, 1.4 million Americans lost their health insurance—over half of those had an annual household income above $75,000, clearly indicating that the majority were middle to upper-middle class. Granted, these are only isolated examples, but they give an indication of what might be happening in the United States.

Third, as we've noted, accumulation is based on externalizing costs. Two of those costs—raw material depletion and toxicity—have natural limits, and it appears that we might be reaching them. Global warming, ozone rupture, destruction of the rain forests, and land degradation from waste are themes with which we are all familiar. Nowhere does the idea of natural limits come out more clearly than in the work of Peter Vitousek, professor of biosciences at Stanford University. Vitousek, Ehrlich, Ehrlich, and Matson (1986) argue that directly (through consumption) and indirectly (through toxic waste), human beings presently use up about 40% of the world's net primary production (NPP), which represents the rate of production of biomass that is available for consumption by all plants and animals. In other words, of the total amount of energy available for life on this planet, human beings use 40% of it. Predicting the Earth's long-term ability to support human life is difficult to calculate, because it depends on the wealth of the population and the kinds of technologies supporting it, but we can see that humans use up a hugely disproportionate amount of the Earth's resources (we are but one of some 5–30 million animal species on the planet), and we can see that the resources of the Earth are finite.

But limits aren't the only concern; toxic waste has been going on for years. Typically, firms take the cheapest way of handling waste—dump it on someone else's or public property—until public outcry motivates governments to pass laws restricting dumping. But the laws are not retroactive and it appears difficult to assign responsibility. The result is that government, not industry, tends to pay for the bulk of cleanup. According to an article in the *Washington Post*, "The number of toxic or hazardous sites requiring federal attention continues to grow, and Congress will have to spend at least $14 billion to $16.4 billion over the coming decade just to keep pace with the problem" (Pianin, 2001, p. A19).

Structural and Cultural Signs of the End

Wallerstein argues that world-systems enter a time of chaos during transition periods. How things change or into what form is not predictable. A world-system runs its cyclical courses through the Kondratieff wave, with periods of growth and stagnation, finally ending in collapse. A new configuration emerges out of this rubble, but, unlike Marx, Wallerstein offers no clear predictions. However, Wallerstein does argue that the uprising of 1968 marked the beginning of the end of the current world-system. We can see not only the clear marks of the dialectical cycles near the end of a 150-year Kondratieff wave, we can also see that the structural supports upon which capitalism has been built are limited and nearing exhaustion.

There are also cultural and structural signs that indicate the system is in the uncertainty of transition. Wallerstein points to two cultural signs: the introduction of complexity theory in science and postmodern theory in the social sciences. In the past 15 years or so, a significant number of physical scientists and mathematicians have turned against the causal predictability of Newtonian physics, which postulated a universe run according to universal laws—laws that in all time and in every place could explain, predict, and control the physical features of the cosmos.

Currently, many scientists are saying that Newtonian physics is a special case of reality; it fits only in circumstances that are clearly circumscribed or limited. The tools of science must therefore incorporate more flexible schemes with wider scopes of application. Thus today we hear of complexity theory, chaos theory, strange attractors, fuzzy logic, and so on. Wallerstein's (1995) point is this: "The natural world and all its phenomena have become historicized" (p. 486). That is, the scientific view of the universe has historically changed: The old science was built on a mechanistic, linear view of the universe; the new science is not linear or mechanistic.

The idea of a historicized science is an oxymoron, at least from the initial perspective of science. Science assumed that the universe is empirical and operates according to law-like principles. These principles could be discovered and used by humans to understand, predict, and control their world. Science was in the business of producing *abstract* and *universal* truths, not truths that only hold under certain conditions. The historicity of society has always been an argument against the possibility of social science, precisely because the factors that influence human behavior and society change according to the context. The hard, laboratory sciences have now become susceptible to the same critique: According to complexity theory, all knowledge is contextual and contingent, and nothing is universal and certain. "Hence the new science raises the most fundamental questions about the modernity of technology" (Wallerstein, 1995, p. 486).

The scene in the social sciences has followed suit and become even less certain than it was before. In the past 25 years, the most vocal and influential voice in the social sciences has been postmodernism (see Chapter 16 of this volume). Postmodernism in its most radical form, as it was brought into the social sciences, argues that the social world in technologically advanced societies is a virtual or hyper-real world. The cultural signs, symbols, and images that we use aren't connected to any social reality. Most of them come not from real social groups in face-to-face interaction, but are, in fact, produced by media and advertising concerns.

As a result of this cultural fragmentation and the new doubts in science, all grand narratives are held in distrust. Grand- or *metanarratives* are stories that attempt to embrace large populations of people. Typically, grand narratives are generated by political groups (as in nationalism and national identities). In their place, postmodernism advocates *polyvocality*, or many voices. Postmodernism argues that all voices are equal and should be given equal weight. These voices are of course linked to specific groups, such as men, women, blacks, Chicanos, and all the subdivisions within the groups, such as bisexual-Chicano-Catholic-males. There is thus an ethical dimension to postmodernism: "It is a mode of rejecting the modernity of technology on behalf of the modernity of liberation" (Wallerstein, 1995, p. 487).

The two structural signs that indicate we are in a time of chaotic transition are financial speculation and worldwide organization of social movements. There has been limited success in rolling back costs and reducing the press on profits, but not nearly what was needed or hoped for. As a result, capitalists have sought profit in the area of financial speculation rather than production. Many have taken great profits from this kind of speculation, but it also "renders the world-economy very volatile and subject to swings of currencies and of employment. It is in fact one of the signs of increasing chaos" (Wallerstein, 2004, p. 86).

On the political scene, since 1968 there has been a shift from movements for electoral changes to the "organization of a movement of movements" (Wallerstein, 2004, p. 86). Rather than national movements seeking change through voting within the system, radical groups are binding together internationally to seek change within the world-system. Wallerstein offers the World Social Forum (WSF) as an example. It is not itself an organization, but rather a virtual space for meetings among various militant groups seeking social change.

Another indicator of this political decentralization is the increase in terrorist attacks worldwide. The terrorist groups themselves are decentralized, non-state entities, which makes conflict between a state like the United States and these entities difficult. Nation-states are particular kinds of entities defined by a number of factors, most importantly by territory, rational law, and a standing military. These factors and the political orientation they bring mean that nation-states are most efficient at confronting other nation-states, ones with specified territories, which legitimate rational law, and have modern militaries. Almost everything about the terrorist groups that the United States is facing is antithetical to these qualities of the nation-state. The United States is a centralized state and the terrorists are decentralized groups. These differences in social structure and relation to physical place make it extremely difficult for the United States to engage the terrorists—there is no interface between the two—let alone defeat or make peace with them.

But more than that, the attacks of September 11 have energized politically right-wing groups in the United States. It has allowed them to cut ties with the political center and "to pursue a program centered around unilateral assertions by the United States of military strength combined with an attempt to undo the cultural evolution of the world-system that occurred after the world revolution of 1968 (particularly in the fields of race and sexuality)" (Wallerstein, 2004, p. 87). This, along with attempts to do away with many of the geopolitical structures set in place after 1945 (like the United Nations), has "threatened to worsen the already-increasing instability of the world-system" (p. 87).

What will follow the 400-year reign of capitalism is uncertain. World-systems theory, as Wallerstein sees it, is meant to call our attention to thinking in structural time and cyclical processes; it is meant to lift our eyes from our mundane problems so that we can perceive the world-system in all its historical power to set the stage of our lives; it is intended to give us the critical perspective to have eyes to see and ears to hear the Marxist dynamics still at work within the capitalist system; and, finally, it is intended to spur us to action.

However, Wallerstein is not saying that these changes are beyond our ability to influence or control. Rather, he means that "fundamental change is possible . . . and this fact makes claims on our moral responsibility to act rationally, in good faith, and with strength to seek a better historical system" (Wallerstein, 1999, p. 3). According to Wallerstein (1999), because the system is in a period of transition where "small inputs have large outputs" (p. 1) and "every small action during this period is likely to have significant consequences" (Wallerstein, 2004, p. 77), we must make diligent efforts to understand what is going on; we must make choices about the direction in which we want the world to move; and we must bring our convictions into action, because it is our behaviors that will affect the system.

> We can think of these three tasks as the intellectual, the moral, and the political tasks. They are different, but they are closely interlinked. None of us can opt out of any of these tasks. If we claim we do, we are merely making a hidden choice. (Wallerstein, 2004, p. 90)

Summary

- Wallerstein sees his work more in terms of a type of analysis than a specific theory. His point is that it is the principles of analysis that drive the theorizing rather than the other way around. There are two main features of Wallerstein's perspective: globality and historicity. Globality conceptualizes the world in system terms, which cut across cultural and political boundaries. Historicity sees history in terms of structural time and cyclical time within the structures, rather than focusing on events, people, and linearity.

- In terms of theory, Wallerstein takes a Marxist approach. He focuses on the division of labor, exploitation, and the processes of accumulation and overproduction. In Marxist theory, exploitation is the chief source of profit. Thus, capitalists are intrinsically motivated to increase the level of exploitation. Since wages tend to go up as capitalist economies mature, reducing the level of exploitation and profit, there is a constant tendency to export exploitation to nations that have a less developed capitalist economy, thus increasing the worldwide division of labor.

- Capitalist accumulation implies that capital is invested for the purpose of creating more capital, which in turn is invested in order to create more capital. In modern capitalism, this process of accumulation is augmented by the state. The state specifically bears the costs associated with transportation, toxicity, and the exhaustion of materials. More powerful states additionally provide conditions that facilitate quasi-monopolies, thus increasing capitalists' profits and the rate of accumulation.

- Overproduction is endemic to capitalism as well. Because they are driven by the capitalist need for accumulation, commodification (the process through which material and nonmaterial goods are turned into products for sale) and production are intrinsically expansive. Capitalists will continue to create new and produce existing commodities until the market will no longer bear it, thus creating more supply than demand.

- Taken together, the processes of exploitation and the division of labor and the dynamics of accumulation and overproduction create a scenario in which there is a continual movement of products and labor from more powerful to less powerful nations.

- In the world-economy, there are four types of nations: the core, semi-periphery, the periphery, and external areas. In general, exploitation and mass production of least-profitable goods move from the core to the external areas. However, because this is a system, there is also a move of nations as they transition from external to peripheral to core. Eventually, there will be no more areas to exploit with low-profit mass production, which will lead to system breakdown.

- The world-economy thus tends to go through cycles of expansion, depression, and breakdown. These cycles reach a crisis about every 150 years. According to Wallerstein, the world is now in its fourth phase of world-economies. The last phase began in 1917, with the United States as the world-economy's core nation. Wallerstein marks the beginning of the end of this phase at the social upheavals of 1968. In addition to the social movements, the world-economy entered a cycle of depression that was particularly harsh and lasted for about 20 years. While the world-economy is actively trying to come back from this economic depression, there are three factors that are inhibiting this attempt: the system limits to exploitation, the middle class squeeze, and the limited ability of states to pick up externalized costs. Thus, Wallerstein argues that the world-system is on the brink of collapse and is currently experiencing the chaotic period that always precedes such an end.

TAKING THE PERSPECTIVE—WORLD SYSTEMS THEORY

Wallerstein prefers the word *globality* to *globalization*. The reason for this is that the term is generally thought of in ahistorical, market economy terms. For example, the 2001 Nobel Prize winner in Economic Sciences, Joseph E. Stiglitz (2003), defines *globalization* as follows:

> the closer integration of the countries and peoples of the world which has been brought about by the enormous reduction of costs of transportation and communication, and the breaking down of artificial barriers to the flows of goods, services, capital, knowledge, and (to a lesser extent) people across borders. (Stiglitz, 2003, p. 9)

Notice that in this definition the focus is on the market flow of goods, services, capital, and so forth; there is no mention of system (other than "closer integration") nor is there any sense of history. The latter two are of specific concern to Wallerstein and world-systems theorists because without the ideas of history and system the descriptions of globalization are atheoretical (without theory). World-systems analysis, on the other hand, can be theoretical precisely because it understands the phenomena using the general dynamics of systems theory that are able to account for historical changes and predict future outcomes.

Wallerstein intentionally uses the hyphen in world-systems theory to emphasize that he is talking about systems that constitute a world or a distinct way of existing. This approach looks at society as an interrelated whole, with every internal part systemically influencing the others. A systems approach additionally places emphasis on the relationship between the system and its environment. Thus, world-systems analysis argues that nations or collectives change in response to systemic factors that press upon it from the outside. For example, according to world-systems analysis, Peru isn't "modernizing" because it is something every nation will do; Peru is modernizing because it is caught in a global capitalist system that is pressuring it to change. Thus, world-systems analysis focuses on factors that cut across cultural and political boundaries and create an "integrated zone of activity and institutions which obey certain systemic rules" (Wallerstein, 2004, p. 17).

If social actors such as nations, institutions, and groups are related to each other through a specific system, then the history of that system is extremely important for understanding how the system is working presently. Wallerstein picked up the notions of structural time and cyclical process from French historian and educator Fernand Braudel (1981–1984). Braudel criticized event-dominated history as being too idiographic and political; this is the kind of history with which we are most familiar. The prefix "idio" specifically refers to the individual or one's own. Idiographic knowledge, then, is focused on unique individuals and their events. An example of this event history approach is to understand U.S. history in terms of things like Abraham Lincoln and the Civil War and Martin Luther King Jr. and the civil rights movement. Such an understanding doesn't see changes through history as the result of systematic social facts, but, rather, it perceives historical change as occurring through unique events and political figures— in other words, idiographic history is atheoretical.

(Continued)

(Continued)

Braudel felt that this kind of history is dust and tells us nothing about the true historical processes. Yet Braudel also criticized the opposite approach, nomothetic knowledge. The word *nomothetic* is related to the Greek word *nomos*, which means law. The goal in seeking nomothetic knowledge, like that of science, is to discover the abstract and universal laws that underpin the physical universe. According to Braudel, when nomothetic knowledge is sought in the social sciences, it more often than not creates mythical, grand stories that legitimate the search for universal laws instead of explaining historical social history.

Wallerstein's idea of *historicity* lies between the ideographic focus on events and the law-like knowledge of science. Rather than focusing on events, Wallerstein's approach concentrates on the history of structures within a world-system. For example, capitalism is a world-system that has its own particular history. There have always been people who have produced products to make a profit, but the capitalism of modernity, the kind that Weber (1904–1905/2002) termed "rational capitalism," is unique to a particular time period. An account of rational capitalism from its beginnings, from around the 16th century, that would include all the principal players (such as nations, firms, households, and so forth) and their systemic relations is what Wallerstein has in mind.

Historicity thus includes the unique variable of time. In taking account of world-systems rather than event history, historicity is centered upon structural time and the cyclical time within the structures. Wallerstein is telling us that structures have histories, and it is the history of structures with which we should be concerned, rather than events, because structures set the frames within which human behavior and meaning take place. Structures have life spans, they are born and they die, and within that span there are cyclical processes.

One other point is important in defining the world-systems perspective: unidisciplinarity. With unidisciplinarity, the world-systems' critique is aimed at the political underpinning of knowledge. Wallerstein argues that the configuration of the modern university system corresponds to the political systems of the age. Modernity brought a new world, one driven by markets, political states, and societal change. New academic disciplines came into existence to understand and control these arenas through the new knowledge of science. Thus, societies and economies were seen to be subject to law-like principles because science became the knowledge of most worth. At the core of the social sciences was the idea that modernity is the touchstone against which all other social forms would be tested. Thus, anthropology and Orientalism (the study of the Orient as distinct from the West) came into existence to measure, understand, and make distinct those other worlds from modernity. When the world politically divided again in 1945, the university changed as well. The world divided into first-, second-, and third-world countries. The world was seen developmentally, with two forms of development politically competing— capitalism and communism. The universities developed area studies so that the knowledge of the university would be politically useful and relevant.

Against this political division of knowledge, world-systems proposes *unidisciplinarity*. The prefix *uni* means singular, as in unicycle. Rather than implying the bringing together of the disciplines, the term instead denotes the denial of the disciplines altogether. As Wallerstein (1999) notes,

If there were historically emergent and historically evolving processes in the world-system, what would lead us to assume that these processes could be separated into distinguishable and segregated streams with particular (even opposed) logics? The burden of proof was surely on those who argued the distinctiveness of the economic, political, and sociocultural arenas. (p. 195)

To reiterate, unidisciplinarity is not multidisciplinarity. The multidiscipline approach, common in American universities today, still maintains the distinctions among the disciplines. World-systems advocates a holistic approach, one that not only sees the world as a totality, but that also sees knowledge as a whole. World-systems analysis, then, transcends sociology, political science, and economics. It takes a longer view than does conventional history and divides the world not in response to political needs and configurations but according to structural time and cyclical processes.

The Network Society:
Manuel Castells (1942–)

Theorist's Digest
Concepts and Theory: Information Technology
    Power, Politics, and Class in the Network Society
Concepts and Theory: Networks, Identities, and Democracy
    The Network Society and the Crisis in Democracy
Summary
Taking the Perspective—Information Theory

There's a lot that is familiar in Wallerstein's theory. He continues to talk about capitalism in terms of commodification, exploitation, and the relations of production—it's the global division of labor that connects us. And nation-states continue to play a significant role especially in facilitating capitalist growth; and capitalism is still centered on production. All of these issues can be found in Marx's theory; in fact, the basic theoretical move that Wallerstein makes is to move Marxian dynamics from the national to international level. But what if society is no longer based on our usual ideas of social structure, capitalist production, and political states? What if there's another system, one that was utterly outside the comprehension of classical theorists such as Marx, Weber, and Durkheim? What if rather than empirical, concrete reality being supremely important, it is something less tangible and more virtual in terms of time and space? What if the ideas of American, German, or Mexican society are less viable than ever before? What if civil society and democratic nations are no longer feasible? These are the possibilities that Manuel Castells asks us to consider.

THEORIST'S DIGEST

Brief Biography

Manuel Castells (1942–) was born in La Mancha, Spain, and grew up in Valencia and Barcelona. In college, he studied law and economics and received his PhD in sociology and another in human sciences from the University of Paris–Sorbonne in 1967. While in Paris, he was a political activist, fighting against Franco's dictatorship. He taught sociology at the University of Paris from 1967 to 1979. In 1979, he took a professorship at the University of California, Berkeley; then, in 2003, he moved to the University of Southern California Annenberg School for Communication. Castells has written 22 books, coauthored 21, and has over 100 articles published in academic journals. His most influential works are his trilogy, *The Information Age: Economy, Society, and Culture,* which has been translated into over 23 languages. Among his many awards and distinctions is the C. Wright Mills Award from the American Society for the Study of Social Problems, the Robert and Helen Lynd Award from the American Sociological Association, the National Medal of Science from Catalonia, and the Lifelong Research Award from the Committee on Computers and Information Technology of the American Sociological Association.

Central Sociological Questions

Castells' early work focuses on the issue of urban space. He uses a Marxian approach to understand how social conflicts transform the urban landscape. This initial concern with space and politics lead him to consider how both are affected by information technologies. In the work we focus on here, Castells asks, How does the intrusion of computer networks impact the space in which people connect and express issues of power and identity?

Simply Stated

Castells argues that computer and information technologies have dramatically impacted human existence. These technologies have lifted out social relationships, the work of capitalism, and political activism from the boundaries of the nation-state. What we mean by society, then, is more in keeping with the dictates of computer networks than the modern ideas of national society and democracy. Importance and power in a network is determined by how much information, symbols, and imagery a position can hold and process. The basis of class has changed as well, from production to managing work and flows of capital. Political activities have also shifted from the content of a political platform to control of image and negative information.

Key Ideas

Keynesian economics, information technology, the logic of networks, annihilation of time and place, power, class, politics, identities, legitimizing identity, resistance identity, project identity, civil society, symbol mobilizers, new democracy

Concepts and Theory: Information Technology

Castells' idea is that the information revolution that began in the 1980s has restructured capitalism and created a global society that is connected via networks. Prior to World War II, the capitalist system had played out its Marxist dynamics and was in a worldwide, inexorable depression—there was no way out. Socialist movements were gaining power globally, and there was a good chance that capitalism would have collapsed had it not been for the war. During the Great Depression of the 1930s, John Maynard Keynes (1936) published a new theory of economics. The basic tenet of *Keynesian economics* is that the state can moderate the effects of free market capitalism through controlling interest rates and by investing in the economic infrastructure, thus becoming a major consumer. But, Castells argues, Keynesian economics, just like laissez-faire capitalism before it, had built-in contradictions and limitations, which came to a head by the 1970s and resulted in rampant inflation.

From the 1970s into the 1990s, massive efforts at restructuring capitalism were underway. There were four goals: (1) deepen the logic of profitability; (2) improve the profitability of both capital and labor; (3) globalize commodity and labor markets; and (4) use the state to maximize the profitability of the national economy, even at the cost of social programs and education. Essential to this project was flexibility, such as "just-in-time" (JIT) inventory strategies, and adaptability. Castells argues (2000b) that this attempt at restructuring would have been extremely limited without the new information technology.

By *new information technology*, Castells has in mind computer technologies, both hardware and software, which, when coupled with the Internet, have connected humanity in a way that was up to this point unthinkable. As a result of information technology, space and time have become more abstract and infinitely less meaningful in terms of patterning and organizing social connections. We can, for example, have virtual face-to-face meetings with people in China, England, the United States, and Argentina at the same "time." Further, and perhaps more importantly, information has become the focal point of economic practices and growth. As the name indicates, information technologies act on information. In industrial societies, technologies act on the production process. For example, Ford's assembly-line technology, along with mass-produced, interchangeable parts, broke down the process of making a car into a series of simple tasks that unskilled workers could perform. So profound was the effect of this technology on economic production that it became known as "Fordism."

Information technologies, however, act upon information. As an example, let's consider something that falls a bit outside of Castells' concerns, but that most of us can relate to: music recording and playback. Before the digital age, music was recorded using analog technologies. Analog recording stores music as a continuous wave in or on the media (phonograph record or magnetic tape). It's called analog because the waves imprinted on the media are *analogous* to the sound waves of the music (the same basic idea applies to video recordings). In digital recording, the music is translated into discrete numbers or data. The first step in this information technology was developed in 1937 by British scientist Alec Reeves—he invented Pulse Code Modulation, one of the platforms upon which today's digital technology is based; and every step since then has involved innovations in how technology can store, transmit, and play back information. The production of these technologies for consumption is a secondary move: In a network society, technical innovation is focused primarily on producing and reproducing information—commodification comes later.

The most important informational technologies have focused on computers and communication. Ever since the first digital computer was invented in the early 1940s, each new technology has been directed at storing and using information. Castells argues (2000b) that this move to information technologies is having and will continue to have pervasive effects because human activity is based on information. There have been three major technological advances that have fundamentally influenced knowledge and information: the alphabet (written language), the printing press, and the computer. We know that the effects of the first two advances were tremendous. Civilization itself is indebted to written language, and the advent of the printing press led to the rise and spread of the Protestant Reformation, the Renaissance, and the Scientific Revolution. In addition, because the first commercially viable printed book was the Bible, and there was no comparable text in Asian countries, mechanized printing did not take hold as rapidly there, which in turn facilitated the European advantage over the East in the Industrial Revolution and technological domination. The printing press also influenced the way in which people think. The transmission of information changed from artistic expression (with hand printing) to chiefly textual. This shift facilitated the conversion from metaphorical to linear thinking. Castells is concerned with the third technological advancement in communication and information—the computer—and its influence in structuring society.

Power, Politics, and Class in the Network Society

The most significant effect of computer technology Castells sees is that *the logic of networks* will be the basis of the new social system. The idea of a network is rather straightforward. It is a set of interconnected points or "nodes," and nodes are simply places where the threads or paths of the network cross. Networks can be made up of any number of things, like networks of exchange. Castells is concerned with information networks, the nodes of which are points where information is held or processed. This kind of network is possible because of computer and communication technologies, and it is defined by those technologies.

Let's think for a moment about a computer network. Because the basic properties of networks are the same, you can choose any network, such as AIM (America Online Instant Messenger), the network at your place of work, the Internet as a whole, and so on. Networks are open and extremely flexible structures. They can be of almost any size and can change without threatening the balance of the whole. Networks have no center, and they work on the binary inclusion/exclusion model: That is, a node is either in the network or not; if a node ceases to function, it's eliminated and the network is rearranged—for example, your computer can move into or out of a network without affecting the network as such. There is no distance between nodes and no time element; rather than distance, such as between my computer and yours, what matters in networks are restrictions on the flow of information, and time, if used at all, is simply a marker of flow (e.g., when you sent your email). A node becomes important in a network either because it can hold and process information more efficiently, or because it functions as a switch that connects different networks. Once programmed, networks function automatically and impose their logic on all the social actors using it.

Such computerized informational networks have redefined the material basis of life in our society. All animals, including humans, are fundamentally related to time and space, but computing and network technologies have changed that relationship. Rather than the biological clock of human existence, or the mechanical clock of the industrial age, new communication technologies *annihilate time and place.* Rather than the essentialness of place, new information technologies have reoriented us to a space of flows, where exists the "organizational possibility of organizing the simultaneity of social practices without geographic contiguity" (Castells, 2000a, p. 14). Thus, social organization is set free from the confines of time and space. This freedom is so profound in its implications that Castells (2000b) marks the Information Age as the beginning of human history, "if by history we understand the moment when . . . our species has reached the level of knowledge and social organization that will allow us to live in a predominantly social world" (pp. 508–509).

Power in any such network is dramatically reorganized from the hierarchical model of bureaucracies and social inequalities. Power in networks is a function of a node's ability to find, hold, and process information. Nodes that can act as switches between informational networks are power-holders: "Since networks are multiple, the inter-operating codes and switches between networks become the fundamental sources in shaping, guiding, and misguiding societies" (Castells, 2000b, p. 502). More importantly, the informational network has provided the structure for the core activities of a global economy. Currently, the bulk of capital accumulation results from financial flows rather than production. Profit from production and consumption, from organizations and institutions, is extracted and reverted to the financial flows. Capital is then invested globally, following interests of greatest return, which are increasingly based on speculation and money markets rather than real goods and services. Financial flows are thus based on theoretical knowledge and timeliness of information. This "electronically operated global casino" decides the "fate of corporations, household savings, national currencies, and regional economies" (Castells, 2000b, p. 503).

The network society has dramatically affected *class* as well. It results first in capitalism without capitalists. The legal owners of any large business—Marx's definition of capitalists—are found in investment funds and individual portfolios, both of which are subject to networks of speculative management. The corporate managers don't make up a capitalist class either, because they do not control, nor do they know about, the movements of capital in networks of financial flows. Rather than a class that holds and uses capital, the global capital network is a network of networks that "are ultimately dependent upon the non-human capitalist logic of an electronically operated, random processing of information" (Castells, 2000b, p. 505).

The working class has likewise been redefined by the logics of networks. Labor has become exceedingly general. Rather than the specified labor of production, it's labor as a generic part of speculative capitalism—labor becomes a piece on the global chessboard of capital flows. Capital and labor increasingly exist in different spaces and times: capital in the space of flows and the instant/constant time of computerized communication, and labor in the space of places and the time of clocks and daily life. "At its core, capital is global. As a rule, labor is local" (Castells, 2000b, p. 506). What becomes organized through networks is work, rather than labor. The work of organizations is carried on in network fashion. Each contributing member is a node, and the network as a whole can be made up of individuals; segments of businesses; or entire companies, large or small. They can be dispersed over thousands of miles and exist in different clock-time zones. All this and more can be coordinated for a single project, thus forming an informational network. As soon as the project is finished, the nodes are disconnected and reorganized for other work. The work process is thus globally integrated but fragmented locally, resulting in the individuation of labor, increased flexibility, and instability of work.

The organizational logic of communication and informational technologies has reformed *politics* as well. In most places around the world, people now get their information about political candidates through the media, which has become the platform for politics. In a media-saturated environment, capturing attention becomes the single most important scarce resource. Politics thus becomes personalized in the cult of personality, "and image-making is power-making" (Castells, 2000b, p. 507). In the spectacle of image, with a public (an audience) dulled by a constant barrage of images and information, the most effective messages are negative: "assassination of opponents' personalities, and/or of their supporting organizations" (Castells, 2000a, p. 13). Thus, the information of value in politics is anything that will spark a scandal. An entire network revolves around finding, protecting, and leaking this valued information. "Politics becomes a horse race, and a tragicomedy motivated by greed, backstage manoeuvres [sic], betrayals, and, often, sex and violence—a genre increasingly indistinguishable from TV scripts" (p. 13).

Politics cannot but influence the *state*, and the politics of spectacle and reliance on the media undermine its legitimacy and power. In response, personalities begin to build informational networks and systems of deference around themselves, further challenging the legitimacy of the state. State power is also challenged by the global flows of money and information. Part of this has to do with the pure size of capital flows and the volatility of money markets, but more basically, since the nation-state has always been defined in terms of "subordinating to orderly domination . . . a 'territory'" (Weber, 1922/1968, p. 901), the breakdown of time and space (territory) by the network society deeply undermines the power of the state. In response, states partner with other nations and build multinational and international organizational, informational networks, such as the World Trade Organization, NATO, the International Monetary Fund, and so on. The result is that "the new state is no longer a nation-state" (Castells, 2000a, p. 14); rather, it is a network state created out of negotiated decision making and power sharing.

Concepts and Theory: Networks, Identities, and Democracy

For Castells, *identities* are clusters of cultural traits that function to provide meaning for people. In order to see the implications of this, think back to the fundamental attributes of meaning from Chapter 6. Meaning isn't any *thing*—it isn't in an action or a word, it isn't inherent within an experience, nor is it located in any object. Rather, meaning is that which actions, words, and so on express or sign, and signs always point away from themselves—therefore, *meaning is never the thing-in-itself.* And meaning constitutes our reality: "No longer can man confront reality immediately. . . . [It] seems to recede in proportion as man's symbolic activity advances. Instead of dealing with the things themselves, man is in a sense constantly conversing with himself" (Cassirer, 1944, p. 42).

If meaning isn't the actual thing or event, then meaning is achieved or created, and one of the functions of identity is to provide a basis for the construction of biographical narratives of meaning. Castells (2004) defines three different types of identities: The first type, the *legitimizing identity,* is the kind found in the dominant institutions of society. Legitimations are stories or narratives that provide a moral or ethical basis for social power. Legitimizing identities, then, are those around which individuals construct meaning and a sense of self that are related to and legitimate civil society. Obvious examples include the president of the United States, corporate CEOs, male and female genders, heterosexuality, professor, and so on.

The second type in Castells' scheme is *resistance identity.* This type of identity normally comes out of a sense of exclusion from the institutions of civil society and is bound up with the formation of communities of resistance that give members a sense of solidarity and the ability to form countercultures and ideology. These communities and identities can center around such issues as religious views and other status inequities. Because they are resistance identities, they create strong boundaries of inclusion and exclusion and thus work to "exclude the excluders." It's important to note that resistance identities aren't necessarily concerned with social change; they are reactionary and seek to establish an identity where identity has been denied.

This is where the issue of meaning that we talked about above becomes important. Identities provide a meaningful ordering and framework for life. When identities are denied, or controlled to the point of redefining the person, the existential questions of life and purpose come to the forefront—conversely, when identities are unproblematic, the questions of existence are effectively silenced; legitimating identities don't tend to provoke existential questions in those claiming them. Under conditions of exclusion, resistance identities function as cultural, emotional, and psychological strongholds. Their purpose isn't to change, but to proclaim. Often these identities are born out of "the pride of self-denigration" (Castells, 2004, p. 9) and shout back at institutions with proclamations such as "black is beautiful" or "I am woman, hear me roar."

The third type of identity that concerns Castells is the *project identity*. This is an identity associated with social projects of change: "In this case, the building of identity is a project of a different life" (Castells, 2004, p. 10). Project identities produce subjects, but subjects, Castells is very clear about, are not individuals. Webster's (2002) defines *subject* variously as "the material from which a thing is formed," "the theme of a discourse or predication," "something that sustains or is embodied in thought or consciousness," or "something that forms a basis (as for action, study, discussion, or use)." Castells' use of the term *subject* captures all of the above. Subjects are collective actors that form the material of our sense of self and our involvement with the world. These subjects are the themes of the discourse of social change; they are the mental and emotional focus through which identity and meaning are sustained in consciousness; and, especially in the case of project identities, the subject forms the basis for action, study, and discussion.

The Network Society and the Crisis in Democracy

Castells (2004) defines *civil society* as "a set of organizations and institutions, as well as a series of structured and organized social actors, which reproduce . . . the identity that rationalizes the sources of structural domination" (p. 8). While civil society isn't identical with the state, it exists in relation to the state; and the state is the "object of citizenship" (p. 402). However, the state is suffering a crisis of legitimation in the network society. Its sovereignty has been undermined by "global flows and trans-organizational networks of wealth, information, and power" (p. 402); by the spectacle of politics; and by the state's increasing inability to fulfill its commitments to the safety net of minimal benefits, including unemployment, retirement income, health care coverage, insuring bank deposits, and so forth. These effects of the network society have created a crisis of legitimation for the nation-state and, by extension, legitimizing identities and democracy.

There are two important effects growing out of this legitimation crisis. First, "A growing majority of citizens do not feel that democracy will help them very much in addressing the issues that confront them in their daily lives" (Castells, 2004, p. 413). One measure of this is what is commonly called voter apathy. In 1960, about 61 percent of the television sets in the United States were tuned to the October presidential debates, and voter turnout for the presidential election was almost 65 percent of the adult population. By the year 2000, fewer than 30 percent of the televisions tuned to the presidential debates, and voter turnout had dropped to 51 percent (Patterson, 2002).

The second outcome of the legitimation crisis is the ascent of resistance identities. Remember how Castells conceptualizes identities: They function to create meaning. In this case, resistance identities are created to counter the loss of meaning and direction that accompanies the legitimation crisis. To help us get a clear sense of resistance identities in the network society, let's think through the example of gender in Western nations. Prior to the women's suffrage movement of the 1800s and early 1900s, being a "woman" was by and large a legitimizing identity. The identity bound all women together and situated them in the discourse of patriarchy. The identity thus legitimated the family structure as well as the unequal power relations between men and women. The suffrage movements worked to create a project identity committed to gaining equal rights for women, in particular, the right to vote and the right to higher education. In the 1960s, a second wave of feminism emerged to address the unofficial discrimination and inequalities that still existed for women. Equal opportunities for work and political power, equal pay, cultural representations, and control over their bodies were some of the issues. Both the first and second waves of feminism had project identities.

Beginning in the early 1990s, another wave of feminism arose, mostly among young women who had grown up with benefits achieved by the first two waves of feminism. These women also were most affected by the new information and communication technologies. Feminism for these women is different. Rather than having specific political, economic, or social goals, third-wave feminism challenges the definitions of woman, femininity, and feminism, which are seen as creating a sense that all women are essentially the same. All essentializing theories are rejected, including feminist theory, gender theory, conflict theory, and so on. The focus is on deconstructing such totalizing identities and discourses and insisting on diversity. Rather than either a legitimizing or project identity, third-wave feminism denies the possibility of a woman's identity: "Since no monolithic version of 'woman' exists, we can no longer speak with confidence of 'women's issues'; instead, we need to consider that such issues are as diverse as the many women who inhabit our planet" (Dicker & Piopmeier, 2006, p. 107).

While being able to trace the history of feminist identity is enlightening, most resistance identities don't have this evolving background. Today, most resistance identities are formed around such things as religious fundamentalism, geographic region, music styles, and so on. An example that has both region and music is found in Jeff Foxworthy's comments at the 2007 Country Music Television awards ceremony, held in Nashville, Tennessee. Here are a few lines from his speech:

> I like country music because it's about the things in life that really matter. . . . It's about love, family, friends, with a few beers. . . . It doesn't take political sides even on things as ugly as war. Instead, it celebrates the men and women who go to fight 'em. . . . It's about kids and how there ain't nothing like 'em. . . . Country folks love their kids and they will jack you up if you try

> to mess with 'em. . . . Country music doesn't have to be politically correct. We sing about God because we believe in Him. . . . It's real music, sung by real people for real people. The people that make up the backbone of this country. . . . You can call us rednecks if you want, we're not offended, 'cause we know what we are all about. We get up and go to work, we get up and go to church, and we get up and go to war when necessary. (Foxworthy, quoted in Martin, 2007)

Foxworthy defined the country music identity by "building trenches of resistance and survival on the basis of principles different from, or opposed to, those permeating the institutions of society" (Castells, 2004, p. 8). Without specifically saying so, the statement builds strong boundaries of exclusion for anyone outside country music or the values proclaimed, and it simultaneously builds a sense of community and solidarity for country music fans. Within that solidarity, it allows little if any diversity: "In contrast to pluralistic, differentiated civil societies, cultural communes display little internal differentiation" (p. 70). That is one of the qualities of resistance identities: They provide a strong cultural center, a clear sense of right and wrong, a solid ground for meaning.

Resistance identities in the network society are acts of cultural resistance, with no real political or economic goals. Much like a third-wave feminist concerned with expressing gender, Foxworthy's country music fan is concerned with the meanings surrounding identity. They both draw a line in the sand and proclaim, this is who I am. Moreover, as you can see with both examples, resistance identities are individualized. There's a sense of cultural community that accompanies these identities, and there are clear meanings associated with them, but neither of them requires or implies that members actually group together. You can be a country music fan and believe in the boundaries that Foxworthy proclaims, and never once get together with other fans. Further, if and when you do get together, the focus will probably be on music and beer, "With a cheap woman and two timin' man thrown in for spice" (Foxworthy, quoted in Martin, 2007). The center of discussion would probably not be political activism. If you do talk about ideas or values with which you disagree, it likely won't be with any intent of creating a project to bring about change. It will simply be a ritual that generates high levels of emotional energy that will make your identity and beliefs feel more sacred. Resistance identities thus create a strong sense of meaning in a world where meanings are becoming delegitimized and fragmented.

With the sources of legitimizing identities weakened or gone, the shared identities necessary for democracy are no longer present. Further, and this is extremely important to note, project identities in and of themselves are suffering the same fate as legitimizing identities, because both share the same social basis: the civil sphere and democratic government defined by the nation-state. What Castells' theory implies is that that form of society is gone or receding; social connections now are being made through the network society that is not bounded or limited by the state. The structural, systemic bases of participatory democracy as understood from the eighteenth century through the ending decades of the twentieth are gone. And resistance identities by themselves are nothing more than emotional constructs that give individuals and small groups a sense of meaning and purpose.

However, resistance identities can form the basis of new project identities. In fact, Castells (2004) argues that resistance identities could "be *the main potential source* of social change in the network society" (p. 70, emphasis added). These new project identities do not come out of the industrial era's "identities of civil society" (p. 422) but may emerge from the intense interactions around cultural resistance. For example, while there's an emphasis on choice in what passes as gender (expressions of femininity) in third-wave feminism, there are also a good number of third wavers who are deeply involved in political activism, not always for women's rights. So, for instance, a third-wave feminist may have a project identity built around environmental issues—specifically feminist-as-environmentalist—yet at the same time she expresses her gender identity as resistance. However, there is nothing about resistance identities that necessarily imply project identities. Resistance identities thus represent a further danger to the idea of participatory democracy. Rather than creating new project identities, these resistance communes could simply maintain their inward gaze, occupied only with keeping the meaningfulness of their own identities. Castells (2004) ironically characterizes such narcissism as "inducing a process that might transform communal heavens into heavenly hells" (p. 70).

Among the resistance identities Castells (2004) lists as possibilities for project identities are religious communes, ethnicity, gender, territorial identities, environmentalism, and so on. Again, please notice that the content—what the identity is about—is virtually unimportant, in terms of it being the basis of a project identity. The deciding factor between resistance and project identities is the intent to bring change. In other words, project identities have projects. Project identities in the network society, however, don't generally work the same as in industrial society. As we've seen, the network society implies a new form of power. Rather than the political power of civil society, network power resides in codes of information and images of representation. Conflict over power in the network society is a battle for people's minds: "Whoever, or whatever, wins the battle of people's minds will rule, because mighty, rigid apparatuses will not be a match, in any reasonable timespan, for the minds mobilized around the power of flexible, alternative networks" (Castells, 2004, p. 425).

According to Castells, there are two types of *symbol mobilizers,* those social actors able to influence information and imagery. First, there are the Prophets, symbolic personalities that can create information and imagery and mobilize the network. Recent examples include Bono of U2 (and his work on AIDS and developing nation debt forgiveness), Angelina Jolie (protesting use of landmines, helping refugees), and Sting (and his work with Amazonia, helping to save the Amazon rainforests). The second and more important avenue for mobilizing symbols and information around project identities is the decentralized activity of the network itself. The Internet can of course be used to gather people together for rallies, demonstrations, and so on. But its greatest impact is on people's awareness, thinking, and feelings about the project issue. In contrast to the Prophet motif, this "impact on society rarely stems from a concerted strategy, masterminded by a center" (Castells, 2004, p. 427). Decentralized, flexible networks of information and communication around issues of environmentalism, women's lives, sweatshop working conditions, refugees, human rights violations, and so on, produce and distribute news, ideas, insights, explanations, strategies, and images around the world, thus impacting the way people see and interface with the world.

This network of social change is the breeding ground for a *new democracy*. Its form is different, without the "orderly battalions, colorful banners, and scripted proclamations" (Castells, 2004, p. 428) of civil society, and it's thus difficult to recognize. But for the same reason, there is a continuing

> subtle pervasiveness of incremental changes of symbols processed through multiform networks, away from the halls of power. It is in those back alleys of society, whether in alternative electronic networks or in grassrooted networks of communal resistance, that I have sensed the embryos of a new society, labored in the fields of history by the power of identity. (Castells, 2004, p. 428)

Summary

- Castells argues that society and capitalism went through significant restructuring between the 1970s and 1990s. Essential to this restructuring were new information technologies. This new technology lifted capital and social relations from the embeddedness of time and space—they redefined the material basis of human life—and allowed for an almost infinite number of reconstructions. The accumulation of capital shifted then from production to financial flows. Capital is then invested globally, following interests of greatest return, which are increasingly based on speculation and money markets rather than real goods and services.

- The basis of social connections changed and is now subject to the logic of networks. Within this logic, connections are created by nodes rather than people situated in time and place. A node is important because of the amount of information it holds and processes or the way it connects to other elements within the network. Actual people as traditionally understood in terms of a situated lifeworld become of secondary importance: A person becomes important in the network as he or she functions as a network node.

- Thus power in a network is determined by a node's ability to find, hold, and process information and, more importantly, the node's ability to act as a switch between informational networks. Class is established more by a node's capability to organize work or direct flows of speculative capital than by production. Politics in the network society are a function of image-making and negative information, which is able to capture attention in the network. The politics of the state, then, are dependent upon network-based media personalities. The sovereignty of the state is also deconstructed by the importance of global flows of money and information, both of which fall outside the ability of the state to regulate efficiently.

- As a result of these changes in power and politics, the legitimacy of the state is questioned. And as a result of this crisis in legitimation, the majority of citizens no longer believe that traditional democracy addresses the problems faced in daily life. Additionally, resistance identities become increasingly important. In the network society there are three forms of identity: legitimating, resistance, and project. Legitimating and project identities are based on the modern ideal of state based emancipatory politics; the former established and the latter seek to reform the distribution of civil rights. As the centrality of the state and emancipatory politics decline, so do the importance and power of legitimating and project identities. Resistance identities—which are formed around existential questions and meaning— ascend in practice and significance. However, in and of themselves, resistance identities are not political and are individualized, which in turn threatens the possibility of participatory democracy. However, in the network society resistance identities represent the best possibility for the reforming of project identities. Resistance identities can be used to mobilize information and imagery, which can bring incremental changes and shifts in network power.

TAKING THE PERSPECTIVE—INFORMATION THEORY

Castells is one of those unique theorists for whom there is little antecedent and little if any extended work. The focus of this theory is simply too new. However, generally speaking, his concerns are well founded in the history of social theory. From the outset, sociological theorists have been concerned with defining and then analyzing society. As noted in Chapter 1, the idea of society as a macro level entity existing above and influencing face-to-face social situations is distinctly modern. And early sociologists spent a good deal of theoretical energy defining and explicating the dynamics of such an entity; it is most explicitly present in Durkheim's work. That approach is where we get our notions of social structure and institutions. However, all that work had as its background assumption the defining feature of the nation-state—society in modern terms is intrinsically linked to the democratic state defined by territory and the exclusive use of legitimated coercive power. Castells' work, even more than Wallerstein's, proposes a new base for and understanding of society.

Castells is also concerned with identity, which, again, is a central issue of modern theorists. Stuart Hall (1996) notes that identity in the Enlightenment "was based on a conception of the human person as a fully centered, unified individual, endowed with the capacities of reason, consciousness, and action" (p. 597). This sense of identity, then, became the basis of the citizen and national identity; an American, for example, capable of participatory democracy. This notion of identity, as well, was based upon the sovereignty of the state, an institution where the politics of democracy could be played out and legitimated power of the state could be directed toward equality and social justice.

As we've seen, Castells argues for a new and different basis of society and thus identity. Society—social connections—are no longer based on identities that are situated and lived in real time and place. Rather, he argues that the majority of our sociability is created through information technology networks, which transcend national borders and thus redefine power, class, and politics. So, while his concerns are clearly modern and well established, he takes us in new directions and asks that we rethink the ideas that have dominated and led the social sciences for almost 200 years.

(Continued)

(Continued)

In terms of his theoretical approach, Castells means his theory to be used as an analytic heuristic, somewhat like Bourdieu in intent. This approach implies two things. First, unlike Wallerstein, Castells' theory isn't meant to be predictive; rather, it's a way of seeing and analyzing the social world. Second, the theory is a "work in progress open to rectification by empirical research" (Castells, 2000a, p. 6). His work, then, is quite literally intended to provide ideas and concepts "to be used in the building of a sociological theory able to grasp emerging forms of social organization and conflict" (p. 6).

BUILDING YOUR THEORY TOOLBOX

Learning More—Primary and Secondary Sources

- Primary sources for Immanuel Wallerstein: He built his theory through three volumes of historical data (*The Modern World-System*, vols. 1–3). The historical breadth is impressive and convincing, but I would suggest you begin your reading of Wallerstein with his later works:
  - *The End of the World as We Know It: Social Science for the Twenty-First Century*, University of Minnesota Press, 1999.
  - *World-Systems Analysis: An Introduction*, Duke University Press, 2004.
- Wallerstein secondary source:
  - A good chapter-length introduction to this perspective is provided by Christopher Chase-Dunn, "World-Systems Theorizing," in *Handbook of Sociological Theory*, edited by Jonathan H. Turner, Kluwer, 2002.
- Primary sources for Manuel Castells: The foundation of Castell's work is found in his three-volume work concerning the network society:
  - *The Rise of the Network Society, The Power of Identity, and The End of Millennium*.
- Castells secondary sources: Though portions of Castells' work appear in many texts, there are very few secondary sources focused exclusively on him. I can suggest the following:
  - *Manuel Castells (Key Contemporary Thinkers)*, by Felix Stalder, Polity Press, 2006.
  - *Conversations With Manuel Castells*, by Castells and Martin Ince, Polity Press, 2003.

Seeing the Social World (knowing the theory)

- Write a 250-word synopsis of the theoretical perspective of world-systems theory.
- Write a 250-word synopsis of the theoretical perspective used in the network society.

- After reading and understanding this chapter, you should be able to define the following terms theoretically and explain their theoretical importance to world-systems analysis: *modern capitalism, globalization, systems, exploitation, dialectical materialism, division of labor, externalized costs, quasi-monopolies, overproduction, world-empires, world-economies, core states, periphery states, semi-periphery states, Kondratieff waves, world-systems theory.*

- After reading and understanding this chapter, you should be able to define the following terms theoretically and explain their theoretical importance to Castells' theory of the network society: *keynesian economics, information technology, the logic of networks, annihilation of time and place, power, class, politics, identities, legitimizing identity, resistance identity, project identity, civil society, symbol mobilizers, new democracy.*

- After reading and understanding this chapter, you should be able to answer the following questions (remember to answer them *theoretically*):

  ○ What are the central features that link national economies into a global system?

  ○ In what ways do states externalize costs and help create quasi-monopolies?

  ○ What are the Marxian economic dynamics in back of the relationships among the core, semi-periphery, periphery, and external areas? Explain how these dynamics work and how they are related to the demise of capitalism.

  ○ What are Kondratieff waves and how do they factor into global changes?

  ○ Beginning with the events in 1968, explain Wallerstein's crisis of modernity. What are the structural and cultural signs that the system is failing?

  ○ In the face of this crisis, what recommendations does Wallerstein have for political involvement? Be certain to explain his rationale for saying these recommendations will influence the system.

- After reading and understanding this chapter, you should be able to answer the following questions (remember to answer them *theoretically*):

  ○ Explain how three major technological advances have fundamentally influenced knowledge and information. Pay special attention to how the logic of networks has altered the way in which people are socially organized.

  ○ Explain how computer/information technologies have fundamentally altered power, politics, and class.

  ○ Explain how the sovereignty of the state is challenged through computer/information technologies.

  ○ Clarify the differences among legitimizing, resistance, and project identities.

  ○ Explain how civil society has changed as a result of computer and information technologies. In your explanation be sure to explicate the new democracy.

(Continued)

(Continued)

Engaging the Social World (using the theory)

- In reference to his work, Wallerstein (2000) has said, "My intellectual biography is one long question for an adequate explanation of contemporary reality that I and others might act upon" (p. xv). In keeping with Wallerstein, I have only one question to put to you: After reading Wallerstein, how will you engage your world? (Remember, small inputs can have large effects.)

- Use Castell's notions about legitimizing, resistance, and project identities to analyze at least three identities you claim.

- Using your explanation of how civil society has changed, draw out at least three implications for democracy. In other words, how has the possibility of democracy changed as a result of the process involved in the network society?

- Propose a project that would fit into Castells' notion of the new democracy. The project topic can be anything, so pick something you really care about. Using Castells' theory, explain how your project could potentially influence society.

- Speculate about possible effects of Castells' idea of the network society on sociology and other social disciplines.

Weaving the Threads (building theory)

- Using Wallerstein and Castells, explain how democracy and politics have changed as a result of globalization. How has the state been decentered from the social project of modernity? How have political identities and personal practices been redefined?

- How is the modern idea of society challenged by Castells and Wallerstein? How would you now define society?

- In Chapters 13 and 14 I asked you to write an analysis of modern democracy using Habermas and Giddens, respectively. Do the same for Wallerstein and Castells (write a separate analysis for each).

- How has capitalism changed as a result of the network society? Focus your discussion on capital and class.

- Compare and contrast Wallerstein's and Castell's theories in terms of political involvement. Which do you think is more viable and why?

- Compare and contrast Castell's theory of politics and identities with that of Wilson and Chafetz. What does the network society imply about the identities and politics of race and gender?

CHAPTER 16

Upsetting Reality:

Michel Foucault
and Jean Baudrillard

But what if empirical knowledge ... obeyed, at a given moment, the laws of a certain code of knowledge? ... The fundamental codes of a culture ... establish for every man, from the very first, the empirical orders with which he will be dealing and within which he will be at home.

—Foucault, 1966/1994b, pp. ix, xx

The systems of reference for production, signification, the affect, substance and history, all this equivalence to a "real" content, load-ing the sign with the burden of "utility," with gravity—its form of representative equivalence—all this is over with.

—Baudrillard, 1976/1993b, p. 6

Modernity began with a strong sense of what was real. No longer under the dominion of religion, humankind felt free to discover the reality of the empirical world. The Enlightenment was founded on the idea that the universe existed empirically and that science could be used to discover its laws. Science, then, was seen as the purest of languages, able to simply and only reflect empirical reality. We've already looked at many of the developments of the twentieth century that cast doubt on the projects of modernity, and I won't belabor them here. Suffice it to say that by the closing decades of that century reality didn't seem as sure. The idea of the social construction of reality had taken firm hold and we became aware of the influence that mass media can have on culture and language; and in the end language itself came under scrutiny. The theories of the two men in this chapter are probably responsible more than any other for this shift in certainty. Michel Foucault is one of the founding thinkers in poststructuralism, and Jean Baudrillard exemplifies postmodernism better than anyone else. However, losing one's reality can have liberating effects, in some cases (it's always difficult to be definite with either of these perspectives).

I mentioned the linguistic turn in Chapter 12 and in both these theories we have strong statements of this shift. Both of these men approach the issues of signs and language differently, but what I want to point out here is that their work heralds a fundamental shift in the way social theorists think about culture. Rather than understanding culture and language within a social context, such as in symbolic interactions or symbolic markets, texts are understood on their own terms, as social factors in and of themselves. In this perspective, culture and cultural readings become fundamentally important. The radical postmodern thread in this linguistic turn is that readings of texts are themselves seen as texts, which means that since humans are defined through meaning, all we have are texts. Foucault's poststructuralism, on the other hand, sees texts as ways through which power is exercised over individual subjects.

Defining the Possible and Impossible:
Michel Foucault (1926–1984)

Theorist's Digest
Concepts and Theory: The Truth About Truth
  Why So Critical?
Concepts and Theory: The Practices of Power
  The Power of Order
  The Power of Discourse
  The Power of Objectification
Concepts and Theory: Disciplining the Body
  The Discipline of the Human Sciences
  The Discipline of Medicine
  Disciplining Sex
Summary
Taking the Perspective—Poststructuralism

Foucault is a complex thinker and writer. As a result, trying to summarize Foucault's theory can be a frustrating experience. In writing this chapter, I had a continuing sense of incompletion. The more I wrote, the more I felt that I was leaving out. I mention this because I know that what I'm presenting in this book is a pared down version of Foucault. Yet I believe that in focusing on a select few of Foucault's major points, I can convey some sense of what he was trying to accomplish.

Stated succinctly, Foucault is interested in how power is exercised through knowledge or "truth," and how truth is formed through practice (note that with Foucault, we can use knowledge and truth interchangeably). His interest in truth isn't abstract or philosophical. Rather, Foucault is interested in analyzing what he calls *truth games*. His use of "games" isn't meant to imply that what passes as truth in any historical time is somehow false or simply a construction of language. Foucault feels that these kinds of questions can only be answered, let alone asked, after historically specific assumptions are made. In other words, something can only be "false" once a specific truth is assumed, and Foucault is involved in uncovering *how* truth is assumed. Specifically, Foucault's interest in truth concerns the game of truth: the rules, resources, and practices that go into making something true for humans.

The idea of *practice* is fairly broad and includes such things as institutional and organizational practices as well as those of academic disciplines—in these practices, truth is formed. The idea also refers to specific practices of the body and self—these are where power is exercised. Most of us use the word "practice" to talk about the behaviors we engage in to prepare for an event, such as band practice for a show. But practice has another meaning as well. This meaning is clear when we talk about a medical practice. When you go to your physician, you see someone who is "practicing" medicine. In this sense, practice refers to choreographed acts that interact with bodies—sets of behaviors that together define a way of doing something. This is the kind of practice in which Foucault is interested.

THEORIST'S DIGEST

Brief Biography

We should begin this brief biography by noting that Foucault would balk at the idea that we need to know anything about the author in order to understand his work. Further, Foucault would say that any history of the author is something that we use in order to validate a particular reading or interpretation. Having said that, Foucault was born on October 15, 1926, in Poitiers, France. Foucault studied at the École Normale Supérieure and the Institut de Psychologie in Paris. In 1960, returning to France from teaching posts in Sweden, Warsaw, and Hamburg, Foucault published *Madness and Civilization*, for which he received France's highest academic degree, doctorat d'État. In 1966, Foucault published *The Order of Things*,

(Continued)

(Continued)

which became a best-selling book in France. In 1970, Foucault received a permanent appointment at the Collège de France (France's most prestigious school) as chair of History of Systems of Thought. In 1975, Foucault published *Discipline and Punishment* and took his first trip to California, which came to hold an important place in Foucault's life, especially San Francisco. In 1976, Foucault published the first volume of his last major work, *The History of Sexuality.* The two other volumes of this history, *The Use of Pleasure* and *The Care of the Self*, were published shortly before Foucault's death in 1984.

Central Sociological Questions

In Foucault's (1984/1990b) own words, "As for what motivated me.... It was curiosity—the only kind of curiosity, in any case, that is worth acting upon with a degree of obstinacy: not the curiosity that seeks to assimilate what it is proper for one to know, but that which enables one to get free of oneself. After all, what would be the value of the passion for knowledge if it resulted only in a certain amount of knowledgeableness and not, in one way or another and to the extent possible, in the knower's straying afield of himself?" (p. 8). In brief, Foucault was interested in how ideas and subjectivities come into existence and how they limit what is possible. But Foucault's search was not simply academic, though it was that. As the above quote tells us, Foucault sought to understand his own practices "in relationship of self with self and the forming of oneself as a subject" (p. 6).

Simply Stated

Foucault's basic premise is that human reality is language. There's an old adage that says "There are three sides to every story: yours, mine, and the truth." Because language is human reality, Foucault would say that there are only two sides; the truth of any event or thing isn't available to humans because of our deep dependence on and use of language. This implies that any claim to represent the truth (such as my trying to convince you that my story is the right one) is an expression of power. Social power is expressed and imposed through what passes as legitimated knowledge, which orders the world around us, and through discourse, which orders our subjective positions. Modernity brought with it a specific kind of power in that the individual disciplines himself or herself—modern power is practiced from within. Modern power is also distinct in that the person is objectified by these internal practices.

Key Ideas

truth games, counter-histories, archaeology, Genealogy, Episteme, Discourse, governmentality, objectification, panopticon, microphysics of power, medical gaze

Concepts and Theory: The Truth About Truth

Foucault uncovers truth games by constructing what he calls *counter-histories*. When most of us think of history, we think of a factual telling of events from the past. We are aware, of course, that sometimes that telling can be politicized, which is one reason we have "Black History Month" here in the United States—we are trying to make up for having left people of color out of our telling of history. But most of us also think that the memory model is still intact; it's just getting a few tweaks. Foucault wants us to free history from the model of memory. He really doesn't say anything directly about whether any particular history is more or less true; that's not an issue for him. History in all its forms is both part of and generated by discourse. Thus, Foucault's concern is how the *idea* of true history is used. What Foucault wants to produce for us is a *counter-history*—a history told from a different point of view from the progressive, linear, memory model.

The important questions then become, why is one path taken rather than another? Why is the present filled with one kind of discourse rather than others? And what has been the cost of taking this path rather than all the other potentialities? Thus, a counter-history identifies

> the accidents, the minute deviations—or conversely, the complete reversals—
> the errors, the false appraisals, and the faulty calculations that gave birth to
> those things that continue to exist and have value for us; it is to discover that
> truth or being does not lie at the root of what we know and what *we are,* but
> the exteriority of accidents. (Foucault, 1984a, p. 81)

Foucault uses two terms to talk about his counter-history: archaeology and genealogy. Though the distinctions are sometimes unclear, *archaeology* seems to be oriented toward uncovering the relationships among social institutions, practices, and knowledge that come to produce a particular kind of discourse or structure of thought. *Genealogy* may be better suited to describe Foucault's (1984a) work that is concerned with the actual inscription of discourse and power on the mind and body: "Genealogy, as an analysis of descent, is thus situated within the articulation of the body and history. Its task is to expose a body totally imprinted by history and the process of history's destruction of the body" (p. 83). We could say that archaeology is to text what genealogy is to the body. In both cases, there is an analogy to digging, searching, and uncovering the hidden history of order, thought, madness, sexuality, and so on. The hidden history isn't necessarily more accurate— it's simply a counter-story that is constructed more in an archaeological mode than a historical one.

Why So Critical?

What is Foucault's point in constructing counter-histories? Part of what Foucault wants to do with counter-histories is expose the contingencies of what we consider reality, but to what end? Many critical perspectives are based on assumptions of what would make a better society. In other words, there must be something to which the current situation is compared to demonstrate what it is lacking. But Foucault sees it otherwise. For him, the critical perspective in itself is sufficient because it opens up possibilities. In fact, Foucault would argue that a utopian scheme only attempts to replace one system of impoverishment with another. *The point is to keep possibilities always open, to keep people critically examining their life and knowledge system so that they can perpetually be open to the possibility of something else.*

According to Foucault's scheme, an important part of what creates knowledge, order, and discourse is the presence of "blank spaces." Foucault (1966/1994b) pictures knowledge as a kind of grid. The boxes in the grid are the actual linguistic categories, such as mammal, flora, mineral, human, black, white, male, and female. We are familiar with those sections; they form part of our everyday language. However, there is actually a more important part of the grid, the one that creates the order—the blank spaces between the categories. "It is only in the blank spaces of this grid that order manifests itself in depth as though already there, waiting in silence for the moment of its expression" (p. xx). The true power of a discourse or knowledge system is in the spaces between the categories. As Eviatar Zerubavel (1991) notes,

> separating one island of meaning from another entails the introduction of some mental void between them. . . . It is our perception of the void among these islands of meaning that makes them separate in our mind, and its magnitude reflects the degree of separateness we perceive among them. (pp. 21–22)

These spaces are revealed most clearly in transgression. As an illustration, let's think about a little boy of about 3 or 4 years of age. He is a playful boy, playing with the toys he's been given and emulating the role models he sees on TV and among the neighborhood children. But one day his father comes home and finds him playing with a doll. His father grabs the toy away and tells his son firmly that boys do not play with dolls. In this instance, the category of gender was almost invisible until the young boy unwittingly attempted to cross over the boundary or space between the categories. The meaning and power of gender waited "in silence for the moment of its expression."

This idea of space is provocative. A more Durkheimian way of thinking about categories would conceptualize the space between them as a boundary or wall. Using the idea of boundary to think about the division between categories is fruitful: Walls separate and prevent passing. The young boy in our example certainly came up against a wall, and many of us have felt the walls of gender, race, or sexism. But the idea of walls makes the use of categories and knowledge seem objective, as if they somehow exist apart from us, and this is not what Foucault has in mind.

Notice that the boy in our example was unaware of the "wall" until his father showed it to him. From Foucault's position, the wall of gender was erected in the father's gendered practices. Foucault's idea of space helps us think about the practices of power. Space, in this sense, is empty until it is filled—seeing space between categories rather than a wall makes us wait to see what will go there and *how* it goes there. Space is undetermined. Something can be built in space, but the space itself calls our attention to potential. Foucault's research, his critical archaeology, fills in that potential—he tells us how that space became historically constructed in one way rather than any of the other potential ways.

Foucault's counterhistory actually creates a space of its own. On one side, Foucault's archaeology of modernity uncovers the fundamental codes of thought that establish for all of us the order that we will use in our world. On the other side, Foucault sets the sciences and philosophical interpretations that explain why such an order exists. Between these two domains is a space of possibilities, a space wherein a critical culture can develop that sufficiently frees itself "to discover that these orders are perhaps not the only possible ones or the best ones" (Foucault, 1966/1994b, p. xx).

In other words, through the archaeology of knowledge, Foucault wants to not only expose the codes of knowledge that undergird everything we do, feel, and think, he also wants to set loose the idea that things might not be as they are. He wants to free the possibility of thinking something different. That possibility of thought exists in the critical space between—but in this case the space isn't specified, as it is in already existing orders. Foucault doesn't necessarily have a place he is taking us; he doesn't really have a utopian vision of what knowledge and practice ought to be. His critique is aimed at freeing knowledge and creating possibility; it's aimed at creating an empty space that is undetermined.

Concepts and Theory: The Practices of Power

According to Foucault, power isn't something that a person possesses; rather, it is something that is part of every relationship. Foucault tells us that there are three types of domains or practices within relationships: communicative, objective, and power. Communication is directed toward producing meaning; objective practices are directed toward controlling and transforming things—science and economy are two good examples; and practices of power, which Foucault (1982) defines as "a set of actions upon other actions" (p. 220), are directed toward controlling the actions and subjectivities of people. Notice where Foucault locates power—it's within the actions themselves, not within the powerful person or the social structure. Foucault uses the double meaning of "conduct" to get at this insight: Conduct is a way of leading others (to conduct an orchestra, for example) and also a way of behaving (as in "Tommy conducted himself in a manner worthy of his position."). Thus, we conduct others through our conduct.

However, Foucault's intent is not to reduce power to the mundane, the simple organization of human behavior across time and place. Rather, Foucault's point is that power is exercised in a variety of ways, many of which we are unaware. Power, then, becomes insidious. Power acts in the normalcy of everyday life. It acts by imperceptible degrees, exerting gradual and hidden effects. In this way, the exercise of power entices us into a snare that feels of our own doing. But how is power exercised? Where does it exist and how are we enticed? Foucault argues that power is exercised through the epistemes (underlying order) and discourses found in what passes as knowledge. The potential and practice of power exists in these epistemes and discourses that set the limits of what is possible and impossible, which in turn are felt and expressed through a person's relationship with himself or herself, in subjectivities—the way we feel about and relate to our inner self—and the disposition of the body.

The Power of Order

Order is an interesting idea. We order our days and lives; we order our homes and offices; we order our files and our bank accounts; we order our yards and shopping centers; we order land and sea—in short, humans order everything. How do we order things? One of the ways is linguistically: "Indeed, things become meaningful only when placed in some category" (Zerubavel, 1991, p. 5). But a deeper and more fundamental question can be asked: How do we order the order of things? In other words, what scheme or system underlies and creates our categorical schemes? We may use categories to order the world around us, but where do the categories get their order?

To introduce us to this question, Foucault (1966/1994b) tells a delightful story of reading a book containing a Chinese categorical system that divides animals into those "(a) belonging to the Emperor, (b) embalmed, (c) tame, (d) sucking pigs, (e) sirens, (f) fabulous, (g) stray dogs, (h) included in the present classification, (i) frenzied, (j) innumerable, (k) drawn with a very fine camelhair brush, (l) et cetera, (m) having just broken the water pitcher, (n) that from a long way off look like flies" (p. xv). The thing that struck Foucault about this system of categories was the limitation of his own thinking—"the stark impossibility of thinking *that*" (p. xv, emphasis original). In response, Foucault asks an important set of questions: What sets the boundaries of what is possible and impossible to think? Where do these boundaries originate? What is the price of these impossibilities—what is gained and what is lost?

Foucault argues that there is a fundamental code to culture, a code that orders language, perception, values, practices, and all that gives order to the world around us. He calls these fundamental codes epistemological fields, or the episteme of knowledge in any age. Episteme refers to the mode of thought's existence, or the way in which thought organizes itself in any historical moment. An episteme is the necessary precondition of thought. It is what exists before thought and that which makes thought possible. This foundation of thought is not held consciously. It is undoubtedly this preconscious character of the episteme that makes thought believable and ideas seem true.

Moreover, rather than seeing thought and knowledge as results of historical, linear processes, Foucault argues that discontinuity marks changes in knowledge. Most of us think that the knowledge we hold accumulated over time, that we have thrown out the false knowledge and replaced it with true knowledge as we have progressively learned how things work. This evolutionary view of knowledge actually comes from the culture of science. It is the way we *want* to see our knowledge, not necessarily the way it is. Foucault argues that knowledge doesn't progress linearly. Rather, what we know and how we know it is linked to historically specific patterns of behavior, institutional arrangements, and economic and social practices that set the rules and conditions of discourse and the limits of our possibilities. And that historical path is marked by rupture: discontinuities and sudden, radical changes.

Think about this: What is Foucault saying that hasn't been said before? Others have said that knowledge is socially constructed. But Foucault is saying that this idea of rupture implies that knowledge and truth are purely functions of institutional arrangements and practices and not the result of any real quest for truth. Thus, what counts as truth in any age—our own included—comes about through historically unique practices and institutional configurations. This implies not only that knowledge is socially constructed, but also, and more importantly, that *knowledge is nothing more and nothing less than the exercise of power*. This pure power is put into effect through discourse and the taken-for-granted ordering of human life.

The Power of Discourse

Discourse refers to languages and behaviors that are specific to a social issue, such as the discourse of race. In simple terms, a discourse is a way of talking about things. If you want to discuss music with a group of musicians, for instance, there is an acceptable discourse or language that you would use. It would include such words as *key, modes, transposing*, and so on. This discourse would be different from the one you would use to talk about baseball. You wouldn't normally tell your baseball team to hit the field and "tune up," nor would you tell a violinist to "bunt."

Foucault's interest in the idea of discourse is a bit more significant. First, he wants us to see beneath the surface of the word choice between "bunt" and "tune up." Foucault is interested in the rules and practices that underlie the words and ideas that we use. Discourse sets the possibilities of thought and existence. There is an obvious link between language and thought: We think in language. So, a discourse, with its underlying rules and practices, gives us a language with which to think and talk. That's a commonsensical statement, and we might be tempted just to accept it at face value. But using discourse as the basis of thought sets the boundaries of what is possible and impossible for us to think, so it is more profound than it might first appear.

The second thing that discourse does is to determine the position a person or object must occupy *in order to become the subject of a statement*. "I'm a man" is such a statement. For me to be a man, I must meet the conditions of existence that are set down in the discourse of gender. I not only have to meet those conditions for you; I must meet them for me as well, because the discourse sets out the conditions of subjectivity—how we think and feel about our self. Subjects, and the accompanying inner thoughts and feelings, are specific conditions within the discourse. As we locate ourselves within a discourse, we become subject to the discourse and thus subjectively answer ourselves through the discourse.

This work of positioning that discourse accomplishes is one of its most powerful acts. Think about it this way: It is extremely difficult to talk to someone about anything without positioning yourself within a discourse. There are discourses surrounding sports, family, gender, race, class, self-improvement, medicine, mass media, cars, trucks, and on and on. Once you begin to converse using a discourse, you automatically occupy a position within it that tells you how to think, feel, and act. For example, the modern discourse of gender tells me what I can and can't feel as a man. Here's a more provocative example: If you feel "sick," you have already positioned yourself within the modern medical discourse (compare this feeling to magical or religious discourses that define such things as spiritual possessions).

The third thing that Foucault wants us to see about discourse is that it is used instead of coercive force to impose order on a social group. Critically speaking, social order is always a problem for the elite in any society. One way to subjugate a population is through physical coercion. However, the use of force is costly and produces contrary effects. Discourse is used instead of force and is thus characterized by a will to truth and a will to power. In other words, there is political intention behind truth and power. What passes as truth and how truth is validated is dependent upon the discourse. And discourse intrinsically contains a will to power.

Let me give you a dramatic example. The attacks of September 11, 2001, were perpetrated by men who are considered either "terrorists" or "freedom fighters," depending on the discourse that is used. Within these discourses are legitimations and methods of reasoning that create these two different social meanings. Further, the discourses create the subjective experience of all the different peoples involved. The substance of one discourse is captured by the title of the report generated by the U.S. government: "The National Commission on Terrorist Attacks Upon the United States."

Clearly, the discourse in the United States defines the perpetrators as *terrorists* and the subjective experience of those in the United States as being innocently *attacked.* The substance of the other discourse is revealed in the title and opening lines of a document confiscated by the police in Manchester, England, during a search of an Al Qaeda member's home. The title of the document is "Declaration of Jihad," and the opening lines are addressed to "those champions who avowed the truth day and night" (*Al Qaeda Training Manual,* n.d.). One discourse creates the meaning of attack and terrorist; the other creates the meaning of holy war and champion.

The Power of Objectification

For Foucault, then, power is not so much a quality of social structures as it is the practices or techniques that become power as individuals are turned into subjects through discourse. Foucault intends us to see both meanings of the noun "subject": as someone to control, and as one's self-knowledge. Here Foucault's unique interest is quite clear—perhaps the most insidious form of power is that which is exercised by our self over how we think and feel; it is the power we exercise in the name of others over our self.

In an interesting analysis, Foucault uses the state to illustrate both meanings of subject. State rule is usually understood in terms of power over the masses. While this is a true characteristic of the state, Foucault argues that the modern state also exercises individualization techniques that exercise power over the subjectivity of the person. Foucault talks about this form of ruling as **governmentality**: "The government of the self by the self in its articulation with relations to others" (Foucault, 1989, as quoted in Davidson, 1994, p. 119). Governmentality was needed because of the shift from the power of the monarch to the power of the state.

Under a monarchy, the power of the queen or king was absolute and he or she required absolute obedience, but the scope of that control was fairly narrow. The nation-state "freed" people from the coercive control of the monarchy but at the same time broadened its scope of control. The nation-state is far more interested in controlling our behaviors today than monarchies were 300 years ago. In governmentality, the individual is enlisted by the state to exercise control over himself or herself. This is partly achieved through expert, professional knowledge that comes from medicine and the social and behavior sciences. The state supports such scientific research, and the findings are employed to extend control, particularly as the individual uses and consults medicine, psychology, and other sciences.

A fundamental part of Foucault's argument about the practices of power is the historical shift to *objectification*. Obviously, if power is intrinsic to human affairs of all kinds, then people have always exercised power. However, the practice of power became something different and more insidious due to historical changes that objectified the subject of power—the individual person. We can get a picture of this shift in how power is exercised over the person by comparing the roots, primary meanings, and transitive verb forms of *object* and *subject*.

Foucault's work is found in a series of books that provide a counter-history to some of the objectifying power practices in Western societies. These books detail madness and rationality, abnormality and normality, medicine and the clinic, penal discipline and punishment, psychiatry and criminal justice, and the history of sexuality. In general, these works document how you and I exercise power over our bodies and subjectivities. While I don't have the luxury of introducing you to all of Foucault's archaeology and genealogy, it is important for us to talk about a few of his concepts so that you can get a sense of how his theoretical ideas get played out. We'll first be looking at how power is exercised over our body and then over our inner, subjective life.

Concepts and Theory: Disciplining the Body

Foucault's intent in his book *Discipline and Punish* is to map a major shift in the way in which Western society handles crime and criminals. The shift is from punishment and torture to discipline. Foucault paints a graphic comparative picture in the first seven pages of this book. The first part of the picture is an account of the public torture and killing of a man named Damiens on March 2, 1757. Damiens had been convicted of murder and sentenced to having his flesh torn from his body with red-hot pincers, followed by various molten elements (such as lead, wax, and oil) poured into the open wounds. The hand that held the knife with which he had committed the murder was burnt with sulfur. Finally, he was drawn and quartered by four horses and his body burnt to ashes and the ashes scattered to the winds.

The second image in Foucault's picture is a set of 12 rules for the daily activities of prisoners in Paris. The rules covered the prisoners' entire day and included such things as prayer, Bible reading, education, bathing, recreation, and work. These rules were in use a mere 80 years after the public torture of Damiens. The shortness of the time period indicates that the change isn't due to gradual adjustment and progress, but rather to abrupt shifts in knowledge, perception, and power.

Foucault uses this graphic comparison to point out a fundamental change that occurred in Europe and the United States. Most of us would look at these differences and attribute the change to a dawning of compassion and a desire to treat people more humanely. Foucault, on the other hand, looks deeper and more holistically at the shift. This change not only affected the penal system; it was a fundamental social change as well. During this period of time, from the eighteenth to nineteenth centuries (also known as the Enlightenment), science gained its foothold in society. Society as a whole began to embrace what we call *scientism*—the adaptation of the methods, mental attitudes, and modes of expression typical of scientists. Scientism values control, and control is achieved by objectifying the world and reducing it to its constituent parts. The gaze of the scientist is thus penetrating, particularizing, and objectifying. This kind of gaze results in universal technologies that allow humans to regularize and routinize their control of the world.

The shift, then, was not due to society becoming more compassionate and humane; the shift from punishment to discipline was a function of scientism and the desire to more uniformly control the social environment. As Foucault (1975/1995) says, the primary objective of this shift was

> to make of the punishment and repression of illegalities a regular function, coextensive with society; not to punish less, but to punish better; to punish with an attenuated severity perhaps, but in order to punish with more universality and necessity; to insert the *power to punish more deeply into the social body*. (p. 82, emphasis added)

This new way of discipline and control is best characterized by Jeremy Bentham's concept of a panopticon. The word **panopticon** is a combination of two Greek words. The first part, "pan," comes from the word *pantos* meaning "all." The second part comes from the word *optikos* meaning "to see." Together, panopticon literally means "all seeing." There is actually an optical instrument called the panopticon that combines features of both the microscope and telescope, allowing the viewer to see things both up close and far away, thus seeing all.

Jeremy Bentham developed a different kind of panopticon—a building design for prisons. Bentham's panopticon was a round building with an observation tower or core that optimized surveillance. The building was divided into individual prison cells that extended from the inner core to the outer wall. Each cell had inner and outer windows; thus, each prisoner was backlit by the outer window, allowing for easy viewing. "They are like so many cages, so many small theatres, in which each actor is alone, perfectly individualized and constantly visible" (Foucault, 1975/1995, p. 200). The tower itself was fitted with Venetian blinds, zigzag hallways, and partitioned intersections among the observation rooms in the tower. These made the tower guards invisible to the prisoners who were being observed. The purpose of the panopticon was to allow seeing without being seen. Here "inspection functions ceaselessly. The gaze is alert everywhere" (Foucault, 1975/1995, p. 195).

Foucault isn't really interested in the panopticon as such. Rather, he sees the idea of the panopticon as illustrative of a shift in the fundamental way people thought and the way in which power is practiced. In terms of crime and punishment, it involved a shift from the spectacle of torture (which fit well with monarchical power) to regulation in prison (which fits well with the nation-state); from seeing crime as an act against authority to viewing it as an act against society; from being focused on guilt (did he [or she] do it?) to looking at cause (what social or psychological factors influenced the person?); and, most importantly, from punishment to discipline—more specifically, to the self-discipline imposed by the ever-present but unseen surveillance of the panopticon.

Foucault (1975/1995) refers to this kind of control as the *microphysics of power* and sees this as the explicit link between knowledge and power: "There is no power relation without the correlative constitution of a field of knowledge, nor any knowledge that does not presuppose and constitute at the same time power relations" (p. 27). The microphysics of power is exercised or practiced as knowledge is produced, appropriated by groups for use, distributed to the population through education and mass media (such as books, magazines, and the Internet), and then retained internally by those that others want to control.

The Discipline of the Human Sciences

Obviously, all of society was not put into a physical panopticon, but society was placed within a symbolic or institutional system of surveillance. In another word-play, Foucault argues that the discipline associated with panopticon surveillance of the entire population comes from the "disciplines," in particular the human sciences. The modern episteme created the possibility of the human sciences, such as psychiatry, psychology, and sociology. The human has been the subject of thought and modes of control for quite some time, but in every case the human was seen holistically or as part of the universal scheme of things. In the modern episteme, however, mankind becomes the object of study—not as part of an aesthetic whole, but as a thing in its own right.

This discourse of science serves to objectify and control the individual. Psychiatry and psychology used the mechanical model of the universe to gaze inside the psyche of the person; sociology and political science looked at the external circumstances of humanity. Thus, the internal motivations and reasons behind action as well as the external factors became the objects of science in order to fulfill the chief goal of science, which is control. Statistics are used to quantify and categorize; psychotherapy and psychological testing are used to probe and catalog; all of the disciplines and their methodologies are brought into "discipline" in order to fulfill the primary goal of science: to control.

Foucault (1982) finds the human sciences particularly interesting because they are "modes of inquiry which try to give themselves the status of sciences" (p. 208). The human sciences are thus not true science; they only take on the guise of science. The human sciences did not grow out of scientific questions; they grew out of the modern episteme. Simply put, during the time that people began to talk about society and psychology, the kind of knowledge that was seen as real and valuable was science. So, in order to be accepted, the social and behavioral disciplines had to take on the guise of science.

More specifically, Foucault argues that there are three areas of knowledge in the modern episteme: mathematical and physical sciences, life and economic sciences, and philosophy. The human sciences grew out of the space created by these three knowledge systems. Asking scientific questions about things like biology and physics, which have some basis in the objective world, set the stage for those same questions to be asked about the questioner. Further, each of these sciences pursues knowledge in a distinctive manner, each with its own logic. The human sciences, on the other hand, must borrow from each of these because it has no unique domain or methodology. The human sciences stand in

relation to all the other forms of knowledge . . . at one level or another, [they use] mathematical formalization; they proceed in accordance with models or concepts borrowed from biology, economics, and the sciences of language; and they address themselves to that mode of being of man which philosophy is attempting to conceive. (Foucault, 1966/1994b, p. 347)

Therefore, the precariousness or uncertainty of the human sciences isn't due to, "as is often stated, the extreme density of their object" (Foucault, 1966/1994b, p. 348); rather, their uncertainty of knowledge is due to the fact that they have no true method of their own—everything is borrowed. The validity of knowledge is in some way always related to methodology. *What* we know is an effect of *how* we know. Because the human sciences don't have their own methodology, the knowledge generated is without any basis—in the end, it is purely an expression of power that can be explicitly used by the state to control populations but is more generally part of the control people exercise over themselves in modernity.

As such, we generally see and understand ourselves in Western cultures from the human science model. We listen endlessly to public opinion polls and voting predictions, and they become constant topics of conversation for us. We understand the family in terms of such psychosocial models as the "functional family," and we raise our children according to the latest findings. Almost everything that we think, feel, and do is scrutinized by a human science, and we are provided with that knowledge so that we too can understand our own life and its circumstances.

The Discipline of Medicine

But the human sciences are not alone in their objectification of humanity; they are aided by a culture produced by *the medical gaze.* The modern medical gaze is different from that of the eighteenth century. At that time, disease was organized into hierarchical categories such as families, genera, and species. The doctor's gaze was directed not so much at the patient as at the disease—the patient was in some ways superfluous. Diseases transferred to the body when their makeup combined with certain qualities of the patient, such as his or her temperament. Symptoms existed within the disease itself, not the patient. This way of seeing where symptoms live implies that the patient's body could actually get in the way of the doctor seeing the symptoms. For example, if the patient was old, then the symptoms associated with being elderly could obscure the doctor's view of the symptoms associated with the disease. The medical gaze, then, was directed at the disease, not the body.

However, by the nineteenth century, the modern medical gaze had come to locate disease within the patient. Disease was no longer seen to exist within its own world apart from the body; from this new clinical point of view, the patient can't get in the way of the symptoms because the symptoms and disease are the same and exist within the body. This shift in discourse created the *clinical gaze*, an objectifying way of seeing that looks within and dissects the patient. With the clinical gaze, "Western man could constitute himself in his own eyes as an object of science" (Foucault, 1963/1994a, p. 197).

Modern medicine is thus created through a gaze that makes the body an object, a thing to be dissected, either symbolically or actually, in order to find the disease within it. The culture of the clinical gaze helped to create a general disposition in Western society to see the person as an object. This disposition, along with the human sciences, made the practices of power much more effective and treacherous—objects that can be thrown away are much easier to control than subjects that demand continuing emotional and psychic connections.

Disciplining Sex

Thus, bodily regimens of exercise and diet, self-understanding, and regulation of feelings and behaviors all stem from medicine and the human sciences, which Foucault tells us make up the panopticon of modernity. But Foucault is interested in something deeper than the control of the body—he wants to document how we as individuals exercise social power over the way we relate to our own selves. Nowhere is this more clearly seen than in Foucault's counter-history of sexuality. In order to understand Foucault's intent, we will now briefly review Greek and modern ideas of sexuality.

Greek Sexuality

Ancient Greece was the birthplace of democracy and Western philosophy. There was, in fact, a connection between the two. In Athens, in response to an upheaval by the masses against their tyrannical leader, Isagoras, a politician named Cleisthenes introduced a completely new organization of political institutions called democracy (the rule of common people). Through democratic elections, the elite incrementally lost their advantage in the assemblies and the common people ruled. Unfortunately, the masses were susceptible to impassioned speech and ended up making several decisions that conflicted with one another or entailed high costs. In response, philosophers and the politically deposed elite began to search for absolute truth. To them, truth obviously couldn't be found simply through rhetoric; they believed there had to be some absolutes upon which decisions could be based.

Along with other factors, this impetus helped produce the Greek notion of the soul. For the Greek, the idea of the soul captured all that is meant by the inner person: the individual's mind, emotions, ethics, beliefs, and so on. But in reading Plato, it's also clear that the soul was seen to be hierarchically constructed. Within the soul, the mind is preeminent and alone is immortal. The emotions and appetites, though part of the soul, are of lesser import and are mortal. Thus, reason is godlike and education, especially philosophy, is essential for proper discipline.

It is important that we see the emphasis here. The mind, emotions, and bodily appetites are viewed hierarchically, but they are all seen as part of the soul. In order to get a sense of the relationships within the soul, let's take a look at a conversation that Plato (1993) sets up between Socrates and a group of students. These conversations are part of what are more generally referred to as the Socratic dialogues, a literary genre that emerged sometime around the turn of the fourth century BCE. Socrates speaks first:

> "Do you think that it's a philosopher's business to concern himself with what people call pleasures—food and drink, for instance?"
>
> "Certainly not, Socrates," said Simmias.
>
> "What about those of sex?"
>
> "Not in the least. . . ."
>
> "Then it is your opinion in general that a man of this kind is not preoccupied with the body, but keeps his attention directed as much as he can away from it and towards the soul?"
>
> "Yes, it is. . . ."
>
> "Then when is it that the soul attains to truth? When it tries to investigate anything with the help of the body, it is obviously liable to be led astray."
>
> "Quite so."
>
> "Is it not in the course of reasoning, if at all, that the soul gets a clear view of reality?"
>
> "Yes." (pp. 117–118)

Notice how Socrates views sex: It isn't something set aside and special. It is simply seen as a bodily appetite, on a par with eating and drinking. And these aren't a direct concern for the philosopher. If the bodily appetites get in the way of the search for reality or truth, only then are they of concern. The point is to keep the mind free. A person shouldn't be preoccupied with the body, because too much attention on the body and its appetites will take his or her attention away from the quest for truth. This bit of dialogue sets us up well for the way Foucault talks about sex in Greek society.

In Greek society, sexuality existed as *aphrodisia*. This Greek word is obviously where we get our term "aphrodisiac," but it had a much broader meaning for the Greeks. Foucault notes that neither the Greeks nor the Romans had an idea of "sexuality" or "the flesh" as distinct objects. When we think of sex, sexuality, or the flesh, we usually have in mind a single set of behaviors or desires. The Greeks, while they had words for different kinds of sexual acts and relations, didn't have a single word or concept under which they could all fit. The closest to that kind of umbrella term is *aphrodisia*, which might be translated as "sensual pleasures" or "pleasures of love," and more accurately the works and acts of Aphrodite, the goddess of love.

These works of Aphrodite, perhaps like the works of any god or goddess, cannot be fully categorized. To do so would limit the god. This lack of a catalog or objective specification of sexuality is exactly Foucault's point. In modern, Western society, particularly as expressed through Christianity, there is a definite way to index those things that are sexual, or the "works of the flesh." This identifiability is extremely important for the Western mind because sex is a moral issue; it, above all other things, defines immoral practices. So, what counts and doesn't count as sexual is imperative for us, but it wasn't for the Greeks.

The Greeks also employed the idea of *chresis aphrodision* to sexuality: The phrase means "the use of pleasures." The Greeks' use of pleasure was guided by three strategies: need, timeliness, and status. The strategy of need once again highlights Socrates's approach to sexual practices. As we've seen, in Ancient Greece, the relationship to one's body was to be characterized by moderation, but every person's appetites and abilities to cope are different. Thus, the Greek strategy was for the individual to first know his or her need—to understand what the body wants, what its limits are, and how strong the mind is.

The second strategy is timeliness and simply refers to the idea that there are better and worse times to have sexual pleasures. There was a particularly good time in one's life, neither too young nor too old; a good time of the year; and good times during the day, usually connected with dietary habits. The issue of time "was one of the most important objectives, and one of the most delicate, in the art of making use of the pleasures" (Foucault, 1984/1990b, p. 57). The last strategy in the use of pleasures was status. The art of pleasure was adapted to the status of the person. The general rule was that the more an individual was in the public eye, the more he should "freely and deliberately" adapt rigorous standards regarding his use of pleasures.

Rather than seeing sexuality as moral, the Greeks saw it in terms of ascetics. *Ascetics* refers to one's attitude or relationship toward one's self, and for the Greek this was to be characterized through strength. The word comes from the Greek *asketikos,* which literally translated means exercise. The idea here is not simply something we do, as in exercising control; it also carries with it a picture of active training. Here we see the Greek link between masculinity and virility. The virile man in Greek society was someone who moderated his own appetites. He was the man who voluntarily wrestled with the needs of his body in order to discipline his mind. The picture we see is that of an athlete in training. For example, the athlete knows that eating chocolate or ice cream can be very pleasurable. But while in training, the athlete willingly forgoes those pleasures for what he or she sees as a higher good. The result of this training is *enkrateia,* the mastery of one's self. It's a position of internal strength rather than weakness.

Training is always associated with a goal; there is an end to be achieved or a contest to be won. In this case, the aim of the Greek attitude toward sexuality is a state of being, something that becomes true of the individual in the person's daily life. This is the *teleology* or ultimate goal of sexuality, the fourth structuring factor that defines a person's relationship to sex. The goal for the Greek was freedom. We can again see this idea in the conversation with Socrates. Truth and reality were things to be sought after. Too much emphasis on sex, just like eating and drinking, can get in the way of this search. As Socrates (Plato, 1993) said, "surely the soul can reason best when it is free of all distractions such as hearing or sight or pain or pleasure of any kind" (p. 118).

Western Modern Sexuality

The Western, modern view of sex is quite different from the Greek. It is, in fact, quite different from that which developed in the East. Where Eastern philosophy and religion developed a set of practices intended to guide sexual behavior to its highest and most spiritual expression and enjoyment (for instance, Kama Sutra), the West developed systems of external control and prohibitions. Of course, a great deal of the impetus toward this view of sex was provided by the Christian church.

Part of this movement came from Protestantism with its emphasis on individual righteousness and redemption. Rather than being worthy of God because of church membership and sacraments, Protestantism singled the individual out and made his or her moral conduct an expression of salvation and faith. But an important part was also played by the Counter-Reformation, a reform movement in the Catholic Church.

Confession and penance are sacraments in the Catholic Church. They are one of the ways through which salvation is imparted to Christians. The Counter-Reformation increased the frequency of confession and guided it to specific kinds of self-examination, designed to root out the sins of the flesh down to the minutest detail:

> Sex . . . [in all] its aspects, its correlations, and its effects must be pursued down to their slenderest ramification: a shadow in a daydream, an image too slowly dispelled, a badly exorcised complicity between the body's mechanics and the mind's complacency: everything had to be told. (Foucault, 1976/1990a, p. 19)

This was the beginning of the Western idea that sex is a deeply embedded power, one that is intrinsic to the "flesh" (the vehicle of sin par excellence, as compared to the Greek idea of bodily appetites), and one that must be eradicated through inward searching using an external moral code and through outward confession.

While these Christian doctrines would have influenced the general culture, they would have remained connected to the fate of Christianity alone had it not been for other secular changes and institutions beginning in the eighteenth century, most particularly in politics, economics, and medicine. With the rise of the nation-state and science, population became an economic and political issue. Previous societies had always been aware of the people gathered together in society's name, but conceiving of the people as the *population* is a significant change. The idea of population transforms the people into an object that can be analyzed and controlled.

In this transformation, science provided the tools and the nation-state the motivation and control mechanisms (taxation, standing armies, and so on). The population could be numbered and analyzed statistically, and those statistics became important for governance and economic pursuit. The population represented the labor force, one that needed to be trained and, more fundamentally, born. At the center of these economic and political issues was sexuality:

> It was necessary to analyze the birthrate, the age of marriage, the legitimate and illegitimate births, the precocity and frequency of sexual relations, the ways of making them fertile or sterile, the effects of unmarried life or of the prohibitions, the impact of contraceptive practices [and so on]. (Foucault, 1976/1990a, pp. 25–26)

In the latter half of the nineteenth century, medicine and psychiatry took up the sex banner as well. Psychiatry, especially through the work of Freud, set out to discover the makeup of the human mind and emotion, and it began to catalog mental illnesses, especially those connected with sex. It conceptualized masturbation as a perversion at the core of many psychological and physical problems, homosexuality as a mental illness, and the maturation of a child in terms of successive sexual issues that the child must resolve on the way to healthy adulthood. In short, psychiatry "annexed the whole of the sexual perversions as its own province" (Foucault, 1976/1990a, p. 30). Law and criminal justice also bolstered the cause, as society sought to regulate individual and bedroom behaviors. Social controls popped up everywhere that "screened the sexuality of couples, parents and children, dangerous and endangered adolescents—undertaking to protect, separate, and forewarn, signaling perils everywhere, awakening people's attention, calling for diagnoses, piling up reports, organizing therapies. These sites radiated discourses aimed at sex" (pp. 30–31).

All of these factors worked to change the discourse of Western sexuality in the twentieth century. Sex went from the Greek model of a natural bodily appetite that could be satisfied in any number of ways, to the modern model of sex as the insidious power within. At the heart of this change is the confession, propagated by Catholicism and Protestantism and picked up by psychiatrists, medical doctors, educators, and other experts. Confessional rhetoric is found everywhere in a modern society that uses Victorian prudishness as its backdrop for incessant talk about sex in magazines, journals, books, movies, and reality television shows. Notice what Foucault is saying: Repression is used as a source of discourse, and sex has become the topic of conversation—a central feature in Western discourse, and the defining feature of the human animal. Sex is suspected of "harboring a fundamental secret" concerning the truth of mankind (Foucault, 1976/1990a, p. 69).

In the modern discourse of sex, sexuality has become above all an object—a truth to discover and a thing to control. In this, sex has followed the use and development of science in general and the human sciences in particular: "The project of a science of the subject has gravitated, in ever narrowing circles, around the question of sex" (Foucault, 1976/1990a, p. 70). This form of objective control ("biocontrol") over the intimacy of humanity came through science and is linked with the development of the nation-state and capitalism. While capitalism and the nation-state seem to be firmly established and the need for such control not as great, what we are left with is a way of constructing our self as the moral subject of our sexual behavior. We have inherited a certain kind of subjectivity from this discourse, a particular way of relating to our self and sexuality. This legacy of the modern discourse of sexuality sees sex as a central truth of the self, as an object that must be studied and understood. Further, the modern discourse of sexuality tells us that this part of us is intrinsically dangerous. It is at best an amoral creature and at worst a defiling beast that treads upon sacred and moral ground.

Summary

- Foucault takes the position that knowledge and power are wrapped up with one another; each produces and reinforces the other. Power as exercised and expressed through discourse creates the way in which we feel, act, think, and relate to our self. Likewise, the knowledge of any epoch defines what is mentally, emotionally, and physically possible. Foucault sees the practices involved in power and knowledge as games of truth—the use of specific rules and resources through which something is seen as truth in any given age. The games of truth that Foucault is particularly interested in are the ones that involve the practices through which we participate in the domination of our subjectivity.

- Much of Foucault's work is in the form of counter-history. The generally accepted model is that of history as memory: History is our collective memory of events. We also usually think of history as slowly progressing in a linear fashion. Foucault argues that history is far from a memory of linear events—it is power in use. It's a myth that is constructed according to specific values. Foucault proposes a counterhistory, one that focuses on abrupt episodes of change and the way in which knowledge changes in response to various power regimes. Foucault uses an archaeological approach to uncover the practices that are associated with discourse and ways of thinking, and he uses a genealogical approach to uncover how discourse and power are inscribed on the body and mind.

- Foucault argues that the knowledge people hold is based upon historical epistemes, or underlying orders. Foucault uses the term "episteme" to refer to the way thought organizes itself in any historical period of time. Discourses are produced within historical epistemes. A discourse is a way of talking about something that is guided by specific rules and practices, that sets the conditions for our subjective awareness, and that subjugates through a will to truth and power.

- While power is found in all human practice, Foucault is particularly interested in the unique power of modernity. This expression of power is associated with changes in government, medicine, the institution of the human sciences, changes in the Western discourse of sexuality, and changes in the penal system. The change from rule by monarchy to rule by the nation-state demanded a new form of governmentality, one in which the individual watches over his or her own behaviors, and one that increases control while preserving the illusion of freedom. This governmentality was aided by the human sciences through the idea of population, an essentializing and mechanistic model of the person, and the value of expert knowledge. Governmentality was also produced through a new medical "gaze," which located symptoms and disease within the body; panoptical practices in controlling criminality; and changes in sexuality promoted by the Catholic confessional and Protestant individualism. Together, these created a discourse of governmentality that objectifies and controls the individual through his or her own practices.

TAKING THE PERSPECTIVE–POSTSTRUCTURALISM

Obviously most of the theories we've looked at beginning in Chapter 7 have been critical of society in one way or another. This is especially true of Jürgen Habermas whose base is critical theory. Yet there is a fundamental difference between those critiques and the one offered by Foucault. With the others there is a sense of some substance or presence, but with Foucault one gets a sense of absence. For example, with Foucault there isn't truth, only truth games; and there isn't history, just counter-histories. One way to understand this absence is to simply say that Foucault has other concerns, and that undoubtedly is part of it. But there's something deeper, more basic in back of Foucault's approach: Foucault approaches the social world as a poststructuralist.

In order to understand **poststructuralism,** we must first look to structuralism (since the "post" denotes that it comes after structuralism). Structuralism argues that there are deep structures that underlie and generate observable phenomena or events. This is a more radical statement than is usually made when we talk about structure in sociology (such as Parsons' structural-functionalism). For many sociologists, social structures are seen as influencing our lives; they help account for the patterned nature of human action and interaction. But social structures are usually seen as one of several influences. While we can talk about the poles of the debate in terms of structure versus agency, most sociologists acknowledge that interactions, culture, and structure all influence our behavior.

On the other hand, structuralism sees the power of structure as absolute. These structures work below the level of consciousness, and they don't simply influence or even determine our behaviors; they generate, create, and produce them. Everything that we see, think, feel, and do is in reality events or manifestations of the structure. While this may sound depressing to some of us, for structuralists this idea represented a ray of hope. As the linguistic structuralist Claude Lévi-Strauss (1963) put it, "Structural linguistics will certainly play the same renovating role with respect to the social sciences that nuclear physics, for example, has played for the physical sciences" (p. 33). It is the criticism of this belief and hope that forms the core of poststructuralism.

The basic premise of poststructuralism is that language signifies rather than represents. In other words, language doesn't refer to or represent any actually reality—all we have is language. Yet people have always sought a center for language—we have wanted language to be a response to the real world, to be tied down, moored, centered in reality. This center is what brings presence to language. The use of "presence" here functions as a technical term; it implies being or existence. In other words, humans have always sought a center to their linguistic schemes that would make language authentic, true, or real. Ideas such as essence, existence,

(Continued)

(Continued)

substance, subject, transcendence, consciousness, God, man, and so forth have given language a reason for its existence, a firm foundation upon which to stand, and an "invariable presence" (Derrida, 1967/1978, pp. 279–280).

But there are two problems with this idea or desire. First, a center that moors language to some reality is by definition outside of the totality of language. The idea of a monotheistic God is a good example. God is seen to exist outside of time, space, and language, and because of that external existence, believers think that He gives reason for the universe in its totality (including time, space, and language). The clearest expression of this sort of centering is the doctrine of plenary inspiration, the belief that every single word written in the Bible was directly inspired or dictated by God.

However, the external nature of the center reveals a contradiction. A center that is located outside the whole is by definition not inside and thus cannot be at the center of the totality. In other words, language is the totality of human existence—we think, feel, and see linguistically. But humans have always looked outside of language for the center or reason of language. There's part of us that knows this, but we usually ascribe it to being "wrong." We say things like, "People used to talk about the earth being flat, but they were wrong." Poststructuralism wants us to see that there's never a chance of being "right" because those "truths" or "centers" are always and ever, by definition, outside language. What we see in the idea of a center is a desire to master anxiety—anxiety about the human mode of existence. Since this is so, "The entire history of the concept of structure . . . must be thought of as a series of substitutions of center for center" (Derrida, 1967/1978, p. 279). Thus, logically, there is no center to language, no firm foundation upon which to stand.

The second issue that poststructuralists want to bring to our attention is that a rupture has occurred in the history of language. Among all the other critiques of capitalism, race, gender, and so on, there came a time when language itself was critiqued. Writing is a profound process. Through writing, we inscribe or write the world around us. That's what happens when we use language to understand and make meaning out of the physical world and our experiences—we put the meaning on it; the meaning isn't "there" for language to represent. Writing/language is so profound that it writes its own critique. Think of it this way: If you were a linguist and wanted to critique language, what's the only thing you use? You would have to use language; you would write the critique of writing *by writing it*—here language inscribes upon itself. The rupture is that moment in time when language itself was critiqued, and it without question reveals the absolute reflexive nature of language.

Thus, rather than language being centered in an independent reality, language is inherently self-referential, creating a world of oppressive power relations (Foucault's point). The implications of this are that

- Poststructuralism rejects the belief in essentializing ideas that conceptualize the social world or a portion of it as a universal totality—rather, the social world is fragmented and historically specific (general social theories are thus impossible and oppressive).

- Poststructuralism denies the possibility of knowing an independent or objective reality—rather, the human world and knowledge are utterly textual or discursive.

- Poststructuralism discards the idea that texts or language have any true meaning—rather, texts are built around difference and carry a surplus of meaning (humanity is thus left with nothing but interpretation and interpretations of interpretation—this book is an interpretation of others' interpretations of a social world; and as you read, you produce yet another interpretation).

- Poststructuralism rejects the idea of universal human nature developed out of the Enlightenment—rather, the meaning of the human subject is historically specific and is an effect of discourse, with the discourses of an age producing the possible bodies and subjectivities of the person.

Beyond that, Lemert (1990) points us to four uses of poststructuralism in sociology. He says that in the social sciences, we typically solve the problems or questions we pose with "reference to ideas like 'empirical reality'" (p. 244). Poststructuralism shatters the idea of a center; our texts therefore can't legitimately make reference to an empirical reality because every reality for humans is a written (inscribed) one. Thus, what we have isn't an empirical reality; it is a textual reality. What then can we conclude? Lemert gives us four propositions for poststructuralist sociology:

1. That theory is an inherently discursive activity

2. That the empirical reality in relation to which theoretical texts are discursive is without exception textual

3. That empirical texts depend on this relationship to theoretical texts for their intellectual or scientific value

4. That in certain, if not all, cases a discursive interpretation yields more, not less, adequate understanding (p. 244)

The End of Everything:
Jean Baudrillard (1929–2007)

Theorist's Digest
Concepts and Theory: Mediating the World
   Precapitalist Society and Symbolic Exchange
   The Dawn of Capitalism and the Death of Meaning
Concepts and Theory: Losing the World
   Entropy and Advertising
   Simulacrum and Hyperreality
   Sign Implosion
Concepts and Theory: The Postmodern Person
   Fragmented Identities
   Play, Spectacle, and Passivity
Summary
Taking the Perspective—Postmodernism

In August 1990, the United States along with 33 other nations invaded Iraq. The cost of the Gulf War was more than $60 billion and involved over 1 million troops. Though the numbers are still uncertain, it's estimated that well over 100,000 people died as a result of the campaign. Before the invasion, Jean Baudrillard published an article titled "The Gulf War Will Not Take Place." During the campaign Baudrillard published another article, "The Gulf War Is Not Taking Place." After the war, the new piece by Baudrillard was called "The Gulf War Did Not Take Place." He later published a book by the same title: *The Gulf War Did Not Take Place.*

Baudrillard isn't saying that guns weren't fired and people didn't die. Baudrillard's point in this provocative book is that for the world this was a mediated war. The mass media provided continuous television coverage, but that coverage was packaged and presented in such a way as to lure audiences to watch (the medium is the message). The "news," then, was a commodification of what happened on the ground. What the world saw wasn't the reality of the war but a hyperreality designed to stimulate rather than inform: "It is a masquerade of information: branded faces delivered over to the prostitution of the image, the image of an unintelligible distress. . . . It is not war taking place over there but the disfiguration of the world" (Baudrillard, 1995, p. 40).

Baudrillard's striking analysis of the Gulf War is based in a postmodern perspective. Often, postmodernism is confused with poststructuralism, which is Foucault's perspective. And there are some similarities. Both are concerned with culture generally and language particularly, and both argue that culture and language function without any physical or objective reality in back of them. There are, I think, two main differences between them. First, they each locate the reasons for the lack of reality in different places. Poststructuralism generally considers the intrinsic characteristics of language itself, while social postmodernism usually looks to such factors as capitalism and mass media as the culprits.

Second, they each focus on different effects of the state of culture. For instance, Foucault argues that rather than referring to any physical reality, language contains political discourses that function to exercise power over the person. Baudrillard, on the other hand, sees culture as absolutely void of any significance at all, political or otherwise. Any meaning or power in culture has been stripped away by incessant commodification, advertising, and the trivializing effects of mass media.

THEORIST'S DIGEST

Brief Biography

Jean Baudrillard was born in Reims, France, on July 29, 1929. Baudrillard studied German at the Sorbonne University, Paris, and was professor of German for 8 years. During that time, he also worked as a translator and began his studies in sociology and philosophy. He completed his dissertation in sociology under Henri Lefebvre, a noted Marxist-humanist.

Baudrillard began teaching sociology in 1966, eventually moving to the Université de Paris-X Nanterre as professor of sociology. From 1986 to 1990, Baudrillard served as the director of science for the Institut de Recherche et d'Information Socio-Économique at the Université de Paris-IX Dauphine. Beginning in 2001, Baudrillard was professor of the philosophy of culture and media criticism at the European Graduate School in Saas-Fee, Switzerland. Baudrillard is the author of several international best-sellers, among them *Symbolic Exchange and Death, Simulacra and Simulation, Seduction, America,* and *The Gulf War Did Not Take Place.* Baudrillard died March 6, 2007.

Central Sociological Questions

Baudrillard is essentially concerned with the relationship between reality and appearance; this is an issue that has plagued philosophers and theorists for eons. Baudrillard's unique contributions to this problem concern the effects of mass media and advertising. Baudrillard, then, is deeply curious about the effects of mass media on culture and the problem of representation: Have capitalist-driven mass media pushed appearance to the front stage in such a way as to destroy reality? Is there a difference between image and reality in postmodernity?

Simply Stated

Culture is meant to express social meanings and create social relationships, both of which happen through the use of symbols. And symbols work as they are intended when connected to real people in real situations. However, as a result of commodification, advertising, and mass media, cultural symbols have been cut off from their social embeddness and have become free-floating, without any specific social reference. Because human nature is principally oriented toward symbolic meaning, people have been left without any real meaning. This void is filled with mass media and electronic stimulations, which need to be produced in ever more spectacular and plasticine fashion. The person himself or herself is left without any solid, social identities and must cobble together an image-based self.

Key Ideas

postmodern, human nature, symbolic exchange, use-value, exchange-value, sign value, commodity fetish, sign fetish, consumer society, labor of consumption, simulacrum, free-floating signifiers, hyperreality, death of the subject, fragmenting identities

Concepts and Theory: Mediating the World

Precapitalist Society and Symbolic Exchange

Baudrillard's (1981/1994) theory is based on a fundamental assumption: "Representation stems from the principle of the equivalence of the sign and of the real" (p. 6). What Baudrillard means is that it is possible for signs to represent reality, especially social reality. Think about it this way: What is the purpose of culture? In traditional social groups, culture was created and used in the same social context.

For the sake of conversation, let's call this "grounded culture," the kind of culture that symbolic exchange is based on. In a society such as the United States, however, much of our culture is created or modified by capitalists, advertising agencies, and mass media. We'll call this "commodified culture."

Members in traditional social groups were surrounded by grounded culture; members in postmodern social groups are surrounded by commodified culture. There are vast differences in the reasons why grounded versus commodified culture is created. Grounded culture emerges out of face-to-face interaction and is intended to create meaning, moral boundaries, norms, values, beliefs, and so forth. Commodified culture is produced according to capitalist and mass media considerations and is intended to seduce the viewer to buy products. With grounded culture, people are moral actors; with commodified culture, people are consumers. Postmodernists argue that there are some pretty dramatic consequences, such as cultural fragmentation and unstable identities (for a concise statement, see Allan & Turner, 2000).

Beginning with this idea of grounded or representational culture, Baudrillard posits four phases of the sign. The first stage occurred in premodern societies. The important factor here is that language in premodern societies was not mediated. There were little or no written texts and all communication took place in real social situations in face-to-face encounters. In this first phase, the sign represented reality in a profound way. There was a strong correlation or relationship between the sign and the reality it signified, and the contexts wherein specific signs could be used were clear. In this stage, all communicative acts—including speech, gift giving, rituals, exchanges, and so on—were directly related to and expressive of social reality, in something that Baudrillard calls symbolic exchange.

Baudrillard understands **symbolic exchange** as the exchange of gifts, actions, signs, and so on for their symbolic rather than material value. In contrast to Marx, Baudrillard is making the same kind of argument about human nature that Durkheim did: Humans are symbolic creatures oriented toward meaning rather than production. A good example of the value of symbolism in traditional societies is the prevalence of transition rituals, as in the transition from boyhood to manhood. In the ritual of attaining manhood, the actual behaviors themselves are immaterial, whether it is wrapping a sack of fire ants around the hands or mutilating the penis. Any object or set of behaviors can have symbolic value. What matters is what the ritualized actions symbolize for the group. Symbolic exchange formed part of daily life in pre-capitalist societies: the exchange of food, jewelry, titles, clothing, and so on were all involved in a symbolic "cycle of gifts and countergifts" (Baudrillard, 1973/1975, p. 83). Symbolic exchange thus established a community of symbolic meanings and reciprocal relations among a group of people.

Baudrillard also claims that human nature is wrapped up in excess. Like Marx, he sees humanity as capable of creating its own needs. That is, the needs of other animals are set, but the potential needs of humans are without limit. For example, today I "need" an iPod and an HDTV plasma screen, but a few years ago I didn't. And I can't even begin to imagine what I will need five years from now. However, unlike Marx, Baudrillard sees excess as an indicator of human boundlessness.

Wrapped up in this excess is a sense of transcendence: the ability to reach above the mundane, which is in itself a symbolic move.

Thus, in place of Marx's species-being, Baudrillard proposes excess: Rather than being bound up with survival, production, and materialism, human nature is found in excess and exuberance. Douglas Kellner (2003) summarizes Baudrillard's point of view nicely: "Humans 'by nature' gain pleasure from such things as expenditure, waste, festivities, sacrifices and so on, in which they are sovereign and free to expend the excesses of their energy (and thus follow their 'real nature')" (p. 317). Baudrillard argues that these human characteristics were given license and support in pre-capitalist societies. However, the modernist demands of rationality and restraint in the beginning years of capitalism are the antithesis of symbolic exchange and excess.

The second phase of the sign marked a movement away from these direct kinds of symbolic relationships. This stage gained dominance, roughly speaking, during the time between the European Renaissance and the Industrial Revolution. While media such as written language began previous to the Renaissance, it was during this period that a specific way of understanding, relating to, and representing the world became organized. Direct representation was still present, but certain human ideals began to make inroads. Art, for example, was based on observation of the visible world and yet contained the values of mathematical balance and perspective. Nowhere is this desire for mathematical balance seen more clearly than in Leonardo Da Vinci's painting, *Proportions of the Human Figure.* Thinking of some of Da Vinci's other works, such as the *Mona Lisa* and the *The Last Supper,* we can also see that symbols were used to convey mystery and intrigue.

The Dawn of Capitalism and the Death of Meaning

The third phase of the sign began with the Industrial Revolution. This is the period of time generally thought of as modernity. The Industrial Age brought with it a proliferation of consumer goods never before seen in the history of humanity. It also increased leisure time and produced significant amounts of discretionary funds for more people than ever before. These kinds of changes dramatically altered the way produced goods were seen. Here is where we begin to see the widespread use of goods as symbols of status and power. Thorstein Veblen (1899) termed this phenomenon *conspicuous consumption.*

Baudrillard (1970/1998) characterizes this era as the beginning of the **consumer society**. The consumer society is distinctly different from the kind of capitalism that Marx saw himself critiquing. One of Marx's main criticisms was exploitation, and exploitation, you will remember, is based on use-value and exchange-value. *Use-value* refers to the actual function that a product contains, or its material makeup, while *exchange-value* refers to the rate of exchange one commodity bears when compared to other commodities. The interesting thing for Marx is that when reduced to monetary value, exchange-value is much higher than use-value. In other words, you get paid less to produce a product than it sells for, which is exploitation.

Baudrillard counters by arguing that Marx is ironically buying into the basic assumptions of capitalism. Use-value is completely bound up with the idea of products, oriented to a materialist world alone. It is filled with practical use that is used up in consumption and has no value or meaning other than material. Moreover, like species-being, the idea of use-value validates the basic tenets of capitalism—the truth of human life is rooted in economic production and consumption. Exchange-value is materialist as well, because exchange-value is based on human, economic production. The idea of exchange-value also legitimates and substantiates instrumental rationality, the utilitarian calculations of costs and benefits. Rather than critiquing capitalism, Baudrillard sees Marx as legitimating it:

> The Marxist seeks a *good use* of economy. Marxism is therefore only a limited petit bourgeois critique, one more step in the banalization of life toward the "good use" of the social! . . . Marxism is only the disenchanted horizon of capital—all that precedes or follows it is more radical than it is. (Baudrillard, 1987, p. 60, emphasis original)

In place of use- and exchange-values, Baudrillard proposes the idea of sign-value. Commodities are no longer purchased for their use-value, and exchange-value is no longer simply a reflection of human labor. Each of these capitalist, Marxist values has been trumped by signification. In postmodern societies, commodities are now purchased and used more for their sign-value than for anything else.

Baudrillard links sign-value with fetish, another idea from Marx. As you may recall, Marx was very critical of the process of commodification. A commodity is simply something that is sold in order to make a profit. Commodification as a process refers to the way more and more objects and experiences in the human world are turned into products for profit. Increasing commodification leads to *commodity fetish*. Marx used the term *fetish* in its pre-Freudian sense of idol worship. The idea here is that the worshipper's eyes are blinded to the falsity of the idol. Marx's provocative term has two implications that are related to one another. First, in commodity fetish people misrecognize what is truly present within a commodity. By this Marx meant that commodities and commodification are based on the exploitation of human labor, but most of us fail to see it.

Second, in commodity fetish there is a substitution. For Marx, the basic relationship between humans is that of production. But in commodity fetish, the market relations of commodity exchange are substituted for the productive or material relations of persons. The result is that, rather than being linked in a community of producers, human relationships are seen through commodities, either as buyers and sellers or as a group of like consumers. Commodification and its fetish are one of the primary bases of alienation, which, according to Marx, separates people from their own human nature as creative producers and from one another as social beings.

Again, Baudrillard argues that Marx's concern was misplaced and actually motivated by the capitalist economy. Marx's entire notion of the fetish is locked up with species-being and material production. With commodity fetish, we don't recognize the suppressive labor relations that underlie the product and its value, and we substitute an alienated commodity for what should be a product based in our own species-being. In focusing exclusively on materialism, "Marxism eliminates any real chance it has of analyzing the *actual process of ideological labor*" (Baudrillard, 1972/1981, p. 89, emphasis original). According to Baudrillard, ideology isn't based in or related to material relations of production, as Marx argued. Rather, ideology and fetishism are both based in a *"passion for the code"* (p. 92, emphasis original).

Human nature is symbolic and oriented toward meaning. In symbolic exchange, real meaning and social relationships are present. However, capitalism and changes in media have pushed aside symbolic exchange and in postmodernity have substituted sign-value. Moreover, sign-value is based on textual references to other signs, nothing else. The fetish, then, is the human infatuation with consuming sign-vehicles that are devoid of all meaning and reality. Thus, ideology "appears as a sort of cultural surf frothing on the beachhead of the economy" (Baudrillard, 1972/1981, p. 144). Signs keep proliferating without producing substance. This simulation of meaning is what constitutes ideology and fetish for Baudrillard. This implies that continuing to use the materialist Marxist ideas of fetish and ideology actually contributes to capitalist ideology, because it displaces analysis from the issues of signification.

Thus, in the consumer society, social relations are read through a system of commodified signs rather than symbolic exchange. Commodities become the *sign-vehicles* in modernity that carry identity and meaning (or its lack). For example, in modern society the automobile is a portable, personal status symbol. Driving an SUV means something different from driving a Volkswagen Beetle, which conveys something different from driving a hybrid. As this system becomes more important and elaborated, a new kind of labor eventually supplants physical labor, *the labor of consumption.* This doesn't mean the work involved in finding the best deal. The labor of consumption is the work a person does to place himself or herself within, or to "read" the signs of an identity that is established and understood in, a matrix of commodified signs.

The dynamics begun in the third stage of the sign are exacerbated in the fourth, which began shortly after World War II and continues through today. This fourth stage occurs in postindustrial societies. As such, there has been a shift away from manufacturing and toward information-based technologies. In addition, and perhaps more importantly for Baudrillard, these societies are marked by continual advances and an increasing presence of communication technologies and mass media. Mediated images and information, coupled with unbridled commodification and advertising, are the key influences in this postmodernity. The cultural logic has shifted from the logic of symbolic exchange in pre-capitalist societies, to the logic of production and consumption in capitalist societies, and finally now to the logic of simulation. For Baudrillard (1976/1993b), postmodernity marks the end of everything:

> The end of labor. The end of production. . . . The end of the signifier/signified dialectic which facilitates the accumulation of knowledge and of meaning. . . . And at the same time, the end simultaneously of the exchange value/use value dialectic which is the only thing that makes accumulation and social production possible. . . . The end of the classical era of the sign. (p. 8)

Baudrillard (1981/1994) posits that the postmodern sign has "no relation to any reality whatsoever: It is its own pure simulacrum" (p. 6). These kinds of signs are set free from any constraint of representation and become a "play of signifiers . . . in which the code no longer refers back to any subjective or objective 'reality,' but to its own logic" (Baudrillard, 1973/1975, p. 127). Thus, in postmodernity, a fundamental break has occurred between signs and reality. Signs reference nothing other than themselves; they are their own reality and the only reality to which humans refer. These seem like brash and bold claims, but let's look at Baudrillard's argument behind them.

Concepts and Theory: Losing the World

Entropy and Advertising

First, Baudrillard argues that there is something intrinsic in transferring information that breaks it down. This is an important point: Any time we relate or convey information to another, there is a breakdown. So fundamental is this fact that Baudrillard makes it an equation: information = entropy. Baudrillard argues that information destroys its base. The reason for this is twofold. First, information is always *about* something; it isn't that thing or experience itself. Information by definition, then, is always something other than the thing itself. Second, anytime we convey information, we must use a medium, and it is impossible to put something through a medium without changing it in some way. Even talking to your friend about an event you experienced changes it. Some of the meaning will be lost because language can't convey your actual emotions, and some meaning will be added because of the way your friend individually understands the words you are using.

Mass media is the extreme case of both these processes: Social information is removed innumerable times from the actual events, and capitalist mass media colors things more than any other form. One of the reasons behind this coloration is that mass media expends itself on the staging of information. Every medium has its own form of expression—for newspapers it's print and for television it's images. Every piece of information that is gleaned by the public from any media source has thus been selected and formed by the demands of the media. This is part of what is meant by the phrase "the media is the message."

Further, mass communication comes prepackaged in a meaning form. What I mean by that is that information is staged and the subject is told what constitutes his or her particular relationship to the information. The reason for this is that media in postmodernity exist to make a profit, not to convey information. "Information" is presented more for entertainment purposes than for any intellectual ones. The concern in media is to appeal to and capture a specific market segment. That's why Fox News, CNN, and National Public Radio are so drastically different from one another—the information is secondary; the network's purpose is to draw an audience that will respond to appeals by capitalists to buy their goods. The presentation of information through the media is a system of self-referencing simulation or fantasy. Thus, "information devours its own content. It devours communication and the social" (Baudrillard, 1981/1994, p. 80).

There is yet another important factor in this decisive break—advertising: "Today what we are experiencing is the absorption of all virtual modes of expression into that of advertising" (Baudrillard, 1981/1994, p. 87). The act of advertising alone reduces objects from their use-value to their sign-value. For Marx, the movement from use-value to exchange-value entails an abstraction of the former; in other words, the exchange-value of a commodity is based on a representation of its possible uses. Baudrillard argues that advertising and mass media push this abstraction further. In advertising, the use-value of a commodity is overshadowed by a sign-value. Advertising does not seek to convey information about a product's use-value; rather, advertising places a product in a field of unrelated signs in order to enhance its cultural appearance. As a result of advertising, we tend to relate to the fragmented sign context rather than the use-value. Thus, in postmodern society, people purchase commodities more for the image than for the function they perform.

Let's think about the example of clothing. The actual use-value of clothing is to cover and keep warm. Yet right now I'm looking at an ad for clothing in *Rolling Stone* and it doesn't mention anything about protection from the elements or avoiding public nudity. The ad is rather interesting in that it doesn't even present itself as an advertisement at all. It looks more like a picture of a rock band on tour. We could say, then, that even advertising is advertising itself as something. On the sidebar of the "band" picture, it doesn't talk about the band. It says things such as "Jacket, $599, by Avirex; T-shirt, $69, by Energie," and so on. Most of us won't pay $599 for a jacket to keep us warm, but we might pay that for the status image that we think the jacket projects. Baudrillard's point is that we aren't connected to the basic human reality of keeping warm and covered; we aren't even connected to the social reality of being in a rock band (which itself is a projected image of an idealized life). We are simply attracted to the images.

Simulacrum and Hyperreality

Baudrillard further argues that many of the things we do today in advanced capitalist societies are based largely on images from past lives. For example, most people in traditional and early industrial societies *worked with* their bodies. Today, increasing numbers of people in postindustrial societies don't work with their bodies; they *work out* their bodies. The body has thus become a cultural object rather than a means to an end. In **postindustrial** society, the body no longer serves the purpose of production; rather, it has become the subject of image creation: We work out in order to alter our body to meet some cultural representation.

Clothing too has changed from function to image. In previous eras, there was an explicit link between the real function of the body and the clothing worn—the clothing was serviceable with reference to the work performed or it was indicative of social status. For example, a farmer would wear sturdy clothing because of the labor performed, and his clothing indicated his work (if you saw him away from the field, you would still know what he did by his clothing). However, in the postmodern society, clothing itself has become the creator of image rather than something merely serviceable or directly linked to social status and function.

Let's review what we know so far: In times past, the body was used to produce and reproduce; clothing was serviceable and was a direct sign of work and social function. In postmodern society, however, bodies have been freed from the primary burden of labor and have instead become a conveyance of cultural image. The body's "condition" is itself an important symbol, and so is the decorative clothing placed upon the body. Now here is where it gets interesting: In the past, a fit body represented hard work and clothing signed the body's work, but what do our bodies and clothing symbolize today? Today, we take the body through a workout rather than actually working with the body. We work out so we can meet a cultural image—but what does this cultural image represent?

In times past, if you saw someone with a lean, hard body, it meant the person lived a mean, hard life. There was a real connection between the sign and what it referenced. But what do our spa-conditioned bodies reference? Baudrillard's point is that there is no real objective or social reference for what we are doing with our bodies today. The only reference to a real life is to that of the past—we used to have fit bodies because we worked. Thus, in terms of real social life, today's gym-produced bodies represent the past image of working bodies. Further, what does this imply about the clothes we wear? The clothes themselves are an image of an image that doesn't exist in any kind of reality. Baudrillard calls this **simulacrum**, an image of an image of a "reality" that never existed and never appears.

Thus, what we buy today aren't even commodities in the strictest sense. They are what Fredric Jameson calls **free-floating signifiers**—signs and symbols that have been cut loose from their social and linguistic contexts, and thus their meaning is at best problematic and generally nonexistent. In such a culture, tradition and family can be equated with paper plates (as in a recent television commercial) and infinite justice with military retribution (as in the U.S. president's initial characterization of the current Iraq conflict).

Rather than representing, as signs did in the first phase, and rather than creating meaningful and social relations, as symbolic exchange did, commodified signs do nothing and mean nothing. They have no referent and their sign-context—the only thing that could possibly impart meaning—is constantly shifting because of mass media and advertising. As they are, these signs cannot provoke an emotional response from us. Emotions, then, develop "a new kind of flatness or depthlessness, a new kind of superficiality in the most literal sense . . . [which is] perhaps the supreme formal feature of all the postmodernisms" (Jameson, 1984, p. 60).

These free-floating signs and images don't represent reality; they create hyperreality. Part of the hyperreality is composed of the commodities that we've been talking about. But a more significant part is provided by the extravagance of media entertainment, like Las Vegas and Disneyland. **Hyperreality** is a way of understanding and talking about the mass of disconnected culture. It comes to substitute for reality. In hyperreality, people are drawn to cultural images and signs for artificial stimulation. In other words, rather than being involved in social reality, people involve themselves with fake stimulations. Examples of such simulacrum include artificial Christmas trees, breast implants, airbrushed Playboy Bunnies, food and drink flavors that don't exist naturally, and so on.

A clear example of this kind of hyperreality is reality television. Though predated by *Candid Camera,* the first reality show in the contemporary sense was *An American Family,* shown on Public Broadcasting Service stations in the United States in 1973. It was a 12-installment show that documented an American family going through the turmoil of divorce. The show was heavily criticized in the press. Today, reality shows are prevalent. Though the numbers are difficult to document, between 2000 and 2005 there were some 170 new reality shows presented to the public in the United States and Great Britain, with the vast majority being shown in the United States. The year 2004 saw reality programming come of age, as there were nine reality shows nominated for a total of 23 Emmy awards.

The interesting thing about reality programming is that there is no reality. However, it presents itself as a *representation* of reality. For example, the show *Survivor* placed 16 "castaways" on a tropical island for 39 days and asked, "Deprived of basic comforts, exposed to the harsh natural elements, your fate at the mercy of strangers . . . who would you become?" (Survivor Show Concept, n.d.). But the "castaways" were never marooned nor were they in any danger (as real castaways would be). And the game rules and challenges read more like *Dungeons and Dragons* than a real survivor manual, with game "challenges" and changes in character attributes for winning (like being granted "immunity"). So, what do the images of reality programming represent? Perhaps they are representations of what a fantasy game would look like if human beings could really get in one. The interesting thing about reality programming, and fantasy games for that matter, is the level of involvement people generate around them. This kind of involvement in simulated images of non-reality is hyperreality.

The significance of the idea of hyperreality is that it lets us see that people in postmodernity seek stimulation and nothing more. Hyperreality itself is void of any significance, meaning, or emotion. But, within that hyperreality, people create unreal worlds of spectacle and seduction. Hyperreality is a postmodern condition, a virtual world that provides experiences more involving and spectacular than everyday life and reality.

Sign Implosion

Baudrillard characterizes the simulacrum and hyperreality of postmodernity as an implosion. Where in modernity there was an explosion of signs, commodities, and distinctions, postmodernity is an implosion of all that. In modernity, there were new sciences such as sociology and psychology; in postmodernity, the divisions between disciplines have collapsed and instead there is an increasing preference for and growth of multidisciplinary studies. In modernity, there were new distinctions of nationality, identity, race, and gender; in postmodernity, these distinctions have imploded and collapsed upon themselves. Postmodernity is fractal and fragmented, with everything seeming political, sexual, or valuable—and if everything is, then nothing is. Baudrillard claims that this implosion of signs, identities, institutions, and all firm boundaries of meaning has led to the end of the social.

What Baudrillard is saying is that the proliferation, appropriation, and circulation of signs by the media and advertising influence the condition of signs, signification, and meaning in general. In the first stage of the sign, signs had very clear and specific meanings. But as societies and economic systems changed, different kinds of media and ideas were added. In the postmodern age, the media used to communicate information becomes utterly disassociated from any kind of idea of representation. Everywhere a person turns today in a postmodern society, there are media. Cell phones, computers, the Internet, television, billboards, "billboard clothing" (clothing hocking brand names), and the like surround us. And every medium is commodified and inundated with advertising. In postmodernity, we are hard pressed to find any space or any object that isn't communicating or advertising something beyond itself.

All of this has a general, overall effect. Signs are no longer moored to any social or physical reality; all of them are fair game for the media's manipulation of desire. Any cultural idea, image, sign, or symbol is apt to be pulled out of its social context and used to advertise and to place the individual in the position of consumer. As these signs are lifted out of the social, they lose all possibility of stable reference. They may be used for anything, for any purpose. And the more media that are present, and the faster information is made available (like DSL versus dial-up computer connections), the faster signs will circulate and the greater will be the appropriation of indigenous signs for capitalist gain, until there remains no sign that has not been set loose and colonized by capitalism run amok. All that remains is a yawning abyss of meaninglessness—a placeless surface that is incapable of holding personal identity, self, or society.

Let's take a single example—gender. Gender has been a category of distinction for a good part of modernity. Harriet Martineau, the first person to ever use the word "sociology" in print, saw some 80 years before women won the right to vote that the project of modernity necessarily entailed women's rights. So close is the relationship between the treatment of women and the project of modernity for Martineau (1838/2003) that to her it becomes one of the earmarks of civilization: "Each civilized society claims for itself the superiority in its treatment of women" (p. 183). When gender first came up as an issue of equality, specifically in terms of a woman's right to vote, there was little confusion about what gender and gender equality meant. It was common knowledge who women were and what that very distinct group wanted.

But as modernity went on, things changed. In the United States after the 1960s, the single category of gender broke down. Various claims to distinction began to emerge around gender: The experience of gender is different by race, by class, by sexuality, and so on. The category imploded, with all the implicit understandings that went along with it. Today, when confronted by a person who appears to be a woman, the observing individual may be unsure. Is the "woman" really a woman or a man trapped in a woman's body? Or, is the "woman" a transsexual, who has physically been altered or symbolically changed (as with someone like RuPaul)? In postmodernity, the given cues of any category or object or experience cannot be taken at face value as indicative of a firm reality. All of the signs are caught up in a whirlwind of hyperreality.

In postmodernity, very few if any things can be accepted at face value. Meaning and reality aren't necessarily what they appear, because signs have been tossed about by the media without constraint, driven by the need to squeeze every drop of profit out of a populace through the proliferation of new markets with ever-shifting directions, cues, signs, and meanings in order to present something "new."

I've pictured my take of Baudrillard's argument in Figure 16.1. Let me emphasize that my intention with this diagram is simply to give you a heuristic device; it's a way to order your thinking about Baudrillard's theory. One of the best things about postmodern theory is that it is provocative, partly because it isn't highly specified. In one sense, then, this kind of picture stifles the postmodern; there's also a way in which something like this is quite modernist: It seeks to reduce complexity by making generalizations. So, I present this figure with some trepidation, but with the intent of giving you a place to "hang your hat." (In other words, if you're feeling at all lost and uncomfortable, then you need a modernist moment.)

As you can see in the figure, I've divided Baudrillard's thought into three main groups: signification, social factors, and social practices. I see Baudrillard as weaving these themes throughout his opus. And I've organized these ideas around the notion of sign phases. Generally speaking, the first two phases of the sign were fairly well grounded in the social. People were clearly involved in face-to-face social networks, the principal form of labor was material, commodities basically contained use- and exchange-values, and humanity was deeply entrenched in symbolic exchange.

Figure 16.1   Baudrillard's Sign Stages

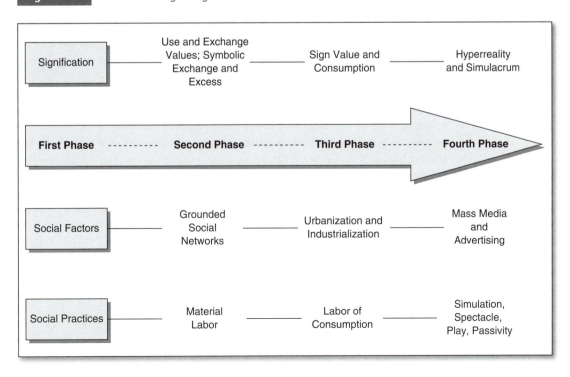

The third phase of the sign came about as the result of capitalism and the nation-state. The strong social factors in this era were urbanization and industrialization; people began to spend increasing amounts of time doing consumption labor; and the value of commodities shifted from use- to sign-value. As communication and transportation technologies increased, mass media and advertising became the important factors in social change. In a world of pure sign, signs no longer signify; it's all hyperreality and simulacrum, the fourth stage of the sign.

Concepts and Theory: The Postmodern Person

Fragmented Identities

Baudrillard envisions the "death of the subject." The subject he has in mind is that of modernity—the individual with strong and clear identities, able to carry on the work of democracy and capitalism. That subject, that person, is dead in postmodern culture. With the increase in mass media and advertising, there has been a corresponding decrease in the strength of all categories and meanings, including identities. What is left is a mediated person, rather than the subject of modernity. As Kenneth Gergen (1991) puts it,

> One detects amid the hurly-burly of contemporary life a new constellation of feelings or sensibilities, a new pattern of self-consciousness. This syndrome may be termed *multiphrenia,* generally referring to the splitting of the individual into a multiplicity of self-investments. (pp. 73–74, emphasis original)

This is an important idea, and one that appears in the work of a number of postmodernists. So let's take a moment to consider it fully.

One of the fundamental ways in which identity and difference are constructed is through exclusion. In psychology, this can by and large be taken for granted: I am by definition excluded from you because I am in my own body. For sociologists, exclusion is a cultural and social practice; it's something we *do,* not something we *are.* This fundamental point may sound elementary to the extreme, but it's important for us to understand it. In order for me to be me, I can't be you; in order for me to be male, I can't be female; in order for me to be white, I can't be black; in order to be a Christian, I can't be a Satanist; ad infinitum.

Cultural identity is defined in opposition to, or as it relates to, something else. Identity and self are based on exclusionary practices. The stronger the practices of exclusion, the stronger will be the identity; and the stronger my identities, the stronger will be my sense of self. Further, the greater the exclusionary practices, the more real will be my experience of identities and self. Hence, the early social movements for equality and democracy had clear practices of exclusion. This gave the people the strength of identity to make the sacrifices necessary to fight.

The twist that postmodernism gives to all this is found in the ideas of cultural fragmentation and de-centered selves and identities. In many ways, the ideas of gender and race are modernist: They collapse individualities into an all-encompassing identity. However, a person isn't simply female, for example—she also has many identities that crosscut that particular cultural interest and may shift her perceptions of self and other in one direction or another. For us to claim any of these identities—to claim to be female, black, male, or white—is really for us to put ourselves under the umbrella of a grand narrative, stories that deny individualities in favor of some broader social category. Grand narratives by their nature include very strong exclusionary tactics.

More to the point, the construction of centered identities is becoming increasingly difficult in postmodernity. Postmodernists argue that culture in postindustrial societies is fragmented. Since culture and identity are closely related, if the culture is fragmented, then so are identities. The idea of postmodernism, then, makes the issues of gender and race very complex. Clear racial and gender identities may thus be increasingly difficult to maintain. The culture has become more multifaceted, and so have identities. This means that we have greater freedom of choice, which we think we enjoy, but freedom of choice also implies that the distinctions between gender and racial identities aren't as clear or as real as they once were. Thus, social movements around race and gender become increasingly difficult to produce in postmodernity.

How, then, are postmodern identities constructed? Zygmunt Bauman (1992) argues that, as a result of de-institutionalization, people live in complex, chaotic systems. Complex systems differ from the mechanistic systems in that they are unpredictable and not controlled by statistically significant factors. In other words, the relationships among the parts are not predictable. For example, race, class, and gender in a complex system no longer produce strong or constant effects in the individual's life or self-concept.

Thus, being a woman, for instance, might be a disability in one social setting and not have any meaning at all in another; likewise, race, class, and gender might come together in a specific setting in unique and random ways. Within these complex systems, groups are formed through unguided self-formation. In other words, we join or leave groups simply because we want to. Moreover, the groups exist not because they reflect a central value system, as a modernist would argue; rather, they exist due to the whim and fancy of their members and the tide of market-driven public sentiment.

The absence of any central value system and firm, objective evaluative guides tends to create a demand for substitutes. These substitutes are symbolically, rather than actually or socially, created. The need for these symbolic group tokens results in what Bauman (1992, pp. 198–199) calls "tribal politics" and defines as self-constructing practices that are collectivized but not socially produced. These neo-tribes function solely as imagined communities and, unlike their premodern namesake, exist only in symbolic form through the commitment of individual "members" to the *idea* of an identity.

But this neo-tribal world functions without an actual group's powers of inclusion and exclusion. It is created through the repetitive and generally individual or imaginative performance of symbolic rituals and exists only so long as the rituals are performed. Neo-tribes are thus formed through concepts rather than actual social groups. They exist as imagined communities through a multitude of agent acts of self-identification and exist solely because people use them as vehicles of self-definition: "Neo-tribes are, in other words, the vehicles (and imaginary sediments) of individual self-definition" (Bauman, 1992, p. 137).

Play, Spectacle, and Passivity

All that we just covered is caught up in the social practices of postmodernity. Opposition is impossible because postmodern culture has no boundaries to push against; it is tantamount to pushing against smoke. Further, the acting subject is equally as amorphous. Thus, according to Baudrillard, there's little place in postmodernity to grab hold of and make a difference. Most things turn out to be innuendo, smoke, spam, mistakes . . . a smooth surface of meaninglessness and seduction. Baudrillard (1993a) leaves us with a few responses: play, spectacle, and passivity.

What can you do with objects that have no meaning? Well, you can play with them and not take them seriously. "So, all that are left are pieces. All that remains to be done is to play with the pieces. Playing with the pieces—that is postmodern" (Baudrillard 1993a, p. 95). How do we play in postmodernity? What would postmodern play look like? Here's an example: People in postmodern societies intentionally engage in fleeting contacts. Consider the case of "flash mobs." According to Wikipedia.com, "A flash mob is a group of people who assemble suddenly in a public place, do something unusual or notable, and then disperse. They are usually organized with the help of the Internet or other digital communications networks" (Flash Mob, n.d.). Sydmob, an Internet group facilitating flash mobs in Sydney, Australia, asks,

> Have you ever been walking down a busy city street and noticed the blank look on people's faces? How about on public transport? That look of total indifference is unmistakable; it's the face of [a] person feeling more like a worker bee than a human being. Have you ever felt like doing something out of the ordinary to see their reaction? (Sydmob, n.d.)

In this play, spectacle becomes important. Georg Simmel, a classical theorist ahead of his time, gives us the same insight. Simmel (1950) argues that

> life is composed more and more of these impersonal contents and offerings that tend to displace the genuine personal colorations and incomparabilities. This results in the individual's summoning the utmost in uniqueness and particularization, in order to preserve his most personal cores. He has to exaggerate this personal element in order to remain audible even to himself. (p. 422)

Echoing Simmel, Zygmunt Bauman (1992) notes that, "to catch the attention, displays must be ever more bizarre, condensed and (yes!) disturbing; perhaps ever more brutal, gory and threatening" (p. xx).

The remaining postmodern practice is a kind of resistance through passivity—refusing to play. There's an old American slogan from the Vietnam era that says, "Suppose they gave a war and nobody came?" This is similar to what Baudrillard has in mind with resistance through passivity. Rather than attempting to engage postmodern culture, or responding in frustration, or trying to change things, Baudrillard advocates refusal or passive resistance. And perhaps like the war that no one shows up for, postmodernity will simply cease.

Summary

• Baudrillard uses Marx's notions of use- and exchange-value to argue that commodities are principally understood in postmodernity in terms of their sign-value.

• Baudrillard proposes four stages of the sign. In the first two stages, the sign adequately represented reality, and social communities were held together through the reciprocity of symbolic exchanges. People were also able to practice "excess"—the boundless potential of humanity—through festivals, rituals, sacrifices, and so on.

• Modernity began in the third phase of the sign with the advent of capitalism and industrialization. Baudrillard characterizes modernity as the consumer society. Within such a society, labor shifts to techniques of consumption with an eye toward sign identification. Modernity also brought rationalization and constraint, the antithesis of symbolic exchange and excess.

• In postmodernity, the increasing presence and speed of mass media, along with ever-increasing levels of commodification and advertising, push all vestiges of meaning out of signs. Mass media tends to empty cultural signs because the natural entropy of information is multiplied and because signification is suppressed in favor of media concerns of production. Advertising pushes this process of emptying further: Advertising sells by image rather than use, which implies that commodities are placed in unrelated sign-contexts in order to fit a media-produced image. These detached and redefined images are pure simulacrum. Postmodern society is inundated by media technology and thus an immense amount of this kind of signification and culture, most of which references and produces a hyperreality.

• Baudrillard's postmodern condition is found in simulation, spectacle, play, and passivity. Baudrillard claims that the central subject of modernity—the person as the nexus of national and economic rights and responsibilities—is dead. In the place of the subject stands a media terminal of fragmented images. What remains is play and spectacle. As signs move ever faster through the postmodern media, their ability to hold meaning continues to disintegrate. Thus, in order to make an impression, cultural displays must be more and more spectacular. In such a climate, the hyperreality of media becomes more and more enticing, with greater emotional satisfaction than real life—but these media images must continue to spin out to ever more radical displays. Playing with empty signs or intentionally disengaging are the only possible responses.

TAKING THE PERSPECTIVE—POSTMODERNISM

In these sections, I try to give you a sense of the theoretical perspective as a whole that an individual theorist is using. However, there's a problem with trying to do this with postmodernism. Recall what Baudrillard said? Systems of reference are gone. So, because culture is fragmented and free-floating for postmodernists, "postmodernism" can't reference any single, cohesive idea. We're not left being silenced, however. Just keep in mind that in this small section I will of necessity (and by definition!) be leaving a good deal out.

The word *postmodernism* was first used in Hispanic literary criticism in the 1930s, it gained currency in the visual arts and architecture by the 1960s and early 1970s, and it made its way into social theory with the French publication of Jean-François Lyotard's *The Postmodern Condition* in 1979 (see Anderson, 1998). As I said, postmodernism is a word that denies its ability to function as a word. There does, however, seem to be one organizing feature: No matter what field we're talking about, postmodernism is always understood in contrast to modernism.

Modernity and *postmodernity* are terms that are used in a number of disciplines. In each the meaning is somewhat different, but it is also generally the same: Modernity is characterized by unity, and postmodernity is distinguished by disunity. In modern literature, for example, the unity of narrative is important. Novels move along according to their plot, and while there might be twists and turns, most readers are fairly confident in how time is moving and where the story is going. Postmodern literature, on the other hand, doesn't move in predictable patterns of plot and character. Stories will typically jump around and are filled with indirect and reflexive references to past styles or stories. The purpose of a modern novel is to convey a sense of continuity in story; the purpose of a postmodern work is to create a feeling of disorientation and ironic humor.

In the social world, modernity is associated with the Enlightenment and defined by progress; by grand narratives and beliefs; and through the structures of capitalism, science, technology, and the nation-state. To state the obvious, postmodernism is the opposite or critique of all that. According to most postmodern thought, things have changed. Society is no longer marked by a sense of hope in progress. People seem more discouraged than encouraged—more filled with a blasé attitude than optimism.

In a late capitalist society, rather than providing a basis of meaning, "Culture has necessarily expanded to the point where it has become virtually coextensive with the economy itself . . . as every material object and immaterial service becomes [an] inseparably tractable sign and vendible commodity" (Anderson, 1998, p. 55). Thus, capitalism has colonized culture and turned meaning into goods that are bought and sold. At the same time, these processes make culture less real. As we saw in the quote from Baudrillard at the beginning of this chapter, signs in advanced capitalism don't represent anything; they have no utility or reality. They are commodified images that serve little more function than to seduce us into consumerism.

The same is true for self and identity: "As an older industrial order is churned up, traditional class formations have weakened, while segmented identities and localized groups, typically based on ethnic or sexual differences, multiply" (Anderson, 1998, p. 62). However, these segmented relationships "pull us in myriad directions, inviting us to play such a variety of roles that the very concept of an 'authentic self' with knowable characteristics recedes from view. The fully saturated self becomes no self at all" (Gergen, 1991, p. 7).

Taken together, then, we can define social postmodernism as a critical form of theorizing that is concerned with the unique problems associated with culture and the subject in advanced capitalistic societies.

BUILDING YOUR THEORY TOOLBOX

Learning More—Primary and Secondary Sources

- Michel Foucault's primary "must reads":
  - *The History of Sexuality, Vol. I: An Introduction,* Vintage, 1990.
  - *The Order of Things: An Archaeology of the Human Sciences,* Vintage, 1994.
  - *Discipline and Punish: The Birth of the Prison,* Vintage, 1995.
  - *The Birth of the Clinic: An Archaeology of Medical Perception,* Vintage Books, 1994.
- Good secondary sources for Foucault:
  - *Michel Foucault,* by Sara Mills, Routledge, 2003.
  - *The Cambridge Companion to Foucault,* edited by Gary Gutting, Cambridge, 1994.
  - *Foucault,* by Gilles Deleuze, University of Minnesota Press, 1988.
- Primary texts for Jean Baudrillard:
  - *For a Critique of the Political Economy of the Sign,* Telos Press, 1981.
  - *The Mirror of Production,* Telos Press, 1975.
  - *Simulacra and Simulation, University* of Michigan Press, 1994.

(Continued)

(Continued)

- Seondary texts for Jean Baudrillard:
  - Jean Baudrillard: *From Marxism to Postmodernism and Beyond,* by Douglas Kellner, Stanford University Press, 1990.
  - *Jean Baudrillard (Routledge Critical Thinkers),* by Richard Lane, Routledge, 2009.

Seeing the Social World (knowing the theory)

- Write a 250-word synopsis of poststructuralism.
- Write a 250-word synopsis of postmodernism.
- After reading and understanding this chapter, you should be able to define the following terms theoretically and explain their theoretical importance to Foucault's theory of power: *truth games, counter-histories, archaeology, genealogy, episteme, discourse, governmentality, objectification, panopticon, microphysics of power, medical gaze.*
- After reading and understanding this chapter, you should be able to define the following terms theoretically and explain their theoretical importance to Baudrillard's theory of postmodernity: *human nature, symbolic exchange, use-value, exchange-value, sign value, commodity fetish, sign fetish, consumer society, labor of consumption, simulacrum, free-floating signifiers, hyperreality, death of the subject, fragmenting identities.*
- After reading and understanding this chapter, you should be able to answer the following questions (remember to answer them *theoretically*):
  - Explain Foucault's connection between power and knowledge. How does he conceptualize power? How does knowledge function as power? What are the unique characteristics of modern power?
  - What does Foucault mean by "the order of things"? Explain how his "counter-histories" are used to expose this order.
  - Define discourse and explain how it provides a subjective position for the speaker.
  - Explain the place of the social sciences (human disciplines) in creating governmentality and the microphysics of power.
  - Describe how sex and sexuality changed between ancient Greek society and modern Western society.
  - How does Baudrillard argue that Marx actually affirms and legitimates capitalism? How does Baudrillard invert Marx's argument?
  - Explain how ideology and fetishism are based on a passion for the code.
  - What are the four stages of the sign? Be certain to explain their characteristics and the social factors that helped bring them about.
  - What is the consumer society? What labor is specific to the consumer society?
  - How do mass media and advertising empty the sign of all meaning and reference?
  - How have social identities imploded in postmodernity? What are the ramifications for political change?
  - Explain why play, spectacle, and passivity make sense in Baudrillard's postmodernity.

Engaging the Social World (using the theory)

- Both Foucault and Baudrillard talk about what it means and what it's like to be you in this society. Go back through this chapter and make two lists, one for Foucault and the other for Baudrillard, that detail the ideas these theorists have about living during this time period. Now go back through the lists and think of examples from your life that illustrate each idea. What insights about your life did you glean? Were you able to think of examples for each idea? How do these different approaches compare and contrast with each other?

Weaving the Threads (building theory)

- Using the index of this book, find the different ways power is defined and used theoretically. Evaluate each of these ways and create a theory of power that you think best explains it. Justify your answer.

- Compare and contrast Foucault's idea of governmentality and Anthony Giddens' notion of the reflexive project of the self. Explain why you think these two ideas are distinct. Together, what do they imply about how we relate to the "self" in modernity?

- Compare and contrast the political implications of Giddens' late-modernity and Baudrillard's postmodernity. Which do you think more accurately reflects the current conditions? Why?

CHAPTER 17

Politics of Identity:

Dorothy E. Smith, Patricia Hill Collins, and Cornel West

I n the first edition of this book, the previous chapter with Foucault and Baudrillard was last, and this chapter came before it. On many levels, shifting the places of two chapters seems insignificant; and, truth be told, it probably is. But it gives me the opportunity to explain the shift, and I think that has importance. Over the past few years, I've been thinking quite a bit about modernity and democracy. As I've studied and thought and interacted with my students, I've become deeply impressed with some powerful changes that have been building over the last couple of decades but appear to be coming to fruition. The tenor of the entire book reflects this sense, as I've repeatedly brought us back to the foundations of the age we live in and the place the social disciplines have in it. I've also brought us back numerous times to consider the person in modernity.

Things are different today than they were in 1776 when this social experiment called democracy began. The world has changed since the emancipatory movements of the nineteenth and early twentieth centuries. And things are different today than they were during the upheavals of the 1960s. The social world that we've seen painted over the last few chapters is the new one; at the very least these artists have given us glimmers of what is happening. In the words of Stephen King, the world's moved on. And in the moving, the person and the politics of the person have changed. While you may not be black or female, the social thinkers in this chapter outline a different kind of politics than was first conceived at the birth of democracy. They tell us more about the political person hinted at in Giddens' and Castells' theories. It's a politics of knowledge and identities. While I wouldn't say that everybody in this chapter fits into Patricia Hill Collins' definition of identity politics, it nonetheless captures an essence that I think they all share: Identity politics encompasses "a way of knowing that sees lived experiences as important to creating knowledge and crafting group-based political strategies. Also, [it is] a form of political resistance where an oppressed group rejects its devalued status" (P. H. Collins, 2000, p. 299).

The point in ending the book with this chapter is that you matter. Who you are and how you express your existence in the world around you matters. It matters because in modernity it's always mattered. As I've said, modernity was founded on a specific idea of the citizen. And I think that the same is true whatever world we're moving into; in fact, if the glimmers of the last few chapters are an indication, then I would say it's even truer today. And the exciting, frightening thing is that I think Giddens is right: There aren't the same kinds of guideposts that traditional and early modern societies provided. We need to find our way together, which is, after all, the meaning behind democracy. The voices in this chapter are powerful. I hope you'll listen and critically think about what they say.

Gendered Consciousness:
Dorothy E. Smith (1926–)

Theorist's Digest
Concepts and Theory: The Problem With Facts
    Not Theory—Method!
    Facts and Texts: The New Materialism
    Defining Standpoint
Concepts and Theory: The Standpoint of Women
    Sociology and the Relations of Ruling
    The Fault Line
Standpoint and Text-Mediated Power
Summary

Gender inequality has been studied by sociologists ever since the time of Harriet Martineau. In 1837 she published her study of America. For Martineau (1837/2005), one of the key tests of civilization and democracy in a society is the condition of women: "If the test of civilization be sought, none can be so sure as the condition of that half of society over which the other half has power" (p. 291). Granted, since that time the topic of gender has come in and out of favor with the discipline as a whole. Nevertheless, it's safe to say that gender inequality as a topic of study has been a central concern since the 1970s, and sociologists have done countless studies and published innumerable articles, books, and essays on the subject since then.

But, what if a good many of them actually worked to suppress women rather than liberate them? Dorothy E. Smith asks us to consider this possibility. She argues that the way in which women are dominated isn't solely through the social structures with which Janet Saltzman Chafetz told us about in Chapter 10. No, gender inequality also works through the social and behavioral sciences as they create *knowledge about women* in opposition to *women's knowledge.* This body of knowledge claims objectivity and thus authority "not on the basis of its capacity to speak truthfully, but in terms of its specific capacity to exclude the presence and experience of particular subjectivities" (Smith, 1987, p. 2). Smith wants to begin with and center social and behavioral research on the actual lived experiences of people and their encounter with texts, rather than on the texts that deny the very voices they claim to express.

THEORIST'S DIGEST

Brief Biography

Dorothy E. Smith was born in Northallerton, Yorkshire, Great Britain, in 1926. She earned her undergraduate degree in 1955 from the London School of Economics. In 1963, Smith received her PhD from the University of California at Berkeley. She has taught at Berkeley, the University of Essex, and the University of British Columbia. She is currently Adjunct Professor at the University of Victoria. In recognition of her contributions to sociology, the American Sociology Association (ASA) honored Smith with the Jessie Bernard Award in 1993 and the Career of Distinguished Scholarship Award in 1999. Her book *The Everyday World as Problematic* has received two awards from the Canadian Sociology and Anthropology Association: the Outstanding Contribution Award and the John Porter Award, both given in 1990.

Central Sociological Questions

Like Foucault, Smith sees that knowledge produced through the social sciences can contain and thus replicate relations of ruling. Smith is centrally concerned with how the daily lives of men and women are quite often different. Yet, when gender is studied from a social scientific perspective, the distinct experiences and knowledge of women are written out. The relations of ruling, then, continue to be exerted even under the guise of gender inequality. "My research concern is to build an ordinary good knowledge of the text-mediated organization of power from the standpoint of women in contemporary capitalism" (Smith, 1992, p. 97).

Simply Stated

Smith argues that the social and behavioral sciences have systematically developed an objective body of knowledge about the individual, social relations, and society in general. This body of knowledge claims objectivity and thus authority "not on the basis of its capacity to speak truthfully, but in terms of its specific capacity to exclude the presence and experience of particular subjectivities" (Smith, 1987, p. 2). Because of this exclusion, social scientific texts are nothing more than an expression of the relations of ruling that continue to oppress women. Smith wants to center research on the actual lived experiences of women, and their encounters with these texts.

(Continued)

Concepts and Theory: The Problem With Facts

As I've done with others, I'm putting Smith's perspective upfront rather than at the end of the chapter. The main reason I'm doing this with Smith is because in many ways her theory and perspective are the same; as you'll see, it's hard to talk of one apart from the other. Plus, she gives us a different account of how gender inequality is achieved than did Chafetz (Chapter 10), again, because she sees the world a bit differently.

Not Theory—Method!

In 1992, *Sociological Theory*, the premier theoretical journal of the American Sociological Association, presented a symposium on the work of Dorothy E. Smith. Though Smith had been publishing for quite some time, her dramatic impact on sociology came with the publications in 1987 of *The Everyday World as Problematic* and in 1990, *The Conceptual Practices of Power*. Being the subject of a special issue in *Sociological Theory* so soon after the publication of two major works attests to the impact that Smith's perspective was having on sociology. Among the commentators in that special issue were Patricia Hill Collins, Robert Connell, and Charles Lemert, each a significant theorist in her or his own right. However, Smith (1992) critiqued each of these theorists as having misinterpreted her work, saying "each constructs her or his own straw Smith" (p. 88).

Of course, Collins, Connell, and Lemert had their own individual issues, but Smith (1992) argues that they universally misconstrued her work as theory rather than method. "It is not . . . a totalizing theory. Rather it is a *method of inquiry*, always ongoing, opening things up, discovering" (p. 88, emphasis original). This is obviously an important point for us to note at the beginning of our discussion of Smith's work. She doesn't give us a general theory, not even a general theory of gender oppression. Smith gives us a method, but it isn't a method in the same sense as data analysis—Smith's is a *theoretical* method. It's a method grounded in a theoretical understanding of the world that results in theoretical insights. Further, for Smith these theoretical insights are themselves continually held up to evaluation and revision.

In general, Smith's work is considered "standpoint theory." As we'll see below, that's a fairly accurate description of what she does. But Smith argues that thinking about standpoint theory theoretically makes the idea too abstract and it defeats the original intent. Like Pierre Bourdieu, Smith is very interested in the practices of power. She is interested in what happens on the ground, "where the rubber meets the road," in the lived experiences of women, more than the abstract words of sociological theory.

Let me give you an example that might help us see the distinction that Smith is making. Not long ago I was talking to a friend of mine who plays and builds drums. We were talking about the special feeling that comes from building the instrument you play. There's a kind of connection that develops between the builder and the wood, a connection that is grounded in the physical experience of the wood. I agreed with what he said and told him that kind of knowledge is called "kinesthetic." But I was painfully aware that there was a real difference between what we were each talking about. He has actually worked with the wood out of which he builds his drum kits; though I play guitar, I have never experienced that kind of connection with my instrument. I had the word for what he was talking about, but he had the actual experience.

Smith is arguing that something happens when we formalize and generalize our concepts. We can quickly move out of the realm of real experience. As such, it is possible for concepts to play a purely discursive role. Just like in my example of kinesthetic knowledge, we can talk about things of which we only have discursive or linguistic knowledge. Thus, I can talk about the intuitive connection that exists between a musician and an instrument that he or she has built, but I have no actual knowledge of it. It's purely theoretical for me.

Obviously, there are no significant consequences of my woodworking example. But in the social world, there can be important ramifications, and that's the point that Smith wants us to see. Standpoint theory isn't a theory per se; it's a method of observation that privileges the point of view of actual people over theoretical, abstract knowledge. That may sound commonsensical and you may agree with it, but Smith would contend that most of what you and I know about the social world is like my knowledge of building a musical instrument.

In thinking about Smith's approach, it is important to note that she doesn't see herself as arguing against abstractions. To one degree or another, theory is usually abstracted. When we talk about theory being abstract, we mean that it is not simply a statement or restatement of the particulars. In a fundamental way, then, most theories and theoretical terms exist outside of the actual situation as generalizations. For example, there is a significant difference between saying "LaToya went to Food Lion to do the food shopping" and "Women generally do the grocery shopping." The first statement is particular; it refers to the behaviors of a specific person at a definite location and time. In that sense, the statement is limited and not theoretically powerful. The second statement, because it is abstract, is more theoretically powerful. Most theory is at least somewhat abstract; it's the best way for us to say something significant about what is going on. Because she focuses on the actualities of lived experience, Smith's standpoint theory can be read to mean that abstractions are themselves bad. But that isn't her intent.

Nor is she interested in simply discrediting or deconstructing the knowledge or relations of ruling. Quite a bit of critical theory is aimed at these issues. For example, chances are good that much of what you've learned in other classes about gender or race is a historical account of how patriarchy or racism came about and how it functions to oppress people. The intent in these courses is to discredit sexism or racism by deconstructing its ideological and historical basis. But discrediting isn't Smith's specific intent either.

Smith argues that in both these cases, abstractions and ideological deconstruction, the critique by itself isn't enough; it doesn't tell the actual story. Theory in both forms plays itself out in the everyday, actual world of people, and that is Smith's concern. Insofar as theory and ideology mean anything, they mean something in everyday life, whether that life is the researcher's or that of ordinary women. Like I said, Smith is interested in where the rubber meets the road. In this case, the "rubber" is made up of theoretical abstractions and ideological knowledge that governs, and the "road" is the actual experiences of women. Thus, Smith isn't interested in doing away with abstractions per se, nor is she simply interested in exposing the relations of ruling; doing so is not enough and it runs the risk of replicating the problem, as we will soon see.

Facts and Texts: The New Materialism

As we've seen in previous chapters, Marx's materialism argues that there is a relationship between one's material class interests and the knowledge one has. Smith proposes a *new materialism,* one where facts and texts rather than commodification produce alienation and objectification. With Marx, commodities and money mediate the relationships people have with themselves and others. That is, we relate and come to understand our self and others through money and products. Marx's theory was specific to industrialized capitalism—the economies of more technologically advanced societies may be different. Some of the important changes include shifts from manufacturing to "service" economies, increases in the use of credentials and in the amount and use of expert knowledge, advances in communication and transportation technologies, exponential increases in the use of advertising images and texts, and so on. In such economies, relationships and power are mediated more through texts and "facts" than commodities and money. Further, just as people misrecognized the reality in back of money and commodities, so today most people misrecognize the relations of power in back of texts and facts. Texts and the facticity that text produces are the primary medium through which power is exercised in a society such as the United States.

Text

Though the idea of text is gaining usage and popularity, it, like culture, is one of the more difficult words to define. Winfried Nöth (1985/1995), in her *Handbook of Semiotics,* says that given that textuality is defined by the researcher, "It is not surprising that semioticians of the text have been unable to agree on a definition and on criteria of their object of research" (p. 331). Smith, however, gives us a broad, clear, and useful definition of "text" that includes three elements:

the actual written words or symbols, the physical medium through which words and symbols are expressed, and the materiality of the text—the actual practices of writing and reading.

Smith is specifically concerned with texts that are officially or organizationally written and read. She gives us the example of two different texts that came out of an incident in 1968 involving police and street people in Berkeley, California. One text came in the form of a letter to an underground newspaper and was written by someone who was marginally involved in the altercation. His text was "written from the standpoint of an actual experience" (Smith, 1990, p. 63) and contained specific references to people, places, times, and events. It was embedded in and expressed actual life experiences as they happened. This was a personal account of a personal experience that reflexively situated the writer in the event.

The other text was the official incident report that came from the mayor's office. The standpoint of this second text is organizational. Rather than being an account of a personal experience, it is written from the point of view of anonymous police officers who are portrayed as trained professionals and organizational representatives. In addition, the official report embedded the text within "sequences of organizational action extending before and after them" (Smith, 1990, p. 64) using reports from police, courts, and probation officers. In other words, the official text brought in many elements that exist outside of the actual situation and experience. In the end, every element of the actual experience was given meaning through these extra-local concepts rather than the experience itself.

Facts

The obliteration of the historical and specific sources is part of the process of creating facts (Smith, 1990, p. 66). The facticity of a statement is thus not a property of the statement itself. A statement simply proposes a state of affairs such as "The earth is flat." For a statement to become fact, there must be a corresponding set of practices that provide its plausibility base—a group of people, beliefs, and practices that give substance to the statement. Facticity, then, "is essentially a property of an institutional order mediated by texts" (p. 79). Facts and texts are organizational achievements, not independent truths of the world. These are the texts and facts in which Smith is interested: the ones that are written and read as part of organizational method and relations of power. They create an objective reality whose existence is dependent upon specific institutionalized practices.

Defining Standpoint

In general, *standpoint theory* addresses the issue of which kind of knowledge carries the greatest value. Most people have a tendency to accept knowledge in a taken-for-granted manner: Knowledge may be incorrect, but those mistakes can be fixed and knowledge progresses onward. Standpoint theory, like Marxian and other critical theories before it, points out that knowledge is specific to social structure and position. In other words, there are many forms of knowledge, but some of them are privileged over others. Obviously, the privileged forms of knowledge benefit the power elite and serve to suppress others.

Standpoint theory argues that groups standing outside the place of privilege actually have a more authentic knowledge of the social system. This is true first because they are in a better position to see the whole system at work. For example, most white people aren't aware that they are not the subject of police scrutiny. Most blacks, on the other hand, have firsthand knowledge of how surveillance works in the shopping malls and streets of America. The second reason it is more authentic is that it intrinsically recognizes the political nature of all knowledge and ways of knowing. Rather than seeing information as pure and free from ethical considerations, standpoint recognizes that all knowledge exists because of a specific kind of sociopolitical configuration of social structures and interests. Further, the use to which information is put is always tainted by values and politics.

As a form of critical knowledge, then, standpoint theory seeks to:

- Privilege the lived experiences of those who are outside the relations of ruling
- Represent the social world from the standpoint of the oppressed
- Make the studies and accounts of disenfranchised groups accessible to those who are the subjects of the studies
- Create knowledge that can be used by the oppressed to subvert and change their social world

Concepts and Theory: The Standpoint of Women

Smith argues that the distinction between abstract knowledge (or text) and lived experience holds for all people, whether male, female, black, white, Chicano, or anyone else. However, women's experience and knowledge is specifically important. Generally speaking, there are a few reasons why this would be accurate. First, as we've already seen, knowledge of oppressed peoples is in some ways truer than that of the ruling groups. Because it crosscuts all other social categories, the oppressive system par excellence is gender. Thus, women's knowledge is uniquely suited to help us see an oppressive structure for what it is.

Another reason to favor women's knowledge is that women are particularly embodied. For example, the beginnings of gender stratification are undoubtedly linked to the control of women's sexuality and bodies. Obviously, these beginnings are clouded by time and are fairly complex. Yet, we can get a sense of how women's inequality and their bodies became linked by looking at a few of these issues. One of the most important factors in establishing this link is the control of wealth. In order to dominate wealth, men had to control inheritance. Until DNA paternity testing became a reality, a man's ability to legitimate his lineage was largely dependent upon exclusive access to the woman; thus, men had to regulate women's sexual behaviors in order to control wealth.

Women's bodies also became important politically in at least two other ways. First, women were used to form political alliances through marriage. Obviously, a man was involved in this marriage, but in Western civilizations it was generally the woman who left her home and became part of her husband's realm. In exchange terms, she was the "good" that was traded, and the quality of that good, in terms of sexual purity, was of utmost importance. Second, women's bodies were used in warfare as a way of demoralizing the enemy, through such things as systematic rape, a practice termed "rape warfare" by Beverly Allen (1996) and "mass rape" by Alexandra Stiglmayer (1994) in their analyses of incidents in Bosnia-Herzegovina.

There is no doubt that women's bodies continue to be a primary site of gender inscription, as countless studies and films (such as Jean Kilbourne's *Killing Us Softly* series) document. For Smith (1987), a woman's body is significant because it "is also the place of her sensory organization of immediate experience; the place where her coordinates of here and now, before and after, are organized around herself as center" (p. 82). Thus, women are likely more aware of and more centered in their bodies than are men.

A third reason for privileging women's experiences is the position they play relative to men and men's relationship to objective text. We'll consider this again in the section on the fault line, but it bears mentioning here. While what Smith is saying about objective knowledge on one hand and subjective experience on the other is true about men, it is also true that women by and large take care of most of the details of life (such as cooking, cleaning, childrearing, and so on). These "details" are what allow "men's life" to be lived. Because women take care of the actualities, men are allowed to think that life is really about the abstract, general knowledge they construct and believe. Women thus typically provide a buffer between men and the actual demands of life, and thus, women's knowledge is more materially real.

Because of her emphasis on standpoint, Smith argues that her project is not an ideological representation or movement. Often when we think of feminism, we think of a social movement with a specific agenda and ideology. While liberation from oppression is certainly part of what Smith (1987) wants to attain, she doesn't offer us "an ideological position that represents women's oppression as having a determinate character and takes up the analysis of social forms with a view to discovering in them the lineaments of what the ideologist already supposes that she knows" (pp. 106–107). Whether it comes from social science or feminism, Smith is concerned about knowledge that objectifies, that starts from a position outside the everyday world of lived experience, as generally sociology does.

Smith gives us an example of walking her dog. When walking her dog, she needs to be careful that he doesn't "do his business" in places that are inappropriate. Smith points out that her behavior in this situation would generally be understood in terms of norms. From the normative perspective, she would simply be seen as conforming to the social norms of walking a dog. However, Smith (1987) contends that the idea of norm "provides for the surface properties of my behavior, what I can be seen to be doing" (p. 155). In other words, the normative approach can only give us a surface or simplistic understanding of what is going on. What is ignored in seeing the norm is "an account of the constitutive work that is going on" (p. 155).

In this case, "constitutive work" refers to the efforts Smith must put forth in conforming to the norm. And in the process of conforming, there are any number of contingencies, including the kind of neighborhood, the type of neighbors, the kind of leash, the breed of dog, the weather, her subjective states, and so on. All of the contingencies require practical reasoning that in turn produces a specific kind of reaction to the norm. The issue for Smith is that the normative account ignores the actual experiences of the person: how, when, and why the individual conforms to, negotiates, or ignores the demands made by the norm.

Disregarding the site of constitutive work is how "the very intellectual successes of the women's movement have created their own contradictions" (Smith, 1992, p. 88). The contradictions arise, according to Smith, as feminism becomes its own theory—a theory that is seen to exist apart from the lived experiences of the women it attempts to describe. For Smith, resistance and revolution do not—indeed, cannot—begin in theory or even sociology. Such a beginning would simply replace the ruling ideas with another set of ruling ideas. In order to create a sociology of women, or to bring about any real social change, it is imperative to begin and continue in the situated perspectives of the people in whom we are interested.

Thus, Smith's intent is to open up the space of actual experience as the site of research. This is exactly what Smith means by the title of her 1987 book, *The Everyday World as Problematic*. Most social research takes on problems that are guided by the literature, the researcher's career, or by the availability of funds. According to Smith, this practice results in a body of knowledge that more often than not only references itself or the relations of ruling that fund it. In Smith's work, it is the everyday world of women that is problematized. It's the actual experience of women that sets the problems and questions of research and provides the answers and theory. "Inquiry does not begin within the conceptual organization or relevances of the sociological discourse, but in actual experience as embedded in the particular historical forms of social relations that determine that experience" (Smith, 1987, p. 49).

Another way to put this issue is that most social research assumes a reciprocity of perspectives. One of the things that ethnomethodology (see Chapter 12) has taught us about the organization of social order at the micro level is that we all assume that our way of seeing things corresponds fairly closely to the way other people see things. More specifically, we assume that if another person were to walk in our shoes, they would experience the world just like we do. This is an assumption that allows us to carry on with our daily lives. It lets us act as if we share a common world, even though we may not and we can never know for sure if we do. According to Smith, social science usually works in this way, too, but she wants us to problematize that assumption in sociology. She wants us to ask, "What is it like to be *that* person in *that* body in *those* circumstances?"

Sociology and the Relations of Ruling

Smith (1990) talks about the practices, knowledge, and social relations that are associated with power as relations of ruling. Specifically, *relations of ruling* include "what the business world calls *management*, it includes the professions, it includes government and the activities of those who are selecting, training, and indoctrinating those who will be its governors" (p. 14, emphasis original). In technologically advanced societies that are bureaucratically organized, ruling and governing take place specifically through abstract concepts and symbols, or text. As Michel Foucault explains, knowledge is power; it is the currency that dominates our age. Authority and control are exercised in contemporary society through different forms of knowledge—specifically, knowledge that objectifies its subjects.

The social sciences in particular are quite good at this. They turn people into populations that can be reduced to numbers, measured, and thus controlled. Through abstract concepts and generalized theories, the social sciences empty the person of individual thoughts and feelings and reduce him or her to concepts and ideas that can be applied to all people grouped together within a specific social type. The social sciences thus create a textual reality, one that exists in "the literature" outside of the lived experience of people.

Much of this literature is related to data generated by the state, through such instruments as the U.S. Census or the FBI's Uniform Crime Reporting (UCR) Program. These data are accepted without question as the authoritative representation of reality because they are seen as *hard data*—data that correspond to the assumptions of science. These data are then used to "test" theories and hypotheses that are generated, more often than not, either from previous work or by academics seeking to establish their names in the literature. Even case histories that purport to represent the life of a specific individual are rendered as documents that substantiate established theoretical understandings.

Thus, most of the data, theory, and findings of social science are generated by a state driven by political concerns, by academics circumscribed by the discipline of their fields, by professors motivated to create a vita (resume) of distinction, or by professionals seeking to establish their practice. All of this creates "textual surfaces of objective knowledge in public contexts" that are "to be read factually . . . as evidences of a reality 'in back of' the text" (Smith, 1990, pp. 191, 107). Therefore, a sociology that is oriented toward abstract theory and data analysis results in a discipline that "is a systematically developed consciousness of society and social relations . . . [that] claims objectivity not on the basis of its capacity to speak truthfully, but in terms of its specific capacity to exclude the presence and experience of particular subjectivities" (Smith, 1987, p. 2).

These concepts, theories, numbers, practices, and professions become relations of ruling as they are used by the individual to understand and control her own subjectivity, as she understands herself to be a subject of the discourses of sociology, psychology, economics, and so on. We do this when we see ourselves in the sociological articles or self-help books we read, in the written histories or newspapers of society, or in business journals or reports. With or without awareness of it, we mold ourselves to the picture of reality presented in the "textual surfaces of objective knowledge."

Smith points out that this process of molding becomes explicit for those people wanting to become sociologists, psychologists, or business leaders. Disciplines socialize students into accepted theories and methods. In the end, these are specific guidelines that determine exactly what constitutes sociological knowledge. For example, most of the professors you've had are either tenured or on a tenure track. Whether an instructor has tenure or not is generally the chief distinction between assistant and associate professors. And when a sociology professor comes up for tenure and promotion, one of the most important questions asked about his or her work is whether or not it qualifies as sociology. Not everything we do is necessarily sociology—it has to conform to specific methodologies, assumptions, concepts, and so on to qualify as sociology.

There is something reasonable about this work of exclusion. If I wrote an article with nothing but math concepts in it, it probably shouldn't be considered sociology. Otherwise there wouldn't be any differences among any of the academic disciplines. However, Smith's point is that there is more going on than simple definitions. Definitions of methods and theory are used by the powerful to exclude the powerless. What counts as sociology and the criteria used to make the distinctions are therefore reflections of the relations of ruling. Sociology and all the social sciences have historically been masculinist enterprises, which means that what constitutes sociology is defined from the perspective of ruling men. The questions that are deemed important and the methods and theories that are used have all been established by men: "How sociology is thought—its methods, conceptual schemes, and theories—has been based on and built up within the male social universe" (Smith, 1990, p. 13).

Let me give you an example to bring this home, one that has to do with race, but the illustration still holds. In the latter part of the 1990s, two colleagues and I were untenured in our department. One of those colleagues is black. All three of us were worried about tenure and promotion—there was quite a bit of contradictory information circulating about how we could get tenure. So we had a meeting with the man who was department head at the time. Each of us had specific concerns. My black colleague's concern was about race. As a result of some of the things the department head said, I asked him point blank: "Will the articles that [my black colleague] has published count for tenure and promotion or not?" The head answered that he wasn't sure because the articles were published in black journals and may not therefore "count as sociology." As you can see, what counts as "sociology" is defined by those in power.

The Fault Line

Smith argues that since the motivations, questions, and data come out of the concerns of those that govern and not the actual experiences of those living under the relations of ruling, masculinist knowledge is by default objective and objectifying—from beginning to end, it stands outside of the actual experience of those other than the ruling. Smith's sociology is thus not specifically concerned with what usually passes as prejudice or sexism, that expressed through negative stereotypes and discrimination. Rather, "We are talking about the consequences of women's exclusion from a full share in the making of what becomes treated as our culture" (Smith, 1987, p. 20).

One of those consequences is the experience of a **fault line** for those women training as social scientists. The idea of a fault line comes from geology where it refers to the intersection between a geologic fault (a fracture in the earth's crust) and the earth's surface. Many fault lines are dramatically visible. (If you've not seen one, use an Internet search engine to find an image of a fault line.) Smith's analogy is quite striking. She is arguing that the fault line for women is conceptual; it occurs between the kind of knowledge that is generally produced in society, specifically through the social sciences, and the knowledge that women produce as a result of their daily experiences. There is a decisive break between the two.

We generally think there are some differences between objective culture or knowledge and the lives that people live. But because the current relations of ruling produce masculinist knowledge, men do not sense a disjuncture between what they live and what they know of the world. Part of the reason for this is that many of the activities of men match up with or correspond to abstract, objectifying knowledge. A male sociologist "works in the medium he studies" (Smith, 1990, p. 17). But even for men, there is still a clear distinction between objective knowledge, "the governing mode of our kind of society" (p. 17), and daily life. Thus, while there may be a correspondence for men, there is also a place "where things smell, where the irrelevant birds fly away in front of the window, where he has indigestion, where he dies" (p. 17). In other words, Smith is arguing that even for men there is a break between objective forms of knowledge and daily life as it is subjectively experienced. The difference is that generally men don't sense the disjunction. But *why* don't men sense or experience it?

The reason, Smith informs us, is that women have traditionally negotiated that break for men. Let's think about the usual distinction between boss and secretary. Generally speaking, the secretary is there to do the menial labor, to take care of the mundane details through which an organization functions, and to keep the boss free from intrusions from the outside world by screening all calls and letters. Think also about the traditional division of labor in the home. Men go to work while women take care of the "small details" of running a household: grocery shopping, cooking, cleaning, and taking care of the kids. Both of these examples picture the mediation role that Smith tells us women play—women intervene between men and the actual lived world and they take care of the actualities that make real life possible. In doing so, they shelter men from the "bifurcation of consciousness" that women experience (Smith, 1987, p. 82).

Standpoint and Text-Mediated Power

Bringing all this together, we end up with a rather new way of doing sociology, one that focuses on the experience of women as it is mediated through various texts, particularly those produced through the relations of ruling. I've diagrammed my take on Smith's ideas in Figure 17.1. As with any such model, especially one constructed to reflect a critical perspective, it is a simplification. But in some ways I think that a simplification is exactly what Smith is after. Her argument entails elements from existentialism, phenomenology, symbolic interactionism, ethnomethodology, and Marxist theory. The argument is thus not simplistic. It is quite

Figure 17.1 Smith's Standpoint Inquiry

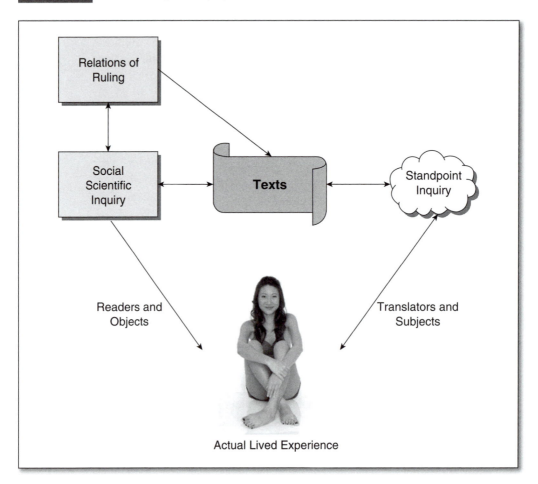

Actual Lived Experience

complex and nuanced and it can and will inspire intricate and subtle thought and research. But her point is rather straightforward—social research and theory need to be grounded in the actual lived experiences of people, particularly women.

The first thing I'd like for you to notice about Figure 17.1 is the central position of both actual lived experience and text. Smith (1992) argues that text forms "the bridge between the actual and discursive. It is a material object that brings into actual contexts of reading a fixed form of meaning" (p. 92). Notice the distinction that Smith is making between the "fixed form" of the text and the "actual context of reading." The actual context is our place of lived experiences. It's a place where life is unfixed, spontaneous, meaningful, and subjective. The text, however, is fixed.

When we become aware of the texts that surround our lived reality, they form the bridge that Smith is talking about. There are two ways through which these texts can influence us. First, we may become directly aware of them, generally through higher education but also through the media. At this point, the discursive text directly enters the everyday life of people. This kind of text is generally authoritative; it claims to be the voice of true knowledge gained through scientific or organizational inquiry. However, as Smith points out, social scientific research is based outside of actual lived experience. Its position outside is in fact what makes this knowledge appear legitimate, at least in a culture dominated by scientific discourse. It is this appearance that prompts us to privilege the objective voice above our own. But there is more to these texts, as you can see from the left side of Figure 17.1.

The relations of ruling have a reciprocal relationship with social scientific inquiry, as noted by the double-headed arrow. We believe that legitimate research produces the only real knowledge, and government finances, directs, and thus defines the kinds of research that are seen as legitimate. Social scientific inquiry then produces the kinds of data and knowledge that reinforce and legitimate the ruling. The single-headed arrow from relations of ruling to text implies the top-down control of knowledge that Marx spoke of: The ruling ideas come from the ruling people, in this case men. The arrow between scientific inquiry and text, however, is two-headed. This means that the questions and theories that social scientific research uses come from the literature rather than the real lives of people. It also implies that social science is in a dialogue with itself, between its texts and its inquiry.

The second way we can become aware of these texts is through social scientific inquiry itself. Have you ever answered the phone and found that someone wanted you to respond to a survey? Or have you ever been stopped in a mall and "asked a few questions" by someone with a clipboard? Have you ever filled out a census survey? Through all these ways and many others, we are exposed to objectifying texts by social scientific inquiry.

Notice that the arrow coming from social scientific inquiry has only one head, going toward the actual world of women, and notice that the arrow has two nouns: *readers* and *objects*. This one-way arrow implies that social scientific research produces both readers and objects. The readers are the researchers; they are trained to read or impose their text onto the actual world. They see the lived experience of women through the texts and methods of scientific research. They come to real, actual, embodied life with a preexisting script, one that has the potential to blind them to the actualities of women. Further, when the questions and methods of science are used to understand women, women are made into objects, passive recipients of social science's categories and facts.

The right side of the model depicts Dorothy Smith's approach. There are two important things to notice. First, there are no relations of ruling controlling standpoint inquiry. Part of this is obvious. As I've mentioned, Smith says that this way of seeing things is applicable to all types of people, but it is particularly salient for women. The reason for its importance for women is that the relations of ruling are masculine in a society such as ours. Men control most of the power and wealth and thus control most of the knowledge that is produced. And while there is a difference between objective knowledge on the one hand and the lived experience of men on the other, women mitigate that discrepancy.

But this issue of ruling isn't quite that clear-cut for Smith. Relations of ruling are obviously associated with men. However, there is a not-so-obvious part as well.

The work of women or feminists (who can be either men or women) can fall prey to the same problem that produces social scientific inquiry. This can happen when women reify the ideas, ideology, or findings of feminist research. Any time research begins outside of the lived experience of embodied people, it assumes an objective perspective and in the end creates abstract knowledge. This is how women's movements "have created their own contradictions." It's possible, then, for women's knowledge to take on the same guise as men's. In Smith's approach, there are no relations of ruling, whether coming from men or women. Standpoint inquiry must continually begin and end in the lived experiences of people.

The other thing I'd like to call your attention to is that all the arrows associated with standpoint inquiry are double-headed. Rather than producing readers and objects, standpoint inquiry creates space for translators and subjects. In standpoint, the lives of women aren't simply read; that is, they aren't textually determined. A researcher using standpoint inquiry is situated in a never-ending dialogue with the actual and the textual. There is a constant moving back and forth among the voice of the subject, the voice of authoritative text, and the interpretations of the researcher. Smith (1992) sees this back-and-forth interplay as a dialectic:

> The project locates itself in a dialectic between actual people located just as we are and social relations, in which we participate and to which we contribute, that have come to take on an existence and a power over against us. (pp. 94–95)

Notice that the dialectic is between actual experience and social relations. Smith is arguing that in advanced bureaucratic societies, our relationships with other people are by and large produced and understood through text. For example, you have a social relationship with the person teaching this class. What is that relationship? To state the obvious, the relationship is that of professor–student. Where is that relationship produced? You might be tempted to say that it is produced between you and your professor, but you would be wrong, at least from Smith's point of view. The relationship is *practiced* between you and your professor, but it is *produced* in the university documents that spell out exactly what qualifies as a professor and a student (remember, you had to apply for admittance) and how professors and students are supposed to act.

This textuality of relationships is a fact of almost every single relationship you have. Of course, the relations become individualized, but even your relationship with your parents (How many books on parenting do you think are available?) and with the person you're dating (How many articles and books have been written about dating? How many dating-related surveys have you seen in popular magazines?) are all controlled and defined through text. However, as we've already seen, Smith argues that even in the midst of all this text, there is a reality of actual, lived experience. Smith is explicitly interested in the dialectic that occurs between abstract, objectifying texts on the one hand, and the lived actualities of women on the other.

We thus come to the core of Smith's project. Recently (2005), Smith has termed this project "institutional ethnography." The "ethnography" portion of the term is meant to convey its dependence upon lived experience. Smith's project, then, is one that emphasizes inquiry rather than abstract theory. But, again, remember that Smith isn't necessarily arguing against abstractions and generalizations. She herself uses abstractions. Notice this quote from Smith (1987) concerning the fault line: "This inquiry into the implications of a sociology for women begins from the discovery of a point of rupture in my/our experience as woman/women within the social forms of consciousness" (p. 49). In it she uses both abstractions and particulars: my/our, woman/women. To say anything about women—which is a universal term—is to already assume and use a theoretical abstraction. Thus, Smith uses abstract concepts, so she isn't saying that in and of themselves they are problematic—the issue is what we do with them. Her concern is for when abstractions are reduced to "a purely discursive function" (Smith, 1992, p. 89). This happens when concepts are reified or when inquiry begins in text: "To begin with the categories is to begin in discourse" (p. 90).

There are, I think, two ways that Smith uses and approaches abstractions. First, in standpoint inquiry, concepts are never taken as if they represented a static reality. Lived experience is an ongoing, interactive process in which feelings, ideas, and behaviors emerge and constantly change. Thus, the concepts that come out of standpoint inquiry are held lightly and are allowed to transform through the never-ending quest to find out "how it works."

The second and perhaps more important way that Smith approaches theoretical concepts is as part of the discursive text that constitutes the mode through which relations of ruling are established and managed. As we've seen, "The objectification of knowledge is a general feature of contemporary relations of ruling" (Smith, 1990, p. 67). A significant principle of standpoint inquiry is to reveal how texts are put together with practices at the level of lived experience. "Making these processes visible also makes visible how we participate in and incorporate them into our own practices" (Smith, 1992, p. 90) and how we involve ourselves in creating forms of consciousness "that are properties of organization or discourse rather than of individual subjects" (Smith, 1987, p. 3).

It's at this point that Smith's use of the word *institutional* is relevant. It signals that this approach is vitally concerned with exploring the influences of institutionalized power relations on the lived experiences of their subjects. **Institutional ethnography** is like ethnomethodology and symbolic interactionism in that it focuses on how the practical actions of people in actual situations produce a meaningful social order. But neither of these approaches gives theoretical place to society's ruling institutions, as Smith's method does. In that, it is more like a contemporary Marxist account of power and text. Thus, institutional ethnography examines the dialectical interplay between the relations of ruling as expressed in and mediated through texts, and the actual experiences of people as they negotiate and implement those texts.

Smith uses the analogy of a map to help us see what she is getting at. Maps assist us to negotiate space. If I'm in a strange city, I can consult a map and have a fair idea of how to proceed. Maps, however, aren't the city and they aren't our experience. Smith (1992) wants sociology to function like a map—a map that gives an account of the person walking and finding his or her way (lived experience) through the objective structures of the city (text). This kind of sociology "would tie people's sites of experience and action into accounts of social organization and relations which have that ordinarily reliable kind of faithfulness to 'how it works'" (p. 94).

Specifically, Smith is interested in finding out just how the relations of ruling pervade the lives of women. These relations, as we've seen, come through texts and researchers. But in most cases, the relations of ruling are misrecognized by women. They are rendered invisible by the normalcy of their legitimacy. Part of what these maps can do, then, is make visible the relations of ruling and how they impact the lived experiences of women.

Smith is also interested in how actual women incorporate, respond to, see, and understand the texts that are written from a feminist or standpoint perspective. This is an important issue. Looking at Figure 17.1, we might get the impression that standpoint inquiry automatically and always produces translators and subjects. That is, it appears as if standpoint inquiry is a static thing, as if once done, the inquiry stands as the standpoint forever. This is certainly not what Smith is arguing. Notice again that double-headed arrow between "Standpoint Inquiry" and "Texts." Once standpoint inquiry is expressed in text, there is the danger that it will be taken as reality and become discursive. Smith's is thus an ongoing and ever-changing project that takes seriously the objectifying influence of text.

> For me, then, the standpoint of women locates a place to begin inquiry before things have shifted upwards into the transcendent subject. Once you've gone up there, settled into text-mediated discourse, irremediably stuck on the reading side of the textual surface, you can't peek around it to find the other side where you're actually *doing* your reading. You can reflect back, but you're already committed to a standpoint other than that of actual people's experience. (Smith, 1992, p. 60, emphasis original)

Summary

• Smith argues that in contemporary society, power is exercised through text. Smith defines text using three factors: the actual words or symbols, the physical medium, and the materiality of the text. It is the last of the three with which Smith is most concerned—the actual practices of writing and reading. Most, if not all, of the texts produced by science, social science, and organizations achieve their facticity by eliminating any reference to specific subjectivities, individuals, or experiences.

• These texts are gendered in the sense that men by and large constitute the ruling group in society. Men work and live in these texts and thus accept them as taken-for-granted expressions of the way things are. Women's experience and consciousness, on the other hand, are bifurcated: They experience themselves within the text, as the ruling discourse of the age, but they also experience a significant part of their lives outside of the text. And it is in this part of women's lives where the contingencies of actual life are met, thus giving these experiences a firmer reality base than the abstract, ruling texts of men. Further, men are enabled to take objective, ruling texts as true because women provide the majority of the labor that undergirds the entire order.

• The bifurcated consciousness becomes particularly problematic for those women trained in such disciplines as business, sociology, psychiatry, psychology, and political science. In these professions, women are trained to write and read ruling texts, ignoring the lived experiences of women at the fault line.

• Smith proposes a theoretical method of investigation (standpoint inquiry, or institutional ethnography) that gives priority to the lived experiences of women. In this scheme, texts are not discounted or done away with; rather, they are put into the context of the embodied, actual experiences of women. Smith thus opens up a site of research that exists in the dialectic interplay between text and women's experience.

Race and Matrices of Domination:
Patricia Hill Collins (1948–)

Theorist's Digest
Concepts and Theory: The Standpoint of Black Women
    Black Feminist Epistemology
    Eurocentric Positivism
    Four Tenets of Black Feminist Epistemology
    Implications of Black Feminist Thought
    Black Intellectuals
Concepts and Theory: Intersectionality and Matrices of
    Domination
    Black Feminist Thought, Intersectionality, and Activism
Summary

Patricia Hill Collins will ask us to see two things. First, inequality in society is a complex matter. It can't simply be reduced to considerations of race or gender. Every person stands at a crossroads that distinguishes him or her from most others. For example, being black, female, middle class, and heterosexual is quite different than being black, female, working class, and lesbian. Collins wants us to see deeper into the workings of inequality than ever before. The second thing that Collins will ask us to see is standpoint. Of course, Dorothy E. Smith asked us to do the same, but Collins wants us to see the value in the standpoint of *black* feminists. In Collins' scheme, a single system isn't enough to explain inequality. Stratification works through matrices of domination, not single systems, and one of the most powerful intersectional standpoints is black women. It's at that point that race and gender meet. As such, it is probably the most powerful beginning point for intersectional analysis.

THEORIST'S DIGEST

Brief Biography

Patricia Hill Collins was born on May 1, 1948, in Philadelphia, Pennsylvania. Collins received her bachelor's degree and PhD in sociology from Brandeis University and a master's degree in social science education from Harvard. Collins served as director of the African American Center at Tufts University before moving to the University of Cincinnati, where she was named the Charles Phelps Taft Distinguished Professor of Sociology in 1996. She is currently at the University of Maryland and holds the Wilson Elkins Professor of Sociology position. Her book, *Black Feminist Thought,* received the Association for Women in Psychology's Distinguished Publication Award, the Society for the Study of Social Problems' C. Wright Mills Award, and the Association of Black Women Historians' Letitia Woods Brown Memorial Book Prize.

Central Sociological Questions

Collins, like Foucault, sees a strong connection between power and knowledge. Certain forms of knowledge can be dominating; other forms of knowledge can be liberating. Collins (2000) wants to "empower African-American women" through knowledge and changing "an individual Black woman's consciousness concerning how she understands her everyday life" (p. x).

Simply Stated

Collins critiques positivism's objective stand, emotional divestment, the idea of value-free research, and growth in knowledge based on debate. In the end, this approach denies ethical considerations and authentic involvement. A black feminist approach to knowing and knowledge counters each of these issues. Collins' research and theory is based on intersectionality, recognizing that people sit at crossroads of multiple systems of power organized around four general domains of power: structural (the interrelationships of social structures), disciplinary (bureaucratic organization and protocol), hegemonic (cultural legitimations), and interpersonal (personal relationships).

Key Concepts

intersectionality; Eurocentric positivism; black feminist epistemology; common challenges/ diverse responses; safe places; self-definition; rearticulation; black feminist intellectuals; matrix of domination; structural, disciplinary, hegemonic, and interpersonal domains of power

Concepts and Theory: The Standpoint of Black Women

Patricia Hill Collins is centrally concerned with the relationships among empowerment, self-definition, and knowledge, and she is particularly concerned with black women—it is the oppression with which she is most intimately familiar. But Collins is also one of the few social thinkers who are able to rise above their own experiences and to challenge us with a significant view of oppression and identity politics that not only has the possibility of changing the world but also of opening up the prospect of continuous change.

For change to be continuous, it can't be exclusively focused on one social group. In other words, a social movement that is only concerned with racial inequality, for example, will end its influence once equality for that group is achieved. What Patricia Hill Collins gives us is a way of transcending group-specific politics that is based upon black feminist epistemology. However, it is vital to note that her intent is to place "U.S. Black women's experiences in the center of analysis without privileging those experiences" (P. H. Collins, 2000, p. 228). Collins is saying that there is something significant we can learn from black women's knowledge that can be applied to social issues generally.

Black women sit at a theoretically interesting point. Collins argues that black women are uniquely situated in that they stand at the focal point where two exceptionally powerful and prevalent systems of oppression come together: race and gender. Collins refers to this kind of social position as **intersectionality:** a place where different systems of domination crisscross. There are obviously other systems that Collins talks about, such as class, sexuality, ethnicity, nation, and age, but it is with black women where these different influences get played out most clearly. Seeing this intersectional position of black women, then, ought to compel us to see and look for other spaces where systems of inequality come together.

Just as important to this possibility of continuous change are the qualities of what Collins variously terms alternative or *black feminist epistemology*. This notion implies that one of the things that has hindered social reform is the emphasis on social, scientific knowledge. In this sense, Collins is a critical theorist who argues that all knowledge is political and can be used to serve specific group interests. Social science is particularly susceptible to this because it simultaneously objectifies its subjects and denies the validity of lived experience as a form of knowing.

Black Feminist Epistemology

Epistemology is the study of knowledge, and we've been thinking a lot about knowledge in this chapter. Marx (1859/1978e) gave us eyes to see that epistemology is a sociological concern: "It is not the consciousness of men that determines their being, but, on the contrary, their social being that determines their consciousness" (p. 4). Patricia Hill Collins argues that the politics of race and gender influence knowledge. In Marxian terms, race and gender are part of our "social being." In order to talk about this issue, and specifically about black feminist knowledge, Collins juxtaposes it with Eurocentric, positivistic knowledge—the kind of knowledge in back of science. But before we get to that, I need to point out that there is more to knowledge than simply information. Knowledge—information and facts—can only exist within a context that is defined through specific ways of knowing and validation.

For example, the "fact" that God created the heavens and earth only exists within the context of a specific religious system. The same is true for any other "facts," scientific or otherwise. Thus, what we know is dependent upon how knowledge is produced and how it is validated as true. The question here becomes, what are the ways of knowing and methods of validation that are specific to Eurocentric, positivistic knowledge? Collins gives us four points. Note that sociology is generally defined as a social science, and insofar as it is a scientific inquiry into social life, it espouses these four points.

Eurocentric Positivism

First, according to the positivistic approach, true or correct knowledge only comes when the observer separates himself or herself from that which is being studied. You undoubtedly came across this idea in your methods class: The researcher must take an objective stand in order to safeguard against bias. Second, personal emotions must be set aside in the pursuit of pure knowledge. Third, no personal ethics or values must come into the research. Social science is to be value-free, not passing judgment or trying to impose values on others. And, fourth, knowledge progresses through cumulation and adversarial debate.

Recall our discussion of scientific theory in the introduction to Section II. Cumulation is that process by which theories are built up through testing and rejecting elements that don't correspond to the empirical world. The ideas that pass the test are carried on, and theory cumulates in abstract statements about the general properties of whatever is being investigated. The goal is to disassociate ideas from the people who spawned them and to end up with pure theory. Thus, scientific knowledge is validated because it is tested and argued against from every angle. The belief is that only that which is left standing is truth, and it is upon those remnants that objective, scientific knowledge will be built.

Four Tenets of Black Feminist Epistemology

Collins gives us four characteristics of alternative epistemologies, ways of knowing and validating knowledge that challenge the status quo. As we discuss these, notice how each point stands in opposition to the tenets of positivistic knowledge.

The first point is that alternative epistemologies are built upon lived experience, not upon an objectified position. Social science argues that, to truly understand society and group life, one must be removed from the particulars and concerns of the subjects being studied. In this way, subjects are turned into objects of study. Patricia Hill Collins' (2000) alternative epistemology claims that is it only those men and women who experience the consequences of living under an oppressed social position who can select "topics for investigation and methodologies used" (p. 258). Black feminist epistemology, then, begins with "connected knowers," those who know from personal experience.

The second dimension of Collins' alternative epistemology is the use of dialogue rather than adversarial debate. As we've seen, knowledge claims in social science are assessed through adversarial debate. Using dialogue to evaluate implies the presence of at least two subjects—thus, knowledge isn't seen as having an objective existence apart from lived experiences; knowledge ongoingly emerges through dialogue. In alternative epistemologies, then, we tend to see the use of personal pronouns such as "I" and "we" instead of the objectifying and distancing language of social science. Rather than disappearing, the author is central to and present in the text. In black feminist epistemology, the story is told and preserved in narrative form and not "torn apart in analysis" (P. H. Collins, 2000, p. 258).

Centering lived experiences and the use of dialogue imply that knowledge is built around ethics of caring, Collins' third characteristic of black feminist knowledge. Rather than believing that researchers can be value-free, Collins argues that all knowledge is intrinsically value-laden and should thus be tested by the presence of empathy and compassion. Collins sees this tenet as healing the binary break between the intellect and emotion that Eurocentric knowledge values. Alternative epistemology is thus holistic: It doesn't require the separation of the researcher from his or her own experiences nor does it require separation of our thoughts from our feelings, or even assume that it is possible to do so. In addition, Patricia Hill Collins (2000) argues that the presence of emotion validates the argument: "Emotion indicates that a speaker believes in the validity of an argument" (p. 263).

Fourth, black feminist epistemology requires personal accountability. Because knowledge is built upon lived experience, the assessment of knowledge is a simultaneous assessment of an individual's character, values, and ethics. This approach puts forth that all knowledge is based upon beliefs, things assumed to be true, and belief implies personal responsibility. Think about the implications of these two different approaches to knowing, information, and truth: On the one hand, information can be objective and truth exists apart from any observer, while on the other hand, all information finds its existence and "truth" within a preexisting knowledge system that must be believed in order to work. The first allows for, indeed demands, the separation of personal responsibility from knowledge—knowledge exists as an objective entity apart from the knower. The second places accountability directly on the knower. Collins would ask us, which form of knowing is more likely to lead to social justice, one that denies ethical and moral accountability or one that demands it?

Implications of Black Feminist Thought

By now we should see that, for Collins, ways of knowing and knowledge are not separable or sterile—they are not abstract entities that exist apart from the political values and beliefs of the individual. How we know and what we know have implications for who we see ourselves to be, how we live our lives, and how we treat others. Collins sees these connections as particularly important for black women in at least three ways.

First, there is a tension between common challenges and diverse experiences. Think for a moment about what it means to center the idea of lived experience. We've already touched upon several implications of this idea, but what problem might arise from this way of thinking? The notion of lived experience, if taken to an extreme, can privilege individual experience and knowledge to the exclusion of a collective standpoint. The possibility of this implication is particularly probable in a society like the United States that is built around the idea of individualism. However, this isn't what Collins has in mind. One doesn't overshadow the other in intersectionality. We'll explore this idea further later, but for now we want to see that each individual stands at a unique matrix of crosscutting interests. These interests and the diverse responses they motivate are defined through such social positions as race, class, gender, sexual identity, religion, nationality, and so on.

Thus, the lived experience of a middle class, pagan, single, gay black woman living in Los Angeles will undoubtedly be different from that of an impoverished, Catholic, married black woman living in a small town in Mississippi. As Patricia Hill Collins (2000) says, "It is important to stress that no homogeneous Black *woman's* standpoint exists" (p. 28, emphasis original). However, there are core themes or issues that come from living as a black woman such that "a Black *women's* collective standpoint does exist, one characterized by the tensions that accrue to different responses to common challenges" (p. 28, emphasis original). In other words, a black women's epistemology recognizes this tension between common challenges and diverse responses, which in turn is producing a growing sensibility that black women, because of their gendered racial identity, "may be victimized by racism, misogyny, and poverty" (P. H. Collins, 2000, p. 26). Thus, even though individual black women may respond differently based on different crosscutting interests, there are themes or core issues that all black women can acknowledge and integrate into their self-identity.

Another implication of black feminist epistemology is informed by this growing sensibility of diversity within commonality: Understanding these issues leads to the creation of safe spaces. *Safe spaces* are "social spaces where Black women speak freely" (P. H. Collins, 2000, p. 100). These safe spaces are of course common occurrences for all oppressed groups. In order for an oppressed group to continue to exist as a viable social group, the members must have spaces where they can express themselves apart from the hegemonic or ruling ideology.

Collins identifies three primary safe spaces for black women. The first is black women's relationships with one another. These relationships can form and function within informal relationships such as family and friends, or they can occur within more formal and public spaces such as black churches and black women's organizations. In this context, Patricia Hill Collins (2000) also points to the importance of mentoring within black women's circles, mentoring that empowers black women "by passing on the everyday knowledge essential to survival as African-American women" (p. 102).

The other two safe spaces are cultural and are constituted by the black women's blues tradition and the voices of black women authors. Such cultural expressions have historically given voice to the voiceless. Those who were denied political or academic power could express their ideas and experiences through story and poetry. As long as the political majority could read these as "fictions"—that is, as long as they weren't faced with the facts of oppression—blacks were allowed these cultural outlets in "race markets." However, these books, stories, and poetry allowed oppressed people to communicate with one another and to produce a sense of shared identity.

There are several reasons why the musical form known as the blues is particularly important for constructing safe spaces and identities for black women. The blues originated out of the "call and response" of slaves working in the fields. It was born out of misery but simultaneously gave birth to hope. This hope wasn't simply expressed in words; it was also more powerfully felt in the rhythm and collectivity that made slave work less arduous. The blues thus expresses to even the illiterate the experience of black America, and it wraps individual suffering in a transcendent collective consciousness that enables the oppressed to persevere in hope without bitterness:

> The music of the classic blues singers of the 1920s—almost exclusively women—marks the early written record of this dimension of U.S. Black oral culture. The songs themselves were originally sung in small communities, where boundaries distinguishing singer from audience, call from response, and thought from action were fluid and permeable. (P. H. Collins, 2000, p. 106)

The importance of these safe spaces is that they provide opportunities for self-definition, and self-definition is the first step to empowerment—if a group is not defining itself, then it is being defined by and for the use of others. These safe spaces also allow black women to escape and resist "objectification as the Other" (P. H. Collins, 2000, p. 101), the images and ideas about black women found in the larger culture.

These safe spaces, then, are spaces of diversity, not homogeneity: "The resulting reality is much more complex than one of an all-powerful White majority objectifying Black women with a unified U.S. Black community staunchly challenging these external assaults" (P. H. Collins, 2000, p. 101). However, even though these spaces recognize diversity, they are nonetheless exclusionary (here we can clearly see the tension that Collins notes). If these spaces did not exclude, they would not be safe: "By definition, such spaces become less 'safe' if shared with those who were not Black and female" (p. 110). Although exclusionary, the intent of these spaces is to produce "a more inclusionary, just society" (p. 110).

This idea leads us to our third implication of black feminist thought: The struggles for self-identity take place within an ongoing dialogue between group knowledge or standpoint and experiences as a heterogeneous collective. Here Collins is reconceptualizing the tension noted above between common challenges and diverse responses. This is important to note because one of the central features of Collins' approach is complexity. Collins wants us to see that most social issues, factors, and processes have multiple faces. Understanding how the different facets of inequality work together is paramount for understanding any part of it. In this case, on the one hand we have a *tension* between common challenges and diverse responses, and on the other hand we have a *dialogue* between a common group standpoint and diverse experiences.

Collins is arguing that changes in thinking may alter behaviors, and altering behaviors may produce changes in thinking. Thus, for U.S. black women as a collective, "The struggle for a self-defined Black feminism occurs through an ongoing dialogue whereby action and thought inform one another" (P. H. Collins, 2000, p. 30). For example, because black Americans have been racially segregated, black feminist practice and thought have emerged within the context of black community development. Other ideas and practices, such as black nationalism, have also come about due to racial segregation. Thus, black feminism and nationalism inform one another in the context of the black community, yet they are both distinct. Moreover, the relationships are reciprocal in that black feminist and nationalist thought influences black community development.

Collins also sees this dialogue as a process of rearticulation rather than consciousness-raising. During the 1960s and 1970s, consciousness-raising was a principal method in the feminist movement. Consciousness-raising groups would generally meet weekly, consist of no more than 12 women, and would encourage women to share their *personal experiences as women.* The intent was a kind of Marxian class consciousness that would precede social change, except that it was oriented around gender rather than class.

Rearticulation, according to Collins, is a vehicle for re-expressing a consciousness that quite often already exists in the public sphere. In rearticulation, we can see the dialogic nature of Collins' perspective. Rather than a specific, limited method designed to motivate women toward social movement, Collins sees black feminism as part of an already existing national discourse. What black feminism can do is to take the core themes of black gendered oppression—such as racism, misogyny, and poverty—and infuse them with the lived experience of black women's taken-for-granted, everyday knowledge. This is brought back into the national discourse where practice and ideas are in a constant dialogue: "Rather than viewing consciousness as a fixed entity, a more useful approach sees it as continually evolving and negotiated. A dynamic consciousness is vital to both individual and group agency" (P. H. Collins, 2000, p. 285).

Black Intellectuals

Within this rearticulation, black feminist intellectuals have a specific place. To set ourselves up for this consideration, we can divide social intellectuals or academics into two broad groups: pure researchers and praxis researchers. Pure researchers hold to value-free sociology, the kind we noted above in considering Eurocentric thought. They are interested in simply discovering and explaining the social world. Praxis or critically oriented researchers are interested in ferreting out the processes of oppression and changing the social world. Black feminist intellectuals are of the latter kind, blending the lived experiences of black women with the highly specialized knowledge of intellectualism.

This dual intellectual citizenship gives black feminist scholars critical insights into the conditions of oppression. They both experience it as a lived reality and can think about it using the tools of critical analysis. Further, in studying oppression among black women, they are less likely to walk away "when the obstacles seem overwhelming or when the rewards for staying diminish" (P. H. Collins, 2000, p. 35). Black feminist intellectuals are also more motivated in this area because they are defining themselves while studying gendered racial inequality.

Finally, Patricia Hill Collins (2000) argues that black feminist intellectuals "alone can foster the group autonomy that fosters effective coalitions with other groups"

(p. 36). In thinking about this, remember that Collins recognizes that intellectuals are found within all walks of life. Intellectual status isn't simply conferred as the result of academic credentials. Black feminist intellectuals think reflexively and publicly about their own lived experiences within the context of broader social issues and ideas.

Black feminist intellectuals, then, function like intermediary groups. On the one hand, they are very much in touch with their own and their peers' experiences as a disenfranchised group; on the other hand, they are also in touch with intellectual heritages, diverse groups, and broader social justice issues.

> By advocating, refining, and disseminating Black feminist thought, individuals from other groups who are engaged in similar social justice projects— Black men, African women, White men, Latinas, White women, and members of other U.S. racial/ethnic groups, for example—can identify points of connection that further social justice projects. (P. H. Collins, 2000, p. 37)

Collins notes, however, that coalition building with other groups and intellectuals can be costly. Privileged group members often have to become traitors to the "privileges that their race, class, gender, sexuality, or citizenship status provide them" (P. H. Collins, 2000, p. 37).

Concepts and Theory: Intersectionality and Matrices of Domination

Collins is best known for her ideas of intersectionality and the matrix of domination. Intersectionality is a particular way of understanding social location in terms of crisscrossing systems of oppression. Specifically, intersectionality is an "analysis claiming that systems of race, social class, gender, sexuality, ethnicity, nation, and age form mutually constructing features of social organization, which shape Black women's experiences and, in turn, are shaped by Black women" (P. H. Collins, 2000, p. 299).

This idea goes back to Max Weber and Georg Simmel. To refresh our memories, Weber's concern was to understand the complications that status and power brought to Marx's idea of class stratification. According to Weber, class consciousness and social change are more difficult to achieve than Marx first thought: Status group affiliation and differences in power create concerns that may override class issues. And, as you'll remember, Simmel was interested in the way the motivations for and patterns of group memberships changed as a result of living in urban rather than rural settings. Simmel noted that people living in cities tend to have greater freedom of choice and the opportunity to be members of more diverse groups than people in small towns. He was specifically concerned with the psychological and emotional effects that these different social network patterns have on people.

There is a way in which Collins blends these two approaches while at the same time going beyond them. Like Simmel, Collins is concerned with the influences of intersectionality on the individual. But the important issue for Collins is the way intersectionality creates different kinds of lived experiences and social realities. She is particularly concerned with how these interact with what passes as objective knowledge and how diverse voices of intersectionality are denied under scientism. Like Weber, she is concerned about how intersectionality creates different kinds of inequalities and how these crosscutting influences affect social change. But Collins brings Weber's notion of power into this analysis in a much more sophisticated way. Collins sees intersectionality working within a matrix of domination.

The **matrix of domination** refers to the overall organization of power in a society. There are two features to any matrix. First, any specific matrix has a particular arrangement of intersecting systems of oppression. Just what and how these systems come together is historically and socially specific. Second, intersecting systems of oppression are specifically organized through four interrelated domains of power: structural, disciplinary, hegemonic, and interpersonal.

The *structural domain* consists of such social structures as law, polity, religion, and the economy. This domain sets the structural parameters that organize power relations. For example, prior to February 3, 1870, blacks in the United States could not legally vote. Although constitutionally enabled to vote after that date, voting didn't become a reality for many African American people until almost a century later with the passage of the Voting Rights Act of 1965, which officially ended Jim Crow laws. Collins' point is that the structural domain sets the overall organization of power within a matrix of domination and that the structural domain is slow to change, often only yielding to large-scale social movements, such as the Civil War and the upheavals of the 1950s and 1960s in the United States.

The *disciplinary domain* manages oppression. Collins borrows this idea from both Weber and Michel Foucault (see Chapter 16): The disciplinary domain consists of bureaucratic organizations whose task it is to control and organize human behavior through routinization, rationalization, and surveillance. Here the matrix of domination is expressed through organizational protocol that hides the effects of racism and sexism under the canopy of efficiency, rationality, and equal treatment.

If we think about the contours of black feminist thought that Collins gives us, we can see that the American university system and the methods of financing research are good examples. Sexism and racism never raise their ugly heads when certain kinds of knowledge are systematically excluded in the name of science and objectivity. This same kind of pattern is seen in the U.S. economy. According to the Bureau of Labor Statistics (2005), in the first quarter of 2005, the average weekly income for white men was $731.00, for white women $601.00, for black men $579.00, and for black women $506.00. In a country that has outlawed discrimination based on race and sex, black women still make on average about 31% less than white men.

In this domain, change can come through insider resistance. Collins uses the analogy of an egg. From a distance, the surface of the egg looks smooth and seamless. But upon closer inspection, the egg is revealed to be riddled with cracks. For those interested in social justice, working in a bureaucracy is like working the cracks, finding spaces and fissures to work in and expand. Again, change is slow and incremental.

The *hegemonic domain* legitimizes oppression. Max Weber was among the first to teach us that authority functions because people believe in it. This is the cultural sphere of influence where ideology and consciousness come together. The hegemonic domain links the structural, disciplinary, and interpersonal domains. It is made up of the language we use, the images we respond to, the values we hold, and the ideas we entertain. It is produced through school curricula and textbooks, religious teachings, mass media images and contexts, community cultures, and family histories. The black feminist priority of self-definition and critical, reflexive education are important steppingstones to deconstructing and dissuading the hegemonic domain. As Patricia Hill Collins (2000) puts it, "Racist and sexist ideologies, if they are disbelieved, lose their impact" (p. 284).

The *interpersonal domain* influences everyday life. It is made up of the personal relationships we maintain as well as the different interactions that make up our daily life. Collins points out that change in this domain begins with the *intra*personal, that is, how an individual sees and understands his or her own self and experiences. In particular, people don't generally have a problem identifying ways in which they have been victimized. But the first step in changing the interpersonal domain of the matrix of domination is seeing how our own "thoughts and actions uphold *someone else's subordination*" (P. H. Collins, 2000, p. 287, emphasis added).

Part of this first step is seeing that people have a tendency to identify with an oppression, most likely the one they have experienced, and to consider all other oppressions as being of less importance. In the person's mind, his or her oppression has a tendency then to take on a master status. This leads to a kind of contradiction where the oppressed becomes the oppressor. For example, a black heterosexual woman may discriminate against lesbians without a second thought, or a black Southern Baptist woman may believe that every school classroom ought to display the Ten Commandments. "Oppression is filled with such contradictions because these approaches fail to recognize that a matrix of domination contains few pure victims or oppressors" (P. H. Collins, 2000, p. 287).

Black Feminist Thought, Intersectionality, and Activism

There are a number of implications for activism that Collins draws out from black feminist thought and the notions of intersectionality and the matrix of domination. The first that I want to point out is the most immediate: Collins' approach to epistemology and intersectionality conceptualizes resistance as a complex interplay of a variety of forces working at several levels—that is, resistance in the four interrelated domains of power that we've just discussed.

This point of Collins' isn't an incidental issue. Remember that part of what is meant by modernity is the search for social equality. In modernity, primary paths for these social changes correspond to Collins' first domain of power. For example, the U.S. Declaration of Independence, Constitution, and Bill of Rights together provide for principal mechanisms of structural change: the electoral process within a civil society guaranteed by the twin freedoms of press and speech and the upheaval or revolutionary process. Though we don't usually think of the latter as a legitimated means of social change, it is how this nation began and it is how much of the more dramatic changes that surround equality have come about (for example, the social movements behind women's suffrage and civil rights).

One of the ideas that comes out of postmodernism and considerations of late modernity is the notion that guided or rational social change is no longer possible. What Collins gives us is a different take on the issues of complexity and fragmentation. While recognizing the complexity of intersectionality and the different levels of the matrix of domination, Collins also sees the four domains of power as interrelated and thus influencing one another. By themselves, the structural and disciplinary domains are most resilient to change, but the hegemonic and interpersonal domains are open to individual agency and change. Bringing these domains together creates a more dynamic system, wherein the priorities of black feminist thought and understanding the contradictions of oppression can empower social justice causes.

Collins' approach also has other important implications. Her ideas of intersectionality and the matrix of domination challenge many of our political assumptions. Black feminist epistemology, for example, challenges our assumptions concerning the separation of the private and public spheres. What it means to be a mother in a traditional black community is very different from what it means in a white community: "Black women's experiences have never fit the logic of work in the public sphere juxtaposed to family obligations in the private sphere" (P. H. Collins, 2000, p. 228). Intersectionality also challenges the assumption that gender stratification affects all women in the same way; race and class matter, as does sexual identity.

In addition, Collins' approach untangles relationships among knowledge, empowerment, and power, and opens up conceptual space to identify new connections within the matrix of domination. The idea of the matrix emphasizes connections and interdependencies rather than single structures of inequality. The idea itself prompts us to wonder about how social categories are related and mutually constituted. For example, how do race and sexual preference work together? Asking such a question might lead us to discover that homosexuality is viewed and treated differently in different racial cultures—is the lived experience of a black gay male different from that of a white gay male? If so, we might take the next step and ask how does class influence those differences? Or, if these lived experiences are different, we might be provoked to ask another question: Are there different masculinities in different racial or class cultures?

As you might be able to surmise from this example, Collins' approach discourages binary thinking and the labeling of one oppression or activism as more important or radical. From Collins' point of view, it would be much too simplistic to say that a white male living in poverty is enjoying white privilege. In the same way, it would be one-dimensional to say that any one group is more oppressed than another.

Collins' entire approach also shifts our understanding of social categories from bounded to fluid and highlights the processes of self-definition as constructed in conjunction with others. Intersectionality implies that social categories are not bounded or static. Your social nearness or distance to another changes as the matrix of domination shifts, depending on which scheme is salient at any given moment. You and the person next to you may both be women, but that social nearness may be severed as the indices change to include religion, race, ethnicity, sexual practices or identities, class, and so forth.

Groups are also constructed in connection to others. No group or identity stands alone. To state the obvious, the only way "white" as a social index can exist is if "black" exists. Intersectionality motivates us to look at just how our identities are constructed at the expense of others: "These examples suggest that moral positions as survivors of one expression of systemic violence become eroded in the absence of accepting responsibility of other expressions of systemic violence" (P. H. Collins, 2000, p. 247).

Here is one final implication of Collins' approach: Because groups' histories and inequalities are relational, understanding intersectionality and the matrix of domination means that some coalitions with some social groups are more difficult and less fruitful than others. Groups will more or less align on the issues of "victimization, access to positions of authority, unearned benefits, and traditions of resistance" (P. H. Collins, 2000, p. 248). The more closely aligned are these issues, the more likely and beneficial are the coalitions. Coalitions will also ebb and flow, "based on the perceived saliency of issues to group members" (p. 248). We end, then, with the insight that inequalities and dominations are complex and dynamic.

Summary

- Collins argues that black women represent a powerful place to begin theorizing about social inequality. Studies and theories in inequality generally focus on one specific issue, such as race or gender. To understand the inequality of black women, however, forces us to be concerned with at least two systems of inequality (gender and race) and their intersections.

- According to Collins, the four qualities of Eurocentric positivism hamper our understanding of how systems of inequality work. These four characteristics are (1) the objective stand, (2) emotional divestment, (3) value-free theory and research, and (4) progress through cumulation and adversarial debate. The four characteristics of black feminist knowledge counter each of these points. Black feminist knowledge is (1) built upon lived experience, (2) emphasizes emotional investment and accountability, (3) honors ethically driven research and theory, and (4) understands intellectual progress through dialogue.

- There are three primary implications of black feminist thought: first, the recognition of the tension between common challenges and diverse responses; second, the creation of safe places that honor diversity; and third, self-identity formed within a continuing dialogue between common challenges and varied experiences. This last implication has importance for rearticulating the public discourse surrounding black women.

- Black feminist intellectuals have a specific place in the construction of black women's identities and the rearticulation of the public sphere. Specifically, black feminists hold a kind of dual intellectual citizenship: They are trained in positivistic methods yet they also have the lived experience of black women. This dual citizenship gives black feminists greater opportunities to forge coalitions with other social justice groups.

- Collins' approach to studying inequality is based on the concepts of intersectionality and a matrix of domination. Intersectionality captures the structured position of people living at the crossroads of two or more systems of inequality, such as race and gender. The different intersectionalities of a society influence the overall organization of power—what Collins refers to as the matrix of domination. These matrices are historically and socially specific, yet they are organized around four general domains of power: structural (the interrelationships of social structures), disciplinary (bureaucratic organization and protocol), hegemonic (cultural legitimations), and interpersonal (personal relationships).

- There are various implications of Collins' approach. First, activism is a complex enterprise that links together different practices in the four domains of power. In other words, activism can involve more than social movements aimed at changing the institutional arrangements of a society. Because there are four domains of power, there can be four fronts of activism. Second, her approach challenges many of the existing political assumptions and opens up new conceptual space for understanding how inequalities work. The ideas of intersectionality and a matrix of domination discourage simple, binary thinking in politics and research. Third, Collins' ideas sensitize us to the fluid nature of social categories, identities, and relations. And, fourth, political coalitions can ebb and flow as different groups align to varying degrees on the issues of power, victimization, and resistance.

Race and Democracy:
Cornel West (1953–)

Theorist's Digest
Concepts and Theory: Black Existence in America
    Black Nihilism
    Crisis in Black Leadership
    Leadership for Equality
Concepts and Theory: The Postdemocratic Age
    Three Antidemocratic Dogmas
    Putting on the Democratic Armor
Summary

There's a way in which Cornel West picks up from where William Julius Wilson left off. Wilson argued that since the civil rights movement in the 1960s, the black population in the United States has been split as never before by class. Most of the changes that have occurred with reference to race have thus benefited rising middle class blacks and have left those African Americans at the poverty level and below as the "truly disadvantaged." West picks up Wilson's theme but moves it more into the realm of culture. Since the 1960s, the upwardly mobile black population in the United States has increasingly become the target of capitalist markets. Not only did capitalists discover a new market when African Americans entered the middle class, they also in a sense tried to make up for lost time. Capitalists have had over two centuries of marketing to whites, but blacks have constituted a strong and viable market for only the past 40 years or so. Given the historical background of the black community in the United States, this concentrated market force has had unique effects on African Americans of all classes.

THEORIST'S DIGEST

Brief Biography

Cornel West was born in Tulsa, Oklahoma, in 1953. He began attending Harvard University at seventeen and graduated three years later, magna cum laude. His degree was in Near Eastern languages and literature. West obtained his PhD at Princeton, where he studied with Richard Rorty, a well-known pragmatist. West has taught at Union Theological Seminary, Yale Divinity School, the University of Paris, Harvard, and is currently at Princeton. Among his most significant works are *Race Matters* and *Democracy Matters: Winning the Fight Against Imperialism*. His recent works include *Keeping Faith: Philosophy and Race in America* and a rap CD, *Never Forget: A Journey of Revelations*.

Central Sociological Questions

Cornel West's life is committed to not only the race question in America, but to the democratic ideals of open and critical dialogue, the freedom of ideas and information, and compassion for and acceptance of diverse others. His passion, then, is to expose antidemocratic energies wherever they may be found. In this chapter he specifically asks two questions: "How has capitalist marketing affected black Americans?" and "How has 9/11 affected democracy in America?"

Simply Stated

West is concerned about race and democracy in the United States. Since the civil rights era of the 1960s blacks have experienced greater political participation and economic upward mobility than ever before. While these changes have had obvious positive effects, they have also worked to weaken traditional black community and create a crisis in black leadership.

(Continued)

(Continued)

Since the 1960s African Americans have been subjected to intense marketing with an ever expanding number of commodities. As a result market moralities have replaced traditional black cultural armor and have created a sense of black nihilism. In response to these threats, West calls for a reenergizing of moral reasoning, coalition strategy, and mature black identity. West is also focused on greater democratic good in the United States. He argues that this has been threatened as a result of 9/11. The threat isn't terrorism but, rather, the American response to terrorism, which has produced antidemocratic dogmas that threaten the very core of democracy. Here West calls for resurrecting Socratic questioning, commitment to prophetic justice, and a tragicomic commitment to hope.

Key Ideas

false consciousness, pragmatism, existentialism, democratic faith, modern capitalist markets, market saturation, black cultural armor, market moralities, ontological wounds, existential angst, black nihilism, politics of conversion, crisis in black leadership, three kinds of leadership styles, racial reasoning, moral reasoning, mature black identity, coalition strategy, postdemocratic age, Constantinian Christianity, Prophetic Christianity, free-market fundamentalism, aggressive militarism, escalating authoritarianism, Socratic questioning, democratic armor, commitment to prophetic justice, tragicomic commitment to hope

Concepts and Theory: Black Existence in America

West gives us two basic structural influences on blacks in the United States: the economic boom and expansion of civil rights for blacks in the 1960s, and the saturation of market forces. In terms of the economic and political well-being of blacks in the United States, West is simply saying that they both increased, particularly during the boom of the 1970s. For example, the U.S. Census Bureau (n.d.) reports that black, male, median income increased from $9,519 in 1950 to $17,055 in 1970, as measured in 2003 dollars. These changes helped define blacks as a viable market group, one with disposable income and market-specific products. In some obvious ways, these changes have benefited the black experience in America. However, the development of black economic markets has also had significant negative effects.

As a way of distributing goods and services, markets have been a part of human history for millennia. *Modern, capitalist markets,* however, have a couple of unique characteristics. Modern capitalism, you'll remember, is defined by the endless accumulation of capital to create more capital. Because capital is its own goal, it's never achieved (capital to generate capital to generate capital and so on endlessly). This drive implies that the need for profit is insatiable and thus continues to increase. Because markets are the mechanism through which profit and capital are gained, modern capitalist markets are intrinsically expansive: They expand vertically (through accessories for an existing product), horizontally (producing new products within a market), and geographically (extending existing markets to new social groups).

A second unique characteristic of modern capitalism is related to the factor of expanding markets: Capitalists are driven to create a never-ending stream of new or different commodities. Keep in mind that commodification is a process that converts more and more of the human lifeworld into something that can be bought and sold, and it creates new "needs" within the consumer. Human beings are not just the only animal capable of economic production; we are also the only species able to create new psychological drives and needs for the new products. There's a sense in which markets are without any morals whatsoever: They aren't restricted by any kind of ethic—they can be used to sell Bibles or guns to terrorists. This quality makes them applicable to any situation or product. However, as we will see, the absence of any ethical restrictions implies and creates a morality of its own. And these market moralities are particularly destructive for black Americans.

Black Nihilism

West characterizes this market expansion into the black community as a kind of *market saturation*. He first argues that the market saturation of the black population has stripped away community-based values and substituted market moralities. Earlier I mentioned that markets are amoral. But this is in a restricted sense only—markets can be used for anything. Markets do, however, convey some specific cultural ideas and sensibilities. In classical theory, for example, Max Weber was extremely interested in how markets and bureaucracies create rational rather than affective culture, and Georg Simmel saw markets as contributing to cultural signs becoming frivolous.

West argues that being a focus for market activity, commodification, and advertising has changed black culture in America. Prior to market saturation, blacks had a long history of community and tradition. They were equipped with a kind of *black cultural armor* that came via black civic and religious institutions. This armor consisted of clear and strong structures of meaning and feeling that "embodied values of service and sacrifice, love and care, discipline and excellence" (West, 1993/2001, p. 24). While this is specific to black Americans, it's important to note that this general shift from community-based traditional culture to less meaningful and more pliable culture was a concern of many social theorists of modernity. We find this idea of cultural shift repeatedly in classical theory. The basic idea is that culture has dramatically changed through processes accompanying urbanization and commodification. Rather than being meaningful, normative, and cohesive, culture is trivialized, anomic, and segmented.

West is making this same kind of argument, so he follows a strong theoretical tradition. West, however, is pointing out that while the dispersion of community and the emptying of culture may have affected much of modern society during the beginning and middle stages of modernity and capitalism, the black community in America wasn't strongly influenced by these changes until after the 1960s. Until then, blacks continued to rely on community-based relations and religiously influenced culture. As a result of the twin structural influences of civil rights and upward mobility, blacks moved out of black communities and churches. The structural bases for cultural armor were weakened as a result.

In place of cultural armor, blacks have since been inundated with the *market moralities* of conspicuous consumption and material calculus. The culture of consumption orients people to the present moment and to the intensification of pleasure. This culture of pleasure uses seduction to capitalize "on every opportunity to make money" (West, 1993/2001, p. 26). It overwhelms people in a moment where the past and future are swallowed up in a never-ending "repetition of hedonistically driven pleasure" (p. 26). Further, the material calculus argues that the greatest value comes from profit-driven calculations. Every other consideration, such as love and service to others, is hidden under the bushel of profit.

As I've mentioned, most of these cultural ramifications of markets and commodification have also been present in other groups. But in West's (1993/2001) opinion, two issues make these effects particularly destructive for blacks. First, black upward mobility and the presence of the black middle class concern only a small sliver of the pie. Most of the black citizens of the United States still suffer under white oppression. The other issue that makes the black experience of market saturation distinct is the "accumulated effect of the black wounds and scars suffered in a white-dominated society" (p. 28). In other words, there is a historical and cultural heritage, no matter how much the immediacy of market saturation and pleasure tries to deny it—much of the history of the United States was built on the oppression of blacks over the 188 years from 1776 to 1964.

Obviously, these two factors influence one another. Healing from past wounds can only take place in a present that is both nurturing and repentant, a place that does not replicate hurts from the past. According to West (1993/2001), this isn't happening for blacks in America: Cultural beliefs and media images continue to attack "black intelligence, black ability, black beauty, and black character in subtle and not-so-subtle ways" (p. 27). And, as noted earlier, black upward mobility is still limited. For example, in 2002 over 30% of black children lived under the poverty line, compared to 12.3% of white children (Statistical Abstract of the United States, 2002).

In the abstract, West's argument so far looks like this: black upward mobility + increased civil rights → weakening of civic and religious community base → substitution of market moralities for cultural armor—all of which takes place within the framework of the black legacy in the United States and continued oppression. "Under these circumstances black existential *angst* derives from the lived experience of ontological wounds and emotional scars" (West, 1993/2001, p. 27, emphasis original). The *ontological wounds* that West is speaking of come from the ways in which black reality and existence have been denied throughout the history of the United States.

In general, *existential angst* refers to the deep and profound insecurity and dread that comes from living as a human being. This idea comes from existentialism. Existentialism starts with the problem of being or existence and argues that the very question or problem creates existence. As far as we know, human beings are the only animal that questions its existence: Why am I here? What's the meaning of life? All other animals simply exist. But human beings ask, and in asking we create human existence as a unique experience. That unique experience is existential angst, worrying over the great questions of life. But this angst can lead to the great transcendences of human life; it can lead to community as we share our existential existence.

West employs the idea of angst to describe the uniquely black experience of living under American capitalism and democracy—under slavery blacks were denied existence as human beings and weren't given civil rights until the 1960s. Further, black experience is deeply historical, yet the past and the future are now buried under the market-driven pleasures of the moment; and black experience is fundamentally communitarian, yet that civic and religious base is overwhelmed by market individualisms; black experience is painfully oppressive, yet it is countered only by increasing target marketing and consumerism. Thus, West argues that the result of market saturation and morality for blacks is a deeply spiritual condition of despair and insecurity. Because blacks no longer have the necessary culture, community, or leadership, this angst cannot be used productively. It is instead turned inward as anger. And this anger is played out in violence against the weak. Righteous anger, turned against the oppressor in hopes of liberation, becomes increasingly difficult to express. **Black nihilism** denies the hope in which this anger is founded. With no viable path, this anger is turned inward and found in black-against-black violence, especially against black women and children.

Crisis in Black Leadership

However, nihilism can be treated. West argues that it is a disease of the soul, one that cannot be cured, as there is always the threat of relapse. This disease must be met with love and care, not arguments and analysis. What is required is a new kind of politics, a *politics of conversion,* which reaches into the subversive memory of black people to find modes of valuation and resistance. Politics of conversion is centered on a love ethic that is energized by concern for others and the recognition of one's own worth. This kind of politics requires prophetic black leaders who will bring "hope for the future and a meaning to struggle" (West, 1993/2001, p. 28). There is, however, a *crisis in black leadership.*

For West, there is a relationship between community and leadership. Strong leaders come out of vibrant communities. With the breakdown of the black community, black leaders don't have a social base that is in touch with the real issues. There is thus no nurturing of critical consciousness in the heart of black America. Rather, much of the new black leadership in America comes out of the middle class. And black middle-class life is "principally a matter of professional conscientiousness, personal accomplishment, and cautious adjustment" (West, 1993/2001, p. 57). West maintains that what is lacking in contemporary black leadership is anger and humility; what is present in overabundance is status anxiety and concerns for personal careers.

West divides contemporary black leaders into two general types—politicians and academics—with *three kinds of leadership styles:* race-effacing managerial leaders, race-identifying protest leaders, and race-transcending prophetic leaders. There are some differences between politicians and academics, but by and large exclusionary, and punitive" (p. 66). Specifically, the rhetoric of Christian fundamentalism is used to legitimate three antidemocratic dogmas: free-market fundamentalism, aggressive militarism, and authoritarianism. In addition, West (2004) argues that the Christian Right is perverting the soul of American democracy, "because the dominant forms of Christian fundamentalism are a threat to the tolerance and openness necessary for sustaining any democracy" (p. 146).

West is a Christian. But he sees vast differences between what he calls Constantinian Christianity and prophetic Christianity. *Constantinian Christianity* is named after the Roman emperor Constantine, who converted to Christianity in 312 CE. The various accounts differ on some of the specifics, but all agree that Constantine received a vision of Christ just before the Battle of the Milvian Bridge. As a result, Constantine commanded that a purple silk banner hanging from a crosspiece on a pike (representing Christ) be placed as his new battle standard. Eventually, because of Constantine, Christianity became the official religion of the Roman Empire. The state then used the church as an instrument of imperial policy, and the church used the state as a means of imposing its religious rule. Constantinian Christianity, then, is a "terrible co-joining of church and state" (West, 2004, p. 148) that robs the church "of the prophetic fervor of Jesus and the apocalyptic fire of that other Jew-turned-Christian named Paul" (p. 147).

West (2004) argues that as a result of the marriage between church and state, Christianity has been invested with an "insidious schizophrenia." On the one hand, there are the Constantinian elements occupied with power, privilege, and possession, a Christianity that has "been on the wrong side of so many of our social troubles, such as the dogmatic justification of slavery and the parochial defense of women's inequality" (p. 149). West argues that the Christian Right, including the Christian Coalition and the Moral Majority, is the shining example of Constantinian Christianity in America.

On the other hand are the elements of prophetic Christianity, most clearly seen in Social Gospel churches. *Prophetic Christianity* holds up wisdom, justice, and freedom for all humanity as its virtues. It isn't concerned with power; it is concerned with promoting equality and respecting and supporting every cultural group's unique heritage and way of life. In making his case for the differences between Constantinian and prophetic Christianity, West (2004) argues that the strongest movements for equality have been led by prophetic Christians, including "the abolitionist, women's suffrage, and trade-union movements in the nineteenth century and the civil rights movement in the twentieth century" (p. 152).

> I do not want to be numbered among those who sold their souls for a mess of pottage—who surrendered their democratic Christian identity for a comfortable place at the table of the American empire while, like Lazarus, the least of these cried out and I was too intoxicated with worldly power and might to hear, beckon, and heed their cries. To be a Christian is to live dangerously, honestly, freely. . . . This is the kind of vision and courage required to enable the renewal of prophetic, democratic Christian identity in the age of the American empire. (West, 2004, p. 172)

Three Antidemocratic Dogmas

Before we begin this section, we should take a moment to define what West means by democracy. *Democracy* is not simply the freedom to vote—the freedom to vote democratically is based on the presence of at least three elements. Together, these elements give democracy a forward vision—the hope of future progress gained through rejecting the shackles of the past and the continual process of enlightenment. The first element of democracy is open and critical dialogue. The democracy of the United States is built upon such dialogue, as is evident in the Declaration of Independence and the First Amendment to the Constitution. The second element is necessitated by the first: the freedom of ideas and information necessary for democratic dialogue and questioning. Democracy cannot exist in an environment where knowledge and thought are hidden in darkness.

Third, the necessity of dialogue and the freedom of ideas imply compassion for and acceptance of diverse others. A democratic government exists in order to preserve the freedoms and rights of diverse others. Any kind of government can protect its borders and provide infrastructure, but West argues that a democratic government is especially well-suited to guard the freedoms of its citizens in the face of oppression. This protection is the defining feature of a democratic government and its sole reason for existence. Note that acceptance is not the same as tolerance. Tolerated voices aren't allowed an equal footing in dialogue. But American democracy goes further than acceptance. In the roots of American democracy there is desire for alternative voices.

West takes seriously the idea that culture can exist and act like a structure. This position implies first that culture can develop autonomously and second that culture can have its own set of effects in concert with or independent of other social structures. In this case, the social structural issues that concern West are the rising plutocracy and the Christian Right. West is also still concerned with the saturation of market forces. In addition, West sees the terrorist attacks of 9/11 as a key event in pushing the United States toward a postdemocratic society.

There are three cultural dogmas with which West is concerned: free-market fundamentalism, aggressive militarism, and escalating authoritarianism. We'll talk about each of these in a moment, but first notice West's use of religious terms. First, these cultural issues are dogmas. While dogma can have a more general meaning, in religious circles it is a technical term with a very specific meaning. Dogmas are officially established religious doctrines. They serve not only to distinguish one belief system from another, but they are also the guiding lights for religious practice. West is telling us that these cultural elements function like religious dogma: They dictate and legitimate certain beliefs and practices. And these beliefs, practices, and legitimations are held to be fundamental to a certain way of life—in this case, the American way of life.

The second religious term that West uses is fundamentalism, and it is used in reference to the first cultural belief: free markets. Interestingly enough, though we may now talk about Islamic fundamentalists, the term was first used in reference to Protestant Christianity. Christian fundamentalism began in the United States against all" (p. 218). This gangsterization of America not only concerns aggres-sive militarism and escalating authoritarianism, it also involves market morali-ties and fetishes that come out of free-market fundamentalism. These dogmas have produced "an unbridled grasp at power, wealth, and status" that have snuffed the democratic light from the very nation that is its chief advocate: "We are experiencing the sad American imperial devouring of American democracy" (West, 2004, p. 8).

Putting on the Democratic Armor

To combat the nihilist threat, to overcome the niggerization and gangsterization of America, West exhorts us to put on the democratic armor. There are three ele-ments to this defensive covering: Socratic questioning, prophetic justice, and tragi-comic commitment to hope. Socrates never wrote a word. What we know of the *Socratic questioning* came to us through Plato, his student. Plato presents the Socratic method as a way of discovering ethical truths. It is a method of inquiry that uses critical questions as its tool—imagine a class where the professor didn't lecture but only asked questions. The purpose of the method is to question every idea until its underlying assumptions are exposed. The assumptions are then questioned in terms of their logical relationship to other assumptions. In this process, those involved agree to accept any answer that is logically reasoned. In other words, what matters most is the process, not the product. There aren't predetermined truths that the "teacher" is attempting to impose. Questioning and logic, then, are both method and goal.

I'm sure you can see why West advocates Socratic questioning as a primary piece in the democratic citizen's armor. Democracy for West is based upon and can only prosper when critical questioning is its driving force. As West points out, critical questioning was the wellspring of America's first document, the Declaration of Independence: Without it, not only would the United States not have been born, but the United States as a truly democratic nation could not continue to exist.

West gives us at least two guidelines for this quest. First, we must engage in a critical and open-minded assessment of the history of every dogma. West takes seriously the structural weight of culture. One of the things that means is that ideas and dogmas do not exist as some kind of soliloquy or solo performance. They have a history. Uncovering that history exposes ideology's contingent and political base. The second guideline that West gives us is the *race lens*. The history of ideas and the race lens go hand in hand. There are a number of frames through which we could uncover the heritage of democratic ideas in America. But the race lens is perhaps the most powerful, because whether we look at the oppression of gays, women, workers, or the near genocide of Native Americans, what we find at the core is "the deeply antidemocratic and dehumanizing hypocrisies of white supremacy" (West, 2004, p. 14).

However, remember West's (2004) purpose in advocating the race lens: to incite critical inquiry. The purpose, then, is not to create "sentimental stories of pure heroes of color and impure white villains"; this would "simply flip the script and tell new lies about ourselves" (p. 15). Rather, using the race lens should unsettle Americans. It should bring into sharp relief the distinctions between Constantinian America and democratic America. It should humble America in the realization that today's dogmas are just as destructive to the democratic spirit as racism. It should make Americans reject dogmas of any kind. According to West, democracy never gets it right; what is right about democracy is its process: "All democracies are incomplete and unfinished" (p. 204). In short, the race lens should prompt never-ending Socratic, pragmatic questioning and parrhesia—freedom of speech.

West points out something extremely important about democracy and freedom of speech. The men who founded America feared the masses or demos. Plato feared the demos as well and advocated the rule of philosopher-kings. These elite feared chaos and anarchy. The masses were seen as uneducated and capable of being easily persuaded. West (2004) tells us that the "genius of the Founding Fathers" of the United States was to still grant and protect Socratic questioning and freedom of speech (p. 211). What this means is that democracy is founded on a tension between elites and the demos, and this tension is always and necessarily there. If either side becomes too dominant (as with the current American plutocracy), the dialogue that democracy is founded on comes to a halt.

Socratic questioning and *commitment to prophetic justice* are intertwined. Many people, when they think of a prophet, conceive of a person telling and fore-telling absolute truth. This is not what West has in mind. West's idea of prophetic vision can't be related to truth because of his notion of Socratic questioning and because of the prominence he gives pragmatism. A commitment to prophetic justice is first a call away from indifference. Prophetic justice is a commitment—it is in its essence engagement. Every example we have of prophets indicates that they are people who are utterly involved—think of John the Baptist or Siddhartha Gautama, the Buddha.

For West (2004), this prophetic commitment is to "justice of an oppressed people" (p. 17). To talk about this justice, West invokes the model of jazz. In jazz, every player has a distinct voice. It isn't like a symphony where individual voices are swallowed up in sections and the presence of the whole. Jazz is based on virtuosity and improvisation within a single melodic structure. All members are playing the same song, but each gives his or her own take. Commitment to justice, then, is first a commitment to polyvocality, the presence and honoring of many voices. True democracy can never oppress or disenfranchise; to the degree that a nation does, it is no longer democratic. The test of democracy is in how many voices are being silenced.

A commitment to justice also implies a commitment to one's own self. This commitment is

> a matter of finding one's own distinctive voice, one's own precious individuality that is not reduced to rugged, rapacious, ragged individualism. But rather is constituted by bouncing up against other voices within a community just like a jazz quartet, where if you haven't found your distinctive voice, it's time for you to practice more. (West, 2000)

Practicing for jazz entails an understanding of music theory so deep that it frees the player to intuitive improvisation. Thus, a democratic commitment to prophetic justice entails a commitment to true and continuous education. Together, polyvocality and self-education create fire—they both produce and validate prophetic speech. Only when a person is committed to diversity in community and to the edification of education can he or she speak. When one is dedicated to this fire, he or she must speak, and in the fire of polyvocality and self-education others will listen.

The third portion of the democratic cultural armor is a *tragicomic commitment to hope*. To explain this armor, West draws on the musical genre of the blues. Most of us know that both blues and jazz came out of black culture, but many of us don't recognize or like to think about the fact that they came out of the black experience of white oppression. Yet this is West's point exactly: Jazz and blues are the freest music forms in America, yet they were created by an enslaved people. Blues specifically gives expression to tragicomic hope.

The blues originated in the back-and-forth call of slaves working the fields. The call at once gave voice to pain and hope to the soul. Grief was expressed in the call, yet the cadence gave rhythm and thus lightness to the work. Individual suffering was expressed, affirmed, and given meaning in a community of sufferers. "The root of blues is the human experience and psyche itself" (Erlewine, 1999, p. v), and its essence is "to stare painful truths in the face and persevere without cynicism or pessimism" (West, 2004, p. 21).

Tellingly, the blues was born out of terrorism: the terrorist suppression of blacks by white supremacist slave owners. West tells us that we are at a crossroads brought about by yet another kind of terrorism: the attacks of 9/11. According to West (2004), we have begun down the wrong road, toward a post-democratic society. Even so, "Our fundamental test may lie in our continuing response to 9/11" (p. 8). America's move toward the road of democracy begins with the blues:

> The blues forges a mature hope that fortifies us on the slippery tightrope of Socratic questioning and prophetic witness in imperial America. . . . This kind of tragicomic hope is dangerous—and potentially subversive—because it can never be extinguished. . . . It is a form of elemental freedom that cannot be eliminated or snuffed out by any elite power. (pp. 216, 217)

Summary

- Since the 1960s, blacks in the United States have on the one hand enjoyed increased economic and political freedoms, but on the other have become the victims of market saturation. Market saturation has changed the primary orientations of blacks. Previously, blacks were strongly oriented to civic and religious institutions and the traditional ties of family and home. Market saturation has infested the black community with market moralities: fleeting hedonistic pleasure and monetary gain. The effects of markets are exaggerated for blacks because of the black heritage in America. The mix of past wounds, the continuing racial prejudice, and market moralities create black nihilism (a sense of hopelessness and meaninglessness associated with living as a black person in the United States).

• West exposes a crisis in black leadership, arguing that most black leaders either fall under the managerial/elitist model or that of protest leaders. With protest leaders, racial reasoning is paramount, which promotes ethics based on skin color alone, rather than on moral or justice issues. West calls on prophetic leaders that will transcend race and return to moral reasoning. These leaders must begin in the community, at the grassroots level, where they can participate in pragmatic community dialogue, build up trust, and maintain accountability.

• West argues that since 9/11, America has entered a postdemocratic age. There are three dogmas that have worked to bring this about: free-market fundamentalism, aggressive militarism, and escalating authoritarianism. To return to democracy, West argues that we must put on the democratic armor: Socratic questioning, prophetic justice, and tragicomic commitment to hope.

BUILDING YOUR THEORY TOOLBOX

Learning More—Primary Sources

- Primary sources for Dorothy E. Smith:
  - Smith, D. E. (1987). *The Everyday World as Problematic: A Feminist Sociology.* Boston: Northeastern University Press.
  - Smith, D. E. (1990). *The Conceptual Practices of Power: A Feminist Sociology of Knowledge.* Boston: Northeastern University Press.
  - Smith, D. E. (2005). *Institutional Ethnography: A Sociology for People.* Walnut Creek, CA: AltaMira Press.
- Primary sources for Patricia Hill Collins:
  - Collins, P. H. (2000). *Black Feminist Thought* (2nd ed.). New York: Routledge.
  - Collins, P. H. (2004). *Black Sexual Politics.* New York: Routledge.
  - Collins, P. H. (2006). *From Black Power to Hip Hop: Racism, Nationalism, and Feminism.* Philadelphia: Temple University Press.
- Primary sources for Cornel West:
  - West, C. (1993). *Race Matters.* New York: Vintage.
  - West, C. (2004). *Democracy Matters: Winning the Fight Against Imperialism.* New York: Penguin.

(Continued)

(Continued)

Seeing the Social World (knowing the theory)

- After reading and understanding this chapter, you should be able to define the following terms theoretically and explain their theoretical importance to Smith's standpoint: *practices of power, new materialism, texts, facticity, standpoint, constitutive work, relations of ruling, fault line, relations of ruling, institutional ethnography.*

- After reading and understanding this chapter, you should be able to define the following terms theoretically and explain their theoretical importance to Collins' theory: *intersectionality; Eurocentric positivism; black feminist epistemology; common challenges/diverse responses; safe places; self-definition; rearticulation; black feminist intellectuals; matrix of domination; structural, disciplinary, hegemonic, and interpersonal domains of power.*

- After reading and understanding this chapter, you should be able to define the following terms theoretically and explain their theoretical importance to West's theories: *false consciousness, pragmatism, existentialism, democratic faith, modern capitalist markets, market saturation, black cultural armor, market moralities, ontological wounds, existential angst, black nihilism, politics of conversion, crisis in black leadership, three kinds of leadership styles, racial reasoning, moral reasoning, mature black identity, coalition strategy, postdemocratic age, Constantinian Christianity, Prophetic Christianity, free-market fundamentalism, aggressive militarism, escalating authoritarianism, Socratic questioning, democratic armor, commitment to prophetic justice, tragicomic commitment to hope.*

- After reading and understanding this chapter, you should be able to answer the following questions (remember to answer them theoretically):

  - Explain how standpoint is more method than theory. How does some feminist work actually defeat standpoint?

  - How are the relations of ruling expressed through social science?

  - What is the new materialism? How does it affect what people accept as true or factual?

  - Explain the differences between the general sociological approach and Smith's.

  - How does the fault line perpetuate gender inequality?

  - Describe Smith's institutional ethnography. How is it dialectical? What do you think the benefits of institutional ethnography would be?

  - Compare and contrast the characteristics of Eurocentric positivism and black feminist epistemology.

  - Explicate the implications of black feminist epistemology.

  - Explain how inequality can best be understood as intersectionality and matrices of domination. In your explanation, be certain to discuss the implications of such an approach.

o What are the three structural forces influencing blacks in America today?

o Why did market saturation affect the black community in unique ways?

o What is black nihilism, where does it come from, and how is it affecting blacks in the United States today?

o Why is there a black leadership crisis? What are politics of conversion?

o What is racial reasoning? How does moral reasoning counter racial reasoning?

o What is West's critique of the Christian Right? How is the Christian Right an example of Constantinian Christianity?

o What are the three elements of democracy?

o How are free-market fundamentalism, aggressive militarism, and escalating militarism creating a postdemocratic age?

o How has the United States as a whole been niggerized and gangsterized?

o What is the democratic armor? How will each piece help overcome the postdemocratic age?

o How does West use the concepts of jazz and blues?

Engaging the Social World (using the theory)

• As a student, how do you see yourself being socialized to the relations of ruling? If you are a woman, do you see bifurcated consciousness in your life? As a sociologist, how will you avoid being trapped and controlled by the relations of ruling?

• In general, what implications do you see of objectified knowledge for the way people view and experience themselves? What are the implications if society were to do away with objective knowledge about social things?

• Discuss the kinds of activism that Patricia Hill Collins' approach includes. In your discussion, be certain to include the four domains of power and the unique place that black feminist intellectuals have in activism.

• Become involved in campus efforts to end discrimination. Check and see if you have an office of multicultural affairs. Find out what other campus organizations are involved in ending discrimination.

• If you're African American, explore how your values and sense of self are impacted by market moralities. If you're not African American, how have market moralities affected you?

• What does West's critique of political leadership imply generally about what we should expect from leaders in a democratic society? Analyze the current national leadership using West's criteria. Think especially about Barack Obama. Where would you place him in West's scheme? Search the Internet to discover West's opinion of Obama.

(Continued)

(Continued)

Weaving the Threads (building theory)

- Evaluate Wilson's class-based proposals using West's theory of black nihilism.

- Synthesize Wilson and West into a general theory of racial inequality.

- Compare and contrast Foucault's and West's theories of subjective experience. How can these theories be brought together to give us greater insight into how individual, subjective experiences are formed in this period of modernity?

- Compare and contrast Foucault's and Smith's ideas about how power is mediated.

- Compare and contrast Smith's idea of the fault line and Chafetz's theory of male micro-resource power.

- Write a two-page analysis of contemporary democracy using West's theory of the post democratic age. After you've finished, use West and the analyses you wrote for Habermas, Giddens, Wallerstein, and Castells to compare, contrast, and evaluate these five theorists on the issue of democracy. Based on your evaluation, synthesize these theories and create a single assessment of the democratic project of modernity. Evaluate the potential for reinvigorating democracy.

Glossary

Account-able: A theoretical idea in ethnomethodology, the term implies that the basic requirement of all social settings is that they be recognizable or accountable as whatever social setting they are supposed to be. Members visibly and knowingly work at making their scenes accountable; this work, in turn, organizes the situation and renders it meaningful and real.

Action theory: In general, any theory that begins and is concerned with individual, social action rather than structure. For Max Weber, action is social insofar as the individual takes into account other people. Weber is specifically concerned with rational action (in his typology—traditional, affective, value-rational, instrumental rational—only value and instrumental are truly rational). Parsons is interested in the conditions under which action takes place (the choice of means and ends constrained by the physical and social environments). Parsons' theory of the social system is built upon his notion of voluntaristic action.

Action types: According to Parsons, there are three kinds of action. Action may be strategic, expressive, or moral. Strategic action (rationally planned) is based on a need for and the value of objective knowledge. Expressive action (emotional or aesthetic) is based on the need for emotional attachment and value of aesthetic sentiments. Moral action (action based on ultimate realities) is based on the need for and belief in evaluative standards. As with any typology, Parsons' action types are intended to be analytical devices rather than predictive theory.

Adaptation: One of four sub-systems in Parsons' AGIL conception of requisite needs; the subsystem that converts raw materials from the environment into usable stuffs (in the body, the digestive system; in society, the economy).

AGIL: Parsons proposes four system needs and argues that every grouping of social units that acts like a system must meet these needs. These four system needs can be remembered by the acronym AGIL: adaptation, the subsystem that converts raw materials from the environment into usable stuffs; goal attainment, the subsystem that motivates and guides the system as a whole; integration, the subsystem that regulates the activities of the systems' diverse members; and latent pattern maintenance, the subsystem that indirectly preserves patterns of behavior that are needed for survival.

Alienation: Alienation is a concept in Marx's theory of the effects of capitalism on consciousness and human nature and is based on the idea that there is an intrinsic connection between the producer and the product. The word itself means to be separated from; it also implies that there is something that faces humans as an unknown or alien object. For Marx there are four different kinds of alienation that is true about the worker: alienation from one's own species-being; alienation from the work process; alienation from the product; alienation from other social beings. Alienation also forms the basis of private property.

Anomie: Anomie is a concept that is used by both Durkheim and Simmel in their theories of modernity. Anomie literally means to be without norms or laws. Because human beings are not instinctually driven, they require behavioral regulation. Without norms guiding behavior, life becomes meaningless. Anomie is a pathology of modernity and tends to occur under high levels of structural differentiation and division of labor when the culture of society does not generalize quickly enough. High levels of anomie can lead to anomic suicide.

Black nihilism: Black nihilism is a theoretical concept from the work of Cornel West. Nihilism in general refers to the idea that human life and existence are meaningless and useless. West uses the idea to describe the African American experience as the result of market saturation. Up until the 1950s, blacks were not considered a viable or large market for capitalism. Since the era of civil rights, however, African Americans have been increasingly targeted: Blacks have been inundated with new commodities and enticed by values of consumerism. Consumerism along with upward mobility for some blacks has weakened the civic and religious community base that has traditionally been the source of strength and validation for blacks living under American apartheid. For West, the main problem is that true equality and justice still do not exist for African Americans: The black life is still one of oppression, yet it is experienced under the shroud of consumerism and the belief that owning more and more commodities is the source of happiness. The loss of community coupled with consumerism and continued oppression has contributed to a growing sense of meaninglessness and loss of purpose for African Americans.

Blasé attitude: The blasé attitude is a concept from Simmel's theory of urbanization. The word "blasé" means "to be uninterested in pleasure or life." According to Simmel, the blasé attitude is the typical emotional state of the modern city dweller. It is the direct result of the increased emotional work and anomie associated with diverse group memberships and increased cognitive stimulation due to the rapidness of change and flow of information.

Bureaucracy: For Weber bureaucracy is a system of organizing people and their behavior that is characterized by the presence of written rules and communication, job placement by accreditation, expert knowledge, clearly outlined responsibilities and authorities, explicit career ladders, and an office hierarchy. The purposes of the bureaucratic form are to rationalize and routinize behavior.

Bureaucratic personality: The bureaucratic personality is an extension of Weber's theory of the rationalization processes intrinsic within bureaucracies, and is the result of extensive use of bureaucratic methods for organization within a society. The bureaucratic personality is characterized by rational living, identification with organizational goals, reliance on expert systems of knowledge, and sequestered experiences (experiences that are removed from social or family life and placed in institutionalized settings).

Civil society: A concept from Jürgen Habermas' critical theory, civil society is a social network of voluntary associations, organizations (especially mass media), and social movements; its purpose is to inform and actualize the public sphere. To function properly, the civil society must be free from control by the state, economy, and religion, and it must exist within a liberal culture that values equality and freedom.

Class: Class is a theoretical concept, broadly used to talk about a social structure that is built around issues of economic production. Class is specifically an issue in modernity and capitalism in that other social positions tended to be more significant in previous eras, such as in feudalism. Karl Marx argued that, under capitalism, class became explicit and the most powerful issue in the stratification of unequal resources. The issue in classical theory is central for Marx and Weber. For Marx, class is the only structure that matters, and it is specifically defined by the ownership of the means of production. In capitalist societies, class bifurcates into owners (bourgeoisie) and workers (proletariat). For Weber, class is one of three systems of stratification, status and power being the other two. Weber also defines class more complexly than does Marx. According to Weber, one's class is defined by the probability of acquiring the goods and positions that are seen to bring inner satisfaction. Class position is determined by the control of property or market position, both of which may be positively, negatively, or medially possessed. In contemporary theory, class is a central issue in Bourdieu's theory of habitus and symbolic violence.

Class consciousness: Class consciousness is a concept from Marx's theory of capitalism. It is the subjective awareness that class determines life chances and group interests. With class consciousness a class moves from a class in itself to a class for itself, a shift from a structured position to a political one. Class-consciousness is one of the prerequisites to social change in Marxian theory and varies directly by the levels of worker communication, exploitation, and alienation.

Collective consciousness: The collective consciousness is a central theoretical issue in Durkheim's theory of social solidarity. It refers to the collective representations (cognitive elements) and sentiments (emotional elements) that guide and bind together any social group. The collective consciousness varies by three elements: the degree to which culture is shared; the amount of power the culture has to guide individual's thoughts, feelings, and actions; its degree of clarity; and by its relative levels of religious versus secular content. Each of these is related to the amount of ritual performance in a collective. According to Durkheim, the collective consciousness takes on a life and reality of its own and independently influences human thought, emotion, and behavior, particularly in response to high levels of ritual.

Colonization of the life-world: A theoretical concept used by Jürgen Habermas to describe the process through which the everyday life of people is taken over by economic and political structures. By definition, the life-world is the primary place of intimate communication and social connections. These functions are overshadowed by the values of money and power that come from the economic and political realms, which in turn reduce true communication and sociability. Life-world colonization tends to increase as social structures become more complex and bureaucratized, and when the state creates a climate of entitlement.

Commodification: Commodification is a theoretical idea in Marxian theory that expresses the process through which material and non-material goods are turned into products for sale. Since commodities are created (nothing by its nature is a commodity); and, because humans have the ability to create subjectively felt needs; and, because modern capitalism is defined by the endless pursuit of more capital; then the process of commodification has no natural limit. Increasing commodification is a result of industrialization and market expansion and directly affects overproduction.

Commodity fetish: A central concept in Marxian theory. In commodity fetish, workers fail to recognize the human factor in products. Creative production is the distinctive trait of humanity. Therefore, all products have an intrinsic relationship to the people who make them. However, in capitalism, the product is owned and controlled by another, and it thus faces the worker as something alien that must be bought and appropriated. In misrecognizing their own nature in the product, workers also fail to see that there are sets of oppressive social relations in back of both the perceived need and the simple exchange of money for a commodity. Moreover, commodities come to substitute for real social relations—under capitalism, people see their lives being defined through commodity acquisition rather than community relations.

Constructivist structuralism: Pierre Bourdieu's theoretical perspective. It's a way of seeing the social world that does away with dualisms such as object/subject and structure/agent. Bourdieu sees a dialectical tension between constructive and structuring social elements. The dialectic indicates that the elements are in tension (structuring and constructing) with one another and that the outcome includes both but is different from either.

Consumer society: A theoretical idea from the work of Jean Baudrillard. Goods and services have always been consumed; it's a basic fact of economic existence. However, in postmodernity, consumption itself drives the economy rather than basic needs and production. Pure consumption has no natural limits—that is, consumption for consumption's sake cannot be satisfied and produces a never-ending demand for new and different commodities. Further, consumption becomes a primary, if not *the* primary, way people define themselves and experience life.

Crosscutting stratification: Weber was the first to explore the idea of crosscutting economic, political influences. More recently Patricia Hill Collins (African American feminist) uses the idea of intersectionality. The basic idea is that systems of race, gender, class, nationality, sexuality, and age crisscross one another at specific social locations that form a matrix of domination. The analytical issue, then, is to empirically discover how these various systems come together for any specific person or group. Collins is specifically concerned with how these systems shape black women's experiences and are, in turn, influenced by black women.

Cultural capital: Cultural capital is a theoretical concept used in Randall Collins' theory of interaction ritual chains and Pierre Bourdieu's theory of class replication. For Collins, cultural capital is defined as the amount of cultural goods—such as knowledge and symbols—that a person has at his or her disposal to engage others in interaction rituals. The more cultural capital is held in common, the more likely people are to interact with one another. But because it is a form of capital, people are also looking for a return on their investment—they hope to take more culture away than what they brought into the interaction. Collins conceptualizes three types of cultural capital: generalized (group specific), particularized (specific to relationships between individuals), and reputational (what is known about the individual). For Bourdieu, there are three kinds of cultural capital: objective (material goods that vary with class), institutionalized (official recognition of knowledge and skills), and embodied (the result of class-based socialization; habitus). Generally, the concept refers to the social skills, linguistic styles, and tastes that one accrues through education and distance from necessity (a measure of how far removed someone is from basic sustenance living). As the levels of education and distance from necessity increase, language, taste, and social skills tend to become more complex and abstract.

Cultural patterns: In Parsons' theory of institutionalization, culture patterns are made up of sets of beliefs, values, and symbols that arise out of people's motivations and values in action. There are three types of cultural patterns: beliefs in cognitive significance, expressive symbolism, and standards of values.

Cultural strain: Cultural strain is a concept in Parsons' theory of social change and revolution. Cultural strain occurs when cultural elements are in conflict one with another, and thus the expectations people have based on cultural values, beliefs, and practices are disrupted. Cultural strain is a natural part of societal growth and reintegration. Social systems that are able to resolve the strains are able to move ahead and become more adaptive; if a society is unable to adapt to the strain, it sets up the possibility of a group experiencing alienation, thus opening the path to revolutionary change.

Culture generalization: Culture or value generalization is a concept in Durkheim's theory of organic solidarity. It's the process through which culture and values become more abstract and are able to transcend specific social groups. As a society experiences greater levels of social diversity, the need for more generalized and transcendent culture and values increases.

Cybernetic hierarchy of control: In Parsons' theory, the cybernetic hierarchy of control argues that all systems are nested, controlled by information and communication, and are at some level self-regulating through information gathered from the environment and the system itself: Systems make internal adjustments based on new information. For human systems, information comes from culture and moves downward through the social, personality, and organic systems. Motivation/energy for action moves from the bottom up: beginning in the biological/organic systems of the human body.

Definition of the situation: Part of symbolic interactionist theory, it refers to the primary meaning given to a social interaction. The definition of the situation is important because it implicitly contains identities and scripts for behavior. Because the definition of the situation is a meaning attribution, it is flexible and negotiable—in other words, people can change it at a moment's notice and with it the available roles and selves.

Dialectic: Dialectic is a theoretical concept that describes the intrinsic dynamic relations within a phenomenon, such as the economy. The term is generally, though not exclusively, used in conflict or critical perspectives. The idea of dialecticism came to sociology through Karl Marx, and Marx, for his part, got the idea from the philosopher Georg Wilhelm Hegel. A dialectic contains different elements that are naturally antagonistic or in tension with one another—this antagonism is what energizes and brings change. Dialectics are cyclical in nature, with each new cycle bringing a different and generally unpredictable resolve. The resolve, or new set of social relations, contains its own antagonistic elements, and the cycle continues.

Discourse: Discourse is a theoretical concept that is widely used but is most specifically associated with the work of Michel Foucault. A discourse is an institutionalized way of thinking and speaking. It sets the limits of what can be spoken and, more importantly, *how* something may be spoken of. In setting these limits, discourses delineate the actors of a field, their relationships to one another, and their subjectivities. Discourses are thus an exercise of power.

Discursive consciousness: A theoretical concept used to understand the hierarchy of the agent (different levels of awareness and thus action) in Anthony Giddens' theory. Discursive consciousness refers specifically to the ability to give verbal accounts or rationalizations of action. It's what we are able to say about the social situation. Discursive consciousness is the awareness of social situations in verbal form.

Disembedding mechanisms: The idea of disembedding mechanisms is a theoretical concept from Anthony Giddens' theory of modernity. Disembedding speaks of processes that lift social relations and interactions out from local contexts, which has implications for time–space distanciation and ontological security. There are two types of mechanisms: symbolic tokens and expert systems.

Division of labor: The way in which work is divided in any economy. It can vary from everyone doing similar tasks to each person having a specialized job. This concept is an important one for most theories of modernity. In previous epochs, labor was more holistic in the sense that the worker was invested in a product from beginning to end. Thus, a shoemaker made the entire shoe. One of the distinctive traits of modernity is the use of scientific management, or *Fordism*, to divide work up into the smallest manageable parts. The division of labor is an important variable for Durkheim, Simmel, Marx, and others. For Durkheim, the division of labor creates specialized cultures for each group that may in turn threaten the cohesiveness of the general culture; for Simmel, the division of labor increases the level of objective culture in any society and it trivializes the meaning surrounding products; for Marx, the division of labor is understood as potentially separating people from species-being (natural or forced; material versus mental).

Documentary method: A theoretical term from ethnomethodology. The documentary method is the activity through which a link is created between an event or object and an assumed meaning structure. It is more than interpretation. Documentary method refers to the actual work that people perform in a social situation that links an event to its interpretation in such a way as to authenticate the correspondence.

Double consciousness: Double consciousness is part of Du Bois' understanding of the black experience in the United States. It generally refers to the experience of one's identity being fragmented into several, contradictory facets. These facets war at and negate one another so that the disenfranchised is left with no true consciousness. As Du Bois (1903/1966a) explains: "One ever feels his twoness,—an American, a Negro; two souls, two thoughts, two unreconciled strivings; two warring ideals in one dark body, whose dogged strength alone keeps it from being torn asunder" (p. 102).

Dramaturgical analogy: Dramaturgy is a theoretical perspective that is most closely associated with the work of Erving Goffman. Dramaturgy uses the analogy of the stage to analyze and understand what people do in social encounters. People are conceived of as actors, sometimes working as teams, who work to convey specific self-impressions to an audience (others present). This work is referred to as impression management. Emphasis is placed on the continual production of a social self, which places moral imperatives on the interaction order.

Effervescence: Emotional energy or effervescence is key theoretical idea in Durkheim's theory of ritual. It is defined as the level of motivational energy an individual feels after participating in a ritual. It varies by the degree of common focus of attention, common emotional mood, and physical co-presence. Emotional effervescence by itself tends to quickly dissolve unless it is given a symbol that represents the high level of emotion. These symbols tend to then be seen as sacred (such as national flags and religious emblems) and are used to prompt further ritual enactment through creating a common focus of attention and emotional mood.

Emergence: Emergence is a theoretical idea used to understand meaning and interaction in Mead's theory of symbolic interaction. To emerge means to rise from or come out into view, like steam from boiling water. Emergent meaning (or self), then, implies that meaning is not intrinsic to any sign or object. Meaning, rather, is a function of social interaction: the meaning of a sign, symbol, non-verbal cue, social object, and so on comes out of (emerges from) social interaction. In this perspective, meaning is thus a very supple thing and is controlled by people in face-to-face interaction, not social structure.

Emotional energy: A theoretical idea that originated with Émile Durkheim and is used by Randall Collins in his theory of interaction rituals. It is defined as the level of motivational energy an individual feels after leaving an interaction. Emotional energy is specifically linked to the level of collective emotion formed in a ritual, and it predicts the likelihood of further ritual performance and the individual's initial involvement within the ritual.

Episteme: Episteme is a theoretical concept from Michel Foucault's theory of knowledge and power. It refers to the fundamental notions of truth and validity that underlie knowledge—it's the hidden order of knowledge. Epistemes organize and are a necessary precondition for thought; they set the boundaries of what is possible and knowable. One important implication is that an episteme will maintain the order produced by a knowledge system even in the face of contradictory events or findings. Epistemes are historically specific and change through rupture rather than linear progress.

Equilibrium: A concern of functionalist theory, equilibrium refers to a state of balance between integrative and disintegrative forces; it implies a social system that maintains certain constancies of patterns relative to its environment. The idea is that a social system must maintain a balance, whether internally or between itself and its environment.

Evolution: Generally speaking, evolution is a scientific theory of the process of continuous change. The process is marked by transformation from simpler, less adaptable forms to more complex. Complexity is usually understood in terms of the number, types, and interrelationships among biological structures within an organism. The basic tenets are the same for social evolution: societies change gradually over time into structurally more complex forms. More complex societies are judged superior by virtue of increased adaptation and survivability.

Evolution of religion: A significant issue in the sociological study of religion is historical change, and the basic tenet of this approach is that religion and society are locked in a kind of reciprocal relationship; as one changes, so does the other. This issue is significant in understanding religion in a democratic society. Harriet Martineau, for example, argued that democracy needed and created "moderate religions," where education and self-actualization are keys. More recently, Robert Bellah argues that many of the ethical and moral dimensions of religion become part of a "civil religion" that is separate from both state and church and is instrumental in not only creating common beliefs but also argument, even conflict, about the meaning of the shared values and goals.

Exploitation: Exploitation is a central concept in Marxian economic theory. In its sparsest terms, exploitation refers to the measurable difference between what a worker gets paid and the amount of product she or he produces. Capitalist profit is based on exploitation (paying the worker less than he or she actually earns). Capitalists are thus dependent upon workers, which, in turn, gives workers a bargaining tool to push for higher wages and benefits. Because of the rising cost of labor in advanced capitalist countries, capitalists are forced to export exploitation to "less developed" countries, where workers will labor for less. These workers, however, will push for better wages and benefits, and the capitalists eventually will have to find other labor markets with cheap labor. Ultimately, according to Marxian theory, this dynamic of exploitation will lead to the demise of capitalism.

Facticity: A theoretical concept found in a number of different social constructivist approaches, facticity refers to the quality of being a fact. Implicit in this concept is the idea that facts are produced; they don't intrinsically exist as facts. Events, objects, and phenomena in general become facts under certain knowledge systems.

False consciousness: False consciousness is a concept in Marxian theories of alienation. False consciousness is more profound than ideology and has two components: First, false consciousness is human self-awareness that is false in its very foundations. It appears that human beings are uniquely aware of their own nature, the essence of what makes humanity different from other species. In false consciousness humankind's awareness of human nature is fictitious and counterfeit. The second element to false consciousness is that humankind is unable to recognize this problem. This second component obviously creates problems for theorists using the idea: How is it possible to overcome false consciousness if we are unaware that it exists in the first place? Generally speaking there are two sorts of answers: the one Marx gives, the structural dialectics of capitalism will create class consciousness, which is a step out of false consciousness. The other answer is that the unhappiness of the human condition implies the problem and that intentionally using critical thinking/theory to deconstruct oppression are the first steps in discovering false consciousness and moving past it.

Fault line: A theoretical concept specific to Dorothy E. Smith's feminist theory. Smith argues that a gap exists between official knowledge—especially knowledge generated through the social sciences—and the experience of women. This fault line is particularly important for understanding how men are unable to see the differences between objective, public knowledge and the reality of day-to-day existence: Women traditionally negotiate or obscure the disjunction for men through their caring for the daily administration of the household, including meeting the sustenance and comfort needs of both men and children.

Field: The field is a theoretical concept from Pierre Bourdieu's constructivist structuralism approach. The concept functions to orient the researcher to an arena of study. Field denotes a set of objective positions and relations that are tied together by the rules of the game and by the distribution of four fundamental powers or capitals: economic, cultural (informal social skills, habits, linguistic styles, and tastes), social (networks), and symbolic (the use of symbols to recognize and thus legitimate the other powers). People and positions are hierarchically distributed in the field through the overall volume of capital they possess. Symbolic and cultural capitals are specifically important: Cultural capital helps to form habitus and thus contributes to the replication of the field, and symbolic capital gives legitimacy and meaning to the empirical field.

Frames: The idea of frames is a theoretical concept in Goffman's analysis of how people experience reality. The analogy is to a film strip and its frames or to the frame of a picture on the wall. In both cases the frame delineates certain features as important by excluding all others. Frames, then, tell people what to pay attention to and thus how to organize their subjective involvement. There are two primary frames: natural and social. These are perceived as solid and factual. These frames may be keyed and thus given different meanings. Keying generally makes a primary frame seem less real. The five keys are make-believe, contests, ceremonies, technical redoings, and regroupings.

Free-floating signifiers: The idea of free-floating signifiers comes from the postmodern writings of Fredric Jameson. In traditional and modern societies, signifiers, or signs, are set and understood within a social or linguistic structure, what is sometimes referred to as a signification chain. In postmodernity, however, the chain or context of signs has been disrupted by machines of reproduction, or mass media. This break in the signification chain indicates that each sign stands alone, or in relatively loose association with fragmented groups of other signs. Signs, then, become free-floating signifiers.

Front: The theoretical idea of a front comes from Erving Goffman's dramaturgy. Front refers to the totality of identity cues offered by an individual in a social encounter. These cues come from setting, manner, and appearance.

Function: The idea of social function comes through analogy from biology. Classic thinkers like Spencer and Durkheim used the analogy of how an organism works to think about society (the *organismic* analogy). A biological creature is made up of different organs, each of which fulfills a need that the animal has, with each and every organ purposefully related to other organs within the body. The idea of social function, then, denotes the necessary contribution a social structure makes, as well as the way the structure is related to other elements in society.

Game stage: The game stage is the second of three stages in Mead's theory of self-formation. It corresponds to the time when children are able to take the role of multiple others separately and can understand rule-based behavior.

Gender: Gender is a social category that is used to establish differences in status, power, class, roles, norms, values, and beliefs. The concept of gender is defined through its relationship with several other categories: sex, socially agreed upon biological criteria; sex category, based on sex criteria but maintained socially through specific displays; gender, the social category that uses sex category to assign differences in practices, subjectivities, status, power, class, norms, values, and beliefs; and gender identity, a person's inner sense of gender.

Generalized media of exchange: A concern for functional theory, specifically Durkheim and Parsons, generalized media of exchange refers to symbolic goods that are used to facilitate interactions across institutional domains. Thus, they are values and symbols that allow different structures to relate one to another; the goods and services exchanged by different institutions.

Generalized other: The generalized other is a theoretical concept used in symbolic interactionism that refers to sets of perspectives and attitudes indicative of a specific group or social type with which the individual can role-take. In the formation of the self, the generalized other represents the last stage in which the child can place herself in a collective role from which to view her own behaviors. It is the time when the self is fully formed as the person takes all of society inside.

Goal attainment: One of four subsystems in Parsons' AGIL conception of requisite needs; the subsystem that motivates and guides the system as a whole (in the body, the mind; in society, government).

Governmentality: Governmentality is a theoretical term from Michel Foucault's theory of knowledge and power. The term refers to a specific kind of institutionalized power. In Foucault's scheme, modernity is unique because of the manner through which states control populations. Generally speaking, in previous ages power and control were exercised upon the individual from without. Governments would actively and directly control the person, when domination was necessary or desired. In contrast, modern states exercise power from within the individual. Governmentality, then, captures the process through which the person participates in her or his own domination—control is exercised within the person by the person.

Gynaecocentric theory: Gynaecocentric theory originated with Lester F. Ward (1841–1913), the first president of the American Sociological Association. Gilman used gynaecocentric theory to argue that women, not men, are the general species type for humans: It is through women that the race is born and the first social connections created. In gynaecocentric theory, men and women have essential sex-specific energies.

Habitus: A central theoretical term from Pierre Bourdieu's theory of class replication. Habitus refers to the cultural capital an individual possesses as a result of his or her class position. Habitus is embodied; that is, it works through the body

Interaction: Interaction is a central theoretical idea in symbolic interactionism. Interaction is the intertwining of individual human actions. In symbolic interactionism, the interaction is the true acting unit in society. According to this view, interaction is not simply the means of expressing social structure or the individual's personality traits; rather, the interaction is the premier social domain and is thus the chief factor through which social structures and individual personalities are created and sustained. Interaction occurs via a three-part process through which meaning, society, and self emerge: the presentation of a cue, the initial response to the cue, and the response to the response. However, the end point of the process generally becomes itself an initial cue for further interaction, starting the process over again.

Intersectionality: Intersectionality is a theoretical concept in Patricia Hill Collins' theory of structured inequality. The basic idea is that systems of race, gender, class, nationality, sexuality, and age crisscross one another at specific social locations that form a matrix of domination. The analytical issue, then, is to empirically discover how these various systems come together for any specific person or group. Collins is specifically concerned with how these systems shape black women's experiences and are, in turn, influenced by black women.

Iron cage of bureaucracy: The iron cage of bureaucracy is an important effect in Weber's theory of bureaucracy and rationalization. There are two ways the idea is used. First, once in place bureaucracies are difficult if not impossible to get rid of: "Bureaucracy is the means of transforming social action into rationally organized action" (Weber 1922/1968, p. 987, emphasis original). Second, while in the beginning of modernity people strove to have a rationally controlled life, the pervasive presence of bureaucratic organization has forced people to rationally control life, to become "narrow specialists without mind" (Weber 1904–1905/2002, p. 124).

Joint action: Joint action is a theoretical term from Blumer's symbolic interactionism that describes the process through which various individual and discrete actions and interactions are brought together to form a meaningful whole. This joining is accomplished symbolically by both individuals and groups and constitutes a significant portion of what is meant by "society." The insight of this concept is that at every point of interaction or joint action there is uncertainty. The implication is that society is emergent.

Latent pattern maintenance: One of four subsystems in Parsons' AGIL conception of requisite needs; the subsystem that indirectly preserves patterns of behavior that are needed for survival (in the body, the autonomic nervous system; in society, education, religion, and family).

Legitimation: Legitimation is a theoretical concept that describes the effects that specific stories, histories, and myths have in granting ethical, moral, or legal status or authorization to social power and relations. Weber tells us that there are two components to any system of legitimation: subjective and objective; and he is specifically concerned with the legitimation of authorities, charismatic, traditional, and rational-legal. The general idea of legitimation is particularly important in contemporary theories of the social construction of reality. In social constructivist theory, there are three levels of legitimation (self-evident, theoretical, and symbolic universes [i.e., religious systems]), each more powerful than the previous. Habermas also uses this idea to talk about the shift from legitimations of capitalism to the state. This change happens as the result of organized capitalism and results in a crisis of legitimation.

Life politics: A theoretical idea from Anthony Giddens' theory of modernity, life politics is an outgrowth of emancipatory politics. Emancipatory politics is concerned with liberating individuals and groups from the constraints that adversely affect their lives—people are thus liberated to make choices. Life politics is the politics of choice and lifestyle. It is concerned with issues that flow from the practices of self-actualization within the dialectic of the local/global, where self-realization affects global strategies. Life politics is dependent upon the individual creating and maintaining inner authenticity.

Lifeworld: The lifeworld is a theoretical concept that came into sociology through the work of Alfred Schutz. The lifeworld refers to the world as it is experienced immediately by each person. It is a cultural world filled with meaning and is made up of the sets of assumptions, beliefs, and meanings against which an individual judges and interprets everyday experiences.

Linguistic market: A theoretical concept from Pierre Bourdieu's theory of class replication, the idea emphasizes the importance of language and social skills in reproducing class. Every time a person speaks with another, there is a linguistic market within which each person has different skill levels and knowledge. These differing levels lead to distinct rewards in the market that in turn announce one's class position. The power of the market is that people tend to sanction themselves because they intuitively understand how their culture and language skills will play out in any given market.

Magic and religion: Magic and religion are ideas Weber uses to understand the evolution of spiritual forms of action and social organization. Magic is based in a naturalistic view of the universe and is concerned with direct manipulation of natural forces; religion, on the other hand, is symbolic and is concerned with rituals that dramatically enact abstract truths. Evolution toward more symbolic forms is associated with professionalization, bureaucratization of government, and technology.

Manifest and latent functions: Elements of functional theorizing specifically introduced by Robert K. Merton. Manifest functions are those known effects of a social structure that lead to integration and equilibrium; latent functions are the hidden or unacknowledged contributions of social structure that lead to integration and equilibrium.

Material dialectic: The material dialectic is the driving force (dynamic) in Marx's understanding of economic and historical change. A dialectic contains different elements that are naturally antagonistic or in tension to one another—this antagonism is what energizes and brings change. In the material world of capitalist production, the primary contradictions are found in exploitation and overproduction. For Marx, the dialectic continues until an economic system in keeping with species-being comes into existence.

Matrix of domination: The idea of matrices of domination comes from Patricia Hill Collins' theory of black feminist epistemology. In general, the notion of a matrix refers to a mass within which something is enclosed. This enclosure is a point of origin or growth (as in the cradle or matrix of civilization). For Collins, the issue is that current society is built of matrices of domination that form around the intersecting issues of race, gender, age, sexuality, nationality, and so on. Any matrix of domination works through four different domains: structural, disciplinary, hegemonic, and intrapersonal.

Means and relations of production: The means of production is a central concept in Marx's theory of capitalism. Simply, the means of production refers to the way in which commodities are produced. However, in Marx's hands the concept comes to denote quite a bit more. Because the basic social fabric is economic in Marxian theory, relations of production are inherent within the means of production. Thus, the means of production—such as capitalism, feudalism, and socialism—determine how people relate to self and others (the relations of production).

Means of production: A central concept in Marx's theory of capitalism. Simply, the means of production refers to the way in which commodities are produced. However, in Marx's hands the concept comes to connote quite a bit more. Because the basic social fabric is economic in Marxian theory, relations of production are inherent within the means of production. Thus, the means of production—such as capitalism, feudalism, and socialism—determines how people relate to self and others (the relations of production).

Mechanical solidarity: Mechanical solidarity is part of Durkheim's typology of society and refers to the kind of social solidarity experienced in traditional societies. Durkheim uses the term "social solidarity" to refer to the level of cultural integration in a society, as measured by the subjective sense of being part of a group (cohesion), the constraint of individual behaviors for the group good (normative regulation), and the level of coordination and control among various social units. In mechanical solidarity, all three of these variables are high. Specifically, people are united by sharing a clear and limited set of common beliefs and sentiments, and through a sense that society (or the group) is more important and viable than the individual person. In addition, people's behaviors are regulated through strong feelings of morality and through repressive law. Mechanical solidarity is dependent upon a limited social network with frequent face-to-face interactions.

Middle-range theories: Middle-range theories are a central component in Robert K. Merton's empirical functionalism. These are theories that are empirically based yet generalized to an intermediate level; that is, they are not completely abstract or empirical. Merton proposed the use of middle-range theories as a method of building sociologically relevant theory, in comparison to the more abstract schemes of such theorists as Talcott Parsons and Karl Marx. Merton's idea was that middle-range theories could be linked together to form more general yet empirically relevant theories.

Militaristic and industrial societies: Militaristic and industrial societies form Spencer's typology of society. Militaristic societies are characterized by a high level of governmental control of social units and mass media, with religion and education working to legitimate the state. Industrial societies are characterized by low levels of government control and high levels of economic freedom; information flows freely and religion and education oriented toward individual expression and exploration. Because it is more adaptive, there is a general tendency for societies to move in the direction of industrial but there are regressive tendencies as well: the industrial-military complex, legitimate threat, and territorial subjects.

Mind: According to Mead, the mind is a social entity constituted through language and role-taking. The mind exists in certain kinds of behavior; specifically, the internalized conversation of linguistic signs and symbols, and the ability to suspend behavior and to rehearse actions. The mind is socially necessary because of its place in human behavior.

Misrecognize: A central concept in Marxian theory. Marxists argue that people fail to see or recognize the relations of production within a commodity or the means of production. Misrecognition is thus a function of ideology and implies that the dominated are blind to their own oppression.

Modalities of structuration: A concept used in Anthony Giddens' structuration, modalities of structuration are the paths through which structure is expressed in social encounters. There are three modalities (interpretive schemes, facilities, and norms) that are linked on the one hand to structures (signification, domination, and legitimation) and on the other to social practices (communication, power, and sanctions). These modalities are socially and culturally specific.

Modes of orientation: The beginning element in Parsons' theory of social action and institutionalization, modes of orientation are the different values (cognitive, appreciative, and moral) and motivations (cognitive, cathectic, and evaluative) that people bring into a situation. They result in identifiable types of action (strategic, expressive, or moral) that in the long run pattern interactions across time and space and result in the taken-for-granted norms, roles, and status positions that constitute social structure and society.

Money: Money is a generalized media of economic exchange. Money can vary in its abstraction. Initially precious metals were used as money—this form of money was valued in and of itself. Later, paper was used as a symbol for gold and silver; this money was more abstract but nevertheless had an objective base. In time the gold and silver in back of paper money was dropped and paper money became pure symbol. Credit and debit cards soon came to function in the place of paper-money. Simmel sees the increasing use and abstraction of money as having both positive and negative effects: It increases personal freedom, rationalization, calculability, as well as increasing the number and extent of exchange relations, continuity between groups and individuals, and trust in the national system. At the same time, the increased use of money decreases the level of emotional attachment that individuals can have to things and other people, and it reduces the level of moral constraint.

Morbid excess in sex distinction: A theoretical concept in Charlotte Perkins Gilman's evolutionary theory of gender. Sex distinctions are those physical and visual cues that make sexes different from one another. Gilman argues that the sex distinctions in humans have been carried to a harmful extreme due to women no longer living in the natural environment of economic pursuit, but, rather, living in the artificial environment of the home that has been established by men. Women have thus been physically and sexually changed by evolution so that they can better survive under patriarchy.

Motives: A motive is the energy within a person that stimulates her or him into action. As part of Parsons' modes of orientation there are three kinds of motives: cognitive, cathectic, and evaluative.

Nation-states: A defining feature of modernity; a nation-state is a socially diverse collective that occupies a specific territory, creates a common history and identity, and whose members sees themselves as sharing a common fate. Nation-states are bureaucratically organized and emphasize mass democracy.

Natural signs and significant gestures: According to Mead, natural signs are signs that have an intrinsic relationship to that which it signifies. The sign and its object naturally go together. In comparison to natural signs, significant gestures are abstract and arbitrary in their relationship to the object. Significant gestures are also reflexive, in that they call out the same response in the sender and receiver. Significant gestures are the central element in Mead's theory of minds, self, and society.

Normative specificity: Norms are behaviors that have some sanction attached to them. The sanctions can be positive (reward) or negative (punishment), and they can be formal (like laws) or informal (generally understood). Normative specificity, then, refers to the degree to which behaviors are specifically regulated (explicit norms for specific behaviors). Normative specificity is high when a group is regulating a large proportion of a person's behaviors. We find this issue in Durkheim, Simmel, and Parsons' theories.

Objective culture: The issue of objective culture is central to Simmel's theorizing. Objective culture must be understood in reference to subjective culture, which is culture that is essentially and wholly meaningful and understood by an individual.

Culture becomes objective as its size, diversity of components, and complexity increase. Among the effects of increasing objective culture are anomie and the blasé attitude.

Ontological security/insecurity: Ontological security is a theoretical concept from Anthony Giddens' structuration theory. Ontology refers to the way things exist and specifically implies that human existence is different from all other forms of existence because of meaning. Meaning is not a necessary or intrinsic feature of any event or object, which implies that human reality is unstable. This intrinsic instability creates an unconscious need for ontological security—a sense of trust in the taken-for-grantedness of the human world. This need motivates humans to routinize and regionalize their practices.

Ontology: A branch of philosophy that is concerned with how things exist. An obvious example is that rocks and people exist differently: One is biological and the other isn't. But ontology is concerned with less obvious, more fundamental questions—in particular, how categories exist. In our case, we are concerned with how society exists—what is its ontological source? Does society exist as an object made up of social facts and structures? Or, does society exist symbolically through the way we create meaning around the idea of society?

Organic solidarity: Organic solidarity is part of Durkheim's typology of social integration, which is measured by the subjective sense of being part of a group (cohesion), the constraint of individual behaviors for the group good (normative regulation), and the level of coordination and control among various social units. Organic solidarity is characteristic of modern societies with a high division of labor, and is created through high levels of mutual dependency (structural, group, and individual), generalized culture, and the presence of intermediate (between the level of society and the level of face-to-face interaction) groups and organizations. Relationships are regulated more through rational-legal means (restitutive law) than moral codes, and people generally have weak attachments to family and tradition. In Durkheim's mind, organic solidarity is more precarious than mechanical and susceptible to various "pathologies" (such as anomie).

Organismic analogy: Analogies are quite often used in sociology as ways of understanding how society works. With an analogy there is resemblance in some particulars between things that are otherwise unlike—and analogies are used to explain from something well-known to something unfamiliar. The organismic analogy is specific to functionalist theorizing and implies that society works like a biological organism in that it has survival needs and evolves to greater complexity. The analogy also implies that society, just like complex organisms, operates like a system of interrelated parts that tend toward stasis or balance, and any derivation from that life-balance is seen as illness or pathology.

Overproduction: In Marx's theory, overproduction is one of the central contradictions of capitalism. Modern capitalism is defined by the endless pursuit of capital accumulation. This essential characteristic of capitalism, coupled with the human capacity to create endless needs, drives ever-expanding markets, commodification, and the use of technology to increase productive output, all of which lead to an overproduction of goods compared to the current demand and, thus, an economic downturn. Every cycle of expansion and downturn is deeper and more widespread. And because there are no natural limits within capitalism to capital accumulation and no limits to the potential for new human needs, these cycles continue until capitalism fails.

Panopticon: Panopticon is a theoretical concept from Michel Foucault's theory of knowledge and power. The panopticon was an architectural design for a prison that allowed for the unobserved observation of prisoners. The idea behind the panopticon is that if prisoners thought they were being watched, even if they weren't, the prisoners themselves would exercise control over their own behaviors. Foucault sees this physical prison as a metaphor for the way control and power are exercised in modernity. He specifically has in mind the self-administered control that comes through the knowledge produced by the social and behavioral sciences as well as medical science.

Phenomenology: Phenomenology is a school of philosophy developed by Edmund Husserl that argues that consciousness is the only experience or phenomenon of which humans can be certain. It seeks, then, to discover the natural and primary processes of consciousness apart from the influence of culture or society. Husserl hoped to create "a descriptive account of the essential structures of the directly given," that is, the immediate experience of the world apart from preexisting values or beliefs. Social phenomenology, on the other hand, argues that nothing is directly given to humans; we experience everything through stocks of language, typifications, and so on. Social phenomenology, then, seeks to explain the phenomena of the social world as they are presented to us. This approach is distinct from most sociology in that phenomenologists reduce phenomena to the simplest terms possible. For example, a structural sociologist will study racial inequality and its effects. Race is simply a given in this kind of approach. A phenomenological approach will take race itself as the most basic problem to explain: How is it that race can be experienced as a given, as something that can be taken-for-granted, as an intersubjective reality? How does "race" present itself to us in just such a way as to appear real, taken-for-granted, and intersubjective?

Play stage: The play stage is one of the three phases in Mead's theory of self-formation. The play stage is the initial stage wherein the child first sees herself as a social object separate from her behaviors. In the play stage, the child literally takes on the role of one significant other and acts and feels toward herself as the other does.

Postdemocratic age: This idea comes from the work of Cornel West. The notion of a postdemocratic age is based on a definition of democracy as a community of involved citizens actively engaged in open and critical dialog, under the condition of the freedom of ideas and information, and oriented toward achieving justice, equity, compassion, and acceptance of diverse others. West argues that the American postdemocratic age has come about principally through the work of the Christian right amplified by the fear generated by 9/11. Three dogmas are associated with this fundamentalist movement, all of which contribute to postdemocracy: free-market fundamentalism, aggressive militarism, and escalating authoritarianism.

Postindustrial: A society wherein the economy has moved from having its base in industry and manufacturing to service and knowledge. In a postindustrial society, knowledge is more important than property, and professionals and technicians are the most important social type. The idea of postindustrial society was popularized by Daniel Bell in his book, *The Coming of Post-Industrial Society*.

Power: Power is a theoretical concept found in many social and sociological theories. The short definition of power is the ability to get others to do what you want. Yet, in terms of how it works and where it resides, power is one of our most difficult and controversial terms. For Anthony Giddens, power is part of every interaction and is defined in terms of autonomy and dependence. The greater our level of autonomy and the greater others' level of dependence, the greater will be our power in an encounter. Thinking of power in this way makes it an outcome rather than a resource that is possessed. It also makes power part of face-to-face encounters rather than part of an obdurate structure or linked to group politics. In structuration theory, power is one result that comes from the use of allocative and authoritative resources. For exchange theorists, power is the result of unequal exchange relations. Power refers to the other individual's or group's ability to recurrently impose its will on a person. There are four conditions of power in Peter Blau's exchange scheme: The power of actor A over actor B is contingent upon (1) B having limited needs; (2) B having few or no alternatives; (3) B being unable or unwilling to use force; and (4) B continuing to value the good or service that A controls. Michel Foucault sees power in two ways; both are hidden rather than overt. First, and most importantly, power is exercised through knowledge. The knowledge that any person holds at any given time is the result of historically specific institutional arrangements and practices. For Foucault, knowledge isn't simply held; it is applied to every aspect of the person's life by the individual. Thus, knowledge exercises control over people's bodies, minds, and subjectivities. The second way Foucault uses the notion of power is in daily encounters with others. In every social encounter, people's actions influence other actions; these practices enact the social discourse or knowledge and serve to guide and reinforce one another.

Practical consciousness: Practical consciousness is a concept from Anthony Giddens' theory and refers to what people know or believe about social situations and practices but can't verbally explain. It is the basis for the routinization of daily life, which, in turn, provides ontological security. One important ramification of practical consciousness is that it implies that behavior is often directed by non-conscious intuition and that the reasons given for action (discursive consciousness) can have a separate interactional function.

Pragmatism: Pragmatism is a school of philosophy that argues that the only values, meanings, and truths humans hold onto are the ones that have practical benefits. These values, meanings, and truths shift and change in response to different concrete experiences. Pragmatism forms the base for many American social theories, most specifically symbolic interactionism.

Primary groups: A theoretical concept from Charles Horton Cooley and symbolic interactionism. Primary and secondary groups vary by length of time of association, purpose, degree of involvement, and intimacy. Primary groups stay together for long periods of time and tend to be open, honest, and emotionally based. Primary groups will have stronger influence on individual thoughts, feelings, and behaviors.

Private property: Private property is a distinctly modern, capitalist concept and a major idea in Marx's theory of capitalism. For Marx, the quality of "private" property can only be understood through the idea of alienation. Private property can only exist when the worker is first alienated from his or her humanity (species-being).

Problem of routinization: Routinization is the process through which something is made habitual or routine. The concept is most closely associated with Weber's theory of bureaucratization—the purpose of bureaucracy is to routinize actions. The problem of routinization, however, is somewhat different. The problem of routinization occurs after the charismatic leader dies. Because charismatic authority is rooted in an individual, when that individual is gone the authority must be made routine, either through traditional or rational-legal authority.

Professionalization: Professionalization is a concept in Weber's theory of religious evolution. In its most simple form, professionalization occurs when a person or group is paid to do specific work. This move frees these people from basic concerns of sustenance. Professionals are thus able to elaborate (more abstract and complex) and control their specific fields, thus protecting their vested interests.

Public sphere: The public sphere is a theoretical construct from the critical work of Jürgen Habermas. It is an imaginary community or virtual space where a democratic public "gathers" for dialogue. With the idea of the public sphere, Habermas is arguing that a true democratic process demands an active, public dialogue that takes place outside the influence of government or the economy. To function properly, the public sphere demands unrestricted access to information and equal participation of all members.

Race-preservation: The idea of race-preservation is part of Gilman's evolutionary theory of gender relations. Race-preservation stimulates the natural selection of skills that promote the general welfare of the collective; however, because women have been removed from the natural environment by male-dominated society, race-preservation skills are deemphasized and the evolutionary system is out of balance—motivations for self-preservation dominate.

Rationalization: According to Weber, rationalization is the main defining dynamic of modernity. It is the process through which spirituality, tradition, moral values, and affective social ties are replaced by rational calculation, efficiency, and control.

Reification: Reification captures the idea that concepts and ideas may be treated as objectively real things. In social science generally, reification can be seen as a methodological problem because of the tendency to ascribe causation to ideas, as in gender causing inequality. In critical theory, reification is taken further and refers to the process through which human beings become dominated by things and become more thing-like themselves. Marx specifically argued that ideas that do not naturally spring out of species-being can only appear real through reification (making something appear real that isn't); all ideology is reified and the furthest reach of reification is the idea of God.

Requisite needs: The concept of requisite needs is an essential assumption of the functionalist perspective. Requisite needs are requirements that every system must meet in order to survive. Because every system has the same needs, functionalists argue that all systems can be understood using the same set of ideas.

Ritual: Rituals are the key to Durkheim's theory of social solidarity. In Durkheimian theory, rituals are patterned sequences of behavior that re-create high levels of co-presence, common emotional mood, and common focus of attention. In Durkheim's scheme, rituals function to create and reinvigorate a group's moral boundaries and identity. Collins uses the same basic theory to explain a number of issues: interaction ritual chains, the macro–micro link, and social exchange.

Role conflict: Roles are behavioral expectations that are attached to status positions and groups. According to Simmel, role conflict occurs when behavioral expectations of two different roles clash or contradict one another. The more complex one's web of group affiliations, the more likely is role conflict.

Role-taking: Role-taking is the central mechanism in Mead's theory of the self, through which an individual is able to get outside of her or his own actions and take them as a social object. Specifically, role-taking is the process through which an individual puts herself in the position (role) of another for the express purpose of viewing herself from that other person's role.

Secondary elaborations of belief: A theoretical concept from ethnomethodology's understanding of the reflexive nature of human organization and reality. Secondary elaborations of belief are prescribed, legitimating accounts that explain away any piece of empirical data that contradicts how reality is assumed to function, as when the Azande's oracle fails, or the Christian doesn't received an answer to prayer, or the scientist's experiment doesn't yield expected results.

Secondary groups: From Charles Horton Cooley and symbolic interaction. Primary and secondary groups differ by length of time of association, purpose, degree of involvement, and intimacy. Secondary groups are those that do not last long, that tend to be goal rather than emotion based, and people in the groups tend not to reveal personal matters.

Self- and Race-Preservation: The ideas of race-preservation and self-preservation are part of Gilman's evolutionary theory of gender relations. Race-preservation stimulates the natural selection for skills that promote the general welfare of the collective; and self-preservation motivates the natural selection for skills that protect the individual. Self-preservation and race-preservation skills ought to balance one another. However, because women have been removed from the natural environment by male dominated society, the self-preservation skills are over-emphasized and the evolutionary system is dysfunctional.

Self: The self is a theoretical idea that describes various features of the individual. According to symbolic interactionist theory, the self is a social object, a perspective, a conversation, and a story. The self is seen as arising from diverse role-taking experiences. It is thus a social object in that it is formed through definitions given by others, especially the generalized other, and is a central meaningful feature in interactions. The self is a perspective in the sense that it is the place from which we view our own behaviors, thoughts, and feelings. It is an internal conversation through which we arrive at the meaning and evaluation we will give to our own behaviors, thoughts, and feelings. This conversation is ongoing and produces a story we tell ourselves and others about who we are (the meaning of this particular social object). The self is initially created through successive stages of role-taking and the internalization of language. The self continually emerges, is given meaning, and is furnished with stability or flexibility through patterns of interactions with distinct groups and generalized others. The idea of the self is also prominent in Goffman's dramaturgy (the presentation of self) and Giddens's understanding of modernity (the reflexive project of the self).

Self-preservation: Part of Gilman's evolutionary scheme, self-preservation motivates the natural selection of skills that protect the individual. Self-preservation and race-preservation skills ought to balance one another; however, because women have been removed from the natural environment by male-dominated society, the self-preservation skills of women are overemphasized and the evolutionary system is disequilibrated.

Setting: Setting is a theoretical concept from Goffman's dramaturgical perspective. Settings are composed of physical sign equipment that is semi-permanently attached to physical locations. The physical props of the setting cue people to a limited number of possible definitions and self-identities. Settings thus stabilize encounters. They are part of the front that people manage.

Sexuo-economic relations: In Gilman's evolutionary theory of gender inequality, sexuo-economic relations occur when sex relations and economic relations overlap fundamentally. In a society where women's workforce participation is limited, the structures of economy and family are confounded; sex distinctions between men and women are accentuated and unbalanced; sex itself becomes pathologically important to people; women become consumers par excellence; and men are alienated from their work.

Simulacrum: A theoretical concept most closely associated with the postmodern work of Jean Baudrillard. The word itself simply refers to a representation or simulation. For example, a statue of Karl Marx has a similar appearance to, and thus represents or simulates, Marx. Baudrillard argues that, in postmodernity, most cultural images and signs do not have an actual reference and thus don't represent or simulate anything. Further, simulacra in postmodernity are simply images of images that never existed in the first place. The Disneyland ride "Pirates of the Caribbean" is a good example. Pirates certainly existed, but never in the form presented at the Disney ride: The ride is an idealized version of the fantasy of pirates given life in such novels as *Peter Pan*. So, the ride is an image of an image that doesn't truly represent. But the slide of simulacrum doesn't end there: Disney produced a movie based on the ride. The movie is thus an image of an image of an image, which never referred to anything real in the first place.

Social action typology: Social action is defined by Max Weber as any individual action that takes into account other people or has some value attached to it; value in this case is socially defined. In order to understand action, Weber constructed an ideal typology with four categories: instrumental-rational action is behavior that is guided by means–ends considerations; value-rational action is behavior that is motivated by and makes sense from the perspective of some system of values (like religion); traditional action is behavior that is motivated by custom and long-practiced routines; and, finally, affectual action is motivated and guided by situationally provoked emotions. This general concern of Weber's forms the basis of action theory and Talcott Parsons' explication of the unit act.

Social differentiation: Social differentiation is a concept in Durkheim's theory of modernity. Specifically, it is the level of cultural diversity in any society: People become different from one another in response to increases in the division of labor and structural differentiation, both of which increase the level of particularized culture.

Social exchange: According to Peter Blau, exchange refers to those voluntary social actions in which people engage that are dependent upon some present or future reward from others. The concept of exchange does not encompass all behavior. It particularly does not address those choices and preferences influenced by personality preferences, social position and experience, coercion, morals, or irrational emotions. Social exchange is distinct from economic exchange in that social exchanges lack specificity and social meaning, they build trust over long periods of time, and social benefits are less detachable from the source of the benefits.

Social facts: The concept of social facts is the foundation of Durkheim's empirical approach to sociology. Durkheim argues that the facticity of society is created by its felt influence. Society appears to unavoidably influence the individual from the outside. The social facts of society are external to and coercive of the individual. Durkheim uses the existence of social facts to argue in favor of a scientific approach to understanding society.

Social forms: Social forms are Simmel's basic perspective of social life. A form is a patterned mode of interaction through which people meet personal and group goals; forms exist prior to the interaction and provide rules and values that guide the interaction and contribute to the subjective experience of the individual; forms also imply social types—types of people that occupy positions within a social form (examples: stranger, adventurer, competitor, miser).

Social institutions: Social institution is a key concept in many macro-level theories of society. For most sociologists, social institutions are collective moral sets of predetermined meanings, values, legitimations, and scripts for behavior that resist individual agency and are perceived to meet the survival needs of a society. The main institutions studied by sociologists are family, education, religion, law, government, and the economy.

Social objects: The idea of social objects is a theoretical concept in symbolic interactionist theory. Social objects are anything in an interaction that we call attention to, attach legitimate lines of behavior to, and name. In this sense, the self and one's own feelings and thoughts can become social objects, as well as the more obvious "objects" in the environment.

Social solidarity: Social solidarity is Durkheim's term for the level of integration in a society. Generally speaking, integration is the blending and organizing of separate and diverse elements into a more complete, balanced whole. Social solidarity specifically refers to the subjective sense of group membership individuals have, the constraint of individual behaviors for the group good, and the organization of social units and groups. Durkheim argues that social solidarity is different in modern rather than traditional societies.

Social structure: Social structure is a central idea for sociology. The notion of structure is an answer to the problem of patterned human behavior. People tend to act in predictable ways across time and space even though humans are not directed by instinct and are assumed to have free will. Thus, there are two fundamental characteristics of structures: Structures are made up of connections; and structures create and sustain predictable patterns and shapes. Structures are usually understood as existing outside the individual (objective) and having the force necessary to conform the person's behaviors to social expectations; structures are thus responsible for the general patterns we see in society. However, some theorists argue that there are other forces at work and that the idea of social structure is wrong-headed.

Social system: Seeing society as a set of interrelated parts that function together to create integration and equilibrium. Systems can be smart or dumb (ability to take in and adjust to information) and open or closed (exposure to external forces); systems may also contain feedback and feed-forward effects as well as mechanisms that produce equilibrium; according to Parsons, social systems may be large (entire societies) or small (face-to-face interactions), are distinguished by boundaries between the system and its environment, and are controlled cybernetically.

Sociological ambivalence: A theoretical concept from Robert K. Merton's understanding of functionalism, sociological ambivalence is an effect of structural relations. In sociological ambivalence, the structured, normative role expectations of a social position are contradictory.

Species-being: Species-being is one of Karl Marx's basic assumptions about human nature. The idea links the way humans as a species survives with human consciousness. According to Marx, every species is unique because of and defined by the way it as a biological organism exists. Humans exist and survive through creative production. Human consciousness, then, is created as people see the humanity in the world that has been economically produced. False consciousness and ideology increase as humans fail to perceive the intrinsic link to production.

Spirit of capitalism: Weber's term to capture the cultural values and beliefs that undergird rational capitalism. There are at least three values and beliefs in the spirit of capitalism: life should be rationally organized to maximize profit; economic work is the most important thing we can do with our time and we must be diligent in our work; things of true value are quantifiably measured.

Status: Status is one of three systems of stratification in Weber's theory. Status is social honor or esteem that is hierarchically arranged. Status is generally associated in modern societies with different levels of education or career, distinctive lifestyles, and/or family traditions and history.

Structural differentiation: Structural differentiation is a concept generally found in evolutionary or functionalist explanations of social change. It is the process through which the behaviors associated with social networks of roles, norms, and status positions that are associated with requisite needs are acted out in different places and at different times. In societies with high levels of structural differentiation, the requisite functions are carried out in distinct and separate institutions.

Structuration theory: A theoretical perspective developed by Anthony Giddens. The perspective is more an analytical framework—or ontological scheme—than a complete theory. Structuration tells the theorist-researcher what kinds of things exist socially and what to pay attention to. Structuration denies the existence of structure and free agency (seen as a false dualism) and argues that these generally reified concepts form an active duality: two parts of the same thing. In order to act, social actors must use known rules and resources. Giddens conceptualizes rules (normative rules and codes of signification) and resources (authoritative resources and allocative resources) as structural elements, which means that actors constitute or enact structure through their agency. Giddens applies this concept to the issue of time–space distanciation. Thus, in structuration, local interactions are linked with distant others through the use of known rules and resources. This way of seeing things avoids the reification of agency or structure, places the structuring (patterning) elements within the observable interaction, and encourages a historical sociology. The latter is important for Giddens as he explains the ways through which modern society stretches out time and space, or links local interactions with distant ones, and allows him to explicate some of the unique features of modernity.

Surplus labor: A theoretical concept from Marx's understanding of capitalism. According to Marx, surplus labor is the amount of labor a worker performs for which she or he does not get paid. It's the difference between the worker's pay and the value of the products he or she produces. Surplus labor is equivalent to the level of exploitation and is the source of capitalist profit. There are two main types of surplus labor: absolute surplus labor, a method of increasing profit by increasing the number of hours a worker works; and relative surplus labor, increased exploitation through industrialization.

Symbolic capital: Symbolic capital is a theoretical concept from Pierre Bourdieu's theory of class replication and refers to socially legitimated symbolic power of definition. Bourdieu argues that social groups and status positions exist empirically and symbolically; but it is the symbolic that gives groups and positions meaning and legitimacy. This power of definition is thus an important factor in creating the social world. Symbolic capital varies by social credentials, which generally come through education and political office.

Symbolic exchange: Symbolic exchange is an idea from Jean Baudrillard's theory of postmodernism that he uses as a comparison point for the pure sign-value of postmodern culture. In more traditional societies, when communication was closely tied to human interaction in social groups, symbols carried meaning. The symbols that people used arose from and represented real-life concerns and experiences. In contrast, much of postmodern culture has been created for or trivialized by mass media and advertising. These signs, rather than symbols, do not and cannot represent any kind of real social existence. Thus, cultural signs in postmodernity carry no meaning, are free-floating (released from all social context and linguistic structure), and are simply used by mass media and people in endless fields of play.

Symbolic violence: Symbolic violence is a theoretical concept from Pierre Bourdieu's theory of class replication that refers to the self-sanctioning that occurs in linguistic markets.

The situation: In simple terms, there are four possible sites of social and behavioral research: the individual, the interaction or social situation, social structures, and social or global systems. While some sociologists see these as levels of analysis, others are convinced that the social situation is the only truly empirical space available to sociologists. Herbert Blumer (1969), the man who systematized Mead's theory, argues that the only acting unit is the interaction and that any time we appeal to psychological or social structures as the impetus behind human behavior, "The human being becomes a mere medium through which such initiating factors operate to produce given actions" (p. 73). Harold Garfinkel (1967), the founder of ethnomethodology (a new perspective in sociology), says that what we mean by "society" is an ongoing achievement of people in observable situations—everything we mean by the social is in truth simply the methods we use in face-to-face encounters. Erving Goffman (1983), the founder of dramaturgy (another new perspective), argues that what we get from people who study anything other than the situation "is somebody's crudely edited summaries" (p. 9) and that the interaction order achieved through the presentation of self is our most stable and routine social entity. For Randall Collins (2004), the ideas of structures and systems are simply heuristic devices, aids to discovery, and that the interaction rituals people perform in face-to-face situations are the true essence of society.

The spirit of capitalism: The spirit of capitalism is a key factor in Weber's explanation of rational capitalism. The spirit of capitalism refers to the cultural values and beliefs that make rational capitalism possible: the belief that life should be rationally organized, that economic work is the most valued of all action, and that quantification is the true estimate of value and worth.

The web of group affiliations: The web of group affiliations is a concept developed by Georg Simmel (1908/1955) that describes social networks in modernity. In traditional societies, an individual's web of social connections was determined by birth and tradition (organic motivation). In modern societies, group membership is based on free choice (rational motivation). The more modern a person's web of group affiliations is, the more likely it is that she or he will develop a unique personality and experience anomie, role conflict, and a blasé attitude.

Time–space distanciation: Time–space distanciation is a theoretical concept from Anthony Giddens' structuration approach. This concept reformulates the problem of social order by focusing on the stretching out of time and space rather than the patterning of behaviors. Generally speaking, concentrating on how behaviors are patterned has resulted in an emphasis on either structure or agency. Giddens sees this distinction as a false dualism, and focusing on time–space distanciation avoids this issue. Specifically, time–space distanciation refers to the process through which local social interactions are linked to distant ones either through time (as in future with past interactions) or geographic space (as in an interaction in New York City with one in Los Angeles), thus ordering society.

Traditional and rational capitalism: Traditional and rational capitalism are Weber's ideal typology of capitalism; in traditional capitalism, profit is limited by traditional and affective ties; in rational capitalism, the pursuit of profit is unlimited and pursued for its own sake. Rational capitalism is a major force in the quantification of human relationships.

Unanticipated consequences: The idea of unanticipated consequences is a theoretical concept from Merton's functionalism. According to Merton, purposeful social action can have unexpected consequences. These kinds of effects of social action can accumulate and lead to structural change. Ideas like this allow Merton to move functionalism into a more dynamic realm.

Unit act: In Parsons' theory of institutionalization, the unit act denotes the entire set of conditions under which actions take place, including the means and conditions of action. The unit act is an analytical device that calls attention to certain features in the social environment.

Urbanization: Urbanization is an important factor in Simmel's theory of modernity and is defined as the process through which more and more of a given population moves from rural settings to the city. Urbanization increases in response to capitalism generally and industrialization specifically. It results in such things as higher levels in the division of labor, increases in the use of money and the size and velocity of exchanges and markets, rational versus organic group memberships, overstimulation, increasing social diversity, and so on.

Use-value: According to Marx, use-value is determined by the use or utility any commodity has. It is expended or consumed through use. The term is understood in relation to exchange-value, and later in relation to Baudrillard's notion of sign-value.

Values: Values are collective cultural systems that rank social objects in terms of relative worth. Parsons argues that social interaction and exchange would be virtually impossible without shared values; as such, values are one of the primary ingredients in modes of orientation. In Parsons' theory, there are three types of values: cognitive, appreciative, and moral.

Voluntaristic action: In Parsons' theory, voluntaristic action is the idea that people make rational decisions to maximize benefits in social and physical environments that limit means and ends. Specifically, the social environment restricts action through sets of values and norms. Yet at the same time, these limitations also enable rational actors to meet goals, because the values and norms that have been seen as most effective have been institutionalized in status positions.

Web of group affiliations: The web of group affiliations is a theoretical concept developed by Georg Simmel to describe social networks: the number, frequency, and intensiveness of relationships among people. Simmel is particularly concerned with why people join groups—variation by motivation. Simmel argues that the motivation behind group membership changes as a society moves from traditional to modern. Organic motivation is prevalent in traditional society and indicates that group membership is based on either family ties or previously established social relations. In modern society, however, motivation for group membership is based on free choice rather than family ties or previously established social relations.

References

Al Qaeda training manual. Retrieved October 27, 2004, from http://www.usdoj.gov/ag/ trainingmanual.htm

Alexander, J. C. (1985). Introduction. In J. C. Alexander (Ed.), *Neofunctionalism.* Beverly Hills, CA: Sage.

Alexander, J. C. (1998). *Neofunctionalism and after: Collected readings.* Malden, MA: Wiley-Blackwell.

Allan, K., & Turner, J. H. (2000). A formalization of postmodern theory. *Sociological Perspectives, 43*(3), 363–385.

Allen, B. (1996). *Rape warfare: The hidden genocide in Bosnia-Herzegovina and Croatia.* Minneapolis: University of Minnesota Press.

Alway, J. (1995). *Critical theory and political possibilities: Conceptions of emancipatory politics in the works of Horkheimer, Adorno, Marcuse, and Habermas.* Westport, CT: Greenwood Press.

Anderson, P. (1998). *The origins of postmodernity.* London: Verso.

Bandura, A. (1977). *Social learning theory.* New York: General Learning Press.

Barker, C. (2008). *Cultural studies: Theory and practice* (3rd ed.). Los Angeles: Sage.

Barthes, R. (1967). *Elements of semiology* (A. Lavers & C. Smith, Trans.). London: Jonathan Cape. (Original work published 1964)

Baudrillard, J. (1972). *For a critique of the political economy of the sign.* St. Louis, MO: Telos Press. (Original work published 1981)

Baudrillard, J. (1975). *The mirror of production* (M. Poster, Trans.). St. Louis, MO: Telos Press. (Original work published 1973)

Baudrillard, J. (1987). When Bataille attacked the metaphysical principle of economy. *Canadian Journal of Political and Social Theory, 11*(3), 57–62.

Baudrillard, J. (1993a). *Baudrillard live: Selected interviews* (M. Gane, Ed.). New York: Routledge.

Baudrillard, J. (1993b). *Symbolic exchange and death* (I. H. Grant, Trans.). Newbury Park, CA: Sage. (Original work published 1976)

Baudrillard, J. (1994). *Simulacra and simulation* (S. F. Blaser, Trans.). Ann Arbor: University of Michigan Press. (Original work published 1981)

Baudrillard, J. (1995). *The Gulf War did not take place* (P. Patton, Trans.). Bloomington: Indiana University Press.

Baudrillard, J. (1998). *The consumer society: Myths and structures* (C. Turner, Trans.). London: Sage. (Original work published 1970)

Bauman, Z. (1992). *Imitations of postmodernity.* New York: Routledge.

Becker, H. (1963). *Outsiders: Studies in the sociology of deviance.* New York: Free Press.

Benford, R. D., & Snow, D. A. (2000). Framing processes and social movements: An overview and assessment. *Annual Review of Sociology, 26,* 611–639.

Bentham, J. (1996). *An introduction to the principles of morals and legislation* (J. H. Burns & H. L. A. Hart, Eds.). New York: Oxford University Press. (Original work published 1789)

Bernstein, J. M. (1991). Introduction. In T. Adorno (Ed.), *Culture industry.* London: Routledge.

Blau, P. M. (1968). Social exchange. In David L. Sills (Ed.), *International encyclopedia of the social sciences.* New York: Macmillan.

Blau, P. M. (1995). A circuitous path to macrostructural theory. *Annual Review of Sociology, 21,* 1–19.

Blau, P. M. (2003). *Exchange and power in social life.* New Brunswick, NJ: Transaction.

Blau, P. M., & Meyer, M. W. (1987). *Bureaucracy in modern society* (3rd ed.). New York: McGraw-Hill.

Blumer, H. (1969). *Symbolic interactionism: Perspective and method.* Berkeley: University of California Press.

Blumer, H. (1990). *Industrialization as an agent of social change: A critical analysis.* Chicago: Aldine.

Bonacich, E. (1972). A theory of ethnic antagonism: The split labor market. *American Sociological Review, 37,* 547–559.

Bourdieu, P. (1984). *Distinction: A social critique of the judgment of taste* (R. Nice, Trans.). Cambridge, MA: Harvard University Press. (Original work published 1979)

Bourdieu, P. (1985). The genesis of the concepts of *habitus* and of *field. Sociocriticism, 2*(2), 11–29.

Bourdieu, P. (1989). Social space and symbolic power. *Sociological Theory, 7*(1), 14–25.

Bourdieu, P. (1990). *The logic of practice* (R. Nice, Trans.). Stanford, CA: Stanford University Press. (Original work published 1980)

Bourdieu, P. (1991). *Language and symbolic power* (J. B. Thompson, Ed.; G. Raymond & M. Adamson, Trans.). Cambridge, MA: Harvard University Press.

Bourdieu, P. (1993). *Outline of a theory of practice* (R. Nice, Trans.). Cambridge, UK: Cambridge University Press. (Original work published 1972)

Bourdieu, P., & Wacquant, L. J. D. (1992). *An invitation to reflexive sociology.* Chicago: University of Chicago Press.

Business and Professional Women's Foundation. (2004). *101 facts on the status of women.* Retrieved May 9, 2005, from http://www.bpwusa.org/i4a/pages/index.cfm?pageid=3301

Calhoun, C. (2003). Pierre Bourdieu. In G. Ritzer (Ed.), *The Blackwell companion to major contemporary social theorists.* Malden, MA: Blackwell.

Calhoun, C., Gerteis, J. Moody, J., Pfaff, S., & Virk, I. (2002). Introduction to part V. In C. Calhoun, J. Gerteis, J. Moody, S. Pfaff, & I. Virk (Eds.), *Contemporary sociological theory.* Oxford, UK: Blackwell.

Cassirer, E. (1944). *An essay on man.* New Haven, CT: Yale University Press.

Castells, M. (2000a). *The end of millennium* (2nd ed.). Malden, MA: Blackwell.

Castells, M. (2000b). *The rise of the network society* (2nd ed.). Malden, MA: Blackwell.

Castells, M. (2004). *The power of identity* (2nd. ed.). Malden, MA: Blackwell.

Chafetz, J. S. (1990). *Gender equity: An integrated theory of stability and change.* Newbury Park, CA: Sage.

Charon, J. M. (2001). *Symbolic interactionism: An introduction, an interpretation, an integration* (7th ed.). Upper Saddle River, NJ: Prentice Hall.

Chodorow, N. (1978). *The reproduction of mothering: Psychoanalysis and the sociology of gender.* Berkeley: University of California Press.

Cohen, A., Baumohl, B., Buia, C., Roston, E., Ressner, J., & Thompson, M. (2001, January 8). This time it's different. *Time, 157*(1), 18–22.

Collins, P. H. (2000). *Black feminist thought: Knowledge, consciousness, and the politics of empowerment* (2nd ed.). New York: Routledge.

Collins, R. (1975). *Conflict sociology.* New York: Academic Press.

Collins, R. (1979). *The credential society: An historical sociology of education and stratification.* San Diego, CA: Academic Press.

Collins, R. (1986a). Is 1980s sociology in the doldrums? *American Journal of Sociology, 91,* 1336–1355.

Collins, R. (1986b). *Max Weber: A skeleton key.* Newbury Park, CA: Sage.

Collins, R. (1986c). *Weberian sociological theory.* Cambridge: Cambridge University Press.

Collins, R. (1987). Interaction ritual chains, power and property: The micro–macro connection as an empirically based theoretical problem. In J. C. Alexander, B. Giesen, R. Münch, & N. J. Smelser (Eds.), *The micro–macro link.* Berkeley: University of California Press.

Collins, R. (1988). *Theoretical sociology.* San Diego, CA: Harcourt Brace Jovanovich.

Collins, R. (1989). Sociology: Proscience or antiscience? *American Sociological Review, 54,* 124–139.

Collins, R. (1993a). What does conflict theory predict about America's future? *Sociological Perspectives, 36*(4), 289–313.

Collins, R. (1993b). Emotional energy as the common denominator of rational action. *Rationality and society, 5,* 203–230.

Collins, R. (2004). *Interaction ritual chains.* Princeton, NJ: Princeton University Press.

Collins, R. (2009). *2011 Annual Meeting.* Retrieved November 29, 2009, from http://www.asanet.org/cs/root/leftnav/meetings/future_meetings/2011_annual_meeting_theme

Comte, A. (1898). The positive philosophy of Auguste Comte (Trans. H. Martineau). London: Bell & Sons. (Original work published 1854)

Condon, W. S., & Ogston, W. D. (1971). Speech and body motion synchrony of the speaker-hearer. In D. D. Horton & J. J. Jenkins (Eds.), *Perception of language.* Columbus, OH: Merrill.

Cook, K. (1978). Power, equity and commitment in exchange networks. *American Journal of Sociology, 43,* 712–739.

Cooley, C. H. (1998). *On self and social organization* (H. Schubert, Ed.). Chicago: University of Chicago Press.

Coser, L. A. (1956). *The functions of social conflict.* Glencoe, IL: Free Press.

Coser, L. A. (2003). *Masters of sociological thought: Ideas in historical and social context* (2nd ed.). Prospect Heights, IL: Waveland Press.

Dahrendorf, R. (1959). *Class and class conflict in industrial society.* Stanford, CA: Stanford University Press. (Original work published 1957)

Dahrendorf, R. (1968). *Essays in the theory of society.* Stanford, CA: Stanford University Press.

Dahrendorf, R. (1989). *Straddling theory and practice: Conversation with Sir Ralf Dahrendorf.* Retrieved May 5, 2006, from http://globetrotter.berkeley.edu/Elberg/Dahrendorf/dahrendorf2.html

Danto, A. C. (1990). The hyper-intellectual. *New Republic, 203*(11–12), 44–48.

Davidson, A. I. (1994). Ethics as ascetics: Foucault, the history of ethics, and ancient thought. In G. Gutting (Ed.), *The Cambridge companion to Foucault.* Cambridge, UK: Cambridge University Press.

deGroot Redford, G., & Kinosian, J. (2008). Your brain on exercise: How breaking a sweat can make you smarter. *AARP The Magazine, 51*(2A), 26.

Denzin, N. (1992). *Symbolic interactionism and cultural studies: The politics of interpretation.* Oxford, UK: Blackwell.

Denzin, N. (1993). *The alcoholic society: Addiction and recovery of the self.* New York: Transaction.

Derksen, L. (2010). Micro/macro translations: The production of new social structures in the case of DNA profiling. *Sociological Inquiry, 80*(2).

Derrida, J. (1978). *Writing and difference* (A. Bass, Trans.). Chicago: University of Chicago Press. (Original work published 1967)

Dicker, R., & Piopmeier, A. (2006). Catching a wave: Reclaiming feminism for the 21st century. In L. Heywood (Ed.), *The Women's movement today: An encyclopedia of third-wave feminism.* Westport: CT: Greenwood Press.

Drake, J. (1997). Review essay: Third Wave feminisms. *Feminist Studies, 23*(1), 97–108.

Du Bois, W. E. B. (1996a). The souls of black folk. In E. J. Sundquist (Ed.), *The Oxford W. E. B. Du Bois reader.* New York: Oxford. (Original work published 1903)

Du Bois, W. E. B. (1996b). Darkwater. In E. J. Sundquist (Ed.), *The Oxford W. E. B. Du Bois reader.* New York: Oxford. (Original work published 1920)

Du Bois, W. E. B. (1996c). The propaganda of history. In E. J. Sundquist (Ed.), *The Oxford W. E. B. Du Bois reader.* New York: Oxford. (Original work published 1935)

Du Bois, W. E. B. (1996d). In black. In E. J. Sundquist (Ed.), *The Oxford W. E. B. Du Bois reader.* New York: Oxford. (Original work published 1920)

Durkheim, É. (1938). *The rules of sociological method* (G. E. G. Catlin, Ed.; S. A. Solovay & J. H. Mueller, Trans.). Glencoe, IL: Free Press. (Original work published 1895)

Durkheim, É. (1957). *Professional ethics and civic morals* (C. Brookfield, Trans.). London: Routledge.

Durkheim, É. (1961). *Moral education: A study in the theory and application of the sociology of education* (E. K. Wilson, Trans.). New York: Free Press. (Original work published 1903)

Durkheim, É. (1984). *The division of labor in society* (W. D. Halls, Trans.). New York: Free Press. (Original work published 1893)

Durkheim, É. (1993). *Ethics and the sociology of morals* (R. T. Hall, Trans.). Buffalo, NY: Prometheus. (Original work published 1887)

Durkheim, É. (1995). *The elementary forms of the religious life* (K. E. Fields, Trans.). New York: Free Press. (Original work published 1912)

Emerson, R. (1972). Exchange theory part I: A psychological basis for social exchange; Exchange theory part II: Exchange relationships and network structures. In J. Berger, M. Zelditch & B. Anderson (Eds.), *Sociological theories in progress.* New York: Houghton Mifflin.

Engels, F. (1978). The origin of the family, private property, and the state. In R. C. Tucker (Ed.), *The Marx–Engels reader.* New York: W.W. Norton. (Original work published 1884)

Erlewine, M. (1999). Foreword. In M. Erlewine, V. Bogdanov, C. Woodstra, C. Doda, & S. T. Erlewine (Eds.), *All music guide to the blues: The experts' guide to the BEST BLUES recordings.* San Francisco: Backbeat.

Fanon, F. (1967). *Black skins, white masks* (C. L. Markmann, Trans.). New York: Grove Press. (Original work published 1952)

Fanon, F. (2004). *The wretched of the earth* (R. Philcox, Trans.). New York: Grove Press. (Original work published 1961)

Fine, G. A. (1987). *With the boys: Little league baseball and preadolescent culture.* Chicago: University of Chicago Press.

Fine, G. A., & Manning, P. (2003). Erving Goffman. In G. Ritzer, (Ed.), *The Blackwell companion to major contemporary social theorists* (pp. 34–62). Oxford, UK: Blackwell.

Fisher, S. (1973). *Body consciousness.* London: Calder & Boyars.

Flash mob. (n.d.). *Wikipedia.* Retrieved June 8, 2005, from http://en.wikipedia.org/wiki/Flash_mob

Flyvbjerg, B. (2001). *Making social science matter: Why social inquiry fails and how it can succeed again.* Cambridge, UK: Cambridge University Press.

Footnotes. (2009). *2010 ASA Annual theme.* Retrieved November 29, 2009, from http://www.asanet.org/footnotes/septoct08/2010_theme.html

Foucault, M. (1982). The subject and power. In H. L. Dreyfus & P. Rabinow (Eds.), *Michel Foucault: Beyond structuralism and hermeneutics.* Brighton, UK: Harvester Press.

Foucault, M. (1984a). Nietzsche, genealogy, history. In P. Rabinow (Ed.), *The Foucault reader.* New York: Pantheon.

Foucault, M. (1984b). Space, knowledge, and power. In P. Rabinow (Ed.), *The Foucault reader.* New York: Pantheon.

Foucault, M. (1984c). On the genealogy of ethics: An overview of work in progress. In P. Rabinow (Ed.), *The Foucault reader.* New York: Pantheon.

Foucault, M. (1990a). *The history of sexuality, volume I: An introduction* (R. Hurley, Trans.). New York: Vintage. (Original work published 1976)

Foucault, M. (1990b). *The history of sexuality, volume 2: The use of pleasure* (R. Hurley, Trans.). New York: Vintage. (Original work published 1984)

Foucault, M. (1994a). *The birth of the clinic: An archaeology of medical perception* (A. M. Sheridan Smith, Trans.). New York: Vintage. (Original work published 1963)

Foucault, M. (1994b). *The order of things: An archaeology of the human sciences.* New York: Vintage. (Original work published 1966)

Foucault, M. (1995). *Discipline and punish: The birth of the prison* (A. Sheridan, Trans.). New York: Vintage. (Original work published 1975)

Fromm, E. (1955). *The sane society.* New York: Henry Holt.

Fromm, E. (1961). *Marx's concept of man.* New York: Continuum.

Garfinkel, H. (1967). *Studies in ethnomethodology.* Cambridge, UK: Polity Press.

Garfinkel, H. (1974). On the origins of the term "ethnomethodology." In R. Turner (Ed.), *Ethnomethodology: Selected readings.* Harmondsworth, UK: Penguin Education.

Garfinkel, H. (1996). Ethnomethodology's program. *Social Psychology Quarterly, 59*(1), 5–21.

Gergen, K. J. (1991). *The saturated self: Dilemmas of identity in contemporary life.* New York: Basic Books.

Giddens, A. (1986). *The constitution of society.* Berkeley: University of California Press.

Giddens, A. (1990). *The consequences of modernity.* Stanford, CA: Stanford University Press.

Giddens, A. (1991). *Modernity and self-identity: Self and society in the late modern age.* Stanford, CA: Stanford University Press.

Giddens, A. (1992). *The transformation of intimacy: Sexuality, love, and eroticism in modern societies.* Stanford, CA: Stanford University Press.

Gilman, C. P. (1975). *Women and economics: A study of the economic relation between men and women as a factor in social evolution.* New York: Gordon Press. (Original work published 1899)

Gilman, C. P. (2001). *The man-made world.* New York: Humanity Books. (Original work published 1911)

Global Exchange. (1998, September). *Wages and living expenses for Nike workers in Indonesia, September 1998.* Retrieved December 22, 2004, from http://www.globalexchange.org/campaigns/sweatshops/nike/

Goffman, E. (1959). *The presentation of self in everyday life.* Garden City, NY: Anchor Books.

Goffman, E. (1961). *Asylums: Essays on the social situation of mental patients and other inmates.* Garden City, NY: Anchor Books.

Goffman, E. (1963a). *Stigma.* New York: Touchstone.

Goffman, E. (1963b). *Behavior in public places.* New York: Free Press.

Goffman, E. (1967). *Interaction ritual: Essays on face-to-face behavior.* New York: Pantheon.

Goffman, E. (1977). The arrangement between the sexes. *Theory and Society, 4,* 301–331.

Gramsci, A. (1971). *Selections from the prison notebooks.* London: Lawrence & Heinemann. (Original work published 1928)

Habermas, J. (1984). *The theory of communicative action, vol. 1: Reason and the rationalization of society* (T. McCarthy, Trans.). Boston: Beacon. (Original work published 1981)

Habermas, J. (1987). *The theory of communicative action, vol. 2: Lifeworld and system: A critique of functionalist reason* (T. McCarthy, Trans.). Boston: Beacon. (Original work published 1981)

Hall, S. (1996). The question of cultural identity. In Stuart Hall, David Held, Don Hubert, & Kenneth Thompson (Eds.), *Modernity: An introduction to modern societies.* Malden, MA: The Open University.

Harrison, F. (1913). Introduction. In H. Martineau (Trans.), *The positive philosophy of Auguste Comte.* London: G. Bell.

Havens, J. J., & Schervish, P. G. (2003). *Why the $41 trillion wealth transfer estimate is still valid: A review of challenges and questions.* Retrieved August 31, 2004, from http://www.bc.edu/research/swri/meta-elements/pdf/41trillionreview.pdf

Heritage, J. (1984). *Garfinkel and ethnomethodology.* Cambridge, UK: Polity Press.

Hochschild, A. R. (1983). *The managed heart: Commercialization of human feeling.* Berkeley: University of California Press.

Hofstadter, D. R. (1985). *Metamagical themas: Questing for the essence of mind and pattern.* New York: Basic Books.

Homans, G. C. (1950). *Human group.* New York: Harcourt Brace Jovanovich.

Homans, G. C. (1958). Social behavior as exchange. *The American Journal of Sociology, 63*(5), 597–606.

Homans, G. C. (1961). *Social behavior: Its elementary forms.* New York: Harcourt, Brace & World.

Homans, G. C. (1964). Bringing men back in. *American Sociological Review, 29*(5): 809–818.

Homans, G. C. (1987). Behaviourism and after. In A. Giddens & J. Turner (Eds.), *Social theory today.* Stanford: Stanford University Press.

hooks, b. (1989). *Talking back: Thinking feminist, thinking black.* Boston: South End Press.

Horkheimer, M. (1993). *Between philosophy and social science: Selective early writings* (G. F. Hunter, M. S. Kramer, & Torpey, Trans.). Cambridge: MIT Press.

Horkheimer, M. (2004). *Eclipse of reason.* London: Continuum.

Horkheimer, M., & Adorno, T. W. (1972). *Dialectic of enlightenment.* New York: Herder & Herde.

Income, Poverty, and Health Insurance Coverage in the United States. (2008). Retrieved November 12, 2009, from http://www.census.gov/prod/2009pubs/p60-236.pdf

Jacobs, R. (2006). Civil society. In John Scott (Ed.), *Sociology: The key concepts.* London: Routledge.

Jameson, F. (1984). *The postmodern condition.* Minneapolis: University of Minnesota Press.

Johnson, A. G. (2000). *The Blackwell dictionary of sociology: A user's guide to sociological language* (2nd ed.). Malden, MA: Blackwell.

Kagan, H. L. (2008, March). Why did my patient develop a taste for paper? *Discover.*

Kanter, R. M. (1977). *Men and women of the corporation.* New York: Basic Books.

Kellner, D. (2003). Jean Baudrillard. In G. Ritzer (Ed.), *The Blackwell companion to major contemporary social theorists.* Malden, MA: Blackwell.

Kennickell, A. B. (2003). *A rolling tide: Changes in the distribution of wealth in the U.S., 1989–2001.* Retrieved August 27, 2004, from http://www.federalreserve.gov/pubs/feds/2003/200324/200324pap.pdf

Kozol, J. (1991). *Savage inequalities: Children in America's schools.* New York: Crown.

Kuhn, M. H. (1964). Major trends in symbolic interaction theory in the past twenty-five years. *Sociological Quarterly, 5*(1), 61–84.

Kuhn, M. H., & McPartland, T. S. (1954). An empirical investigation of self-attitudes. *American Sociological Review, 19*(1), 68–76.

Lemert, C. (2000). W. E. B Du Bois. In G. Ritzer (Ed.), *The Blackwell companion to major social theorists.* Malden, MA: Blackwell.

Lemert, E. M. (1951). *Social pathology: A systematic approach to the theory of sociopathic behavior.* New York: McGraw-Hill.

Lemert, E. M. (1967). *Human deviance, social problems, and social control.* Englewood Cliffs, NJ: Prentice Hall.

Lengermann, P. M., & Niebrugge-Brantley, J. (2000). Early women sociologists and classical sociological theory: 1830–1930. In G. Ritzer (Ed.), *Classical sociological theory* (3rd ed.). Boston: McGraw-Hill.

Lévi-Strauss, C. (1963). *Structural anthropology.* New York: Basic Books.

Lidz, V. (2000). Talcott Parsons. In G. Ritzer (Ed.), *The Blackwell companion to major social theorists.* Malden, MA: Blackwell.

Lilley, S. J., & Platt, G. M. (1994). Correspondents' images of Martin Luther King, Jr: An interpretive theory of movement leadership. In T. R. Sarbin & J. I. Kitsuse (Eds.), *Constructing the social.* Newbury Park, CA: Sage.

Lipset, S. M. (1962). Harriet Martineau's America. In H. Martineau, *Society in America.* New Brunswick, Transaction Publishers.

Luckmann, T. (1973). Philosophy, science, and everyday life. In M. Natanson (Ed.), *Phenomenology and the social sciences.* Evanston, IL: Northwestern University Press.

Luhmann, N. (1982). *The differentiation of society* (S. Holmes & C. Larmore, Trans.). New York: Columbia University Press.

Luhmann, N. (1989). *Ecological communication* (H. Bednarz Jr., Trans.). Chicago: Chicago University Press. (Original work published 1986)

Luhmann, N. (1995). *Social systems* (J. Bednarz Jr. & D. Baecker, Trans.). Stanford, CA: Stanford University Press. (Original work published 1984)

Lukács, G. (1971). *History and class consciousness: Studies in Marxist dialectics* (R. Livingstone, Trans.). London: Merlin. (Original work published 1923)

Lynch, M. (1997). *Scientific practice and ordinary action: Ethnomethodology and social studies of science.* Cambridge: Cambridge University Press.

Mahar, C., Harker, R., & Wilkes, C. (1990). The basic theoretical position. In R. Harker, C. Mahar, & C. Wilkes (Eds.), *An introduction to the work of Pierre Bourdieu.* London: Macmillan.

Marcus, M. (2005). Indiana's manufacturing advantage. *In context, 6*(4). Retrieved August 11, 2006, from http://www.incontext.indiana.edu/2005/july/1.html

Marshall, G. (1998). *A dictionary of sociology* (2nd ed.). Oxford, UK: Oxford University Press.

Martin, E. (2007). *Jeff Foxworthy's passionate, show-stopping speech at the CMT awards.* Retrieved September 3, 2009, from http://www.freerepublic.com/focus/f-news/1821089/posts

Martineau, H. (2003). *How to observe morals and manners.* New Brunswick, NJ: Transaction Press. (Original work published 1838)

Marx, K. (1977). *Capital: A critique of political economy, vol. 1* (E. Mandel, Trans.). New York: Vintage. (Original work published 1867)

Marx, K. (1978a). Economic and philosophic manuscripts of 1844. In R. C. Tucker (Ed.), *The Marx-Engels reader.* New York: Norton. (Original work published 1932)

Marx, K. (1978b). The German ideology. In R. C. Tucker (Ed.), *The Marx-Engels reader.* New York: Norton. (Original work published 1932)

Marx, K. (1978c). Contribution to the critique: Introduction. In R. C. Tucker (Ed.), *The Marx-Engels reader.* New York: Norton. (Original work published 1844)

Marx, K. (1978d). Theses on Feuerbach. In R. C. Tucker (Ed.), *The Marx-Engels reader.* New York: Norton. (Original work published 1888)

Marx, K. (1978e). A contribution to the critique of political economy. In R. C. Tucker (Ed.), *The Marx-Engels reader.* New York: Norton. (Original work published 1859)

Marx, K. (1995). Economic and philosophic manuscripts of 1844. In E. Fromm (Trans.), *Marx's concept of man.* New York: Continuum. (Original work published 1932)

Marx, K., & Engels, F. (1978). Manifesto of the Communist Party. In R. C. Tucker (Ed.), *The Marx-Engels reader.* New York: Norton. (Original work published 1848)

Maturana, H. R., & Varela, F. J. (1991). *Autopoiesis and cognition: The realization of the living.* New York: Springer.

Maynard, J. (Ed.). (1996). *Through Indian eyes.* Washington, DC: Reader's Digest.

McCready, S. (Ed.). (2001). *The discovery of time.* Naperville, IL: Sourcebooks.

Mead, G. H. (1925). The genesis of the self and social control. *International Journal of Ethics, 55,* 255–277.

Mead, G. H. (1934). *Mind, self, and society: From the standpoint of a social behaviorist* (C. W. Morris, Ed.). Chicago: University of Chicago Press.

Mead, G. H. (1938). *The philosophy of the act.* Chicago: University of Chicago Press.

Mehan, H., & Wood, H. (1975). *The reality of ethnomethodology.* New York: Wiley.

Menand, L. (2001). *The metaphysical club: A story of ideas in America.* New York: Farrar, Straus & Giroux.

Merriam-Webster. (2002). *Webster's third new international dictionary, unabridged.* Retrieved March 31, 2006, from http://unabridged.merriam-webster.com

Merton, R. K. (1967). *On theoretical sociology: Five essays, old and new.* New York: Free Press.

Merton, R. K. (1976). *Sociological ambivalence and other essays.* New York: Free Press.

Milgram, S. (1974). *Obedience to authority: An experimental view.* New York: Harper& Row.

Mills, C. W. (1956). *The power elite.* New York: Oxford University Press.

Morris, C. W. (1962). Introduction: George H. Mead as social psychologist and social philosopher. In C. W. Morris (Ed.), *Mind, self, and society from the standpoint of a social behaviorist.* Chicago: University of Chicago Press.

National Academy of Sciences. (1995). *National science education standards.* Retrieved August 20, 2004, from http://www.nap.edu/readingroom/books/nses/html/action.html

National Urban League (2009). State of black America. Retrieved November 12, 2009, from http://www.nul.org/newsroom/publications/soba

Nöth, W. (1995). *Handbook of semiotics.* Bloomington: Indiana University Press. (Original work published 1985)

Oakes, G. (1984). Introduction. In *Georg Simmel on women, sexuality, and love.* New Haven, CT: Yale University Press.

Orwell, G. (1946). *Shooting an elephant and other essays.* New York: Harcourt.

Outhwaite, W. (2003). Jürgen Habermas. In G. Ritzer (Ed.), *The Blackwell companion to major contemporary social theorists.* Malden, MA: Blackwell.

Parsons, T. (1949). *The structure of social action* (2nd ed.). New York and London: Free Press.

Parsons, T. (1951). *The social system.* London: Free Press.

Parsons, T. (1961). Culture and the social system. In T. Parsons (Ed.), *Theories of society: Foundations of modern sociological theory* (pp. 963–993). New York: Free Press.

Parsons, T. (1966). *Societies: Evolutionary and comparative perspectives.* Englewood Cliffs, NJ: Prentice Hall.

Parsons, T. (1990). Prolegomena to a theory of social institutions. *American Sociological Review, 55*(3), 319–339.

Parsons, T., & Shils, E. (Eds.). (1951). *Toward a general theory of action.* Cambridge, MA: Harvard University Press.

Patterson, T. E. (2002): *The vanishing voter: Public involvement in an age of uncertainty*. New York: Alfred A. Knopf.

Perinbanayagam, R. S. (2000). *The presence of the self*. Lanham, MD: Rowman & Littlefield.

Perinbanayagam, R. S. (2003). Telic reflections: Interactional processes, as such. *Symbolic Interaction, 26*(1), 67–83.

Pianin, E. (2001, July 10). Superfund cleanup effort shows results, study reports. *Washington Post,* p. A19.

Plato. (1993). *The last days of Socrates* (H. Tredennick & H. Tarrant, Trans.). London: Penguin.

Plummer, K. (1998). Herbert Blumer. In Rob Stones (Ed.), *Key sociological thinkers.* New York: New York University Press.

Rawls, A. (2003). Harold Garfinkel. In G. Ritzer (Ed.), *The Blackwell companion to major contemporary social theorists.* Malden, MA: Blackwell.

Ray, L. (Ed.). (1991). *Formal sociology: The sociology of Georg Simmel.* Aldershot, UK: Elgar.

Ritzer, G. (1998). *The McDonaldization thesis.* London: Sage.

Ritzer, G. (2004). *The McDonaldization of society* (Rev. ed.). Thousand Oaks, CA: Pine Forge.

Ritzer, G., & Goodman, D. (2000). Introduction: Toward a more open canon. In G. Ritzer (Ed.), *The Blackwell Companion to major social theorists.* Malden, MA: Blackwell.

Roy, W. G. (2001). *Making societies.* Thousand Oaks, CA: Pine Forge.

Rule, J. B. (2003). Lewis Coser: 1913–2003. *Dissent.* Retrieved May 5, 2006, from http://www .dissentmagazine.org/article/?article=470

Sacks, H. (1995). *Lectures on conversation.* Malden, MA: Wiley-Blackwell.

Said, E. W. (1994). *Culture and imperialism.* New York: Vintage.

Said, E. W. (2003). *Orientalism: Western concepts of the Orient* (Preface to the 25th anniversary ed.). New York: Vintage.

Sanderson, S. K. (2005). Reforming theoretical work in sociology: A modest proposal. *Perspectives 28*(2), 1–4.

Schutz, A. (1967). *The phenomenology of the social world* (G. Walsh & F. Lehnert, Trans.). Evanston, IL: Northwestern University Press.

Simmel, G. (1950). *The sociology of Georg Simmel* (K. H. Wolff, Ed. & Trans.). Glencoe, IL: Free Press.

Simmel, G. (1955). *Conflict and the web of group affiliations.* New York: Free Press. (Original work published 1908)

Simmel, G. (1959). *Essays on sociology, philosophy, and aesthetics [by] Georg Simmel [and others]: Georg Simmel, 1858–1918* (K. H. Wolfe, Ed.). New York: Harper & Row.

Simmel, G. (1971). *Georg Simmel: On individuality and social forms* (D. N. Levine, Ed.). Chicago: University of Chicago Press.

Simmel, G. (1978). *The philosophy of money* (T. Bottomore, & D. Frisby, Trans.). London: Routledge & Kegan Paul.

Simmel, G. (1997). *Essays on religion* (H. J. Helle, Trans. & Ed.). New Haven, CT: Yale University Press.

Smith, A. (1937). *An inquiry into the nature and causes of the wealth of nations.* New York: Modern Library. (Original work published 1776)

Smith, D. E. (1987). *The everyday world as problematic: A feminist sociology.* Boston: Northwestern University Press.

Smith, D. E. (1990). *The conceptual practices of power: A feminist sociology of knowledge.* Boston: Northeastern University Press.

Smith, D. E. (1992). Sociology from women's experience: A reaffirmation. *Sociological Theory, 10*(1), 88–98.

Smith, D. E. (2005). *Institutional ethnography: A sociology for people.* Lanham, MD: AltaMira Press.

Index

About the Author

Kenneth Allan received his PhD in sociology from the University of California, Riverside (1995), and is currently Associate Professor of Sociology at the University of North Carolina at Greensboro (UNCG). Before moving to UNCG, he directed the Teaching Assistant Development Program at the University of California, Riverside, and coedited *Training Teaching Assistants,* 2nd edition (1997), published by the American Sociological Association. In addition to teaching classical and contemporary theory at UNCG, Allan also regularly teaches graduate pedagogy courses and oversees the department's online iSchool program, which currently offers university-level courses to over 2,000 high school students per year. Allan's research areas include theory, culture, and the self. He has authored several other works in the area of theory, including *The Meaning of Culture: Moving the Postmodern Critique Forward, Explorations in Classical Sociological Theory: Seeing the Social World,* and *Contemporary Social and Sociological Theory: Visualizing Social Worlds.*

Supporting researchers for more than 40 years

Research methods have always been at the core of SAGE's publishing program. Founder Sara Miller McCune published SAGE's first methods book, *Public Policy Evaluation*, in 1970. Soon after, she launched the *Quantitative Applications in the Social Sciences* series—affectionately known as the "little green books."

Always at the forefront of developing and supporting new approaches in methods, SAGE published early groundbreaking texts and journals in the fields of qualitative methods and evaluation.

Today, more than 40 years and two million little green books later, SAGE continues to push the boundaries with a growing list of more than 1,200 research methods books, journals, and reference works across the social, behavioral, and health sciences. Its imprints—Pine Forge Press, home of innovative textbooks in sociology, and Corwin, publisher of PreK–12 resources for teachers and administrators—broaden SAGE's range of offerings in methods. SAGE further extended its impact in 2008 when it acquired CQ Press and its best-selling and highly respected political science research methods list.

From qualitative, quantitative, and mixed methods to evaluation, SAGE is the essential resource for academics and practitioners looking for the latest methods by leading scholars.

For more information, visit **www.sagepub.com**.